Dictionary of Literary Biography

Dictionary of Literary Biography Documentary Series

Dictionary of Literary Biography Yearbooks

1980 edited by Karen L. Rood, Jean W. Ross, and Richard Ziegfeld (1981)

1981 edited by Karen L. Rood, Jean W. Ross, and Richard Ziegfeld (1982)

1982 edited by Richard Ziegfeld; associate editors: Jean W. Ross and Lynne C. Zeigler (1983)

1983 edited by Mary Bruccoli and Jean W. Ross; associate editor Richard Ziegfeld (1984)

1984 edited by Jean W. Ross (1985)

1985 edited by Jean W. Ross (1986)

1986 edited by J. M. Brook (1987)

1987 edited by J. M. Brook (1988)

1988 edited by J. M. Brook (1989)

1989 edited by J. M. Brook (1990)

1990 edited by James W. Hipp (1991)

1991 edited by James W. Hipp (1992)

1992 edited by James W. Hipp (1993)

1993 edited by James W. Hipp, contributing editor George Garrett (1994)

1994 edited by James W. Hipp, contributing editor George Garrett (1995)

1995 edited by James W. Hipp, contributing editor George Garrett (1996)

1996 edited by Samuel W. Bruce and L. Kay Webster, contributing editor George Garrett (1997)

1997 edited by Matthew J. Bruccoli and George Garrett, with the assistance of L. Kay Webster (1998)

1998 edited by Matthew J. Bruccoli, contributing editor George Garrett, with the assistance of D. W. Thomas (1999)

1999 edited by Matthew J. Bruccoli, contributing editor George Garrett, with the assistance of D. W. Thomas (2000)

2000 edited by Matthew J. Bruccoli, contributing editor George Garrett, with the assistance of George Parker Anderson (2001)

Concise Series

Concise Dictionary of American Literary Biography, 7 volumes (1988-1999): *The New Consciousness, 1941-1968; Colonization to the American Renaissance, 1640-1865; Realism, Naturalism, and Local Color, 1865-1917; The Twenties, 1917-1929; The Age of Maturity, 1929-1941; Broadening Views, 1968-1988; Supplement: Modern Writers, 1900-1998.*

Concise Dictionary of British Literary Biography, 8 volumes (1991-1992): *Writers of the Middle Ages and Renaissance Before 1660; Writers of the Restoration and Eighteenth Century, 1660-1789; Writers of the Romantic Period, 1789-1832; Victorian Writers, 1832-1890; Late-Victorian and Edwardian Writers, 1890-1914; Modern Writers, 1914-1945; Writers After World War II, 1945-1960; Contemporary Writers, 1960 to Present.*

Concise Dictionary of World Literary Biography, 10 volumes projected (1999-): *Ancient Greek and Roman Writers; German Writers; African, Caribbean, and Latin American Writers; South Slavic and Eastern European Writers.*

Dictionary of Literary Biography® • Volume Two Hundred Fifty-Three

Raymond Chandler
A Documentary Volume

Raymond Chandler
A Documentary Volume

Edited by
Robert F. Moss

A Bruccoli Clark Layman Book
The Gale Group
Detroit • San Francisco • London • Boston • Woodbridge, Conn.

Advisory Board for
DICTIONARY OF LITERARY BIOGRAPHY

John Baker
William Cagle
Patrick O'Connor
George Garrett
Trudier Harris
Alvin Kernan
Kenny J. Williams

Matthew J. Bruccoli and Richard Layman, Editorial Directors
Karen L. Rood, Senior Editor

Printed in the United States of America

ISBN 0-7876-5247-4

10 9 8 7 6 5 4 3 2 1

For Jennifer

Contents

Plan of the Series

The advisory board, the editors, and the publisher of the *Dictionary of Literary Biography* are joined in endorsing Mark Twain's declaration. The literature of a nation provides an inexhaustible resource of permanent worth. Our purpose is to make literature and its creators better understood and more accessible to students and the reading public, while satisfying the needs of teachers and researchers.

To meet these requirements, *literary biography* has been construed in terms of the author's achievement. The most important thing about a writer is his writing. Accordingly, the entries in *DLB* are career biographies, tracing the development of the author's canon and the evolution of his reputation.

The purpose of *DLB* is not only to provide reliable information in a usable format but also to place the figures in the larger perspective of literary history and to offer appraisals of their accomplishments by qualified scholars.

The publication plan for *DLB* resulted from two years of preparation. The project was proposed to Bruccoli Clark by Frederick G. Ruffner, president of the Gale Research Company, in November 1975. After specimen entries were prepared and typeset, an advisory board was formed to refine the entry format and develop the series rationale. In meetings held during 1976, the publisher, series editors, and advisory board approved the scheme for a comprehensive biographical dictionary of persons who contributed to literature. Editorial work on the first volume began in January 1977, and it was published in 1978. In order to make *DLB* more than a dictionary and to compile volumes that individually have claim to status as literary history, it was decided to organize volumes by topic, period, or

*From an unpublished section of Mark Twain's autobiography, copyright by the Mark Twain Company

genre. Each of these freestanding volumes provides a biographical-bibliographical guide and overview for a particular area of literature. We are convinced that this organization—as opposed to a single alphabet method—constitutes a valuable innovation in the presentation of reference material. The volume plan necessarily requires many decisions for the placement and treatment of authors. Certain figures will be included in separate volumes, but with different entries emphasizing the aspect of his career appropriate to each volume. Ernest Hemingway, for example, is represented in *American Writers in Paris, 1920–1939* by an entry focusing on his expatriate apprenticeship; he is also in *American Novelists, 1910–1945* with an entry surveying his entire career, as well as in *American Short-Story Writers, 1910–1945, Second Series* with an entry concentrating on his short fiction. Each volume includes a cumulative index of the subject authors and articles.

Since 1981 the series has been further augmented by the *DLB Yearbooks,* which update published entries, add new entries to keep the *DLB* current with contemporary activity, and provide articles on literary history. There have also been nineteen *DLB Documentary Series* volumes which provide illustrations, facsimiles, and biographical and critical source materials for figures, works, or groups judged to have particular interest for students. In 1999 the *Documentary Series* was incorporated into the *DLB* volume numbering system beginning with *DLB 210, Ernest Hemingway.*

We define literature as the *intellectual commerce of a nation:* not merely as belles lettres but as that ample and complex process by which ideas are generated, shaped, and transmitted. *DLB* entries are not limited to "creative writers" but extend to other figures who in their time and in their way influenced the mind of a people. Thus the series encompasses historians, journalists, publishers, book collectors, and screenwriters. By this means readers of *DLB* may be aided to perceive literature not as cult scripture in the keeping of intellectual high priests but firmly positioned at the center of a nation's life.

DLB includes the major writers appropriate to each volume and those standing in the ranks behind them. Scholarly and critical counsel has been sought in deciding which minor figures to include and how full their entries should be. Wherever possible, useful references are made to figures who do not warrant separate entries.

Each *DLB* volume has an expert volume editor responsible for planning the volume, selecting the figures for inclusion, and assigning the entries. Volume editors are also responsible for preparing, where appropriate, appendices surveying the major periodicals and literary and intellectual movements for their volumes, as well as lists of further readings. Work on the series as a whole is coordinated at the Bruccoli Clark Layman editorial center in Columbia, South Carolina, where the editorial staff is responsible for accuracy and utility of the published volumes.

One feature that distinguishes *DLB* is the illustration policy—its concern with the iconography of literature. Just as an author is influenced by his surroundings, so is the reader's understanding of the author enhanced by a knowledge of his environment. Therefore *DLB* volumes include not only drawings, paintings, and photographs of authors, often depicting them at various stages in their careers, but also illustrations of their families and places where they lived. Title pages are regularly reproduced in facsimile along with dust jackets for modern authors. The dust jackets are a special feature of *DLB* because they often document better than anything else the way in which an author's work was perceived in its own time. Specimens of the writers' manuscripts and letters are included when feasible.

Samuel Johnson rightly decreed that "The chief glory of every people arises from its authors." The purpose of the *Dictionary of Literary Biography* is to compile literary history in the surest way available to us—by accurate and comprehensive treatment of the lives and work of those who contributed to it.

The *DLB* Advisory Board

Introduction

In his May 1948 *Harper's* article, "The Guilty Vicarage," W. H. Auden wrote of Raymond Chandler, "I think Mr. Chandler is interested in writing, not detective stories, but serious studies of a criminal milieu . . . [H]is powerful but extremely depressing books should be read and judged not as escape literature, but as works of art." Scholars frequently cite Auden's article as an important early recognition of Chandler's literary value, but it also underscores the critical challenge that Chandler faced throughout his writing career. Detective stories, in the view of Auden and his contemporaries, were by definition escapist and subliterary; because Chandler's books showed artistic merit, they must have been something other than detective stories.

The truth, however, is that Chandler's novels are excellent detective stories *and* serious works of literature. He wrote seven of the best novels in the American hard-boiled tradition, establishing some conventions that others would imitate and overcoming the limitations of genre publishing to earn a wide popular and literary audience both in the United States and abroad. His writing is memorable, moreover, because he wrote lyrical and evocative prose, and his characters and scenes are depicted vibrantly and compellingly. His novels are works of perceptive social realism that capture and interpret American life between 1939 and 1959. The writing endures.

Born in Chicago in 1888, Raymond Chandler was raised in England and started writing in the first decade of the twentieth century, contributing poems, essays, and sketches to London literary magazines. In 1912, at the age of twenty-four, he decided that he could not make a living as a writer and moved to Los Angeles to begin a career as a businessman. Twenty years later—after rising to become a vice president and director of a conglomerate of small oil companies and being fired for alcoholism and erratic behavior—he returned to professional writing to support himself and his wife. He chose the detective pulps as his market, in part because he could be paid while learning the genre and in part because he believed that the detective story offered him a chance to turn a popular form into art. The tension between the conventional requirements of

the genre and Chandler's artistic aspirations shaped and defined his professional career.

Chandler was an immediate success in the pulp market. His first story, "Blackmailers Don't Shoot" (December 1933), was accepted by *Black Mask* magazine, the most prestigious of the detective pulps. His greatest influence was Dashiell Hammett, a fellow *Black Mask* writer and one of the originators of the American hard-boiled detective story. Chandler admired Hammett for overturning the genteel conventions of the traditional British mystery and writing about murder in a gritty, realistic fashion. To Hammett's objective, hard-boiled style, Chandler added a biting wit and a distinctive use of the American vernacular. Within two years his stories were featured on the covers of *Black Mask,* and he was recognized as a leading pulp writer. In 1939, after a six-year apprenticeship, Chandler published his first novel, *The Big Sleep,* which introduced private detective Philip Marlowe.

Chandler initially intended writing detective novels to be the first stage in a diverse career. He planned to finish three or four Philip Marlowe novels quickly and earn from them enough money to support himself while writing nonmystery novels and "fantastic stories"—realistically told short stories based upon an unrealistic premise such as magic or invisibility. Because of the nature of the mystery and general fiction markets, however, Chandler was unable to achieve these goals. His first novel and the three that followed—*Farewell, My Lovely* (1940), *The High Window* (1942), and *The Lady in the Lake* (1943)—sold well, but the detective genre was financially limited, with five to ten thousand copies being considered strong sales. Until the mid 1940s authors received the majority of their income from hardcover sales. The subsidiary rights market was small, limited to screen and prepublication serial rights; and the paperback industry had yet to develop as an important source of income for novelists. To earn what Chandler considered an acceptable living from his novels alone, a writer would have to publish a book every six months—a pace Chandler never tried to achieve.

In 1943 Chandler turned to Hollywood to earn the money he could not make from his novels. He was fascinated by the movie industry and his quick study of the craft of screenwriting brought him early success. His collaboration with Billy Wilder on *Double Indemnity* (1944)–Chandler's first movie–earned the pair an Academy Award nomination for best screenplay. Within three years he was commanding a top salary as a screenwriter and was able to win unique concessions, such as being allowed to work at home and have scripts accepted sight unseen. In important ways, however, Chandler was fundamentally at odds with the life of a writer in the movie industry. He chafed against the phoniness of the studios and, as a shy person, never became confortable with Hollywood social life. Most significantly, he resented the impinging of the studio upon his autonomy as a writer and detested giving up control of his scripts to directors and dialogue polishers. In 1948, eager to return to novel writing, he began looking for a way out of the studios.

Chandler's tenure in Hollywood had effectively ended his literary production: he had not completed a single work of prose fiction in almost six years. During this fallow time, though, the literary market was changing. Paperback publishing grew rapidly after the end of World War II, and paperback reprint rights became a substantial source of income for authors. By 1949 Chandler was earning between $15,000 and $25,000 a year from the paperback royalties on his first four novels. In addition, he was able to sell the screen rights to his novels for increasingly higher sums, and radio and television began expressing an interest in purchasing his works. The clerical work required for these new business dealings occupied much of his average workday, but Chandler was now financially able to live on the proceeds of fiction writing alone.

At the same time that his financial situation was improving, Chandler's literary reputation was beginning to grow. After the war a small number of critics in both the United States and England began arguing that Chandler's novels were more than escapist fare and should be read as works of literature. In Britain his reputation quickly spread, and by the end of the 1940s Chandler had achieve a large audience outside the ranks of mystery fans. His popularity grew more slowly in the United States, where he sold fewer books than in Britain and was snubbed by many of the most influential critics.

In 1949 Chandler published his fifth book, *The Little Sister,* and resumed a career as a full-time novelist. During the 1950s he focused on maintaining and expanding his literary reputation, and in 1953 he published *The Long Goodbye,* the longest and most personal of his novels. By this point Chandler had achieved an international following; his books were available in more than a dozen foreign languages, including Swedish, Finnish, Polish, and Portuguese. Readers abroad found Chandler's works to be not only exciting detective stories but also vital examples of American culture, novels that portrayed a glamorous world of gangsters, crooked politicians, and dissolute movie queens.

Following the death of his wife in 1954, Chandler began to decline emotionally and physically and, during the last five years of his life, fell into depression. He wrote only one more novel, *Playback* (1958), a work that he transformed from an original unproduced screenplay. At his death in 1959 Chandler was widely regarded as America's foremost detective novelist. His reputation as a writer of serious literature grew posthumously, and by the 1970s he was the subject of dozens of scholarly books and articles. Today, Chandler is recognized as both an icon of popular culture and as an important American writer.

Raymond Chandler achieved this reputation for several reasons. As a novelist, he helped develop the American hard-boiled genre and is acclaimed by many as the country's greatest detective writer. As a stylist, he accurately captured the American language and created stories that are vivid and evocative in their narrative detail. As a realist, he chronicled three decades of life in Los Angeles, rendering the city in a richness and breadth unachieved by any other writer.

DLB 253: Raymond Chandler: A Documentary Volume chronicles the career of the author, from his days as an aspiring man of letters in London to his life as a professional novelist and literary celebrity. It is the story of an intriguing personality–a shy man who could be at turns kind and irascible; an American who was raised in England and instilled with Victorian moral values but found a home in the glamorous, decadent city of Los Angeles; a classically educated poet who took as his medium a popular form. Most of all, it is the story of a professional writer keenly devoted to his craft who, after long years of struggle and patient study of the literary markets, achieved commercial success and established an enduring reputation as a great American novelist.

–Robert F. Moss

Acknowledgments

This book was produced by Bruccoli Clark Layman, Inc. George Parker Anderson was the in-house editor.

Production manager is Philip B. Dematteis.

Administrative support was provided by Ann M. Cheschi, Amber L. Coker, and Angi Pleasant.

Accountant is Ann-Marie Holland.

Copyediting supervisor is Sally R. Evans. The copyediting staff includes Phyllis A. Avant, Brenda Carol Blanton, Melissa D. Hinton, Charles Loughlin, Rebecca Mayo, Nancy E. Smith, and Elizabeth Jo Ann Sumner. Freelance copyeditor is Jennie Williamson.

Editorial associates are Michael S. Allen, Michael S. Martin, and Pamela A. Warren.

Database manager is José A. Juarez.

Layout and graphics supervisor is Janet E. Hill. The graphics staff includes Karla Corley Brown and Zoe R. Cook.

Office manager is Kathy Lawler Merlette.

Photography supervisor is Paul Talbot. Photography editor is Scott Nemzek.

Digital photographic copy work was performed by Joseph M. Bruccoli.

The SGML staff includes Jaime All, Frank Graham, Linda Dalton Mullinax, Jason Paddock, and Alex Snead.

Systems manager is Marie L. Parker.

Typesetting supervisor is Kathleen M. Flanagan. The typesetting staff includes Jaime All, Patricia Marie Flanagan, Mark J. McEwan, and Pamela D. Norton. Freelance typesetter is Wanda Adams.

Walter W. Ross did library research. He was assisted by Jaime All, Steven Gross, and the following librarians at the Thomas Cooper Library of the University of South Carolina: circulation department head Tucker Taylor; reference department head Virginia W. Weathers; Brette Barclay, Marilee Birchfield, Paul Cammarata, Gary Geer, Michael Macan, Tom Marcil, Rose Marshall, and Sharon Verba; interlibrary loan department head John Brunswick; and interlibrary loan staff Robert Arndt, Hayden Battle, Barry Bull, Jo Cottingham, Marna Hostetler, Marieum McClary, Erika Peake, and Nelson Rivera.

The completion of this volume would not have been possible without the kind assistance of the following people: Paul Fletcher at the Dulwich College Archives; Grainne Fox at Ed Victor, Ltd.; Jim Moske at the New York Public Library; Jennie Rathbun at the Houghton Reading Room, Harvard University; Paul Schultz at the Thomas Cooper Library, University of South Carolina; and Robert Trogdon at Kent State University.

I am grateful once again to Dr. Matthew J. Bruccoli for his editing and mentorship, to Judy Baughman and Park Bucker for their assistance and support, and most of all to my wife, Jennifer, for her patience and encouragement.

Permissions

McCarthy, "Detective Fiction," *The Sunday Times,* London (29 October 1944) © Times Newspapers Limited, 1944; Cyril Ray, "The Unconventional Mr. Chandler Comes to Town," *The Sunday Times,* London (21 September 1952) © Times Newspapers Limited, 1952.

University of California Los Angeles
Photo of the *Rex* gambling ship, from *Los Angeles: An Illustrated History* by Bruce Henstell; and photos of Cissy Chandler, Raymond Chandler in a World War I uniform, Chandler with other Black Mask writers, Chandler and Billy Wilder, Chandler and Taki the Cat and Chandler putting on gloves. Courtesy of the Department of Special Collections, Charles E. Young Research Library, UCLA.

University of California Press
Charles Gregory, "The Long Goodbye," *Film Quarterly* 26, no. 4 (Summer 1973): 46–48, copyright © 1973 The Regents of the University of California. Reprinted by permission; Joseph McBride, excerpt from *Hawks on Hawks* (Berkeley: University of California Press, 1982),

copyright © 1982 The Regents of the University of California. Reprinted by permission; Dorothy Gardiner and Kathrine Sorley Walker, "Extract from Notes Dated 1950 About the Screenplay Strangers on a Train" in *Raymond Chandler Speaking* (Boston: Houghton Mifflin, 1962), pp. 133–135, copyright © 1997 The Regents of the University of California. Reprinted by permission.

University of North Carolina Press
Excerpt from *Down These Mean Streets A Man Must Go: Raymond Chandler's Knight* by Philip Durham. Copyright © 1963 by the University of North Carolina Press. Used by permission of the publisher.

University of Texas Press
Rats Behind the Wainscoting: Politics, Convention, and Chandler's "The Big Sleep" by Peter J. Rabinowitz from Texas Studies in Literature and Language 22:2, pp. 224–245. Copyright © 1980 by the University of Texas Press. All rights reserved.

Raymond Chandler
A Documentary Volume

Dictionary of Literary Biography

Books by Raymond Chandler

See also the Chandler entries in *DS 6: Hardboiled Mystery Writers: Raymond Chandler, Dashiell Hammett, Ross Macdonald* and *DLB 226: American Hard-Boiled Crime Writers.*

BOOKS: *The Big Sleep* (New York: Knopf, 1939; London: Hamilton, 1939);

Farewell, My Lovely (New York: Knopf, 1940; London: Hamilton, 1940);

The High Window (New York: Knopf, 1942; London: Hamilton, 1943);

The Lady in the Lake (New York: Knopf, 1943; London: Hamilton, 1944);

Five Murderers (New York: Avon, 1944);

Five Sinister Characters (New York: Avon, 1945);

The Finger Man and Other Stories (New York: Avon, 1947);

The Little Sister (London: Hamilton, 1949; Boston: Houghton Mifflin, 1949);

The Simple Art of Murder (Boston: Houghton Mifflin, 1950; London: Hamilton, 1950);

The Long Good-Bye (London: Hamilton, 1953; Boston: Houghton Mifflin, 1954);

Playback (Boston: Houghton Mifflin, 1958);

Raymond Chandler Speaking, edited by Dorothy Gardiner and Kathrine Sorley Walker (London: Hamilton, 1962; New York: Houghton Mifflin, 1962);

Killer in the Rain (London: Hamilton, 1964; Boston: Houghton Mifflin, 1964);

Chandler Before Marlowe, edited by Matthew J. Bruccoli (Columbia: University of South Carolina Press, 1973);

The Blue Dahlia: A Screenplay, edited by Bruccoli (Carbondale and Edwardsville, Ill.: Southern Illinois University Press, 1976; London: Elm Tree Books, 1976);

The Notebooks of Raymond Chandler and English Summer, edited by Frank MacShane (New York: Ecco, 1976; London: Weidenfeld & Nicolson, 1977);

Raymond Chandler's Unknown Thriller: The Screenplay of Playback. (New York: Mysterious Press, 1985);

Poodle Springs, by Chandler and Robert B. Parker (New York: Putnam, 1989; London: Macdonald, 1990).

LETTERS: *Raymond Chandler Speaking,* edited by Dorothy Gardiner and Katherine Sorley Walker (Boston: Houghton Mifflin, 1962);

Letters: Raymond Chandler and James M. Fox, edited by James Pepper (Santa Barbara, Cal.: Neville & Yellin, 1978);

Selected Letters of Raymond Chandler, edited by Frank MacShane (New York: Columbia Univeristy Press, 1981);

The Raymond Chandler Papers, edited by Tom Hiney and Frank MacShane (London: Hamish Hamilton, 2000; New York: Atlantic Montly Press, 2000).

Raymond Chandler (23 July 1888 – 26 March 1959)

Raymond Chandler:
A Chronology of His Life and Writings

1888

23 July   Raymond Thornton Chandler is born in Chicago, Illinois. He is the only child of Florence Dart Thornton Chandler, an Irish emigrant, and Maurice Benjamin Chandler, a Pennsylvania Quaker who works for the railroad.

1889–1894

Chandler is taken by his mother to spend summers in Fitt, Nebraska, with his aunt Grace Thornton.

1895

Chandler's parents divorce; he moves to London with his mother, where they live with his grandmother Annie Thornton and aunt Ethel Thornton.

1900

Fall   Chandler enters Dulwich College, a respected public school.

1905

April   Chandler leaves Dulwich and travels to Paris to study French.

1906

Chandler moves to Munich, Germany, to continue language studies.

1907

20 May   Chandler returns to England and becomes a naturalized British subject.

June   Chandler passes the Civil Service exam and becomes a clerk for the Admiralty, a position he quits after six months.

1908

Chandler leaves the Admiralty to attempt a career as a man of letters.

19 December   Chandler publishes his first poem, "The Unknown Love," in *Chambers's Journal.*

1909–1911

Chandler works briefly as a reporter for the London *Daily Express*. He contributes poems, sketches, essays, and translations to the *Westminster Gazette* and *The Academy*.

1912

Chandler returns to America. He lives briefly in St. Louis and Omaha before moving on to the Los Angeles area, where he is employed in a series of odd jobs, which include stringing tennis rackets for a sporting goods store and working on an apricot ranch.

1913

Chandler enrolls in a night-school bookkeeping course and finds work as a bookkeeper and accountant at the Los Angeles Creamery.

1916

Chandler lives with his mother, who had come over from England, at 311 Loma Drive in downtown Los Angeles.

1917

August   Chandler enlists as a private in the Canadian army.

November   Chandler is assigned to the 7th Battalion, Canadian Expeditionary Force, and is posted to England.

1918

March   Chandler serves three months at the front in France.

July   Chandler is transferred to England, attached to the Royal Air Force, and attends aviation training school.

13 December   Chandler is promoted to Acting Sergeant.

1919

20 February   Chandler receives discharge.

Chandler moves to San Francisco, where he takes a position in an English bank. He then returns to Los Angeles.

Chandler begins an affair with Cissy Pascal, a married woman nearly eighteen years his senior, who was born Pearl Eugenie Hurlburt in Perry, Ohio.

1920

20 October   Cissy divorces her husband. Chandler delays marrying Cissy because his mother disapproves.

1922

Chandler takes a bookkeeping job with Dabney Oil Syndicate; he eventually rises to the position of vice president.

1924

January   Chandler's mother dies.

6 February   Chandler marries Cissy.

1925–1931

The Chandlers move frequently around Los Angeles. He begins to drink heavily and have affairs, sometimes with the women in his office. He also disappears occasionally for days at a time and begins to make suicide threats.

1932

Chandler is fired from Dabney Oil Syndicate for drinking and absenteeism. He begins receiving an allowance of $100 a month from Edward Lloyd, whom he had helped with a lawsuit, and devotes himself to his writing.

1933

Chandler spends five months writing "Blackmailers Don't Shoot."

December   "Blackmailers Don't Shoot," Chandler's first pulp story, is published in *Black Mask*.

1934

July   "Smart-Aleck Kill" is published in *Black Mask*.

October   "Finger Man," in which Chandler first uses a first-person narrator, is published in *Black Mask*.

1935

January   "Killer in the Rain" is published in *Black Mask*.

June   "Nevada Gas" is published in *Black Mask*.

November   "Spanish Blood" is published in *Black Mask*.

1936

January   "Guns at Cyrano's" is published in *Black Mask*.

March   "The Man Who Liked Dogs" is published in *Black Mask*.

May   "Noon Street Nemesis" is published in *Detective Fiction Weekly*. The story is later published as "Pick-Up on Noon Street" in *The Simple Art of Murder* (1950).

June   "Goldfish" is published in *Black Mask*.

September   "The Curtain" is published in *Black Mask*.

1937

January	"Try the Girl" is published in *Black Mask*.
November	"Mandarin's Jade" is published in *Dime Detective*. Chandler switched to *Dime Detective* after Joseph Shaw was dismissed as the editor of *Black Mask*.

1938

January	"Red Wind" is published in *Dime Detective*.
March	"The King in Yellow" is published in *Dime Detective*.
Spring	Chandler begins writing *The Big Sleep,* featuring detective Philip Marlowe. In a process he calls "cannibalization," he makes use of "Killer in the Rain," "The Curtain," and a small portion of "Finger Man," rewriting whole scenes while tightening his prose and enriching his descriptions. He completes the novel in three months.
June	"Bay City Blues" is published in *Dime Detective*.

1939

January	"The Lady in the Lake" is published in *Dime Detective*.
6 February	*The Big Sleep,* Chandler's first novel, is published by Alfred A. Knopf in an initial print run of five thousand copies. The first English edition is published in March by Hamish Hamilton.
April	"Pearls Are a Nuisance" is published in *Dime Detective*.
August	"Trouble Is My Business" is published in *Dime Detective*.
May	The Chandlers rent a cabin near Big Bear Lake.
September	Chandler volunteers for the Canadian Army but is turned down because of his age.
November	"The Bronze Door," a fantastic story, is published in *Unknown*.
December	"I'll Be Waiting" is published in *The Saturday Evening Post*.
December	The Chandlers move to 1265 Park Row, La Jolla, California.

1940

January	The Chandlers move briefly to Monrovia, California, and then to Arcadia, California.
1 October	*Farewell, My Lovely* is published by Knopf in an initial print run of 7,500 copies. The first English edition is published the same month by Hamish Hamilton.
October	The Chandlers move to 449 San Vincente Boulevard, Santa Monica, California.
Fall	Chandler begins writing *The High Window*.

1941

July	RKO pays Chandler $2,000 for the movie rights to *Farewell, My Lovely. The Falcon Takes Over,* the first movie version of *Farewell, My Lovely,* is released in 1942. *Murder, My Sweet,* the second movie version, is released in 1944.
September	"No Crime in the Mountains," Chandler's last pulp story, is published in *Detective Story*.

1942

March | Chandler finishes *The High Window*.

May | 20th Century-Fox pays Chandler $3,500 for the movie rights to *The High Window*. *Time to Kill*, the first movie version of *The High Window,* is released in 1943, and *The Brasher Doubloon,* a second movie version, is released in 1947.

Summer | The Chandlers move to Idyllwild, California.

17 August | *The High Window* is published by Knopf in an initial print run of 6,500 copies. The first English edition is published in February 1943 by Hamish Hamilton.

1943

Summer | Chandler signs a contract to collaborate with Billy Wilder on the screen adaptation of James M. Cain's *Double Indemnity* (1943).

Summer | The Chandlers move to 6520 Drexel Avenue, Los Angeles.

1 November | *The Lady in the Lake* is published by Knopf in an initial print run of six thousand copies. The first English edition is published in October 1944 by Hamish Hamilton.

December | "The Simple Art of Murder" is published in *The Atlantic Monthly;* the essay was republished in *Third Mystery Companion,* edited by A. L. Furman (1945). Chandler revised the essay for inclusion in *Art of the Mystery Story,* edited by Howard Haycraft (1946); this revised version was subsequently published in *Finger Man and Other Stories* (circa 1946; published 1947) and as an appendix to *The Simple Art of Murder* (1950).

1944

April | *Double Indemnity* is released and becomes a success. Chandler later is nominated for an Academy Award for the screenplay.

Chandler continues to work as a contract screenwriter at Paramount, contributing to *And Now Tomorrow* and *The Unseen*.

1945

Chandler writes *The Blue Dahlia* for Paramount.

July | Chandler begins working on the screenplay for *The Lady in the Lake* but leaves M-G-M before the screenplay is finished. Steve Fisher completes the work, and Chandler refuses to have his name connected to it.

November | "Writers in Hollywood" is published in *The Atlantic Monthly*.

1946

May | Chandler begins working on a screenplay of Elizabeth Sanxay Holding's *The Innocent Mrs. Duff* for Paramount but leaves before completing it because of disagreements with the studio.

June | *The Blue Dahlia* is released. Chandler later receives an Edgar award from the Mystery Writers of America and is nominated for an Academy Award for the screenplay.

August | The movie version of *The Big Sleep* is released by Warner Bros.

The Chandlers move from Los Angeles to La Jolla.

November | Chandler breaks off his connection with his literary agent, Sydney Sanders.

1947

Spring   Chandler begins writing the screenplay to *Playback* for Universal; he completes it in early 1948, but the movie is not produced.

July   "Critical Notes" is published in *The Screen Writer*.

1948

Chandler signs with Brandt and Brandt literary agency.

March   "Oscar Night in Hollywood" is published in *The Atlantic Monthly*.

April   Chandler switches publishers from Alfred A. Knopf to Houghton Mifflin.

October   "10 Greatest Crimes of the Century" is published in *Cosmopolitan*.

1949

April   "The Little Sister," a prepublication abridgement of *The Little Sister,* is published in *Cosmopolitan*.

24 June   *The Little Sister* is published by Hamish Hamilton (U.K.). The first American edition is published 26 September by Houghton Mifflin in an initial print run of 12,500 copies.

1950

15 April   "The Simple Art of Murder" is published in *The Saturday Review of Literature*. This article was later published as the "Introduction" to *The Simple Art of Murder.*

July   Chandler begins work with Alfred Hitchcock on the movie version of Patricia Highsmith's *Strangers on a Train.* Hitchcock becomes unhappy with Chandler's work, and Czenzi Ormonde replaces Chandler as the screenwriter.

19 September   *The Simple Art of Murder* is published by Houghton Mifflin in an initial print run of eight thousand copies. The first English edition is published 24 November by Hamish Hamilton.

1951

Chandler begins writing *The Long Goodbye.*

June–August   "Professor Bingo's Snuff" is published as a serial in the June, July, and August issues of *Park East.* The story also appears serially in *Go* (June–July 1951).

1952

February   "Ten Per Cent of Your Life" is published in *The Atlantic Monthly*.

August   The Chandlers visit England, where they spend the next three months.

November   Chandler breaks off his relationship with Brandt and Brandt.

Cissy Chandler's health worsens.

1953

27 November   *The Long Good-Bye* is published in Great Britain by Hamish Hamilton. The first American edition is published 18 March 1954 by Houghton Mifflin with an initial print run of ten thousand copies.

1954

12 December   Cissy Chandler dies.

1955

January   Chandler drinks heavily and suffers from severe depression.

22 February   Chandler attempts suicide and is confined to a county hospital, then moved to a private sanatorium.

March   Chandler sells his house in La Jolla and spends a few weeks in New York City.

12 April   Chandler sails for England. During the trip he learns that he has won the Edgar award from the Mystery Writers of America for *The Long Goodbye*.

Summer   Chandler meets Helga Greene, who later becomes his literary agent.

September   Chandler's residential permit expires, and he returns to the United States.

November   Chandler returns to London.

December   Chandler is hospitalized for two weeks and diagnosed with a form of malaria.

1956

May   Chandler returns to the United States to avoid paying the heavy taxes that he has accumulated by remaining illegally in England.

Chandler is hospitalized in New York City for alcoholism and exhaustion.

June   Chandler returns to La Jolla, taking an apartment at 6925 Neptune Place.

1957

Chandler begins reworking "English Summer," a story he had written nearly twenty years before, then puts the story aside to work on transforming the screenplay *Playback* into a novel.

Chandler becomes involved in a tax dispute with British authorities and decides not to return to England as planned.

August   Chandler is hospitalized again for drinking.

December   Chandler finishes *Playback*.

1958

February   Chandler returns to London for the first half of the year.

30 March   "The Terrible Dr. No.," a review of Ian Fleming's *Dr. No,* is published in the *London Sunday Times*.

May   Chandler is hospitalized in London for drinking.

10 July   *Playback* is published by Hamish Hamilton (U.K.). The first American edition is published by Houghton Mifflin in October in an initial print run of six thousand copies.

August   Chandler returns to La Jolla, resumes heavy drinking, and is periodically hospitalized.

Fall   Chandler becomes involved in disputes over the disposition of his will as well as in problems involving domestic and secretarial help.

| October/ November | An abridgement of *Playback* is published in *Suspense;* it also appears in *Personality* (4 December 1958, 18 December 1958, 1 January 1959, 15 January 1959). |

1959

February	Chandler is again hospitalized and there proposes marriage to Helga Greene, who accepts.
Spring	"The Detective Story as an Art Form" is published in *The Crime Writer*.
March	Chandler travels to New York to accept the presidency of Mystery Writers of America.
23 March	Chandler falls ill with pneumonia and is hospitalized.
26 March	Chandler dies in the Scripps Clinic, La Jolla, California. He is buried in the Mount Hope Cemetery in San Diego.

1.
Chandler Before the Pulps, 1888–1932

A Child of Two Countries

Raymond Thornton Chandler was born in Chicago on 23 July 1888. His father, Maurice Chandler, was from Pennsylvania and worked as a civil engineer for a Western railway company. His mother, Florence Thornton Chandler, was Anglo-Irish; she immigrated in the early 1880s to the United States and initially lived with her sister Grace and her husband Ernest Fitt in Plattsmouth, Nebraska, a town near the railway center of Omaha. Chandler's parents were married in Laramie, Wyoming, in 1887 and set up house in Chicago; they divorced when their only child was seven years old, and mother and son moved to London to live with her relatives. What little is known about Chandler's childhood has been gleaned from letters and interviews from much later in his life. The following letter excerpts present

Chandler's memory of his early days in Nebraska and his impressions of his family in England and Ireland.

In a 20 November 1944 letter to Charles Morton, an editor at The Atlantic Monthly *with whom business correspondence had taken a personal turn, Chandler recalled spending summers with the Fitts. "Ak-Sar-Ben," Nebraska spelled backward, is a social and philanthropical society; "Bryan" is a reference to William Jennings Bryan, a midwestern orator who ran unsuccessfully for the presidency in 1896, 1900, and 1908.*

I had an uncle in Omaha who was a minor politician–crooked, if I am any judge of character. I've been there a time or two. As a very small boy I used to be sent to spend part of the summer at Plattsmouth. I remember the oak trees and the high

Chandler's birth certificate (Cook County Clerk, Cook County, Illinois)

Chandler as a child. Written at the top of the picture is "Alfred and Raymond Chandler relaxing."

inspector or something, at least in name. He is dead now. I remember him very well. He used to come home in the evening (in the Plattsmouth period) put the paper on the music rack and improvise while he read it. I have read somewhere that Harold Bauer used to play his programmes through while reading a paper, but I always thought him a dull pianist, so it didn't surprise me. My uncle had talent, but no musical education. He had a brother who was an amazing character. He had been a bank clerk or manager in a bank in Waterford, Ireland (where all my mother's people come from, but none of them were Catholics) and had embezzled money. He cleaned out the till one Saturday and, with the help of the Masons, escaped the police net to the continent of Europe. In some hotel in Germany his money was stolen, or most of it. When I knew him, long after, he was an extremely respectable old party, always immaculately dressed, and of an incredible parsimony. He once invited me to dinner and to the Ak-Sar-Ben festivities. After the dinner he leaned over and in a confidential whisper said: "We'll each pay for our own." Not a drop of Scotch blood anywhere either. Pure

wooden sidewalks beside the dirt roads and the heat and the fireflies and walking-sticks and a lot of strange insects and the gathering of wild grapes in the fall to make wine and the dead cattle and once in a while a dead man floating down the muddy river and the dandy little three-hole privy behind the house. I remember Ak-Sar-Ben and the days when they were still trying to elect Bryan. I remember the rocking chairs on the edge of the sidewoak in a solid row outside the hotel and the tobacco spit all over the place. And I remember a trial run on a mail car with a machine my uncle invented to take on mail without stopping, but somebody beat him out of it and he never got a dime.

—*Selected Letters of Raymond Chandler,* pp. 33–34

* * *

In a 1 January 1945 letter to Morton, Chandler's reminiscence about Ernest Fitt led him to consider his Anglo-Irish roots.

My doubtfully honest uncle's (by marriage only) name was Ernest Fitt, and he was a boiler

Florence Thornton Chandler

Chandler in Ireland, circa 1896. As a boy, Chandler spent his summers in Waterford, Ireland, visiting his mother's relatives.

middle-class Protestant Irish. I have a great many Irish relatives, some poor, some not poor, and all Protestants and some of them Sinn Feiners and some entirely pro-British. The head of the family, if he is still living, is a very wealthy lawyer who hated the law, but felt obliged to carry on his father's firm. He had a housekeeper who came of a county family and did not regard my uncle (the lawyer one) as quite a gentleman because he was a solicitor. She used to say: There are only four careers for a gentleman, the Army, the Navy, the Church and the Bar. A barrister was a gentleman, but not a solicitor. This in spite of the fact that his son was a lieutenant in the Royal Navy and another of his relatives was Adjutant-General of the Royal Marines. With her he never lived down being a solicitor. An amazing people, the Anglo-Irish. They never mixed with Catholics socially. I remember playing on a cricket team with some of the local snobs and one of the players was a Catholic boy who came to the game in an elaborate chariot with grooms in livery; but he was not asked to have tea with the rest after the game. He wouldn't

have accepted, of course. People over here don't understand the Irish at all. A third of the population of Eire is Protestant, and it is by far the best educated and most influential third. Almost all the great Irish rebels were Protestants, and the whole tone of their present nation is Calvinistic rather than Catholic. I grew up with a terrible contempt for Catholics, and I have trouble with it even now. My uncle's snob housekeeper wouldn't have a Catholic servant in the house, although they were probably much better than the trash she did have. What a world! The rather amusing development in my uncle's case was that he took unto himself a Jewish mistress in London, raised her son, who was an illegitimate get of a couple of Sassoons, had two illegitimate children himself, and then married her. *But he never took her to Ireland!* I could make a book about these people, but I am too much of an Irishman myself ever to tell the truth about them.

—*Selected Letters of Raymond Chandler,* pp. 41–42

Two views of Dulwich College, one of the better public schools (private preparatory schools) in England, located in a London suburb (courtesy of the Governors of Dulwich College)

Dulwich College

In the fall of 1900, at the age of twelve, Chandler entered Dulwich College, where he received not only a classical education but also rigorous moral instruction. Arthur H. Gilkes, the head-master, sought to instill firm Christian values and a gentlemanly code of conduct in his students, and this moral atmosphere had a strong influence on Chandler's character. Gilkes's beliefs and per-sonality were described by Dulwich alumnus H. V. Doulton in these excerpts from his introduction to Gilkes and Dulwich: 1885–1914, *a school history published in honor of the headmaster.*

Dr. Welldon once said, wittily but truly, that the moment you met Gilkes you recognized that you were in the presence of a bigger man than yourself! With his Olympian build, he could not, indeed, fail to be a commanding figure in any gathering, but it required only a brief experience to realize that his majestic body was only the framework of a great personality. He was the most dignified man I have ever known. Entirely free from exaggeration of any kind, either of speech or gesture, he had a mind of striking originality, but his thoughts were clothed in words so simple, that you were continually wondering how the truth they expressed had hitherto escaped you. He had a beautiful voice which he used with great art, rarely lifting it, even in great assemblies, above the ordinary pitch, but always reaching the most distant parts of his audience. He *compelled* attention. With his imposing figure, and the majestic calm in which he moved, he was naturally regarded with awe by both boys and masters, but in the end, in most cases, this feeling changed to something warmer. and I, for one, came as near to loving him as was possible; possible, because there must always be something in the relations of a headmaster to his staff which must stop short of complete intimacy, and in Gilkes's case, one never got over the feeling that he was built of different and finer stuff than other men.

. . . .

He always took our forms in translation, and his visits—not perhaps quite such surprises as was supposed to be the case—were eagerly awaited by boys and masters alike. One most valuable thing he introduced was the practice of "Slips," which consisted of a few short questions on the prepared lesson, the answers to which were written and examined rapidly, so that if a boy had neglected his work, it was difficult for him to escape detection. Every boy had to have a notebook; this, he thought, helped to keep his attention. He always insisted on a strictly literal translation (I am, of course, speaking of my own form, Lower V), and woe betide a boy who served up an ill-digested note! "Together with

Arthur H. Gilkes, Headmaster of Dulwich College from 1885 to 1914

dawn appearing" was his rendering of an Homeric phrase; the translation does not sound very nice, but it does at least secure that a boy has understood clearly the meaning and relation of three Greek words, whereas "better English" might contain the seed of future error.

Gilkes's industry was amazing. The late Master, Mr. George Smith, who succeeded him, told me that on his appointment Gilkes gave him his time-table, and he was staggered to see that the teaching hours alone were practically those of a full-time form master. Besides Sixth Form work and his occasional visits to all the forms in turn, he regularly took work, English or Divinity, on all sides other than the Classical, so that he was constantly meeting all the senior boys of the School. He took boarders' "Prep," two hours in Hall twice a week—the four house masters doing one night each, and the extra lesson, two hours every Saturday afternoon, the staff sharing the corresponding duty on Wednesdays, which worked out for us at twice a year. I doubt if any headmaster in the world ever made such a division of labour. There was the weekly lesson for the Prefects, and their essays to be looked over; this was done partly in the evenings, fifteen minutes being given to each, and

Chandler as a student at Dulwich College

One of his rules we regretted on purely musical grounds—treble solos were absolutely taboo. This was a great musical loss, but he feared that to bring a young boy into prominence in this way was dangerous. He hated conceit, and thought this was at the bottom of most faults of character. Even his literary judgments were coloured by this conviction. "Cicero," he told the Sixth, "had a large plant of conceit growing in his heart, and he watered it every day." He was never, despite his keenness for the cricket, quite happy when a comparatively junior boy was tried in the XI; any junior who trespassed on a part of the ground reserved for seniors, was sure of a good "slating,' and what we should now, perhaps, welcome as an "expression of personality," Gilkes, I expect, would have often labelled "a disagreeable piece of self-assertion." But the difficulties caused by the occasional conflict of convenience and principle, were as nothing compared to the value of the encouragement he gave to every form of school activity.

. . . .

Discipline he considered to be the very corner-stone of the whole edifice. Very rarely did a masters' meeting, held regularly twice a term, pass without reference to "Points of Discipline," and though, perhaps, we got a little bored with hearing the same things so often, each man thinking, of course, that it was his neighbour who was being "got at," yet quite often enough we were uncomfortably conscious that he was getting under our guard. He was never tired of telling us that the best lesson was useless without discipline, by which he did not mean merely that the boys must not throw the inkpots about, but that a master must ensure that the attention of the whole class was kept active and alert. His own powers in this respect were remarkable: he could make himself most interesting, often by some quaint and original turn given to quotation or anecdote, and could see and hear everything. His control of a large audience was absolute : if a boy but whispered to his neighbour, the Master would break off and call on the boy by name to keep silent. If a boy appeared at Prayers in Hall in a garment of too bright a hue, he was liable to be haled out and sent to change. Boys were expected to go about in an orderly way, and to dress quietly. Punctuality was insisted on most strongly, both for boys and masters; if a master were late for his class, as likely as not he would find the Head standing in the passage, gazing reproachfully at his watch; if he were very late, he would probably find the Master sitting in his chair and the lesson started.

We had very few official punishments. Flogging were few and far between, and were used solely for very serious offences. There was an "Extra Lesson"

there were between twenty and thirty of them. Out of school hours there was not a single school activity that he did not encourage by his presence; gym., shooting, O.T.C., music, boxing—he found time for all. And there was nothing perfunctory about his visits: the boys knew he was really interested in what they were doing, and were thus greatly helped in their efforts to serve the School. We had four music practices every week: Gilkes attended them all. The choir practice, perhaps, demanded most from the boys, as the practice came at the end of a full day's work, and they had no instruments or apparatus to help to keep them interested. When, about half-time, the Master's tall figure was seen striding into the Hall, it had the effect of a trumpet-call to attention. At all rehearsals he was present throughout.

Page from the Dulwich library register for 1904, showing that Chandler checked out William Makepeace Thackeray's Vanity Fair *on 4 November. Other pages from the register reveal that Chandler borrowed Charles Lamb's* The Essays of Elia, *Thackeray's* The History of Henry Esmond, Esq., *and Thomas Carlyle's* Sartor Resartus *(courtesy of the Governors of Dulwich College).*

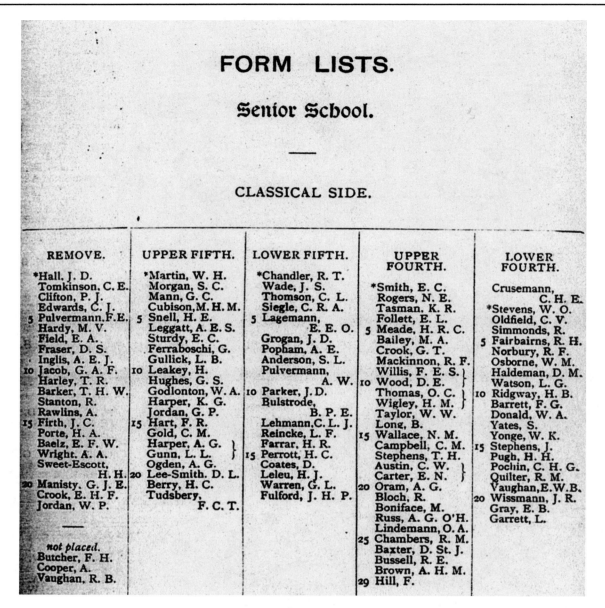

FORM LISTS.

Senior School.

—

CLASSICAL SIDE.

REMOVE.	UPPER FIFTH.	LOWER FIFTH.	UPPER FOURTH.	LOWER FOURTH.
*Hall, J. D.	*Martin, W. H.	*Chandler, R. T.	*Smith, E. C.	Crusemann, C. H. E.
Tomkinson, C. E.	Morgan, S. C.	Wade, J. S.	Rogers, N. E.	*Stevens, W. O.
Clifton, P. J.	Mann, G. C.	Thomson, C. L.	Tasman, K. R.	Oldfield, C. V.
Edwards, C. J.	Cubison, M. H. M.	Siegle, C. R. A.	Follett, E. L.	Simmonds, R.
5 Pulvermann, F. E.	5 Snell, H. E.	5 Lagemann, E. E. O.	5 Meade, H. R. C.	5 Fairbairns, R. H.
Hardy, M. V.	Leggatt, A. E. S.	Grogan, J. D.	Bailey, M. A.	Norbury, R. F.
Field, E. A.	Sturdy, E. C.	Popham, A. E.	Crook, G. T.	Osborne, W. M.
Fraser, D. S.	Ferraboschi, G.	Anderson, S. L.	Mackinnon, R. F.	Haldeman, D. M.
Inglis, A. E. J.	Gullick, L. B.	Pulvermann, A. W.	Willis, F. E. S. }	Watson, L. G.
10 Jacob, G. A. F.	10 Leakey, H.	10 Parker, J. D.	10 Wood, D. E. }	10 Ridgway, H. B.
Harley, T. R.	Hughes, G. S.	Bulstrode, B. P. E.	Thomas, O. C. }	Barrett, F. G.
Barker, T. H. W.	Godlonton, W. A.	Lehmann, C. L. J.	Wigley, H. M. }	Donald, W. A.
Stanton, R.	Harper, K. G.	Reincke, L. F.	Taylor, W. W.	Yates, S.
Rawlins, A.	Jordan, G. P.	Farrar, H. R.	Long, B.	Yonge, W. K.
15 Firth, J. C.	15 Hart, F. R.	15 Perrott, H. C.	15 Wallace, N. M.	15 Stephens, J.
Porte, H. A.	Gold, C. M.	Coates, D.	Campbell, C. M.	Pugh, H. H.
Baelz, E. F. W.	Harper, A. G. }	Leleu, H. J.	Stephens, T. H.	Pochin, C. H. G.
Wright, A. A.	Gunn, L. L. }	Warren, G. L.	Austin, C. W. }	Quilter, R. M.
Sweet-Escott, H. H.	Ogden, A. G.	Fulford, J. H. P.	Carter, E. N. }	Vaughan, E. W. B.
	20 Lee-Smith, D. L.		20 Oram, A. G.	20 Wissmann, J. R.
20 Manisty, G. J. E.	Berry, H. C.		Bloch, R.	Gray, E. B.
Crook, E. H. F.	Tudsbery, F. C. T.		Boniface, M.	Garrett, L.
Jordan, W. P.			Russ, A. G. O'H.	
			Lindemann, O. A.	
			25 Chambers, R. M.	
not placed.			Baxter, D. St. J.	
Butcher, F. H.			Bussell, R. E.	
Cooper, A.			Brown, A. H. M.	
Vaughan, R. B.			29 Hill, F.	

Christmas 1903 Form Lists for Dulwich College, showing Chandler ranking first in the Lower Fifth form (courtesy of the Governors of Dulwich College)

on half-holidays, but this, again, we were supposed to use very sparingly, and only where an offence had been committed involving disgrace, such as lying, cheating, or really gross idleness. Gilkes was very insistent about this, and the offence being serious, the Master was presumed to have reflected seriously before inflicting the punishment. Therefore when a boy's name was once in "the Book," in the boy had to go, no matter if his master had relented, or had been "got at" in the meantime. Departure from these principles provided a very common text for "Points of Discipline" at Masters' meetings. For the rest, we had to keep the boys in ourselves, or set written punishments, which were supposed to be short, insistence being laid on the work's being written as perfectly as possible. I am afraid this was a counsel of perfection, but it did us good to be reminded that impositions take a good deal longer to do than to set, and that the fewer the punishments, the better the discipline usually was. Still, it was remarkable how we got along without punishments; the work was good and the discipline was good, and it was the personality of the Master, influencing both masters and boys, which was responsible for this state of things. His own simple but dig-

House photograph of the Classical Lower Fifth at Dulwich, midsummer 1903. Chandler is circled
(courtesy of the Governors of Dulwich College).

nified bearing, his quiet utterance, and the complete absence of anything like posing, kept before the boys the idea that orderliness and manliness were not incompatible.

There were two offences that he treated with severity—smoking and swearing; he never actually expelled a boy for smoking, though it was often said that he did so. If a "smoker" was expelled, he was expelled for disobedience, deliberate and repeated, and the same fate awaited anyone who deliberately and repeatedly broke any other school rule; obviously this must always apply or discipline would disappear altogether. But there is no doubt that his attitude to smoking did arouse prejudice against him. I believe his objection was mainly based on medical grounds: in any case, his ideas were not so singular as people thought, and perhaps still think—Hawtrey, the great Headmaster of Eton, said that smoking was a beastly habit of which "no gentleman would be guilty," while Bradley, another of the great Headmasters, practically forbade the Marlborough masters to smoke at all. Gilkes always stopped visitors whom he saw smoking on the field, and often gave offence, especially to visiting cricket teams. With regard to the playing fields, the custom at

schools varies, but he was certainly going rather far when he told a master that he wished to resign his post if he met him smoking in the road.

Swearing angered him more than any other offence: he was said to have told a prefect that he would sooner see him dead than hear him swear! So strong was his feeling that he could hardly bring himself to utter "swear-words" when he came across them in works of literature. Here is another extract from the letter previously quoted: "He was reading that scene in 'Macbeth' when he came to the words 'Out damned spot.' He stopped, and said with that half humorous, very impressive little stammer of his, 'I am afraid I must say it,' and then said it with a peculiar emphasis which somehow seemed to me to combine his own dislike of the word, with a terrifying revelation of Lady Macbeth's despair." Once when the School XV was playing a match, I saw him march on to the football ground and give a most terrible dressing down to the captain of the opposing team who had very audibly and grossly offended.

Even mild slang was to him an unnecessary abuse of language: if you spoke of "Matric" or "Exam," he would as often as not correct you,

In a 3 December 1957 letter to Wesley Hartley, a California teacher who had sent him questions, Chandler recalled the education he received at the school and afterward.

I was educated at Dulwich College, an English Public School, not quite on a level with Eton and Harrow from a social point of view, but very good educationally. In my time they had two "sides," a Modern Side intended mostly for boys who expected to go into some sort of business, and a Classical Side for those who took Latin and Greek and expected to go to Oxford or Cambridge. I went up the Modern Side to the top and then switched down to the lowest form (class) in the senior school on the Classical side. I went up that to the form next to the Sixth, the top form. You usually stay in the Remove, as they call it, for a year before being sent on to the Sixth. I left school at seventeen—the usual leaving age then was before one's twentieth birthday, which was compulsory, I mean one had to leave before the 20th. birthday.

After this I had six months each in Paris and Germany. In Paris at school and in Germany with a private tutor. I could speak German well enough then to be taken for a German, but not now, alas, and the language has changed a lot (but I don't think the Germans will ever change). French one never speaks well enough to satisfy a Frenchman. Il sait se faire comprendre is about as far as they will go. Or Il parle très bien le français, mais (a shrug) l'accent—horrible!

—*Selected Letters of Raymond Chandler*, p. 458

C·CLARE
Hofphotograph   FREIBURG i/B
                             Holzmarktplatz 10.

Chandler as a young man in Germany

repeating the word very deliberately, but with a humorous expression which utterly removed all offensiveness. He objected to anything colloquial in reports, nor was the smart epigram encouraged. One of the most amusing and illuminating hours I ever spent was once when I was filling up House reports in his study. He was himself going through the School reports, and from time to time would read out one with comments not very flattering to the master responsible for it. One term we were singing an Irish piece in the choir: the word "Divil"—to an Irishman, merely a compliment or form of endearment—occurred frequently; it had always to be expunged.

This fastidiousness in the use of language—due probably to the fact that he was partly of Quaker origin—and his insistence on minute points of discipline, earned him, with people who did not take the trouble to understand his motives, the reputation of being faddy and finicking. Others were inclined to resent the control which he asserted over the boys even when away from the School—a difficulty which cannot arise in a boarding school. It was to some parents an intolerable interference for the school to claim authority even in a boy's own home, and it was difficult, if not impossible, to enforce the claim; nevertheless, the fact that it was made helped to establish the principle that, though day boys, they were yet members of a great institution, and that membership involved loyal obedience to rules, and a responsibility for the good name of the School. Gilkes thought that for the boys to meet just for work and play and then to separate and be free of all constraint, so far as the School was concerned, would be to impair the most valuable and most distinctive thing a public school has to teach—a proper sense of discipline, which is not for times and places, but is an all-pervading principle of the good life, both at school and afterwards.

A London Writer

Following his departure from Dulwich, Chandler traveled in Europe to study languages, then returned to England and took a clerk's job with the British Admiralty. He left this position after six months and decided to pursue a career writing essays and poems for London journals.

In this excerpt from his 11 December 1950 letter to his English publisher and friend Hamish Hamilton, Chandler recalled the difficulties he had in trying to make his way as a writer in London.

J. A. Spender was editing the *Westminster Gazette* in the days when I worked for it. I got an introduction to him from a very charming old boy named Blennerhassett, a landed proprietor in Ireland, a barrister with, I think, a House of Lords' practice. It seems to me that I have written to you about him before. He was the sort of man who could make a frightened young nobody feel at ease in the company of the cream of patrician society. Spender put me up for the National Liberal Club in order that I might have the use of its reading room, and I used to browse through the French and German papers looking for odd paragraphs and news items which could be translated and adapted for a column the *Westminster Gazette* ran. Spender thought I could make six guineas a week out of this, but I don't think I ever made more than about three. I wrote quite a lot of verses for him also, most of which now seem to me deplorable, but not all, and a good many sketches, mostly of a satirical nature—the sort of thing that Saki did so infinitely better. I still have a couple of them somewhere, and they now seem to me very precious in tone. But I suppose they weren't so bad, considering how little valid experience I had to back them up. Of course Naomi Royde-Smith may have been connected with the Westminster at that time, but I never personally came into contact with her. As a matter of fact, I had only the most limited personal contact with Spender. I would send the stuff in, and they would either send it back or send me proof. I never corrected the proof, didn't even know whether I was expected to. I simply took it as a convenient form of acceptance. I never waited for them to send me the money but appeared regularly on a certain day each week at their cashier's office and received payment in gold and silver, being required to affix a penny stamp in a large book and sign my name across it by way of receipt. What a strange world it seems now! I suppose I have told you of the time I wrote to Sir George Newnes and offered to buy a piece of his trashy but successful weekly magazine called *Tit-Bits*. I was received most courteously by a secretary, definitely public school, who regretted that the publication was not in need of capital, but said that my approach

had at least the merit of originality. By the same device I did actually make a connection with *The Academy,* then edited and owned by a man named Cowper, who had bought it from Lord Alfred Douglas. He was not disposed to sell an interest in his magazine, but pointed to a large shelf of books in his office and said they were review copies and would I care to take a few home to review. I wonder why he did not rather have me thrown down his murky stairs; perhaps because there was no one in the office who could do it since his entire editorial staff seemed to consist of one placid middle-aged lady and a mousy little man, named Vizetelly, who was (I believe) the brother of another and more famous Vizetelly—the one who was arrested in New York in connection with an obscenity complaint over the American publication of the translation of *Madame Bovary.* I met there also a tall, bearded, and sad-eyed man called Richard Middleton, of whom I think you may have heard. Shortly afterwards he committed suicide in Antwerp, a suicide of despair, I should say. The incident made a great impression on me, because Middleton struck me as having far more talent than I was ever likely to possess; and if he couldn't make a go of it, it wasn't very likely that I could. Of course in those days as now there were popular and successful writers, and there were clever young men who made a decent living as free lances for the numerous literary weeklies and in the more literary departments of the daily papers. But most of the people who did this work either had private incomes or jobs, especially in the civil service. And I was distinctly not a clever young man. Nor was I at all a happy young man. I had very little money, although there was a great deal of it in my family. I had grown up in England and all my relatives were either English or Colonial. And yet I was not English. I had no feeling of identity with the United States, and yet I resented the kind of ignorant and snobbish criticism of Americans that was current at that time. During my year in Paris I had run across a good many Americans, and most of them seemed to have a lot of bounce and liveliness and to be thoroughly enjoying themselves in situations where the average Englishman of the same class would be stuffy or completely bored. But I wasn't one of them. I didn't even speak their language. I was, in effect, a man without a country. Having passed third (and first on the classical list) in an open civil service examination, I could have had a life-long and perfectly safe job with six weeks' vacation every year and ridiculously easy hours. And yet I thoroughly detested the civil service. I had too much Irish in my blood to stand being pushed around by suburban nobodies. The idea of being expected to tip my hat to the head of the department struck me as verging on the obscene. All in all, perhaps I ought to have stayed in Paris, although I never really liked the French. But you didn't exactly have to like the French to be at home in Paris. And you could always like some of them. On the other hand, I did like the Germans very much, that is the South Germans. But there wasn't much sense living in Germany, since it was an open secret, openly discussed, that we would be at war with them almost any time now. I suppose it was the most inevitable of all wars. There was never any question about whether it would happen. The only question was when.

—*Selected Letters of Raymond Chandler,* pp. 248–250

Of the poems published by Raymond Chandler between 1908 and 1912, twenty-seven have been located and collected by Matthew J. Bruccoli in Chandler Before Marlowe *(1973). The following poems show the romantic sensibility and chivalric themes that are typical of Chandler's early writing.*

In a 1955 interview published in Twentieth Century Authors, *Chandler recalled, "My first poem was composed at the age of nineteen, on a Sunday, in the bathroom, and was published in* Chambers's Journal. *I am fortunate in not possessing a copy, but I can remember some of it and I think it would go over well if recited by Margaret O'Brien." "The Unknown Love" is the first Chandler poem to appear in* Chambers's Journal; *it was published in the 19 December 1908 issue.*

The Unknown Love

When the evening sun is slanting,
When the crickets raise their chanting,
And the dewdrops lie a-twinkling on the grass,
As I climb the pathway slowly,
With a mien half proud, half lowly,
O'er the ground your feet have trod I gently pass.

Round the empty house I wander,
Where the ivy now is fonder
Of your memory than those long gone away;
And I feel a sweet affection
For the plant that lends protection
To the window whence you looked on me that day.

Was it love or recognition,
When you stormed my weak position
And made prisoner my heart for evermore?
For I felt I long had known you,
That I'd knelt before the throne you
Graced in Pharaoh's days or centuries before.

Though your face from me was hidden,
Yet the balm was not forbidden
On your coffin just to see the wreath I sent.
Though no word had passed between us,
Yet I felt that God had seen us
And had joined your heart to mine e'en as you went.

Let them talk of love and marriage,
Honeymoon and bridal carriage,
And the glitter of a wedding à la mode!
Could they understand the union
Of two hearts in dear communion
Who were strangers in the world of flesh and blood?

In my eyes the tears are welling
As I stand before your dwelling,
In my pilgrimage to where you lived, my fair.
And ere I return to duty
In this world of weary beauty,
To the stillness of the night I breathe my prayer:

When the last great trump has sounded,
When life's barque the point has rounded,
When the wheel of human progress is at rest,
My beloved, may I meet you,
With a lover's kiss to greet you,
Where you wait me in the gardens of the blest!

R. T. CHANDLER.
—*Chandler Before Marlowe,* pp. 3–4

* * *

The Wheel.

The world expends its useless might,
The heaving nations toil and fight,
The dizzy thinker peers for light,
The day doth follow day and night,
    Is there no rest from anything?

The lover gives another heart,
The merchant finds another mart,
The young men have their lives to start,
The old reluctantly depart,
    Is there no rest from anything?

The gloomy sigh that life is pain,
The buoyant call each day a gain,
The doubter cries that nought is plain,
The cynic sneers that hope is vain,
    Is there no rest from anything?

The worshippers their gods appease,
The tortured sinner moans for ease,
The speed of things doth not decrease,
The Wheel of Things doth never cease,
    Is there no rest from anything?

What is the end of toil and thought?
What is the jewel we have sought?
What is the work that we have wrought?
Can nothingness end but in nought?
    Can there be rest from anything?

"Fool! rest shall come when stones can feel,
Fool! rest shall come when poisons heal,
Fool! rest comes not at thy appeal,
Fool! thou art bound upon the Wheel,
    There is no rest from anything!"

R. T. CHANDLER.

Poem published in the 26 March 1909 issue of the
Westminster Gazette

This poem was published in the 2 June 1909 issue of Westminster Gazette.

The Quest

I sought among the trampling herds of men
    That choke the cities of the east and west.
The proudest mansion and the foulest den
    I entered, seeking wisdom yet unguessed.
I searched them through unpausing, without rest,
    Until the bricks and plaster of each wall
Became transparent at my thought's behest,
    But still I could not hear the Master's call.

I wandered on the moorland and the fen,
    I climbed the mountain to its silent crest,
I watched the robin redbreast and the wren
    Choose out the leaves wherewith to build a nest.
I looked upon the plain by dawn caressed,
    I saw its contours gaunt beneath night's pall.
All nature told her tale at my behest,
    But still I could not hear the Master's call.

I thought to keep all knowledge in a pen,
    All human hardship was to me a test,
There seemed naught undiscovered to my ken,
    But that I sought I found nowhere expressed.
I left my learning for a maiden's breast,
    I scorned my wisdom to become her thrall,
Blasphemed my task at her unspoke behest,
    But still I could not hear the Master's call.

She spurned the love which all my soul possessed,
    She threw it down and jested at its fall.
I laughed and turned to recommence my quest,
    And in the laugh I heard the Master's call.

                      R. T. CHANDLER
                –*Chandler Before Marlowe, pp. 14–15*

                        * * *

This poem was first published in the 1 March 1912 issue of Westminster Gazette.

The King

The night doth cut with shadowy knife
In half the kingdom of the sun;
The red dawn meets with her in strife;–
Vassal of mine I hold each one.

The sailors chant beside the mast,
The tempest lash the riven foam,
But I, the King, am striding fast
Before the prow, to guide it home.

I am the lover wed to tears,
I am the cynic cold and sage,
I am the ghost of noble years,
I am the prophet lapp'd in rage.

I am the fane no longer trod
That moulders on the wild hill-brow;
I am the fresh and radiant god
To whom the young religions bow.

Perfection woo'd in many a guise
Is in my charge, a stabled beast;
The myriad moons look from my eyes;
The worlds unnam'd sit at my feast.

My glance is in the splendid noon,
The golden orchid blown of heat;
My brow is as the South lagoon,
And all the stars are at my feet.

The lost waves moan: I made their song.
The lost lands dream: I wove their trance.
The earth is old, and death is strong;
Stronger am I, the true Romance.

                    R. T. CHANDLER
             –*Chandler Before Marlowe, pp. 46–47*

When Chandler began writing for The Academy in 1911, he contributed essays on art, literature, and culture. Eight of these essays were located by Bruccoli and published in Chandler Before Marlowe. The three examples below show Chandler's dealing with the issues of pretension, realism, and the idea of the hero—themes that resurfaced in his detective fiction some thirty years later.

This essay was first published in the 19 August 1911 issue of The Academy.

The Genteel Artist
The Academy, 81 (19 August 1911): 250

Perhaps there was once a day when the artist was a man of toil, capable of vying in industry with the farm labourer and of excelling him in most things else. One likes, for example, to think of those mediæval gilders and carvers and stainers as sitting all day from dawn till dusk by leaded panes in queer old silent houses, plying their tasks with relentless perseverance, careless of the weather and the antics of history. One likes to think of them taking frugal meals beside their work, munching an apple while putting the finishing touches to a gilded devil, holding the tankard with one hand and the brush with the other. One feels sure that when the night came they went to bed with a very pleasant weariness, slept soundly, and did not lie awake wondering how they had managed to foozle at the eighth green. No doubt their pleasures were simple; and the invention of some slight artistic device was the joy of many weeks. They lived quiet lives and died quiet deaths, leaving behind them arts which we mimic with a vain superficiality.

Cover for the issue of The Academy *that included Chandler's essay "The Genteel Artist." Chandler contributed to the journal in 1911 and 1912.*

No doubt, like all enthusiasts, they were capable of quarrelling violently over very small details. No doubt they were on occasion careless of their morals, and rather neglected to arrange the universe and to populate Valhalla according to their private moods. They had their faults, being human; but when we turn from them to their successors of these days, how very favourable to them is the comparison! How very garish seem the surroundings of the prosperous ladies and gentlemen who paint our successful pictures and write our successful books; the pleasant people who sit in padded chairs before mahogany writing-tables, wielding gold-banded fountain pens or dictating in a leisurely manner over a choice cigar or cigarette!

There appeared once, in one of those popular articles on contemporary painters which have long been a feature of a certain magazine, the portrait of a gentleman standing elegantly before the easel upon which one of his own creations reposed. A spotless silk handkerchief peeped from his pocket, his cuffs were stiff and white as if they had only just left the haberdasher's, his beard was as trim as an aristocratic shrubbery, the crease in his trousers was perfect, the cut of his coat ideal, the radiance of his shoes all that dreams could desire. He had a negligent air, as of being about to do something interesting with a perfect ease and politeness. A cigarette drooped from the corner of his mouth, and his half-closed eyes seemed more intent upon the floating smoke than on anything else in this transient world. In the background were rich curtains and expensive furniture. Beneath his feet was a thick carpet upon which presumably no spot of paint had ever fallen. And the sum total of one's idea of this gentleman was that he was in no danger of producing a great painting. He might be a charming companion, he was more than well-groomed, and he was very possibly more than usually clever. But the beholder felt quite sure that he was not a great artist. He had never felt the sweet bitterness of the garret, he had never dreamed a day away on a hillside, he had never shuddered at a vision or wept over a fantastic sorrow. Or, if he had, at a simpler age, done any of these things, the experience had left no mark, and had not made him any more cunning in his work.

The story goes, it is true, of one great painter of a past century who always attired himself for his easel as if for a fashionable gathering, in the stiffest of ruffs, the richest of velvet, and the most costly lace. And it is easy to sympathise with his attitude. He looked upon his art as something to be attempted only in a perfect purity of mind and body; he clad himself for his work as the bride for her wedding or the young girl for her first Communion. And if any such sentiment was present in the breasts of our modern genteel artists and writers, one could welcome it and approve. But to them their art is a business or a whim or a side issue of some sort, a thing to do for a couple of hours in the evening before dinner. It would never be permitted to interfere with a social function or a motor-excursion. It would never

cause its devotees to miss a meal or to bundle a friend out of the room with a vigorous rudeness. It would never produce exhaustion or the sweat of a terrible toil. Its creators do not weep like Dickens over their imaginary deathbeds nor tremble like Poe at the horror of their own visions. They do not sit for impotent hours over a blank sheet, nor revile all created things because they cannot attain the impossible. So far from being a religion their art is scarce even a profession; it is merely an exercise. They may gather fortunes, but they are never more than dilettanti, and the poorest hack of Grub-street or the most utterly forgotten carver of Ghent is their better.

Art is not the be-all and end-all even of this present life, and it is possible for the artist to take himself and his work far too seriously. One would not have every poet and painter possessed of devils; but surely a touch of fanaticism makes for great achievement. Art has, in these days, real and apparent enemies which it never had in ages of infinitely less widespread culture, and the artist who aspires to the meagrely-rewarded success of true distinction will get through the easier if he be lightly touched with fanaticism. Nothing in a man of character breeds this healthy fanaticism more certainly than a little hardship and want of luxury. Other things being equal, one feels that a great poem is more likely to be written on a deal table than on an article of inlaid rosewood. The genius in the garret may have an uncomfortable time in many ways, but he has one great advantage over his more luxurious rivals—he is compelled to throw himself body and soul into his work. He must live with it entirely. All moods and all hours must contribute their inspiration to it, all sensations of the mind and body must wait upon it, every thought and impression must carve some line, however faint, in its ideal structure. The night spreads her wings about it, all the colours of the sun light it up, all the noises of the city, all the voices of Nature are somehow echoed in it. It lies as close to life as any work of man may lie, and in the result, be it failure or success, it has not lacked attention. The garreteer, whether he eventually dies famous or completely unknown, has been worthy of his craft. But the genteel artist, in his expensive study or studio, smiled upon by electric lights, flattered by costly mirrors, embraced by Russia-leather chairs, can seldom make any such claim. His successes are usually mere *tours de force,* like juggling with billiard balls, noteworthy only because they amuse and because not everyone can imitate them. He turns out a novel or a painting as neatly and as coldly as the machine turns out the packed ounce of tobacco, and probably in the general scheme of things the three products are of similar value.

R. T. CHANDLER.
—*Chandler Before Marlowe,* pp. 55–58

* * *

The Remarkable Hero

The Academy, 81 (9 September 1911): 322

The time is not distant beyond the memory of living men when the hero of a typical novel had to be, if not a person of title, at any rate a man of tolerable family. If, in the days of his affluence, he did not possess a valet, or if when leaving home under a cloud he could not bestow his last sovereign on a head gardener, he was not likely to have many admirers. The snobbishness of those days was not greater than the snobbishness of these, but it was far simpler and more straightforward. It demanded quite honestly, on behalf of the middle-class reader, to mix with its social betters. No doubt it was perfectly right; if a man cannot choose his company even in novels things are in a bad way. But, however that may be, the distinction of the hero of that time was on the side of birth and breeding. He might be compelled by circumstances to associate with coal-heavers, but even when his coat was shiny at the elbows the cabmen called him "My lord." When be told the landlady of his humble lodging that he had come into a marquisate and forty thousand a year, she always reminded him that she had known him at the first for a "real gent." His brains might be of feeble quality—indeed they usually were—but his manners were of the best. He might not know how to counter the most childish plot, but he invariably knew what to do with his hands in a drawing-room, a problem which has puzzled more people than ever troubled about the riddles of life and death.

In these days, however, good breeding is usually left as a minor perquisite to the villain. The hero may, as far as his social position is concerned, be anybody. He may drop his aspirates, he may be a boor, he may be ignorant of the most elementary rules of polite behaviour. Common honesty is not in the least a necessity to him. If he is fiendishly ugly, his adventures are all the more piquant. He may even be deformed, and his Life will sell in tens of thousands. He may squint, he may be club-footed, he may wear ready-made clothes, he may smoke in church, he may shoot foxes, he may browbeat women and patronise old men, he may do any of those forbidden things, for doing the least of which we would cut our dearest friends, and yet he may charm voracious multitudes. We care nothing for his clothes, nor his manners nor his antecedents nor his actions; in these respects we are all-tolerant. But there is one quality which we demand in him: he must be a remarkable person. It matters very little in what his fate lies, whether in art, finance, sport, politics, exploration, swindling, or throat-cutting, but his intellect must be of the cast of great men.

The superficial reason is not very far to seek. Satirised out of his old, honest, matter-of-fact reverence for rank and wealth, the commonplace reader has to satisfy his inborn humility looking up to an intellectual superior. Forbidden to act the flunkey to the aristocrat, he allows himself to adore the prima donna, the brilliant statesman, the swaggering freebooter, or the subtle master of intrigue. As he can no longer delight in the conversation of a duke, he accepts instead the conversation of an eminent house-breaker. And seeing that, however slight his knowledge of aristocratic circles might have been, his acquaintance with men of genius is even slighter—he is seldom able to detect the fraud which is so often played upon him. He may have a shrewd conception of how a duke would behave in a given situation, but a man of genius is above laws, and his actions are therefore incalculable. So the reader takes, with shut eyes and open mouth, whatever the journeyman novelist cares to offer him in the way of inspired heroes. He is unaware that the great detective whom he so much admires is as unlike any possible great detective as he is unlike a Patagonian anteater; these mysterious and incomprehensible actions pass not, as they should, for the well-meaning, but rather futile, efforts of an uninspired writer to simulate inspiration, but for the unfathomable deeds of a demigod. The more extraordinary they are, the more convinced is the reader of his hero's genuineness. In the result, one reads of a great realistic author who studies his situations by kidnapping people, and forcing them to act for him; one finds a great thief who lives, surrounded by *objets d'art,* in a castle in the middle of a sea-girt rock; one finds a great poet who, by way of seeking inspiration, wanders like a mad-man over the face of the earth for several months, then, returning home, scribbles for four days without stopping, and finally falls dead over his completed masterpiece. The convenience for a second-rate author of a public which accepts such creations may easily be estimated. If extravagane be a sign of genius, then it is infinitely easier to portray genius than mediocrity. The man in the street is quite capable of judging his kind, but to judge the weird antics of an inspired soul he has only the unreliable experience of nightmares. He can but devour and hold out his innocent hands for more. So the curious fashion grows, until the remarkable becomes more common than the commonplace; an amusing development enough, if one does not pause to reflect how swiftly this highly-seasoned fare can destroy any lingering taste for the products of a restrained and disciplined art.

[Unsigned]
—Chandler Before Marlowe, pp. 59–61

January 6, 1912   THE ACADEMY   5

REALISM AND FAIRYLAND

FAIRYLAND is Everyman's dream of perfection, and changes, dreamlike, with the mood of the dreamer. For one it is a scene of virgin, summery Nature undefiled by even the necessary works of man. For another it is a place where there exist no codes, conventions, or moral laws, and where people love or hate at sight, having their virtues and vices writ large upon them. For another it is a champaign dotted with fine castles, in which live sweet ladies clad in silk, spinning, and singing as they spin, and noble knights who do courteous battle with each other in forest glades; or a region of uncanny magic, haunting music, elves and charmed airs and waters. For still another it may be an anarchy of the beautiful touched with terror, tenanted by spirits who must be propitiated with cakes left on the window-sill and soft words spoken up the chimney at night. No two minds see fairyland alike or demand like gifts from it, and to the same fancy it alters from day to day, as the winds change which blow about a house, and with as little apparent reason. Nevertheless it gives by contraries so accurate a reflection of life that the spirit of an age is more essentially mirrored in its fairy-tales than in the most pains-taking chronicle of a contemporary diarist.

The visions of what is called idealism are only reflections of fairyland and its experiences; they share with the scenes of that wonderful domain the merit of telling the truth about those who see them, and of telling it the more clearly because unconsciously. Yet there have arisen in the last half-century, more or less, certain long-faced, earnest, intent, and seemingly very daring people, who inform us sadly that we must look dull facts in the face if we would see truth, that we must not delude ourselves with rosy dreams or golden castles in Spain. By way of showing us how to proceed they rake over the rubbish-heaps of humanity in its close alleys and noisome slums to find fragments of broken moral crockery, to nose out the vices of unfortunate people, to set upon them the worst possible interpretation for the social system, and, by the simple process of multiplication, to construct from them what they consider typical human beings. Determining to hide nothing, and to show every side of life impartially, they forget that the things which necessarily strike them most in their impartial survey and appear most emphatic in their work are mere offal of the senses; as a man with a delicate sense of smell would find unpleasant odours the chief feature of life in a hovel of disease. Boldly declaring that they will cast aside all factitious optimism, they automatically choose the dark aspect of all things in order to be on the safe side; as a result unpleasantness becomes associated in their minds with truth, and if they wish to produce a faultlessly exact portrait of a man, all they need do is to paint his weaknesses and then, for the sake of propitiating the instinct of kindness left by some oversight in their hearts, to explain that his shortcomings are the inevitable consequences of a mistaken scheme of life. There remains only to set down the man thus portrayed in a *milieu*, the dulness, sordidness, and stuffiness of which is "reproduced" with a monotonous and facile elaboration hitherto unknown in art, and a masterpiece of realism is obtained. It is hardly surprising that when such stuff is given to tired and overworked men and women with unsteady nerves as a study for their leisure hours, it is apt to cause a certain flavour of despondency and pessimism to become

characteristic of the time, with the social result that if any difficult problem of life clamours to be solved those best equipped for solving it have utterly lost all youthful hope and cheer and have no energy for the labour. They pass on with sighs, leaving the task to bureaucrats and party politicians.

It is an old sneer, no doubt, that realism is a picker-up of life's refuse, and it may be just that any point of view which belongs to a large class of people should find representation in art. But it has never been proved to the satisfaction of the most reasonable and easily convinced visionary that the realistic is a definite point of view. For in truth it is only the mood of every man's dull and depressed hours. We are all realists at times, just as we are all sensualists at times, all liars at times, and all cowards at times. And if it be urged that for this very reason, because it is human, realism is essential to art, the obvious answer comes, that this claim entitles it at most to a niche in the temple, not as at present to a domination of the whole ritual, and that truth in art, as in other things, should not be sought by that process of exhaustion encouraged so fatally in our age by the pedants of science, and by their fallacy that it may be discovered by considering all the possibilities: a method which surrenders intuition and all the soul's fine instincts to receive in exchange a handful of theories, which, compared with the infinite forms of immortal truth known to the gods, are as a handful of pebbles to a thousand miles of shingly beach.

Faulty as its philosophy is, however, the realistic creed which dominates our literature is not due so much to bad theories as to bad art. To be an idealist one must have a vision and an ideal; to be a realist, only a plodding, mechanical eye. Of all forms of art realism is the easiest to practise, because of all forms of mind the dull mind is commonest. The most unimaginative or uneducated person in the world can describe a dull scene dully, as the worst builder can produce an ugly house. To those who say that there are artists, called realists, who produce work which is neither ugly nor dull nor painful, any man who has walked down a commonplace city street at twilight, just as the lamps are lit, can reply that such artists are not realists, but the most courageous of idealists, for they exalt the sordid to a vision of magic, and create pure beauty out of plaster and vile dust.

R. T. C.

A LOST LITERARY ART

By J. E. PATTERSON

WHERE are they?—those old correctors of men's excesses, women's foibles, the warpings of the times, the nonsensical vagaries of "Movements," and the leeway of a nation's tendencies—where are they? Those strenuous wielders of the lash of satire, who cared for no man that did not act aright, who feared no dishonest organisation no matter how powerful, and respected nothing that did not make for British integrity and general welfare—where are they? Gone, alas! with the wigs, the snuff-boxes, and the coloured clothes of our grandfathers. Yes, gone; and the nation is left the poorer for their going. Of course, they had to go; that they could not last indefinitely was a mere unit in the common order of things. Of that it were puerile and useless

Chandler's fifth contribution to The Academy

Jacques Barzun, a literary critic and professor at Columbia University, wrote the introductory essay for Chandler Before Marlowe. *In "The Young Raymond Chandler" Barzun assesses Chandler's early poems and essays and identifies themes that would be refined later in Chandler's detective fiction.*

As an essayist, Chandler is known to the general public solely as the author of "'The Simple Art of Murder." This sentimental piece glorifying the tough American tale and its hero has been much reprinted because it expresses a number of emotions that continue to haunt the insecure American mind: hostility to things English, resentment against both convention and corruption, and self-pity over the common lot, mixed with the illusion of self-reliance in the effort to down surrounding evils.

One of the interesting results of going back to Chandler's early essays and verse is to find the germs of these attitudes in a young writer who was not reared in America and who harbored them many years before the disillusionment of the Great Depression. But before one looks at these early records of feeling and opinion, it is only right to bear in mind one critical fact: whereas the "philosophy" of Philip Marlowe, the Galahad-detective, deserves only a smile when inspected in essay form, it is dramatically right for a hero in his situation, private and professional; and as such it is a splendid source of motive power in the great tales of Chandler's maturity.

Nor should the reader conclude that Chandler was nothing more than a story-teller. In the letters and other writings of his novelistic period that have been published and anthologized, he shows himself a better and sterner mind than in his war-horse essay on fictional murder. He is never an exact critic, but he often manages some detachment from his sense of wrong, and what he says suggests that he has read and reflected on literature at large, and not merely English and American detective fiction.

Now, thanks to the enterprise and devotion of Mr. Matthew Bruccoli, Chandler's admiring readers can round out their picture of the man and his mind, a mind that I think will seem in retrospect quite representative of the age. What is unusual about it is that its characteristic traits were in evidence well before Marlowe, before the Marxist Thirties, before the invention of Southern California as the natural theater of crime and concentrated vulgarity.

About Chandler's verses there is little to say except that they are without merit of any kind. The most searching detection does not discover one line capable of sticking in the memory, even when the author lifts whole phrases from Blake or Wordsworth. Only three pieces (one of them quite late and presumably inspired by the death of his wife) show any knowledge of contemporary diction and technique. What strikes us in the reading is the recurrent theme of being weighed down by some unnamed tyranny and the equally frequent defiance of it by the heroic ego. The poet calls upon Art or Thought or some other underdog entity to make war upon the resistless conspiracy of material interests. The verse, in short, contains in essence the root idea of all the later tales.

Now it is true that the primacy of art and beauty was a favorite theme of the Symbolist period in which Chandler came of age. But when be began to publish, the Nineties had *established* the superiority of art over commerce and politics and there was no reason, except in Chandler's inner self, for feeling put upon. That (as Marlowe might say) is the fishy bit that provides us with a clue.

Turn next to the essays, and observe that the first three, all in the last months of 1911, sound the note of angry dissent: "The Literary Fop," "The Genteel Artist," and "The Remarkable Hero" exhibit as many aspects of resentment tinged with envy, the target being the esthete. A literature of refinement is hateful to the young Chandler, and it is he who in connection with it raises the spectre of "the barricades." His later assumption that whatever is elegant is both sissyfied and corrupt underlies these short but effective diatribes, even though literature, not life, is their ostensible object.

For the positive side, we need only refer to "Realism and Fairyland," in which "life's refuse" (= realism) is embraced and equated with what is truly human, besides being representative of "a large class of people." Populism, realism, and moral egalitarianism are declared the premises of true art. By moral egalitarianism I mean the proposition that "We are all realists at times, just as we are all sensualists at times, all liars at times, and all cowards at times." This would be hard to prove, especially as to realism and sensuality, but as a political philosophy for novels of crime and corruption, it is perfect.

I do not want to spoil the reader's pleasure by going on and making a demonstration out of what should remain a suggestion, a quick look at the natural bent of Chandler's mind from his earliest days in literature. But two other small points are relevant and corroborative. One is the care and compression of the young man's prose. Chandler at 23 is in command of his means and enjoys putting things just so—even when he derides "the Phrasemaker." The other point is his insistence on one or two ideas, whether in verse or prose. That is unusual in so young a writer. The obsessive character of his thought, which gives the novels much of their power, is right here, full force, in these youthful pages, so happily gathered and restored to our inquisitive but sympathetic glance.

—*Chandler Before Marlowe*, pp. ix–xii

In addition to sketches and essays, Chandler also contributed unsigned book reviews to The Academy. *In a letter looking back on his days as a reviewer, he recalled, "I seldom got the best books to review, and in fact the only one of importance I got my hands on was* The Broad Highway *(Jeffrey Farnol) for whose author, then unknown, I am glad to say I predicted an enormous popularity. I reviewed Elinor Glyn and how. Like all young nincompoops I found it very easy to be clever and snotty, very hard to praise without being ingenuous." The following two reviews were first published in the 18 March 1911 issue of* The Academy.

Untitled Review of Jeffrey Farnol's *The Broad Highway*

It is possible that Mr. Jeffrey Farnol has not read "Lavengro," or that, having read it, he had yet no idea of making his present hero a recreation of George Borrow's romantic picture of himself. Yet Lavengro was an unusual person, not to be confounded with the common ruck of men, and it would be hard to believe that one who reflects many of his characteristic traits so closely as does Peter Vibart should have no connection with him. Firstly, as if to clinch the matter, Mr. Farnol has put his hero in the same epoch, amid similar scenes, and has made him what Lavengro was above all things—a wanderer. So good a reflection of Lavengro is Peter Vibart, indeed, that he possesses the same disabilities as that romantic but inestimable person. Mr. Farnol tries to fill him with a great love-passion, but the thing is impossible; the man who loves Charmian in the second part of "The Broad Highway" is not the Peter Vibart of the first half, but an ordinary moonstruck hero of sentimental romance, a creature of hothouse moods and unnatural speeches.

For the detailed account of his adventures we must refer the reader to the book itself, and he will be a person of very jaded appetite indeed who does not relish the freshness, the quietness, and the queer Borrow touch about Peter's encounter with the boastful pugilist, "Cragg by name and craggy by nature," and with the farmer who coveted his waistcoat, but with whom Peter refused to breakfast because his would-be host could not believe that that magnificent article of attire had cost 40s. in London. Then there was the affair of the insolent dandies, the duel in which Peter for the first time caught a distant glimpse of his cousin, the rescue of a damsel in distress from two offensive abductors, and her restoration to her lover, the meeting with the madman who was dogging Peter with murderous intent, and many other roadside happenings.

With the opening of the second part comes the entry of Charmian into the haunted cottage, on a night of storm, and pursued by Maurice Vibart. With him Peter does furious battle in the darkness, and at length sends him away unconscious in his own post-chaise.

With these events, too, comes the degeneration of the story in manner though not, perhaps, in plot. The old solemn Borrow touch is gone, and with it the subtly humorous conversations and the atmosphere of pure romance. In their stead we have all the feverishness and over-rapidity of the second-rate sensational writer. The love passages of Charmian and Peter are forced and wearisome, and the doings of Black George, when maddened by jealousy, are told with that gloomy extravagance which suggests disordered nerves in the writer. Mr. Farnol regains something of his former quiet incisiveness in narrating Peter's escape from justice, when, the madman having at last found and killed his enemy, Peter suspects Charmian of the crime, and takes it upon himself; but the end, with its almost hysterical reconciliation of Peter and Charmian, who is, of course, the Lady Sophia Sefton of Cambourne, is but feeble stuff. It is impossible not to regret deeply the defects of the second half of Mr. Farnol's book, yet the first half is really very good. It is fine work of an uncommon order, and not merely a promise of future worth. We judge Mr. Farnol to be a young writer, and we do not at all regret his occasional crudeness, since it is merely undisciplined strength. But he must learn to avoid the feverish touch; that more than anything is death to true romance.

[Unsigned]
—Chandler Before Marlowe, pp. 85–86

* * *

Untitled Review of Elinor Glyn's *The Reason Why*

The frontispiece to Mrs. Glyn's latest novel is, in a way, a far better criticism of it than anything a hasty reviewer can write. It depicts a well-preserved lady of tall stature and voluptuous outlines throwing aside a fur cloak lined with amethyst silk in order to display a sort of bathing costume of sapphire blue, which appears to be her only garment. This article of attire reveals a quantity of white and rather pasty skin, an equally white and pasty face, with a ruby smear for a mouth, and two large, but not at all inscrutable, eyes. In the ears are pearl drops of such size as to be immediately set down as false, and the whole vision is surmounted by a badly-made wig of violent auburn hue.

Such is Zara, Countess Schulski, as seen by the powerful imagination of the enthusiastic illustrator. As a matter of fact, Zara is very beautiful and virtuous, and twenty-three years old, none of which truths one would gather from her portrait. She is driven, in order to provide for a delicate little brother, who is a musical prodigy, to enter upon a mercenary marriage with Tristram Lorrimer Guiscard Guiscard, twenty-fourth Baron Tancred, of Wrayth, in the county of Suffolk. She has been married already to some awful scoundrel of a foreigner, whose toy she was, and has consequently but a poor opinion of men. Owing to a misunderstanding of Tristram's (if we dare allude to a nobleman of such very ancient lineage by his Christian name) reasons for marrying her, which is the fault of her uncle, a millionaire with a house in Park-lane and a private lift, she treats Tristram coldly, and there is a scene after the wedding in which he swears she shall go down on her bended knees before he will speak words of love to her again. Gradually she falls in love with him, but she is pale as death all the while. Aristocratic society flutters in admiration about her, remarking upon her troubled looks. Tristram becomes wilder and wilder, loses all taste for his food, suspects her of infidelity, and departs for the Soudan. But the financier, meantime reformed by the softer passion, allows Zara to explain matters which she promised to conceal, and she reaches Tristram's rooms in London just in time to fall into his arms and murmur, "Tu sais que je t'aime."

Mrs. Glyn writes with an enormous amount of sensuous zest, which suggests that she really believes her work to be worth doing. It is this quality that lifts her out of the sea of bad fiction to a position of some notoriety, but to the critical reader it only condemns her, in the literary sense, the more securely.

[Unsigned]
–*Chandler Before Marlowe*, pp. 87–88

A New World

In this excerpt from his 10 November 1950 letter to Hamilton, Chandler describes his prospects and activities in California.

I arrived in California with a beautiful wardrobe, a public school accent, no practical gifts for earning a living, and a contempt for the natives which, I am sorry to say, has in some measure persisted to this day. I had a pretty hard time trying to make a living. Once I worked on an apricot ranch ten hours a day, twenty cents an hour. Another time I worked for a sporting goods store, stringing tennis rackets for $12.50 a week, 54 hours a week. I taught myself bookkeeping and from there on my rise was as rapid as the growth of a sequoia.

–*Selected Letters of Raymond Chandler*, p. 236

Los Angeles and War

In 1912, at the age of twenty-three, Raymond Chandler decided he had no future as a London man of letters. He borrowed £500 from his uncle Ernest Thornton and sailed to the United States, where he hoped to establish a career in business. He lived briefly in St. Louis and Omaha, then moved to California, which would be his home for the rest of his life.

After completing a bookkeeping course, Chandler took a job as an accountant for the Los Angeles Creamery, and his mother came from England to live with him. The Chandlers became part of an informal social group that gathered regularly at the home of Warren and Alma Lloyd, a couple Chandler had met on his Atlantic crossing, for musical evenings and discussions of literature and philosophy. Included in this group were Julian Pascal, a concert pianist and composer, and his wife, Cissy.

In August 1917, after the United States entered World War I, Chandler and the Pascals' son, Gordon, traveled to Vancouver, British Columbia, to enlist in the Canadian army. In an autobiographical statement for Twentieth Century Authors, *Chandler explained that he chose the Canadian forces over the American because, having only recently arrived from England, "it was still natural to me to prefer a British uniform." He was assigned to the 50th Regiment—also known as the Gordon Highlanders—trained at Victoria, British Columbia, and sailed to England in November. In England, Chandler was stationed at Seaford on the Sussex coast for three months, then was assigned as a replacement to the Seventh Battalion of the Canadian Expeditionary Force. He arrived behind the lines in France on 18 March 1918.*

Little is known about Chandler's experience at the front. He mentioned his military service only briefly in letters, writing, for example, to his Australian friend Diedre Gartrell in July 1957 that "once you have had to lead a platoon into direct machine-gun fire, nothing is ever the same again." During the fall and winter before Chandler arrived, the Seventh Battalion had seen some of the fiercest trench fighting of the entire war at the Battles of Vimy Ridge and Passchendaele. In spring 1918, however, the battalion was stationed behind the lines in a reserve position and saw little or no action. In June 1918 Chandler was transferred from the Seventh Battalion back to England. He had applied for a commission in the Royal Air Force and was posted to the school of aviation at Waddington, but the war ended before he completed his training.

Chandler in his Canadian Expeditionary Force uniform, Seaford, England

This sketch, published in MacShane's biography of the author, is Chandler's only known attempt to write about combat. The date of the composition is unknown.

Trench Raid

The strafe sounded a lot heavier than usual. The candle stuck on the top of his tin hat guttered from something more than draught. The rats behind the dugout lining were still. But a tired man could sleep through it. He began to loosen the puttee on his left leg. Someone yelled down the dugout entrance and the beam of an electric torch groped about on the slimy chalky steps. He swore, retied his puttee and slithered up the steps. As he pushed aside the dirty blanket that served for a gas curtain the force of the bombardment hit him like the blow of a club at the base of the brain. He grovelled against the wall of the trench, nauseated by the din. He seemed to be alone in a universe of incredibly brutal noise. The sky, in which the calendar called for a full moon, was white and blind with innumerable Very lights, white and blind and diseased like a world gone leprous. The edge of the parados, lumpy with the dirt from a recent housekeeping, cut this whiteness like a line of crazy camels against an idiotic moonrise in a nightmare. Against the emptiness [word

uncertain] of the night, a nose cap whined down nearby with a slow intimate sound, like a mosquito. He began to concentrate on the shells. If you heard them they never hit you. With a meticulous care he set himself to picking out the ones that would come near enough to be reckoned on as a possible introduction to immortality. To these he listened with a sort of cold exhausted passion until a flattening of the screech told him they had gone over to the support lines. Time to move on. Mustn't stay too long in one place. He groped round the corner of the bay to the Lewis gun post. On the firing step the Number One of the gun crew was standing to with half of his body silhouetted above the parapet, motionless against the glare of the lights except that his hand was playing scales on the butt of the gun.

—*The Life of Raymond Chandler*, pp. 29–30

Chandler in the uniform of the Gordon Highlanders regiment

50th Regt. Reinforcements C.E.F.

Naturalised British subject ORIGINAL

ATTESTATION PAPER.

No. 2025271

Folio.

CANADIAN OVER-SEAS EXPEDITIONARY FORCE.

QUESTIONS TO BE PUT BEFORE ATTESTATION.
(ANSWERS.)

1. What is your surname?	CHANDLER
1a. What are your Christian names?	RAYMOND THORNTON
1b. What is your present address?	127 So. Vendome St Los Angeles, Cal. U.S.A
2. In what Town, Township or Parish, and in what Country were you born?	Chicago, Ill U.S.A.
3. What is the name of your next-of-kin?	MRS. FLORENCE D. CHANDLER
4. What is the address of your next-of-kin?	127 SOUTH VENDOME ST LOS ANGELES, CAL. U.S.A
4a. What is the relationship of your next-of-kin?	MOTHER
5. What is the date of your birth?	July 23rd 1888
6. What is your Trade or Calling?	Journalist
7. Are you married?	No.
8. Are you willing to be vaccinated or re-vaccinated and inoculated?	Yes
9. Do you now belong to the Active Militia?	No.
10. Have you ever served in any Military Force? If so, state particulars of former Service.	No.
11. Do you understand the nature and terms of your engagement?	Yes
12. Are you willing to be attested to serve in the CANADIAN OVER-SEAS EXPEDITIONARY FORCE?	Yes
13. Have you ever been discharged from any Branch of His Majesty's Forces as medically unfit?	No.
14. If so, what was the nature of the disability?	
15. Have you ever offered to serve in any Branch of His Majesty's Forces and been rejected?	No.
16. If so, what was the reason?	

DECLARATION TO BE MADE BY MAN ON ATTESTATION.

I, Raymond Thornton Chandler, do solemnly declare that the above are answers made by me to the above questions, and that they are true, and that I am willing to fulfil the engagements by me now made, and I hereby engage and agree to serve in the Canadian Over-Seas Expeditionary Force, and to be attached to any arm of the service therein, for the term of one year, or during the war now existing between Great Britain and Germany should that war last longer than one year, and for six months after the termination of that war provided His Majesty should so long require my services, or until legally discharged.

R. T. Chandler (Signature of Recruit)

Date...........191. Gordon Pascal (Signature of Witness)

OATH TO BE TAKEN BY MAN ON ATTESTATION.

I, Raymond Thornton Chandler, do make Oath, that I will be faithful and bear true Allegiance to His Majesty King George the Fifth, His Heirs and Successors, and that I will as in duty bound honestly and faithfully defend His Majesty, His Heirs and Successors, in Person, Crown and Dignity, against all enemies, and will observe and obey all orders of His Majesty, His Heirs and Successors, and of all the Generals and Officers set over me. So help me God.

R. T. Chandler (Signature of Recruit)

Date...........191. Gordon Pascal (Signature of Witness)

CERTIFICATE OF MAGISTRATE.

The Recruit above-named was cautioned by me that if he made any false answer to any of the above questions he would be liable to be punished as provided in the Army Act.

The above questions were then read to the Recruit in my presence.

I have taken care that he understands each question, and that his answer to each question has been duly entered as replied to, and the said Recruit has made and signed the declaration and taken the oath

before me, at.................this...........day of...........191.

Charles A. Forsythe (Signature of Justice)

M. F. W. 23.
750 M.—1-17.
Lt. Q. 1773-30-841.

N.B.—ATTENTION IS DRAWN TO THE FACT THAT ANY PERSON MAKING A FALSE ANSWER TO ANY OF THE ABOVE QUESTIONS IS LIABLE TO A PENALTY OF SIX MONTHS' IMPRISONMENT.

Front and back of Chandler's Attestation Papers, which were completed when he enlisted in the Canadian Army in August 1917. The address listed on these papers, 127 South Vendome Street, was the home of Julian and Cissy Pascal (courtesy of National Archives of Canada).

Description of *Raymond Thornton Chandler* On Enlistment.

Apparent Age *29* years .... months. (To be determined according to the instructions given in the Regulations for Army Medical Services.)	**Distinctive marks, and marks indicating congenital peculiarities or previous disease.** (Should the Medical Officer be of opinion that the recruit has served before, he will, unless the man acknowledges to any previous service, attach a slip to that effect, for the information of the Approving Officer).

Height .... *5* ft. *9* ins.

Chest measurement. { Girth when fully expanded .... *37* ins.
Range of expansion .... *5* ins.

Complexion .... *Fresh*

Eyes .... *Hazel*

Hair .... *Dark Brown*

Religious denominations. {
Church of England .... *Yes*
Presbyterian ....
Methodist ....
Baptist or Congregationalist ....
Roman Catholic ....
Jewish ....
Other denominations ....
(Denomination to be stated.)

Vision R: D. *20*   L: D. *20*
Hearing R. *W*   L. *W*

CERTIFICATE OF MEDICAL EXAMINATION.

I have examined the above-named Recruit and find that he does not present any of the causes of rejection specified in the Regulations for Army Medical Services.

He can see at the required distance with either eye; his heart and lungs are healthy; he has the free use of his joints and limbs, and he declares that he is not subject to fits of any description.

I consider him* *fit* for the Canadian Over-Seas Expeditionary Force.

Date .... 191 .

Place ....

Medical Officer.

*"Insert here "fit" or "unfit."

NOTE.—Should the Medical Officer consider the Recruit unfit, he will fill in the foregoing Certificate only in the case of those who have been attested, and will briefly state below the cause of unfitness:—

MOBILIZATION CENTRE
VICTORIA

Pres.
Member
Member

CERTIFICATE OF OFFICER COMMANDING UNIT.

.... *Raymond Thornton Chandler* having been finally approved and inspected by me this day, and his Name, Age, Date of Attestation, and every prescribed particular having been recorded, I certify that I am satisfied with the correctness of this Attestation.

Charlish Dorsythe Lieut. Col. (Signature of Officer)
O.C 50th Regt. Reinforcements C.E.F.

Date .... *14th August* 1917.

2nd DEPOT BATT. B.C. REGT.

Fill in Only.—Unit, Number, Rank and Name.

M. F. W. 54. (A. F. B. 103.)

250.m—7/16.
H. Q. 177/39-820.

Casualty Form—Active Service.

Unit, Regiment or Corps. 2nd DEPOT BATT. B.C.E.F. REGT.

Regimental No. 2025271. Rank. Private. Name. Raymond Thornton Chandler

C.E.F. Soflo

Enlisted (a) 14/8/17. Terms of Service (a) .... Service reckons from (a) .... 14/8/17.

Date of appointment to present rank. ....

Numerical position on roll of N.C.Os. }

Extended .... Re-engaged ....

Qualification (b) ....

Report		Record of, promotions, reductions, transfers, casualties, etc., during active service, as reported on Army Form B 213, Army Form A. 36, or in other official documents. The authority to be quoted in each case.	Place	Date	Remarks taken from Army Form B 213, Army Form A. 36, or other official documents.
Date	From whom received				
no record	Taken on strength Victoria 14/8/17				
	Embarked	Halifax	26.11.17	Nominal Roll
	Disembarked	Liverpool	9/12/17	
	TAKEN ON STRENGTH OF 1st CAN. RES. BATTN.	Seaford	8.12.17	A.II.327
	PROCEEDED ON DRAFT TO 7...BATT Seaford		8 - MAR 1918	M290 57 ks
				L.J. Withlut Captain, Adjutant, 1st Canadian Reserve Battalion.
	ON STRENGTH 7TH BATTN CAN BASE DEPOT		8/3/18	Pt. 11 No. 31 dl
	JOINED UNIT,		11.3/18	0223
	Transfit to England apposed to B.C. Rea. repn. Seaford. for the purpose of obtaining a commission in the R.A.F.		11.6.18	O.G (2148/369 (o) 4.26.18.

(a) In the case of a man who has re-engaged for, or enlisted into Section D. Army Reserve, particulars of such re-engagement or enlistment will be entered.
(b) e.g. Signaller, Shoeing Smith, etc., etc., also special qualifications in technical Corps duties.

[P.T.O.

CERTIFIED CORRECT.
8 - MAR 1918
CAN. RECORDS, LONDON.

16.3.18. 7 Bn
6.6.18. O.G.

Chandler's Casualty Form for his service in the 50th Regiment. This form tracks the assignments, casualties, and promotions received by a soldier during his term of service (courtesy of the National Archives of Canada).

Report		Record of promotions, reductions, transfers, casualties, etc., during active service, as reported on Army Form B. 213, Army Form A. 36, or in other official documents. The authority to be quoted in each case.	Place	Date	Remarks taken from Army Form B. 213, Army Form A. 36, or other official documents.
Date	From whom received				
8-7-18		T.O.S. B.C. Reg. Depot.			
10-12-18	B.C.R.D.	Command to all Distribution Depot R.A.F. London. Appointed 2/Lieut.	Seaford	11-6-18	Pt.2.D.O. 162.
31-12-18	"	Ceases to be on Command to R.A.F. London & Detailed to Depot Coy.	"	11-6-18	" 897
15-1-19	"	T.O.S. on posting to Reg.	Seaford	24-12-18	Pt.2.D.O. 311
			"	10-1-19	" 15
15-1-19	1/W.R.R.	attached from B.C.R.D. (cadre)	Seaford	14-1-19 Pr 2 do 7/2	
22-1-19	1/W.R.R.	Ceases to be attached from B.C.R.D. proceeding for R. Embarkation pending Return to Canada	Seaford	21-1-19 Pr 2 do	

For O.C. B.C. REGL. DEPOT.

Liverpool 27.F.B.R.C.S. Canada 1919

Adjutant, 1st Canadian Reserve Battalion.

M. F. W. 54. (A. F. B. 10).
500M.—9-18
H. Q. 1172-39-9/0.

Fill in only.—Unit, Number, Rank and Name.

Casualty Form—Active Service.

Unit, Regiment or Corps. ..50.♭.Res..Regt.....(2ⁿᵈ.Deptᵗ B...B.C.Rᵍᵗ.)..

Regimental No. 2025271. Rank. Pte. Name. Chandler. R. Raymond...Thornton....

Enlisted (a). 14.8.17. Terms of Service (a). O. A. W. Service reckons from (a) 14.8.17.

Date of promotion to } present rank .... Date of appointment } to lance rank ....

Numerical position on } roll of N. C. Os. ....

Extended .... Re-engaged. .... Qualification (b). ....

Date	Report		Record of promotions, reductions, transfers, casualties, etc., during active service, as reported on Army Form B. 213, Army Form A. 36, or in other official documents. The authority to be quoted in each case	Place	Date	Remarks taken from Army Form B. 213, Army Form A. 36, or other official documents
		From whom received				
10.2.19	OVERSEAS		T.O.S. DISTRICT DEPOT XI	HASTINGS PARK VANCOUVER, B.C.	1.2.19	D.O. Pr. 11 50. 1919
	DISCHARGED		DEMOBILIZATION	VANCOUVER, B.C.	30/9/19	D.O. 53/324 v. of 24/2/19
						M. Maclean
						(for O.C. District Depot X¹

a) ¹n the case of a man who has re-engaged for, or enlisted into Section D, Army Reserve, particulars of such re-engagement or enlistment will be entered.
(b) e.g. Signaller, Shoeing Smith, etc., etc., also special qualifications in technical Corps duties.

[P.T.O.

38

Florence and Raymond Chandler

Chandler at a California beach in the 1920s

Cissy

Not long after he returned from the war, Chandler and Cissy Pascal announced that they had fallen in love with each other. Born Pearl Eugenie Hurlburt in 1870, Cissy was eighteen years older than Chandler. As a young woman, she had moved from her hometown of Perry, Ohio, to New York City to study music. In 1897 she married a salesman named Leon Brown Porcher, whom she divorced seven years later. In 1911, she married her second husband, a pianist named Goodrich Bowen who used the professional name Julian Pascal, and moved with him to Los Angeles.

The Pascals filed for divorce on July 10, 1919. Chandler's mother disapproved of the match between her son and Cissy because of the great difference in their ages. For this reason, Chandler postponed marriage. Florence Chandler died in January 1924, and Raymond and Cissy Chandler were married the next month.

Cissy Chandler

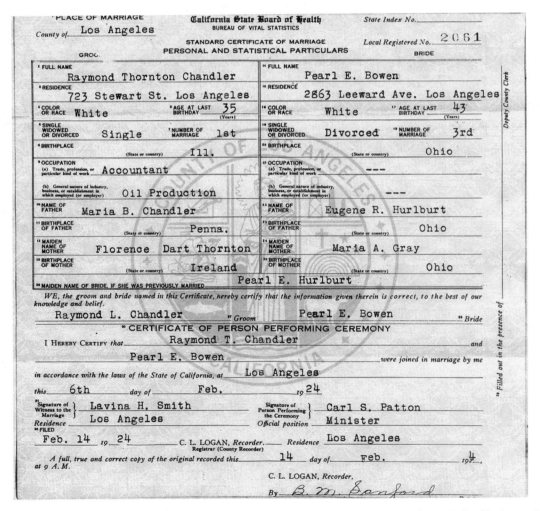

Raymond and Cissy Chandler's marriage certificate. Though Cissy listed her age as forty-three on this document, she was in fact fifty-three at the time of the marriage (Registrar-Recorder/County Clerk, County of Los Angeles).

These two panoramic photographs show Hollywood in 1912 (top), the year Chandler arrived in the city, and 1923 (bottom) (courtesy of the Library of Congress, Prints and Photographs Division).

The Growth of Los Angeles

During the first two decades that Chandler lived in Los Angeles, the city experienced the greatest population boom in America's history. The boosterism and excitement surrounding the growth of the city is captured in a 23 December 1923 article in The World's Work, *"The World's Greatest City–in Prospect":*

Has the population of Los Angeles reached 1,000,000? Is it the first city on the Pacific Coast to attain real metropolitan proportions? . . . But this is only the beginning. That Los Angeles is the metropolis of the Pacific Coast is already apparent, but its destiny is something far more splendid than that. It is to be not only America's largest city; it is to be the biggest city on earth.

The Oil Business

In the early 1920s Chandler left the Los Angeles Creamery to become an accountant for the Dabney Oil Syndicate, a holding company for more than a dozen smaller drilling firms. Though he disliked the ethics of the oil business, which he felt was dominated by corrupt opportunists, Chandler succeeded in the industry. He was soon promoted to auditor and then vice president of the Dabney's South Basin Oil Company, earning a salary of $1,000 a month. He managed the company's Los Angeles office and handled the paperwork for its contracts and purchases. Chandler's career in the oil industry lasted almost ten years. Although he would later say that he lost his job because of the Depression, his termination resulted from his personal conduct. By the late 1920s he started to drink heavily and behave erratically. He had a series of affairs with office secretaries, sometimes disappearing with them for binges that lasted for days at a time. He was fired in 1932.

Toward the end of his life, in a 5 May 1957 letter to his agent, Helga Greene, Chandler looked back on this period and recounted some of his experiences in the oil industry.

I was an executive in the oil business once, a director of eight companies and a president of three, although actually I was simply a high-priced employé. They were small companies, but very rich. I had the best office staff in Los Angeles and I paid them higher salaries than they could have got anywhere else, and they knew it. My office door was never closed, everyone called me by my Christian name, and there was never any dissension, because I made it my business to see that there was no cause for it. Once in a while, not often, I had to fire someone—not someone I had picked myself, but someone who had been imposed upon me by the big man—and that I hated terribly, because one never knows what hardship it may mean to the individual. I had a talent for picking out the capabilities of people. There was one man, I remember, who had a genius for filing. Others were good at routine jobs but had no initiative. There were secretaries who could remember everything and secretaries who were wonderful at dictation and typing, but whose minds were really elsewhere. I had to understand them all and use them according to what they were. There was one girl, not pretty and not too bright, who could have been given a million dollars in cash, and a month later, without being asked, she would have known the number of every bill and listed it, and would have, at her own expense, taken a safe deposit box to keep the money in. There was a lawyer on salary in our office (I didn't approve of the idea, but was overruled by the Board) who was very acute but also very unreliable, because he drank too much. I found out just how to use his brain, and he said often and publicly that I was the best office manager in Los Angeles, and probably one of the best in the world. (Eventually, he crashed a police car and I had to get him out of jail.) When I hadn't been long with the firms we had an embezzler. His method would only be possible in a badly organized office. But I found him out and at his trial I had to sit beside the Assistant D.A. and tell him what questions to ask. The damn fool didn't know his own case.

. . . .

I always somehow seemed to have a fight on my hands. At one time I employed six lawyers; some were good at one thing, some at another. Their bills always exasperated the Chairman; he said they were too high. I always paid them as rendered because they were not too high, in the circumstances. Business is very tough and I hate it. But whatever you set out to do, you have to do as well as you know how.

I remember one time when we had a truck carrying pipe in Signal Hill (just north of Long Beach) and the pipe stuck out quite a long way, but there was a red lantern on it, according to law. A car with two drunken sailors and two girls crashed into it and filed actions for $1000 apiece. They waited almost a year, which is the deadline here for filing a personal injury action. The insurance company said, "Oh well, it costs a lot of money to defend these suits, and we'd rather settle." I said, "That's all very well. It doesn't cost you anything to settle. You simply put the rates up. If you don't want to fight this case, and fight it competently, my company will fight it." "At your own expense?" "Of course not. We'll sue you for what it costs us, unless you pay without that necessity." He walked out of the office. We defended the action, with the best lawyer we knew, and he proved that the pipe truck had been properly lighted and then we brought in various bar men from Long Beach (it took money to find them, but it was worth it) and that they had been thrown out of three bars. We won hands down, and the insurance company paid up immediately about a third of what they would have settled for, and as soon as they did this I cancelled the policy, and had it rewritten with another company.

Perhaps all this sounds a little hard-boiled. But I wasn't like that really at all. I was just doing what I thought was my job. It's always been a fight, hasn't it? Everywhere you go, everything you do—it all takes it out of you. It takes more out of me than it did once, but still I have the same feeling.

—*Selected Letters of Raymond Chandler*, pp. 443–445

Chandler at the Dabney-Johnston oil wells, Signal Hill, 1920s

In 1923 The Saturday Evening Post *published a series of articles by Albert W. Atwood on the oil industry in Los Angeles. In this excerpt from "Mad From Oil," he describes the ballyhoo that was used to promote investment in oil ventures and captures the boom-town atmosphere of Los Angeles in the 1920s.*

. . . the oil boom in Southern California in the last two years has been distinctive in that all the major discoveries were made at the gates of a great city. Never in the entire history of the oil industry has it been so easy to look upon and invest in oil wells, drilling, flowing and pumping. All that any resident of the city needed, to feast the eyes upon this magic source of wealth, has been two or three hours' time, together with a seat in an automobile or the price of a short interurban ride.

Naturally, the fields have been visited by untold thousands of tourists and newcomers with leisure time and surplus money. But in the throngs who have ridden out every day are many who can

hardly be classed in either category. Wealth from oil appeals to no one age, sex, class or group. It has a universal appeal, this possibility of sudden wealth; it strikes a responsive chord in every breast.

. . . .

One salesman estimated that as many as 5000 or 6000 people go out to the oil fields on free rides on a single day. I have seen 300 or 400, and in one case 500, people in a single tabernacle, all brought out free, fed free and lectured to free. Women go from house to house day after day, offering the occupants free rides either to the oil fields, to new real-estate subdivisions or to other enterprises selling stock or lots or units. There are houses whose doorbells are rung every day by canvassers offering free rides. One can ride as far and as often as one chooses, and in practically any direction.

. . . .

Chandler at the Bureau of Mines and Oils Annual Banquet, Biltmore Hotel, Los Angeles, in March 1927

Atwood reports on a promoter's bus trip to the oil fields. E. L. Doheny, mentioned in the first paragraph, owned a mansion that may have served as a model for the Sernwood home in The Big Sleep *(1939).*

We had certainly chosen the Four-B route to wealth from oil—busses, barkers, ballyhoo and boobs. At any rate, the trip was planned to thrill people with the idea of wealth, to hammer in the desire for money, to make us as avaricious as possible. First we passed the old wells in the city itself, brought in by E. L. Doheny— "the multimillionaire," as the barker bawled it out, with emphasis on the "multi." Then we were landed plump on the Pasadena street of wealth, with loud references to the homes of chewing-gum magnates and movie stars. From there we were driven through one of the old oil fields, from which the Baldwin estate has derived such great wealth.

But here we were at last in Santa Fé Springs itself, having gone only twice as far as necessary to reach the place. Now we were passing the famous Bell property, and here we could see the ruins of a rig which had been blown to pieces a few days before from the terrific pressure of gas. Frantically the barker shouted a few salient facts about the great oil field. Meanwhile we were fast

moving on beyond proved territory. We turned into a field through a grand entrance and stopped in front of a tent. Flags were flying and other huge busses were arriving and discharging their loads. We disentrained and were herded into the tent, or tabernacle, with great promptness.

Inside, at one end was a platform, a table and a blackboard, with maps of the oil fields. In front of the platform were rows upon rows of long, rough dining tables and benches, capable of holding perhaps 500 people. Over each table was a sign bearing the name of a section or suburb of Los Angeles, and we seated ourselves according to the place we were supposed to come from.

Shortly the salesman bore down upon us, bearing huge cups of coffee, coarse sandwiches and cookies. We were urged again and again to eat hearty, that "there is more where this came from." The atmosphere was certainly one of the most hearty and excessive hospitality; and it was, indeed, beautiful to see a well-dressed salesman, who would be disgusted at less that fifty dollars a day in commissions while the picking was good, wait upon toil-begrimed workmen and sad-looking women with smelly babies.

Lest the writer be accused of looking a gift horse in the mouth, it should be said in all seriousness that there are literally thousands of persons who spend most of their time in taking free bus rides, eating free lunches and going where the best hot lunches are to be found. I however, am unlucky. Despite careful inquiry of newspaper men, the State Corporation Department and other authorities, I never succeeded, on several trips of this kind, in picking out an oil investment which provided a hot lunch. Always I had a cold and clammy lunch. But there is consolation in the statement made by one investigator, that the chicken dinners never consisted of chicken, anyway, but of sea gulls.

As one sat at luncheon, there was plenty to look at. Through the open flap of the tent, the buildings of the state insane asylum could be seen at a little distance, and a squad of inmates marched from one building to another in what seemed to be a lock step. But the people in the tent were more worth studying. Many bore upon their faces and persons unmistakable signs of both ignorance and poverty, although they were of no one class or group. For the most part, however, they were a sad aggregation of humanity, a lot of culls, as it were, brought together by the powerful forces of curiosity and greed.

Observers of this promotional aspect of the oil boom maintain that the investors are mostly women, and elderly. Altogether, the writer visited seven tents, containing from fifty to 500 people each, and spent from fifteen minutes to several hours in each. The people were of all descriptions, but it is probable that the predominant type was the elderly or middle-aged female, bearing every sign of a monotonous and mediocre life.

. . . .

A sort of master of ceremonies mounted the platform and introduced the promoter, who also was to give the lecture. He was introduced as never having been in a losing venture.

"I am not a minister, a doctor, a professor or a judge," he began. "But I will tell my story as best I can. I am a plain American citizen." [Loud applause from the salesmen mobilized on the rear seats, and a little from the elderly lady prospects.]

This reference to the various professions was a knock at other promotion outfits that employ ex-clergymen, judges, and the like, to lecture to the tent loads. In one or two cases, men of former prominence are engaged in this occupation, and it is said that one of them was paid $1000 a week for a time.

"I am an idealist," went on the lecturer. "I can accomplish anything if I try hard enough, and so can you. Strong men decide for themselves and so must you. Five per cent of the men in this country have nearly all the money. Why is that? Because they have the courage to act right now, because they are positive and decisive.

"People say to me, 'This proposition is probably all right, but I want to wait until tomorrow to think it over.' But

there is no tomorrow. What we call tomorrow will be another day. We sleep between today and tomorrow, and recently I looked up the meaning of sleep in Webster's dictionary. What do you think it said? Temporary death.

"As we were passing an oil well the other day an old lady on the bus whispered to her husband, but I heard her, 'Why, I guess that's oil, after all!' Then she explained that she wanted to write to her son back in Bangor, Maine, before investing.

"'But, madam,' I said, 'what does he know about oil? There is none in Maine.'

"'He runs a drug store,' she replied, 'and sells castor oil.'" [Mild laughter.]

The lecturer then went on at great length about the evils of fear, and how fear keeps people from making investments. He told us that the first well in Pennsylvania is still producing, and predicted higher prices for oil; which, of course, was perfectly safe, because he put no time limit on his prediction.

But in the main, his long talk consisted of purely hypnotic exhortation, in an almost semireligious, Billy Sunday, camp-meeting vein.

"Be masters of your own destinies. Don't you know that people are poor because they are in bondage to fear and doubt, because they do not think for themselves, because they let the banks make 100 per cent with their money and they make only 4 per cent?"

Finally he had finished, and before his words had died away an employe in the back of the tabernacle was shouting out the names and prices of various oil units on the Los Angeles market, and another was writing them on the blackboard, all in imitation of the excitement of a broker's office.

But almost before the lecturer had spoken has last word the salesmen were down upon us, at our very elbows, peering into our faces, and the real slaughter had begun.

—*The Saturday Evening Post*, 14 July 1923,
pp. 10, 11–12

"They say that oil is a gamble; but life is too. Death is the only thing in which there is no gamble. You are crazy if you don't gamble. If you haven't sense enough to take a chance, the booby house over there is for you. Talk about chances, why, there was a time when you could have bought lots on Pershing Square for fifty-dollars. If you are willing to come in without doubts and fears, come ahead; if not, stay out, we will sell it to others. I don't believe you are taking any more chances on this well than if you bought government bonds."

—Promoter, quoted by Atwood in
"Mad From Oil," p. 94

2.
Apprenticeship and *The Big Sleep*, 1933–1939

After he was terminated by the Dabney Oil Syndicate, Chandler decided to return to writing for a living. In part because he had provided them with information for a lawsuit against Dabney, Edward and Paul Lloyd, the sons of his old friends, gave Chandler a $100 monthly allowance for living expenses as he tried to establish a career as a writer.

Between 1933 and 1937 Chandler published eleven stories in Black Mask, *edited by Joseph T. Shaw. When Shaw left the magazine in 1937, Chandler switched to* Dime Detective, *which was edited by Ken White, and published seven of his stories there between 1937 and 1939. Although Chandler did not have as close a personal relationship with White as he had with Shaw, White's magazine paid better than* Black Mask—*approximately $400 a story—and accepted stories such as "Pearls are a Nuisance," which burlesqued the conventions of hard-boiled fiction.*

The Pulp Market

Though he was paid only a penny a word for his first story, "Blackmailers Don't Shoot," its publication in the December 1933 issue of Black Mask *was a significant accomplishment for Chandler. He started his pulp-fiction career with the most prestigious of the detective magazines. In the following excerpt from his memoir* The Pulp Jungle *(1967) Frank Gruber, a writer who started his career at about the same time as Chandler, recalls the pulp-fiction market in New York in the 1930s.*

There were in existence in 1934 some one hundred fifty pulp magazines. . . . The Ace of Aces, the goal of all pulp writers, was *Black Mask*. The elite of the elite were the *Black Mask* writers. They were followed by the writers of *Adventure, Short Stories, Argosy,* and *Detective Fiction Weekly.*

The prestige of these magazines wasn't determined necessarily by the rate of payment to authors. *Black Mask* was reputed to pay two cents a word to start, with a scale rising to around four cents a word. *Detective Fiction Weekly* and *Argosy* were said to pay Max Brand five cents a word and numerous writers received around three cents a word. For that matter, *Dime Western* and *Dime Detective,* although not rated with the elite, paid a few writers as high as three cents a word: Walt Coburn, Harry F. Olmsted and perhaps one or two more.

The base rate of pay at the majority of the pulp magazines was one cent a word. The fringe publishers paid less,

but at Standard, Popular, Street & Smith and Munsey the usual pay was one cent a word.

The average pulp magazine of one hundred twenty-eight pages contained sixty-five thousand words. Since many of the magazines, such as *Argosy, Detective Fiction Weekly, Love Story, Western Story, Wild West Weekly,* were weeklies, the total market for stories was considerably greater than one hundred fifty times sixty-five thousand words.

There were also a number of semimonthly publications, such as *Ranch Romances* and *Short Stories.* Roughly, these weeklies and semimonthlies brought the total pulp market to about two hundred fifty copies of sixty-five thousand words per month. On a yearly basis some one hundred ninety-five million words were needed to fill the hungry maws of the pulps. At the base rate of one cent a word, this meant a total outlay of almost two million dollars per year for stories.

There were in and around New York some three hundred pulp writers who had made their marks and who descended periodically upon the several dozen editors to peddle their words. Perhaps another thousand established writers mailed in their wares from all parts of the country, and the world, for that matter. L. Patrick Greene, a regular contributor to *Short Stories,* lived in South Africa, and Max Brand, the king of kings of the pulps, had lived in Florence, Italy, for a dozen years. California alone boasted of no less than a hundred established pulp writers, including such giants as Erle Stanley Gardner, Walt Coburn and Harry Olmsted.

These twelve hundred to thirteen hundred pulp writers who made their livelihoods from writing for the pulps, some very good livelihoods, some meager, were by no means the entire competition in the pulp field. Nineteen thirty-four was still a Depression year and in the Depression there were literally thousands of people unemployed at their regular vocations, who turned to writing in the desperate hope that this might be the means of getting off WPA. Most of these were rank amateurs, but still many, many were gifted enough to sell an occasional story. They accounted for perhaps ten per cent of all the stories published in the pulps.

—*The Pulp Jungle,* pp. 20, 23–25

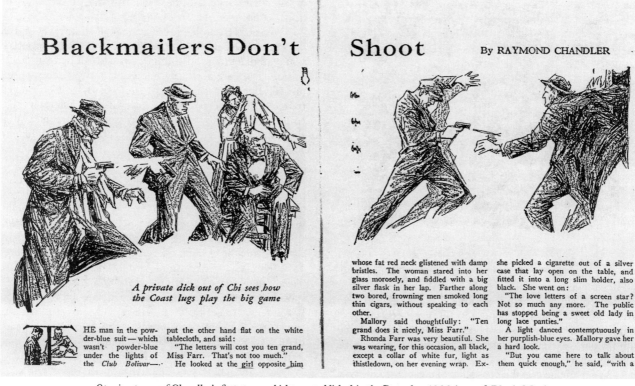

Opening pages of Chandler's first story, which was published in the December 1933 issue of Black Mask

---

Getting Started

In his 3 December 1957 letter to schoolmaster Wesley Hartley, Chandler recalled using Erle Stanley Gardner as a model when he returned to writing.

[A]lthough I did a lot of writing as a young man in London . . . I couldn't write fiction to save my life. I couldn't get a character in or out of a room, I couldn't even get his hat off. I learned to write fiction by a method which I have recommended to other young struggling writers I tried to help, but no soap. Everything they did had to be for sale. What I did was take a novelette, I think it was by Gardner, and make a detailed synopsis of it. From this synopsis I wrote the story, then compared it with the original to see where he, Gardner, had got an effect and I had got nothing. I did this over and over again with the same story. I think I did learn a great deal that way. My first novelette for the *Black Mask* took me five months to write, and I got $180 for it. Another device I used, especially for the pulp field, was to write a straight story and then rewrite so that it *seemed*, just seemed, like something else. I concentrated on the detective story because it was a popular form and I thought the right and lucky man might finally make it into literature.

—Selected Letters of Raymond Chandler, p. 459

Shaw and *Black Mask*

Black Mask *was the leading detective pulp for two reasons. It published the most talented writers in the field, including Dashiell Hammett, Erle Stanley Gardner, Raoul Whitfield, and Carroll John Daly. It also published a distinctive style of hard-boiled detective fiction. Joseph T. Shaw, the editor of the magazine during the late 1920s and 1930s, attempted to describe this style in his introduction to* The Hard-Boiled Omnibus, *a collection of short stories originally published in* Black Mask.

Introduction

We had recently returned from a five-year sojourn abroad during and following the First World War. Happening upon a sporting magazine, to which we had haphazardly contributed in years past, we were curious enough to investigate the remarkable change that had taken place in its format and appearance. We found the miracle man to be Ray Holland, a six-foot stalwart who, in addition to his familiarity with the birds and beasts, knew also the vital difference between the functions of an editor who knows his stuff and that of a publisher not so gifted. Ray also had the personality to enforce recognition of his knowledge and to keep the breach open. Hence, the success of the magazine.

In friendly conversation we were asked to edit another magazine in the same group: *Black Mask*, a detec-

Joseph T. Shaw

tive story magazine. Before that, we had never seen a copy, had never even heard of the magazine. We had not even a bowing acquaintance with the "pulps." Yet we always held that a good story is where you find it regardless of author-fame or medium of publication. It has been said that with proper materials available, a good mouse trap can be built anywhere.

We meditated on the possibility of creating a new type of detective story differing from that accredited to the Chaldeans and employed more recently by Gaborieau, Poe, Conan Doyle—in fact, universally by detective story writers; that is, the deductive type, the cross-word puzzle sort, lacking—deliberately—all other human emotional values.

Obviously, the creation of a new pattern was a writer's rather than an editor's job. Consequently, search was made in the pages of the magazine for a writer with the requisite spark and originality, and we were amazingly encouraged by the promise evident in the work of one. Not that his pattern was different from that of others, but he told his stories with a new kind of compulsion and authenticity.

So we wrote to Dashiell Hammett. His response was immediate and most enthusiastic: *That is exactly what I've been thinking about and working toward. As I see it, the approach I have in mind has never been attempted. The field is unscratched and wide open.*

It was apparent that Mr. Hammett shared our hope for a medium in which he could achieve his aim while developing his talent into a highly skillful instrument. We pointed out that this particular medium—the magazine mystery story—was both constrained and restrained. We felt obliged to stipulate our boundaries. We wanted simplicity for the sake of clarity, plausibility, and belief. We wanted action, but we held that action is meaningless unless it involves recognizable human character in three-dimensional form.

Dashiell Hammett had his own way of phrasing this: *If you kill a symbol, no crime is committed and no effect is produced. To constitute a murder, the victim must be a real human being of flesh and blood.*

Simple, logical, almost inevitable. Yet, amazingly, this principle had been completely ignored by

crime writers—and still is, in the deductive type of mystery story.

In physics, an explosion sends out sound waves. But if there are no ears within their range, there is no sound. If you read of a thousand aborigines wiped out by earthquake or flood, you are abstractly interested, but you are not disturbed. But let a member of your own family be even remotely threatened and you are at once intensely concerned, emotionally aroused. This is true in real life. Why shouldn't it hold true in fiction, which must create the illusion of reality?

It was on this philosophic concept that we began to shape the magazine we wanted, the kind of story it would print.

The formula or pattern emphasizes character and the problems inherent in human behavior over crime solution. In other words, in this new pattern, character conflict is the main theme; the ensuing crime, or its threat, is incidental.

For a clear demonstration of this pattern, consider *The Thin Man* by Dashiell Hammett, and *The Big Sleep,* by Raymond Chandler. In approach and structure, both are singularly alike, since both adhere closely to the pattern. Otherwise they are as dissimilar as any two novels, which demonstrates the infinite variety attainable under this pattern. Neither can be tagged "just another detective story."

In both, characters, in full three dimensions, and character conflict are set up. The main crime and its victim are off-stage, and, while the solution of the crime is woven into the pattern of each story, it by no means constitutes the essence of the story. In fact, strip the crime from each book, and you still have a thrilling story, a test which the deductive type of mystery story could scarcely meet.

A London publisher wrote us that he recognized in our magazine a new school in writing, differing from anything else American, and unlike anything English. He accredited the *Black Mask* group of writers with its inception and accomplishment. We believe it was Mr. McKeogh, writing in the *New York World-Telegram,* who stated that all plots and props in detective stories had been used and abused, and there could be nothing new except treatment; and he, too, gave credit to the *Black Mask* writers for this innovation.

Such distinctive treatment comprises a hard, brittle style—which Raymond Chandler, one of its most brilliant exponents, declares belongs to everybody and to no one—a full employment of the functions of dialogue, and authenticity in characterization and action.

To this may be added a very fast tempo, attained in part by typical economy of expression which, probably, has had definite influence on writing in other fields. As Mrs. Harry Payne Burton said: "Hammett and his confrères have shown our authors how to attain the shortest distance between two points; and are we glad!"

The contributors of this brittle style were, notably, Hammett, Raymond Chandler, Raoul Whitfield, George Harmon Coxe, Roger Torrey, Forrest Rosaire, Paul Cain, Lester Dent, among others. It was rather extravagantly tagged as the "hard-boiled" school, and it was imitated

throughout the "pulp" field. There is, however, this difference of distinction. While many *Black Mask* characters were
admittedly "hard-boiled," the appellation belonged to the
characters rather than to the school of writing. Style and
treatment were something else again.

These writers observed the cardinal principle in creating the illusion of reality: they did not make their characters
act and talk tough; they allowed them to. They gave the stories over to their characters, and kept themselves off the
stage, as every writer of fiction should. Otherwise, as Raymond Chandler puts it, that most powerful factor, melodrama, becomes "used as a bludgeon and not as an art"—
and loses ten-fold its effectiveness.

They did not themselves state that a situation was
dangerous or exciting; they did not describe their characters
as giants, dead-shots, or infallible men. They permitted the
actors in the story to demonstrate all that to the extent of
their particular and human capabilities. Moreover, as they
attained their skill, they wrote with greater and greater
restraint, careful of over-exaggeration in a word of their own
where text demanded their descriptive contribution, adher-
ing to the sound principle that whatever arouses the incredu-
lity of a reader—no matter how true to life—has exactly the
same effect as that which could not possibly happen. As a
consequence, they wrote convincingly.

Long is the roster of the contributors to the magazine's
individual type of crime fiction. Many who saw their first stories in print there have since risen to the heights in this and
other fields of literature. It was often said, in that period, that
their product, in its best examples, was several years ahead of
its time. These writers were blazing new paths.

Most of the writers who together produced this magazine have since contributed the most skilled and successful
crime novels written in the past decade, and have also contributed enormously to the best Hollywood has to offer in
the mystery field. Hammett and Chandler are outstanding
examples. There are a score of other writers who contributed their share to make the *Black Mask* group outstanding,
writers who favored us with their first work and have since
come into national recognition. We would like to mention
them all individually, as we so clearly remember them. We
would like to include in this volume examples of each one's
work, but in both cases space forbids.

We make only one final point. We do not, and we
cannot, claim credit either for the original work of these
Black Mask writers or for their success. It is our conviction
that no one person can bring forth successful writing from
another. A discerning editor may help toward skill and
craftsmanship, but application of that skill and the thought
behind it are the sole properties of the writer himself. And
so, without any further introduction from me, meet the artists who made *Black Mask* what it was, a unique magazine
and a new influence in American literature.

Joseph T. Shaw
—*The Hard-Boiled Omnibus*, pp. v–ix

Chandler on Shaw

*Shaw had little influence on the style or themes of Chand-
ler's fiction; he wrote that Chandler "came to us full-fledged;
his very first stories were all that could be desired." Chandler found in Shaw, however, an editor who both encouraged
him in his writing and valued the type of stories he was trying to create. Chandler read a prepublication version of* The
Hard-Boiled Omnibus *and recorded his reaction to
Shaw's introduction in the following January 1946 letter to
Gardner. Though he criticizes Shaw for taking too much
credit for the* Black Mask *formula, Chandler reflects upon
the qualities that made Shaw a good editor.*

I have always received from Shaw the definite
impression (borne out by his projected introduction
to his projected anthology) that he invented the
hardboiled dick story with a ready assist from Hammett. Certainly nothing of Shaw's own fiction that I
have seen has any such germs in it. It's about the
deadest writing I ever saw, on a supposedly professional level. I don't know what Hammett was writing before he and Shaw had the brainwave, but it is
now obvious to me and would have been earlier if I
had really done any serious thinking on the subject,
that it did not happen all at once. There must have
been experiments and discussions and a need to get
an okay from the boss. Shaw's gifts as an editor
seem to me now to be exactly what you rate them.
He was a warm editor and always seemed to have
time to write at length and to argue with you. To
some of us I think he was indeed a genuine inspiration in that, just as you say, we wrote better for him
than we could have written for anybody else. The
proof of that is that some writers we both know
have never reached the standard again that they
attained in the *BM* under Shaw. I also agree with
you that he was blind to any kind of writing he did
not think the best at the moment. I don't believe
Cornell Woolrich or Cleve Adams ever made the
BM under his editorship, although both were probably far better men than some of his regulars. Norbert Davis also, who took his murders rather lightly
when allowed, made the *BM* only two or three
times. He said Shaw was too fussy for him and took
the whole thing too seriously. I'm quite sure Shaw
would never have published a story I once wrote
kidding the pants off the tough dick story, but Ken
White did.

—*Selected Letters of Raymond Chandler,*
pp. 67–68

Chandler on Flower Arrangement

Perhaps as a diversion from his pulp work, Chandler wrote the following two letters to the editor of the Los Angeles bibliophile magazine The Fortnightly Intruder. *They are the earliest published Chandler correspondence to be located.*

                                        15 June 1937

Sirs:

Your essay on flower arrangement is priceless, as much so as the typography of your sheet, but to what audience in heaven's name do you address yourselves? You are precious, you write in a dead language, and in the delicate and occasionally sterile tones of the Eighteenth Century. You are of a pretty wit and a soothing yet deadly irony. Are there people who admire such fanciful tricks? I have lived in this city for some twenty-five years and now I find you, apparently also of its citizenry, dwelling with Chinese calm in a past that was even then as improbable as the novels of Richardson. Occasionally, also, as dull.

Your little paper one receives with pleasure, and yet with a certain discomfort, like a voice from an ancient chimney on a gusty October night. One hears death in it, and is tired of hearing death in so many things. You are decadent in an environment which, for all its fancy pants, is still provincial. You have the deadly smoothness of an old pistol grip.

It is only a few short years since I was told, with more emphasis than hope, that the American gentleman did not spit. Doth he not so? I thought, then someday I shall meet him. Of course I did, but not so soon as I thought.

Who, except those by life already defeated and wasting in the twilight, has any taste for such writing as yours? I ask to know. Perhaps we are on the verge of a classic revival. God knows I am very tired of talking without moving my lips. But I'm a little afraid you are received too much with kindness, too little with understanding, that you come as a nostalgia for the Age of Culture (whatever that is, and may it rot, if it must be called by that odious word), and that you are accepted with that bewildered desperation which the Ladies of the Friday Morning Club reserved for the visiting English novelists of the tepid years before the War.

You too, Sirs, I should like to think of with gardenias in your morning coats, with grey-striped trousers of impeccable vicuna, with parted hair, and with the soft birdsong of the Oxford close in your gentle throats. But I'm afraid you wear corduroy pants and talk the flat language of the dehydrated New Englander. It is almost certain to be so. This American mind has its peculiar thinness. It acquires learning only by losing blood.

I wish you success—and can not, alas, predict it. Sirs, Your Obedient Humble Servant,

                                        R.C., Esqr.

                        —*Selected Letters of Raymond Chandler,*
                                        pp. 1–2

                                        1 July 1937

You do kid rather easily, don't you, pals? That I state a case against you is bosh. I pay you grave compliments and you mistake them for sneers. I call you precious, being precious myself. As to the corduroy pants, the remark was dated. It slipped out of my 1928 Anthology.

That you should have pride in your purer American heritage of language seems to me a slight thing. Latin became corrupt, but French is a sharper language than Latin ever was. The best writing in English today is done by Americans, but not in any purist tradition. They have roughed the language around as Shakespeare did and done it the violence of melodrama and the press box. They have knocked over tombs and sneered at the dead. Which is as it should be. There are too many dead men and there is too much talk about them.

But all this is beside the point, and still I lack the information for which I wrote to you the first time. It was kind of you to answer so soon, and at all. But who reads you? One knows, roughly, what sort of people read the *Post, Esquire, Terror Tales, New Republic, Mercury,* and the grand old man of Arlington Street, the *Atlantic.* But one suspects in the last case, where there is definite intention to preserve clarity of thought and expression and to exclude the sophisticated gimcracks of the cocktail mob, not only a paucity of support—which is a fact—, but a large element of snob readers whose minds are marionettes as completely as the fans of _____ or the followers of _____.

You see, I have lived here so long. I have perhaps been unfortunate, but I have not met the people who would like your kind of writing, unless someone first told them they must like to be saved.

                                        R.C., Esq.

                        —*Selected Letters of Raymond Chandler,*
                                        pp. 2–3

Detective Stories

Title	First Publication	Protagonist	Occupation
"Blackmailers Don't Shoot"	*Black Mask* (Dec. 1933)	Mallory	private detective
"Smart-Aleck Kill"[1]	*Black Mask* (July 1934)	Mallory	private detective
"Finger Man"[2]	*Black Mask* (Oct. 1934)	unnamed	private detective
"Killer in the Rain"[3]	*Black Mask* (Jan. 1935)	unnamed	private detective
"Nevada Gas"	*Black Mask* (June 1935)	Johnny DeRuse	gambler
"Spanish Blood"	*Black Mask* (Nov. 1935)	Sam Delaguerra	policeman
"Guns at Cyranos"[4]	*Black Mask* (Jan. 1936)	Ted Malvern	ex-private detective
"The Man Who Liked Dogs"[5]	*Black Mask* (Mar. 1936)	Carmady	private detective
"Noon Street Nemesis"	*Detective Fiction Weekly* (30 March 1936)	Pete Anglich	police officer
"Goldfish"[6]	*Black Mask* (June 1936)	Carmady	private detective
"The Curtain"[7]	*Black Mask* (September 1936)	Carmady	private detective
"Try the Girl"[8]	*Black Mask* (Jan. 1937)	Carmady	private detective
"Mandarin's Jade"[9]	*Dime Detective* (Nov. 1937)	Johnny Dalmas	private detective
"Red Wind"[10]	*Dime Detective* (Jan. 1938)	Johnny Dalmas	private detective
"The King in Yellow"	*Dime Detective* (Mar. 1938)	Steve Grayce	hotel detective
"Bay City Blues"[11]	*Dime Detective* (June 1938)	Johnny Dalmas	private detective
"The Lady in the Lake"[12]	*Dime Detective* (Jan. 1939)	Johnny Dalmas	private detective
"Pearls are a Nuisance"	*Dime Detective* (Apr. 1939)	Walter Gage	playboy
"Trouble is My Business"[13]	*Dime Detective* (Aug. 1939)	Johnny Dalmas	private detective
"No Crime in the Mountains"[14]	*Detective Story* (Sep. 1941)	John Evans	private detective
"Marlowe Takes on the Syndicate"[15]	*London Daily Mail* (6–10 April 1959)	Philip Marlowe	private detective

Notes

1 When the story was reprinted in the collection *The Simple Art of Murder* (1950), Chandler changed the protagonist's name to Johnny Dalmas.
2 Protagonist's name changed to Philip Marlowe in *The Simple Art of Murder*.
3 Incorporated into *The Big Sleep* (1939).
4 Protagonist's name changed to Ted Carmady in *The Simple Art of Murder*.
5 Incorporated into *Farewell, My Lovely* (1940).
6 Protagonist's name changed to Philip Marlowe in *The Simple Art of Murder*.
7 Incorporated into *The Big Sleep*.
8 Incorporated into *Farewell, My Lovely*.
9 Incorporated into *Farewell, My Lovely*.
10 Protagonist's name changed to Philip Marlowe in *The Simple Art of Murder*.
11 Incorporated into *The Lady in the Lake* (1940).
12 Incorporated into *The Lady in the Lake*.
13 Protagonist's name changed to Philip Marlowe in *The Simple Art of Murder*.
14 Incorporated into *The Lady in the Lake*.
15 Reprinted under the title "Wrong Pigeon" in *Manhunt* (Feb. 1969); "The Pencil" in *Argosy* (Sep. 1965); and "Philip Marlowe's Last Case" in *Ellery Queen's Mystery Magazine* (Jan. 1962).

Non-Detective Stories

Title	First Publication
"I'll Be Waiting"	*The Saturday Evening Post* (14 Oct. 1939)
"The Bronze Door"	Unknown (Nov. 1939)
"Professor Bingo's Snuff"	*Park East* (June, July, & Aug. 1951)

Cover for the issue of Black Mask *that included*
Chandler's third crime story

Chandler and Depression-Era Los Angeles

In the following essay Roy Meador discusses the origins of
Chandler's pulp writing.

Chandler in the Thirties
Apprenticeship of an Angry Man
Roy Meador
Book Forum, 6, no. 2 (1982): 143–153

When the 1930s began, Raymond Chandler was a well-paid oil company executive in Los Angeles. When the 30s ended, he was unemployed, economically harassed, and yet vastly better off than when the decade started. In 1939, after a struggle during the 30s to master fiction writing, Chandler published *The Big Sleep,* introduced Philip Marlowe, and found a literary career ahead, his for the grasping. Chandler's harvest following the drudgery of the 30s was approval from readers in many languages, attention from critics for doing new things with detective stories, wide recogni-

tion of his success in straddling the border between mysteries and mainstream literature, and opportunities to get rich in Hollywood.

"What greater prestige can a man like me have," Chandler wondered in a 1945 letter, "than to have taken a cheap, shoddy, and utterly lost kind of writing and have made of it something that intellectuals claw each other about?"

The clawing persists. Raymond Chandler's books are in print and readily accessible. Writers of his generation with stronger claims to durability in their heyday—John P. Marquand, Kenneth Roberts, Nobel laureates Pearl Buck and Sinclair Lewis come to mind—are less discussed and analyzed as well as tougher to locate. Ask around. Are there many readers, writers, professors, critics, or travelers in waiting rooms who never heard of Chandler and his eminent gumshoe Marlowe? Chandler, Marlowe, and the Coast city they loved, revealed, and methodically bludgeoned show signs of continuing vitality and long survival.

The crossroad year for Raymond Chandler was 1932 when he was 44 years old. The Depression and his personal circumstances served as a whirlwind to lift Chandler abruptly and start him off in a direction strange and alien compared with his activities in the 1920s. Behind him was a background that included birth in Chicago (July 23, 1888), growing up in England, studying classics at Dulwich Public School, toiling as a London jack-of-all-letters, picking apricots and stringing tennis rackets in Los Angeles before World War I, leading a combat platoon in the war, marrying Pearl Eugenie Hurlburt who was 17 years his senior, and laboring in Los Angeles during the 1920s as the president of companies owned by Dabney Oil Syndicate.

In 1932 California orchards produced fruit, but three dozen oranges sold for a dime. Few had the dime. At Los Angeles as in other cities, silent throngs waited at garbage dumps to search refuse for food. Millions awakened that year from America's dream of eternal prosperity. The nation approached 5 million unemployed, and over a fourth of the banks closed by fall. The Republicans nominated Herbert Hoover, and the Democrats sentenced Franklin Roosevelt to the presidency and the task of restoring confidence. In a climate of economic paralysis, even movie attendance fell. Walter Gifford, President of American Telephone and Telegraph and head of the Organization on Unemployment Relief, offered an inspired update of Marie Antoinette's suggestion that the masses should eat cake. Gifford suggested distributing free movie tickets to the poor. If times were bad and people hungry, let them go to the movies. In 1932 as well, Raymond Chandler lost his job.

Advertisement in the January 1935 issue of Black Mask. *Chandler later incorporated* "Killer in the Rain" *into his first novel,* The Big Sleep *(1939).*

Later he blamed the Depression. Actually he was fired for drinking heavily, recurrent binges, absenteeism, and calling the office at odd hours threatening to leap from the window of a Los Angeles hotel. Such anomalies led to his dismissal. Chandler would recall his business years with overlapping pride and distaste. He claimed to have the best office staff in Los Angeles because of his talent for picking people, yet "business is very tough and I hate it," he wrote in 1957.

Several theories are put forward to account for Chandler's reckless behavior: frustration in marriage to an aging wife, chronic shyness driving him to seek release from inhibitions through alcohol, dissatisfaction with business forcing actions to make dismissal inevitable. After losing his job, Chandler quickly proved he could stop drinking and had the will power to commit himself at the age of 44 to a task demanding self-discipline, hard work, and courage.

To survive, millions of Americans that year waited in unemployment and bread lines, knocked on doors, applied for relief, sold apples, joined the Marines, hopped freight trains, hitchhiked toward any rumor of work, became prostitutes, begged, borrowed, or stole. Chandler did none of these things. He remained home and methodically taught himself the arcane craft of writing fiction professionally. Seven years later he published a celebrated first novel. Those who strive in their middle years to swim literary rapids with nervous typewriters and shaky resolutions can take heart from Raymond Chandler's 1932 example. Philip Marlowe, the same as Social Security and bank deposit insurance, is a direct result of Depression-era troubles. If Chandler had continued to manage the best office staff in Los Angeles, it is doubtful that Marlowe would ever have patrolled the "mean streets" of Los Angeles or maintained his lonely vigils in the "nights of a thousand crimes."

Chandler was shocked by his dismissal and later said the event "taught me not to take anything for granted." He wrote disparagingly of his ten years as "the factotum of a corrupt millionaire." The experience did not produce an anti-business bias in his writing, although the hypocrisies of the rich apparently rankled. "Philip Marlowe and I do not despise the upper classes because they take baths and have money. We despise them because they are phoney," he wrote.

After 1932, Chandler never returned to the business world. His only periods of employment were brief, peevish intervals on Hollywood payrolls as a screenwriter in the 1940s. In 1932, out of work and short of funds with the Depression tightening its embrace, instead of seeking another job, Chandler resurrected a dormant suspicion that he could make money writing. A 1950 letter to his British publisher Hamish Hamilton recalls the start:

Wandering up and down the Pacific Coast in an automobile, I began to read pulp magazines, because they were cheap enough to throw away and because I never had at any time any taste for the kind of thing which is known as women's magazines. This was in the great days of the *Black Mask* (if I may call them great days) and it struck me that some of the writing was pretty forceful and honest, even though it had its crude aspect. I decided that this might be a good way to try to learn to write fiction and get paid a small amount of money at the same time. I spent five months over an 18,000 word novelette and sold it for $180. After that I never looked back, although I had a good many uneasy periods looking forward.

(*Raymond Chandler Speaking*)

For the rest of the decade with Depression sulking in the world outside, Chandler persisted in the struggle to make himself a professional writer. He turned unemployment into artistic opportunity, but life without a regular salary was not easy in Los Angeles during the 1930s. The Chandlers lived on savings, a small monthly allowance from former colleagues Chandler had supported in a law suit against Dabney Oil Syndicate, and modest income from his sales to pulp magazines. The Chandlers were better off than many; but after years of prosperous comfort, Depression hard times were an unaccustomed ordeal. Chandler reminisced when the times were past:

I never slept in the park, but I came damn close to it. I went five days without anything to eat but soup once, and I had just been sick at that. It didn't kill me, but neither did it increase my love of humanity. The best way to find out if you have any friends is to go broke. The ones that hang on longest are your friends.

(Letter to James Sandoe, December 15, 1948)

With their furniture stored, during the 1930s the Chandlers lived in rented quarters, moving frequently from one Los Angeles area to another. They changed residences nine times in ten years. The reason was Chandler's nerves, however, not poverty. At one place the children were noisy, at another the traffic distracted. Sometimes the neighbors were difficult or the climate was inhospitable.

Wandering from abode to abode, Chandler in the 30s absorbed the whole of Los Angeles through his pores. He added to his already substantial knowledge of the city until his familiarity with the area was encyclopedic, covering the mood, look, temper, moral attitudes, and social realities of the place. His pulp stories and Marlowe novels confirm that Chandler was not simply a Los Angeles resident. He was a scientist dissecting a native society and recording detailed notes. He classified the facts and resonances of Southern California with the precision of a cultural historian and anthropologist combined. Los Angeles is a pervasive background in Chandler's work of the 30s and his later work based on the 30s. He used the city as an

A "WHITE" ISSUE IN JUNE

HOLD everything!

Believe it or not we are reluctant to express our own, editorial feeling toward a given story, even one by any of the tried-and-true favorite writers of the magazine. Once on a time we did say that we had never seen a better detective story in print or manuscript form than **"MALTESE FALCON,"** and the fame and wealth that came to **Dashiell Hammett** seem to have justified our enthusiasm.

In the case of a comparatively new writer, however, it is possible to speak without suspicion of favorable prejudice. But in place of telling it ourselves, we will let two writers, unacquainted with each other, contributors to other markets, tell it for us. These two writers called at widely separated intervals. The first spoke of "the best story he had ever seen published in America." The second mentioned "the best story he had ever read in **BLACK MASK.**" And both referred to identically the same story, one by **Raymond Chandler**, published in **BLACK MASK** some months ago.

The point is that **"NEVADA GAS,"** by **Raymond Chandler**, is the lead novelette in the June issue, and it is our humble opinion that **"NEVADA GAS"** is the best work, by and large, that **Mr. Chandler** has yet given us. Just let us say, mildly, that you are going to get one great kick out of **"NEVADA GAS"** next month, and we won't be accused of overstatement.

Why, you know **Hugh Candless**, you have seen and listened to his perfect type; and **George Dial** and **Johnny De Ruse**, maybe. And **Francine Ley**? Well, we won't say anything about **Francine**; she has a way of speaking for herself. And we doubt if **Zaparty** or **Mops Parisi** is on your calling list.

It's dollars to doughnuts that you'll read **"NEVADA GAS"** more than the once and find something which the excitement and the rush of action made you miss the first time over. And that, by the way, was an old trick in the work of **Dash Hammett**, wasn't it?

Advertisement in Black Mask *for Chandler's fifth story published in the magazine and the cover for the number in which it appeared. The editors were promoting Chandler as the successor to Hammett.*

integral and atmospheric presence so that his works surpass textbooks and maps in revealing the truth and texture of Los Angeles during pre-war, pre-freeway, pre-smog days. Lawrence Clark Powell wrote about the first four Marlowe novels that became Chandler's principal dividends from his toils and observations of the 30s:

> We find in his "Big Four" a glittering mosaic of greater Los Angeles from San Bernardino to the sea . . . What distinguishes his treatment of Los Angeles from that of most novelists is his wealth of precise observation and power of description . . . Not only does Chandler describe environment with poetical realism, his people are vividly alive, even the most minor such as bartenders, elevator men, and parking lot attendants. His major characters, especially detectives, are gloriously real and threaten to walk off the page into our own lives. He created an enthralling human menagerie. Read Chandler and then go downtown to the Central Library and sit on a bench in the park. His characters will pass by, and some may even sit down beside you.
>
> (Lawrence Clark Powell, *California Classics*)

The "Big Four" hailed by Powell are *The Big Sleep, Farewell, My Lovely, The High Window,* and *The Lady in the Lake.* The first two were written in the 30s and the others early in the 40s. All four give us Philip Marlowe in his finest hours with a Los Angeles setting and a 30s mood.

Los Angeles in the 1930s was not a sleepy village as Marlowe describes it in *The Little Sister.* The city he sentimentally recalls there is adrift somewhere in the past, kept alive through the remembering words of Raymond Chandler:

> I used to like this town. A long time ago. There were trees along Wilshire Boulevard. Beverly Hills was a country town. Westwood was bare hills and lots offering at eleven hundred dollars and no takers . . . Los Angeles was just a big dry sunny place with ugly homes and no style, but goodhearted and peaceful. It had the climate they yap about now. People used to sleep out on porches.

In this passage, Chandler's memory was turning back a calendar of decades rather than years to early in the century. The Los Angeles of hustle and threat that Marlowe faced in the 30s was rather different. *Colliers* reported in 1938 that Los Angeles had 600 brothels, 300 gambling houses, 1,800 bookies, and 23,000 one-armed bandits. It was a city with ample work for Marlowe and the tough Chandler detectives who prepared the way for him in the 1930s pulps: Mallory, Johnny DeRuse, Carmady, John Dalmas, Steve Grayce, Pete Anglich. These were the tough and harassed protagonists of Chandler's pulp apprenticeship in the 30s.

Why the pulps? They were ubiquitous, popular, and greedy for stories from any competent writers who could help satisfy the national appetite by the 1930s for approximately 200 million words annually. The typical pulp had 120 pages, 7 x 10 inches in size, with showy covers and long stories written to a formula that emphasized brisk action, gripping suspense, and an atmosphere of violence and peril. Over a thousand pulp writers, a third of them in Manhattan, wrote fast to meet deadlines and earn their penny a word. Pulp specialists such as Erle Stanley Gardner churned out stories in a few days and often published under pseudonyms. Chandler's output was minuscule compared with such fiction speed demons. From the start he worked painstakingly. He had something more than immediate income as an objective.

The pulps in the 1920s and 1930s provided a valuable training ground for many writers, especially the major pulp alumni led by Dashiell Hammett and Raymond Chandler. After assessing the pulp field, Chandler selected *Black Mask* as his model and target. This proved his taste and literary savvy. *Black Mask,* founded by H. L. Mencken and George Jean Nathan to earn capital for *Smart Set,* under editor Captain Joseph T. Shaw began demonstrating in the 1920s that literature can happen on wood pulp paper as well as slick paper.

Black Mask ran Dashiell Hammett's first story in 1922 and the September 1929-January 1930 issues contained *The Maltese Falcon,* featuring Marlowe's deadly and distinguished forerunner in the private eye vocation, Sam Spade. Chandler wrote of this seminal creation, "an art which is capable of it is not 'by hypothesis' incapable of anything. Once a detective story can be as good as this, only the pedants will deny that it *could* be even better."

Chandler analyzed the work of Hammett and others with the fidelity scholars typically reserve for erudite prospecting in the pages of a Shakespeare or Joyce. In 1932 when he started, Chandler was a 44-year old undergraduate attending *Black Mask* university with that magazine's hard-boiled contributors as the faculty. Chandler rewrote stories in his own words and compared with the originals. He told Erle Stanley Gardner about his results with a Gardner novelette: "In the end I was a bit sore because I couldn't try to sell it. It looked pretty good."

Chandler's synopses and annotations tutored him in the methods and tough manners of pulp detective stories. George Eliot called popular fiction "spiritual gin," but little could be labeled spiritual about the pulps, though gin was perhaps apropos. Chandler wrote that "the demand was for constant action; if you stopped to think you were lost. When in doubt have a man come through a door with a gun in his hand."

When he was ready to stop "playing the sedulous ape," after laborious writing and rewriting, Chandler finished and submitted his first story, "Blackmailers Don't Shoot." Captain Shaw promptly acknowledged its quality and published the novelette in the December 1933 issue of

Black Mask. The payment of $180 worked out to a rate of about $1 per day. Chandler needed to sell at least ten such stories annually to come within nibbling distance of an austere living, but he continued to write as if each story was not an ephemeral pulp but an overture to literature. He exercised care that was an unheard of luxury among pulp professionals. Obstinate rewriting was an epicurean affectation for writers trying to make a living.

Chandler sold one story in 1933, two in 1934, three in 1935, five in 1936, two in 1937, three in 1938, and five in 1939. The three stories sold to *Dime Detective* in 1938 earned $1,275. During part of 1938, Chandler worked on *The Big Sleep,* an essential investment in the future but no immediate help as a source of funds. By contrast, across town in the film colony, Fred Astaire's 1937 salary was $271,711, Marlene Dietrich's was $370,000, and Louis B. Mayer's was $1,161,753.

When he completed *The Big Sleep,* Chandler worked several months on a second novel, only to scrap the results. A December 1939 letter states:

> I had to throw my second book away, so that leaves me
> with nothing to show for the last six months and possi-
> bly nothing to eat for the next six. But it also leaves the
> world a far far better place to live in than if I had not
> thrown it away.

(Selected Letters of Raymond Chandler)

Scrapping work that might have produced income underscores Chandler's stubborn integrity as a writer even before he was established. As the Depression decade ended and the 40s began, Chandler labored with that familiar occupational torment of authors—the second novel. In April 1940, he finished *Farewell, My Lovely* which broodingly portrays the Los Angeles scene of the 1930s insistently and poetically. Later, as he had thrown away an early version of his second novel, Chandler in a sense also threw away the city that spawned his detective and gave direction to his private vision.

After the 30s, wartime boom and postwar growth transformed Southern California into a plush megalopolis Philip Marlowe would never quite fit or call home. Marlowe's true city is always Los Angeles with a 1930s frown, venal, sweaty before air conditioning, dangerous. In *The Long Goodbye,* a disillusioned Marlowe realizes "there aren't any safe places" left in "the big angry city" where "twenty-four hours a day somebody is running, somebody else is trying to catch him. Out there in the night of a thousand crimes . . . A city no worse than others, a city rich and vigorous and full of pride, a city lost and beaten and full of emptiness."

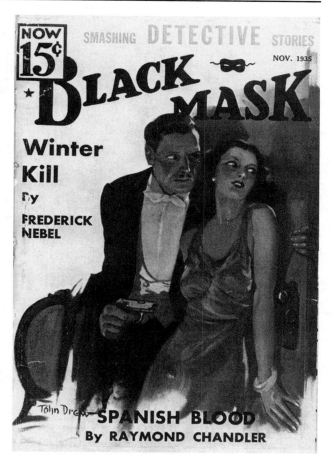

Cover for the issue featuring Chandler's sixth Black Mask *story*

Chandler demonstrated that it is not essential to admire a place to write about it memorably. A 1939 Chandler letter complains that there is a touch of the desert about everything in California and the minds of the people. "I'm sick of California and the kind of people it breeds," he wrote. Such statements could also signal weariness with a rough decade and hanging on until better days arrived. Those days came in the 1940s, and Chandler used screenwriting profits to buy a house in La Jolla. He claimed not to miss the city, but Marlowe showed the loss. In *Playback* (1958), Marlowe is a shadow image of himself without the city as a dynamic, mobile stage for his performance. He is a man whose significance depends on a specific place which seems to have been misplaced. In a 1956 letter Chandler acknowledged the city's importance:

> I know now what is the matter with my writing or not
> writing. I've lost any affinity for my background. Los
> Angeles is no longer my city . . . To write about a place
> you have to love it or hate it or do both by turns, which is

Photograph from the First West Coast Black Mask *Get-Together, 11 January 1936. This dinner was the only occasion on which Chandler and Dashiell Hammett met. Pictured are, seated left to right, Arthur Barnes, John K. Butler, W. T. Ballard, Horace McCoy, and Norbert Davis; standing are Raymond J. Moffatt, Chandler, Herbert Stinson, Dwight Babcock, Eric Taylor, and Hammett.*

usually the way you love a woman. But a sense of vacuity and boredom—that is fatal.

(*Selected Letters of Raymond Chandler*)

Chandler's attitude in the 30s was ambivalent. Then he both loved and loathed the city, which can be a potent mixture of emotions for creating the special tensions of literature. From the start, Los Angeles served Chandler as a vital backdrop. His first detective, Mallory in "Blackmailers Don't Shoot," comes to Los Angeles from Chicago on a case and stays. Mallory's successors including Marlowe keep Los Angeles their permanent beat.

A parallel Chandler concern from the start was to get the most from the American language, which he claimed to learn as a foreign language after returning to the country of his birth with a British education. Captivated by the Possibilities of the American language, Chandler insisted it "could say almost anything."

All I wanted to do when I began writing was to play with a fascinating new language, to see what it would do as a means of expression which might remain on the level of unintellectual thinking and yet acquire the power to say things which are usually only said with a literary air. . . . I wrote melodrama because when I looked around me it was the only kind of writing I saw that was relatively honest and yet was not trying to put over somebody's party line.

(*Raymond Chandler Speaking*)

In stories and novels, Hemingway had vividly illustrated the special power of this "new language." James M. Cain had also revealed its possibilities for mystery and sus-

pense fiction in his 1934 novel set in Southern California, *The Postman Always Rings Twice,* whose narrator Frank Chambers is a primitive Marlowe ancestor in language if not character. Following Hemingway's large-booted lead, Chandler used ordinary American slang and vernacular with extraordinary skill to achieve graceful, robust, unexpected effects. Though a disciple of Hammett, Chandler noted Hammett's failure to venture far with the language and its flexible potential. In "The Simple Art of Murder," Chandler wrote, "The American language . . . can say things he did not know how to say, or feel the need of saying. In his hands it had no overtones, left no echo, evoked no image beyond a distant hill." In a letter to John Houseman, Chandler spoke late in life about his fun with the language and his severed connection with the city:

I could write a bestseller, but I never have. There was always something I couldn't leave out or something I had to put in . . . I have had a lot of fun with the American language; it has fascinating idioms, is constantly creative, very much like the English of Shakespeare's time, its slang and argot is wonderful, and so on. But I have lost Los Angeles. It is no longer the place I knew so well and was almost the first to put on paper. I have that feeling, not very unusual, that I helped create the town and was then pushed out of it by the operators. I can hardly find my way around any longer.

(From a Memoir by John Houseman included with *The Blue Dahlia, A Screenplay*)

Chandler in the 30s sought to make both language and locale accurate and appropriate for his stories. These

1930s pulp efforts are fast-paced, sport a tough milieu, and obey the tradition of laying on the violence; but they contain many early intimations of the simile-rich Chandler style that distinguishes the Marlowe novels and elevates them from escapist thrillers to art. Frank MacShane in *The Life of Raymond Chandler* calls it a miracle, considering the author's financial straits, that from 1933 to 1938 his work steadily improved.

His pulps of the 30s eventually proved to be astute investments of time and effort. The stories have been resurrected from their wood pulp archives and reprinted. Many of them served as raw materials for the Marlowe novels. In *The Big Sleep,* Chandler used material from the 1935 and 1936 *Black Mask* stories, "Killer in the Rain" and "The Curtain." He displayed similar frugality with his literary capital from the Depression years by skillfully metamorphosing other pulp novelettes into Marlowe novels, all prominent today among the small group of mysteries hailed as important and accepted as literature.

Style, language, and site are important in mystery stories, but the detective is the prime mover in the equation. Chandler's detectives from the 1933 Mallory through Marlowe show a pattern of evolution from pulp-primitive to Marlowe-sophistication; but Chandler's men have certain character traits in common, especially a commitment to ethical and professional work, loyalty to clients, sympathy for underdogs, and a day's work for a day's pay ($25 per day and expenses plus eight cents a mile in Marlowe's early cases). Chandler's detective returns the fee if he can't deliver. He stubbornly applies his author's British public school principles as he painfully lives up to what are no doubt the most famous lines ever published and republished about a private eye:

> Down these mean streets a man must go who is not himself mean, who is neither tarnished nor afraid . . . He must be, to use a rather weathered phrase, a man of honor—by instinct, by inevitability, without thought of it, and certainly without saying it. He must be the best man in his world and a good enough man for any world.
>
> ("The Simple Art of Murder")

Chandler's detective is committed to social justice because social injustice was a grim fact of American life in the 1930s. When Tom Joad says goodbye to Ma, telling her that he will be wherever there's a fight so hungry people can eat, it seems not implausible that Tom Joad, on the run, changes his name to Philip Marlowe and opens an office in Los Angeles. Both men are crusaders, and Steinbeck's saga of the Okies and *The Big Sleep* appeared about the same time early in 1939. Two other lasting California documents appeared that year: Huxley's *After Many A Summer Dies the Swan* and West's *The Day of the Locust.* Among these four 1939 books with a claim on the

Cover for the issue featuring Chandler's tenth Black Mask *story*

present, *The Big Sleep* is probably familiar to more people than the three other classics combined. It has established as permanent a toehold in American culture as Bogart's twitch. Marlowe in *The Big Sleep* is, of course, the definitive Chandler detective, encompassing the others and reaching out to new dimensions. Marlowe is the archetypal private eye, a knight-errant equipped to cope with 20th century urban dragons. The same as Hamlet, he occupies a world badly out of joint and has the nontransferrable duty to set it right.

Marlowe is a loner, as dedicated and nearly as celibate as an Irish priest. He is a man of the 30s in his thirties, a graduate student of hard times. He works all hours and greets beatings or bullets as occupational hazards. Examine Edward Hopper's 1942 painting, "Nighthawks," showing a city lunch counter at midnight. A man and woman drink coffee. Another man, alone in the heart of loneliness, sits with his back to us, rehashing a dangerous day. That man could be Marlowe. He goes home eventually to his bachelor apartment, i.e, monastic cell. If his bed is occupied by a corrupt female such as Carmen Sternwood, he throws her out and remakes the bed with

Cover for the issue of Black Mask *that includes Chandler's story "Try the Girl," his last story about a private detective named Carmady*

compromise with corruption, battle gangsters and police, remain "a lonely man, a poor man, a dangerous man," while polishing up the American dream. "Marlowe is a failure," Chandler admitted. "In the long run I guess we are all failures or we wouldn't have the kind of world we have." Chandler knew his detective-crusader could not win, not permanently. The cities of America in the 1930s were not programmed for automatic happy endings. Police Captain Gregory in *The Big Sleep* tells Marlowe:

> I like to see the law win . . . That's what I'd like. You and me both lived too long to think I'm likely to see it happen. Not in this town, not in any town half this size in any part of this wide, green, and beautiful U.S.A. We just don't run our country that way.

Marlowe sees no reason to argue, but he keeps trying to make it happen, perpetually quixotic. Chandler made his detective responsible for an impossible moral struggle and a modern Crusade in the homes, offices, alleys, and streets of Los Angeles. Marlowe calls it a place dedicated to the principle that "law is where you buy it." We have scant reason to wonder that Chandler's man goes to bed "full of whiskey and frustration" and sometimes feels "as empty of life as a scarecrow's pockets." "I don't like it," says Marlowe, "but what the hell am I to do? I'm on a case. I'm selling what I have to sell to make a living. What little guts and intelligence the Lord gave me and a willingness to get pushed around in order to protect a client."

From his first pulp story, Chandler hoped to transcend the conventional mystery format and to write scenes that would "leave an afterglow." Defining a classic as writing that surpasses the possibilities of its form, Chandler believed no such classics of crime and detection had been written, "which is one of the principal reasons why otherwise reasonable people continue to assault the citadel."

He was never satisfied with his own results in the 30s or later, but he granted the power of stories in the *Black Mask* tradition. Though primitive and predictable, they packed a wallop and generated "the smell of fear."

> Their characters lived in a world gone wrong, a world in which, long before the atom bomb, civilization had created the machinery of its own destruction, and was learning to use it with all the moronic delight of a gangster trying out his first machine gun. The law was something to be manipulated for profit and power. The streets were dark with something more than night.
>
> (Raymond Chandler, 1950 Introduction to *Trouble Is My Business*)

clean sheets. "This was the room I had to live in. It was all I had in the way of a home . . . I couldn't stand her in that room any longer." At the soul's dark hour of three a.m., he drinks alone and plays a solitary game of chess. Soon with the new day, new problems. They won't be easy.

Marlowe, Los Angeles knight of the 30s, must be a special man, because his jobs are far outside the safe and tame boundaries of the normal. In the 1930s, failure and fear suddenly became avenues of life in America for people who had never met such strange enemies before. Raymond Chandler sent Marlowe to battle them. If he cannot right now turn social defeat into victory, Marlowe brings the consolation that there are worse things than defeat, and tomorrow is another day for another try. In the 1930s, something had gone awry, and the times called for a combination Zorro-Lochinvar-Shadow to cauterize public evil. Chandler gave Marlowe the assignment. He must keep honest and aloof, refuse to

Cover for the June 1938 issue of Dime Detective Magazine, *which included a story Chandler later incorporated into his novel* Farewell, My Lovely *(1940)*

When the 30s ended, so did Chandler's apprenticeship. He was ready for his Marlowes of the 40s, for Hollywood, for Depression's end. In 1945 he paid income taxes of nearly $50,000. "Pretty awful for a chap who was gnawing old shoes not too many years ago." In the 30s he found what he wanted to do and learned how to do it. Now we go to Chandler to gauge the look, meaning, and symptoms of the 30s in urban places. These lessons have value. They explain human responses to trouble through the insights, truth, and singular beauty of literature by a writer who traveled beyond a distant hill and leaves an afterglow. "Pulp paper never dreamed of posterity," wrote Chandler, but his 30s struggles bestowed on his own pages the birthright of long life.

Looking Back

In 1950 twelve of Chandler's short stories were reprinted in a collection titled The Simple Art of Murder. *In his introduction to the volume Chandler looked back on the stories he had written during the 1930s and commented on what he was trying to achieve with his fiction.*

Some literary antiquarian of a rather special type may one day think it worth while to run through the files of the pulp detective magazines which flourished during the late twenties and early thirties, and determine just how and when and by what steps the popular mystery story shed its refined good manners and went native. He will need sharp eyes and an open mind. Pulp paper never dreamed of posterity and most of it must be a dirty brown color by now. And it takes a very open mind indeed to look beyond the unnecessarily gaudy covers, trashy titles and barely acceptable advertisements and recognize the authentic power of a kind of writing that even at its most mannered and artificial, made most of the fiction of the time taste like a cup of luke-warm consommé at a spinsterish tearoom.

I don't think this power was entirely a matter of violence, although far too many people got killed in these stories and their passing was celebrated with a rather too loving attention to detail. It certainly was not a matter of fine writing, since any attempt at that would have been ruthlessly blue-penciled by the editorial staff. Nor was it because of any great originality of plot or character. Most of the plots were rather ordinary and most of the characters rather primitive types of people. Possibly it was the smell of fear which these stories managed to generate. Their characters lived in a world gone wrong, a world in which, long before the atom bomb, civilization had created the machinery for its own destruction, and was learning to use it with all the moronic delight of a gangster trying out his first machine gun. The law was something to be manipulated for profit and power. The streets were dark with something more than night. The mystery story grew hard and cynical about motive and character, but it was not cynical about the effects it tried to produce nor about its technique of producing them. A few unusual critics recognized this at the time, which was all one had any right to expect. The average critic never recognizes an achievement when it happens. He explains it after it has become respectable.

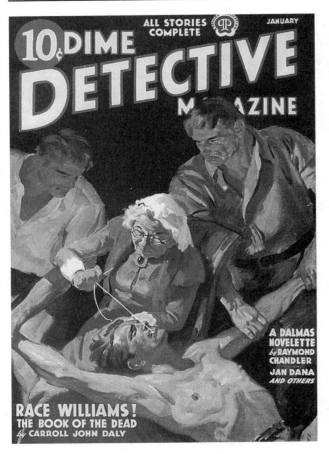

Cover for the January 1939 issue of Dime Detective Magazine, *which included Chandler's story "The Lady in the Lake"*

The emotional basis of the standard detective story was and had always been that murder will out and justice will be done. Its technical basis was the relative insignificance of everything except the final denouement. What led up to that was more or less passage-work. The denouement would justify everything. The technical basis of the *Black Mask* type of story on the other hand was that the scene outranked the plot, in the sense that a good plot was one which made good scenes. The ideal mystery was one you would read if the end was missing. We who tried to write it had the same point of view as the film makers. When I first went to work in Hollywood a very intelligent producer told me that you couldn't make a successful motion picture from a mystery story, because the whole point was a disclosure that took a few seconds of screen time while the audience was reaching for its hat. He was wrong, but only because he was thinking of the wrong kind of mystery.

As to the emotional basis of the hard-boiled story, obviously it does not believe that murder will

out and justice will be done—unless some very determined individual makes it his business to see that justice is done. The stories were about the men who made that happen. They were apt to be hard men, and what they did, whether they were called police officers, private detectives or newspaper men, was hard, dangerous work. It was work they could always get. There was plenty of it lying around. There still is. Undoubtedly the stories about them had a fantastic element. Such things happened, but not so rapidly, nor to so close-knit a group of people, nor within so narrow a frame of logic. This was inevitable because the demand was for constant action; if you stopped to think you were lost. When in doubt have a man come through a door with a gun in his hand. This could get to be pretty silly, but somehow it didn't seem to matter. A writer who is afraid to overreach himself is as useless as a general who is afraid to be wrong.

As I look back on my own stories it would be absurd if I did not wish they had been better. But if they had been much better they would not have been published. If the formula had been a little less rigid, more of the writing of that time might have survived. Some of us tried pretty hard to break out of the formula, but we usually got caught and sent back. To exceed the limits of a formula without destroying it is the dream of every magazine writer who is not a hopeless hack. There are things in my stories which I might like to change or leave out altogether. To do this may look simple, but if you try, you find you cannot do it at all. You will only destroy what is good without having any noticeable effect on what is bad. You cannot recapture the mood, the state of innocence, much less the animal gusto you had when you had little else. Everything a writer learns about the art or craft of fiction takes just a little away from his need or desire to write at all. In the end he knows all the tricks and has nothing to say.

As for the literary quality of these exhibits, I am entitled to assume from the imprint of a distinguished publisher that I need not be sickeningly humble. As a writer I have never been able to take myself with that enormous earnestness which is one of the trying characteristics of the craft. And I have been fortunate to escape what has been called "that form of snobbery which can accept the Literature of Entertainment in the Past, but only the Literature of Enlightenment in the Present." Between the one-syllable humors of the comic strip and the anemic subtleties of the litterateurs there is a wide stretch of country,

I'LL BE WAITING

By RAYMOND CHANDLER

ILLUSTRATED BY HY RUBIN

Al took his hand out of his pocket and stretched it against Tony's chest. He gave him a light lazy push. "Get her out of there."

AT ONE O'CLOCK in the morning, Carl, the night porter, turned down the last of three table lamps in the main lobby of the Windermere Hotel. The blue carpet darkened a shade or two and the walls drew back into remoteness. The chairs filled with shadowy loungers. In the corners were memories like cobwebs.

The frown passed and a miniature of a smile quirked at the corners of his lips. He sat relaxed, a short, pale, paunchy, middle-aged man with long, delicate fingers clasped on the elk's tooth on his watch chain; the long delicate fingers of a sleight-of-hand artist, fingers with shiny, molded nails and tapering first joints, fingers a little spatulate at the

the watch chain. At one moment he was leaning back relaxed, and the next he was standing balanced on his feet, perfectly still, so that the movement of rising seemed to be a thing imperfectly perceived, an error of vision.

He walked with small, polished shoes delicately across the blue carpet and under the arch. The music

Opening page of "I'll Be Waiting" in the 14 October 1939 issue of The Saturday Evening Post, *Chandler's only story sale to the slick-magazine market. Although such magazines paid much better than the pulps, Chandler considered their formulas for plots and characters to be unrealistic and dishonest, and he refused to write more fiction for them.*

in which the mystery story may or may not be an important landmark. There are those who hate it in all its forms. There are those who like it when it is about nice people ("that charming Mrs. Jones, whoever would have thought she would cut off her husband's head with a meat saw? Such a handsome man, too!"). There are those who think violence and sadism interchangeable terms, and those who regard detective fiction as sub-literary on no better grounds than that it does not habitually get itself jammed up with subordinate clauses, tricky punctuation and hypothetical subjunctives. There are those who read it only when they are tired or sick, and, from the number of mystery novels they consume, they must be tired and sick most of the time. There are the aficionados of deduction (with whom I have had words, see pp. 977–992) and the aficionados of sex who can't get it into their hot little heads that the fictional detective is a catalyst, not a Casanova. The former demand a ground plan of Greythorpe Manor, showing the study, the gun room, the main hall and staircase and the passage to that grim little room where the butler polishes the Georgian silver, thin-lipped and silent, hearing the murmur of doom. The latter think the shortest distance between two points is from a blonde to a bed.

No writer can please them all, no writer should try. The stories in this book certainly had no thought of being able to please anyone ten or fifteen years after they were written. The mystery story is a kind of writing that need not dwell in the shadow of the past and owes little if any allegiance to the cult of the classics. It is a good deal more than unlikely that any writer now living will produce a better historical novel than *Henry Esmond,* a better tale of children than *The Golden Age,* a sharper social vignette than *Madame Bovary,* a more graceful and elegant evocation than *The Spoils of Poynton,* a wider and richer canvas than *War and Peace* or *The Brothers Karamazov.* But to devise a more plausible mystery than *The Hound of the Baskervilles* or *The Purloined Letter* should not be too difficult. Nowadays it would be rather more difficult not to. There are no "classics" of crime and detection. Not one. Within its frame of reference, which is the only way it should be judged, a classic is a piece of writing which exhausts the possibilities of its form and can hardly be surpassed. No story or novel of mystery has done that yet. Few have come close. Which is one of the principal reasons why otherwise reasonable people continue to assault the citadel.

"Cannibalized" Stories

In 1938, after five years writing stories for the pulp magazines, Chandler began work on his first novel. For the plot, he drew upon material used in his pulp stories. In the following excerpt from the introduction to Killer in the Rain *(1964), a collection of Chandler's short stories, Philip Durham explains the technique Chandler used to combine earlier stories into* The Big Sleep.

When Raymond Chandler published *The Big Sleep,* his first of seven novels, in 1939, he did what multitudes of writers had done before him : he re-used some of his earlier material. Unlike most writers, however, re-using previously published stories left him with an uneasy feeling. Once a story was used in a novel it became—to use his word—'cannibalized'.

. . . .

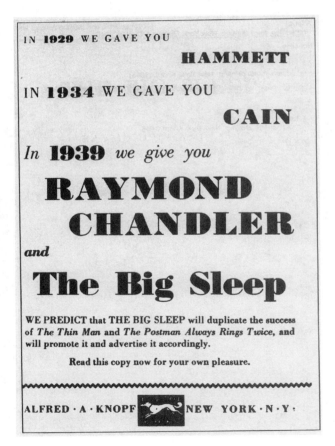

Front wrapper of the review copy of The Big Sleep. *This wrapper reflects Knopf's promotional strategy of linking Chandler to Hammett and James M. Cain, two celebrated hard-boiled writers also published by Knopf (Bruccoli Collection, Kent State University).*

A substantial part of Chandler's first novel, *The Big Sleep* (1939), was made from 'Killer in the Rain' (*Black Mask,* January 1935) and 'The Curtain' (*Black Mask,* September 1936); the second novel, *Farewell, My Lovely* (1940), made extensive use of 'The Man Who Liked Dogs' (*Black Mask,* March 1936), 'Try the Girl' (*Black Mask,* January 1937), and 'Mandarin's Jade' (*Dime Detective Magazine,* November 1937); and the fourth novel, *The Lady in the Lake* (1943), relied on 'Bay City Blues' (*Dime Detective Magazine,* November 1937), 'The Lady in the Lake' (*Dime Detective Magazine,* January 1939), and 'No Crime in the Mountains' (*Detective Story Magazine,* September 1941).[1]

Turning short stories into cohesive novels tested the extent of Chandler's skill. It meant combining and enlarging plots, maintaining a thematic consistency, blowing up scenes, and adapting, fusing, and adding characters.

To illustrate Chandler's method of combining and enlarging plots, one can see in *The Big Sleep,* for example, how the author drew from 'The Curtain' for Chapters 1–3, 20, 27–32 and from 'Killer in the Rain' for Chapters 4, 6–10, 12–16. With the exception of small bits borrowed from 'Mandarin's Jade' and 'Finger Man', Chapters 5, 11, 17–19, 21–26 were added. Ten chapters were drawn from 'The Curtain', eleven were taken from 'Killer in the Rain', and eleven were almost all new material. The twenty-one borrowed chapters, however, were expanded considerably beyond their original state in the short stories.

In 'The Curtain' Dade Winslow Trevillyan killed Dudley O'Mara, his stepfather, but to shield the family Dade's mother had O'Mara's body disposed of, leaving the impression that the missing man had pulled down the curtain. In 'Killer in the Rain' young Dade's counterpart is Carmen Dravec; both are psychopathic. In *The Big Sleep* young Dade Trevillyan and Carmen Dravec are fused into Carmen Sternwood, the twenty-year-old girl who had 'little sharp predatory teeth, as white as fresh orange pith and as shiny as porcelain.' Carmen Sternwood, the thumb-sucking psychopath, committed the murder which had been performed in 'The Curtain' by Dade Trevillyan. The central portion of the novel, largely added, linked the two short stories together, but throughout the novel the plots of the two stories were neatly woven into a unified whole.

Knopf newspaper advertisement for The Big Sleep

At times Chandler lifted whole passages, changing only a word here and there to improve the syntax or vary a mood. More frequently, however, he blew up scenes for the novel. An example is the greenhouse scene, which accounts for approximately 1,100 words in 'The Curtain', but is enlarged to 2,500 words in *The Big Sleep*.

In miniature the transformation developed as follows: forty-two words from 'The Curtain',

The air steamed. The walls and ceiling of the glass house dripped. In the halflight enormous tropical plants spread their blooms and branches all over the place, and the smell of them was almost as overpowering as the smell of boiling alcohol.

became eighty-two words in *The Big Sleep:*

The air was thick, wet, steamy and larded with the cloying smell of tropica orchids in bloom. The glass walls and roof were heavily misted and big drops of moisture splashed down on the plants. The light had an unreal greenish colour, like light filtered through an aquarium tank. The plants filled the place, a forest of them, with nasty meaty leaves and stalks like the newly washed fingers of dead men. They smelled as overpowering as boiling alcohol under a blanket.

Both passages are intense and vivid. The selection from 'The Curtain' achieves its effectiveness through terseness, while the selection from the novel allowed the author to create a mood through the use of hyperbole and striking similes.[2]

A Parallel Passage

For his description of Eddie Mars's Cypress Club in The Big Sleep, *Chandler borrowed and revised a passage from his pulp story "Finger Man," which was published in* Black Mask *in October 1934. When compared, the passages indicate how Chandler revised his prose in his novels.*

"Finger Man"

It was about ten o'clock when the little yellow-sashed orchestra got tired of messing around with a rhumba that nobody was dancing to. The marimba player dropped his sticks and got a cigarette into his mouth almost with the same movement. The boys sitting down reached for glasses under their chairs.

It was a good crowd for a Tuesday. The big, old-fashioned room had been a ballroom in the days when Las Olindas was thirty miles by water from San Angelo, and that was the only way anyone went to it. It was still a beautiful room, with damask panels and crystal chandeliers.

I leaned sidewise against the bar, which was on the same side of the room as the orchestra stand. I was turning a small glass of tequila around on the top of the bar. All the business was at the center one of the three roulette tables.

The Big Sleep

It was about ten-thirty when the little yellow-sashed Mexican orchestra got tired of playing a low-voiced, prettied-up rhumba that nobody was dancing to. The gourd player rubbed his finger tips together as if they were sore and got a cigarette into his mouth almost with the same movement. The other four, with a timed simultaneous stoop, reached under their chairs for glasses from which they sipped, smacking their lips and flashing their eyes. Tequila, their manner said. It was probably mineral water. The pretense was as wasted as the music. Nobody was looking at them.

The room had been a ballroom once and Eddie Mars had changed it only as much as his business compelled him. No chromium glitter, no indirect lighting from behind angular cornices, no fused glass pictures, or chairs in violent leather and polished metal tubing, none of the pseudomodernistic circus of the typical Hollywood night trap. The light was from heavy crystal chandeliers and the rose-damask panels of the wall were still the same rose damask, a little faded by time and darkened by dust, that had been matched long ago against the parquetry floor, of which only a small glass-smooth space in front of the little Mexican orchestra showed bare. The rest was covered by a heavy old-rose carpeting that must have cost plenty. The parquetry was made of a dozen kinds of hardwood, from Burma teak through half a dozen shades of oak and ruddy wood that looked like mahogany, and fading out to the hard pale wild lilac of the California hills, all laid in elaborate patterns, with the accuracy of a transit.

It was still a beautiful room and now there was roulette in it instead of measured, old-fashioned dancing. There were three tables close to the far wall. A low bronze railing joined them and made a fence around the croupiers. All three tables were working, but the crowd was at the middle one. I could see Vivian Regan's black head close to it from across the room where I was leaning against the bar and turning a small glass of bacardi around on the mahogany.

A First Novel

The Big Sleep *was published in the United States on 6 February 1939 by Alfred A. Knopf, with a first printing of five thousand copies. Knopf's plan for marketing the book was to declare Chandler the heir to Hammett and Cain, two successful hard-boiled novelists also in the Knopf stable. The firm promoted* The Big Sleep *heavily, giving it the most advertising for any of its detective novels since Hammett's* The Thin Man *in 1934. This campaign included large advertisements in* The New York Times *and on the cover of* Publishers Weekly.

Raymond Chandler

has had that type of career which is commonly referred to as "checkered." Born in Chicago of an Irish mother and an American father, he went early to England, where eventually he attended Dulwich College. After completing his education in France and Germany, he turned first to school-teaching as a profession, but soon gave that up in favor of writing. He became successively a book-reviewer, poet, paragraph-writer, and essayist. Following the war, in which he served with the Canadian Infantry, he came to the United States, where he has been variously occupied ever since in such capacities as accountant, tax expert, oil executive, and pulp writer. *The Big Sleep* is his first novel.

the big sleep

Not since Dashiell Hammett first appeared has there been a murder mystery story with the power, pace, and terrifying atmosphere of this one. And like Hammett's this is more than a "murder mystery": it is a novel of crime and character, written with uncommon skill and in a tight, tense style which is irresistible.

The center of the plot is a family: an old, paralyzed ex-soldier, who made a fortune in oil; his two beautiful daughters—one a gambler, the other a degenerate; and a strangely missing son-in-law. Around such a family, with all its money, its vices, and its hidden scandals, it was inevitable that there should cluster blackmailers, gangsters, and purveyors of forbidden thrills. There are violence and shameful things in the family's history, but the detective—shrewd, strong, incorruptible, the healthy force amid the shadows and the whispers—who started out to break a blackmail case and ended up to his neck in a series of mysterious murders, clears the atmosphere and leaves the reader content that justice, though of an unexpected sort, will after all be done.

BORZOI MYSTERIES

DASHIELL HAMMETT OMNIBUS

Three murder-mystery novels in one volume by the man whom Alexander Woollcott has called the greatest American detective-story writer. The works included are *Red Harvest, The Dain Curse,* and *The Maltese Falcon.*

THE BIG SLEEP
by Raymond Chandler

Not since Dashiell Hammett first appeared has there been a murder-mystery story with the power, pace, and terrifying atmosphere of this one. And like Hammett's this is more than a "murder mystery": it is a novel of crime and character, written with uncommon skill and in a tight, tense style which is irresistible.

CAUSE FOR ALARM
by Eric Ambler

This one is about Nicholas Marlow, engineer, who accepted the post of Milan representative of an English machinery firm and immediately became entangled in a web of international intrigue and espionage. Because he had nerve and shrewdness—and luck, however, he succeeded in putting a kink in the Rome-Berlin axis.

FOUR FRIGHTENED WOMEN
by George Harmon Coxe

All Murdock had to do was go down to the home of Ted Bernard, the radio comedian, and get some pictures of him and of his week-end guest, Irene Alexander, who was still one of America's movie sweethearts. The next morning the actress's nude body was found in her bedroom—and Murdock was one of the chief suspects. All of which makes Murdock's best case, for this time he is not just a smart newspaper man, but a man fighting to save his own skin.

TRENT INTERVENES
by E. C. Bentley

Here is Trent carrying on with his "cases" with his usual competence and aplomb, though Mr. Bentley is too good an artist to make him invariably successful. There are a round dozen of "cases" in this collection, each one full of excitement, provocation, and final satisfaction.

THREE STAR OMNIBUS

Three great murder-mystery stories in one volume—*Trent's Last Case* by E. C. Bentley, *Green Ice* by Raoul Whitfield, and *The Middle Temple Murder* by J. S. Fletcher.

ALFRED A. KNOPF · PUBLISHER · N·Y

Dust jacket for the first American edition of The Big Sleep, *published in 1939*
(Bruccoli Collection, Kent State University)

When Chandler converted short stories into a novel he needed a greater array of characters for the longer form. The manner in which he adapted, fused, and added characters for *The Big Sleep* was again a test of the author's literary ingenuity. Of the twenty-one characters in *The Big Sleep* seven were drawn directly from 'The Curtain,' six were taken from 'Killer in the Rain', four were composites from the two stories, and four were new creations.

The fusing of Dade Trevillyan and Carmen Dravec into Carmen Sternwood, and the fusing of General Dade Winslow of 'The Curtain' and Tony Dravec of 'Killer in the Rain' into General Guy Sternwood of *The Big Sleep* are examples of technical competence.

More important, however, was Chandler's development of the detective-hero. Philip Marlowe, the consistent hero throughout all of his novels, first appeared in *The Big Sleep* in 1939. But he had been conceived in 'Blackmailers Don't Shoot' in 1933.

. . . .

When Chandler published 'Killer in the Rain', his fourth story, in 1935, he was still experimenting with his principal character, a nameless first person narrator. In the next of these three stories the detective operated under the name of Carmady, and in the following three he was John Dalmas. By 1941 in 'No Crime in the Mountains' he appeared as John Evans, but in the meantime he had become the Philip Marlowe of Chandler's novels.

1. *Farewell, My Lovely* also used a small part from 'Trouble Is My Business'; *The High Window* drew a small portion from 'The King in Yellow'; and *The Long Good-bye* used a small bit from 'The Curtain'. It might also be noticed that on occasion Chandler borrowed from one short story for another. In 'No Crime in the Mountains', for instance, the description of Constable Barron is essentially the same as the description of Constable Tinchfield in Chapter IV of 'The Lady in the Lake'.

2. *Farewell, My Lovely* and *The Lady in the Lake* were put together in a manner quite like that described here for *The Big Sleep*. The technique, of course, was worked with variations. When, for example, Chandler incorporated the short story 'The Lady in the Lake' into the novel of the same name, he gave a completely different twist to a portion of the plot. In the short story Melton was a murderer, but in the novel, as Kingsley, he had nothing to do with murder. In 'Try the Girl', as another example, Mrs. Marineau shot Skalla, who died with Beulah holding his hand. When this story was developed in *Farewell, My Lovely*, Beulah (Velma)—who had already betrayed Skalla (Malloy)—was the one who killed the big man.

American Reviews of *The Big Sleep*

As was the case for his next three books, The Big Sleep *was reviewed as a genre novel in columns dedicated to mystery fiction. Though mostly positive, these brief reviews focused on the toughness of the tone and the sordidness of its plot and characters. The following reviews are typical of the reception Chandler's first novel received in the United States.*

Will Cuppy's review appeared in his column titled "Mystery and Adventure."

This unusual first novel should stir up a lot of valuable discussion. It can boast of an admirable hard-boiled manner, it contains several characters who will scare you with their extraordinary brands of wickedness, and the nightmare atmosphere is the real thing in spots. In our opinion, though, Mr. Chandler has almost spoiled it with a top-heavy cargo of lurid underworld incident, and he should therefore be stood in a corner and lectured upon the nature and suitable use of his talents. Two of the leading persons are Carmen and Vivian Sternwood, fast and far from righteous West Hollywood heiresses. As their father, paralyzed old General Sternwood, says: "Neither of them has any more moral sense than a cat. Neither have I. No Sternwood ever had." They're mixed up with the killing of a book racketeer, blackmail, more murder, and such folks as Eddie Mars (gambler), Joe Brody (crook) and Blonde Agnes (in person). Phil Marlowe is a slick sleuth in the Hammett tradition. It's a much better than average tough item; we're only saying that it might have been better with less high-pressure plot—but, then, it would have been another story. Moreover, Mr. Chandler deserves a medal for his handling of some wicked scenes; we shudder to think what some of our bad young bafflers would have done with them.
—*New York Herald Tribune Books*, 5 February 1939, p. 12

* * *

Under the title "February Mysteries" the reviewer for Time *noted, "Of last month's 22, the following stood out as best bets."* The Big Sleep *was one of a handful of novels briefly described.*

Detective Marlowe is plunged into a mess of murderers, thugs and psychopaths who make the characters of Dashiell Hammett and James Cain look like something out of Godey's Lady's Book.
—*Time* (6 March 1939): 63

* * *

The courtyard at Greystone, Beverly Hills, California. The Sternwood mansion in The Big Sleep *is based in part on this house, which was built by oilman Edward L. Doheny for his son, Edward Jr., in 1922 (courtesy of the Library of Congress, Prints and Photographs Division, Historic American Buildings Survey).*

The New Republic *was one of the few magazines in which Chandler's novel was not considered in the context of genre. In "New Books: A Reader's List," the reviewer briefly discussed a memoir of D. H. Lawrence, a book critical of the high regard of scientists and their work, and an historical study of "anti-Catholic, anti-foreign" sentiment in the United States before coming to* The Big Sleep, *the last book on his list.*

Some of the day's best commercial prose was served up by Black Mask, a pulp magerzoon, while Captain Shaw was at its head. This Chandler, like Dashiell Hammett before him, is a graduate (*cum laude*) of Black Mask; and it goes without saying that his first novel is something a good deal more than a who-done-it. If you have any feeling for subtle workmanship, don't give it the go-by.

—*The New Republic*, 98 (15 March 1939): 56

Chandler on the American Reception

Alfred A. Knopf sold ten thousand copies of The Big Sleep. *Although Chandler received only $2,000 from these sales, his novel was considered a commercial success in the mystery field. At the time, the average detective novel sold fewer than three thousand copies and only a handful of titles exceeded sales of five thousand. On 19 February 1939, two weeks after the American publication of* The Big Sleep, *Chandler wrote the following letter to Alfred A. Knopf, in which he reacted to the reception of his first novel and discussed his plans for future work.*

The Sternwoods, having moved up the hill, could no longer smell the stale sump water or the oil, but they could still look out their front windows and see what had made them rich. If they wanted to.

—*The Big Sleep*

Two views of the Horatio Court Apartments, Los Angeles. A distinctive architectural feature of Los Angeles, the bungalow court, in which small bungalows or apartments are arranged around a narrow central courtyard, appears frequently in Chandler's novels. In The Big Sleep, *Marlowe pursues one of A. G. Geiger's customers to "a narrow tree-lined street with a retaining wall on one side and three bungalow courts on the other" (Courtesy Library of Congress, Prints and Photographs Division, Historic American Buildings Survey).*

Dear Mr. Knopf:—

Please accept my thanks for your friendly letter and please believe that, whether you wrote to me or not, I should have written to thank you for the splendid send-off you are trying to give me. Having been more or less in business a great part of my life, I have some appreciation of what this involves, even though I know nothing of the publishing business.

Mr. Conroy wrote to me twice that you had said something about my getting to work on another book and I answered him that I wanted to put it off until I had an idea what kind of reception this one would get. I have only seen four notices, but two of them seemed more occupied with the depravity and unpleasantness of the book than with anything else. In fact the notice from the *New York Times,* which a clipping agency sent me as a come-on, deflated me pretty thoroughly. I do not want to write depraved books. I was aware that this yarn had some fairly unpleasant citizens in it, but my fiction was learned

Alfred A. Knopf in 1940

Not since Dashiell Hammett first appeared has there been a murder mystery story with the power, pace, and terrifying atmosphere of this one. And like Hammett's this is more than a "murder mystery": it is a novel of crime and character, written with uncommon skill and in a tight, tense style which is irresistible.

The centre of the plot is a family: an old, paralyzed ex-soldier, who made a fortune in oil; his two beautiful daughters—one a gambler, the other a degenerate; and a strangely missing son-in-law. Around such a family, with all its money, its vices, and its hidden scandals, it was inevitable that there should cluster blackmailers, gangsters, and purveyors of forbidden thrills. There are violence and shameful things in the family's history, but the detective—shrewd, strong, incorruptible, the healthy force amid the shadows and the whispers—who started out to break a blackmail case and ended up to his neck in a series of mysterious murders, clears the atmosphere and leaves the reader content that justice, though of an unexpected sort, will after all be done.

We recommend this novel with enthusiasm. In our opinion it will repeat the success of *The Postman Always Rings Twice*.

Selected Thrillers, Spring 1939

THE HAND OF KORNELIUS VOYT
by OLIVER ONIONS

Sober and convincing, yet mystifying and macabre, this extraordinary novel displays its author's brilliant ability in its highest degree. 7s 6d net

LAM TO THE SLAUGHTER
by A. A. FAIR

The greatest find amongst detective stories in the past decade. This is a mystery-sensation novel with a difference. It has wit, punch, toughness and ingenuity. 7s 6d net

THE BIG SLEEP
by RAYMOND CHANDLER

A murder mystery story with power, pace, and terrifying atmosphere a novel of crime and character, written with uncommon skill and in a tense style which is irresistible. 7s 6d net

HAMISH HAMILTON
90 Great Russell Street, London, WC1

Dust jacket for the first British edition of The Big Sleep, *published in March 1939. Hamish Hamilton was the British publisher for all of Chandler's novels (Bruccoli Collection, Kent State University).*

Newspaper advertisement for the English edition of The Big Sleep

terday. They have Humphrey Bogart playing the lead, which I am in favor of also. It only remains to convince Warner Brothers.

As to the next job of work for your consideration, I should like, if you approve, to try to jack it up a few more notches. It must be kept sharp, swift and racy, of course, but I think it could be a little less harsh—or do you not agree? I should like to do something which would not be automatically out for pictures and which yet would not let down whatever public I may acquire. *The Big Sleep* is very unequally written. There are scenes that are all right, but there are other scenes still much too pulpy. Insofar as I am able I want to develop an objective method—but slowly—to the point where I can carry an audience over into a genuine dramatic, even melodramatic, novel, written in a very vivid and pungent style, but not slangy or overly vernacular. I realize that this must be done cautiously and little by little, but I think it can be done. To acquire delicacy without losing power, that's the problem. But I should probably do a minimum of three mystery novels before I try anything else.

Thank you again and I do hope that when the returns are in, you will be not too disappointed.

—*Selected Letters of Raymond Chandler*, pp. 3–5

English Reviews of *The Big Sleep*

Although Chandler first gained critical recognition in England, British reviewers were no more receptive to The Big Sleep *than were their American counterparts. These reviews show that British critics saw Chandler only as a writer of tough, racy thrillers and found little literary merit in his writing.*

Milward Kennedy's review appeared under the title "Nightmare of Crime."

The Americans have discovered the thrill-value of decadence. They mix it with gangsterdom; and Raymond Chandler further spices the concoction by introducing into his nightmare a decent but tough detective, who takes whatever comes because that is how he earns his living, but does not lose his sense of values. Marlowe is employed by a crippled old aristocrat because a daughter (the degenerate, not the gambler) is being blackmailed. Very soon he is taking risks, of all sorts, in investigating not only blackmail but murder—risks from clients, police, racketeers, and others; and all too soon, for me, he has explained an affair that must surely bewilder any European.

in a rough school, and I probably didn't notice them much. I was more intrigued by a situation where the mystery is solved by the exposition and understanding of a single character, always well in evidence, rather than by the slow and sometimes long-winded concatenation of circumstances. That's a point which may not interest reviewers of first novels, but it interested me very much. However, there's a very good notice in today's *Los Angeles Times* and I don't feel quite such a connoisseur of moral decay as I did yes-

Chandler's First Paperback

In 1942, Avon Books published a twenty-five-cent edition of The Big Sleep, *the first of Chandler's books to appear in paperback form. Paperback publishing was a new industry, the first modern paperback line being introduced in 1939 by Pocket Books. Paperback reprints became a major source of income for Chandler as the industry developed after the war, but during the early 1940s the sums paid were trivial. Chandler received a royalty of only $500—a penny a copy—from the first Avon edition. The following letter from Chandler to Alfred A. Knopf discusses the new paperback edition as well as his and Cissy's coping with wartime rationing in Cathedral City.*

The first paperback edition of a Chandler novel (Bruccoli Collection, Kent State University)

Cathedral City,
Calif.
February 8th. 1943

Dear Mr. Knopf:

Thanks for yours of Jan 14th. and it was friendly, understanding and welcome, as always. Thank you also for the two-bit edition of *The Big Sleep.* I looked into it and found it both much better and much worse than I had expected—or than I remembered. I have been so belabored with tags like tough, hardboiled, etc., that it is almost a shock to discover occasional signs of almost normal sensitivity in the writing. On the other hand I sure did run the similes into the ground.

William Irish is a man named Cornell Woolrich, an author under his own name, and one of the oldest hands there are at the pulp detective business. He is known in the trade as an idea writer, liking the tour de force, and not much of a character man. I think his stuff is very readable, but leaves no warmth behind it.

No, I don't think the sinus condition is clearing up. This place bores me. But I've just about been talked into sticking out the mountains and the desert for another year. After that to hell with the climate, let's meet a few people. We have a one-store town here, and the meat situation would make you scream. On Wednesday morning the guy opens at 7 A.M. and all the desert rats are there waiting for him to give out numbered tickets. Anybody who delays long enough to wash his face is automatically classed as parasitic and gets a high number, if he gets one at all. On Thursday at 10 the inhabitants bring their bronchitis and halitosis into the store and park in front of the meat counter and the numbers are coonshouted. When we, having a very late number, kick our way up to the collapsed hunk of hamburger we are greeted with a nervous smile that suggests a deacon caught with his hand in the collection plate, and we leave bearing off enough meat for the cat. This happens once a week and that is all that happens, in the way of meat.

Of course we go to Palm Springs. If we didn't, I should not be writing this letter. I should be out in the desert trying to dig up a dead gopher. We happened on a rib roast a couple of weeks back, just walked in and said hello, and there the damn thing was. We ate for six nights running, behind drawn curtains, chewing quietly, so the neighbors wouldn't hear.

There are a bunch of great guys in Washington, high-minded and pure, but once in a while I hunger for a touch of dirty Irish politics.

I hope I get a book out fairly soon. I am trying to think up a good title for you to want me to change.

Yours sincerely,

Raymond Chandler

—*Selected Letters of Raymond Chandler,* pp. 23–25

"THE BIG SLEEP" is well told. Marlowe, the narrator, reveals his own character and the others too—as nasty and incredible, some of them, and yet as real as the creatures that live under stones in your garden. There is atmosphere and there is violent action, and each is exciting. There is a touch of sentiment to give an unexpected bitter flavour at the end. It is a book to be read at a sitting; but it is not Sunday-school literature.

—*The Times* (London), 8 March 1939, p. 8

* * *

In his column titled "Death With A Difference," Ralph Partridge reviews a dozen novels, coming last to books by Chandler and George Harman Coxe.

I have reserved *The Big Sleep* and *The Frightened Women* to the last, as my judgments on the merits of American tough thrillers is by now hopelessly impaired by addiction. The only question you can ask a dope fiend about the composition of his dope is whether it gives him an authentic kick. As there are adulterated products in circulation I can guarantee these two are full strength blends of sadism, eroticism and alcoholism. If you like to pretend you read the stuff for any reason but sordid mental intoxication, these ingredients are crystallised around a central thread of detection. But if you take your medicine straight, you'll never notice it.

—*The New Statesman and Nation*, (10 June 1939): 909

* * *

In "The Big Shots," a review article in which he discusses twelve novels, Nicholas Blake begins by referencing the "revered names" represented—H. C. Bailey, Margery Alligham, Ellery Queen, and R. C. Woodthorpe—and asserting that "these big shots are beaten to the draw by a comparative unknown." The first novelist the reviewer elevates is Patrick Quentin, not Raymond Chandler.

The Big Sleep, as its title suggests, is American and very, very tough after the *Thin Man* fashion. Almost everyone in the book, except the detective, is either a crook or wonderfully decadent, and the author spares us no blushes to point out just how decadent they are. "We're all grifters," says one of them. The action is tightly knit and fast-moving, however, and there is some charming dialogue.

—*The Spectator*, (31 March 1939): 558

Edition of Chandler's first novel that was distributed free to American military personnel during World War II
(Bruccoli Collection, Thomas Cooper Library, University of South Carolina)

3.
Early Novels, 1939–1944: *Farewell, My Lovely;*
The High Window; and *The Lady in the Lake*

A Welter of Work

After The Big Sleep *was published, Chandler began working on his next novel. He had finished his first book in only three months, but he found it much harder to complete works through the rest of his career. In the spring and summer of 1939 he worked intermittently on two different novels and several short stories, all of which were eventually published. In a 6 July 1951 letter to his lawyer Leroy Wright, written in response to an income tax issue, Chandler described his work during this period.*

Now the novel *The Lady in the Lake* was based on two novelettes called "Bay City Blues," published in June, 1938, and *The Lady in the Lake,* published January 1939. But in order to demonstrate method, I think it might be necessary to go beyond this. *The Big Sleep* was written in the spring of 1938 and was based on two novelettes called "Killer in the Rain," published January, 1935, and "The Curtain," published September, 1936. Included in this book also was a fairly long sequence taken from a novelette called "The Man who Liked Dogs," published March, 1936. *Farewell, My Lovely* was based on two novelettes called "Try the Girl," published January, 1937, and "Mandarin's Jade," published November, 1937. In the early part of 1939, that is to say up to April 12, I seem except for fumbling around with plots to have been writing novelettes and short stories. There is evidence of about four of them, not involved in this case, being written or partly written in that time. On April 12 I have an entry "Page 10–'The Girl from Brunette's'" with a question mark after it. This is evidently *Farewell, My Lovely,* because almost immediately the title was changed to "The Girl from Florian's" on April 18, when I'd reached page 52. Florian's is the Negro dive on Central Avenue involved in the beginning of the book. There is on March 31 an entry called "Page 14–'Law is Where You Buy It.'" That apparently died right there and frankly I'm not sure what it refers to, since later in

the year in the diary there is some evidence that I switched the titles around and applied this particular title to more than one book, although the idea of the title evidently derives from the story "Bay City Blues." That is a story which happens in a town so corrupt from the law enforcement point of view that the law is where you buy it and what you pay for it. To resume, on April 23 I am at page 100 with the notation "First lap–'The Girl From Florian's.'" On April 29 I am at page 127 and there is a reference to a

Raymond Chandler in 1939 (Herald Examiner Collection/ Los Angeles Public Library)

Since all plans are foolish and those written
down are never fulfilled, let us make a plan,
this 16th. day of March 1939, at Riverside, Calif.

Got bellfaio'. Mart 1942

For the rest of 1939, all of 1940, spring of
1941, and then if there is no war and if there is
any money, to go to England for material.

Detective novels (<u>Law Is Where You Buy It</u>)
Based on ~~Jade~~, The Man Who
Liked Dogs, Bay City Blues.
Theme, the corrupt alliance of
police and racketeers in a
small California town, outwardly
as fair as the dawn.

<u>The Brashear Doubloon</u>, a bur-
lesque on the pulp novelette,
with Walter and Henry. Some
stuff from Pearls are a Nuisance
but mostly new plot.

<u>Zone of Twilight</u> A grim witty
story of the boss politician's
son and the girl and the blending
of the upper and underworlds.
Material, Guns at Cyrano's,
Nevada Gas.

Chandler's plan for future work that was typed into his notebooks by his wife, Cissy, who appended a note suggesting that it was unrealistic. The plan called for Chandler to produce three more detective novels in the space of two years, then turn his attention to non-mystery projects. Although it would take him much longer than he anticipated, Chandler did complete most of the works laid out in the plan. "Law Is Where You Buy It" became The Lady in the Lake *(1943); "The Brasher Doubloon" was completed as* The High Window *(1942); and two of the fantastic stories, "The Bronze Door" and "Professor Bingo's Snuff," were published in magazines. Though he would work throughout his career on expanding his short story "English Summer" into a dramatic novel, he never completed the project (Bodleian Library, Oxford University).*

2

If advisable, try Goldfish for material for a fourth.

Dramatic novel   English Summer. A short, swift, tense, gorgeously written story verging on melodrama, based on my short story. The surface theme is the American in England, the dramatic theme is the decay of the refined character and its contrast with the ingenuous honest utterly fearless and generous American of the best type.

Short-long stories   A set of six or seven fantastic

Seven From the Stars
Seven from Nowhere.
Seven Tales from do.

stories, some written, some thought of, perhaps one brand new one. Each a little different in tone and effect from the others. The ironic gem, the Bronze Door, the perfect fantastic atmosphere story The Edge of the West, the spooky story, Grandma's boy, the farcical story, The Disappearing Duke, the Allegory Ironic, the Four Gods of Bloon, The pure fairytale The Rubies of Marmelon.

'3'

The three mystery stories should be finished in
the next two years, by end of 1940. If they make
enough for me to move to England and to forget
mystery writing and try English Summer and the
Fantastic Stories, without worrying about whether
these make money, I tackle them. But I must have two
years money ahead, and a sure market with the
detective story when I come back to it, if I do.
If English Summer is a smash hit, which it should be,
properly written, written up to the hilt but not
overwritten, I'm set for life. From then on I'll
laternate the fantastic and the dramatic until I
think of a new type. Or may do a suave detective
just for the fun.

       Dear Raymio, you'll have fun looking at
this maybe, and seeing what useless dreams you had.
Or perhaps it will not be fun.

girl named Anne Riordan who appears as a character in *Farewell, My Lovely*. This sort of thing goes on intermittently to May 22, when I'm at page 233, with a notation, "This story is a flop. It smells to high heaven. Think I'll have to scrap it and try something new." After that for several days I seem to have been toying with a story called "Tony Gets Out." I think this eventually developed into the short story called "I'll Be Waiting." On May 29 there is a notation "Tomorrow get out draft of 'The Girl From Florian's.'" On May 30 I evidently did this because I am checking the draft up to page 87, but that's as far as it goes. I didn't like it. Now come the entries, although this foregoing explanation is going to be necessary later on. On June 1, "Page 4—'Murder Is a Nuisance.'" This in itself means nothing except there is a mention of a character named Adrian Fromsett who is a character in *The Lady in the Lake* book and nowhere else. Next day, June 2, I'm at page 10 and I'm calling it *The Lady in the Lake*. This apparently died on me, because on June 5 I wrote 18 pages of a novelette called "Goldfish," but immediately dropped that for the time being. There are many notations that show that I didn't feel well. On June 12 I'm up to page 30; June 13, page 50; June 14, Page 60, and here is a notation "Leave photo of Fromsett, "which seems to indicate what I am writing; June 15, page 71; June 16, page 127; June 17, page 148; June 18, page 169; June 19, page 191, and the damned thing is now called "The Golden Anklet." Now this ties it clearly to *The Lady in the Lake* because on the chapter headings of *The Lady in the Lake* novelette, inserted by the magazine editor, (I never used chapter headings myself) was "The Golden Anklet," and a golden anklet does figure in the story. June 20 I am at page 203, I'm now calling it "Deep and Dark Waters." That title is self explanatory. On June 28 I'm up to page 337. On June 29 there is this notation, "Tragic realization that there is another dead cat under the house. More than three-quarters done and no good." This certainly refers to the draft of *The Lady in the Lake,* by whatever provisional title I might happen to have been calling it at the time. Now I write on half sheets of paper, turned endwise, and they figure out about six to a thousand words. Therefore 337 of these pages would make about 55,000 words of rough script, which is a very substantial hunk even though all done within a month.

. . . .

The year 1940, partly from reasons of health and still more from the state of the world, seems to have contained an abnormal amount of vacillation. By the end of November I had made less real progress than I sometimes would make in a week. I also puttered with at least three other stories only one of which was ever finished. The end of the year finds me having written 157 pages of the novelette "No Crime in the Mountains." I bring all these matters up just to show that I never worked on just one thing at a time for very long. *But* eventually somehow I would finish practically all these projects, no matter how long it took nor how many things I did in the meantime.

—*Selected Letters of Raymond Chandler*, pp. 281–283

A Second Novel

As had been the case since he lost his oil industry job in the 1930s, Chandler continued to move frequently while working on his first four novels. In the summer of 1939 the Chandlers rented a cabin at Big Bear Lake, a mountain resort about fifty miles east of Los Angeles. The area was then just becoming a popular tourist destination, but Chandler was still able to find a reasonably priced escape from the heat and noise of the city. In the following two letters to Blanche Knopf he reports his progress on his second novel, tentatively titled "The Second Murderer." Sydney Sanders, mentioned in the first letter, was Chandler's literary agent from the 1930s until 1946.

Box 481 Big Bear Lake Calif
August 23rd. 1939

Dear Mrs. Knopf:

The effort to keep my mind off the war has reduced me to the mental age of seven. The things by which we live are the distant flashes of insect wings in a clouded sunlight. But——

I enjoyed meeting you so much. There is a touch of the desert about everything in California, and about the minds of the people who live here. During the years when I hated the place I couldn't get away, and now that I have grown to need the harsh smell of the sage I still feel rather out of place here. But my wife is a New Yorker, and that 95 with unlimited humidity doesn't appeal much either.

If I could write another 12,000 words I should have a draft of a book finished. I know what to write, but I have momentarily mislaid the urge. However by the end of September, as you said, there should be something for you to wrinkle your very polite nose at. It's rather a mixed up mess that will run 75,000 words but I'll likely cut it at least 5000 and perhaps more. It will take me a month to shape it up. The title, if you should happen to approve, is *The Second Murderer*. Please refer to King Richard III, Act 1, Scene IV.

Blanche Knopf in 1940

Second Murderer:	What, shall we stab him when he sleeps?
First Murderer:	No; then he will say 'twas done cowardly when he wakes . . . How dost thou feel thyself now?
Second Murderer:	'Faith, some certain dregs of conscience are yet within me.

However the joker is that the second murderer is ——— ?

Sanders has been impressing on me the dire necessity of so contriving a detective story that it might be serialized. This is only horse sense, even though good serials seldom make good novels. I do not think this particular opus is the one he is looking for. In fact, I'm very sure of it. I'm not sure anyone is looking for it, but there's a law against burning trash up here during the fire hazard.

Yours very truly,

Raymond Chandler
—Selected Letters of Raymond Chandler, pp. 9–10

* * *

Box 581 Big Bear Lake Calif.
September 15th. 1939

Dear Mrs. Knopf:

Thank you for your letter. I have finished a rough, and I am sorry I mean rough, draft of the book and am now sitting back in a haze of expensive cigar smoke admiring myself. There's a lot to be done on it yet and I am afraid you can't count on it by the end of this month, nor at the earliest before the end of next. Some scenes have to be written in, some dropped, some this and that. It is rather a mess. If you think so, you will have no complaint from me. It is about 80,000 words at present and I don't know how it will end up, probably about 75,000.

I guess even smart people in the publishing business are whittling their wits with the carving knife by now. But I think there is going to be a mild boom in detective stories. But better writers will have to write them. I don't think the average American detective story is nearly good enough—from the writing point of view.

I won't talk about the War, because I am not neutral and don't pretend to be.

Yours most sincerely,

Raymond Chandler
—Knopf papers, Harry Ransom Humanities Research Center, University of Texas at Austin

---

Despite the progress made on "The Second Murderer" during the summer of 1939, Chandler was not pleased with the draft and soon set it aside to work on other projects. During late 1939 and early 1940 Chandler was distracted by illness, the developing world war, and problems finding a suitable home. In December 1939 he and Cissy moved into furnished rooms in La Jolla, California, an exclusive beach town just north of San Diego. A month later, convinced that the damp weather was causing rheumatism in his arm, Chandler decided to move to Monrovia, a small city at the edge of the San Gabriel Mountains. Within a few months the noise of their neighbors compelled the Chandlers to move once again, this time to Arcadia, California, where they would stay through the fall of 1940.

Chandler finished Farewell, My Lovely *in May 1940. Before its publication he wrote to George Harmon Coxe, a fellow* Black Mask *author, discussing his feelings about the war and the upcoming publication of his novel. He also responded to Agatha Christie's* And Then There Were None *(1940), which Coxe had recommended.*

1155 Arcadia Avenue   Arcadia Calif.   June 27th, 1940
Dear George:

Your letter sounds rather gloomy. If so, forget it. The English Channel, even at its narrowest point, is worth fifty Maginot lines, and the English troops are at least equal to the Germans and the British colonials are far better. The job of landing in England enough shock troops, tanks and guns to overrun the country is probably a military possibility, but it is infinitely more difficult than anything the Nazis have yet attempted. Probably Hitler would rather have destroyed or captured the British army in Flanders than anything else in the world, and he had all the cards, but he failed. As for bombing, it will be bad, but it will work both ways. If Hitler uses gas on England, it will be used on Germany. If he bombs London, Berlin will be bombed. And the British night bombers are better than the German, because the British have made a specialty of night bombing for twenty-five years. And on top of all this the English civilian population is the least hysterical in the world. They can take an awful pounding and still keep on planting lobelias. I think the worst that can happen would be a negotiated peace, very different from a surrender. Its ultimate effect would no doubt be to make England a second-class power, but that is rather sure to happen anyhow. And if there comes a reasonably free Europe, what does it matter?

People in this country are hysterical with fear because they think that Hitler will take England in a month, grab the British navy, organize 350 millions of Europeans into a coherent whole and then face down the USA without even moving a pawn. I can't see it. Hitler gave Germany a tremendous shot in the arm when it needed it very badly. For that he deserves a lot of credit. But the Germans are fundamentally just as decent as we are and the prospect of fighting endless wars on short rations for nothing but the personal aggrandizement of a nasty little man and his gang of Gestapo is going to look sour to

them after a little while. At least, that is the way I look at it.

What this has done to the writer as writer is bad enough. What it has done to the book business I guess we shall both find out rather soon. I still cling to the opinion that in times like these a good strong detective story is a godsend. I see you are going to be back in the good old Black mask. I guess that is a good idea, but I don't think I am going to try to follow you. I think, if this new book of mine has reasonable success, that I shall struggle along those lines for a while. But I don't think I'll beat my brains out trying to use material from old novelettes any more. It's really frightfully hard work.

On your recommendation and that alone I read Agatha Christie's And Then There Were None, and after reading it I wrote an analysis of it, because it was blurbed as the perfect crime story, incapable of dishonesty by reason of the way it was constructed. As entertainment I liked the first half and the opening, in particular. The second half got pallid. But as an honest crime story, honest in the sense that the reader is given a square deal and the motivation and mechanisms of the murders are sound—it is bunk. The fundamental conception of the book in particular annoyed me. Here is a judge, a jurist, a man with a touch of sadism but withal a passion for exact justice, and this man condemns to death and murders a group of people on nothing but hearsay evidence. In no case did he have a shred of actual proof that any one of them had actually committed murder. In every case it was merely someone's opin-

The gambling ship Rex, *which during the late 1930s Tony Cornero anchored off the coast of Santa Monica, outside the three-mile limit of the state's legal jurisdiction. Cornero advertised his floating casino widely in Los Angeles papers, and it became a popular nighttime attraction. Water taxis ferried gamblers, including many Hollywood celebrities, from the Santa Monica Pier out to the ship. Cornero's enterprise flourished until 1939, when California attorney general Earl Warren raided the ships and destroyed the gambling equipment. Chandler used the* Rex *as the model for the gambling ship* Montecito, *which appears in the closing chapters of* Farewell, My Lovely.

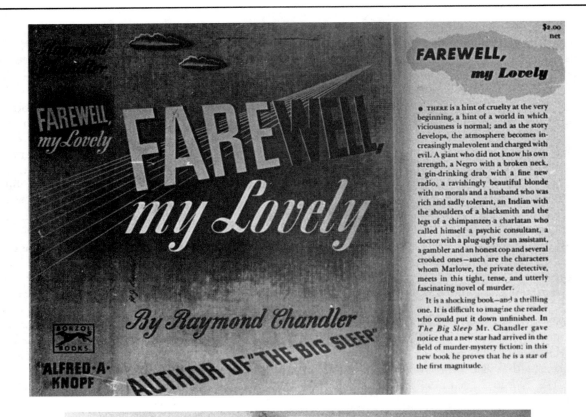

Dust jacket for the first American edition of Chandler's second novel, 7,300 copies of which were published on 1 October 1940. The British edition of the novel was also published in October (Bruccoli Collection, Kent State University).

ion, or a possible, even probable, inference from circumstances. But proof, even absolute inner conviction, simply did not exist. Some of these people admit their crimes, but this is all after the murders were planned, the judgment entered, the sentence pronounced. In other words it is as complete and shameless a bamboozling of the reader as ever was perpetrated. And I won't go into the mechanism of the crimes, most of which were predicated on pure chance, and some actually impossible. They also show an abysmal ignorance of lethal drugs and their action. But I'm very glad I read the book because it finally and for all time settled a question in my mind that had at least some lingering doubt attached to it. Whether is possible to write a strictly honest mystery of the classic type. It isn't. To get the complication you fake the clues, the timing, the play of coincidence, assume certainties where only 50 per cent chances exist at most. To get the surprise murderer you fake character, which hits me hardest of all, because I have a sense of character. If people want to play this game, it's all right by me. But for Christ's sake let's not talk about honest mysteries. They don't exist.

Time out while I take a long breath.

The title of my book is not The Second Murderer, and that was not the title I had in mind when I was talking to you. I used that for a while as a working title, but I didn't like it, although Mrs. Knopf did. I didn't know it had been announced under that name. When I turned the manuscript in they howled like hell about the title, which is not at all a mystery title, but they gave in. We'll see. I think the title is an asset. They think it is a liability. One of us has to be wrong. I suppose, since they are in the business, it should be I. On the other hand I have never had any great respect for the ability of editors, publishers, play and picture producers to guess what the public will like. The record is all against them. I have always tried to put myself in the shoes of the ultimate consumer, the reader, and ignore the middleman. I have assumed that there exists in the country a fairly large group of intelligent people, some formally of good education and some educated by life, who like what I like. Of course the real trouble is that you can be read by an enormous number of people who don't buy any books. My book is supposed to come out in August. The proofs were a bloody mess. I've just finished them and don't feel at all that they are a clean job yet.

All the best,
Ray
—Coxe Papers, Beinecke Rare Books and Manuscript Library, Yale University

The American Reception of
Farewell, My Lovely

In October 1940 Farewell, My Lovely *was published in the United States by Knopf and in England by Hamish Hamilton. In both countries, reviews of the book were brief and somewhat condescending, showing that Chandler was still being treated as nothing more than a genre writer. The following notices are typical of the critical response to the novel.*

This review appeared in Will Cuppy's "Mystery and Adventure" column. Although the reviewer admits to not having read The Big Sleep, *it had been favorably noted in an earlier column.*

All set to sneer loftily at another tough item, billed as "a shocking book—And a thrilling one," this department soon succumbed to what struck us as the real thing in wickedness and the best hard-boiled mystery in ages. (We were entirely dumb about Mr. Chandler, having missed his earlier thriller, "The Big Sleep," which was probably fine.) As for Moose Malloy, a frightful gigantic killer looking for his long-lost sweetheart, Velma Valento, you can take him as a figure of fun if you choose, but you should be wallowing earnestly in the tale by the fifth chapter, believing every word. That's where you meet Jessie Florian, as vicious a dipsomaniac as you could wish, and from there on you may baffle yourself with a terrific mystery girl (wife of a multi-millionaire), the necklace of Fei Tsui jade, blackmail, more murders and assorted crime of a nature to give you pause. All of which is narrated with a grand line of lowdown lingo and brutal moods by Philip Marlowe, private investigator. There is brisk action everywhere, even when you might expect a brief pause for repairs or a meditative sigh. "I bent to pick it up. She tried to kick me in the face." That was Jessie all over. One of the minor characters is named Hemingway. Grade A.
—*New York Herald Tribune Books,* 6 October 1940, p. 25

* * *

Farewell, My Lovely *was the last of four novels given a brief notice in "A Reader's List."*

By the author of "The Big Sleep," which was a fast, tough detective story with excellent dialogue and a screwy plot. This new one is faster and tougher and the plot is better too. Mr. Chandler is a neat craftsman and writes like a breeze. A good time will be had by all.
—*The New Republic,* 103 (7 October 1940): 482

Chandler had hoped that the sales of Farewell, My Lovely *would exceed those of his first novel, but both he and Knopf were disappointed with the results. Despite a strong advertising campaign, advance sales for the book were small—only 2,900 copies—and Knopf did not sell out its first printing of 7,500 copies. Chandler wrote the following letter to Blanche Knopf, in which he discusses the American reception of the novel.*

449 San Vicente Boulevard
Santa Monica, Oct. 9th. [1940]

Dear Mrs. Knopf:

The above address will be good for six months, I hope.

Thanks for yours of October 1st. which only just caught up with me. I am terribly sorry about the title and all that, and because the advance sales disappointed us, but you must remember that I didn't refuse to change the title, I just couldn't think of another one, you gave me no time at all, and although I said I liked the title, that should not have made you go against your business judgment. Everyone I know likes the title very much, but of course they are not in the trade. And I still think *'Zounds, He Dies* was a good title. If I had had some of the time the book was being prepared, I'm sure I could have come up with something that would have satisfied you. But you caught me off base and got me rattled.

Personally, and in this I am born out by one professional opinion, I think the handicap of the title will be only temporary and that if the sales do not do anything, it will really be for some other cause. For instance, the war. A woman out here who runs a string of rental libraries in and around Hollywood told a friend of mine that one of her branches had ten copies of the book out and that she hardly ever bought more than two copies of a mystery story. She said she thought this was in part due to a "very marvelous" review in the *Hollywood Citizen-News* of Sept 21st. I hope you have seen this. Evidently they jumped the gun on the publication date. Of course it would have only a local influence, but the mere fact

Advertisement in the 6 October 1940 issue of The New York Times

that a critic who confessedly does not like mystery stories and thinks they are mostly tripe should take this book seriously as a piece of writing is worth an awful lot to me. Because I am not innately a hack writer.

Syd Sanders sent me a cut of your advertisement in the *New York Times*. I don't see how you can afford it. If that doesn't start something, what's the use?

> With kindest regards,
> Raymond Chandler
> —*Selected Letters of Raymond Chandler*, pp. 18–19

Chandler here responds to Coxe's writing him about the publication of Farewell, My Lovely. *In the first paragraph he refers to Frederick Lewis Nebel, a fellow* Black Mask *author. At the end of the letter he alludes to the novelette "No Crime in the Mountains"—his last story for the pulp magazines.*

> 449 San Vicente Boulevard
> Santa Monica Calif Nov 5th. 1940

Dear George:

Thanks for your letters and for sending me the N.Y.Times ad that Knopf put out on my book. I wish they wouldn't be quite so blatant in their advertising. Thanks also for the report of remarks made by Nebel, very nice of him and all that. As you say, much better give the bitter with the sweet.

Still from The Falcon Takes Over *(RKO, 1942), the first movie to be made from a Chandler novel. Starring George Sanders (right), the movie was based on* Farewell, My Lovely, *but it was changed considerably in order to fit the characters into RKO's Falcon series. In the movie Sanders plays Gay Lawrence, also known as The Falcon, a playboy who solves crimes in his spare time. Alan Jenkins (left) played Goldy Locke, the Falcon's chauffeur and comic sidekick. Chandler sold* Farewell, My Lovely *to RKO in July 1941 for $2,000—a deal he later called "a contract of almost unparalleled stupidity on the part of my New York agent" because it included all movie rights and kept Chandler from earning any money from future movie versions of the novel.*

I don't think I have written to you since we were in Arcadia. It got too hot for us there, so we went up to Big Bear Lake for a while and didn't like it any more. The place is getting so built up that it is no longer the place it was even two years ago when we first spent a summer there. Funny thing civilization. It promises so much and what it delivers is mass production of shoddy merchandise and shoddy people.

So we went away from there and came back to the ocean and are now living in an apartment with our own furniture out of storage, or as much of it as we could get into four rooms.

How's the writing racket by you? By me it's pretty much of a blank. I'm trying to write a pulp story just to feel I'm doing something, but I no longer seem to be any good at it.

All the best,

R

C

—Coxe Papers, Beinecke Rare Books and Manuscript Library, Yale University

Apology!

Circumstances have recently made it impossible to keep pace with the demand for the following titles :

THE LAST DAYS OF PARIS by Alexander Werth
8s. 6d. net (3rd Printing)
TIME'S HARVEST, by Dorothy Charques
9s net (2nd Printing)
THUNDER ROCK, by Robert Ardrey
5s. net (3rd Printing)

We have pleasure in assuring our friends in the trade that fresh supplies are now available, and that all outstanding orders are being fulfilled as rapidly as possible.

We also have pleasure in announcing that ANGELA THIRKELL'S novel, *Cheerfulness Breaks In* (7s. 6d. net), is available in a second large printing, and that RAYMOND CHANDLER'S super-thriller *Farewell, My Lovely* (successor to *The Big Sleep*, 7s. 6d. net) has just been published according to schedule.

On Friday next, the 25th, we are publishing OTTO D. TOLISCHUS'S remarkable analysis of Hitlerism, *They Wanted War* (10s. 6d. net)—a book which is already high on the American best-seller lists.

HAMISH HAMILTON

Advertisement in the 17 October 1940 issue of The Bookseller

English Reviews of *Farewell, My Lovely*

This brief mention of Chandler's novel appeared in "Fresh Bloods," a review article in which eight mystery novels were considered.

Farewell, My Lovely, if you like the tough, sexy American thriller, will suit you all right; the dialogue crackles, the killer kills, the girls are good value, the action covers a great deal of ground and hard knocks at terrific speed.

—*The Spectator,* 165 (22 November 1940): 558

* * *

Fiction is sometimes described as a way of escape from reality. The "tough" American story is perhaps rather a way of escape from civilisation. Some readers, however, may find a sort of fearful joy in an introduction to a world in which no one seems to have much idea of self-respect, where whisky can be a man's sole sustenance, where the really nice young ladies remark, "I would like to be kissed, damn you!" where, in fact, the general standards resemble those of the jackal and the ape. Mr. Raymond Chandler's "Farewell, My Lovely," is, however, a favourable specimen of its class. The writing is often picturesque and vivid, though often, too, incomprehensible to the mere Englishman, the plot is clever and well constructed, and Mr. Chandler does try to give some semblance of humanity even to his most brutal characters.

—*Manchester Guardian,* 10 December 1940, p. 7

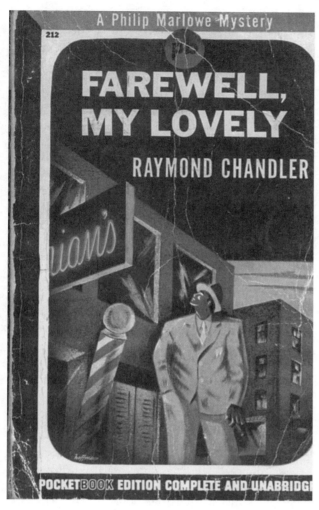

*First paperback edition for Chandler's second novel,
published in 1943*

The Brashear Doubloon and *The High Window*

By the spring of 1942 Chandler was completing a novel with the working title "The Brashear Doubloon," which is the name of a stolen coin that provides the catalyst for the murder plot. He wrote to Blanche Knopf to announce his reluctant completion of the manuscript, which was published as The High Window.

12216 Shetland Lane
Los Angeles, Calif.
March 15th. 1942

Dear Mrs. Knopf:

Your letter, kind and charming as always, reaches me at a very bad time. I'm afraid the book is not going to be any good to you. No action, no likable characters, no nothing. The detective does nothing. I understand that it is being typed, which seems like a waste of money, and will be submitted to you, and

I'm not sure that that is a good idea, but it is out of my hands. At least I felt that you should be relieved of any necessity of being kind to me in a situation where kindness is probably not of any use. About all I can say by way of extenuation is that I tried my best and seemed to have to get the thing out of my system. I suppose I would have kept tinkering at it indefinitely otherwise.

The thing that rather gets me down is that when I write something that is tough and fast and full of mayhem and murder, I get panned for being tough and fast and full of mayhem and murder, and then when I try to tone down a bit and develop the mental and emotional side of a situation, I get panned for leaving out what I was panned for putting in the first time. The reader expects thus and thus of Chandler because he did it before, but when he did it before he was informed that it might have been much better if he hadn't.

However all this is rather vain now. From now on, if I make mistakes, as no doubt I shall, they will not be made in a futile attempt to avoid making mistakes.

Most sincerely,
Raymond Chandler
—*Selected Letters of Raymond Chandler,* p. 20

In The High Window *Chandler incorporated details of a real-life murder case into his story. The following article discusses the case and how it relates to Chandler's novel.*

Cracking the Cassidy Case
Robert F. Moss
The Raymond Chandler Web Site

"Don't forget this is a murder case, Marlowe."

"I'm not. But don't you forget I've been around this town a long time, more than fifteen years. I've seen a lot of murder cases come and go. Some have been solved, some couldn't be solved, and some could have been solved that were not solved. And one or two or three of them have been solved wrong. Somebody was paid to take a rap, and the chances are it was known or strongly suspected. And winked at. But skip that. It happens, but not often. Consider a case like the Cassidy case. I guess you remember it, don't you?"

Breeze looked at his watch. "I'm tired," he said. "Let's forget the Cassidy case. Let's stick to the Phillips case."

I shook my head. "I'm going to make a point, and it's an important point. Just look at the Cassidy case. Cassidy was a very rich man, a multi-millionaire. He had a grown up son. One night the cops were called to his home and young Cassidy was on his back on the floor with blood all over his face and a bullet hole in the side of his head. His secretary was lying on his back in an adjoining bathroom, with his head against the second bathroom door, leading to a hall, and a cigarette burned out between the fingers of his left hand, just a short burned out stub that had scorched the skin between his fingers. A gun was lying by his right hand. He was shot in the head, not a contact wound. A lot of drinking had been done. Four hours had elapsed since the deaths and the family doctor had been there for three of them. Now, what did you do with the Cassidy case?"

Breeze sighed. "Murder and suicide during a drinking spree. The secretary went haywire and shot young Cassidy. I read it in the papers or something. Is that what you want me to say?"

"You read it in the papers," I said, "but it wasn't so. What's more you knew it wasn't so and the D.A. knew it wasn't so and the D.A.'s investigators were pulled off the case within a matter of hours. There was no inquest. But every crime reporter in town and every cop on every homicide detail knew it was Cassidy that did the shooting, that it was Cassidy that was crazy drunk, that it was the secretary who tried to handle him and couldn't and at last tried to get away from him, but wasn't quick enough."

The narrator is Philip Marlowe, Raymond Chandler's hard-boiled private eye. The scene is from *The High Window*, Chandler's third novel. The cops—Breeze and Spangler—are leaning on Marlowe, trying to get him to tell who he's working for, but Marlowe won't play ball. He goes on talking, giving more and more detail about the Cassidy case, until Breeze cuts him off:

> "Make your point."
> I said: "Until you guys own your own souls you don't own mine. Until you guys can be trusted every time and always, in all times and conditions, to seek the truth out and find it and let the chips fall where they may—until that time comes, I have a right to listen to my conscience, and protect my client the best way I can."

The scene is stock detective story stuff: crooked cops, civic corruption, rich men buying off the law, and the honest private detective who'll ensure justice is served. Lt. Breeze isn't too impressed by Marlowe's story, but his younger partner Spangler is. Later he tells Marlowe, "Say, I'd like to read up on that Cassidy case. . . . Sounds interesting. Must have been before my time."

"It was a long time ago," Marlowe says. "And it never happened. I was just kidding."

But neither Marlowe nor Chandler were kidding.

Shortly after midnight on Sunday, February 17th, 1929, the Beverly Hills Police Department and the Los Angeles District Attorney were called to Greystone, a thirty-five-room mansion on twelve and a half acres of land. They found two men dead. One was Edward L. Doheny, Jr., the thirty-six-year-old son of a multimillionaire oilman. The other was Hugh Plunkett, the son's confidential secretary. Both had been shot through the head by bullets from a single .45 calibre pistol.

Doheny, dressed only in underwear and a silk bathrobe, lay on his back on the carpet of a luxurious first-floor bedroom. A bullet had penetrated his skull from ear to ear. Blood criss-crossed his face in a grid-like pattern and pooled around his head on the carpet. Plunkett's corpse was twelve feet away, sprawled spread-eagle on his stomach, in the hallway just beyond the bedroom door.

Dr. E. C. Fishbaugh, a prominent Beverly Hills society doctor and personal physician to the Doheny family, was the primary witness to the events that evening. Hugh Plunkett, he said, had been suffering from "a nervous disease." On the afternoon of Saturday, February 16th, Plunkett had come to Greystone for a conference with Dr. Fishbaugh and Edward L. Doheny, Jr., who were trying to persuade the secretary to admit himself to a sanitarium. Plunkett refused. That night Dr. Fishbaugh went to a Hollywood theater to watch a comedy show. Around 10:30 P.M. he received a telephone message that he was urgently needed at the Doheny mansion to try to relieve Plunkett, who was suffering from throat pain and hysteria. When he arrived at Greystone, Fishbaugh was met at the front door by Mrs. Doheny, whom he described as calm and in good spirits. "She greeted me," Fishbaugh said in his statement to the District Attorney,

> and when I asked where her husband was she said he was in a guest room to the left of the hall leading from the front entrance.
> Mrs. Doheny and I started down the hall side by side. Suddenly, through the half-opened door which partitions the hallway, I saw Plunkett walking toward us. 'You stay out of here!' he shouted. Then he slammed the door shut. A moment later we heard a shot.
> I sent Mrs. Doheny back to the living room. Then I pushed the door open and saw Plunkett lying on his face opposite the door to the bedroom.

Fishbaugh went past Plunkett's body and into the guest room, where he found Doheny dead, a chair overturned beside him. In his statement, he said he heard only one shot, the one right after Plunkett slammed the hallway door. Mrs. Doheny reported that earlier she had heard a noise that might have been a gunshot, but at the time thought that it was "someone turning over some furniture or something." She had heard no quarrelling between her husband and his secretary.

After she and Dr. Fishbaugh discovered the corpses, Mrs. Doheny called her two brothers, Warren and Clark Smith, and her brother-in-law, Anson Lisk. Lisk lived in a house on the estate and arrived at the Doheny home after only a few minutes. The Smith brothers followed not long after, and they phoned the Beverly Hills police and District Attorney Buron Fitts, who showed up around midnight. A little after 2 A.M. Fitts's investigators were on the scene.

The crime occurred too late to make the Sunday morning papers, but it was reported in Monday editions across the country, including the front page of *The New York Times.* The murder of a wealthy man is always newsworthy. But, Edward L. Doheny, Jr. was more than just a wealthy man.

His father, Edward, Sr., could have been a character out of a Horatio Alger story. He was born in Wisconsin in 1856, the son of Irish-Catholic immigrants. At fifteen, Doheny graduated from high school (as class valedictorian), then took a job as a mule driver for a U.S. government surveying party in Arizona and New Mexico. He learned the basics of surveying, but soon turned to prospecting for gold and silver in the deserts and mountains of the Southwest.

Fourteen years later, in 1892, Doheny was in Los Angeles, California. He had made a good bit of money prospecting, but a series of failed ventures left him broke. He was still looking for his big chance, and when it came he seized it with both hands. Doheny was walking down a Los Angeles street when he saw a wagon filled with oozing, dark black earth. He asked the driver what the load was and learned that it was *brea,* Spanish for tar, and that it had come from the Westlake Park area. Doheny knew that where there was tar there was oil. He and a partner leased some land in Westlake, hired a driller, and struck oil at 225 feet. The Doheny strike sparked the Los Angeles petroleum boom. Over the next decade 1,500 wells were drilled in and around the city. By 1912 the region was producing 4.4 million barrels a year. Doheny himself owned eighty-one oil wells in the city, and he quickly expanded his operation throughout the state of California. The rush for oil was the first step in the transformation of Los Angeles from a small western city to a major American metropolis. Edward L. Doheny was, in a sense, one of the city's founding fathers.

Sometime during the 1880s, Doheny had married his first wife, a woman named Carrie about whom little is known. His only son, Edward, Jr., was born in 1894. Doheny apparently separated from Carrie around the turn of the century, and on August 22, 1900 he married his second wife, Estelle. In 1901 they bought a mansion at Number Eight Chester Place, the city's most prestigious street. Doheny and his wife completely redecorated the house, buying a glass dome from Tiffany, marble columns from Italy, and a gold-lacquer Steinway piano. Estelle Doheny became an avid collector of jewels, orchids, paper weights, and books. The family owned a 400-acre ranch in Beverly Hills—where they would later build their son's mansion—as well as a yacht and a park containing domesticated deer, monkeys, and parrots. It was in this world that Edward L. Doheny, Jr. ("Ned" to his friends) was raised.

Ned Doheny entered Stanford in 1912 and a year later transferred to the University of Southern California to study law. In June 1913 he married Lucy Smith, the daughter of a vice president of the Santa Fe Railroad Company. When he graduated from USC in 1916, Ned became a vice-president in his father's company. He served as a lieutenant in the Navy during World War I, then returned to Los Angeles to continue in the oil business.

Ned found a valuable assistant in Hugh Plunkett, a man who—like the elder Doheny— had made a success of himself through hard work and a little luck. Plunkett was born in Kansas and moved to Los Angeles with his family in 1912. He found work as a tire changer at a service station owned by W. H. Smith, the father of Ned Doheny's fiancee. Plunkett regularly worked on vehicles belonging to the Doheny family, and when Ned and Lucy were married in 1913, he was hired as a family chauffeur. He gradually rose in the family's confidence, and by the 1920s was overseeing the operations of Ned Doheny's household. Plunkett had a hand in many of the details of the construction of Greystone, including signing checks on Doheny's account to pay contractors' bills—bills running into the hundreds of thousands of dollars.

It was at this time that Ned Doheny, his father, and Hugh Plunkett became embroiled in one of the most notorious political scandals in American history: Teapot Dome.

The roots of the scandal lay in the efforts of private companies to have access to Naval Oil Reserves, federal lands set aside to ensure the military an adequate supply of fuel during wartime. Woodrow Wilson's administration opposed such private leases, but the climate changed when Warren Harding was elected President in 1920. In 1922, Albert B. Fall, Harding's Secretary of the Interior and an old friend of Edward Doheny, secretly leased the Teapot Dome

Reserve to Harry F. Sinclair's Mammoth Oil Company and the Elk Hills Reserve to Doheny's Pan-American Petroleum Company. There was no competitive bidding for the contracts, and the day after Doheny signed the initial papers he received a telephone call from Fall, telling him to go ahead and send the "loan" they had previously discussed. Ned Doheny and Hugh Plunkett withdrew $100,000 in cash from Ned's account at the Blair and Company brokerage house, put it in a little black bag, and delivered it to Albert Fall at the Wardman Park Hotel in Washington. Harry Sinclair had worked out a similar arrangement with Fall, giving him some $260,000 in Liberty bonds.

The deals remained secret until after Warren Harding's death in August 1923, when Calvin Coolidge began an investigation into Fall's activities. The Senate Committee on Public Lands and Surveys called for hearings on the Naval Reserve leases, and the scandal was soon made public. Fall, Sinclair, and Doheny were called to testify before the committee, and they were eventually indicted on charges of bribery and conspiracy to defraud the government. The court proceedings lasted almost a decade, and the investigations sparked by the Teapot Dome scandal soon uncovered widespread corruption in Harding's administration, making it a contender with Ulysses S. Grant's for the most graft-ridden in U.S. history.

Two civil cases resulted in the cancellation of the Naval Reserve leases, but in a criminal trial Doheny was acquitted of conspiracy to defraud the government. There was still one more charge to face: criminal bribery. Albert Fall was scheduled to be tried on October 7, 1929. If Fall were acquitted, Doheny, Sr. would effectively be acquitted as well. If not, Doheny would have to stand trial on his own in March 1930. Ned Doheny and Hugh Plunkett were both slated to be witnesses in Fall's trial. Neither lived to testify.

On the Monday after the murder/suicide, the *Los Angeles Times* devoted three pages to the investigation, complete with a detailed summary of Dr. Fishbaugh's statement to the district attorney, accounts of Ned Doheny's and Hugh Plunkett's lives, and a half-page diagram of the crime scene and Plunkett's apparent movements. District Attorney Buron Fitts announced that he was launching "a sweeping investigation of the events surrounding the slaying of Edward L. Doheny, Jr." The case seemed poised to join the Snyder-Grey and Leopold-Loeb murders as one of the most sensational crimes of the 1920s.

It never did. The next day, Tuesday, February 19th, the *Times* gave only a single column to the story. Less than twenty-four hours after announcing a "sweeping investigation," Fitts declared that "since the person responsible for the tragedy was dead," no inquest would be held. The death certificates were signed, and the case was closed as a homicide and a suicide. The remainder of the article discussed the plans for Ned Doheny's funeral and the emotional state of the family.

The last paragraph revealed one new fact not known the day before: Ned Doheny had not died immediately when shot by Plunkett but rather lived "until a moment after Dr. Fishbaugh rushed into the room at the sound of the shot with which the secretary ended his own life." The detail seemed trivial and irrelevant. Wednesday's paper contained a modest account of Ned Doheny's funeral, and then nothing more was said about the case. The curtain had been rung down.

Not everyone was satisfied with the official accounts of the deaths. One such skeptic was Leslie T. White, a newly-hired investigator for the District Attorney's office. The Doheny murder offered White his first taste of really "big stuff," and he dove into the case with zeal. White's account of the investigation is recorded in his 1936 autobiography, *Me, Detective*, a book that was published with little fanfare and almost immediately faded into obscurity. His memoir, though, gives a unique, unauthorized version of the events at Greystone on the night of February 17th, 1929, and the details don't quite match up with the official story. White recalled being summoned to the Doheny mansion at 2:00 A.M. There he found D. A. Fitts, the Beverly Hills police, and a scene much like that described in the newspapers: Ned Doheny dead on his back in the guest room and Plunkett face-down in the hallway outside. White went to work gathering physical evidence and interviewing witnesses. Dr. Fishbaugh, Mrs. Doheny, and the household staff had had a sizeable amount of time to recover their composure between the firing of the shots and the arrival of the police. Their testimony, White later wrote, "dovetailed with remarkable accuracy." They had heard a disturbance, gone to investigate, and had been met at the hallway door by Plunkett, who slammed the door and, a moment later, ended his own life. But, according to White, one witness

> . . . reported that the shots, all of them, had been fired in quick succession—within a full second . . .
>
> "One—two—three!" she described it.
>
> This story did not quite fit the physical facts as I found them, and with a shock, I began to suspect that something was wrong.

When he examined Plunkett's body on the floor, furthermore, White found that the left hand held a ciga-

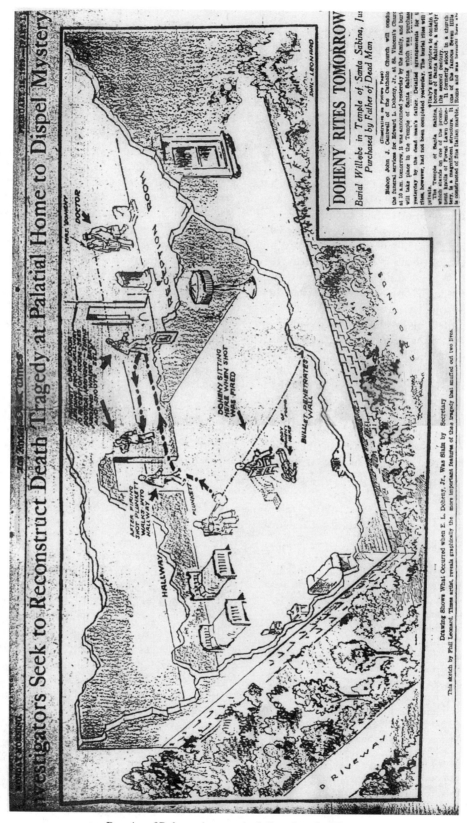

Drawing of Doheny crime scene in the Los Angeles Times

rette "in such a way that it would have been impossible for him to have opened the door and threatened witnesses as they so testified. He had the gun in his right, by their story."

White uncovered more suspicious evidence after he took the bodies to the morgue for examination. "I found powder burns," he wrote, "around the bullet-hole in Doheny's head, proving the gun was held less than three inches away at the moment it was fired. I found no such markings on Plunkett's head." At the crime scene, White had discovered the murder weapon under Plunkett's body. Though Plunkett had been dead for several hours, the gun was still warm. White test-fired the weapon many times, but found that "it did not heat up to any noticeable extent." There were no fingerprints on the gun, and White was at a loss to explain how it could have stayed so warm for so long. White's initial hypothesis was that Plunkett had not killed Doheny at all and that there was something "warped" about the case.

White continued his investigation through the night, and in the morning reported to District Attorney Fitts. He confessed his suspicions about the witnesses' stories, but admitted he was reluctant to tamper with a family as powerful as the Dohenys. White recalled that Fitts reddened and snapped, "There isn't a man in the United States that's big enough to stop me from conducting a criminal investigation." Fitts seemed determined to push the inquiry further and summoned several of the witnesses—including Dr. Fishbaugh—to the Hall of Justice for questioning.

At this session, Fitts did most of the talking, with White interrupting only once to ask a few questions, which brought an odd response:

> "Doctor, you were in the house at the time the shooting took place and you rushed into the bedroom within a matter of seconds thereafter. Is that correct?"
> He nodded affirmatively.
> "Doheny was dead when you arrived?"
> He again nodded.
> "And the body was not disturbed in any way?"
> "It was not disturbed."
> "Then, Doctor, as an experienced physician, will you kindly explain how blood could run *up* from the ears and cross back and forth over the face of a man who never moved off his back?"
> The physician hesitated. He was trapped and he knew it. In a low voice he admitted that young Doheny had lived for approximately twenty minutes after the shooting and during that time they had picked him up, then replaced him on the floor.

White does not make much of Dr. Fishbaugh's changing his story, merely adding it to the list of suspicious details. But, the revelation that Doheny did not die until well after he was shot was reported in newspapers on Tuesday, February 19th. Its appearance in the press lends credence to Leslie White's story. At the very least, it seems that there was certainly something "warped" about the Doheny case.

One of the most curious elements of the crime is that it occurred only a short time before Ned Doheny and Hugh Plunkett were scheduled to testify in the Albert Fall bribery case. The Dohenys, by their own admission, had been trying for several weeks to convince Plunkett to enter a sanitarium. In an official statement released the day after the shooting, the Doheny family lawyer claimed, "a few weeks ago Plunkett showed signs of a nervous breakdown." This explanation of madness was faithfully reported in the press, though no one outside the Doheny family and their employees provided any evidence of this instability. Plunkett's ex-wife told reporters that she never saw signs of insanity in her former husband, though he was occasionally subject to fits of anger.

Plunkett was not the only witness unable to testify in the bribery trial. Ned McLean, who had been a witness in the earlier Senate Committee hearings, apparently went insane as well. At the time of Fall's trial, McLean was confined to an asylum.

Had nothing further come of the murder/suicide, it would have remained a curious historical anecdote. But something further did come of it: it was picked up by Raymond Chandler.

In February 1929, Chandler had yet to write a single word of detective fiction. He was forty years old and an executive in the California oil business.

. . . .

It is unclear exactly how much Chandler knew about the Doheny family. None of his letters from before 1938 survive. What little is known about Chandler's years in the oil business has been reconstructed from his comments in letters written later in his life and from interviews with several of his business colleagues (conducted in the 1970s by Frank MacShane, Chandler's biographer). Doheny's name is absent from these sources, but Chandler—as an executive in the California oil industry—certainly knew who Doheny was and, more than likely, had met him at one time or another.

So how, then, did Chandler get his information about the Doheny/Plunkett case, information that he incorporated into *The High Window*? There are several possibilities.

The first is that he learned much of it from his colleagues in the oil business. The crime, after all, not only received front-page coverage in the Los Angeles

Fitts Pushes Inquiry Into Doheny Murder

SCENE STUDIED TO GET CLEWS

Reconstruction of Crime at Mansion Sought

Doctor Tells of Arrival and of Hearing Shot

Both Bodies Then Found in Adjoining Rooms

Victim of Murderous Frenzy and His Slayer

Both Dead as Result of Tragedy in Mansion
Theodore Hugh Plunkett (left) and Edward Laurence Doheny, Jr. (right)

(Continued from First Page)

away from the section where Doheny's body lay in the mansion guest chamber, slammed a door between himself and Dr. Fishbaugh and Mrs. Doheny, who had met the physician at the door and then fired a bullet into his own brain.

More than an hour elapsed after the tragedy before Mr. Doheny, Sr., was informed. He immediately walked across the short intervening distance between the two homes, and to the tragedy-filled room.

The white-haired father gazed down on his son lying in the disordered room, and collapsed For a time it was feared the shock was too much for him. He recovered his composure, however, and assured friends that he would face the situation as stoically as he could.

Subsequent investigation and interrogation of members of the family disclosed that when Mrs. Doheny smilingly greeted Dr. Fishbaugh at the door of her home, which was opened by Night Watchman Morris, her husband lay dead at the hands of his secretary, unknown to her.

By a comparison of time between the telephone call placed at the theater for Dr. Fishbaugh, his arrival and Plunkett's self-destruction, Fitts last night definitely placed the time of young Doheny's slaying at 10:55 o'clock.

Mrs. Doheny Jr., had heard the muffled report of the shot that killed her husband, but believed it to be an object of overturned furniture and thought nothing of the incident, she told Dr. Fishbaugh.

INSTANT DEATH

Almost instant death struck Plunkett when the bullet plowed through his brain, according to the physician. From the sound of shot until he reached the body was only a matter of seconds, yet the secretary was dead.

The death weapon fell from his hand when Plunkett fell and was found under his breast.

The body was lying partly on the left side. The right arm was stretched out and empty, while the left was doubled back down the side, and the lifeless fingers held a still smoldering, half-smoked cigarette. Before the cigarette was taken from the dead man's fingers it had burned a small portion of the skin.

Following the all-afternoon inquiry, and the questioning of members of the Doheny staff of servants, Dist.-Atty. Fitts said:

"This investigation is just an additional check on the information gathered early Sunday morning at the scene by Chief Investigator Wheeler and Identification-Expert White from my office; Capt. Bright and his assistants from the Sheriff's office and Chief of Police Blair of Beverly Hills.

"So far there isn't a thing that has developed that detracts from

wood Play House from my maid at 10:30 o'clock and was told to go to the Doheny home immediately," Dr. Fishbaugh said after he had made a statement to Fitts.

"Upon my arrival there one of the watchmen, whose name I do not know, let me in the house. I have a key to the iron gates in front of the estate.

"As I entered Mrs. Doheny was standing in the middle of the hallway approximately eight feet back from the door, and greeted me.", he continued.

In answer to the physician's question as to where Mr. Doheny was, Mrs. Doheny informed Dr. Fishbaugh her husband was in the guest room, on the first floor, to the left of the hall leading from the front entrance.

SHOT HEARD

"Both Mrs. Doheny and I started down the hall side by side. A door, which partitions the hall, was slightly ajar, and I saw Plunkett walking toward it.

"'You stay out of here,'" he shouted at me and slammed the door shut. I then heard a shot.

"'You go back,' I told Mrs. Doheny, and she returned to the living-room, which is approximately seventy-five feet from the guest room where the tragedy occurred.

"I pushed the door open and saw Plunkett lying in his face opposite the door to the bedroom where I later found Mr. Doheny. Plunkett, to the best of my recollection, was fully clothed.

ONLY ONE REPORT

"The door to the bedroom was open and when I looked in I saw Mr. Doheny lying on his back a chair overturned between him and

sion of the Sheriff's office, and his two chief aides, Harry Brewster and Dave Crousborn, were called.

B. E. Dayton, manager of the Beverly Mills mortuary, arrived at the mansion at 4 a.m. and an hour later removed both victims to the undertaking parlor.

An examination there disclosed that Mr. Doheny had been shot from the left side a fraction of an inch above the ear, the bullet piercing his head and emerging from the right side one and three-quarters inches above the ear.

SLEEPING POWDERS

The second bullet from the heavy-caliber gun plowed almost an identical path through the killer's brain excepting that he shot himself from the right sight of the head.

According to Dr. Fishbaugh, Plunkett often was an overnight guest in the Doheny home and usually occupied the guest room where young Doheny was murdered.

"I have never treated Mr. Doheny in that room and believe he probably went there to talk over the removal of Plunkett to a hospital for rest," the physician said.

"For the past six months the secretary, has been suffering from nervous trouble and because he was unable to sleep, he had been taking very strong sleeping powder."

Police investigators said Mr. Doheny apparently had prepared for bed when Plunkett arrived at the house. This was the latter's second visit to the Doheny home during the evening, the first one occurring about 7 o'clock.

When found Doheny was dressed in a green silk night robe with a dressing gown over it.

While officials said they are convinced that it was temporary insanity that drove the trusted fam-

vestigators pictured Doheny sitting in a chair near one of the twin beds, counseling his ailing friend.

As far as officers can determine, Plunkett probably fired without warning while pacing the floor. Doheny's body, with the hole torn through his head by the death-dealing missile, apparently slowly toppled from the chair to the floor, the chair overturning as he fell.

The four servants who appeared before Dist.-Atty. Fitts yesterday were unable to shed any light on the tragedy other than to substantiate the accounts related by Mrs. Doheny and Dr. Fishbaugh. They knew of the efforts of Mr. Doheny and the physician to send Plunkett to a hospital. Morris, the watchman who opened the door for Dr. Fishbaugh, said he did not hear the first shot fired by the slayer.

Besides the watchman, Alfred Doar, butler, Mrs. Ingril Doar, maid to the children, and Kate Walker, maid, were questioned by the prosecutor.

How many minutes passed after he fired the first bullet from the gun until he used the second to take his own life, cannot be determined with any degree of accuracy, investigators said, but it probably was only a few.

Mrs. Doheny was unable to fix definitely the time when she heard what she believed to be overturning furniture, but she said she thinks it was no more than a few seconds before Dr. Fishbaugh rang the doorbell.

CHILDREN ASLEEP

Upstairs the five children of Mr. and Mrs. Doheny were sleeping unaware of the tragedy being enacted below them.

Early yesterday morning the chil-

Los Angeles Times, *18 February 1929, page 3*

papers, but it involved major players in the California oil industry. Even if Chandler himself did not have close ties to the Doheny family, he certainly knew people who did.

A more likely source is Leslie White's memoir *Me, Detective.* After Chandler lost his job in the oil industry in 1932–fired because of drinking problems, absenteeism, and a series of affairs with office secretaries–he listed himself in the Los Angeles Directory as a writer and began teaching himself the craft of fiction. Unlike Dashiell Hammett, who had been a Pinkerton detective before turning to writing, Chandler had no first-hand experience in crime investigation. He learned, instead, by reading mystery stories and books on firearms, police methodology, cross-examination, and toxology. A book such as *Me, Detective,* which was published in the middle of Chandler's apprentice period, would have been an ideal addition to his library.

Chandler could have gotten some of his facts–such as the positions of the bodies and the presence of the family doctor at the scene–from newspaper accounts, but many of the Cassidy case details appear only in White's book. Doheny's head, for instance, showed a contact wound and Plunkett's did not–a seeming contradiction of the official story that Plunkett was the one who did the shooting. Chandler incorporates as well the detail of the cigarette that was found in the secretary's left hand, burned down to the point of scorching the skin. In Chandler's version, Marlowe says that four hours elapsed between the shootings and the time the police were called. Newspaper accounts of the crime, though, repeatedly state that the shooting took place between 10 and 11 P.M. and that the Beverly Hills Police were on the scene by midnight–a one- or two-hour gap. The most likely explanation for this discrepancy is that Chandler was working primarily from the account in *Me, Detective.* White reports that he was called to Greystone at 2:00 A.M., but he makes no mention of when the regular police were called. The four-hour figure seems an easy assumption for Chandler to have made.

There remains one further possibility for Chandler's source: he could have heard the story from Leslie White in person. In 1932, the same year Chandler was fired from the oil business, White resigned as a D.A.'s investigator. Like Chandler, he decided to pursue a career in fiction writing. White got his start writing for the pulp magazines, and he published some five hundred stories and articles and twenty books over the next thirty years. He also wrote screenplays for Hollywood, a profession Chandler would share in the 1940s. Los Angeles pulp writers maintained a fairly close network during the Depression, and White and Chandler were both friends with Erle Stanley Gardner (the creator of Perry Mason). There is no record that the two ever met, but considering the circumstances of their careers it seems likely that they would have known each other. If so, Chandler could have gotten first-hand dope on the Dohney murder from the man who had actually been there.

The connections among the Doheny family, Leslie White, and Raymond Chandler are compelling, but they do not provide a concrete explanation of what happened that night in 1929 at the Doheny mansion. Marlowe's question to Detectives Breeze and Spangler is a good one: what do you do with the Cassidy case?

The full story will never be told. Leslie White seemed content to let the case slide, to chalk it up as merely another example of the power of wealth buying exemption from legal and public scrutiny. Dan La Botz, the biographer of Edward L. Doheny, Sr., connects the murder/suicide with the prospect of Hugh Plunkett's testifying against the Dohenys in the upcoming Albert Fall bribery trial, but he shies away from laying any definite blame for the crime. Both writers seem content to portray the murder/suicide as "fishy" and let it go at that.

What really matters about the Cassidy/Doheny case is not who shot whom or even whether there was a connection with the ongoing Teapot Dome scandal. The fact remains that there was more than enough evidence of funny business for the D.A. to launch an in-depth investigation and for the newspapers to make a scandal out of the shootings. That never happened. Instead, because of the power of the Doheny oil money, the case was brought to a hasty close and a blanket of silence fell over the press.

The murder/suicide, nevertheless, has a lasting legacy in American culture. The Doheny case lies not only beneath the novels of Raymond Chandler but, because of Chandler's position as one of the founding fathers of the hardboiled detective story, beneath the mystery genre as well. The patterns established by Chandler in his Marlowe novels were picked up by the writers who followed him and have worked their way into movies and television. They have become stereotypes.

Chandler insisted in his letters and essays that he took the existing form of the murder mystery and made it realistic, taking it out of English rose gardens and vicarages and putting it down in the mean streets where crimes really happened. "The realist in murder," Chandler wrote,

> writes of a world in which gangsters can rule nations and almost rule cities, in which hotels and apartment

Identification card for the investigator whose account of the Doheny case was published in his 1936 autobiography (from Lester White's Me, Detective)

houses and celebrated restaurants are owned by men who made their money out of brothels, in which the screen star can be the finger man for a mob, and the nice man down the hall is a boss of the numbers racket; a world where a judge with a cellar full of bootleg liquor can send a man to jail for having a pint in his pocket, where the mayor of your town may have condoned murder as an instrument of money making, where no man can walk down a dark street in safety because law and order are things we talk about but refrain from practicing.

Chandler was a disillusioned romantic, an English public schoolboy who grew up to learn that the world is not governed by a gentlemen's code—and was outraged by that lesson. And, certainly, it would be foolish to claim that Los Angeles was nothing more than a teeming underworld of sin and corruption. But, there were real, concrete reasons for Chandler to have made these conclusions. At the time that he was exploring and learning about the city, Los Angeles truly was controlled by an untouchable circle of rich men. The police and the press were under the thumbs of wealth and criminal syndicates, and law could be bought for the right price.

Buron Fitts, the District Attorney who led the abortive investigation into the Doheny slayings, had been elected as a reformer. In 1928, Fitts had been appointed by the state attorney general as a special prosecutor against Asa Keyes, the incumbent Los

Angeles D.A., who was indicted on charges of criminal conspiracy to give and receive bribes. Fitts's prosecution was successful, and he used the publicity to get himself elected as Keyes's successor.

Whatever reformist zeal the new D.A. had at the beginning of his tenure—and Leslie White claimed that Fitts made a "valiant attempt to get at the truth" in the Doheny murder—he soon learned that the powers controlling Los Angeles were too strong to be bucked. Fitts quickly became a part of the machine. During his decade in office he earned a reputation as a man who would protect his friends—and anyone else with enough money—from the threat of prosecution.

In 1934, Fitts was indicted on twenty-one charges, including perjury and bribe-taking, though a jury acquitted him in 1936. Fitts's connections in Hollywood were strong as well. He received lavish gifts from producers and stars and could be depended on to allow celebrities to avoid scandalous trials. Budd Schulberg, the son of a studio mogul and a screenwriter during Fitts's era, remembers that, "Buron Fitts was completely in the pocket of the producers. You could literally have somebody killed, and it wouldn't be in the papers."

The Doheny case was one of the first of Fitts's many concessions to the political influence of money. And he wasn't alone. His career followed the standard pattern for public officials in Los Angeles. Between

1915 and 1940, every mayor, district attorney, and county sheriff elected ran on a reform platform; each was either run out of office within two years or became just as corrupt as the man who preceded him. These office holders walked a tight rope between, on the one hand, the interests of conservative businessmen (supported by Harry Chandler, the publisher of the *Los Angeles Times*) and, on the other, the entrenched network of organized crime.

The police force served more often to protect major racketeers from upstart competitors than to eradicate crime. Cops routinely trampled on constitutional rights–arresting without warrants, framing reform leaders, brutalizing prisoners, and protecting vice interests. An observer–like Chandler–who had lived in the city for several decades would have witnessed a continual parade of anti-vice campaigns and reform tickets, each of which made a lot of noise and each of which accomplished next to nothing. Little wonder then that both Chandler and White concluded that it was the system as a whole that was corrupt and that there was little an individual–no matter how honest–could do to change it.

These conclusions can be seen in the way Chandler portrays the police in his novels. Commentators have often remarked that Chandler filled his stories with cops who are brutal and dishonest, but that is not exactly the case. Very few of Chandler's policemen are seriously corrupt. Most are tough, hard-working family men trying their best to do an honest job despite the corruption of the system. And that, ultimately, is what Chandler's novels are about: not crime, not sex, not murder, but rather the struggles of a lone individual with a sense of honor and propriety trying to function in a world hostile to honesty. Chandler was not a reformer. He was, by nature, quite conservative. He never advocated a program for social change. If his letters are any indication, Chandler had little interest in politics and did not heavily research real-life corruption. His crime stories, rather, functioned more as a metaphor for his bitter view of modern life as a whole.

Chandler in many ways seems to have viewed himself as a Marlowe-like figure. His experiences with the Dabney Syndicate convinced him that the oil business was little more than a racket, yet he took pride in his own performance as an executive and office manager. Chandler once bragged in a letter, "I always somehow seemed to have a fight on my hands." He recalled an incident where a car collided with one of the company's trucks and the passengers sued for damages. The insurance company wanted to settle, but Chandler insisted on taking the case to court. He won. In another incident, in which the firm pressed charges against an embezzler, Chandler claimed that at the trial he "had to sit beside the Assistant D.A. and tell him what questions to ask. The damn fool didn't know his own case."

Chandler approached the writing business with the same attitude. He chose to write for the detective pulps because it offered the possibility of writing honest fiction. On the other hand, the slick magazines (such as *The Saturday Evening Post*) showed a "fundamental dishonesty in the matter of character and motivation." Chandler characterized rental libraries as a "racket" and fulminated about having to split paperback and film royalties fifty-fifty with his publisher. Literary agents were corrupt leeches who, as he entitled a scathing essay, took "Ten Percent of Your Life."

Chandler closed one of his letters about his struggles in the oil industry by saying, "Perhaps this sounds a little hard-boiled. But I wasn't like that really at all. I was just doing what I thought was my job. It's always been a fight, hasn't it?" The words could very well be Philip Marlowe's.

Chandler's detective is not an heir to the lone cowboy of the western. Marlowe is an honest man fighting to salvage a few scraps of justice out of a corrupt world, but he cannot succeed. Ultimately, the honest individual is powerless in the face of the corrupt system. Marlowe tries to keep his integrity untarnished, but his cases take him repeatedly into situations where his code of conduct can no longer function. As he says at the end of *The Big Sleep,* "I was a part of the nastiness now."

The Cassidy case is only a very small part of one of Chandler's seven novels, a mere three-page digression in the middle of the story. But, he returns to it at the end of the book. Breeze gives Marlowe some leeway to operate on the murder of Anson Phillips, and after Marlowe solves the mystery, he and Breeze get together to wrap things up:

> "Remember that Cassidy case you were howling about to Spangler and me that night in your apartment?"
>
> "Yes."
>
> "You told Spangler there wasn't any Cassidy case. There was–under another name. I worked on it."
>
> He took his hand off my shoulder and opened the door for me and grinned straight into my eyes.
>
> "On account of the Cassidy case," he said, "and the way it made me feel, I sometimes give a guy a break he could perhaps not really deserve. A little something paid back out of the dirty millions to a working stiff–like me–or you. Be good."

It's not much of a moral victory, but in a city like Los Angeles, Chandler seems to be saying, it's about as good as an honest man can do.

The Angel's Flight funicular railway in downtown Los Angeles. In The High Window Marlowe parks "at the end of the street, where the funicular railway comes struggling up the yellow clay bank from Hill Street" (Library of Congress).

Interior of the Bradbury Building, a Los Angeles landmark with distinctive open-grill elevators. Because of these elevators, some commentators have identified the Bradbury Building as the model for Chandler's Belfont Building (Library of Congress).

Victorian-era houses in the Bunker Hill District. Though it had once been one of Los Angeles's most exclusive neighborhoods, by the 1940s Bunker Hill had fallen into disrepair and its elegant homes had been converted into low-rent rooming houses (Library of Congress).

Dust jacket for the first American edition of Chandler's third novel, which had a first print run of 6,500 copies, published on 17 August 1942
(Bruccoli Collection, Kent State University)

Still from Time to Kill *(20th Century-Fox, 1942), the second movie to be made from a Chandler novel. Based on* The High Window, *the story, like* The Falcon Takes Over, *was modified to fit into an existing detective series. Lloyd Nolan (right) starred as Michael Shayne, a character originally created by Brett Halliday. Chandler was paid $3,500 for the screen rights to his novel.*

The American Reception of *The High Window*

As had been the case with Farewell, My Lovely, *the sales and reception of* The High Window *disappointed both Chandler and Knopf. The book sold fewer than six thousand copies and received the same brief, dismissive reviews as had Chandler's previous novels.*

THE HIGH WINDOW, by Raymond Chandler. Private Detective Philip Marlowe, a tough guy in spite of his fancy manners, is called in on a case in Pasadena which hinges on an Early American coin and includes four murders and a bit of blackmail. The police take one point of view, Marlowe takes another, and his client disagrees with both. This obviously doesn't lead to harmony. For those who like their mysteries hard-boiled.

–"Mystery and Crime," *The New Yorker,*
18 (22 August 1942): 48

* * *

Right now we regard Raymond Chandler as the pick of the hard-boiled mystery scribblers. He strikes a reasonable and highly-entertaining balance between the way most people talk and the kind of hardness that just makes you tired. This rare blend pertains unto Philip Marlowe, sleuth, whose line of conversation and general technique as narrator should amuse and edify most fans. Marlowe is one of the laconic school, with a special breeziness that cheers this department considerably. Says he to a lady who sniffs at his lingo: "I'm not tough. Just virile." First, he's hired by Mrs. Elizabeth Murdock, a Pasadena screwball, to find her early American doubloon, perhaps swiped by Linda, her daughter-in-law. So Marlowe starts looking for Lois Magic, now married to Alex Morny, but chummy with Lou Vannier. Speaking of talk, Lou's consists largely in calling, "Here, Heathcliff! Here, Heathcliff!" Heathcliff is a cocker spaniel. Says Lois to Lou: "Shut up! The dog hates your guts." The murder is solved in grand style, without the use of liquor. Will wonders never cease?
–*New York Herald Tribune Books,* 23 August 1942, p. 17

Dust jacket for an Australian edition, published in 1943 (Bruccoli Collection, Thomas Cooper Library, University of South Carolina)

On 22 October 1942, Chandler vented his frustrations over The High Window *in a letter to Blanche Knopf.*

Cathedral City, California
October 22nd. 1942

Dear Mrs. Knopf:

Thank you very much for writing to me about the sales of my last story, and many thanks also for your kind invitation to lunch. But alas, I'm down here in the desert 130 miles from Beverly Hills and I'm afraid I simply can't make it this time. I'm trying to bake out a sinus condition which has been weakening me for years. Don't expect any luck, but felt it had to be tried. I hope you and Mr. Knopf are well and are bearing up under the many cares of these times.

So sorry you are feeling badly about the sales of *The High Window*. Last time you were out here you told me 4000 copies was the ceiling on a mystery. Either you were just saying that to comfort a broken heart or you are now repining for nothing at all. Why should it sell any more? And why should you spend so much advertising, and such very demanding advertising? I don't know anything about promotion, but when Mr. Knopf was out here he gave me the figures on what had been spent advertising *FML,* and to me they seemed very high. I said: "Can you afford it?" He said: "No." But you keep on doing it. Why? *The High Window* was not the striking and original job of work that could be promoted into anything of consequence. Some people liked it better than my other efforts, some people liked it much less. But nobody went into any screaming fits either way. I'm not disappointed in the sales. I think it did well to get by at all. I am sure Sanders thinks so. I hope the next will be livelier and better and faster, because, as you know very well, it is the pace that counts, not the logic or the plausibility or the style. I have just been reading a book called *Phantom Lady,* by William Irish, whoever that is. It has one of those artificial trick plots and is full of small but excessive demands on the Goddess of Chance, but it is a swell job of writing, one that gives everything to every character, every scene, and never, like so many of our overrated novelists, just flushes the highlights and then gets scared and runs. I happen to admire this kind of writing very much. I haven't seen the book advertised anywhere and such reviews as I have seen of it

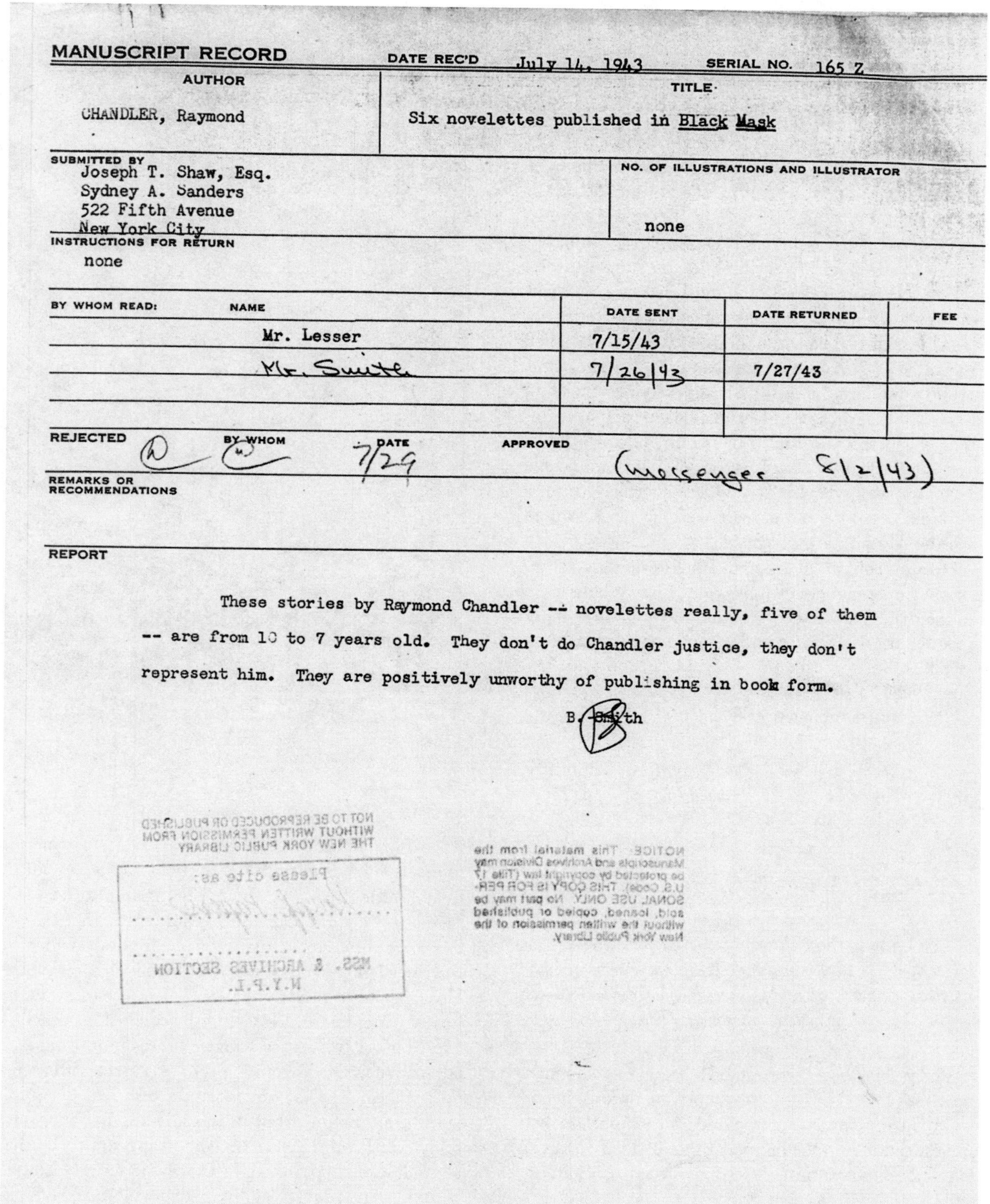

MANUSCRIPT RECORD   DATE REC'D   July 14, 1943   SERIAL NO.   165 Z

AUTHOR	TITLE
CHANDLER, Raymond	Six novelettes published in Black Mask

SUBMITTED BY	NO. OF ILLUSTRATIONS AND ILLUSTRATOR
Joseph T. Shaw, Esq. Sydney A. Sanders 522 Fifth Avenue New York City	none

INSTRUCTIONS FOR RETURN
none

BY WHOM READ:	NAME	DATE SENT	DATE RETURNED	FEE
	Mr. Lesser	7/15/43		
	Mr. Smith	7/26/43	7/27/43	

REJECTED	BY WHOM	DATE	APPROVED	
		7/29	(messenger 8/2/43)	

REMARKS OR
RECOMMENDATIONS

REPORT

These stories by Raymond Chandler -- novelettes really, five of them -- are from 10 to 7 years old. They don't do Chandler justice, they don't represent him. They are positively unworthy of publishing in book form.

B. Smyth

Knopf reader's report rejecting six of Chandler's Black Mask *stories, which had been submitted for publication in book form. The proposed volume was offered by Joseph T. Shaw, the former editor of* Black Mask, *who was a representative in Sydney Sanders's agency. The rejection of these stories— which were later published in hardbound volumes by Houghton Mifflin—contributed to Chandler's growing dissatisfaction with Knopf (The New York Public Library).*

show a complete unawareness of the technical merits of the book. So what the hell.

But as I said I do hope the next one will be better and that one of these days I shall turn one out that will have that fresh and sudden touch that will click. Most of all perhaps, in my rather sensitive mind, I hope the day will come when I won't have to ride around on Hammett and James Cain, like an organ grinder's monkey. Hammett is all right. I give him everything. There were a lot of things he could not do, but what he did he did superbly. But James Cain—faugh! Everything he touches smells like a billygoat. He is every kind of writer I detest, a faux naif, a Proust in greasy overalls, a dirty little boy with a piece of chalk and a board fence and nobody looking. Such people are the offal of literature, not because they write about dirty things, but because they do it in a dirty way. Nothing hard and clean and cold and ventilated. A brothel with a smell of cheap scent in the front parlor and a bucket of slops at the back door. Do I, for God's sake, sound like that? Hemingway with his eternal sleeping bag got to be pretty damn tiresome, but at least Hemingway sees it all, not just the flies on the garbage can.

Heigho. I think I'll write an English detective story, one about Superientendent Jones and the two elderly sisters in the thatched cottage, something with Latin in it and music and period furniture and a gentleman's gentleman: above all one of those books where everybody goes for nice long walks.

Yours most sincerely,

Raymond Chandler
—*Selected Letters of Raymond Chandler*, pp. 21–23

Cover for the first paperback edition of Chandler's third novel, published in 1945

American Reviews of *The Lady in the Lake*

The Lady in the Lake was published in the United States by Alfred A. Knopf on 1 November 1943. The following reviews indicate that after four years and four novels, Chandler was still critically neglected as a mere mystery writer in the United States.

Philip Marlowe, who stands head and shoulders above most of the rough-and-ready private dicks in fiction, solves an intricate murder case which started out as a routine investigation into the disappearance of a lady in a California mountain summer resort. Tough, beautifully organized, and with a great deal more meat on its bones than the usual story of this type.
—"Mystery and Crime" *The New Yorker*,
19 (6 November 1943): 108

* * *

Philip Marlowe, tough Los Angeles private detective gets mixed up with the darndest folks, few of them lovable and many of them downright tramps. There seems to be some truth in his statement that he would like to be different. "But," says he, "nobody will let me—not the clients, or the cops, nor the people I play against. However hard I try to be nice, I always end up with my nose in the dirt and my thumb feeling for somebody's eye." First, Mr. Derace Kingsley hires him to find Crystal, his wife, who is young, pretty, reckless with men and inclined to shoplift when drunk. She has disappeared from a mountain cabin near Little Fawn Lake, but the body Marlowe finds in the water appears to be that of Muriel Cress, wife of the philandering caretaker. Another corpse is Chris Lavery, a professional home-wrecker, and what about Dr. Almore's carryings-on with a certain lady? Passions run riot in this saga of sinful California. Swift, with satisfactory clew chasing.
—Will Cuppy, "Mystery and Adventure," *New York Herald Tribune Books*, 7 November 1943, p. 30

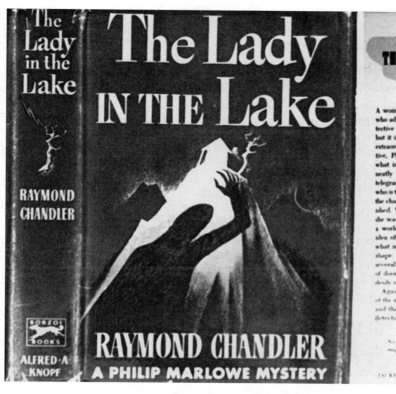

Dust jacket for the first American edition of Chandler's fourth novel (Bruccoli Collection, Kent State University)

The Criminal Record

The Saturday Review's Guide to Detective Fiction

Title and Author	Crime, Place, and Sleuth	Summing Up	Verdict
THE WILD MAN MURDERS *Theodora DuBois* (Crime Club: $2.)	The sleuthing McNeills—husband and wife—solve fatal-push-murder and tangle with a tough outfit.	Ebullient mixture of murder and subversive activities, with the detectives getting some rough handling before it all ends.	Pleasant
THE LADY IN THE LAKE *Raymond Chandler* (Knopf: $2.)	Mr. Marlowe, Calif shamus, undertakes to find vanished wife of perfume maker and runs into several murders.	About as tough as they come—plus an air-tight plot, interesting characters, copious action, and ace-high writing.	Extra good
THE MYSTERY OF SWORDFISH REEF *Arthur W. Upfield* (Crime Club: $2.)	Australian sleuth, Napoleon Bonaparte, swaps bush for ocean in hunt for boat and its occupants.	"Bony" does customarily excellent job of deducing and reveals prowess as fisherman as well. An early Upfield of considerable merit.	O. K.
MEAT FOR MURDER *Lange Lewis* (Bobbs-Merrill: $2.)	Hollywood scenic artist found dead in courtyard of outlandish palazzo. Detective Tuck and asst. Brigid solve it.	Plenty of fantastic local color, raft of exotic characters, believable sleuth, and speedy doings all the way.	—If you like Hollywood yarns
LOOK YOUR LAST *John Stephen Strange* (Crime Club: $2.)	Murder of man wanted in Congressional inquiry starts Barney Gantt on trail of killings with international ramifications.	First-class mystery, good characters, puzzle that holds to the end, serious touches of value, and oceans of action.	Swell!

Review of The Lady in the Lake *from* The Saturday Review of Literature, *6 November 1943. "The Criminal Record" grid, which ran weekly in the magazine, indicates the lack of respect accorded detective fiction during the 1940s.*

Mr. Marlowe, forthright and uninhibited California shamus (private detective), is hired to trace the missing wife of a perfume manufacturer, encounters three murders, trades punches with the police, and finally drives a tragic and cunningly concealed killer to his death. An astringent, hard-bitten, expertly constructed and convincingly characterized story of the just-tough-enough school.

–"Mysteries in November" *Time*
42 (6 December 1943): 104

English Reviews of *The Lady in the Lake*

Because of World War II, the publication of The Lady in the Lake *was delayed in Great Britain. Hamish Hamilton finally brought out the first English edition of the novel in October 1944, almost a year after the American edition was published.*

Marlowe, Mr. Raymond Chandler's sentimental hard-boiled detective, is commissioned to find a missing woman in *The Lady in the Lake*. Derace Kingsley has many good reasons for actively loathing his wife; she has always made plenty of trouble for him, being that

A Hamish Hamilton advertisement for The Lady in the Lake

type of woman; to Marlowe she is the cause of plenty more. There is her tiresome obstructionist playboy friend, then there is the corpse discovered near her country shack. Indeed, the more Marlowe discovers the more difficult the affair becomes. Why are the police so touchy about the death of her friend, Mrs. Almore? And just why is Dr. Almore so upset because Marlowe calls on the glamour-bug, Lavery? Mr. Chandler solves these mysteries and many others. His people, for all their tough nastiness, are recognisable as human beings; this quality, so marked in the novels of Simenon, is all too rare in tough crime stories. Mr. Chandler tells his story at a good pace, the two or three threads he leaves hanging add a pleasing touch to the whole. Strongly recommended to the Cheyney fans.

–John Hampton, "Fiction," *The Spectator,*
17 November 1944, p. 466

* * *

Cover for the edition of Chandler's fourth novel that was distributed free to American military personnel in 1945
(Bruccoli Collection, Thomas Cooper Library, University of South Carolina)

Though relegated to the mystery pages in most British periodicals, The Lady in the Lake *was noticed by Desmond MacCarthy, the influential literary critic for the London* Sunday Times, *and reviewed in his regular weekly column on 29 October 1944. The review was negative, but it was significant that in England, Chandler's books were being given attention by critics of "serious" fiction. Chandler responded to this review by saying, "in view of the fact that he [MacCarthy] does only one article a week . . . and devoted it all to one of mine, I am less concerned with his strictures than what he did with his space. . . ."*

Of one thing I feel sure: Mr. Raymond Chandler must be a great swell in the detective-fiction line; and in saying that I guess I am giving myself away. Yes, I write this week as an outsider; and whatever interest my comments upon "The Lady in the Lake" may prove to have, they cannot be those of a real connoisseur.

It has been a matter of regret to me that I have been unable to share a source of diversion accessible to the vast majority of my contemporaries, my fellow intellectuals included. Nor has it been for want of trying. I have embarked on hundreds of who-dun-its. If staying in a house well stocked with them, I may still carry three with me to bed in hope that one of them . . . But although I quite frequently enjoy the discovery of the corpse, the arrival of the detective and the preliminary stages of the investigation, my interest seems to diminish as the story proceeds. Again and again and again I have found the solution to be only a kind of clever excuse for having postponed revelation.

* *
*

Consequently, for a good many years past I have opened only detective novels which promised me some entertainment of another kind by the way, in addition to exciting my curiosity about the identity of the criminal; either by interesting me in the setting or in the characters concerned. Among these the detective himself is for me all important, and I must thrill with cosy pleasure at the idea of such a man. This seems to be also a popular demand,

Pocket Book № 154,597,753

Raymond Chandler

389

Another Philip Marlowe Mystery

The LADY IN THE LAKE

COMPLETE & UNABRIDGED

Cover for the first commercial paperback edition, published the year after the Armed Services edition

But, of course, the type of detective most fitting to any particular crime-story depends upon the degree of realism with which crime itself is treated in it. In stories which only play with the idea of murder you can introduce a Sherlock Holmes and thus increase the gaiety of nations. But if you are really going to try to portray the ugly queer callousness of real criminals, your detective and his methods must be also correspondingly real. Now the recent success of M. Simenon's crime stories and his detective, M. Maigret, illustrates the truth of this. So, up to a certain point, does this new story by Mr. Chandler.

"The Lady in the Lake" is brutally realistic. Here and there I found it ugly. Now, I do not object in the least to finding my sensibilities rasped, when it is clearly understood between me and the author that we are out together to explore human nature and discover how beastly things happen in this world. Then the more ruthless he is the more I am inclined to respect him. Anyhow, I shudder and learn. But I object if the obvious purpose of his book is only to entertain me by unravelling false clues and surprise me by the unexpected ingenuity and superhuman endurance of his detective. I become also contemptuous if behind a hard surface of skilfully maintained matter-of-factness, which on occasion spares one nothing in the way of horrid detail, I detect an arrant sentimentalism about "toughness" and an indifference to adequate motivation. The murderer is identified as a member of the police.

> He said: "I still ain't heard who killed Muriel." I said: "Somebody who thought she needed killing, somebody who had loved her and hated her, somebody who was too much of a cop to let her get away with any more murders, but not enough of a cop to pull her in and let the whole story come out."

"Too much of a cop" . . . "not enough of a cop"! Such is the psychology in a book which aims on every page at attaining the acme of direct actuality! It is most efficiently written; the story travels at an exhilarating speed. It is a brilliant who-dun-it, but its realism is only bluff.

It is hard to guess how long sentimental toughness is likely to be a dominating note in American fiction. Here Kipling introduced the literary convention of remaining sternly dry-eyed, while slamming the door upon emotion in such a way that we knew he was sobbing on the landing; but it did not catch on. There is, however, something flattering to a huge, defiantly and self-consciously democratic public in the notion that brutality is really a sign of a capacity for tenderness, and self-assertion an augury of fellow feeling. So perhaps in America sentimental toughness may rule the roost for another twenty years. If Communism gets hold of English fiction we may expect the same here.

—Sunday Times (London), p. 3

for who has failed to observe the efforts on the part of such novelists to meet it by making their detectives fascinating? Look at the creator of Lord Peter Wimsey, what charms and accomplishments has she not lavished on him! But, alas, for me in vain I can't swallow an aristocratic detective. He shocks me like a fine animal with two heads. I don't want a detective to be handsome and charming; impressive yes, but thanks to intellectual power and aloofness, courage, ingenuity and presence of mind; or, if he is a professional, to his thorough knowledge of his business. You can make him, in addition, an expert chess-player, or, like Sherlock Holmes, a man who loves the violin, or, maybe, one much respected also in the quiet world of conchology for his exhaustive knowledge of barnacles. These little touches may serve to make him appear more admirable. But you must not load him with Fortune's favours, this incidentally turning the exercise of his astonishing gifts into a mere frivolous sideshow in his own life. If he is a rich man who gets somehow mixed up in criminal mysteries, then let him be like A. E. W. Mason's Mr. Ricardo—the friend of Hanaud—an amiable sybarite, also rather slow-witted.

4.
The Hollywood Years, 1943–1947

A Hollywood Contract

In the summer of 1943, four years after beginning his career as a novelist, Chandler turned to Hollywood for income. His first contract was with Paramount Pictures—at a rate of $750 a week—to collaborate with director Billy Wilder on the movie version of James M. Cain's Double Indemnity, *which was released in 1944. The movie established the reputation of the Austrian-born Wilder in Hollywood. Chandler was represented in Hollywood by H. N. Swanson, who recalled how he became Chandler's agent in his memoir,* Sprinkled with Ruby Dust *(1989).*

One day I had a call from Joseph Sistrom, a producer at Paramount Studios. He told me about a situation in which he thought I could be of help. Sistrom had signed a contract with Raymond Chandler after having read some of his stories in a detective magazine, *Black Mask*. I had just sold James Cain's *Double Indemnity* to the studio. It was to be produced as a film, with Billy Wilder as director. Sistrom's idea was to have Raymond Chandler write the screenplay.

Sistrom said, "Chandler doesn't know a thing about screenplay writing, but it doesn't matter. He knows the kind of people Cain wrote about. He's eager to try his hand at the material and would take the two or three hundred a week the studio would probably offer him. Will you be his agent and get him a proper deal here?"

"I don't know how he writes," I said. "I'd have to be aware of what he does."

"No problem there," Sistrom replied. "I'll get you some of his *Black Mask* stories and you'll see what I've been talking about."

I read the Chandler stories and I was intrigued. I took Ray into Paramount's business office, turned down the $250 a week they offered him and came out the door with a ten-week contract at $750 a week. Ray did a top-rate job and got his first screenplay credit.

—Sprinkled with Ruby Dust, pp. 83–84

The Marathon Street gate to Paramount Studios, where Chandler worked between 1943 and 1946

Chandler and Billy Wilder at Paramount during the writing of
Double Indemnity

Working on *Double Indemnity*

Although they produced a successful screenplay, the working relationship between Chandler and Wilder was not a good one. Wilder recalled his collaboration with Chandler in the following interview with Ivan Moffatt, "On the Fourth Floor of Paramount."

Wilder: It's a very peculiar thing, you know, in all the forty years plus that I have been in Hollywood, when people have come up and asked questions—newspaper men, researchers, or letters from all over the place—the two people that I've been connected with whom everyone is most interested in are Marilyn Monroe and Raymond Chandler. There is some kind of fascination, as well there might be, because they were both enigmas. I knew them well—I made two pictures with Monroe and I wrote and lived on the fourth floor of Paramount for a long time with Chandler—and they were, indeed, enigmas.

I had been a writer at Paramount, teamed with Charles Brackett on many pictures. I had been writing for Mitchell Leisen and Lubitsch—all kinds of things—and one day Joe Sistrom, who was on the production staff there, and was indeed to be the producer of the picture I made with Chandler (though he did not take any credit because he was very insulted that they only wanted to give him the associate-producer credit and he said 'get lost') well, he brought me a story from the old *Liberty* magazine, which is long since deceased. James M. Cain, who had written a most successful novel called *The Postman Always Rings Twice* and who was very much *en vogue,* wrote a short story in two or three or four instalments for *Liberty* magazine called 'Double Indemnity'; and it was in texture, and even in content, an echo of the much better *The Postman Always Rings Twice* (which was owned by MGM and done after *Double Indemnity* with Garfield and Miss Turner; it was a very poor picture, if I say so myself, as shouldn't—the better novel made the poorer picture).

Now Mr Sistrom came and said 'Read that' ['Double Indemnity'], and I read it, and I got very, very excited about it and Charles Brackett, with whom I had been working, was off on some other thing, so it just worked out that I was free—by this time I was already a director, having directed *The Major and the Minor* and *Five Graves to Cairo*—and Sistrom said, 'Well, who do you want to work with on the script?' And I said, 'Let's take Cain.' But Cain—and this is very Hollywood—was working at Fox on a picture called *Western Union,* so Sistrom said, 'Look, there is another writer around town, who writes kind of good—good dialogue and sharp characters—he is a sort of mystery writer who graduated from the *Black Mask* magazine, as has Dashiel Hammett and a lot of other very good writers, and he has sort of the smell of Southern California, where *Double Indemnity* plays—Los Feliz Boulevard and the Pasadena Station and insurance companies downtown and so on.'

Well, we called for Mr Chandler, who appeared in the office of Mr Sistrom. He had never been inside a studio; he had never worked on a picture; he had no idea what the hell the whole thing was about. Sistrom asked him to read the story, which he did, and he came back and said yes, he would like to do it, could he see what a screenplay looked like? So we gave him a screenplay. He had that idiotic idea, you know, that if you know about 'fade in' and 'dissolve' and 'close-up' and 'the camera moves into the keyhole' and so on, that you have mastered the art of writing pictures. He had no idea how these things were done. I remember well what he said: 'I would be interested if you think I am the right man; but this is already Tuesday; I cannot promise you the script until next Monday.' And we looked at him as though he was a maniac. He didn't know that he was going to work with me. Then he said: 'I want a thousand dollars.' We just looked at each other.

He left and he did indeed come back on Monday, having done about eighty pages of script. It was eighty pages of technical drivel–you know, fade-ins and dissolves and all very fancy and full of things he had seen in movies and had found out through the script we had shown him. And we said, 'All right, relax Mr Chandler, this is the way it's going to happen. You will be working with Mr Wilder, who is a writer too; you will be writing together.' He was sort of taken aback. It wasn't the thing for a man who was a novelist to have a collaborator. Then he repeated that he wanted a thousand dollars. We said, 'None of that thousand dollar shit. You are going to get 750.' And he said, '750, I will not work for 750.' We said, 'No, relax, 750 a *week*. Just relax, you are going to get 750 a week.' And he said, 'Oh, really? Then it only goes two or three weeks?' And we said, 'No, fourteen weeks. You don't know how scripts are written.'

And that is the way it started and he sat down and we started working. But as we all know, and he would be the first person to tell you, he was a very peculiar, a sort of rather acid man, like so many former alcoholics are. He was on the wagon, and he was also married to a woman who was considerably older than he was. Suddenly discipline sort of came into his life, because he had to come in the morning and we would write every day, and I would be pacing up and down, and we would have yellow pads. But he didn't really much like me, ever.

Moffat: Why not?

Wilder: Well, to begin with there was my German accent. Secondly I knew the craft better than he did. I also drank after four o'clock in the afternoon and I also, being young then, was fucking young girls. All those things just threw him for a loop. But I thought that he had an enormous talent and we got along fine. Except one day, after about the first three weeks, I remember, Mr Chandler did not show up, and I was waiting and waiting–he should have showed up at nine–and finally at around eleven-thirty or twelve, I went up to Sistrom and I said, 'Shall we find out what happened to Chandler? He didn't show up.' And he said, 'I will tell you what happened to Chandler, he has sent me a letter.' It

was a letter of complaint against me: he couldn't work with me any more because I was rude; I was drinking; I was fucking; I was on the phone with four broads, with one I was on the phone–he clocked me–for twelve and a half minutes; I had asked him to pull down the Venetian blinds–the sun was beating into the office–without saying 'please'. A whole list of complaints. Se we got him to come in, and said, 'Come on, cut out that shit, come on for Christ's sake, we don't have court manners here.' And I apologized: I will never talk, I will never drink in your presence, and so on. And we finished the script. But in a book of little paragraphs that were put together about Chandler later, he said that he had a miserable time with me because I was a son-of-a-bitch. However, he said that all he ever knew about pictures was what he had learned from me. So there was a kind of resentment. Subsequently he stayed on.

Moffat: Stayed on in what way?

Wilder: He stayed on at Paramount and wrote about three or four more pictures, but not with me anymore.

Moffat: Had you read any of his work?

Wilder: I did read some before I met him. I read *The Brasher Doubloon* which was re-titled, and I read two or three of his novels. They were no great structural things. They had nothing to do with the Conan Doyle or Agatha Christie type of superb plotting. They weren't even as well plotted as Dashiel Hammett; but, by God, a kind of lightning struck on every page. How often do you read a description of a character who says that he had hair growing out of his ear long enough to catch a moth? Not many people write like that; and the dialogue was good, and the dialogue was sharp.

Moffat: How soon after you worked together did he start to learn about scripts?

Wilder: Well, there was not much to learn, because I would just guide the structure and I would also do a lot of the dialogue, and he would then comprehend and start constructing too. I told him very quickly, 'Look, I'm going to direct the picture so none of that fade-in and none of those camera tricks: just let's write characters and situations and words.' And he learned that. And he was just an extraordinary man, you know.

Moffat: What did Chandler think of *Double Indemnity?*

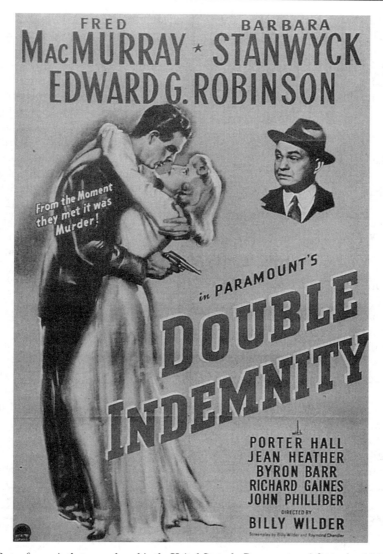

Poster for movie that was released in the United States by Paramount on 6 September 1944

In Double Indemnity, *insurance salesman Walter Neff and his lover Phyllis Dietrichson, played by Fred MacMurray and Barbara Stanwyck, murder her husband for the money from a life insurance policy with a double indemnity clause.*

Walter Neff

You'll be here too?

Phyllis

I guess so, I usually am.

Walter Neff

Same chair, same perfume, same anklet?

Phyllis

I wonder if I know what you mean.

Walter Neff

I wonder if you wonder.

Wilder: In the first preview that we had in West-wood Village, James Cain was standing in the lobby and he put his arms around me and said that it was the first time that somebody had done a good job on any of his stuff, and he kissed me. Chandler sneaked out because he did not want to be seen with his wife.

Moffat: Why?

Wilder: Because she was a grey-haired lady.

Moffat: He was ashamed of her, was he?

Wilder: People would kind of turn to him and say 'Oh, is this your mother?' You know, that kind of situation.

Moffat: Was she sort of a mother figure?

Wilder: No, she was a mother image, she *looked* like a mother. When I did see him he would kind of growl. He was a very difficult man.

Moffat: Bad tempered?

Wilder: Yes, bad tempered–kind of acid, sour, grouchy–I don't know. There was just something about him, you know. But I much preferred *that* to somebody who is light of foot, graceful, full of jokes, but totally incompetent, you know. Give me a collaborator like Chandler any day.

Moffat: Did he like the story to start off with?

Wilder: Yes, he liked the story. That's why he agreed to do it. Of course he was not too complimentary about Cain, and we improved it quite a bit. Cain didn't have that kind of sting in his dialogue. Also I must say that Chandler's great strength was a descriptive one. There are very few people who can get the flavour of California. It's very peculiar, you know, that the only person who caught the Californian atmosphere in prose was an Englishman–Chandler. And the only person who caught it on canvas was also an Englishman by the name of Hockney. No one else can paint California; he can.

Moffat: But why, after all, the film was a tremendous success and a tremendous classic, why didn't you and he work again together?

Wilder: I was kind of on a loan-out, you know. I was cheating on Charles Brackett. I came back and we did *Lost Weekend* right after this. As for *Double*

Indemnity it was extraordinarily difficult to cast because, in those days, for a big star to play a murderer or a murderess–though Barbara Stanwick instantly knew that it was a great part, and she volunteered–was nearly impossible. I went crazy looking for a man to play the part. I went to every single star at Paramount and nobody would touch it. I remember I went one day, in my despair, and told the story of the film to George Raft. And he was sitting there looking bewildered and he kind of interrupted me once in a while and then he said, 'When do we have the lapel?' And I said, 'What?' And he said, 'Well, go on.' And I went on, and then he asked again, 'Where's the lapel?' And he would not explain to me what this meant until I came to the end, and he said, 'Oh, no lapel.' I said, 'What is the lapel?' He said, 'You know, at a certain moment you turn the hero's lapel and it turns out that he's an FBI man or a policeman or someone who works for the government–a good guy really.'

Moffat: They call that a lapel?

Wilder: Yes.

Moffat: I've never heard that, have you?

Wilder: Never.

Moffat: The trouble with George Raft is that he didn't have a lapel. He got kicked out of England for not having one.

Wilder: Ultimately I got Mr Fred McMurray to play the part. It wasn't easy. He said, 'Look, Christ, I'm doing comedy. I'm a saxophone player, I do little comedies with Carole Lombard.' I said, 'You've got to take this big step,' and I finally talked him into it. Later he said that it was the favourite part he'd ever played. He's a very nice guy, and I like him very much, and a very good actor. There are also two of the best scenes that I've ever shot in my whole life still in the vaults at Paramount–one was the execution of Fred McMurray in *Double Indemnity*.

Moffat: You mean to say they executed him in the movie?

Wilder: Yes, I shot a whole scene in the gas chamber, which we never needed. Everything was reconstructed very authentically. We completely rebuilt the gas chamber and we had the bucket and the pellets dropping in the gas, and outside that

Newspaper advertisement for the movie that was nominated for seven Academy Awards, including best screenplay and best director

glass door, you know, where the doctor has got the stethoscope through that thing listening to see whether he is alive or not. And there are some spectators, and he looks and sees Edward G. Robinson watching, and there's a look between the two, and then Robinson leaves and strikes a match on the nail of his thumb. But then the scene was unnecessary. We ended it when he collapses and you hear, in the distance, the sound of the ambulance or of the police car. That was the end of the picture.

Moffat: There was that lovely scene in the film when Edward G. Robinson is detailing all the different kinds of suicide. Who did that one?

Wilder: We wrote it together. But that was not the difficult bit. The difficult bit was to memorize it. Robinson did that in one day, one and a half pages of it.

Moffat: To get back to Chandler—you may not have worked amicably but you worked equally?

Wilder: Yes, we worked well. We would discuss a situation. Once we had the broad outline, we added to and changed the original story and arrived at certain points of orientation that we needed. Then we would start scene by scene, and we started with dialogue, and then with transition. And he was very good at that, just very, very good.

Moffat: Did you ever laugh together?

Wilder: Very rarely. He would just kind of stare at me. I was all that he hated about Hollywood. He'd never seen an animal like this before.

Moffat: Also you were much younger.

Wilder: I was much younger. And he was kind of bewildered, you know; and I was much more at ease with the medium because this was the first piece of pottery he had ever done, and by this time I had done thousands of pieces of pottery—pots to piss in, pots with Mexican designs, every kind of pot went through my hands. But for him, it was a new medium.

Moffat: What effect do you suppose working with you on *Double Indemnity* had on his life, and on his career? He hadn't been involved in movies before then.

Wilder: I guess he could never find his way back to novel writing. He could not sit down any more unless he sort of smelled some kind of activity and studio companionship. You remember how it was on the fourth floor of Paramount—writers sitting around drinking coffee or pinching secretaries' asses, or whatever it was. He found it very difficult, I guess, to go back to a lonely life with just a wife and a typewriter and to switch back again to a completely different medium. And he was making exceedingly good money, not the sort of money that you have to wait for while you are writing a novel—this was instant weekly money.

It's a very peculair thing, the business about serious writers who have followed the lure of Hollywood. Very few of them took it seriously; to them it was easy

money, and they always pooh-poohed it. And they were always slightly ashamed. I'm talking now about Scott Fitzgerald, whom I knew—he was also on the fourth floor at Paramount. And Faulkner, he spent some time there.

Moffat: When did you last see Chandler?

Wilder: Must have been shortly after *Double Indemnity,* because I did *Lost Weekend* and lost sight of him. Then there was the war and, when I came back, he was around, I saw him, but we were not too chummy, ever.
    —*The World of Raymond Chandler,* pp. 44–51

Chandler recalled working with Wilder in his 10 November 1950 letter to Hamish Hamilton.

I went to Hollywood in 1943 to work with Billy Wilder on *Double Indemnity.* This was an agonizing experience and has probably shortened my life; but I learned from it as much about screen writing as I am capable of learning, which is not very much.

    —*Selected Letters of Raymond Chandler,* p. 237

Reviews of Paramount's *Double Indemnity*

Chandler and Wilder were nominated for an Academy Award for best screenplay, and Double Indemnity *established Chandler as an important new screenwriter. The movie lost out in the Oscar competition, however, as the musical comedy* Going My Way *won seven awards, including Best Picture, Best Original Story, and Best Screenplay.*

Double Indemnity *is now considered to be a classic of film noir—a genre of tough, fatalistic movies, generally crime stories, that developed in the 1940s. At the time of the movie's release, the critical response was mixed. While some reviewers found the story implausible and disturbing, others praised the movie as an original thriller. The following reviews reflect the divided reception of the movie.*

The Current Cinema: Blood and Premiums
John Lardner
The New Yorker (16 September 1944): 53

A pretty good murder melodrama has come to town, named "Double Indemnity." I have an idea that Paramount, which launched it, takes a certain artistic pride in the fact that the two leading charac-

Still from Double Indemnity; *Fred MacMurray (left) as Walter Neff and Edward G. Robinson as Barton Keyes*

Walter Neff
Know why you couldn't figure this one, Keyes? I'll tell ya. The guy you were looking for was too close. Right across the desk from ya.

Barton Keyes
Closer than that, Walter.

Walter Neff
I love you, too.

ters, played by Fred MacMurray and Barbara Stanwyck, are heels who behave antisocially throughout and die violent deaths at the finish. This, you understand, is not the kind of thing fan clubs are accustomed to, and a producer who runs such a chance with the public's sweet tooth is no doubt entitled to bask at his desk in a glow of prestige while assistants wring his hand in shifts and say "Chief, you are game as a pebble."

Be that as it may, there is another point about "Double Indemnity" which strikes me as even more unusual. That is the nature of its treatment of the insurance industry and those predatory types among us who buy insurance. Taking up the message of the James Cain novel on which it was based, the picture, without so much as blinking, shows insurance as a deadly war between beneficiaries, felonious to a man, and the company, which fights tooth and nail in defense of its capital holdings. The true giant of the battle, and therefore of the film, is Edward G. Robinson, the company's claims inspector, a gentleman tortured by the thought that a client may get away with something but practically infallible in forestalling such a calamity. When Mr. Robinson, told that the police are giving up their investigation of the death of a policyholder, says scornfully, "Sure, it's not their money," he sounds the keynote of the struggle. He is very entertaining, I should add, and not a little convincing.

It appears that sentinels as keen as this can be duped only by someone on the inside, who knows all the angles—by choice, an insurance salesman. Personally, I have done business with three or four salesmen who were, like Mr. MacMurray in the picture, genial and fair-spoken and absolute mother lodes of human knowledge and special information. It now occurs to me that if I had wanted to commit a perfect crime, and I won't say I didn't, I should have consulted one of them on the spot. That is what Miss Stanwyck does with Mr. MacMurray. She is anxious to dispose of her husband, at a profit, and Mr. Mac-Murray puts his unique resources at her service with a readiness which weakens the picture somewhat, for, though Miss Stanwyck's beauty is great and the temptation to outwit one's employer may be equally so, the salesman's character, as written and acted, does not make his crime wholly credible. Apart from this fault, "Double Indemnity" is a smooth account of sordid minds at work, and compromises with sweetness and light only at well-spaced intervals. There are one or two especially good moments, as when Mr. Robinson, sharing Mr. Cain's relish for this sort of detail, intones as he would a hymn the statutory variations of suicide.

* * *

Hard-as-Nails Dept.
Manny Farber
The New Republic, 111 (24 July 1944): 103

The most neatly machined movie since "The Miracle of Morgan's Creek," and the meanest one since "The Maltese Falcon" (without being as good as either), is a murder melodrama called "Double Indemnity," which was taken from a James Cain story in which a good-bad insurance salesman and an all-bad Los Angeles housewife figure up a nearly foolproof way to kill the wife's husband and collect his insurance. At the end their crime is so nearly cracked by the insurance company's claims manager (Edward G. Robinson), and the two of them (Fred MacMurray and Barbara Stanwyck) have become so distrustful, sick to death and jealous of one another that they try to shoot each other to death. The whole bloody business is told by MacMurray in a flashback as he confesses into his friend's, the claims manager's, dictaphone.

The film is one in which the only people who aren't deceiving someone are either ferociously soured on life, or as dyspeptic and wry as the claims manager, or too foolish to bother with; the manner of getting on with one another, either in conversation, lovemaking or gunplay, is intended to produce an effect like that of two trains hitting head-on. Their conversation—the joint work of James Cain, Raymond Chandler and Billy Wilder—is as fancy and metaphorical as I have ever heard in a movie, so that sometimes they sound like detective-story writers turned gangster. For instance, when the hero wants to say that he must think something over, he says, "I'll have to drive it around a while," when he feels the conversation is positively finished he says, "That tears it." The motto that the wife and he use to describe how their partnership has to be is "It's got to be straight down the line." This produces some embarassingly cute, candyish talk, as well as a good deal that is accurately and fatly descriptive.

The film on its own level is a smooth, talented job of writing and directing, with some very bright, realistic perceptions of the kind of people and places that rarely get into American movies, and some adequate playing—especially by the monolithic MacMurray, who is less that way than he has ever been, by Tom Powers as the soured husband, and by Robinson, who is a mousy creature, but an aggressive, masterful sleuth. However, it leaves me on the cold side of interested.

It seems to me to be slick, slight, arty and visually synthetic. The first murder is dependent on successfully projecting enough sex between the wife and the insurance agent to make a convincing murderer out of a man who is really too smart to murder anyone; the last two depend on successfully working up enough jealousy between them, hatred and fear of each other's suspected deceit, and concern on the man's part for the woman's step-daughter, to make their foolhardy turning on each other credible. The love affair seems too slight to drive the man into murder and to give the picture the great sense of passion and evil it needs, and which Cain himself often gets. Miss Stanwyck's brand of sulky, aloof coldness doesn't seem big enough, and isn't given a chance to make its evil quality effective. Their falling-out and everything else about the ending has a phony ring.

The characters of the two murderers are in general taken far too much for granted, and the very conscious attempt the picture makes to be bluntly and perceptively realistic, from the hero's match-sucking habit to the way Robinson slobbers his drink when he is excited, is a success to the degree that it is less synthetic than most Hollywood films, but it is certainly not less enough. Without going into the reasons for this for the fiftieth time, I can point out that the Russian film, "They Met in Moscow," is scene for scene more real-seeming and meaningful as realism, without making nearly so pretentious an attempt to be. I recommend "Double Indemnity," though, because the level of the work in it seems to me to be higher than it generally is in Hollywood, for the ingenuity and presentation of its first murder and a lot if information about an interesting business—insurance.

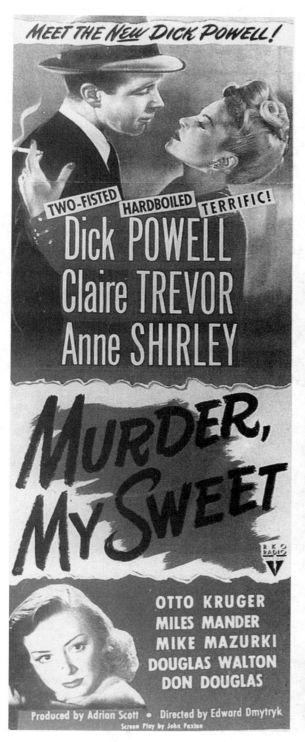

Murder, My Sweet

In 1944 RKO released Murder, My Sweet, *its second screen version of* Farewell, My Lovely. *This movie was more faithful to Chandler's novel than RKO's first,* The Falcon Takes Over, *and it was a major release, not a B movie. The role of Philip Marlowe was played by Dick Powell, an unusual casting choice. Powell had long played romantic leads in musical comedies, but he was trying to establish a new image as a tough-guy leading man.*

Poster and magazine advertisement for the second movie version of Chandler's Farewell, My Lovely

The opening scene of Murder, My Sweet *in Florian's bar. The movie changed what was a black bar in Chandler's book to a white nightclub. Dick Powell (left) as Philip Marlowe; Mike Mazurki (right) as Moose Malloy.*

Marlowe discovers a corpse in Murder, My Sweet

Sweet and Lovely Mayhem

Although the movie adaptation of Raymond Chandler's popular whodunit, "Farewell, My Lovely" was produced, previewed, and even advertised under its original title, RKO-Radio chiefs had a sneaking suspicion that the ambiguous title plus Dick Powell in the leading role sounded like another screen musical.

Some intensive spadework by Audience Research, Inc., an offshoot of the Gallup poll, confirmed this suspicion and, after a hurried huddle, the producers back-tracked with a new label, "Murder, My Sweet." Perhaps both the pollers and the producers might have gone farther and done a little better but, under any other name, this brass-knuckled thriller would prove an absorbing and stimulating exercise, comparing favorably with "Double Indemnity."

Murder Multiplied: Considering such occupational handicaps as the Hays Office and Hollywood's reluctance to retail the lowdown on low life, the screen play is gratifyingly faithful to its source. The story begins when Marlowe (Dick Powell), a case-hardened private detective, is picked up by the Los Angeles police on suspicion of murder. From then on the pattern of "Murder, My Sweet" is a flashback in which the impecunious operative picks up two lucrative jobs in one day. The first is to locate the missing sweetheart of a Neanderthal numbskull (Mike Mazurki) who lost track of her while he was in jail. The other finds him playing reluctant bodyguard to a gigolo who has an appointment with a blackmailer.

Rampant is the word for mayhem in "Murder, My Sweet." By the time Marlowe has matched murders with motives, he has been beaten, drugged, cajoled, and generally pushed around by a large number of complicated folk including a frightened, gin-drinking slattern (Esther Howard), an unctuous psychologist (Otto Kruger), a doddering millionaire (Miles Mander), the rich man's hard-boiled darling (Claire Trevor), and his troubled daughter (Anne Shirley).

"Murder, My Sweet" is a gaudy tale but a neat one. The film's sets are realistically back alley; the actors plausible in their psychopathic variations. Several times before this Dick Powell has tried to break with his June-mooning on the screen. Judging from his current version of a hard guy in a tough spot, Powell, if he doesn't want to, will never have to sing for a sound track again.

—Newsweek, 25 (26 February 1945): 100

Dust jacket for a 1945 reprint of Farewell, My Lovely, *a tie-in for the movie* Murder, My Sweet. *During the 1940s World Publishing brought out both* The Big Sleep *and* Farewell, My Lovely *in their Tower Books line of inexpensive hardcovers that sold for 49¢ (Bruccoli Collection, Kent State University).*

The Worth of Detective Fiction

Though pleased by the success of Double Indemnity, *Chandler made it clear that he considered novel writing to be his primary career. He took his screenwriting seriously and made a studied effort to learn the craft, but he intended to use the money he earned from Hollywood to live on while writing books. With his salary from* Double Indemnity *Chandler rented a house at 6520 Drexel Avenue—a modest neighborhood just south of Hollywood. He and Cissy lived there for two years—their longest period of residence since Chandler lost his job in the oil industry.*

Chandler's initial intention was to work six months on screenwriting and then take six months off to focus on novels. In January 1944, after he had completed work on Double Indemnity *but before the movie was released, Chandler received a letter from James Sandoe, a librarian at the University of Colorado and a detective-fiction enthusiast, inquiring about Chandler's old pulp stories. In his response Chandler reflects on the current state of the detective-fiction market. The letter marked the beginning of a fifteen-year correspondence between the two men.*

Paramount Pictures Inc.
5451 Marathon Street
Hollywood 38, Calif.
January 26, 1944

Dear Mr. Sandoe:

Thank you for your very kind letter of January 12th. Somewhere put away with my papers in storage I have a complete list of all the stuff I have ever had published in this country. All the earlier stories were written for *Black Mask* when Joe Shaw was editor. The Avon Book Co. is bringing out a twenty-five cent edition in the spring sometime containing five of these novelettes. If they sell them they will probably publish others. As to your being able to obtain these old pulp magazines with stuff of mine in them, I doubt it very much. A friend of mine in Kansas City has been trying to build up a collection for years and has offered as much as two dollars a copy without any success.

What you say about me and Cain is very nice. It has always irritated me to be compared with Cain. My publisher thought it was a smart idea because he had a great success with *The Postman Always Rings Twice,* but whatever I have or lack as a writer I'm not in the least like Cain. Cain is a writer of the faux naif type, which I particularly dislike.

You are certainly not without company in your wish that "something could be done about the disadvantages of the redlight segregation of detective stories from 'novels' by the reviews." Once in a long while a detective story writer is treated as a writer, but very seldom. However, I think there are a few very good reasons why this is so. For example: (a) Most detective stories are very badly written. (b) Their principal sale is to rental libraries which depend on a commercial reading service and pay no attention to reviews. (c) I believe the detective story is marketed wrong.

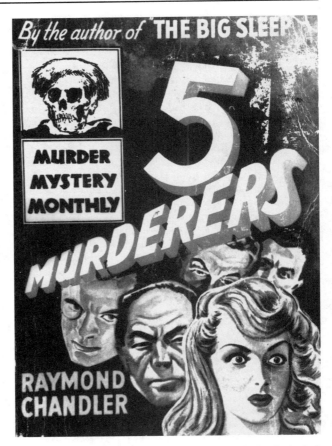

Cover for the first of three Avon Book original paperback collections of Chandler's stories. Published on 3 February 1944 and sold for 25¢ a copy, the collection includes "Goldfish," "Spanish Blood," "Blackmailers Don't Shoot," "Guns at Cyrano's," and "Nevada Gas" (Bruccoli Collection, Kent State University).

It is absurd to expect people to pay any more for it than they would for a movie. (d) The detective or mystery story as an art form has been so thoroughly explored that the real problem for a writer now is to avoid writing a mystery story while appearing to do so. However, none of these reasons, valid or invalid as they may be, changes the essential irritation to the writer, which is the knowledge that however well and expertly he writes a mystery story, it will be treated in one paragraph while a column and a half of respectful attention will be given to any fourth-rate, ill-constructed, mock-serious account of the life of a bunch of cotton pickers in the deep south. The French are the only people I know of who think about writing as writing. The Anglo-Saxons think first of the subject matter, and second, if at all, of the quality.

Thank you again for your letter, and believe me
Yours very truly,
Ray Chandler
—*Selected Letters of Raymond Chandler,* pp. 26–27

In the spring and summer of 1944 Chandler resumed work as a Paramount screenwriter, collaborating with Frank Partos on the screenplay for And Now Tomorrow *(1944) and with Hagar Wilde on* The Unseen *(1945). For both these scripts Chandler's contribution was limited to polishing dialogue, and neither movie achieved either critical or commercial success. Chandler's contract with Paramount expired in September 1944, and he planned to spend his time off working on a fifth Marlowe novel and other literary projects.*

The following letter to Charles Morton, an editor at The Atlantic Monthly, *led to Chandler's writing "The Simple Art of Murder," which was published in the December 1944 issue of* The Atlantic. *In the essay Chandler argues that the traditional British deductive mystery story, typified by Arthur Conan Doyle and Agatha Christie, is stilted and artificial and that the American hardboiled style—typified by Dashiell Hammett—is vibrant, realistic, and has the potential to be real literature. "The Simple Art of Murder" sparked debate among mystery enthusiasts at the time of its publication, and it is now considered the classic defense of the American hard-boiled mystery story. Chandler contributed five more essays to* The Atlantic *during the 1940s and 1950s, and he corresponded regularly with Morton, who, like Sandoe, became one of the friends whom Chandler knew only through letters.*

Paramount Pictures Inc.
5451 Marathon Street
Hollywood, Calif.
July 17, 1944

Dear Mr. Morton:

Sydney Sanders, my agent in New York, wrote to me some time ago saying that you might be interested in having me do a short article on the modern detective story for the *Atlantic*. Naturally I was both flattered and interested by the suggestion.

The last time I had an opportunity I tried to do a rough draft of such an article, only to discover that I hadn't the least idea how to go about it. The trouble seemed to be partly that I hadn't read enough detective stories to be able to indulge in the usual casual display of erudition, and partly that I really don't seem to take the mystery element in the detective story as seriously as I should. The main trouble with most detective stories, as I see it, is that the people who write them are bad writers. But this would not be a very interesting premise for an article. The detective story as I know and like it is a not too successful attempt to combine the attributes of two disparate types of minds; the mind which can produce a coolly thought-out puzzle can't, as a rule, develop the fire and dash necessary for vivid writing.

I am going to have some time off from motion picture work in the near future and I might have a fling at this article. If you have any ideas about what you would like to see me do, it would be a great pleasure to hear from you. I presume the matter of length is also important.

Yours very truly,
Raymond Chandler
—*Selected Letters of Raymond Chandler,* p. 29

Bernard DeVoto

At the end of 1944 two of America's most influential literary critics exchanged salvos in a debate over whether the mystery novel had any literary value. In a 14 October 1944 article in The New Yorker *titled "Why Do People Read Detective Stories?" Edmund Wilson surveyed modern detective novels and concluded that the genre offered little more than poorly written fantasies. Bernard DeVoto responded in his "Easy Chair" column in* Harper's Magazine, *defending the quality of mystery writing and offering Chandler as an example of an excellent prose stylist.*

When Mr. Wilson complains about bad writing in mysteries his scale and comparisons trouble me. I too think that Mr. Stout writes better prose than Mr. Hammett but I cannot agree that Mr. Cain is better still. Besides, is there not a question of function? If distinguished prose as such is what Mr. Wilson wants, let him try Mr. Raymond Chandler. In fact, let him try Mr. Chandler on any ground, for he is one of the best mystery writers now practicing, has carried the Hammett subspecies to a distinction its originator never attained, and in a recent movie greatly improved on Mr. Cain's dialogue. Mr. Carter Dickson and Mr. Dickson Carr writes (the verb is correct) excellent prose, so does H. C. Bailey, so do Margery Allingham and Ngaio Marsh and Dorothy Sayers, so do many others. But though good prose as such is a virtue in mystery stories it is by no means indispensable. The mysteries of Erle Stanley Gardner and A. A. Fair are among the very best there are, but the prose is commonplace; some first-rate mysteries are written in tolerably bad prose. Mr. Wilson is accustomed to a similar phenomenon in novels and would hardly require Theodore Dreiser to write gracefully or forbid Scott Fitzgerald to be rhetorical. In mysteries, as in impure forms of fiction, good writing is not exclusively or even fundamentally good prose. Writing is a means to an end; it is good writing when it furthers that end.
—*Harper's Magazine,* 190 (December 1944): 36

* * *

Edmund Wilson

Wilson, writing in a follow-up article titled "Who Cares Who Killed Roger Ackroyd?: A Second Report on Detective Fiction" maintained his position that detective stories were subliterary rubbish, but he agreed with DeVoto that Chandler was a talented writer.

On the other hand, it seems to me—for reasons that I have suggested in my complaints above—perfectly fantastic to say that the average detective novel is an example of good story-telling. The gift for telling stories is uncommon, like other artistic gifts, and the only one of this group of writers—the writers my correspondents have praised—who seems to me to possess it to any degree is Mr. Raymond Chandler. His "Farewell, My Lovely" is the only one of these books that I have read all of and read with enjoyment. But Chandler, though in his recent article he seems to claim Hammett as his father, does not really belong to this school of the old-fashioned detective novel. What he writes is a novel of adventure which has less in common with Hammett than with Alfred Hitchcock and Graham Greene—the modern spy story which has substituted the jitters of the Gestapo and the G.P.U. for the luxury world of E. Phillips Oppenheim. It is not simply a question here of a puzzle which has been put together but of a malaise conveyed to the reader, the horror of a hidden conspiracy which is continually turning up in the most varied and unlikely forms. To write such a novel successfully you must be able to invent character and incident and to generate atmosphere, and all this Mr. Chandler can do, though he is a long way below Graham Greene. It is only when I get to the end that I feel my old crime-story depression descending upon me again—because here

again, as is so often the case, the explanation of the mysteries, when it comes, is neither interesting nor plausible enough. It fails to justify the excitement produced by the picturesque and sinister happenings, and I cannot help feeling cheated.

—The New Yorker, 20 (January 1945): 62

The publication of "The Simple Art of Murder" and the critical debate over the value of detective stories prompted Dale Warren to write two letters to the editors of prominent literary magazines in which he praised the writing of Chandler. In addition to being a mystery fan, Warren was publicity director of Boston publisher Houghton Mifflin. Three years later he campaigned successfully to get Chandler to move from Knopf to Houghton Mifflin.

Sir:

When I stumbled on my first Raymond Chandler, I decided that this far too little known writer began right where Dashiell Hammett left off, and started wondering where he got his prescription. Later I got a clue in one of his dedications, where he spoke of trying "to get murder away from the upper classes, the week-end house party, and the Vicar's rose garden, and give it back to the people who are really good at it."

Hats off to the *Atlantic* for getting him to go the whole hog in "The Simple Art of Murder" (December issue). Raymond Chandler needs no longer be a mystery. He has put his cards on the table—and all of them aces.

Dale Warren
Boston, Mass.
—Atlantic Monthly, 175 (January 1945): 42

* * *

SIR: I wish that critics who express themselves on the state of the detective story (Judge Lynch and Jacques Barzun in *The Saturday Review,* Edmund Wilson in *The New Yorker,* André Gide in *The New Republic,* etc.), would sample the collected and neglected works of Raymond Chandler ("The Big Sleep," "The High Window," "Farewell, My Lovely," and "The Lady In the Lake"). Some amateurs think of Chandler not only as the olive in the martini but the martini itself.

DALE WARREN
Boston, Mass.
—The Saturday Review of Literature, 28 (20 January 1945): 23

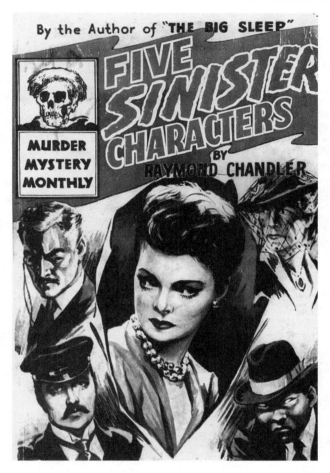

Cover for the second Avon Books collection of Chandler's stories. Published on 14 February 1945, the edition includes "Trouble Is My Business," "Pearls Are a Nuisance," "I'll Be Waiting," "The King in Yellow," and "Red Wind" (Bruccoli Collection, Kent State University).

DeVoto and Wilson's exchange helped gain Chandler visibility among other critics and showed that, even though he had not gained literary acceptance, he was finally being noticed. One of Chandler's earliest American champions was Diarmuid (D. C.) Russell, Irish-born American literary agent and author, who argued forcefully for Chandler's literary value.

The Chandler Books
D. C. Russell
Atlantic Monthly, 175 (March 1945): 123–124

A little over a year ago two friends, almost simultaneously, suggested I might find a new experience by reading the mystery novels of Raymond Chandler. Being mixed up, by nature of my profession, in literary affairs I thanked them enthusiastically and forgot about the matter. Words to me are beautiful and wonderful things, but there are times when they seem as appetizing as a full meal with wines must seem to a gourmet who has just finished an eight-course dinner. In the end one of my friends, a determined fellow, deposited two Chandler novels in my house—thus strategically undermining any possible form of resistance. I now wish to make a public apology to my friends for my delaying tactics, and should like to record my gratitude to Raymond Chandler for what is, indeed, a new experience in mystery novels.

It is a new experience because Chandler writes not out of habit and not with synthetic materials, as do so many mystery writers, but with an artistry of craftsmanship and a realism that can rank him with many a famous novelist. In his hands, words do become beautiful and wonderful things, operating with economy and precision. What a delight it is to come upon a writer who tosses off a good image on almost every page. Here is an old man whose *few locks of dry white hair clung to his scalp like wild flowers fighting for life on a bare rock;* a woman who *looked as if she would have a hall bedroom accent;* cops *in slickers that shone like gun barrels,* a face that *fell apart like a bride's pie crust;* a blonde *to make a bishop kick a hole in a stained glass window;* a voice getting *as cool as a cafeteria dinner* or one *made for talking over an eight party line.*

These have been picked at random by leafing through the pages of Chandler's novels, and I could have found three times as many of equal intensity and caliber if I had taken more time, for Chandler is prodigal in his imagery. If they seem more wisecracks than high-flown literary similes, I will point out that Chandler writes the characteristic American speech and uses characteristic American humor. In doing this he comes closer to literature than other writers who disdain the native brand of thought and language.

If Chandler on the one hand produces a sentence like this: *The eighty-five cent dinner tasted like a discarded mail bag and was served to me by a waiter who looked as if he would slug me for a quarter, cut my throat for six bits, and bury me at sea in a barrel of concrete for a dollar and a half, plus sales tax,* which has all the punch and energy of a drink of neat rye whiskey, it must not be thought that everything he writes is so tough and hard. There are descriptive passages that a poet might envy; and phrases such as *old men with faces like lost battles* or *a lawn flowing like a cool green tide around a rock* or *the surf curled and creamed almost without sound, like a thought trying to form itself on the edge of consciousness* have a beauty which shows that Chandler cannot be pigeonholed merely as an expert in tough language.

There is more of the tough language in Chandler's works than of the other kind, but this is because he writes of a world and order of society in which there is little beauty or serenity. He has a theory about mystery novels which is best explained by one of his own dedications:

> In memory of the time when we were trying to get murder away from the upper classes, the week-end house party and the vicar's rose-garden, and back to the people who are really good at it.

Once in a blue moon...

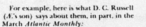

ONCE in a blue moon the public's estimate of a novelist crystallizes into the simple belief: Here, within his chosen field, or certain medium, is a truly great writer. Such a belief seems to be forming in regard to Raymond Chandler, author of *The Big Sleep, Farewell, My Lovely, The High Window,* and *The Lady in the Lake.* Mr. Chandler's four novels, together with his two volumes of novelettes, are usually classified as murder mysteries. But articles about them and their author in the *Atlantic Monthly, Harper's Bazaar* (forthcoming), and elsewhere, and critical opinion generally, indicate beyond a doubt that they are much more than the usual murder mysteries whose chief function is ephemeral entertainment.

RAYMOND CHANDLER

For example, here is what D. C. Russell (Æ's son) says about them, in part, in the March *Atlantic Monthly:*

I should like to record my gratitude to Raymond Chandler for what is, indeed, a new experience in mystery novels. It is a new experience because Chandler writes not out of habit and not with synthetic materials, as do so many mystery writers, but with an artistry of craftsmanship and a realism that can rank him with many a famous novelist. In his hands, words do become beautiful and wonderful things, operating with economy and precision. . . . Chandler writes the characteristic American speech and uses characteristic American humor. In doing this he comes closer to literature than other writers who disdain the native brand of thought and language. . . . He believes, and rightly I think, that most murder stories no longer have any relation to real life—that they have become a literary form and convention remote from realism. . . . Chandler in his works has returned to that world where murder is a commonplace: the world of racketeers in drugs and liquor, in gambling and prostitution: a world in which police and racketeers and politicians are often mixed up in sub-surface alliances. . . . It is strange to meet a murder novel writer who attacks his work with the earnest attention and serious social thought which are supposed to be the prerogative of eminent novelists. This is what Chandler does; and, so doing, he has removed his work from the realm of merely conventional entertainment to the point where it becomes a serious study of a certain kind of American society. This quality, and a grim sense of humor allied with an even grimmer sense of realism ... plus a superb writing ability, have produced five novels which are worth the attention of more readers than just those alone who are interested in the literature of murder.

Then, again, earlier this year Charles W. Morton (who has called Chandler "the top hot-shocker writer of recent years") writing in the *Boston Globe* said:

The year [1944] brought me, also, the growing conviction that the best operator in the business, bar none, is Raymond Chandler. He had a small but ardent following for the past two or three years, but he is about to become a cult. When you can read a private detective yarn a dozen times, and when you find people in general who can quote long excerpts from the author and his characters, that author is obviously getting somewhere.

And Dale Warren, writing in the correspondence columns of the *Saturday Review of Literature,* said:

"Sir: I wish that critics who express themselves on the state of the detective story (Judge Lynch and Jacques Barzun in the *Saturday Review,* Edmund Wilson in the *New Yorker,* André Gide in the *New Republic,* etc.) would sample the collected and neglected works of Raymond Chandler. Some amateurs think of Chandler not only as the olive in the martini but the martini itself."

This is the author whom Erle Stanley Gardner has called "a star of the first magnitude in the constellation of modern mystery writers," and of whom the *Kansas City Star* said some time ago: "When the literary historians some years hence jot down the names of the Americans who developed a distinctive style of mystery story writing, Mr. Chandler will rank high on the list."

What does all this add up to? Certainly, that Raymond Chandler is, first of all, a *writer*—one who uses words consciously as a literary medium—and as such a master of his craft. Second, that he is worth reading not only as an author of murder mysteries but as a *novelist*—whether you ordinarily read mystery stories or not. Third, that his novels may be considered a part of contemporary American *literature,* along with those of such writers as Hammett, Cain, O'Hara, Burnett.

Raymond Chandler has been writing now for about fifteen years. First he published novelettes in the *Black Mask*—novelettes which have recently been collected in the volumes *Five Murderers* and *Five Sinister Characters* (Avon Books). Then in 1939 he published *The Big Sleep,* the first book in which his famous character, Private Investigator Philip Marlowe, appeared: the *Cleveland Plain Dealer's* reviewer said, "I hope it may be the first of a long series, for this fellow knows how to write"). Then followed *Farewell, My Lovely* ("The best hard-boiled mystery in ages"—Will Cuppy), *The High Window* ("A worthy successor to *The Big Sleep* and *Farewell, My Lovely*"—*New Republic*), and *The Lady in the Lake* ("Good news for Chandler fans: The new one is not only as good as, but actually better than his previous books—and that makes it downright superlative. . . . If you don't read another mystery this year, read this one. Golly!"—*Chicago News*).

Meanwhile Private Investigator Marlowe had become "absolute tops among fiction sleuths of recent years," according to the *Boston Globe.*

All these novels, first published as Borzoi Books, enjoyed good sales. They have since been issued in various reprints, which together have sold many hundreds of thousands of copies. *The Big Sleep* was reprinted by Grosset & Dunlap and subsequently in Avon Books; *Farewell, My Lovely* by the World Publishing Company and Pocket Books; *The High Window* by Grosset & Dunlap (World Publishing Company and Pocket Books reprints are forthcoming); and *The Lady in the Lake* by Grosset & Dunlap (Pocket Books reprint forthcoming). In addition, *The Big Sleep* and *Farewell, My Lovely* have been issued together in one volume by the World Publishing Company.

Chandler's books are published in England by Hamish Hamilton, and have been translated into Danish, French, Spanish, and Portuguese.

Many of the Chandler stories have been produced on the radio and are appearing in the movies. *The High Window* was released in January 1943, under the title *Time To Kill* with Lloyd Nolan, by Twentieth Century-Fox. *Farewell, My Lovely* is currently being shown under the title *Murder, My Sweet,* with Dick Powell, Claire Trevor, and Anne Shirley (RKO Radio Pictures). *The Big Sleep* is being filmed by Warners with Humphrey Bogart and Lauren Bacall and will be released later this year. MGM has just bought *The Lady in the Lake.* Also, Chandler has recently won recognition as a screen writer. For about two years he has been working for Paramount, and since his screen adaptation of James M. Cain's *Double Indemnity* he has been one of the most sought after writers in Hollywood.

IN SHORT, Raymond Chandler's career has followed a well-known pattern of success. It is no longer in the making; it is made. His position as an outstanding writer and an unusually successful one is well established.

In recognition of this fact, Chandler's four novels are being reissued in the new Black Widow Thrillers series. *The Big Sleep* has just been published and the others—*Farewell, My Lovely, The High Window,* and *The Lady in the Lake*—will be ready May 14. These are well-made books, bound in good cloth, stamped in gold.

They are available at all bookshops at $2.00 each.
They are Borzoi Books, published in New York by Alfred A. Knopf.

BOOK REVIEW, APRIL 8, 1945.

17

In April 1945 Knopf released reprints of all four of Chandler's novels to date in their Black Widow reprint line. Taking advantage of the recent critical attention given to Chandler, this advertisement emphasizes his literary qualities and promotes him as a writer of importance.

He believes, and rightly I think, that most murder stories no longer have any relation to real life—that they have become a literary form and convention remote from realism. If we were to judge from most murder stories, murders are most prevalent among the middle and upper classes and as often as not are solved, not by the police, but by private individuals possessed of bulging brains and a vast assortment of strange knowledges. It is manifestly ridiculous. Chandler in his works has returned to that world where murder is a commonplace: the world of racketeers in drugs and liquor, in gambling and prostitution; a world in which police and racketeers and politicians are often mixed up in sub-surface alliances. It is not a bad thing that we should be told about the murky depths of our civilization, that this realism should be Chandler's subject, for, as we well know, this is indeed the area of American society in which murder is most frequent.

It is strange to meet a murder-novel writer who attacks his work with the earnest attention and serious social thought which are supposed to be the prerogative of eminent novelists. This is what Chandler does; and, so doing, he has removed his work from the realm of merely conventional entertainment to the point where it becomes a serious study of a certain kind of American society. This quality, and a grim sense of humor allied with an even grimmer sense of realism,—for example, his description of the seedy Fulwider Building in *The Big Sleep*,—plus a superb writing ability, have produced five novels which are worth the attention of more readers than just those alone who are interested in the literature of murder.

I must, as a matter of logic, point out that Mr. Chandler's theory leads him into a rut. If he sticks to it he will also have to stick to writing about a certain type of society and a certain type of people. In time readers will get tired of this. Worse still, even Mr. Chandler will get tired by the monotony of his literary landscape, and his interest in his own work will diminish—I do indeed fancy I see a dimming of vitality in the last two books. There is a point where a theory may become a hindrance, and I should be glad to see Mr. Chandler trying a few experiments. He might meditate on murdering some of the people he secretly thinks ought to be killed off. A fair amount of good literature has consisted of secret desires and thoughts externalized in words.

Mr. Chandler has done his vigorous best to explode the empty convention behind ordinary murder stories, but he ought not to set up a convention for himself. We who read three or four shockers a week can't stand monotony in murder.

Chandler in 1945, working on The Blue Dahlia, *his only original screenplay*

Chandler on Screenwriting

For Chandler, the Wilson-DeVoto debate underscored the difficulty he would have achieving critical respect in the United States. He was being recognized by influential critics as a writer with more talent than the average detective novelist; at the same time, however, the genre in which he was writing was repeatedly dismissed as a mere popular form with little or no literary merit.

In the following letter to Morton, Chandler commented on his recent critical attention, the publication of "The Simple Art of Murder," and his perceptions of Hollywood. He was scheduled to return to Paramount in January, but he had made little progress on his novel during his time off and was reluctant to resume screenwriting. The letter to Morton reveals Chandler's ambiguity toward the motion-picture industry, which he found simultaneously fascinating and offensive.

6520 Drexel Avenue
Los Angeles 38
Dec 18th. 1944

Dear Charles:

Yours of Dec. 14th received and a Merry Christmas to you and the whole idea of Christmas this year has somehow taken on the utter vile commercial falsity of Mother's Day in Peoria.

I saw Mr. De Voto's remarks about Chandler and was of a mind to write to him and ask him to stop using words like "imperatives" and ideas like "functional style" but not to stop slamming people around. But this business of writing, writing to writers, is a career in itself. You end up by having personal thoughts about everyone and speaking your own mind about nothing.

Had a letter from an old unknown friend at the U. of Colorado Library who asks me if my piece in the *Atlantic* was bowdlerized. Which I answered by saying that I had not checked, but had had a vague idea that it had been toned down with an ever so gentle hand here and there, and that of course it had been cut a little, which was my fault. But this just goes to show you that when a man starts to write about the apparatus of intellectualism he begins to use something that sounds like the language of intellectualism, which is a loathsome language. I re-read the *Atlantic* article and was startled to discover that in some thirty years of odd and even living I had learned nothing whatsoever about the English language. It still has me licked. I have old essays written for the *Academy* and sketches written for the *Westminster Gazette* away back when I was an elegant young thing with an Old Alleynian hatband on a very natty basket weave strawhat; they show the same childish petulance and frustrated attempt to be brilliant about nothing.

I cannot complete my piece about screenwriters and screenwriting for the simple reason that I have no honesty about it. I may wake up with a different notion, but you cannot bully me into sending you something I am so deadly unsure about. There are points like these to make, but when you make them you get in a mess. E.g., 1. There is no mature art of the screenplay, and by mature I don't mean intellectual or postgraduate or intelligentsia-little magazine writing. I mean an art which knows what it is doing and has the techniques necessary to do it. 2. An adult, that is dirty or plain-spoken art of the screen, could exist at any moment the Hays Office (Title for an Essay on same: *Dirtymindedness As a Career*) and the local censorship boards would let it, but it would be no more *mature* than *Going My Way* is. 3. There is no available body of screenplay literature, because it belongs to the studios, not to the writers, and they won't show it. For instance, I tried to borrow a script of *The Maltese Falcon* from Warners; they would not lend it to me. All the writer can do is look at pictures. If he is working in a studio, he can get the scripts of that studio, but his time is not his own. He can make no leisurely study and reconstruction of the problems. 4. There is no *teaching* in the art of the screenplay because there is nothing to teach; if you do not know how pictures are made, you cannot possibly know how to write them. No outsider knows that, and no writer would be bothered, unless he was an out-of-work or manqué writer. 5. The screenplay as it exists is the result of a bitter and prolonged struggle between the writer (or writers) and the people whose aim is to exploit his talent without giving it the freedom to be a talent. 6. It is only a little over 3 years since the major (and only this very year the minor) studios were forced after prolonged and bitter struggle to agree to treat the writer with a reasonable standard of business ethics. In this struggle the writers were not really fighting the

motion picture industry at all; they were fighting those powerful elements in it that had hitherto glommed off all the glory and prestige and who could only continue to do so by selling themselves to the world as the makers of pictures. This struggle is still going on, and the writers are winning it, and they are winning it in the wrong way: by becoming producers and directors, that is, by becoming showmen instead of creative artists. This will do nothing for the art of the screenplay and will actually harm those writers who are temperamentally unfitted for showmanship (and this will include always the best of them). 7. The writer is still very far from winning the right to create a screenplay without interference from his studio. Why? Because he does not know how, and it is to the interest of the producers and directors to prevent him from learning how. If even a quarter of the *highly-paid* screenwriters of Hollywood (leaving out all the people who work on program pictures) could produce a completely integrated and thoroughly photographable screenplay, with only the amount of interference and discussion necessary to protect the studio's investment in actors and freedom from libel and censorship troubles, then the producer would become a business co-ordinator and the director would become the interpreter of a completed work, instead of, as at present, the maker of the picture. They will fight to the death against it.

I have a three year contract with Paramount, for 26 weeks work a year, at a vast sum of money (by my standards). Nothing of the above would give particular offense to the studio, but much of it would be deeply resented by many individuals and would involve me in constant arguments which would wear me out. But there is still more to be said, and it is worse yet. A system like this, prolonged over a long period of time, produces a class of kept writers without initiative, independence or fighting spirit; they exist only by conforming to Hollywood standards, but they can produce art only by defying them. Few, very few, of them are capable of earning a living as independent writers, but you will always have to have them, because you will never find enough talent in all Hollywood to make more than one tenth of its pictures even fairly good. Granted that there are too many made; they are going to be made, or the theaters will be dark. Enormous vested interests and the livelihoods of countless thousands of people are involved. Granted again that ninety per cent of Hollywood's pictures are not really worth making; I say that ninety percent of the books and plays and short stories they were made from are not worth seeing or reading, by the same standards. And you and I know those standards are not going to change in our time.

Yet a writer, like me, who has little experience in Hollywood, and presumes to discuss the writers of Hollywood, must either lie, or say that they are largely over-dressed, overpaid, servile and incompetent hacks. All progress in the art of the screenplay depends on a very few people who are in a position (and have the temperament and toughness) to fight for excellence. Hollywood loves them for it and is only too anxious to reward them by making them something else than writers. Hollywood's attitude to writers is necessarily conditioned by the mass of its writers, not by the few who have what it calls integrity. It loves the word, having so little of the quality. Yet it is not fair for me to say in print that the writers of Hollywood are what they are; they have a guild and it may be that in so large an industry they must fight as a group; it is obvious that I have done nothing to help them achieve what they have achieved, and am not likely to, except indirectly, by helping to get out a few pictures a bit above the ruck. It is not even fair to call them overpaid; because other writers as a group are shockingly underpaid; Hollywood is the only industry in the world that pays its workers the kind of money only capitalists and big executives make in other industries. If it is something less than ideal, it is the only industry that even tries for idealism; if it makes bad art, no other makes any art, except as a by-product of money-making. If it makes money out of poor pictures, it could make more money out of good ones, and it knows it and tries to make them. There is simply not enough talent in the world to do it with, on any such scale. Its pictures cost too much and therefore must be safe and bring in big returns; but why do they cost too much? Because it pays the people who do the work, not the people who cut coupons. If it drains off all the writing talent in the world and then proceeds to destroy it by the way it treats it, then why is it able to drain off that talent? Because it knows how to pay for talent. The man who publishes my books has made more out of me than I have out of him, and he has not made it by selling the books, but by cutting himself in on radio and motion picture and reprint rights, which did not cost him a cent. Did he venture anything on the books? Of course not, not a dime. He was insured against loss by the rental libraries. He does not even know how to sell my kind of books, or how to promote them or how to get them reviewed. He just sits there and waits for something to happen, and when it happens, he rubs his hands and cuts himself a nice fat slice of it. But Hollywood pays me a large salary merely to try to write something it can perhaps use. And when I write something that pays, then it tears up my contract and writes a better one. I cannot despise an industry that does this and I cannot say the men in it are bad artists because they do not produce better art. Yet, if I am honest about art, that is the only thing I can say. It is better to say nothing, is it not? At least, for the present.

Phew! I'm exhausted. And what do I know about art anyway? Thank heaven that when I tried to write fiction I had the sense to do it in a language that was not all steamed up with rhetoric. In spite of your kindness and understanding I am beginning to hate you. It took me twenty years to get over writing this sort of twaddle and look at me now!

Ray
—Selected Letters of Raymond Chandler, pp. 35–39

John Houseman, who produced nineteen feature films in Hollywood

Writing *The Blue Dahlia*

When Chandler's screenwriting contract with Paramount resumed in January 1945, he began working on The Blue Dahlia *(1946), a vehicle for Alan Ladd and Chandler's first original screenplay. In the following excerpt from his memoir* Front and Center *(1979), John Houseman, who in the 1940s was establishing himself as a producer in Hollywood, relates the unusual circumstances under which the screenplay was written.*

It was late in 1944 when the management of the Paramount studio came to the horrifying realization that Alan Ladd—the studio's top star and the highest-rated male performer in the U.S.—would be entering the Army in three months' time, leaving behind him not one foot of film for the company to release in his absence. At our next producers' meeting, between the dire threats and fulsome flattery with which Henry Ginsberg was wont to entertain us, he let it be known that anyone who could suggest an Alan Ladd vehicle ready to go into production within a month would earn the eternal gratitude of the Studio and of Barney Balaban, the company's principal shareholder.

That same day, at lunch in one of Lucey's sinister little alcoves, Ray complained of being stuck on a book he was writing and muttered that he was seriously thinking of turning it into a screenplay for sale to the movies. After lunch, we went to his house—a small, Spanish-style stucco bungalow west of Fairfax, where Cissie was lying in a cloud of pink tarlatan, with a broken leg—and I read the first 120 typed pages of his book. Forty-eight hours later Paramount had bought *The Blue Dahlia* for a substantial sum and Ray Chandler was at work on a screenplay for Alan Ladd. I was to produce it, with Joseph Sistrom as my executive producer.

In those lush days it usually took about eighteen months or even more to produce a major film. The average writing time for an adaptation was around five months; for an original, rather more. After that, there was a period of gestation to allow everybody to criticize and tamper with the script; this created the need for revisions, which took as much as another three months. Then came the casting. And while we had not yet reached the fantastic level of titanic negotiation which came later (as the film business began to fall apart), it often took several months to find the right actors for a picture. Finally, a major director having been chosen—who almost certainly demanded rewrites that might take another eight to fifteen weeks—production would start. The average shooting schedule was between seven and twelve weeks, and the editing and scoring took another four or five months after that.

Ray Chandler delivered the first half of his script—about forty-five minutes of film—in under three weeks, at the rate of four or five pages a day. This was no miracle: the situations and the dialogue were already written, with transitions that Ray carried directly into the screenplay. After the first sixty pages had been mimeographed, a shooting date was set—four weeks away. Everyone was astounded and overjoyed.

Our director was one of the old maestros of Hollywood—George Marshall, who had been in movies since their earliest days, first as an actor, then as a director. His most famous picture was *Destry Rides Again,* which, according to him, he had practically created on the set. This and similar successes resulted in a state of mind (which he shared with many of his colleagues at the time) in which the director showed absolutely no respect for the script and made it a point of prestige, justifying his high salary, to rewrite it almost entirely as he went along. It took a lot of earnest talk from me (although, since I was still a beginner, George didn't pay very much attention) and from Joe Sistrom to convince George Marshall that *The Blue Dahlia* was a final script that he was not expected to rewrite or improvise on the set.

Casting proved no serious problem. The leading part, as written by Chandler for Alan Ladd, was perfectly suited to the special qualities of that surprising star, who had played a part, so small that I barely remembered it, in *Citizen Kane* and had continued to work as a stagehand, between acting jobs, until the lucky day on which he was cast in *This Gun for Hire,* in which he played a professional killer with a poignant and desolating ferocity that made him unique, for a time, among male heroes of his day.

As a star, Ladd now had some say in the choice of the persons with whom he worked. Since he himself was extremely short, he had only one standard by which he judged his fellow players: their height. Meeting another actor for the first time during the casting, if his glance hit him or her anywhere below the collarbone, he was sure to explain as soon as we were alone that he didn't think he or she was exactly right for the part, and would I please find someone else.

Veronica Lake was the perfect size for him, but we had trouble over the part of his dissolute wife, in which I had cast my beautiful dark-haired friend Doris Dowling. Since she was a full half-foot taller than Ladd, he made a determined attempt to get rid of her; we placated him in their scenes together by keeping her sitting or lying down. Also in the cast were Bill Bendix, Tom Powers, Will Wright, Howard Da Silva and a whole troupe of those fine, brutal low-life types with whom motion pictures have always been so plentifully populated.

Shooting of *The Blue Dahlia* went well from the start. By the end of our first week we were a day and a half ahead of schedule. In the next fortnight we gained another day. It was not until the middle of our fourth week that a faint chill of alarm invaded the studio when the script girl pointed out that the camera was slowly but surely gaining on the script. We had shot sixty-two pages in four weeks; Mr. Chandler, during that time, had turned in only twenty-two—with another thirty to go.

Ray's problem with the script (as with the book) was a simple one: he had no ending. On page 83 of the shooting script he had reached the following impasse: Ladd's wife had been found shot—in a position that suggested, although it clearly was not, suicide. Our hero was suspected (by the police, but not by anyone else) of having knocked her off in a rage on discovering the dissoluteness of the life she had led during his absence in the South Pacific. Of the members of his bomber crew, one was a dull and devoted friend; the other (Bill Bendix), who had a large silver plate in his head and convenient moments of total aberration, was under serious suspicion, which we were doing everything possible to aggravate. Obviously, he was innocent. There was a

Poster featuring Alan Ladd

villain, lover of the hero's wife: as the main suspect he, too, was clearly above suspicion. There was also the villain's estranged wife (Veronica Lake), who had picked up our hero, one night, on the Pacific Coast highway; but since she had immediately fallen in love with him and he with her, it was quite clear that the murder couldn't possibly be her work. Other characters and suspects included a professional killer, a number of petty crooks, two blackmailers, an ambulance chaser, a house detective, a bartender, and a night watchman, each of whom could very plausibly, with one or two added close-ups and a few planted lines, assume responsibility for the shooting.

I was not worried. Ray had written such stories for years, and I was quite confident that sooner or later (probably later, since he seemed to enjoy the suspense) he would wind up the proceedings with an "artistic" revelation (it was his word) and a caustic last line. But as the days went by and the camera went on chewing its way through the script and still no ending arrived, signs of tension began to appear. Joe Sistrom, who shared my faith in Ray but who was being harassed by the front office, called a couple of meetings to discuss the situation and to review our various suspects. It was during one of these meetings, early one afternoon, that a man came running down the Studio street, stopping at the various windows to shout to the people inside something we could not hear. When he reached us, he shoved his head in and told us that Franklin D. Roosevelt was dead.

I remember that we sat stunned for a while. One by one, we said all the obvious things: how ill He had looked in the photographs from Yalta; how reckless it had been of Him to take that ride in the pouring rain through the New York streets; how He had looked and sounded on that morning of his first inauguration almost exactly twelve years ago—all the things that everyone all over the country was saying in that moment, and would continue to say in the days and the years to come. Finally we fell silent and sat there gloomily for a while. Then, gradually, we drifted back to our story conference; half an hour later, we were deep in the intricacies of *The Blue Dahlia,* looking for the least likely suspect and trying to decide on whom it would be most satisfying to pin the murder. We went through all the tired alternatives, using them to smother the realities of the world outside, and Ray sat listening, only half there, nodding his head, saying little.

Two days later I was sitting in my office when my secretary hurried in to say that Mr. Chandler was outside and was asking to see me. I was not used to this formality, and there was something strange about the way she said it. When Ray came in, he was deadly pale and his hands were trembling. She made him a cup of

coffee and, piece by piece, I heard his story. Late the night before, Ray's agent had called him to say that Mr. Ginsberg would like to see him, privately, in his office, at nine-thirty the next morning. Ray had spent a sleepless night; he was a timorous man, and his agitation was increased by the admonition that he should, under no circumstances, mention the appointment to anyone.

When he appeared in the paneled executive office with its English hunting prints and cream wall-to-wall carpet, Ray was told that the future of Paramount would be seriously imperiled if the balance of *The Blue Dahlia* script was not delivered on time. If it *was*—a bonus of five thousand dollars would be paid at the moment of delivery of the final pages of script.

It was Mr. Ginsberg's calculation, I suppose, that by dangling this fresh carrot before Chandler's nose he was executing a brilliant and cunning maneuver. He did not know his man. He succeeded, instead, in disturbing Ray in three distinct and separate ways: *One*—his faith in himself was destroyed. By never letting Ray share my apprehensions, I had convinced him of my confidence in his ability to finish the script on time. This sense of security was now hopelessly shattered. *Two*—He had been insulted. To be offered an additional sum of money for the completion of an assignment for which he had already contracted and which he had every intention of fulfilling was by Ray's standards a degradation and a dishonor. *Three*—He had been invited to betray a friend and a fellow Public School man. The way the interview had been conducted ("Behind your back, John") filled Ray with humiliation and rage. On leaving Ginsberg's office he had come straight to me in a state of nervous despair: he assured me that his creative mechanism had been wrecked and that he had no choice but to withdraw from a project to which he had nothing more to contribute. I found myself believing him.

After he had gone—to lie down and, later, to discuss the matter with Cissie—I tried to evaluate our situation. The latest word from the sound stage was that we would complete page 93 before night. That left us with thirteen pages of unshot script plus two scenes we had delayed making until we knew who had done the killing. In all, less than seven days' work. And in ten days' time Alan Ladd would vanish beyond hope of recovery into the U.S. Army.

Ginsberg called in the afternoon over the executive intercom and I ignored the call. Joe Sistrom came around, and while he was with me, we received from the sound stage what, in the circumstances, almost seemed like good news. During a scene of mayhem, one of our heavies had let a massive oak table-top fall upon and break another heavy's toe. But when we reached the set, George Marshall told us not to worry;

Still from The Blue Dahlia. *Buzz Wanchek (William Bendix), George Copeland (Hugh Beaumont), and Johnny Morrison (Alan Ladd) play three navy veterans just back from the war.*

he had found a way for the injured heavy to play the rest of his scene from the floor. He also asked where the rest of the pages were.

The next morning, true to the promise he had made me, Chandler appeared in my office, looking less distraught but even grimmer than the day before. He said that after a sleepless and tormented night he had come to the unalterable conclusion that he was incapable of finishing *The Blue Dahlia* script on time—or ever. This declaration was followed by a silence of several minutes during which we gazed at each other, more in sorrow than in anger. Then, having finished his coffee and carefully put down his cup on the floor, Ray spoke again, softly and seriously. After some prefatory remarks about our common background and the esteem and affection in which he held me, he made the following astonishing proposal: I was no doubt aware (or had heard it rumored) that he had for some years been a serious drinker—to the point where he had gravely endangered his health. By an intense effort of will he had managed to overcome his addiction. This abstinence, he explained, had been all the more difficult to sustain because alcohol gave him an energy and a

self-assurance that he could achieve in no other way. This brought us to the crux of the matter; having repeated that he was unable and unwilling to continue working on *The Blue Dahlia* at the studio, sober, Ray assured me of his complete confidence in his ability to finish it at home—*drunk.*

He did not minimize the hazards: he pointed out that his plan, if adopted, would call for deep faith on my part and supreme courage on his, since he would in effect be completing the script at the risk of his life. (It wasn't the drinking that was dangerous, he explained, since he had a doctor who gave him such massive injections of glucose that he could last for weeks with no solid food at all. It was the sobering up that was parlous, the terrible strain of his return to normal living.) This was why Cissie had so long and so bitterly opposed his proposed scheme, till Ray had finally convinced her that duty came before safety and that his honor was deeply engaged, through me, in *The Blue Dahlia.*

My first reaction was one of pure panic. Such is my own insecurity that contact with a human brain that is even slightly out of control frightens, repels and finally enrages me. On that ground alone I was horrified by Ray's proposal. I also knew that if I was mad enough to take this risk, it would have to be entirely my own responsibility and without the Studio's knowledge. At this point Ray produced a sheet of yellow foolscap paper (of the same kind as that on which he had once drawn up his ultimatum to Billy Wilder) and presented me with the list of his basic requirements:

A. Two Cadillac limousines, to stand day and night outside the house with drivers available for:
1. Fetching the doctor (Ray's or Cissie's or both).
2. Taking script pages to and from the studio.
3. Driving the maid to market.
4. Contingencies and emergencies.
B. Six secretaries—in three relays of two—to be in constant attendance and readiness, available at all times for dictation, typing and other possible emergencies.
C. A direct line open at all times to my office by day and the Studio switchboard at night.

I took the paper from him and asked for an hour to think it over. With great courtesy and understanding, Ray agreed. For half an hour I walked the studio streets. I visited the set, where George informed me that he'd be out of script by evening of the following day. I went to Sistrom's office by the back way. I showed him Ray's demands and told him I had decided to take the risk. Joe approved. He said if the picture closed down we'd all be fired anyway. He would give the front office some virus story and immediately requisition the limousines and the secretaries on different charge numbers.

I thanked him and went back down the hall to my office, where Ray was sitting, reading *Variety*. With all the Public School fervor and esprit de corps that I could dredge up from the memory of my ten years at Clifton, I accepted his proposal.

Ray now became extremely happy and exhilarated. It was almost noon, and he suggested, as proof of my faith in him, that we drive to the most expensive restaurant in Los Angeles and tie one on together immediately. We left the studio in Ray's open Packard and drove to Perino's, where I watched him down three double martinis before eating a large and carefully selected lunch, followed by three double stingers. I then drove the Packard, with Ray in it, back to his house, where the two Cadillacs were already in position and the first relay of secretaries at their posts.

Early next morning the limousines were still there, shining in the sun. The drivers had been changed; so had the secretaries. Ray lay, passed out, on the sofa of his living room. On the table beside him was a tall, half-filled highball glass of bourbon; beside it were three typed pages of script, neatly corrected—

Ray's work of the night. As one of the black limousines rushed me back to the studio, I learned what I should have guessed long ago: that the murderer of Doris Dowling was none other than Newell, the house detective. Ray had just given him a death scene:

(Save Film and Win the War![1])

THE BLUE DAHLIA
NEWELL: Cheap, huh? Sure—a cigar and a drink and a couple of dirty bucks—that's all it takes to buy me! That's what *she* thought—(His voice suddenly grows hard and savage) Found out a little different, didn't she? Maybe I could get tired of being pushed around by cops—and hotel managers—and ritzy dames in bungalows. Maybe I could cost a little something. Just for once—even if I do end up on a slab.
(He jerks a gun out of his pocket)
Anybody want to go along with me? It's nice cool country. No offers, huh?
(To Lloyd)
All right, you! Get out of my way.
LLOYD: Sure—anything you say.
(He puts his hand on the knob of the door. There is the sound of a gun shot. Newell staggers)
NEWELL: (As he starts to collapse—keeping himself upright by an effort)
Just a minute, gentlemen—you got me—all—wrong. . . .
(As he falls)

DISSOLVE

I was on the sound stage when a boy on a bicycle arrived with the pages, still damp from the mimeograph machines. George Marshall read them and found them acceptable. I think he had looked forward to saving the day by improvising the last week's work on the set and that he was a little hurt that we preferred the work of a man in an advanced stage of alcoholism to his own. But he behaved admirably. So did everyone else. The film was finished with four days to spare, Alan Ladd went off to the Army, and Paramount made a lot of money.

During those last eight days of shooting, Chandler did not draw one sober breath, nor did one speck of solid food pass his lips. He was polite and cheerful when I appeared, and his doctor came twice a day to give him intravenous injections. The rest of the time, except when he was asleep, with his black cat by his side, Ray was never without a glass in his hand. He did not drink much. Having reached the euphoria that he needed, he continued to consume just enough bourbon to maintain himself in that condition. He worked about a third of the time. Between eight and ten every evening, he sat in Cissie's room and they listened together to the Southern California Gas Company's program of classical music on the radio. The rest of the time was spent in a light sleep, from which he woke in full possession of his faculties to pick up exactly where he had stopped with whichever of the rotating secretaries happened to be with him. He continued until he felt himself growing drowsy again, then dropped back comfortably into sleep while the girl went into the next room, typed the pages and left them on the table beside him to be reread and corrected when he woke up. As his last line of dialogue, Ray wrote in pencil—"Did somebody say something about a drink of bourbon?"—and that's how we shot it.

Ray had not exaggerated when he said that he was risking his life for *The Blue Dahlia*. His long starvation seriously weakened him, and it took him almost a month to recover, during which his doctor came twice a day to administer mysterious, reviving shots that cost him a lot more than the "bonus" he received. During his convalescence he lay neatly dressed in fresh pajamas under a silk robe; when I came to see him he would extend a white and trembling hand and acknowledge my expressions of gratitude with the modest smile of a gravely wounded hero who has shown courage far beyond the call of duty.[2]

1 This phrase occurred on every page of film script from 1942 to 1944.

2 More than twelve years later, Ray wrote from La Jolla—"Do you remember the Blue Dahlia? Not tops of course but I found the script in my store-room the other day and began to read it and I thought it rather good. Of course I was never a really good screenwriter and always knew it. . . ."

In his afterword to the published screenplay Bruccoli reconstructs Chandler's work in The Blue Dahlia *and examines his uneasy relationship with Hollywood.*

Raymond Chandler and Hollywood
Matthew J. Bruccoli
The Blue Dahlia (1976)

A pre-occupation with words for their own sake is fatal to good film making. It's not what films are. It's not my cup of tea, but it could have been if I'd started it twenty years earlier.

    —Chandler to Dale Warren (7 November 1951)

*I am not interested in why the Hollywood system exists . . . I am interested only in the fact that as a result of it there is no such thing as an art of the screenplay, and there never will be as long as the system lasts, for it is the essence of this system that it seeks to exploit a talent without permitting it the right to be a talent. It cannot be done; you can only destroy the tal-*ent, which is exactly what happens—when there is any talent to destroy.

    —Chandler, "Writers in Hollywood" (1945)

. . . most writers in Hollywood are employees. . . . As an individual I refuse to be an employee, but of course I am only an individual.

    —Chandler, "Critical Notes" (1947)

Raymond Chandler occupies a canonized position among twentieth-century detective novelists. Along with Dashiell Hammett and Ross Macdonald, he was one of the big three of hard-boiled fiction; but Chandler has always enjoyed special attention. His style has been justly admired, and he has been accorded considerable serious critical consideration. Indeed, he has been regarded as almost a major writer in some quarters—especially in Europe. Such a judgment is not an absolute distortion, for Chandler clearly merits respect. He, as much as anyone else, took a sub-literary American genre and made it into literature. Hammett did it first, but Chandler did it better.

The genre he worked in was the hard-boiled detective story, which flourished in the late twenties and thirties in the pulp magazines or "dime novels"—especially in *Black Mask* under the editorship of Capt. Joseph Shaw. Here Chandler began publishing in 1933 as a forty-five-year-old unemployed oil company executive. These detective stories as written by Hammett, Cornell Woolrich, Carroll John Daly, George Harmon Coxe, Frank Gruber, Horace McCoy, and Erle Stanley Gardner had certain common elements in addition to the detective hero (sometimes a policeman, sometimes a private eye, sometimes a civilian): a great deal of violence and an attempt to write tough dialogue. Frequently the results were close to self-parody. The heroes absorbed endless beatings, and were often too hard-boiled to believe. The most serious flaw of the school was the tendency of the speech to exaggerate toughness into something unrealistic. How much of the eat-nickels- and-spit-dimes dialogue can be blamed on the influence of Hemingway remains a moot point. Chandler not only made his dialogue believable, he even gave it style. As a writer who had failed as a poet before World War I, he possessed a concern with words, a feeling for good writing, and an obvious pleasure in striking metaphors or similes. But, more than any other element, it was his conception of his hero that distinguished his work from that of the other "Boys in the Black Mask." Chandler's Philip Marlowe is not a thug; he is complex and highly intelligent. Marlowe is the Los Angeles knight imposing a little justice on a corrupt world, handling problems that the agents of the law are too busy, too dumb, or too crooked to deal

Lobby cards for the movie for which Chandler received an Oscar nomination for his original screenplay (Bruccoli Collection, Kent State University)

with.[1] A loner, he makes a bare living while serving his personal code of honor and duty. Philip Marlowe is not greatly different from Hammett's Sam Spade, who appeared in *The Maltese Falcon* (1930), nine years before *The Big Sleep*. Nevertheless, there is the difference that Marlowe is more idealistic and less cynical than Spade, acutely sensitive beneath his tough manner: the anti-romantic hero. It has become a critical commonplace that the private-eye figure–particularly Marlowe–was a response to the corruption of the twenties and the social injustice of the thirties. However, it is not necessary to seek politico-socio causes for Marlowe's concern with honor and justice, which were moral concerns for Raymond Chandler. He was not political, and his work included no political ideas apart from his distrust of power. Remember, Chandler lived in England from age eight to age twenty-four (1896–1912) and received a public school education at Dulwich College. Chandler/Marlowe's code is that of the Edwardian-Georgian gentleman. His hero is an English gentleman transplanted to one of the bizarre colonies, setting an example for the natives.

Raymond Chandler published his first novel *The Big Sleep* in 1939, when he was fifty-one years old. In 1944–at age fifty-six–he commenced as a screenwriter at Paramount for $1,750 per week. Between 1944 and 1951 he worked on at least seven screenplays for Paramount, Warner Brothers, MGM, and Universal. Chandler was most closely involved with Paramount; and in 1945 signed a three-year contract with that studio calling for two scripts a year, for which he received a $50,000 annual guarantee whether or not he delivered the scripts. His Hollywood agent was H. N. "Swanie" Swanson (who also represented F. Scott Fitzgerald, William Faulkner, and John O'Hara). In addition to handling Chandler's services, Swanson also sold six of his novels to the movies–only one of which Chandler worked on.

Chandler's seven years on the payrolls of the studios were largely unsatisfactory, although he earned a great deal of money. In 1947, for example, Universal paid him $100,000 for writing the screenplay version of *Playback*–which was never produced. Although Chandler respected the potential of the movies, he was unable to work comfortably under the mandatory collaborative system. As late as 1948 Chandler called the movies "the only original art the modern world has conceived,"[2] but he disliked most of the people he had to work with, and feuded with his collaborators. He was further annoyed to see his own books butchered by other screenwriters. The only classic movie made from his work, Howard Hawks' *The Big Sleep,* did not involve Chandler.[3]

The earliest movie versions of Chandler's novels were strange attempts to superimpose characters created by other writers on Chandler's plots: *The Falcon Takes Over* (1941) combined *Farewell, My Lovely* with Michael Arlen's "Falcon"; and *Time to Kill* (1942) combined *The High Window* with Brett Halliday's Michael Shayne. Chandler's first screenwriting job at Paramount teamed him with Billy Wilder on James M. Cain's *Double Indemnity* (1944). He disliked both Wilder and the finished product, although the movie was a great success and received an Academy Award nomination for best screenplay. Chandler then collaborated on a pair of undistinguished projects: *And Now Tomorrow* (1944), a sentimental movie about a deaf girl and her doctor; and *The Unseen* (1945), a spooky suspense job. Meanwhile RKO remade *Farewell, My Lovely* as *Murder, My Sweet* (1945) without Chandler, a superior movie directed by Edward Dmytryk, in which Dick Powell was the first Philip Marlowe.

Late in 1944 Paramount had a crisis: Alan Ladd was about to be recalled by the army, and there was no script ready for him.[4] John Houseman's account of how *The Blue Dahlia* was written includes the characteristic elements of Raymond Chandler's personality and work, which may be summarized by the concept of *honor.* In completing this screenplay he did the honorable thing, and honor is what *The Blue Dahlia* is about. Johnny Morrison lives by the code of the hard-boiled Los Angeles knight ("Down these mean streets a man must go who is not himself mean, who is neither tarnished nor afraid . . . if he is a man of honor in one thing, he is that in all things"), the agent of justice functioning apart from the law. It does not occur to Johnny Morrison/Alan Ladd to seek police assistance. His wife has been murdered, and he is obligated to do something about it. She was unfaithful and was responsible for the death of their child in a drunken car accident; nevertheless she was his wife. This sense of honor is even shared by Eddie Harwood, Helen Morrison's lover. A fugitive murderer, Harwood–well played by Howard da Silva–now an elegant quasi-racketeer, is troubled with guilt over his broken marriage to Joyce (Veronica Lake) and recognizes Johnny Morrison's moral superiority. Harwood's gangster partner, Leo, sees these conflicts in him and warns: "Just don't get too complicated, Eddie. . . ."

Houseman's account of the evolution of the plot can be supplemented from Chandler's letters. Chandler did in fact know at the start who the murderer of Helen Morrison was supposed to be: Buzz Wanchek. But at that time the conduct of servicemen in movies had to be cleared with Washington; and the Navy Department ruled that Wanchek, a wounded hero, could not be the murderer. Bad for morale; disrespect for the service.

Still from The Blue Dahlia. *Ladd plays a man falsely accused of murdering his wife, and Veronica Lake plays the woman who helps him find the real killer.*

Therefore Chandler was required to abandon the plot rationale of his screenplay. In June 1946 he complained to James Sandoe, a crime literature specialist:

Yes, I'm through with The Blue Dahlia, it dates even now. What the Navy Department did to the story was a little thing like making me change the murderer and hence make a routine whodunit out of a fairly original idea. What I wrote was a story of a man who killed (executed would be a better word) his pal's wife under the stress of a great and legitimate anger, then blanked out and forgot all about it; then with perfect honesty did his best to help the pal get out of a jam, then found himself in a set of circumstances which brought about partial recall. The poor guy remembered enough to make it clear who the murderer was to others, but never realized it himself. He just did and said things he couldn't have done or said unless he was the killer; but he never knew he did them or said them and never interpreted them.[5]

Hence the absurd trick-shooting scene—supposedly proving that Buzz could not have shot Helen Morrison. Another departure from Chandler's original intention comes at the close of *The Blue Dahlia*. The script ends with the three war buddies looking for a bar after Joyce Harwood drives away: "Did somebody say something about a drink of bourbon?" But in the print of the movie that was released, Buzz and George walk away leaving Johnny with Joyce in a promissory happy-ever-after finish.

Director George Marshall has responded to John Houseman's memoir—mostly substantiating it, but challenging Houseman's statement that he tried to rewrite the screenplay as he shot it:

When the treatment was handed to me exactly as written on yellow foolscap paper, I was so impressed by the material and the quality of writing I remarked to an associate (maybe John himself), that in all the years I had been making films, I had finally found a story which was so beautifully written I could shoot it right from the treatment. . . . Why would I want to re-write something which I had thought so perfect at the beginning? Surely because the material had been put into the script form would be no reason for destroying its inherent value.[6]

The only piece of rewriting that Marshall claims is the scene in which Leo and his thug have kidnapped Johnny Morrison. In the movie version—but not in the screenplay—Leo's toe is broken during the brawl. The injury actually occurred to actor Don Costello while the scene was being shot, so Marshall had to revise the rest of the scene to accommodate Costello/Leo's broken toe. Chandler was not available for this chore because he was at home completing the screenplay. Marshall fully endorsed Chandler's complaints about the Navy Department tampering with the plot.

Although Marshall denies that he tampered with the dialogue, Chandler reported otherwise in a letter to Sandoe:

> . . . it is ludicrous to suggest that any writer in Hollywood, however obstreperous, has a "free hand" with a script; he may have a free hand with the first draft, but after that they start moving in on him. Also what happens on the set is beyond the writer's control. In this case I threatened to walk off the picture, not yet finished, unless they stopped the director putting in fresh dialogue out of his own head. As to the scenes of violence, I did not write them that way at all. . . . The broken toe incident was an accident. The man actually did break his toe, so the director immediately capitalized on it.[7]

Whatever else Marshall may or may not have done to the screenplay, this letter goes a good way toward putting Chandler's complaints against Marshall in perspective. The rights of the matter seem to be that the director had an injured actor and an incommunicado writer, so he improvised lines and action to accommodate the accident and kept shooting. Nevertheless, Chandler objected to even this emergency revision. It appears, then, that what disturbed him was the place of the writer in the movie-making system—which was subservient to the director. Once the camera starts rolling, the movie becomes the director's movie. Chandler understood this and resented it: "There is no such thing as an art of the screenplay."[8]

George Marshall's assessment of the responsibilities of a movie director are instructive for outsiders who tend to lament what this director or that director does to a screenplay by an admired author:

> A director's function is to make as good a film as possible. He must be the guiding force on the stage. He must be able to translate the words as written in the script into a visually entertaining painting; always hoping that it will be the best thing he has ever done. Unfortunately, there are times when the words as written do not fit the people who are to say them. Casting problems have forced the producer to use artists of lesser ability than the ones originally chosen. There are also times when the set does not fit the action called for in the script, so new words are written to overcome the problem; or an injury, as described in the Blue Dahlia. A director must be a master of all trades and he had better well have an answer, and a damn good one, when problems arise.[9]

Chandler was not proud of *The Blue Dahlia,* feeling that the plot change and the incompetent performance of "Miss Moronica Lake" had damaged it. He complained to

Sandoe: "The only times she's good is when she keeps her mouth shut and looks mysterious. The moment she tries to behave as if she had a brain she falls flat on her face. The scenes we had to cut out because she loused them up! And there are three godawful close shots of her looking perturbed that make me want to throw my lunch over the fence"[10] (30 May 1946). Nevertheless *The Blue Dahlia* was a success. It grossed over $2,750,000–a lot of money in those days. Chandler received his second Academy Award nomination for the screenplay, but the Award went to Muriel and Sydney Box for *The Seventh Veil.* The critical reception was predictably mixed. Bosley Crowther of the *New York Times* praised it as entertainment ("a honey of a rough-'em-up-romance"); John McCarten ridiculed it in *The New Yorker;* and John McManus of *PM* found it wanting in relevance. The best review came from James Agee in *The Nation* (3 June 1946): "The picture is as neatly stylized and synchronized, and as uninterested in moral excitement, as a good ballet; it knows its own weight and size perfectly and carries them gracefully and without self-importance; it is, barring occasional victories and noble accidents, about as good a movie as can be expected from the big factories."

The Blue Dahlia is a good–but not a great–movie; certainly not in the same class with *The Big Sleep.* Probably the chief problem is in the casting. Alan Ladd and Veronica Lake are unconvincing, although Ladd's work later improved. But some of the blame for the weakness of the movie belongs to Raymond Chandler. Apart from the problem of the Navy-dictated plot change, the plotting is still weak. Joyce Harwood is not integrated into the action. She picks up Johnny Morrison in her car on a rainy night for no reason and feels an instantaneous commitment to him for no reason. There is no explanation for her behavior toward him before she learns of the murder of Helen Morrison—except, possibly, elective affinity. She is the mandatory Hollywood love interest. Boy must find Girl, whether he needs her or not; and Chandler did not show any originality in handling this requirement.

Chandler never returned to his novel after he converted it into this screenplay. Since the working draft of the novel has not been found, we can only speculate about whether *The Blue Dahlia* was originally conceived as a Philip Marlowe vehicle.

While Chandler was working on *The Blue Dahlia, The Big Sleep* was made at Warner Brothers with Humphrey Bogart as a superb Marlowe. In 1946 Chandler had his first opportunity to work on one of his novels, when MGM teamed him with Steve Fisher on *The Lady in the Lake.* Chandler disliked everything about the project—especially his collaborator—and withdrew, refusing screen credit. This experimental "camera eye" movie was directed by Robert Montgomery who also played the off-screen Marlowe. The idea was that the camera would

Murder! Alan Ladd's Back

The Blue Dahlia, released on 19 April 1946, was a success for Paramount, and they rewarded Chandler for his effort in completing the screenplay, giving a dinner in his honor at Lucey's restaurant and holding a special screening of the movie to which prominent mystery writers were invited. Reviews of the movie, such as the following one from Newsweek, *were strongly favorable as well.*

The gardener—particularly in the season of the seed catalogue—should be warned that the contribution of "The Blue Dahlia" is homicidal rather than horticultural. The film marks Alan Ladd's first screen appearance since his release from the armed services, and he is just as steely eyed and dead-pan as ever, just as free and easy on the draw as he was in "This Gun for Hire" and "The Glass Key." If anything, a little more so.

Although the screen play supplied by Raymond Chandler—an expert in such matters as murder and contributing mayhem—is a little shaky in its logic, "Dahlia" has everything else required for a tough and suspenseful thriller. Chandler tailored the play specifically to fit Ladd's gun smoke and snarls.

Three fliers return to Los Angeles from overseas duty with the Navy. Hugh Beaumont is the protective type. William Bendix, his special charge, has a steel plate in his skull and "blacks out" when the going gets noisy. Ladd, who has other problems, leaves his buddies briefly to drop in on his wife (Doris Dowling) and discovers that she is not the girl he left behind him.

Repacking his bag but forgetting his service gun, Ladd walks out into the rain. He accepts a lift from a sympathetic blonde (Veronica Lake), who talks a lot while driving toward Malibu but is uncommunicative as to her name, age, and occupation. More communicative is a radio broadcast the next morning that reports the murder of the flier's wife and indicates that the husband is suspect No. 1.

The rest of the film is the unlikely story of Ladd's adventures playing detective while avoiding the Los Angeles police. At one time or another the list of suspects includes Howard da Silva, the owner of a swanky night club (the Blue Dahlia, incidentally); da Silva's partner and their hired plug-uglies; Miss Lake, who turns out to be da Silva's estranged wife; and a mealy-mouthed house detective (Will Wright). By his own admission, even the shell-shocked Bendix is a candidate for the gas chamber.

It won't matter if you solve the case before the police do. The action is swift and sadistic. The players, including Tom Powers as a welcome change from the standard cinema cop, carry on with surprising restraint and more conviction than the circumstances warrant.

—*Newsweek*, 27 (22 April 1946)

serve as the narrator and would therefore photograph only what Marlowe could see. Then in 1947 Fox remade *The High Window*—again without Chandler's participation—as *The Brasher Dubloon* with George Montgomery as the fourth Marlowe.

After abortive jobs on *The Innocent Mrs. Duff* (Paramount, 1946) and *Playback* (Universal, 1947?)—both unproduced—Chandler received a choice assignment in 1950 to work with Alfred Hitchcock at Warner Brothers on Patricia Highsmith's *Strangers on a Train*, but this project turned into another failure from Chandler's point of view. Here is Hitchcock's report of the collaboration:

. . . our association didn't work out at all. We'd sit together and I would say, "Why not do it this way?" and he'd answer, "Well, if you can puzzle it out, what do you need me for?" The work he did was no good and I ended up with Czenzi Ormonde, a woman writer who was one of Ben Hecht's assistants. When I completed the treatment, the head of Warner's tried to get someone to do the dialogue, and very few writers would touch it. None of them thought it was any good.[11]

Chandler reluctantly accepted joint screen credit with Ormonde. *Strangers on a Train* was Chandler's last Hollywood writing job. After his death in 1959, four more movies were made from his novels. *The Little Sister* became *Marlowe* in 1969, with James Garner playing a quizzical Philip Marlowe. An atrocious parody of *The Long Goodbye* was written by Leigh Brackett and directed by Robert Altman; Elliot Gould was the transmogrification of Marlowe in this offense. Robert Mitchum reincarnated Marlowe twice: *Farewell My Lovely* (sans comma, 1975) and *The Big Sleep* inexplicably reset in England (1978).

"There's always some lousy condition," Monroe Stahr says in *The Last Tycoon*. That Raymond Chandler worked to little purpose in Hollywood can in large part be blamed on the conditions of movie-making. But blame also attaches to Chandler, whose contempt for the professionals rendered him incapable of collaborating with them comfortably, even when he was assigned to work with the best in the business. Indeed, this contempt was hardly distinguishable from self-contempt.

When he was in the position to write *The Blue Dahlia* alone, he had to anesthetize himself.

1. This view of Chandler's work has been developed by Philip Durham in *Down These Mean Streets a Man Must Go* (Chapel Hill: University of North Carolina Press, [1963]).

2. "Oscar Night in Hollywood," *Atlantic Monthly* (March 1948).

3. The screenplay for *The Big Sleep* was by William Faulkner, Leigh Brackett, and Jules Furthman. There is an undocumented anecdote that at one point Faulkner sent a message to Chandler asking whether the Sternwood chauffeur had committed suicide or had been murdered, and Chandler replied that he didn't know.

4. "In less than two weeks I wrote an original story of 90 pages. All dictated and never looked at until finished. It was an experiment and for one subject from early childhood to plot-constipation, it was rather a revelation. Some of the stuff is good, some very much not."–Chandler to Charles W. Morton, 15 January 1945, in Kathrine S. Walker and Dorothy Gardiner (Eds.), *Raymond Chandler Speaking* (Boston: Houghton Mifflin, 1962).

5. Chandler Collection, UCLA Library.

6. Letter to Matthew J. Bruccoli, 16 December 1974.

7. 2 October 1947, Chandler Collection, UCLA Library.

8. "Writers in Hollywood," *Atlantic Monthly* (November 1945).

9. To Matthew J. Bruccoli, 16 December 1974.

10. Chandler Collection, UCLA Library.

11. François Truffaut, *Hitchcock* (New York: Simon & Schuster, 1967), pp. 142–143.

Making *The Big Sleep*

At the same time that The Blue Dahlia *was being filmed at Paramount, Howard Hawks was directing his movie version of* The Big Sleep *(1946) at Warner Brothers. Chandler sold the screen rights to his novel for $20,000, his first substantial movie sale. The screenplay was written by Faulkner, Leigh Brackett, and Jules Furthman; Humphrey Bogart and Lauren Bacall were cast in the leading roles. Hawks recalled the filming of* The Big Sleep *in the following interview with Joseph McBride, which was published in* Hawks on Hawks *(1982).*

Bogey was one of the best actors I've ever worked with. He was a far cry from the actors today, who are a little bit on the dilettante side. There was Bogey with a homely face and everything, and people adored him. When I started to work with him I said, "Why don't you ever smile?" "Oh," he said, "I got a bum lip." He had a lip that was badly cut up, and I think the nerves were cut. And I said, "Well, the other night when we got drunk you certainly were smiling and laughing a lot." He said, "Do you think I can?" And I said, "You'd better if you're gonna work with me." He became so much more attractive when he smiled.

Did you have any trouble with him?

I had trouble the first day with Bogart. I think I grabbed him by the lapels and pushed his head up against the wall, and said, "Look, Bogey. I tell you how to get tough, but don't get tough with me." He said, "I won't." Everything was fine from that time on. He had

a couple of drinks at lunch, and that's what caused it. Stopped that.

Don Siegel, who was working in the montage department at Warner Brothers when you were directing there, said that you were the only director he ever saw who knew how to handle Bogart. Because you seemed to make Bogart feel that he was part of the creative process of making the film as opposed to just being an actor in it. Was that true?

Yeah, I think that's true. He certainly could do anything that you asked him to do, and he also took criticism without a murmur. We'd start a sequence, and he'd turn around and say, "What do you think of that?" And I'd say, "Duller than hell." He'd say, "Well, what do you mean?" I'm thinking, for instance, about one scene in *The Big Sleep*. We had a bookstore built on a street; we made Bogart going inside. We hadn't done the scene in the bookstore. I said, "I don't know what the hell we're gonna do when we get inside. I've got a good girl in there, she's pretty strong, and *look* at you. If it's as dull as that, we're gonna have a couple of bad scenes. I think the only way to go in would be in a different character. Just so it would be fun when we got in." "Oh," he said, "what can you think of?" I said, "I don't know, can you play a fairy?" He said, "Start your cameras." He came up in front of the store, looked in, put on some glasses, pushed the brim of his hat up, and went in as quite an effeminate character, started lisping something. The girl inside looked at him, and we had a lot of fun making a scene that didn't mean anything,

Howard Hawks, director of The Big Sleep *(Herald Examiner Collection/Los Angeles)*

Posing as an effeminate bibliophile, Marlowe investigates Geiger's rare-book shop in The Big Sleep. *Humphrey Bogart as Marlowe and Sonia Darren as Agnes Lozelle.*

just because Bogart was willing to take any kind of a chance. The whole relationship was that way. [Although Hawks may have forgotten, the character's feigned effeminancy was also in the book. What he and Bogart did was to elaborate on it. In the book, Marlowe comments as he enters the bookstore: "I had my horn-rimmed sunglasses on. I put my voice high and let a bird twitter in it."] And then that led us into another thing. We had another bookstore to go into. There was a darn good-looking girl that I'd seen the day before doing her first scene. She turned out pretty good—it was Dorothy Malone. At the end of this scene I think she said, "Is that all you want?" He kinda looked at her and said, "Well, I could use a drink." She went over and took a sign on the door and turned it so it read "Closed For The Day." And she said, "I just happen to have a bottle." She was so nervous getting the drink that she was just shaking. So we stopped for lunch, and I had the property man pour a piece of lead to put in the bottom of the glass so that she could hold it. And, you know, people remember that scene. That wasn't the way it was written at all. We just did it because the girl was so damn good-looking. It taught me a great lesson, that if you make a good scene, if we could do some-

thing that was fun, the audience goes right along with you.

It seems that you were more concerned with the relationship between Bogart and Bacall than with anything else in the film.

Definitely. So was he. After we took *To Have and Have Not* out to preview it, it went over so well that Jack Warner, riding back, said, "We'd better do another picture with those two people. Do you know a story?" I said, "Yeah." "What's it like?" I said, "Something like *Maltese Falcon*." He said, "Will you buy it and make it?" I never saw him again till we finished the picture and showed it to him in the projection room, and he bought my interest right then and there.

Did you buy the book with your own money or with the studio's money?

I'm very pleased to say I bought that one with my own money. Made five hundred percent on it. The writers [Faulkner, Brackett, and Furthman] passed the script on to me and said, "There are a lot of things that don't make sense." I said, "Good. Let's try it and see whether the audience likes that."

When you were making the film, didn't you send a telegram to Raymond Chandler at one point asking him to explain what was happening in the story?

Magazine advertisement featuring Bogart and Lauren Bacall. The Big Sleep *was the second movie the couple made together.*

her of three in my
ells me on the second
aughing, as if anything
ving readers

aforementioned Good
of your hand." But
oward larger character
ns, unobtrusively but
irie Nocturne still
o the swank
ction, there is forever
nich Scrooge scoffs at
considers and dabs on
otchety naysayer alive

ance presents the
problematic as they
r several books' worth
whole physiognomy

er know or need to
natic sea skipper,
only secret of her life
l come home to stay

I asked him to explain who killed so-and-so. He wired back and said it was George somebody. I said it couldn't be George; he was down at the beach at that time. He wired back and said, "Then I don't know either." Actually, we didn't care. It was the first time I made a picture and just decided I wasn't going to explain things. I was just going to try and make good scenes.

It's a revolutionary thing you did, because it became the method of modern films that people don't care if the plot makes sense if it's fun. Today it's almost getting to the point of being overdone. But you were the first to really be bold enough to do that.

It's just my way of telling a story.

You made the film in 1944, and the servicemen saw it before the war was over, but the American public at home didn't see the film until 1946. And I believe that you added some scenes with Bogart and Bacall before it was released to the theaters.

Jack Warner said, "I got such a great reaction from people, Howard. You ought to have more scenes with those two people." I said, "*You* talk to them. If they can't behave themselves, if they have to get mushy all the time, I'm not going to stick around and make scenes with them." They decided they could perform. I had some horses running at Santa Anita, and I said, "I'm going to miss the races," so I went off and wrote some scenes of Bogart and Bacall talking about a jockey who came from behind and all that kind of thing. The audience liked those scenes too.

That's one of the most outrageous examples of double-entendre I've ever seen in a Hollywood film, talking about sex in terms of horse racing. I'm amazed you got that past the censors.

They said they were gonna object to it, and then they thought it over and decided they liked it so much that they were gonna let it go. What they objected to was stuff that was made with the intention of being lewd, and they said I never did that, so they let me get away with murder. The end of the story was done by the censors. They read the script, and they didn't care for the end Chandler wrote. They said, "Howard, you can't get away with this." And I said, "OK, you write a scene for me." And they did, and it was a lot more violent, it was everything I wanted. I made it and was very happy about it. I said, "I'll hire you fellows as writers." They wrote the scene where Bogart sent a fellow out the door to get shot. That isn't exactly new, but it worked. They had vagaries about censorship. I was able to talk most of the censors out of it. In *I Was a Male War Bride,* the whole idea was Cary Grant and Ann Sheridan got married and tried for six reels to get into bed and didn't make it until they passed the Statue of Liberty coming into New York Harbor. They said, "Howard, you can't get away with this." And I said, "Well, you're the boss." They called me the next day and said, "We got together and decided it was so much fun that you can leave it all in."

You also got away with murder in the way you depicted the Martha Vickers character in The Big Sleep, *sucking her thumb and things like that.*

We had a great start for that little girl, where Bogart said, "Somebody ought to housebreak her." I made her sit around almost a day trying little things, taking a piece of hair and bringing it down and looking at it, you know. Because I didn't want her to be Stella Stevens or somebody like that. I wanted her to be a well-dressed little girl who just happened to be a nymphomaniac.

—Hawks on Hawks, pp. 102–106

Reviews of Hawk's *The Big Sleep*

Although The Big Sleep *is now considered a classic of film noir, it was released to mixed reviews. One of the most common complaints about the movie, echoed in both the reviews below, was that the plot was too complex and confusing.*

"The Big Sleep" mixes violence and "smart" wisecracks along with its suspense, and manages to achieve quite a scarey effect. Producer-director Howard Hawks knows how to build up a scene cinematically so that it reaches a tense climax. The main trouble with this picture, outside of its trying too hard, is that its story is too cryptic. It gathers a good cast portraying a lot of unpleasant people, works up a series of very exciting episodes, but never adds up as a whole. One doesn't know whether to blame William Faulkner and Leigh Brackett who wrote the script, or Raymond Chandler who wrote the original novel, or Mr. Hawks who should have held the pieces together. In any case, even the title is without meaning, and you're never sure just what's up. The cast seem to be enjoying themselves—in a negative sort of way. Humphrey Bogart is tougher than ever as the private dick hired to track down a guy who disappeared. He is hindered on his job mainly by his client's two daughters: the younger (Martha Vickers) a nymph given to dope and unattractive companions, the elder (Lauren Bacall) determined to protect the younger no matter how far she has to go to do it. Various seamy characters wander in and out of the confusion—and most of them don't wander out on their own free will. Perhaps the film makers were kept so busy covering up the shady goings-on of these people that they covered up the plot too. I guess the actors, also, were pretty much in the dark about what they were doing; but it's awfully exciting.

—Philip T. Hartung, "The Screen," The Commonweal, *44 (6 September 1946): 504*

* * *

Still from The Big Sleep; *Bogart as Marlowe, Bacall as Vivian Rutledge, and John Ridgely as Eddie Mars*

"The Big Sleep" is an unsentimental, surrealist excitement in which most of the men in Hollywood's underworld are murdered and most of the women go for an honest but not unwilling private sleuth (Humphrey Bogart). Coinciding with the special prominence of the private detective in Hollywood movies, he has been tagged with the special name of "shamus." Lest there be friction between thieves and shamuses, script-writers have been equally thoughtful about holdup artists, so that their black deeds have been Disneyfied with the name "caper." The plot of "The Big Sleep," which winds as crazily as a Greenwich Village street and involves so many secondary crimes and criminals that figuring it out makes you faint, starts with the underpaid shamus signing up to stop the blackmailing of a tough millionaire's depraved, thumb-sucking daughter (Ann Vickers) by a dealer in pornographic books. That night two people you and the detective haven't seen before are murdered before they get a chance to show their faces on the screen and a six-year-old unsolved disappearance of an Irish patriot is brought to your already hysterical attention. The rest of the movie puts Bogart through some dozen more exotic and brutal situations until at the end, with unusu-

ally refreshing self-effacement, he admits he can tell the police just about all that happened.

There is a fantastic quality about all this excitement due to the apparent lack of integration between crimes, the sudden appearances of bizarre underworld figures and their more sudden, startling disappearances into the murky environment. It all has the feeling of an opium smoker's fantasy, and, incidentally, there's some of that in the film, too. With six murders in the plot, this nightmarish affair becomes less vital as you try to decide what motivates the people, whose chauffeur kills the inept blackmailer, who is having "the big sleep," who the perverted bookseller is—a foppish man with a mustache or a florid old man with a glass eye—what the exact relationship is between the widowed heiress and a classy gambler who operates a crime world by remote control. "The Big Sleep," though, is witty and sinister, and in an odd way is a realistic portrayal of big-city life with "Arabian Nights" overtones.

The detective's job takes him through Hollywood's underworld, which is made up of a classy crook whose cruelty is limitless, and a down-at-the-heel lot with comic faces and angelic souls. The chief impression you get of their world is that the pay is rotten, the

Poster for a mid-1950s re-release of the film noir classic

people—especially the women—are uninhibited and no one lives to middle age. The locale is particularly seedy and pressed in on all sides by drab concrete. Gangster movies are increasingly coming to be stereotypes. Although the drab, blurred city streets are good, they are too familiar to be arresting. But far more than the usual skill is shown in the way the director (Howard Hawks) handles the human element. He is particularly adept in graphically suggesting voyeurism and other forms of sexuality without running afoul of the Johnston office.

The more inspired work occurs where the exotic subject matter is woven with straight naturalism—one of the best scenes has to do with the hiring of the detective by a tough Southern general (writer William Faulkner may have been responsible for this) and who, after a life passionately devoted to pleasure, is living in a hothouse where he grows orchids. The scene is set up in such a super-realistic way it reminds you of an old-fashioned photograph.

"The Big Sleep" would have been a more effective study of nightmarish existence had the detective been more complicated and had more curiosity been shown about his sweetheart's relation to the crime. Lauren Bacall, performing phlegmatically, creates a large empty space in the movie. Though Bogart turns in another jolting performance as well as some good comedy, his detective is a limited, dull person, who seems to have little sympathy with the sub-rosa world with which he must always be associated. A fine bit performance is turned in by Louis Jean Heydt as an incompetent crook who is fully aware of his shortcomings.

—Manny Farber, "Journey Into the Night," *The New Republic* (23 October 1946): 351

Hollywood Frustrations and Fame

In July 1945 Chandler accepted a three-month job with Metro-Goldwyn-Mayer (M-G-M) to write the screenplay for a movie version of The Lady in the Lake. *At first he intended to keep the script faithful to his novel, but he quickly realized that he was tired of the story and had no desire to simply rework the same material in a new form. At the end of his thirteen-week contract Chandler had written only a preliminary script that deviated considerably from the original novel. M-G-M assigned Steve Fisher to complete the screenplay, and Chandler considered the final version so bad that he refused to accept a screen credit for it.*

Chandler's contract with Paramount called for him to return to work at the studio in January, but he demanded more amenable working terms, such as receiving a flat fee for writing a script (with no deadlines) rather than being paid for a predetermined number of weeks. Paramount rejected these conditions, and

Chandler refused to report for work. The studio denied Chandler's request to cancel his contract and instead placed him on suspension. It was not until May 1946 that the dispute was resolved. Chandler's last project with Paramount was the screenplay of The Innocent Mrs. Duff, *based on a novel by Elizabeth Sanxay Holding, which Chandler had persuaded the studio to purchase. At the end of the summer, his contract with Paramount complete, Chandler left the screenplay unfinished, and it was never produced.*

At the same time he was involved in the dispute with Paramount, Chandler was reassessing the sales history of his novels. His books were beginning to be distributed widely in paperback, and he was growing increasingly dissatisfied with the payment he received for reprint rights. An author generally earned a royalty of 10 percent of the cover price for hard-copy books, but paperback publishers typically paid only 1¢ for each 25¢ copy sold. In addition, authors usually had to split this royalty with the publisher of the original hardback edition. For writers such as Chandler, whose books sold far better in paperback than in cloth, this situation was infuriating, particularly since he was growing tired of working in Hollywood and was seeking enough income from book sales to allow him to quit writing screenplays. Chandler discusses his frustrations with Hollywood and the paperback market in the following letter to Blanche Knopf.

6520 Drexel Ave.
Los Angeles 36, Calif.
Mar 27 1946

Dear Blanche:

Thanks for your note, and it's always a pleasure to hear from you. I got pretty well into a Marlowe story but ran into a bad spell of flu and have been dragging myself around ever since. Also I am in trouble with Paramount and may have to go back and finish a couple of jobs for them. Short of an action to cancel the contract, there seems no other way to deal with the situation. And even an equity action takes time and money and is uncertain. I have developed a peculiar phobia about contracts, seem unable to function as a free man when tied up in any way. All very silly, no doubt, but there it is. The mere fact that sometime I must go to a studio to do a job of work seems to prevent my doing anything valid for myself. Hollywood is a trying place in many ways, but at least they pay you for your work.

I don't understand this reprint situation at all. There is a body of opinion that seems to regard the royalities the Pocket Book people are paying as something like outright theft. I do not understand why a publisher should collect three times as much *in royalities* on a writer's books as the publisher pays the writer out in royalties on the original edition. I have a feeling that a situation has developed which needs airing. Why is it not explained? Is it right that a sale of a million copies of a two-bit reprint should bring the man who created the material sold a matter of $7500?

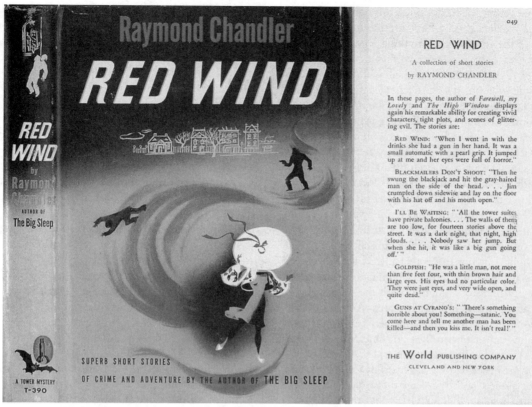

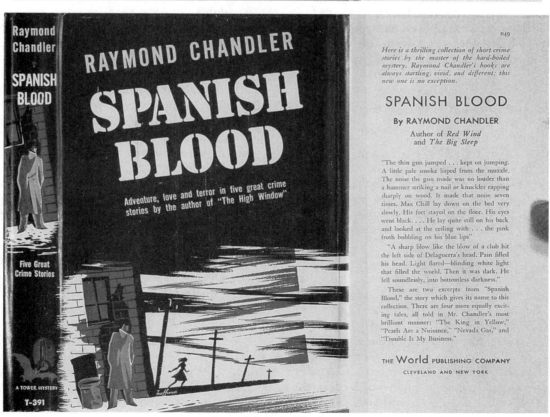

Dust jackets for Tower Book editions of Chandler's stories. Both volumes were published in 1946 (Bruccoli Collection, Kent State University).

This needs an answer. I do not think it *is* right. I think the author on *all* reprints should have a minimum royalty of ten percent of the retail price. Anything less has me wondering what goes on. No wonder writers accept the conditions of Hollywood and say to hell with bookwriting. Leave it to the women. It's all mechanics and promotion anyway. As I told my friend Morton of the *Atlantic* not long ago, the technique of marketable fiction has become almost entirely epicene. It won't be long now until somebody invents a machine to write novels. How often do I pick up a book and say, "This was written by an individual unlike any other individual, a unique person."? Practically never.

But don't take me too seriously. I am becoming a pretty sour kind of citizen. Even Hemingway has let me down. I've been rereading a lot of his stuff. I would have said here is one guy who writes like himself, and I would have been right, but not the way I meant it. Ninety per cent of it is the godddamndest self-imitation. He never really wrote but one story. All the rest is the same thing in different pants—or without different pants. And his eternal preoccupation with what goes on between the sheets becomes rather nauseating in the end. One reaches a time of life when limericks written on the walls of comfort stations are not just obscene, they are horribly dull. This man has only one subject and he makes that ridiculous. I suppose the man's epitaph, if he had the choosing of it, would be: Here Lies A Man Who Was Bloody Good in Bed. Too Bad He's Alone Here. But the point is I begin to doubt whether he ever was. You don't have to work so hard at things you are really good at—or do you?

I thank you.

Ray

—Selected Letters of Raymond Chandler, pp. 71–73

Chandler's novels and screenplays had earned him a reputation as one of America's leading detective writers. In July 1946 Pageant Magazine *published novelist Irving Wallace's "He Makes Murder Pay," a profile of Chandler that emphasizes his recent success in Hollywood and in the paperback market.*

No other living writer can bring to gat-and-gore fiction quite the same degree of mayhem as Raymond Chandler. The literary cocktail he dispenses has a savage kick and a tart flavor all its own. Critics agree that he is one of the most skillful operators in the business since Conan Doyle invented Sherlock Holmes. Hollywood also agrees. Chandler's annual income from murder on the screen and between covers is around $100,000.

His career of fictional crime began one summer night 12 years ago, the way literary careers begin in romantic novels. On a vacation in California, oil executive Chandler picked up a detective magazine just before going to bed. By page 50 he was fretful. "Hell's bells," he said to his wife. "I can write better stuff than this." "Well, why don't you?" she mumbled, and went soundly to sleep. At dawn she found him furiously writing.

For five months he wrestled with the same story, an 18,000-word shocker titled *Blackmailers Don't Shoot. Black Mask* magazine, a pulp whose graduates include Dashiell Hammett and Erle Stanley Gardner, bought it for $180. Chandler quit the oil business for murder at one cent a word.

Selling every story he wrote, he averaged $50 a week for six years. Then, in 1939, he clicked with his first Philip Marlowe novel, *The Big Sleep*. It's still his favorite because, he says, "It's my ambition to write a mystery story without one word of explanation at the end. In *The Big Sleep* I almost succeeded."

In 1940 came his biggest seller, *Farewell My Lovely;* in 1942 *The High Window;* in 1943 *Lady in the Lake*. First issued by publisher Alfred A. Knopf, each of these sold 10,000 copies, a big figure for detective fiction, which in the $2 edition is bought mostly by rental libraries. But the 25-cent reprints of all four Chandler books are flirting with the million mark.

Public and publishers have one complaint against Chandler: there isn't enough to go around. Three hundred crime novels are published annually in the United States. Erle Stanley Gardner has written 44 in a decade. Leslie Charteris has piloted the Saint through 30. Of Chandler's there are only four. But whereas most whodunits are hastily read and promptly forgotten, the Chandler spell lingers on.

Contrary to publishing custom, his murder fiction has been reissued for connoisseurs in a handsome $2 edition. It has been published in England, France, Denmark, Spain, Portugal and Latin America. It has been dramatized on the radio and sold to the movies. RKO fashioned *Farewell My Lovely* into a taut and distinctive melodrama with the title *Murder, My Sweet*. First filmed as a dismal quickie, *The High Window* is being expensively remade by 20th Century-Fox, starring Fred MacMurray. MGM expects to assign Spencer Tracy and a fat budget to *Lady in the Lake*. Lauren Bacall and Humphrey Bogart star in Warners' *The Big Sleep*.

Chandler's most recent movie was a one-man job, *The Blue Dahlia*. While writing it he carried tension, suspense and mounting terror right into the studio and established a solid Hollywood reputation for eccentricity. He turned in the script piece by piece and prowled around muttering at schedule-crazed executives, "What do you think ought to happen next?" With only a few scenes left to shoot, no one in the studio knew the ending. Front-office nerves were snapping when Chandler, at the last minute, delivered the killer to the camera.

Except for such pleasures, Chandler thinks the lot of the screen writer is a foul one: "He's treated like a cow—something to milk dry and send out to graze." Yet Chandler loves Hollywood: "Anyone who doesn't is either crazy or sober."

He has his own home there, a modest bungalow. When he takes a walk, the neighbors look up from their newspapers and lawn mowers to nod. The bemused passer-by with the baggy tweeds, horn-rimmed spectacles, fat brown pipe and slight stoop looks like a graying professor with something on his mind. But there's probably nothing on his mind—nothing but a murder and a sexy redhead sitting in his detective's lap and a butler silently offering doped cigarets.

Everyday reality is Chandler's refuge from the exotic world of his fancy. His close friends are plain people; he avoids the Hollywood crowd. "I dislike actors," he says flatly. He also "loathes" drunks, bridge and golf. He doesn't care for children: "I love to hear the patter of little feet going *away* from me." His likes extend to tea and travel, music, reading, walking and an 18-pound Persian cat.

Chandler was born in Chicago. His mother was Anglo-Irish, his father American. A divorce sent Chandler to England with his mother. He grew up there, now claims he is American and has a long-standing argument with the State Department which claims he is British.

After a classical education at Dulwich College, London, Chandler tried reporting. He failed dismally. The creator of a master sleuth could never track down a news lead: "I always got lost."

Chandler was placing essays and book reviews and collecting rejection slips on his short stories when World War I projected him into the Canadian infantry and later into the Royal Flying Corps.

Back in America in the '20s, he strung tennis rackets, was in turn accountant and tax expert, then landed a handsome job in oil. In 1924 he married Pearl Hulburt, a New Yorker. They're still very much married.

When Chandler moved in on murder, he set out to raise the mystery story to the level of genuine literature. He has succeeded in producing action-filled narratives distinctive for good writing. His dialogue is low American—brash, unsentimental, crackling with wit. His characterizations, often in Marlowe's words, are studded with electric images:

"eyes like strange sins"; "a smile I could feel in my hip pocket"; a voice "that grew icicles."

On almost every page there are phrases a poet might envy: "old men with faces like lost battles"; "the surf curled and creamed, almost without sound, like a thought trying to form itself on the edge of consciousness."

Every character who steps into Chandler's lurid world is unforgettably described.

The cigaret girl "wore an egret-plume in her hair, enough clothes to hide behind a tooth pick, one of her long beautiful naked legs was silver and one was gold. She had the utterly disdainful expression of a dame who makes her dates by long distance."

The crooked cop: "a windblown blossom of some two hundred pounds with freckled teeth and the mellow voice of a circus barker . . . the kind of cop who spits on his blackjack at night instead of saying his prayers . . ."

Chandler has injected into the world of detective fiction a shot of vibrant life. He has tried, he says, "to get murder away from the upper classes, the week-end house party and the vicar's rose garden and back to the people who are really good at it." His terrain is the seamy underworld of Los Angeles and surrounding California. His people are real people: a few of them honest; many of them shabby, cruel, depraved; some of them with a streak of good in the bad.

These people hate and kill because violence is their norm, not (as in the conventional mystery) just a secret vice masked by blameless years on the stock exchange. They kill, not with the studied refinement of amateurs, but with the impromptu skill of professionals using the tools of their trade: pistols, knives, blackjacks and poisons. Their everyday business is dope and pornography and crooked gambling joints, and if they have a hobby it is blackmail.

It is a sordid world, the world of Raymond Chandler. But down these mean streets there goes a man, Chandler avers, who is not himself mean—the 33-year-old private detective Marlowe, college graduate and bachelor who gets bedeviled by aphrodisiacs, blondes and his clients' daughters. Chandler has this to say of him:

"He is neither tarnished nor afraid. He must be a complete man and yet an unusual man. He must be, to use a rather weathered phrase, a man of honor . . . I think he might seduce a duchess and I am quite sure he would not spoil a virgin.

"He is a relatively poor man, or he would not be a detective at all. . . . He will take no man's money dishonestly and no man's insolence without a due and dispassionate revenge. He is a lonely man . . ."

In creating situations and drama for Marlowe, Chandler often starts from a true story he happens to overhear. "I learn something too hot for the papers to publish," he says, "and it starts me thinking and then my imagination takes over." It is said that his first novel, revolving about a fat homosexual who ran a rental library of pornography, had its basis in unprintable fact.

Chandler's adverse critics—who are few—complain that Marlowe is a one-syllable man; that his tales are twice-told, never varying from a pat formula; that his prose is one part slang, one part suspense and one part sex; that even Einstein couldn't follow his plots with any degree of comfort.

Chandler fans concede only the fourth charge. It is all too true that in the Master's inventive hand the skeins of crime become tangled, that there is more of sound and fury than logic in Marlowe's probings into human depravity. But, they would add, Chandler has pace and drive; he is honest and colorful and supremely entertaining. And what more can you ask?

Chandler himself has no delusions of grandeur but he's sure he'll stay in business. "People will continue to read mysteries," he predicts. "Maybe because regular novels are no longer satisfying as stories. Or maybe it's the inner sadism in people. Or maybe Somerset Maugham is right—that everyone is fascinated by mysteries because murder is the one irrevocable crime. Murder is final. You can get back the jewels, but never a human being's life."

—*Pageant Magazine*, 2 (July 1946): 126–129

Chandler was eager to complete a fifth novel and return to a career as a full-time novelist. Hamish Hamilton, his English publisher, had been prodding him for information on his next novel, and Chandler replied on 6 October 1946.

La Jolla
October 6th. 1946

Dear Jamie:

Your letter of September 30th. makes me rather uneasy. "A new Philip Marlowe story by Raymond Chandler, tentatively called *The Little Sister*, and dealing with some rather queer characters in Hollywood, not to mention an innocent little girl from Kansas, who may or may not be quite as innocent as she looks." That's about all I could tell you at the moment.

I have what you people called "a thing" about discussing or writing about anything I haven't licked. I'm never sure I shall lick it. I might blow up completely about page 250 (which means the silly little triple-spaced half pages I type on) and shelve the whole project.

Three years in Hollywood leaves its mark. My kind of writing takes a certain quality of high spirits and impudence. I'm a tired character, a battered pulp writer, an out of work hack. Also, as a mental hazard I might mention that although it seems to me almost mandatory as a business move that I should do a Marlowe story, I have a couple of other notions I'd much rather be trying to work out.

My title may not be very good. It's just the best I can think of without straining. I have peculiar ideas about titles. They should never be obviously provocative, nor say anything about murder. They should be rather indirect and neutral, but the form of words should be a little unusual. I haven't achieved this here. However, as some big publisher once remarked, a good title is the title of a successful book. Offhand, nobody would have thought *The Thin Man* a great title. *The Maltese Falcon* is, because it has rhyme and rhythm and makes the mind ask questions.

As to publishers, I wonder if they know anything about titles. Knopf made me change the title of *The High Window*, but I see Twentieth Century-Fox has restored the original title. Knopf objected strenuously to *Farewell, My Lovely*, and this, according to my Hollywood friends (who are a pretty good judge of these things) is one of the great titles of pure magic that rarely come along. Knopf still feels, I think, that the title hurt the sales of the book. Perhaps he is right. But Pocketbooks didn't find it any disadvantage.

Oh yes, the book will run in length, I hope, not more than 70,000 words, perhaps less.

I never really solved my agent problem. I still feel much about the same about agents as a class: that they are often a nuisance and sometimes do very stupid things. But living down here in La Jolla, and not being able to face a regular secretary around the house, I don't see how I could function without an agent. The thing about agents that really annoys me is not that they make mistakes, but that they never admit them.

All the best,
Ray

—*Selected Letters of Raymond Chandler*, pp. 80–81

A New Home

By the fall of 1946 Chandler was ready to leave Hollywood. He and Cissy decided to move to La Jolla, California, a prosperous beach town just north of San Diego. For $40,000 they purchased a large house at 6005 Camino de la Costa, which would be their home for the next eight years. On 2 October 1946 Chandler described their move to Dale Warren.

. . . I (we) have moved to La Jolla permanently, or as permanently as anything can be nowadays. If I do any more work for Hollywood, which I probably shall, I can do nine tenths of it here anyway. That is, if I can find a secretary. We live close beside the sounding sea—it's just across the street and down a low cliff—but the Pacific is usually very sedate. We have a much better home than an out-of-work pulp writer has any right to expect.

—Selected Letters of Raymond Chandler, p. 79

Chandler's house at 6005 Camino de la Costa, La Jolla, California

San Diego journalist Neil Morgan interviewed Chandler when he first moved to La Jolla, and the two later became friends. Morgan recalls his first impressions of Chandler in this excerpt from his essay titled "The Long Goodbye."

Chafing at the restraints of film writing ("I imagine everyone out to meet Samuel Goldwyn this side of paradise," he said, typically. "I've heard he feels so good when he stops"), he retreated from Hollywood in 1946 to a house on Camino de la Costa in La Jolla. It was the kind of house in the kind of village to which a man might go when he had tried to be a public person and knew he had failed. I found him there in 1946 when I was a 22-year-old newspaper reporter.

Chandler's house seemed out of place along this street of private beaches and pretentious rich. It was on a rise overlooking one of the cliffs where swimmers and divers find public access: a white stucco bungalow with brick steps up from the sidewalk, a shaded courtyard with potted geraniums, fuchsias in hanging baskets, and purplish bougainvillea creeping along the eaves. It was a caricature of Chandler's Southern California. Inside, his study was lined with books more often found in the studies of pro-

fessors of English literature. His desk and typewriter were littered. Pipes were abandoned with their ashes beside his reading chair, and ashtrays teetered on stacks of open books. The long living room, dominated by a Steinway concert grand, led to a picture window looking over the sparkling surf line that hooks and twists around Point Loma.

Chandler was gracious that first afternoon. He was, after all, at the crest. His first four big novels had been written. He was full of future work, but only one major book would lie ahead—*The Long Goodbye,* which most critics found softer than the first four.

That day Chandler hastened to describe Jolla as a boring, gilded suburb "entirely proper . . . a town of arthritic billionaires and barren old women." His overriding impulse, he went on, was to stand naked at high noon on the main business street and shout four-letter words. When I had gotten that down, he poured us a couple of drinks and sat back looking pleased with himself. It was his warning shot to the community that he might better be left alone, and he was.

—California Magazine, 7 (June 1982): 161

The High Window on Screen

Twentieth Century-Fox's movie version of The High Window, *released in 1947, used Chandler's original title for the novel, which he had changed at the suggestion of Knopf. "The Brasher Doubloon" is the stolen rare coin that is the catalyst for the plot.*

Still from The Brasher Doubloon; *from left to right, Florence Bates as Mrs. Murdock, Nancy Guild as Merle Davis, and George Montgomery as Marlowe*

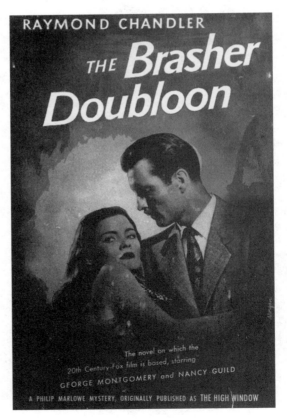

Poster and dust jacket for the World reprint tie-in for The Brasher Doubloon

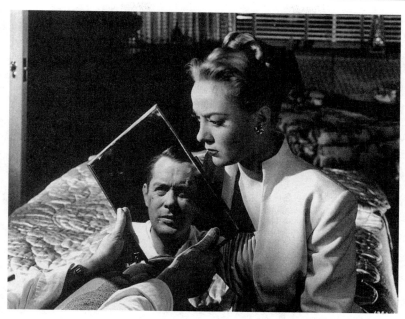

Still from Lady in the Lake; *Robert Montgomery (visible in mirror) as Marlowe and Audrey Totter as Adrienne Fromsett*

Montgomery's *Lady in the Lake*

M-G-M released their screen version of The Lady in the Lake *in 1947. The film's director and star, Robert Montgomery, decided to use an experimental "subjective camera" point of view for the movie, in which almost the entire film was shot as if seen through the eyes of Philip Marlowe, who was visible only in reflections, such as when he passed in front of a mirror. Chandler thought this technique a cheap gimmick, and it furthered his disapproval of the movie. His sentiment was echoed by many of the movie's reviews, such as the following one in* The Commonweal.

Moviegoers whose preferences run to melodrama peppered with violence will find a large assortment of films of this type coming up soon. Of the four reviewed below, "*Lady in the Lake*" is by far the most unusual. Its screenplay, written by Steve Fisher from the novel by Raymond Chandler, has been directed by Robert Montgomery who employs a technique not new to movies but one seldom used so extensively. The story is told by Detective Phillip Marlowe in the first person and is filmed from his point of view so that he and the camera are one. Consequently, although you hear him a great deal, you see Marlowe (played by Robert Montgomery) only in a few sequences when he talks directly to the audience or during the action of the film when he happens to pass before a mirror. This tricky technique involves some unorthodox movie acting, in that the actors talking to Marlowe look right into the camera. This is seldom done in good cinema. Consequently you also become identified with the camera and with

Marlowe—and then suddenly it dawns on you that you are Robert Montgomery and a very good actor at that. I don't know how women in the audience are going to react to this, especially since Marlowe is subjected to some pretty rough treatment at times (the camera even sees stars) and at other times Marlowe and the camera get very amatory over lovely Audrey Totter. Male audiences will no doubt find all this an interesting experience.

I must admit, however, that the extraordinary technique in "Lady in the Lake" is rather wearing (you work throughout the entire picture) and occasionally it distracts your attention from the story. Perhaps this does not matter too much, as the plot, not one of Chandler's best, is on the vague side. You may even have a little difficulty in keeping clues, characters and motives straight, but the suspense is swell and the whole piece is loaded with vicarious thrills and breezy wisecracks. Devotees of Phillip Marlowe may become worried that their favorite hard-boiled dick is going soft because he talks so much about writing a book called "If I Should Die Before I Live." Actually he sticks to detecting and gets in and out of his usual jams. Besides Miss Totter, the camera, and Montgomery's voice, the cast includes Lloyd Nolan, Tom Tully, Jayne Meadows and others, all understandingly directed by Montgomery. To him and to Producer George Haight should go huzzahs and support for their sincere attempt to give us something different in cinema.

—*The Commonweal*, 45 (31 January 1947)

SLEUTH AND HEROINE MEET IN MIRRORED OFFICE

MOVIE OF THE WEEK:
Lady in the Lake

The camera becomes the hero in a Robert Montgomery murder picture

The camera, which in most films is an omnipresent but innocuous recorder of action, has been assigned a new and interesting function in M-G-M's *Lady in the Lake*. In this movie, which is based on a tough, gory book by Raymond Chandler, it substitutes for the hero. Instead of watching the hero from a point of vantage, the audience sees all the action through his eyes (*i.e.* the camera's lens). When he sits, the camera dips appropriately; when he asks for a drink, a glass is thrust right at the camera (*below*). The actor himself (Robert Montgomery) is never visible except fragmentarily when he acts as narrator, extends his hand (*right*) or fleetingly passes a looking glass (*above*).

Lady itself is a shrewdly worked-out murder story in which a woman editor hires a hard-boiled private detective named Phillip Marlowe to investigate the disappearance of her boss's wife. In the ensuing 103 minutes Marlowe is twice beaten up, stumbles over four murders and falls in love. There is plenty of tough talk and violent incident, but the plot is still fairly easy to follow, an accomplishment especially praiseworthy after the recent rash of wilfully opaque thrillers (*The Blue Dahlia*, *The Big Sleep*). Montgomery reads his long off-stage part with satisfactory rudeness. In her first big part Audrey Totter, though she employs many of Bette Davis' mannerisms, plays with competence the editor who hires Marlowe. She is not the lady of *Lady*'s title, however. That female is in the lake, dead as a smoked herring, from start to finish.

WHEN DRINK IS OFFERED to the hero, through whose eyes story is told, glass is thrust right at camera.

WHEN A TELEGRAM IS HANDED Editor Fromsett (Audrey Totter) by Detective Marlowe (Robert Montgomery), the hand is the camera's. Soon the onlooker unconsciously begins to identify himself with Marlowe.

A photo spread in Life *magazine*

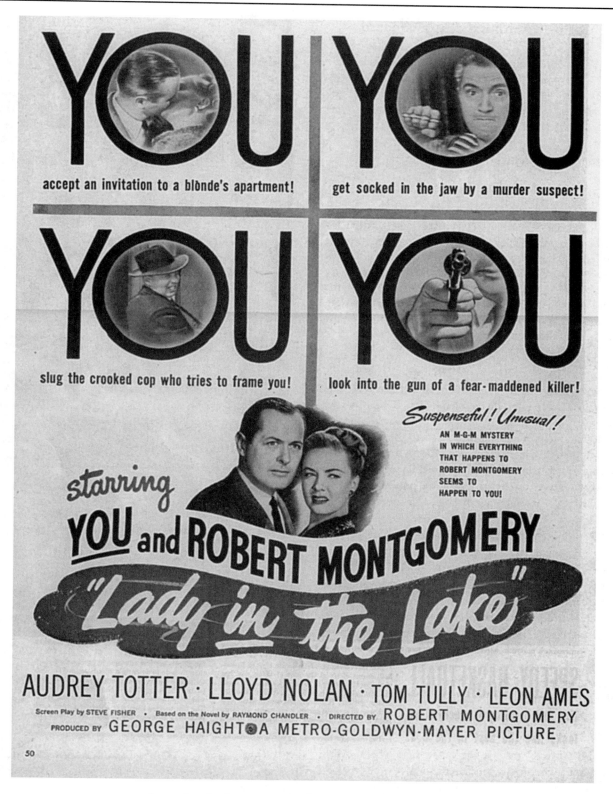

A magazine advertisement promoting the camera-eye technique of the movie

Marlowe as an Existentialist Hero

The following article appeared in the May/June 1947 issue of The Partisan Review, *a left-wing intellectual magazine. Though Chandler was pleased that his work was being taken seriously, he scoffed at such critical commentary for being pretentious and shallow.*

A Cato of the Cruelties

R. W. Flint

Partisan Review, 14 (May/June 1947): 328–330

Raymond Chandler has, in the past, written for the *Atlantic* on the ethics of Hollywood, just as the late Wendell Willkie once wrote on ethics in general for *The American Scholar.* There has been enough respectability in the wares of these two successful specialists in the American ethos to suit the upper-middlebrow market, and enough authenticity in their attitudes to cover the objections of litterateurs.

Philip Marlowe, private dick, is our myth, the closest thing to flesh and blood that Hollywood has recently seen fit to apotheosize. Who, then, is this Marlowe and what is his mighty line? To be solemn first, Philip Marlowe is as much of the existentialist hero as modern America has stomach for. We've become used to the French version, but the term, like pragmatism, means a *way* of philosophizing rather than a body of doctrine. It's a fruitful term, and we should try to salvage it from the purely cultic interpretation that is threatening, through fear more than anything else, to discredit its legitimate use. Marlowe is the American middle-class Existentialist, the People's Existentialist, you might say, insofar as his function cuts across class lines. The marks of his integrity are a searing doubt as to the motives of his fellow countrymen—popularized by Bogart with literary antecedents in Lardner and many others—and a profound awareness of fate. But the red badge that sets him apart is an almost Biblical faith in the value of decision. He is forever rolling the stone uphill—a little too sentimental and self-pitying for a true Stoic, but an existentialist nonetheless. Whatever the alternatives, Marlowe acts and acts alone: his life is all decision—a blind inevitable moral energy plowing through the wildest ambiguities always into the heart of insecurity and danger.

Marlowe's world is the laissez-faire liberal world turned inside-out—a jungle of predatory creatures making amusing patterns out of their guilt and boredom, and desperately lonely. On the surface, nothing happens for obvious reasons. If external amiability isn't faked, it's at least better to assume so until told otherwise. Underneath this casual cruelty—the convention set by Cain, Hammet, et

Cover for the last of three Avon Book original paperback collections of Chandler's stories. Published on 15 April 1947, this collection included the title story and two more stories—"The Bronze Door" and "Smart-Aleck Kill"—as well as a revised version of "The Simple Art of Murder," the essay that was originally published in The Atlantic Monthly (Bruccoli Collection, Kent State University).

al.—move the tides of human destiny and decision, as crude as the surface is intricate and ambiguous.

The Marlowe epics screen better than they read, and I suspect it's because Chandler strains too much in the books to be arty, although he is often brilliantly successful in patches. His conventions admirably suit the movies where the camera, if it's alert, establishes the proper sense of desolation—that miasmic, Dantesque background of California roadways, police stations, office buildings, and fake interiors in which Chandler specializes.

We have come a long way from Holmes to here. The plot is complex and we are still thrown a few clues from time to time, but suspense grows now out of a human rather than a literary situation; it is continuous rather than cumulative, like life in a Camus novel or in modern "crisis" theology. Our hero is no longer the wizard, the mental giant, the latter-day Paracelsus: he is not even the intellectual master of the situation. Where Holmes needed all the glamor he could muster to make Victorian respectability seem worth an elaborate defense, Marlowe lives by the light of his sentimental but genuine humanity: he's the fall-guy, *der reine Narr,* Parsifal-Cassandra whom nobody believes because he has no aces up his sleeve.

In another of his functions, that of father-confessor, he departs radically from the fiction detective tradition. His goodness is obvious enough to become a catalyst in a corrupt society—the great strength that is intended to compensate for his lack of subtlety and the conventional insouciance. Everyone confesses his basic sickness as well as his immediate troubles to Marlowe. In the current Chandler film, *Lady in the Lake,* for example, the weak capitalist, in Marlowe's healing presence, is strong enough to throw over his vicious secretary and confess his loneliness; the crooked cop can't look at Marlowe without a self-revealing yen to "work him over"; the old people confess their utter exhaustion and fear; the slick playboy knocks Marlowe cold for telling the truth, but is soon recompensed by being shot full of holes in his shower by a former sin; and finally, we have the vicious secretary herself, still the superb, capable American Girl whom we have come to know so well from the tradition that starts, perhaps, in Henry James and enters the crime milieu in Nora of *The Thin Man,* but is omnipresent in such creatures as the wooden young lady in *All the King's Men,* and Isabel Bolton's final hypostatization as the "European" paragon of *Do I Wake or Sleep.* The Girl is Marlowe's greatest challenge and his greatest conquest; to her, like Hamlet to his mother, Marlowe "must be cruel, only to be kind"—the therapy of harshness which Marx also prescribes for our bourgeois ills.

A comparison of Marlowe's state of mind and that of the follower of Marx would be suggestive. Both have the attitude of a Jewish prophet toward a bad world: both are proximately tough to counter a degenerate laissez-faire that has learned to use sham-morality brilliantly, but both are ultimately tender and apocalyptic. I don't claim to find any political sophistication in Chandler: I merely suggest the implications of his theory of man, which he would doubtless deny. Leftism in general, insofar as it has popular attributes in America, seems to have settled temporarily on the *PM* level of pervasive general "concern" mixed with a folksy, sexy assertion of man's finiteness and dependence on nature. It's a mixture too usually dismissed by the exacerbated intellectual who, however, welcomes the image of Marlowe as a sign of "vitality" in the movies.

Chandler on Hollywood

In this essay Chandler uses the occasion of the Academy Awards ceremony in Hollywood to discuss the tension in the motion picture industry between commercial ballyhoo and serious art.

Oscar Night in Hollywood
The Atlantic Monthly, 181 (March 1948): 24–27

1

Five or six years ago a distinguished writer-director (if I may be permitted the epithet in connection with a Hollywood personage) was co-author of a screen play nominated for an Academy Award. He was too nervous to attend the proceedings on the big night, so he was listening to a broadcast at home, pacing the floor tensely, chewing his fingers, taking long breaths, scowling and debating with himself in hoarse whispers whether to stick it out until the Oscars were announced, or turn the damned radio off and read about it in the papers the next morning. Getting a little tired of all this artistic temperament in the home, his wife suddenly came up with one of those awful remarks which achieve a wry immortality in Hollywood: "For Pete's sake, don't take it so seriously, darling. After all, Luise Rainer won it twice."

To those who did not see the famous telephone scene in *The Great Ziegfeld,* or any of the subsequent versions of it which Miss Rainer played in other pictures, with and without telephone, this remark will lack punch. To others it will serve as well as anything to express that cynical despair with which Hollywood people regard their own highest distinction. It isn't so much that the awards never go to fine achievements as that those fine achievements are not rewarded as such. They are rewarded as fine achievements in box-office hits. You can't be an All-American on a losing team. Technically, they are voted, but actually they are not decided by the use of whatever artistic and critical wisdom Hollywood may happen to possess. They are ballyhooed, pushed, yelled, screamed, and in every way propagandized into the consciousness of the voters so incessantly, in the weeks before the final balloting, that everything except the golden aura of the box office is forgotten.

The Motion Picture Academy, at considerable expense and with great efficiency, runs all the nominated pictures at its own theater, showing each picture twice, once in the afternoon, once in the evening. A nominated picture is one in connection with which any kind of work is nominated for an award, not necessarily acting, directing, or writing; it may be a purely technical matter such as set-dressing or sound work. This run-

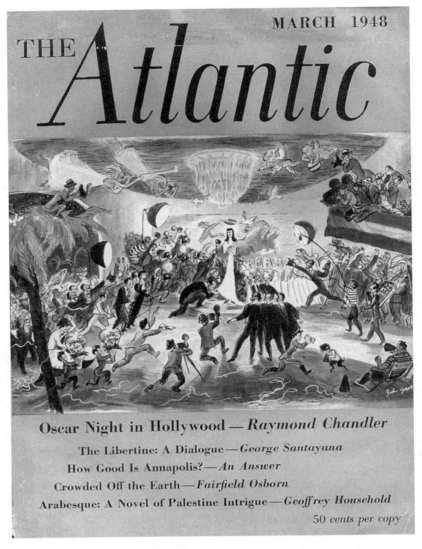

Cover for the issue that includes Chandler's fourth essay for the magazine

ning of pictures has the object of permitting the voters to look at films which they may happen to have missed or to have partly forgotten. It is an attempt to make them realize that pictures released early in the year, and since overlaid with several thicknesses of battered celluloid, are still in the running and that consideration of only those released a short time before the end of the year is not quite just.

The effort is largely a waste. The people with the votes don't go to these showings. They send their relatives, friends, or servants. They have had enough of looking at pictures, and the voices of destiny are by no means inaudible in the Hollywood air. They have a brassy tone, but they are more than distinct.

All this is good democracy of a sort. We elect Congressmen and Presidents in much the same way, so why not actors, cameramen, writers, and all the rest of the people who have to do with the making of pictures? If we permit noise, ballyhoo, and bad theater to influence us in the selection of the people who are to run the country, why should we object to the same methods in the selection of meritorious achievements in the film business? If we can huckster a President into the White House, why cannot we huckster the agonized Miss Joan Crawford or the hard and beautiful Miss Olivia de Havilland into possession of one of those golden statuettes which express the motion picture industry's frantic desire to kiss itself on the back of its neck? The only answer I can think of is that the motion picture is an art.

I say this with a very small voice. It is an inconsiderable statement and has a hard time not sounding a little ludicrous. Nevertheless it is a fact, not in the least diminished by the further facts that its ethos is so far pretty low and that its techniques are dominated by some pretty awful people.

If you think most motion pictures are bad, which they are (including the foreign), find out from some initiate how they are made, and you will be astonished that any of them could be good. Making a fine motion picture is like painting "The Laughing Cavalier" in Macy's basement, with a floorwalker to mix your colors for you. Of course most motion pictures are bad. Why wouldn't they be? Apart from its own intrinsic handicaps of excessive cost, hypercritical bluenosed censorship, and the lack of any single-minded controlling force in the making, the motion picture is bad because 90 per cent of its source material is tripe, and the other 10 per cent is a little too virile and plain-spoken for the putty-minded clerics, the elderly ingénues of the women's clubs, and the tender guardians of that godawful mixture of boredom and bad manners known more eloquently as the Impressionable Age.

The point is not whether there are bad motion pictures or even whether the average motion picture is bad, but whether the motion picture is an artistic medium of sufficient dignity and accomplishment to be treated with respect by the people who control its destinies. Those who deride the motion picture usually are satisfied that they have thrown the book at it by declaring it to be a form of mass entertainment. As if that meant anything. Greek drama, which is still considered quite respectable by most intellectuals, was mass entertainment to the Athenian freeman. So, within its economic and topographical limits, was the Elizabethan drama. The great cathedrals of Europe, although not exactly built to while away an afternoon, certainly had an aesthetic and spiritual effect on the ordinary man. Today, if not always, the fugues and chorales of Bach, the symphonies of Mozart, Borodin, and Brahms, the violin concertos of Vivaldi, the piano sonatas of Scarlatti, and a great deal of what was once rather recondite music are mass entertainment by virtue of radio. Not all fools love it, but not all fools love anything more literate than a comic strip. It might reasonably be said that all art at some time and in some manner becomes mass entertainment, and that if it does not it dies and is forgotten.

The motion picture admittedly is faced with too large a mass; it must please too many people and offend too few, the second of these restrictions being infinitely more damaging to it artistically than the first. The people who sneer at the motion picture as an art form are furthermore seldom willing to consider it at its best. They insist upon judging it by the picture they saw last week or yesterday; which is even more absurd (in view of the sheer quantity of production) than to judge literature by last week's ten best-sellers, or the dramatic art by even the best of the current Broadway hits. In a novel you can still say what you like, and the stage is free almost to the point of obscenity, but the motion picture made in Hollywood, if it is to create art at all, must do so within such strangling limitations of subject and treatment that it is a blind wonder it ever achieves any distinction beyond the purely mechanical slickness of a glass and chromium bathroom. If it were merely a transplanted literary or dramatic art, it certainly would not. The hucksters and the bluenoses would between them see to that.

But the motion picture is *not* a transplanted literary or dramatic art, any more than it is a plastic art. It has elements of all these, but in its essential structure it is much closer to music, in the sense that its finest effects can be independent of precise meaning, that its transitions can be more eloquent than its high-lit scenes, and that its dissolves and camera movements, which cannot be censored, are often far more emotionally effective than its plots, which can. Not only is the motion picture an art, but it is the one entirely new art that has been evolved on this planet for hundreds of years. It is the only art at which we of this generation have any possible chance to greatly excel.

In painting, music, and architecture we are not even second-rate by comparison with the best work of the past. In sculpture we are just funny. In prose literature we not only lack style but we lack the educational and historical background to know what style is. Our fiction and drama are adept, empty, often intriguing, and so mechanical that in another fifty years at most they will be produced by machines with rows of push buttons. We have no popular poetry in the grand style, merely delicate or witty or bitter or obscure verses. Our novels are transient propaganda when they are what is called "significant," and bedtime reading when they are not.

But in the motion picture we possess an art medium whose glories are not all behind us. It has already produced great work, and if, comparatively and proportionately, far too little of that great work has been achieved in Hollywood, I think that is all the more reason why in its annual tribal dance of the stars and the big-shot producers Hollywood should contrive a little quiet awareness of the fact. Of course it won't. I'm just daydreaming.

2

Show business has always been a little overnoisy, overdressed, overbrash. Actors are threatened people. Before films came along to make them rich they often had need of a desperate gaiety. Some of these qualities prolonged beyond a strict necessity have passed into the Hollywood mores and produced that very exhausting thing, the Hollywood manner, which is a chronic case of spurious excitement over absolutely nothing. Nevertheless, and for once in a lifetime, I have to admit that Academy Awards night is a good show and quite funny in spots, although I'll admire you if you can laugh at all of it.

If you can go past those awful idiot faces on the bleachers outside the theater without a sense of the collapse of the human intelligence; if you can stand the hailstorm of flash bulbs popping at the poor patient actors who, like kings and queens, have never the right to look bored; if you can glance out over this gathered assemblage of what is supposed to be the elite of Hollywood and say to yourself without a sinking feeling, "In these hands lie the destinies of the only original art the modern world has conceived"; if you can laugh, and you probably will, at the cast-off jokes from the comedians on the stage, stuff that wasn't good enough to use on their radio shows; if you can stand the fake sentimentality and the platitudes of the officials and the mincing elocution of the glamour queens (you ought to hear them with four martinis down the hatch); if you can do all these things with grace and pleasure, and not have a wild and forsaken horror at the thought that most of these people actually take this shoddy performance seriously; and if you can then go out into the night to see half the police force of Los Angeles gathered to protect the golden ones from the mob in the free seats but not from that awful moaning sound they give out, like destiny whistling through a hollow shell; if you can do all these things and still feel next morning that the picture business is worth the attention of one single intelligent, artistic mind, then in the picture business you certainly belong, because this sort of vulgarity is part of its inevitable price.

Glancing over the program of the Awards before the show starts, one is apt to forget that this is really an actors', directors', and big-shot producers' rodeo. It is for the people who *make* pictures (they think), not just for the people who work on them. But these gaudy characters are a kindly bunch at heart; they know that a lot of small-fry characters in minor technical jobs, such as cameramen, musicians, cutters, writers, soundmen, and the inventors of new equipment, have to be given something to amuse them and make them feel mildly elated. So the performance was formerly divided into two parts, with

an intermission. On the occasion I attended, however, one of the Masters of Ceremony (I forget which—there was a steady stream of them, like bus passengers) announced that there would be no intermission this year and that they would proceed immediately to the *important* part of the program.

Let me repeat, the *important part of the program.*

Perverse fellow that I am, I found myself intrigued by the unimportant part of the program also. I found my sympathies engaged by the lesser ingredients of picture-making, some of which have been enumerated above. I was intrigued by the efficiently quick on-and-off that was given to these minnows of the picture business; by their nervous attempts via the microphone to give most of the credit for their work to some stuffed shirt in a corner office; by the fact that technical developments which may mean many millions of dollars to the industry, and may on occasion influence the whole procedure of picture-making, are just not worth explaining to the audience at all; by the casual, cavalier treatment given to film-editing and to camera work, two of the essential arts of film-making, almost and sometimes quite equal to direction, and much more important than all but the very best acting; intrigued most of all perhaps by the formal tribute which is invariably made to the importance of the writer, without whom, my dear, dear friends, nothing could be done at all, but who is for all that merely the climax of the *unimportant* part of the program.

3

I am also intrigued by the voting. It was formerly done by all the members of all the various guilds, including the extras and bit players. Then it was realized that this gave too much voting power to rather unimportant groups, so the voting on various classes of awards was restricted to the guilds which were presumed to have some critical intelligence on the subject. Evidently this did not work either, and the next change was to have the nominating done by the specialist guilds, and the final voting only by members of the Academy of Motion Picture Arts and Sciences.

It doesn't really seem to make much difference how the voting is done. The quality of the work is still only recognized in the context of success. A superb job in a flop picture would get you nothing, a routine job in a winner will be voted in. It is against this background of success-worship that the voting is done, with the incidental music supplied by a stream of advertising in the trade papers (which even intelligent people read in Hollywood) designed to put all other pictures than those advertised out of your head at balloting time. The psychological effect is very great on minds conditioned to thinking of merit solely in terms of box office and bally-hoo. The members of the Academy live in this atmosphere, and they are enormously suggestible people, as are all workers in Hollywood. If they are contracted to studios, they are made to feel that it is a matter of group patriotism to vote for the products of their own lot. They are informally advised not to waste their votes, not to plump for something that can't win, especially something made on another lot.

I do not feel any profound conviction, for example, as to whether *The Best Years of Our Lives* was even the best Hollywood motion picture of 1946. It depends on what you mean by best. It had a first-class director, some fine actors, and the most appealing sympathy gag in years. It probably had as much all-around distinction as Hollywood is presently capable of. That it had the kind of clean and simple art possessed by *Open City* or the stalwart and magnificent impact of *Henry V* only an idiot would claim. In a sense it did not have art at all. It had that kind of sentimentality which is almost but not quite humanity, and that kind of adeptness which is almost but not quite style. And it had them in large doses, which always helps.

The governing board of the Academy is at great pains to protect the honesty and the secrecy of the voting. It is done by anonymous numbered ballots, and the ballots are sent, not to any agency of the motion picture industry, but to a well-known firm of public accountants. The results, in sealed envelopes, are borne by an emissary of the firm right onto the stage of the theater where the Awards are to be made, and there for the first time, one at a time, they are made known. Surely precaution could go no further. No one could possibly have known in advance any of these results, not even in Hollywood where every agent learns the closely guarded secrets of the studios with no apparent trouble. If there are secrets in Hollywood, which I sometimes doubt, this voting ought to be one of them.

4

As for a deeper kind of honesty, I think it is about time for the Academy of Motion Picture Arts and Sciences to use a little of it up by declaring in a forthright manner that foreign pictures are outside competition and will remain so until they face the same economic situation and the same strangling censorship that Hollywood faces. It is all very well to say how clever and artistic the French are, how true to life, what subtle actors they have, what an honest sense of the earth, what forthrightness in dealing with the bawdy side of life. The French can afford these things, we cannot. To the Italians they are permitted, to us they are denied. Even the English possess a freedom we lack. How much did *Brief Encounter* cost? It would have cost at least

a million and a half in Hollywood; in order to get that money back, and the distribution costs on top of the negative costs, it would have had to contain innumerable crowd-pleasing ingredients, the very lack of which is what makes it a good picture.

Since the Academy is not an international tribunal of film art it should stop pretending to be one. If foreign pictures have no practical chance whatsoever of winning a major award they should not be nominated. At the very beginning of the performance in 1947 a special Oscar was awarded to Laurence Olivier for *Henry V,* although it was among those nominated as best picture of the year. There could be no more obvious way of saying it was not going to win. A couple of minor technical awards and a couple of minor writing awards were also given to foreign pictures, but nothing that ran into important coin, just side meat. Whether these awards were deserved is beside the point, which is that they were minor awards and were intended to be minor awards, and that there was no possibility whatsoever of any foreign-made picture winning a major award.

To outsiders it might appear that something devious went on here. To those who know Hollywood, all that went on was the secure knowledge and awareness that the Oscars exist for and by Hollywood, their purpose is to maintain the supremacy of Hollywood, their standards and problems are the standards and problems of Hollywood, and their phoniness is the phoniness of Hollywood. But the Academy cannot, without appearing ridiculous, maintain a pose of internationalism by tossing a few minor baubles to the foreigners while carefully keeping all the top-drawer jewelry for itself. As a writer I resent that writing awards should be among these baubles, and as a member of the Motion Picture Academy I resent its trying to put itself in a position which its annual performance before the public shows it quite unfit to occupy.

If the actors and actresses like the silly show, and I'm not sure at all the best of them do, they at least know how to look elegant in a strong light, and how to make with the wide-eyed and oh, so humble little speeches as if they believed them. If the big producers like it, and I'm quite sure they do because it contains the only ingredients they really understand—promotion values and the additional grosses that go with them—the producers at least know what they are fighting for. But if the quiet, earnest, and slightly cynical people who really make motion pictures like it, and I'm quite sure they don't, well, after all, it comes only once a year, and it's no worse than a lot of the sleazy vaudeville they have to push out of the way to get their work done.

Of course that's not quite the point either. The head of a large studio once said privately that in his candid opinion the motion picture business was 25 per

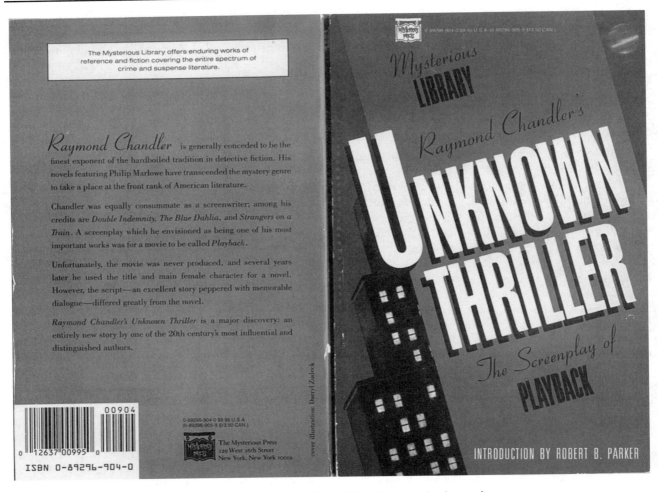

Cover for the 1985 paperback edition of Chandler's unproduced screenplay

cent honest business and the other 75 per cent pure conniving. He didn't say anything about art, although he may have heard of it. But that *is* the real point, isn't it?—whether these annual Awards, regardless of the grotesque ritual which accompanies them, really represent anything at all of artistic importance to the motion picture medium, anything clear and honest that remains after the lights are dimmed, the minks are put away, and the aspirin is swallowed? I don't think they do. I think they are just theater and not even good theater. As for the personal prestige that goes with winning an Oscar, it may with luck last long enough for your agent to get your contract rewritten and your price jacked up another notch. But over the years and in the hearts of men of good will? I hardly think so.

Once upon a time a once very successful Hollywood lady decided (or was forced) to sell her lovely furnishings at auction, together with her lovely home. On the day before she moved out she was showing a party of her friends through the house for

a private view. One of them noticed that the lady was using her two golden Oscars as doorstops. It seemed they were just about the right weight, and she had sort of forgotten they were gold.

A Second Original Screenplay

Though he was determined to return to novel writing, in the spring of 1947 Chandler was offered a screenplay deal he could not refuse: $4,000 a week to write an original screenplay for Universal. In addition to the remarkable salary, the contract guaranteed Chandler a share of the profits, the freedom to work at home, and a commitment from the studio to accept the script unseen. He was scheduled to finish the script, titled "Playback," by August, but he had difficulties with the plot and did not submit the final version to the studio until early 1948. By this time Universal was having financial troubles and was concerned about the potential cost of the production. The movie was cancelled, but Chandler's work was not completely lost; he rewrote the story in the 1950s and published it as a novel.

5.
The Return of a Novelist, 1947–1952:
The Little Sister

Chandler was eager to return to novel-writing as a full-time career after he finished the Playback screenplay for Universal. As he worked on the script at his home in La Jolla, he assessed his publishing arrangements and determined a set of changes he felt necessary to be able to live without income from Hollywood. In November 1946 he ended his association with Sydney Sanders, who had been his agent since the 1930s. Chandler was dissatisfied with the prices Sanders had negotiated for the movie rights to his novels and felt Sanders knew little about creating a literary reputation. Chandler allowed H. N. Swanson, his Hollywood representative, to handle his books in the interim, but he knew he needed an experienced literary agent to represent his interests.

Chandler in La Jolla with his cat, Taki, circa 1948

MEMORANDUM

TO Mr. Dale Warren, Boston   FROM Hardwick Moseley, NYO   DATE 1/17/47

SUBJECT

Where are we now with Raymond Chandler? Do I see Sidney Saunders, or not? I talked to Paul, and he seemed very interested. I knew Chandler by the title FAREWELL, MY LOVELY. Please talk this over with Paul and make up your minds. I feel very strongly about him, and I should like to have him as much as any other mystery writer in the country. He's wonderful!

[handwritten note] Dale: I talked to Moseley this morning. He will HM discuss it further on Wed.

Memo from Hardwick Moseley, sales manager of Houghton Mifflin, to Dale Warren, the firm's publicity director. Warren, a mystery fan, had corresponded with Chandler, and he judged from the author's letters that he was interested in finding a new publisher. The "Paul" mentioned in the memo is Paul Brooks, president of Houghton Mifflin (Houghton Library, Harvard University, b MS Am 1925 [347]).

In May 1948 Chandler approached Brandt & Brandt, one of the leading New York literary agencies. The clients of the firm included E. E. Cummings, John Dos Passos, John P. Marquand, and James Gould Cozzens, and Chandler hoped that the agency would be able to help position him as a writer of serious literature. Brandt & Brandt accepted Chandler as a client, and he was assigned to Bernice Baumgarten, often reputed to be the best literary agent in the business. One of the first issues Chandler took up with Baumgarten was whether to change American publishers. He was displeased with Knopf, whom he believed took too large a share of his subsidiary rights payments and did not promote his books effectively, and was interested in finding a publisher who would not package him as a genre writer. While Baumgarten searched for new publishers, Chandler focused on completing his fifth novel, The Little Sister (1949), on which he had been working intermittently since his days at Paramount.

Changing Publishers

Chandler chose Houghton Mifflin to be the American publisher of his next novel. In his negotiations with the firm, Chandler argued unsuccessfully for a larger percentage of the reprint royalties for his books. Chandler nevertheless signed with Houghton Mifflin because he felt they would promote his books properly. The following undated memo from Dorothy de Santillana, an editor at the firm, to Dale Warren summarizes Chandler's requirements.

Bernice Baumgarten summoned me to her office to receive a long harangue from Raymond Chandler as to the conditions he would impose on his new publisher. Our advance of $4000 is not tempting but would be accepted for two reasons: first, because Chandler does not depend on book advances to do his writing; second, because he is passionately determined to secure one thing in his new contract: this one thing is control of reprint rights. Chandler feels very strongly that Knopf, who has never got for him a commensurate trade edition sale, has profited enor-

Raymond Chandler

6005 Camino de la Costa, La Jolla, Californi

May 11th, 1948

Mr. Carl Brandt
101 Park Avenue
New York.

Dear Mr. Brandt:

Come Michaelmas, or thereabouts, I shall be in need of a literary agent. The purpose of this is to enquire whether your office would be interested.

At the moment there is nothing much to do. I would have a radio program, if I had had the right kind of people after it at the right time. But I don't think much couldbe done now. I have a mystery novel half finished. The writing is of an incomparable brilliance, but something has went wrong with the story. An old trouble with me. The brain is very very tired. I have lately finished a screenplay for Universal-International, want to finish this mystery and do another novel which has a murder in it but is not a mystery. MondayI am going north for a month.

What I want to do and what I do are not always of the same family. There is, of course, the usual collection of minor troubles, suchoas Portuguese rights, Italian rights, Peaguin bookrights to a bunch of novelettes not published in England (and perhaps not worth publishing.) These are annoying things, but not lucrative. I have no ambitions as a slick writer.

My references are poor. I was eight years with Sydney Sanders who

would be delighted to warn you against me, unless he deemed it undiplomatic. After leaving Sanders I tried working through my Hollywood agent, H.N. Swanson, a good fellow and a nice fellow, with whom I am on excellent terms, but not quite in the right setting except for picture work, at which I have no doubt he is excellent.

You are a stranger to me and I can't very well let my hair down, but neither should I want you to be too much in the dark. I am not a completely amiable character any more than I am a facile and prolific writer. I do most things the hard way, and I suffer a good deal over it. There may not be a lot of mileage left in me. Five years of fighting Hollywood has not left me with many reserves of energy. Whether I have had any success your Hollywood representative will be able to tell you, and if you should happen to ask him, Iaam hoping that for once he will (whoever he is, and I don't know) keep it

to himself.

Yours very truly,

Chandler's letter in which he introduces himself to Carl Brandt; he later became a client of the Brandt & Brandt literary agency.

mously—and to Chandler's mind unethically—from Chandler's enormous reprint sales.

Here is the publishing story on Chandler: THE BIG SLEEP. Trade edition, 11,202 copies. Avon Books 300,000. FAREWELL MY LOVELY. Trade edition 10,241, World Reprint (49¢) 63,000, Pocket Books well over 1 million. THE HIGH WINDOW. 9000 trade, 3000 Grosset (75¢), 53,000 World (49¢), Pocket Books over 400,000. This, by the way, is considered Chandler's poorest book. LADY IN THE LAKE, 1944. Trade 13,558, Grossett (75¢) just under 10,000, Pocket Books 383,000 and heavy continuing sales. Chandler now writes directly for Avon and has an arrangement with them by which the short things he does for them will never be issued in trade edition. This means that Pocket Books is his reprint market and a tremendous one. He wishes a clause in his contract, one guaranteeing protection of the Berne Convention copyright (simultaneously in Canada) and on his reprints he wishes a guarantee of 1¢ a copy before the publisher receives anything at all up to 150,000 copies, after which the publisher may receive ½¢ on each copy.

Hardwick on the telephone and in conjunction with Henry Laughlin says absolutely "*no*" to this, although he had a pleasant dinner with Chandler at which Chandler talked as if Houghton Mifflin were already his publisher. Lovell too feels definitely that we cannot establish any such precedent as this in regard to giving away our reprint rights.
—transcribed from original document, Houghton Library, Harvard University, bMS Am 1925 (347)

TUESDAY, NOVEMBER 19, 1940

LOS ANGELES EXAMINER · · · · A PAPER FOR PEOPLE

Wine, Women, Trips Bring Jail Probe of Bugsy Siegel

Central Figures in of Prisoner's Many

Slaying Suspect Met Film Star 'Outside,' Officer Says

(Continued From Page One)
been attired in clothing laid out for him by a private valet, or "gentleman's gentleman," he chose from among fellow jail inmates, to the offices of his attorney, Byron C. Hanna.

Favors accorded the murder suspect by the county jail physician, Dr. Benjamin Blank, who was his shipmate during the fantastic treasure-hunting and mutiny-marred cruise of the "hell ship" Metha Nelson, two years ago.

A luncheon, during one of the trips outside, at Lindy's Restaurant, Wilshire boulevard bar and cafe, at which the alleged slayer and his deputy sheriff escort were joined by Wendy Barrie, beautiful British motion picture star.

Special meals, featuring roast pheasant, served to Siegel by the

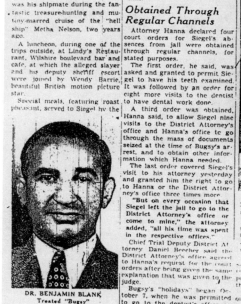

DR. BENJAMIN BLANK
Treated "Bugsy"

jail chef after the birds had been sent to the jail by a friend of Bugsy's, who shot them in Canada.

A diet, devised by Dr. Blank, which includes not one item of the regular jail fare.

The charge that Siegel, for "favors rendered," has made it a practice to "pay off certain jail attaches like a slot machine."

The further charge that Siegel has the freedom of the jail, wanders around "as if he owned the place," and frequently is permitted to sleep in one of the twin beds in Dr. Blank's quarters.

Claim Captain's Quarters Used

The assertion that during the absence of Captain Clem Peoples, chief jailer, Siegel was allowed to go into the captain's quarters to entertain a woman visitor, and that during this tete-a-tite a trusty served Siegel and his visitor soft drinks spiked with whisky.

seizing Siegel's private documents at the time of his arrest, the District Attorney had appropriated valuable data which Mr. Hanna could obtain, in the absence of the documents, only from Siegel himself.

"I am determined to learn whether the orders were abused. If I find this to be the case I will know what action to take."

Obtained Through Regular Channels

Attorney Hanna declared four court orders for Siegel's absences from jail were obtained through regular channels, for stated purposes.

The first order, he said, was asked and granted to permit Siegel to have his teeth examined. It was followed by an order for eight more visits to the dentist to have dental work done.

A third order was obtained, he said, to allow Siegel nine visits to the District Attorney's office and Hanna's office to go through the mass of documents seized at the time of Bugsy's arrest, and to obtain other information which Hanna needed.

The last order covered Siegel's visit to his attorney yesterday and granted him the right to go to Hanna or the District Attorney's office three times more.

"But on every occasion that Siegel left the jail to go to the District Attorney's office or come to mine," the attorney added, "all his time was spent in the respective offices."

Chief Trial Deputy District Attorney Daniel Beecher said the District Attorney's office agreed to Hanna's request for the court orders after being given the same explanation that was given to the judge.

Bugsy's "holidays" began October 7, when he was permitted to go to the dentist's office on the first court order obtained by Hanna.

On his first trip Siegel's custodians were Deputy Sheriffs James Pascoe and R. K. Etienne. Later, Pascoe alone escorted the rollicking gangster on the expeditions.

Tells How Bugsy Met Film Star

Pascoe told of the Wendy Barrie incident.

"It was on November 8," he said, "and Siegel and I were returning from the dentist's office. As we passed Lindy's, he said he was hungry.

"I said to Siegel, 'There's Wendy Barrie.' He said, 'Bring her over.' I did, and they had quite a chat."

Miss Barrie, however, had a slightly different version

A DEPUTY SHERIFF, escorting "Bugsy" Siegel about town, says the slaying suspect met film star Wendy Barrie, above, in a

Wilshire boulevard bar and cafe. Miss Barrie said she knew the deputy sheriff, had only met "Bugsy" once.

true, you can rest assured I'll blow the roof off the Hall of Justice before this is over with," he declared.

The sole duty of the jailer, he said, ... to see that orders of the court are carried out, and that prisoners are back in jail when they are supposed to be.

But the serving of expensive outside food and cigars to prisoners violates his rules, Peoples said, and he intends to check all the circumstances involved.

The Sheriff will take up the inquiry personally when he returns to Los Angeles tomorrow.

The investigations in progress, it was learned, are centering around these points:

1. What went on besides dentistry and conferences with the lawyer during the trips to the world of the free?

Did Siegel Join in Wild Parties?

2. Was Siegel allowed to participate in wild parties?

3. If so, who were his companions?

In addition to the other lavish privileges, Siegel, it was learned, has ready access to the jail telephones for incoming and outgoing calls.

Moreover, it was asserted in jail circles, the dentistry was merely an excuse. Dr. L. E. Multer, jail dentist, declaring he had examined Siegel's teeth and found

in the morning at his leisure, rap smartly on the tank door and hand a fistful of 50 cent cigars to the turnkey, who obligingly ushers him out.

His specially tailored uniforms with nickel lapels, are fresh every day, the clothes just wearing being cleaned and pressed while he is adorned by his "other" suit.

Although jail rules prohibit a prisoner from spending more than $5 a week, Siegel, it is declared, is permitted to keep on deposit whatever amount he wishes, this pin money fund running up to $150 a week.

Takes All Meals in Jail Hospital

Ostensibly, Siegel still is an inmate of the so-called "high power" tank. He is, however, taking all of his meals in the jail hospital, on orders of Blank, who declared:

"Mr. Siegel is a sick man. He has liver trouble, colitis, and kidney trouble."

A jail nurse, however, said in his opinion Siegel is in "100 per cent good health."

Jail records showed that Bugsy's trips outside were listed as follows:

October 7, 1 p. m. to 3:15 p. m.; October 11, 10 a. m. to 1:35 p. m.; October 14, 9:40 a. m. to 1:50 p. m.; October 17, 9:30 a. m. to 2 p. m.; October 21, 9 a. m. to

in the attic of his mansion in Holmby Hills, last August, after District Attorney Fitts asserted ly obtained evidence that Bugsy long a playtime of wealthy Hollywood luminaries, had actively participated in the slaying of Greenberg last Thanksgiving Eve.

Two New York hoodlums, former members of the infamous "Murder, Inc." ring, testified before the county grand jury in the case. One, Abe "Kid Twist" Reles, said he was present at the Greenberg slaying. The other, Al Tannenbaum, declared he was present at the conference in Brooklyn when Siegel assertedly volunteered to "take care" of Greenberg.

Greenberg, once a slugger and armorer for Lepke, was slain because he had attempted to extort $5000 from his erstwhile boss under a threat to "sing" to the law about the activities of Lepke, then a fugitive but now imprisoned.

Frank Carbo, now being sought, was named as the actual killer of Greenberg, leaping, according to Reles, from a car

On 19 November 1940 the Los Angeles Examiner *ran a front-page exposé of mobster Bugsy Siegel's being allowed passes to leave the county jail, where he was being held for the murder of Harry Greenberg, a small-time gangster. Though supposedly going to visit his attorney and to see a dentist, Siegel was spotted by reporters as he ate lunch with actress Wendy Barrie at Lindy's Restaurant. The incident was the seed for the plot of* The Little Sister, *in which Orrin Quest photographs a mobster named Steelgrave dining with actress Mavis Weld when he is supposed to be in jail.*

RAYMOND CHANDLER 6005 Camino de la Costa · La Jolla, California

March 26, 1949

Dear Mrs. Holton:

I'm sending my only copy of LS by air express today. I guess Brandt and Brandt have a copy in their office. I certainly hope so. But Jamie Hamilton already has the book in page proofs.

No dedication. No front matter from me, unless you want to vary the usual protection clause on the back of the title page by saying that "The people and events in this book are not entirely fictional. Some of the eventshappened, although not in this precise time or place, and certain of the characters were suggested by real persons, both living anddead. The author regrets any resemblance to reality that may be found in the pages of his books, andhe particularly regrets that he has on accasion made use of the names of real localities. He admits with shame that there actually is a place called Hollywood and a place called Los Angeles. It has streets a nd he has named some of them. It has a police departmentandhe has referred to it. Los Angles County has a District Attorney and said District Attorney has an office. To all of these matters the author has alluded. How careless of him! He should have called Los Angeles Smogville. He should have called its police department its Ministry of Corrections. Its District Attorney he might more admirably have referred to as the Master of the Rolls, and the office of this functionary might have been placed on an imaginary island somewhere off the coast of an imaginary state in an imaginary country. The characters in the story might, for additional security, have been referred to by letters of the Greek alphabet. "

Yours very truly,

Chandler delivered the final draft of The Little Sister *to Houghton Mifflin on 26 March 1949, and he included with it this note to Nina Holton in the firm's production department. The second paragraph is a facetious response to several letters Chandler had received in the past that criticized him for incorporating real people and places into his stories. Houghton Mifflin liked the mock disclaimer so much that they used it in promotional material for the book.*

The Little Sister Abridgement

Carl Brandt sold prepublication serial rights for The Little Sister *to* Cosmopolitan, *which published an abridged version of the novel in the April 1949 issue.* Cosmopolitan *paid a large sum for the abridgment—$10,000—but Chandler was unhappy with the results. He shared his reaction with Brandt in a letter dated 3 April 1949.*

6005 Camino de la Costa • La Jolla, California
April 3rd. 1949

Dear Carl:

My first experience with an abridgement is rather startling. I didn't read the thing in Cosmo through, I should live so long, but I read enough to convince myself that it was an error I sincerely hope never to have to repeat. I expected them to leave out almost everything that made the story any good, and I know within the space they could hardly do otherwise. I did not quite expect them to interpolate stuff that was not in my book—I'm not giving chapter and verse, partly because from your point of view it will probably not seem important and anyhow I have now no copy of the script, having sent mine to Mrs. Holton. Nor did I quite expect them to change the status of a senior detective-lieutenant attached to the Homicide Detail to "Officer French" the lowest rank on the force andone NEVER used to describe a dick. An 'officer' is always a uniformed man. There is, of course, variance in usage of rankin various police departments. In San Francisco for example an inspector is the lowest rank of detective officer, in Los Angeles one of the highest. In L.A. until very recently all dicks attached to Homicide ranked as Lieutenants, temporary status, although some wereof the perma-

Los Angeles City Hall, which appears in The Little Sister *and other Chandler works*

nent rank of sergeantsand some mere patrolmen, but while serving with Homicide, they were always referred to as Lieut. So and So. Like brevet rank in the army. Lately, however some of them have been called sergeants, probably their permanent rank. The last actual research I did was in 1945 while writing the Blue Dahlia, the first story incidentally which betrayed to they public the fact that the head man of the Homicide Bureau, then a very nice guy called Thad Brown (Captain), did not even have a private office. His desk was set right next to that of a female secretary and his door was always open. Outside there was a bare largish roomin which the dicks lounged about and quite literally did not have enough chairs to sit down in all at once. The entrance to this was a dutch door (whichwe didn't use in the film) and both of those rooms together would have fitted easily into our living room. This was positively all the boys had to work with and out of. This wasn't a top notch film by any means, largely because Veronica Lakecouldn't play thelove scenes and too much had to be discarded, but it did show the verymeager accommodations the homicide boys have to make do with. They actually built the two rooms and the hall outside to scale, and some of the shots got a cluttered effect that was right. But of course nobody sees this stuff in films. A very good cop picture I saw recently called HE WALKED BY NIGHT shows some

excellent technical stuff, but the shots inside Police Headquarters are much too spacious. You got the impression of a very complex and highly efficient organization staffe d by innumerable men. As a matter of fact they are a pretty dumb bunch who operate about on the mental level of plumbers.

Well, I guess the boys in the magazine racket know their business. I can't imagine what sort of people read these magazines anyhow. I can't read them. There's a sort of cheap gloss over everything that I find as sickening as bad perfume.

Yours,
Ray
—Bodleian Library, Oxford University

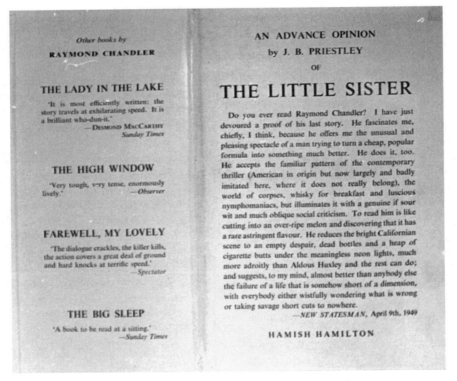

Dust jacket of the first British edition of Chandler's novel that was published by Hamish Hamilton in June 1949
(Bruccoli Collection, Kent State University)

English Reviews of *The Little Sister*

Because of delays caused by Chandler's finding a new American publisher, The Little Sister *was published first in England by Hamish Hamilton on 24 June 1949. The reception in Britain showed that Chandler's reputation had matured during his tenure in Hollywood. The reviews were mostly positive, and many reviewers argued for the literary value of Chandler's work. Hamish Hamilton sold twenty-six thousand copies of the book, making it Chandler's highest selling novel in the United Kingdom.*

Raymond Chandler writes far too little. He is the supreme craftsman of the tough American detective story and more worth reading than the rest of them put together, yet it is four years since his last book. In "The Little Sister" (Hamish Hamilton, 5s 6d) there is Philip Marlowe, Mr. Chandler's private detective, drawn into a welter of crime by a girl from the Middle West. She offers him all the money she has—some 20 dollars—to investigate the disappearance of her brother. The search leads him to dope dens, shady hotels, blackmailers, bullying cops, glamorous film stars, and he finds himself involved in several murders. It is Hollywood at its shadiest and although he would appear to be telling just another tough yarn, Mr. Chandler, the critic, is there all the time.

—"Crime and Detection," *Daily Telegram and Morning Post,*
1 July 1949, p. 6.

* * *

With a whoop of delight we notice that nestling in the middle of our parcels this time has been a new Raymond Chandler. We suspend our function as a reviewer and carry him off to a deck-chair to read him in three hours dead. Mr. Chandler has three hours off you with the speed and precision with which his hero Philip Marlowe had a knife and a Luger off an ugly customer in a boarding-house. This is to say that he has the three hours before you know you've started, just as he had the knife off the customer before you realised that he'd just had a Luger off him too. Remembering sadly that in a fiction review we are meant to be concerned with "important literature, we decide to exclude Chandler. But it is difficult to suppress a subversive thought that any man who can so effectively compel one to read his book, even though it is only about an improbable hard-boiled Hollywood where sleeping men sprout ice-picks from the backs of their necks, must have a real literary quality.

—Robert Kee, "Fiction," *The Spectator* (22 July 1949): 122

RAYMOND CHANDLER'S

The Little Sister

With his first novel for over four years, the author of *The Big Sleep, Farewell My Lovely, The High Window,* and *The Lady in the Lake,* shows that both he and Philip Marlowe, his famous private investigator, are still on top of their form.

Book Society Recommend.

8s. 6d. net

His earlier books were praised by critics as eminent as :

W. H. AUDEN : 'His powerful books should be read and judged, not as escape literature, but as works of art.'

J. B. PRIESTLEY : 'He seems to me the best American detective story writer in the tough and tense Dashiell Hammett tradition.'

DESMOND MACCARTHY : 'Most efficiently written; a brilliant who-dun-it.'

ELIZABETH BOWEN : 'A craftsman so brilliant, with an imagination so wholly original, that no consideration of modern American literature ought to exclude him.'

HAMISH HAMILTON

An English advertisement for Chandler's fifth novel

American Reception of *The Little Sister*

Eager to advance Chandler's reputation as a literary writer, Houghton Mifflin planned an ambitious publicity campaign for The Little Sister. *The following notice from Publishers' Weekly summarized the firm's plans.*

HOUGHTON MIFFLIN: Raymond Chandler will make his debut as a Houghton Mifflin author with "The Little Sister," the fifth Philip Marlowe novel (*PW,* May 7). Promotion will feature quotations from J. B. Priestly, Alistair Cooke, Elizabeth Bowen and W. H. Auden. Several important interviews are planned to coincide with publication.

Trade ads have appeared in *PW,* and are scheduled for the *Retail Bookseller, Latest Books* and *Bookshop News.* Houghton Mifflin will also take large space in general media, with big ads in New York, Boston, Phildelphia, Chicago, in addition to announcement ads in other cities across the country. Special attention will be given to California, the author's home.

Part of "The Little Sister" appeared in the April issue of *Cosmopolitan.* The book has been taken by the Mystery Guild.

—Publishers' Weekly,
(3 September 1949): 1081–1082

Advertisement in the 2 October 1949 issue of The New York Times Book Review

2 PARK STREET, BOSTON 7, MASS.   FOR RELEASE

RAYMOND CHANDLER and THE LITTLE SISTER
September 15
Houghton Mifflin Company

Raymond Chandler is the man who has tried to get murder fiction away from the upper classes, the weekend houseparty and the vicar's rose garden, and turn it back to the people who are good at it.

You'll meet some of the people who are good at it in THE LITTLE SISTER coming September 15 from Houghton Mifflin at $2.50.

<u>Like the Little Sister herself</u>: "Nobody ever looked less like Lady Macbeth. She was a small, neat, rather prissy looking girl...with rimless glasses. On her smooth brown hair was a hat that had been taken from its mother too young."

<u>Like the house dick</u>: "His standard of ethics would take about as much strain as a very tired old cobweb."

<u>Like the man</u> who "wore a Charvet scarf you could have found in the dark by listening to it purr."

<u>Like the girl</u> who "smelt the way the Taj Mahal looks by moonlight, and who looked as if it would take a couple of weeks to get her dressed."

<u>Like Philip Marlowe</u> the shamus (private dick) who "felt like a page from yesterday's calendar crumpled at the bottom of the wastebasket."

The story is "as restful as a split lip." It all takes place in "California. The department store state. The most of everything and the best of nothing...Where the great, fat, solid Pacific trudges into the shore like a scrubwoman going home."

This is the world where the boys talk and spit without ever bothering the cigarettes that live in their faces, where they make drinks in glasses tall enough to stand umbrellas in, where girls are almost as hard to get as a haircut, where you meet nice people with and without ice picks in their necks. This is the world which Raymond Chandler describes in THE LITTLE SISTER with that particular brand of vernacular which makes him seem like a divinely appointed recording angel to the tough guy.

Houghton Mifflin press release for The Little Sister

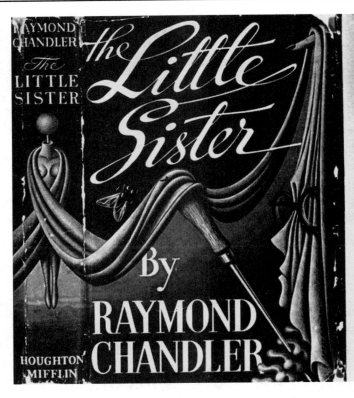

The Little Sister

by *Raymond Chandler*

Some days he's the two-gun kid from Cyanide Gulch and others he's only an ectoplasm with a private license. But to readers of *The Big Sleep, Farewell, My Lovely, The High Window,* and *The Lady in the Lake,* he's Philip Marlowe — Marlowe with an "e" — the most exciting high-velocity private investigator in the business.

Raymond Chandler brings him back alive in the fifth of his tense, taut, tightly meshed novels, although at the end the "little sister," a mousy receptionist to a medico back in Manhattan, Kansas, has the redoubtable Marlowe feeling like a page from yesterday's calendar crumpled at the bottom of the wastebasket. When the reader, too, comes up for air, he doesn't know whether he's been on a two-day reefer jag, or given a mauling by the Bay City cops, or blinded by the neon lighted slum called Hollywood.

What he does know is that Marlowe is still in the groove, that his sardonic humor is running free, that his cynicism is so hard that it bounces. His is a world where a man can talk and spit without ever bothering the

continued on back flap

cigarette that lives in his face, where they make their drinks in glasses tall enough to stand umbrellas in, where a girl may smell like the Taj Mahal looks by moonlight but don't let that fool you if she has a phony Spanish accent and rides heavy on the *Amigo* stuff. It didn't trip Marlowe — in the end, that is.

In *The Little Sister,* Chandler is again master of his own brand of vernacular and sets it down as if he were a divinely appointed recording angel to the tough guy. Few writers have bagged more superlatives and held them with a firmer grasp. *Sui Generis* is not the expression to toss around lightly; it fits the creator of Philip Marlowe as the cartridge fits the chamber of a .32.

Raymond Chandler is the brave man who rescued murder from the vicar's rose garden and gave it back to the people who are really good at it. Beneath its high entertainment value, his work has a sharp bite and a deep cut and displays a frightening knowledge of human motivations, most of them unlovely. In addition to his four novels and collected shorts, his fine California hand can be traced to some of the fastest paced movies of the past decade. "Philip Marlowe, Private Detective" — based on his unquenchable character — is a popular radio feature. Chicago born, Chandler had his schooling in England, France, and Germany. Before turning writer he sampled most of the respectable professions.

Jacket by Boris Artzybasheff

Raymond Chandler

Here's Marlowe

"A California ocean. California, the department-store state. The most of everything and the best of nothing. Here we go again. You're not human tonight, Marlowe. All right. Why would I be? I'm sitting in that office, playing with a dead fly and in pops this dowdy little item from Manhattan, Kansas, and chisels me down to a shopworn twenty to find her brother. He sounds like a creep but she wants to find him. So with this fortune clasped to my chest, I trundle down to Bay City and the routine I go through is so tired I'm half asleep on my feet. I meet nice people, with and without ice picks in their necks. I leave, and I leave myself wide-open too. Then she comes in and takes the twenty away from me and gives me a kiss and gives it back to me because I didn't do a full day's work. So I go see Dr. Hambleton, retired (and how) optometrist from El Centro, and meet again the new style in neckwear. And I don't tell the cops. I just frisk the customer's toupee and put on an act. Why? Who am I cutting my throat for this time? A blonde with sexy eyes and too many door keys? A girl from Manhattan, Kansas? I don't know. All I know is that something isn't what it seems and the old tired but always reliable hunch tells me that if the hand is played the way it is dealt the wrong person is going to lose the pot. Is that my business? Well, what is my business? Do I know? Did I ever know? Let's not go into that. You're not human tonight, Marlowe. Maybe I never was or ever will be. Maybe I'm an ectoplasm with a private license. Maybe we all get like this in the cold half lit world where always the wrong thing happens and never the right."

Dust jacket of the first American edition of The Little Sister *(Bruccoli Collection, Kent State University)*

Houghton Mifflin published The Little Sister *in the United States on 26 September 1949. The firm promoted the book heavily, and its advertisements touted Chandler's literary qualities with a selection of quotations from writers and critics such as W. H. Auden, Elizabeth Bowen, and Diarmuid Russell. The American reception of the novel, however, was mixed. Some periodicals gave the book only a brief treatment in their generic mystery columns; those that gave it more thorough attention generally judged it to be inferior to Chandler's first four novels. The following review is typical of the ambivalence toward Chandler's work expressed by American reviewers.*

Philip Marlowe, Raymond Chandler's "private eye" runs up against a new type of female this time. She comes from Manhattan, Kansas—not New York—she wears prim brown suits and rimless glasses, no make-up and no jewelry. Her name is Orfamay Quest, and she's looking for her brother Orrin who has disappeared. Piqued by her very quaintness, Marlowe undertakes the search and quickly finds himself involved with a bunch of typical Chandler characters. They consist of marijuana peddlers and smokers; movie actresses with traces of nymphomania; night-club proprietors with a criminal record, and a gang from Cleveland who have developed the art of stabbing with an ice-pick to beautiful perfection.

A number of murders take place before Marlowe runs the case to its conclusion.

This is one of Chandler's most ambitious mysteries, but not by any means one of his best. He's overextended himself this time with an elaborate and too pretentious prose style.

—"Mystery and Adventure," *New York Herald Tribune Book Review,* 9 October 1949, p. 14

Newsweek used the publication of The Little Sister *as an occasion to run an article about the business of mystery publishing in general.*

Murder Business

Newsweek (31 October 1949): 69–70

Philip Marlowe and Sam Spade have a great deal in common. Both are private detectives working in the lower levels of California society. Both are attractive to and attracted by lady clients. Both get terribly beaten up by their enemies and terribly browbeaten by the cops. Neither appears in many stories (Spade is the hero of two; Marlowe of five).

Spade is the creature of Dashiell Hammett; Marlowe of Raymond Chandler.

It well may be that if Spade had never lived, neither would have Marlowe. For the mantle of Hammett as leader of the "hard-boiled" mystery writers has surely descended on the shoulders of Chandler. And, therefore, for those who like yeggs well done, the publication of Chandler's "The Little Sister" has about the same réclame as would, for another literary set, Ernest Hemingway's long-expected novel.

"The Little Sister," the present Chandler book, dealing as usual with sin in Los Angeles, enmeshes Marlowe with some movie people and their relatives who get mixed up with marijuana and blackmail. Maybe Chandler fans won't like his new tale as well as they have liked others of his. Maybe they will. Either way, Chandler's success has been impressive. Including pocket-sized reprints, as well as regular trade editions, his four previous books since 1939 have sold a total of nearly 3,000,000 copies.

All of which leads the discerning reader to wonder about mystery-writing and -publishing in general. For thrillers account for one-fifth of the fiction titles published in the United States in a year and enjoy a guesstimated readership of 250,000,000.

Vicarious Mayhem: The "hard-boiled school" of Chandler and Hammett and their followers, popular as it is, is not the foremost. The biggest seller, as well as the biggest producer of detective fiction in the past decade, has been the prolific Erle Stanley Gardner, whose suave, quick-thinking attorney-hero Perry Mason has become even more of a nationally known figure than his creator. In 1948 alone Gardner's books sold 7,315,487 copies. His total sales to date, in regular editions and reprints, come to the staggering total of 35,872,035 copies. It is perhaps significant that Gardner's formula is a combination of puzzle (who done it?), action (his hero usually finds the bodies while they're warm), and legal fireworks.

But like the food and clothing industries, mystery stories have to cater to all tastes, and, besides the aforementioned, the output can be roughly divided as follows:
▸The pure "puzzle" school, in which the reader and author match wits to see who can discover first who poured the arsenic into the old lady's tea. This one still has its faithful following behind authors like Ellery Queen, John Dickson Carr, Agatha Christie, and Rex Stout. Their sleuths—Queen, Gideon Fell, Hercule Poirot, and Nero Wolfe—are aspiring heirs of the great and memorable Sherlock Holmes.
▸"Suspense" stories, built around the pursuit or frustration of a known malefactor, or escape from some fate worse than death. Helen MacInnes's "Suspicion"

and the Eric Ambler stories of skulduggery-plus-international intrigue fall under this heading.

▶A spreading rash of psychological "thrillers." In these the question is not who done it, but why? The sleuths are usually young and personable practitioners of the new mental medicine and only rarely, as in the case of Helen Eustis's "The Horizontal Man," is the job done with any evidence of a real grasp of the subject.

▶The school of debonair dabblers in crime or punishment, usually set against English drawing-room backgrounds, with lords and ladies mingled in mayhem, blackmail, or larceny with the denizens of the underworld. Here belong Leslie Charteris's "Saint" stories and Dorothy L. Sayers's Lord Peter Wimsey whimsies. There are a lot of people who like this sort of thing. Leslie Charteris's books, published by Doubleday, draw the respectable sale of 15,000 in regular editions, plus large reprints. Dorothy L. Sayers's "Busman's Honeymoon," written in 1937, has sold a total of 400,000 copies.

▶A large body of mystery fiction dominated by middle-aged lady sleuths who generally operate in a pleasant domestic atmosphere. This is the field, largely plowed by women both as authors and readers, led by Mary Roberts Rinehart, Mignon Eberhart, and Leslie Ford.

▶Since writers, critics, and readers in mystery fiction all take their work and themselves very seriously, humor has not been a notable ingredient in the stew. The funniest sample was a frank take-off, Elliot Paul's "Hugger-Mugger in the Louvre" of a few years back. The most successful regular practitioner who uses humor as her main device is Craig Rice, who wows some of her audience some of the time but leaves a lot of other people cold.

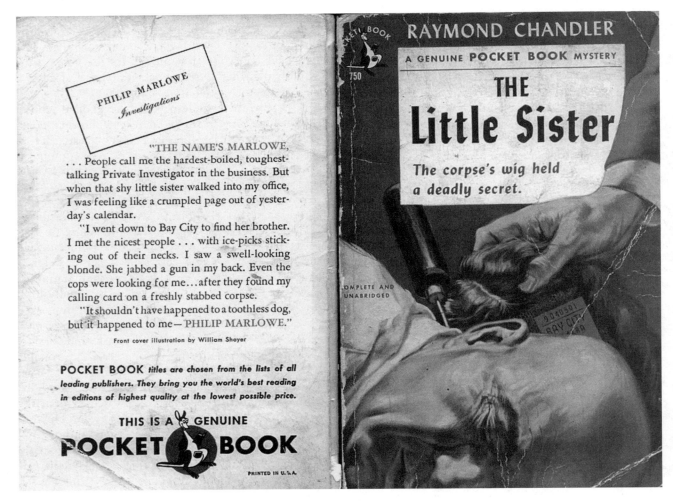

First paperback edition of The Little Sister *(1950)*

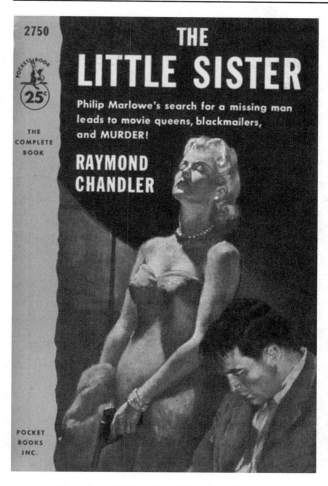

2750

POCKET BOOK
25¢

THE
COMPLETE
BOOK

THE LITTLE SISTER

Philip Marlowe's search for a missing man leads to movie queens, blackmailers, and MURDER!

RAYMOND CHANDLER

POCKET
BOOKS
INC.

Cover for a 1957 reprint of Chandler's fifth novel

Mass Murder: Whatever form they adopt to amuse, mystery stories as a whole are big business. Since publishers are often either coy about sales figures or else are sometimes prone to exaggeration, it is not possible to produce any exact statistical summary. But rough estimates based on available figures produce some staggering conclusions:

▸About 250 mystery titles are published each year by the regular trade publishers with an average printing, say, of 4,500 copies, of which the great bulk goes to circulating libraries. This represents a total of 1,125,000 copies. In the circulating-library business they figure that each book gets about 50 readings before it is retired. If this is true, the regular trade editions of mystery stories each year pass through the hands of about 50,000,000 readers.

▸The 25-cent reprint houses like Dell, Pocket Books, Avon, and Bantam Books put out just under 150 mystery titles each year. According to their varied and sometimes flexible claims, these titles are selling in the neighborhood of 40,000,000 copies a year, which, at an estimated five readers apiece, reach 200,000,000 people.

▸There are three large mystery book clubs which among them claim 140,000 members, each of whom is said to read from one to three mysteries apiece every 30 days.

Few mystery writers share in the prosperity that these figures suggest. After Erle Stanley Gardner there are perhaps ten or fifteen big moneymakers in the business. Below them comes a layer of 30 or 40 writers who clear about $10,000 a year. Of the 200-odd other established mystery-story writers, the great bulk have to eke out their incomes from other sources and are lucky to make $5,000 a year. Below them crowd the mass of the hopeful who seldom get printed at all. (Simon & Schuster's Inner Sanctum editor receives more than 250 manuscripts a year, from which she chooses only twelve.)

The multimillion circulation of the 25-cent reprints is not as profitable for the writer as it sounds. He usually gets no more than 1 cent per book. Few mystery-story writers can get by with only one book a year, and these are the lucky ones who sell serial rights to one of the slick magazines for up to $3,500 or $5,000 and make a further sale to the movies for anywhere between $5,000 and $10,000.

Like most other trades, the mystery-writing craft has organized itself. There is the Mystery Writers of America, Inc., which carries on its activities under the slogan of "Crime Does Not Pay—Enough." Besides instructing its members on the details of poisons and police methods, it works to improve contract arrangements and prices.

Neither Pity nor Fear. The social psychologist can find much to chew on in the field of mystery fiction. He can discover in it great splashy and bloody gobs of the violence, masochism, and sadism of life. He might even discover that in all their various forms these stories are popular because they offer a form of resolution in a time of unresolved conflicts. The mystery-story reader, whether he sits in the White House or in a mill-town shack, can pick up his latest acquisition with the soothing certainty that whatever the violence, whatever the problem, it is going to be unraveled, the obscure made clear, the issue settled, the crime avenged, and the guilty person punished. This, in our time, is a solace not to be taken lightly.

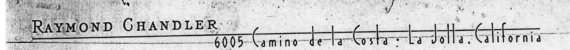

RAYMOND CHANDLER   6005 Camino de la Costa · La Jolla, California

Nov 15, 1949

Dear Bernice:

Thanks for the HM contract and I don't think I ought to take the advance until I have turned in all the material, do you? I have found a copy of No Crime in the Mountains in my 1945 Tax file. I have a refund claim for that year pending and this story is part of the evidence. (It all turns on the interpretation of Section 109 (b)). I should have remembered that. It's rather discouraging to recall how very shipshape everything was a couple of years ago and what a mess it is now.

I suppose from the proper point of view--the kind of book and so on--the sales of LS are fairly good, but I can't feel much encouraged. With all that publicity and all that advertising money (surely out of line for this kind of book) one might have expected more. I think Knopf would have done just as well, because it appears to me that the sales are more or less automatick, even if they stand up against returns. It seems to me that apart from some very extraordinary circumstance you just can't buck the rental library habit. Even I, who have a special interest in them and can afford them, seldom buy mysteries. Why should the average reader plank down two and a half for something he can rent for ten or fifteen cents? If he wants to read it again he knows there will be reprints within a few months or a year. The value simply isn't there. Incidentally I doubt very much Newsweek's information that Leslie Charteris' books sell 15000 in their trade editions. I'd put it at no more than half that. The book business must be maddening to those in the manufacturing and selling end of it.

Taking the whole picture I have no complaint. It wasn't a very good book, although it contained some good writing. The plot didn't have enough lift or imagination and there was too much writing around the edges, too much decoration. I ought to be able to do much better. But even at that when all the returns are in it will be worth around $25,000. Any writer ought to be more than content with that. If I am not, it must be that Hollywood has spoiled me. If I can get (and I still can, I think) $50,000 for a picture script, I suppose I think I ought to get as much for a book, which is far more work. On the other hand when you have a book you have a book; when you have a motion picture script, you have a hole in the air.

Yours always,

NOV 17 1949

Letter from Chandler to Bernice Baumgarten discussing the sales and reception of The Little Sister
(Bodleian Library, Oxford University)

Collecting *The Simple Art of Murder*

The Little Sister sold sixteen thousand copies in the United States—Chandler's best American sales to date, but still a smaller figure than he had hoped. Houghton Mifflin wanted to follow up on the novel with a collection of Chandler's short stories, which he began assembling in the fall of 1949. In order to emphasize Chandler's series character, Dale Warren proposed he change the name of the detective character in all the stories to Philip Marlowe. In this letter to Warren, Chandler responds to the request and discusses the selection of stories for the volume.

6005 Camino de la Costa • La Jolla, California
Dec 22, 1949

Dear Dale:

The stories are being copied double-space on regular 8 X 11 paper. Those on the list you sent me, omitting Blackmailers Don't Shoot, The Bronze Door and No Crime in the Mountains. I've licked this last one up to the final blowOff scene and that won't jell. Kind of a pity too because I always liked the story for its moral—never try to lick a man in his own backyard. But there are twelve stories without it and you would come out with about 215,000 words including introductions. Is that enough?

I am enclosed a very good first carbon of Pick-Up on Moon Street, revised as best I could from memory. You will probably want to have this copied again for the print, if you like the story. At my expense, naturally. This is the only copy I have.

I think the 'the' should be omitted from FINGER MAN, but not from THE KING IN YELLOW.

Have done nothing yet on the intro, but will soon. I see no reason why it could not be published in a mag if I do it right. I'm sure Fred Allen would be kind to me. I'm not so sure about Charlie Morton any more. He revealed a bitter streak in his make up and it might give him pleasure to push my teeth in.

As to the drinking in Pearls Are a Nuisance, of course that was part of the burlesque, but you edit it to suit yourself. I don't care greatly. Bernice has never commented on this story. The opening chapter is the bad part of it. I had to rewrite it and somehow the rewriting disimproved it. It was considered too whimsical before.

As to the use of Marlowe's name, it seems to me that it might be substituted for all the first per-
son names (Except Pearls are etc.) i.e. Finger Man, Trouble is My Business, Red Wind, Goldfish. The third person stories are not Marlowe.

When was he born? If you go by The Big Sleep he was born about 1900. But since he can't get any older than about 38, obviously by poetic convention I have to keep his birthadjusted. This doesnot worry me at all, since the whole basis of this kind of story is a kind of fantasy. I have never been able to understand the criticism made by some idiots that real private detectivesare not like those of fiction. I know exactly what real private detectives are like., but they wouldn't be of any use to me. It seems to me that these things are as unimportant as for example MGM's version of the Los Angeles Homicide Bureau in Scene of the Crime, a picture which had an air of being a documentary without ever for a moment being one.

The chapter divisions are mostly as I wrote them, except that I always used numbers only, no 'chapter', no roman numerals. Editors of magazines fix this to suit themselves. Some of them just skip a line to show a chapter, some use figures, some chapters, some Arabic some Roman. If you express a preference I'll try to adjust the script accordingly. I feel the same way about the order of the stories; you are the best judge. The only time I ever paid any attention to this I felt that, assuming you could tab the three best stories, one, two, three: Two should open the book, Three end it, and One come towards the middle. Definitely I think the 'I' stories should be scattered. Just for a quick rundown I suggest an order something like this. FINGER MAN, SMART-ALECK KILL, GUNS AT CYRANO'S, GOLDFISH, THE KING IN YELLOW, PEARLS ARE A NUISANCE, TROUBLE IS MY BUSINESS, I'LL BE WAITING, NEVADA GAS, RED WIND, SPANISH BLOOD. Or better to end with a Marlowe story perhaps.

I've been having shingles, not bad, but annoying enough. I seem to be crumbling slowly. This house is for sale, not because we don't like it, but because we cannot get any decent help, and have just about decided none is obtainable here. Have had some really awful experiences. So I don't think we can get away for very long, especially as we hope to go to England in the spring.

—transcribed from the original document,
Houghton Library, Harvard University

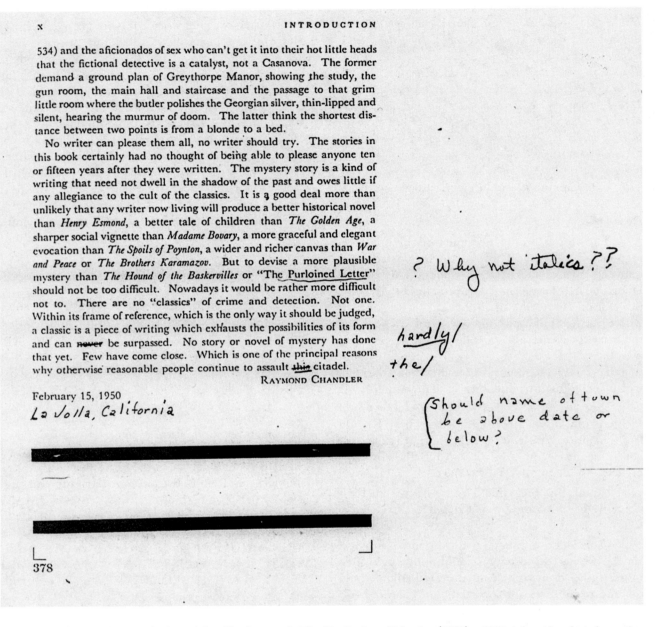

x INTRODUCTION

534) and the aficionados of sex who can't get it into their hot little heads that the fictional detective is a catalyst, not a Casanova. The former demand a ground plan of Greythorpe Manor, showing the study, the gun room, the main hall and staircase and the passage to that grim little room where the butler polishes the Georgian silver, thin-lipped and silent, hearing the murmur of doom. The latter think the shortest distance between two points is from a blonde to a bed.

No writer can please them all, no writer should try. The stories in this book certainly had no thought of being able to please anyone ten or fifteen years after they were written. The mystery story is a kind of writing that need not dwell in the shadow of the past and owes little if any allegiance to the cult of the classics. It is a good deal more than unlikely that any writer now living will produce a better historical novel than *Henry Esmond*, a better tale of children than *The Golden Age*, a sharper social vignette than *Madame Bovary*, a more graceful and elegant evocation than *The Spoils of Poynton*, a wider and richer canvas than *War and Peace* or *The Brothers Karamazov*. But to devise a more plausible mystery than *The Hound of the Baskervilles* or "The Purloined Letter" should not be too difficult. Nowadays it would be rather more difficult not to. There are no "classics" of crime and detection. Not one. Within its frame of reference, which is the only way it should be judged, a classic is a piece of writing which exhausts the possibilities of its form and can never be surpassed. No story or novel of mystery has done that yet. Few have come close. Which is one of the principal reasons why otherwise reasonable people continue to assault this citadel.

RAYMOND CHANDLER

February 15, 1950
La Jolla, California

? Why not italics ??

hardly/
the/

[Should name of town be above date or below?

378

Page proofs for Chandler's introduction and the table of contents for The Simple Art of Murder *(1950), with his holograph and typed corrections; this introduction was published by* The Saturday Review of Literature *on 15 April 1950 under the title "The Simple Art of Murder," creating enduring confusion between this piece and Chandler's more famous essay with the same title, which was originally published in* The Atlantic *in November 1944 and was included as one of the selections in the 1950 story volume. Chandler's typed corrections to the table of contents provide the magazine and year in which each story was first published (Bodleian Library, Oxford University).*

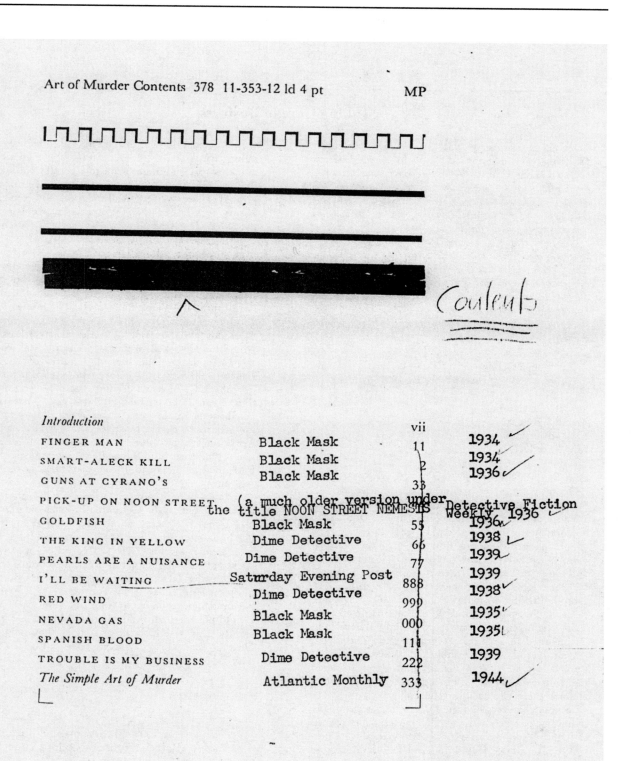

Art of Murder Contents 378 11-353-12 ld 4 pt   MP

Couleut

Introduction		vii	
FINGER MAN	Black Mask	11	1934
SMART-ALECK KILL	Black Mask	2	1934
GUNS AT CYRANO'S	Black Mask	33	1936
PICK-UP ON NOON STREET (a much older version under the title NOON STREET NEMESIS)	Detective Fiction Weekly		1936 1936
GOLDFISH	Black Mask	55	1936
THE KING IN YELLOW	Dime Detective	66	1938
PEARLS ARE A NUISANCE	Dime Detective	77	1939
I'LL BE WAITING	Saturday Evening Post	888	1939
RED WIND	Dime Detective	999	1938
NEVADA GAS	Black Mask	000	1935
SPANISH BLOOD	Black Mask	11	1935
TROUBLE IS MY BUSINESS	Dime Detective	222	1939
The Simple Art of Murder	Atlantic Monthly	333	1944

Taking Care of Business

During the first half of 1950 Chandler found much of his time consumed by business matters such as handling requests for rights to reprint his stories, to translate his novels, and to produce radio and television versions of his stories. In these negotiations Chandler was concerned with expanding his audience, improving his literary reputation, and maintaining the commercial value of his fiction.

In July 1950 Chandler accepted a contract to write the screenplay for Alfred Hitchcock's Strangers on a Train. *Though reluctant to do any more work for Hollywood, Chandler accepted the contract in part because of its large salary— $2,500 a week—and in part because he wanted to work with Hitchcock, a director he admired.*

In the following letter to Baumgarten, Chandler addresses pressing professional issues.

6005 Camino de la Costa • La Jolla, California
September 13, 1950

Miss Bernice Baumgarten
Brandt & Brandt
101 Park Avenue
New York 17, N.Y.

Dear Bernice:

Here is a copy of a letter sent to me by Miss Jo Stewart, of the Sanders Agency, received by her from a Mrs. Pollard, Permissions Department, Doubleday & Company. You will probably want to handle it. I should have turned this down even if the material were not otherwise contracted for. I don't like the anthology racket even when there is a fair payment for the rights, which there very seldom is. The "some difficulty with Raymond Chandler", referred to in the first paragraph of Mrs. Pollard's letter, was a forthright refusal on my part to allow the story to be included in a British edition of their anthology, since it had never been published in that country. It took a lawyer to stop them because they claimed there had been an offer and acceptance, and I claimed there had been no such thing.

Sydney Sanders had the human, but occasionally irritating, conviction that a buck was a buck even though by holding onto it, it might grow into a portrait of Alexander Hamilton. And he would dispose of anthology rights in the most freehanded manner without consulting me at all. This got to be very irritating. It apparently never entered the man's head that this material might acquire a certain value, and that the anthologists were simply stealing it for peanuts. I guess writers really expect too much of agents. It is rather unfair to expect an agent to take the long view when he has no certainty of being around when the long view becomes a close-up, if it ever does.

I'm still slaving away for Warner Brothers on this Hitchcock thing, which you may or may not have heard about. Some days I think it is fun and other days I think it is damn foolishness. The money looks good, but as a matter of fact it isn't. I'm too concientious and, although I do not work nearly as fast as I would have worked twenty years ago, I still work a good deal faster than the job requires or has any right to expect. For the most part the work is boring, unreal, and I have no feeling that it is the kind of thing I can do better than anybody else. Suspense as an absolute quality has never seemed to me very important. At best it is a secondary growth, and at worst an attempt to make something out of nothing.

As I have heard nothing about that fantastic story, I assume that it is dead. I wish that it had never been sent out.

I had a wire this morning from a lady called Janice O'Connell, of the Columbia Broadcasting System in New York, asking about television rights for a one-hour show on their Studio One program, with kinescope, from THE KING IN YELLOW. I wired back that they should get in touch with you. I would not consider less than a thousand dollars, but the question I submit for your consideration is whether it would not be better to hold out altogether. Why should not these stories sometime be sold as a package for a television series, as long as they hold out? On the other hand, if you prefer to put it that way, why should they?

With kindest regards,
Ray

—transcribed from original document,
Bodleian Library, Oxford University

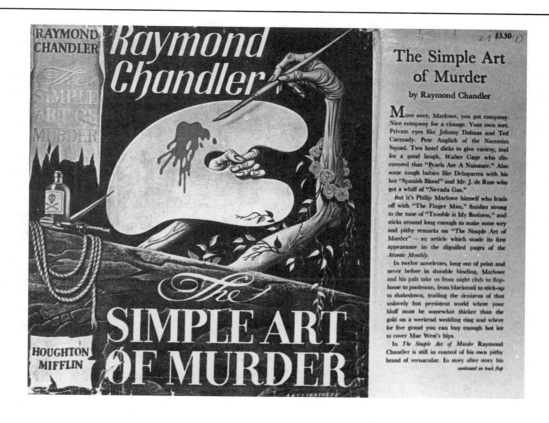

Dust jacket of the first edition of The Simple Art of Murder, *a collection of Chandler's pulp stories from the 1930s*
(Bruccoli Collection, Kent State University)

The Carr Review

Houghton Mifflin published The Simple Art of Murder *on 19 September 1950. The volume sold well for a short story collection, with advanced sales topping five thousand copies, and it was widely reviewed.* The New York Times Book Review *assigned the book to John Dickson Carr, himself a writer of the type of deductive mysteries derided by Chandler in the title essay, who wrote the following stinging review.*

With Colt and Luger
John Dickson Carr
The New York Times Book Review, 24 September 1950, p. 36

IN 1946 Mr. Chandler revised and reprinted an essay called "The Simple Art of Murder." It appeared also in Avon Books. It now turns up for the fourth time in his new book of twelve old novelettes. Since he likes the essay so well, it may be best to consider this piece of naïveté on its own.

His thesis is that murder must become realistic. It must be taken out of the Venetian vase and dropped into the alley. It must be handled by men who understand it, who use the Luger and the Colt for real reasons, undismayed by violence, all raw-head and bloody-bones. Besides, he says, this makes the writing of a detective story good fun.

Now we must not become entangled in the dreary old argument about realism. Anything is real if it seems real. Mr. Chandler sometimes writes fluently and well. He falls into a fit of screaming hysterics only when he considers the formal English detective story and the Detection Club of London. These, he confesses, get him down. In his excitement he pulverizes two English novels, one published in 1913 and the other in 1922. Yet he swears it's no different today and attempts to pulverize everybody else in sight, including a number of Americans who are low-minded enough not to write as he does. Their plots, he says, are artificial, stilted, impossible and dull. The dastards *will* write about curare and hand-wrought dueling pistols. They know nothing about police work, nothing about violence, nothing about real life.

HE is pitiless, this austere fellow. He will not even allow English writers the negative virtues of background or culture. They speak in what Mr. Chandler calls the "conversational accent"—as opposed, perhaps, to the nonconversational accent?—of Surbiton or Bognor Regis. They write about dukes and Venetian vases, but they don't know a thing about dukes or Venetian vases either.

Now this, I confess, somewhat puzzles me. There is nothing wrong with Surbiton or Bognor Regis, unless

Mr. Chandler's soul hides much snobbery. Still, since I have been a member of the Detection Club for fifteen years, I would soothe and comfort him.

He is quite right. The club contains only one peer of the realm, one baronet, one O. B. E., and two lowly knights. There isn't a duke in it. Mr. Chandler, who modestly claims affinity with Aeschylus and Shakespeare, will have to debate only with Miss Sayers (it would brighten my declining years to hear this) and perhaps a dozen others: including Sir Norman Kendal, formerly Assistant Commissioner of the Criminal Investigation Department, Metropolitan Police. And, of course, these people know nothing of violence, especially those who lived in London and were on duty from 1940 to 1945.

YET we must return to Mr. Chandler's essay. "The cool- headed constructionist," he says, "does not also come across with lively characters, sharp dialogue, a sense of pace and an acute sense of observed detail." Well, that is a matter for debate on both sides of the Atlantic. Such writers as Edgar Allan Poe, Nathaniel Hawthorne, Mark Twain, Charles Dickens, Wilkie Collins, Robert Louis Stevenson, Thomas Hardy, Joseph Conrad, John Galsworthy, Hugh Walpole, G. K. Chesterton—all of whom joyously wrote bloods as well as detective stories—were cool-headed constructionists. Can we allow them none of the other virtues as well?

"The fellow who can write you a vivid and colorful prose," says Mr. Chandler, "simply can't be bothered with the coolie labor of breaking down unbreakable alibis." In plain words, this hypothetical fellow won't work. He can't be bothered to learn craftsmanship, as Poe did and Stevenson did. Aside from the hypothetical, Mr. Chandler has emphasized his own dislike for plot-construction. The realistic method, he says, has freed him from "an exhausting concatenation of insignificant clues,"—raised eyebrows department—and he can now let the characters work out the story for themselves.

Here we see the main weakness in Mr. Chandler's novels. From the first page he goes whooping along at high speed, magnificently if somewhat confusedly, until he reaches the last chapter. There he takes one sweet spill into a net. He thrashes wildly, but he can't get out; he can't explain why his characters acted as they did, and he can't even talk intelligibly. This, presumably, is realism.

Mr. Chandler is a serious-minded man, and it would be unjust not to take him seriously. Few writers have been more mannered (I do not say ill-mannered) or more uneven. His similes either succeed brilliantly or fall flat. He can write a scene with an almost suffocating vividness and sense of danger—if he does not add three words too many and make it funny. His virtues are all there. If, to some restraint, he could add the fatigue of construction and clues (the writer he most admires, Mr. Hammett, has never disdained clues and has always given them fairly)—then one day he may write a good novel.

I SAY nothing of new ideas or plot-twists, because Mr. Chandler does not have them. He will never disturb the laurels of Mr. Queen or Mr. Gardner or Mr. Stout. Perhaps it is best to let him alone, and offer no suggestions. In his new book, "The Simple Art of Murder," few of the novelettes are new. Yet many are good and two are first-class. When he forgets he cannot write a true detective story, when he forgets to torture words, the muddle resolves and the action whips along like a numbered racing-car.

"Pickup on Noon Street" is a fine study in terror, moving from reality to a hideous unreality and back again. I put it second only to the story beginning as a burlesque with two noble characters—Walter Gage and Henry Eichelberger—and ending in an admirably sardonic surprise-twist.

In "Goldfish" he tried a plot device, with sad results; but the characters are so well done that we could wish all but two were not knocked off in gunplay before the end. If the stories burst and foam with blood, where is the criticism in that? Philip Marlow is not the only detective—the sleuths range from hotel dick to amateurs.

Yet, it is an admirable collection. Mr. Chandler will do even better when he discovers that you cannot create an American language merely by butchering the English language.

Though Chandler made no public response to Carr's attacks, he was angered and offended by the review. He vented his irritation in the following letter to Warren. By this point he had completed work on the script of Strangers on a Train, *and his letter to Warren also discusses his strained relationship with Hitchcock.*

6005 Camino de la Costa • La Jolla, California
October 4, 1950

Mr. Dale Warren
Houghton Mifflin company
2 Park Street
Boston 7, Massachusetts

Dear Dale:

I have a letter from you somewhere, but I can't find it. Anyhow thanks for the book THE INJUSTICE COLLECTORS, which my wife read with great pleasure. She especially liked the two stories called "The Miracle" and "The Unholy Three." Don't hit me, I'll get around to reading it myself. The one I really want from you is the one on Scott Fitzgerald, if it is good. I don't want to see Fitzgerald messed around by some eager beaver who is trying to soften up a buck. But of course you wouldn't publish anything like that. Or would you?

I finally got done with Mr. Hitchcock. Had several talks with him and he seemed very amiable, with a well-masked conceit of his own talents and a very polite manner to us hired hands. But from the time I began to write the actual screenplay until I sent in the final scenes and since then, I have not even spoken to him on the telephone. This is strange doings. Either he loathes the script or he is mad about something. Even in Hollywood, where a producer loves you to death until the end of the job and can't recognize you on the street the next day, this is carrying things pretty far. I could perhaps explain it by conjecturing from a remark he made. I was looking at his script of THE STAGE DOOR, and I asked him how much of it was really his work. He said about eighty per cent. So it may be that he regards the writer's job as just rough work for him to polish up. If so, he suffers from the common Hollywood delusion that a second-guesser is better than the man who gave him the thing to second guess. And again, it may be that they paid me so much money they don't think they have to be polite.

We all think THE SIMPLE ART OF MURDER is a fine piece of bookmaking. My wife does not like the cover. I explained to her that it was just to catch the yokels, but she won't agree. She likes covers with conventional designs or plain typography, the sort of thing Gollancz introduced in England. So do I as a matter of fact, but I never kibitz a publisher, although I recognize that he is often a sucker for his own racket. The trouble with my wife is that she has too much good taste for this generation. She thinks your publicity is wrong too. She says the one thing you keep telling the public is what they already know, and the thing you don't tell them, that you should tell them, is that if Chandler is any good at all, it's in spite of his being tough and not because of it. Opinions expressed on this program, you understand, are not necessarily those of the sponsor.

I get it from a pal back East that I got a stinking bad review in the NEW YORK TIMES from one John Dickson Carr, about as stinking as the one

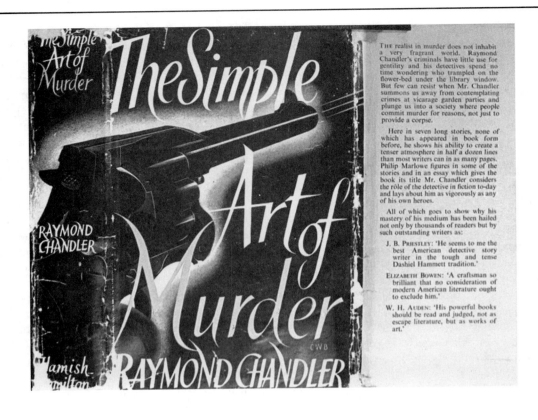

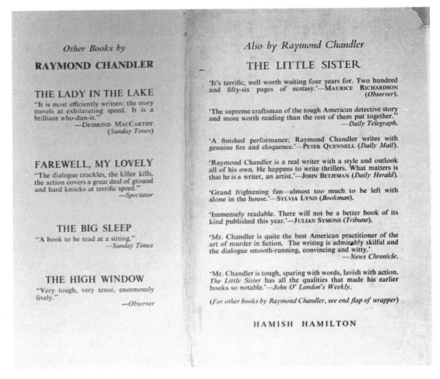

Dust jacket for the first English edition of Chandler's fourth collection of his stories (Bruccoli Collection, Kent State University)

I got from Anthony Boucher. TIME speaks of his taking "deadly aim" at me. I have not seen the review. Obviously people like Boucher and Carr are committed in advance to disliking me, because they are well aware that I regard their kind of detective story as apt to be a crashing bore, even when it is a good deal better written than they could ever write it. The only thing deadly is the assumption that the proper man to review a book is somebody who is drooling for a chance to get his knife into the writer, a snide theory of criticism, which can taste nothing but its own bile. If they don't like my opinions, why don't they sit down and refute them on the same level instead of waiting until I write something else and then take their spleen out on that? I could write a better defense of the deductive mystery than they could. I would be slightly handicapped, because after years of seeking I have not found one single specimen that will stand the kind of analysis it predicates. I have asked people to tell me about one. I don't say there isn't one. I only say I haven't been able to find it. Their whole métier, and it isn't too bad in the hands of fairly talented people (which I don't think Carr and Boucher are—certainly not Boucher), is founded on the correct interpretation of clues. Their stock in trade is analysis, deduction, logic, whatever you call it, so they say. And these are the very things their stories can't stand. Invariably, the basic situation is basically implausible; or the characters are faked into situations which they would never get into; or the motivations are switched at the end to provide the denouement; or there is false under or over emphasis; or the essential clue is buried so deep under a mass of trivialities that only a German historian could find it; or else the interpretation takes so much special knowledge that only a scientific freak could evaluate it. A lot of the books are very readable, some are even re-readable, practically all the Freemans and Sayers, for example. But they are readable, not because they are exercises in logic and deduction, but for entirely different values. With people like Carr and Boucher you don't get those different values. I can't find them anyhow. They write dull, colorless prose, and their detectives are obnoxious show-offs, or neat appearing youths in Brooks Brothers clothes and Woolworth brains. There ought to be a few ethics in this reviewing business. If I were offered a book by Mr. John Dickson Carr—supposing I reviewed books at all—would I jump at the chance because I knew I was going dislike it and would have a field day being nasty about it? I'd say no thanks, I'm not the man for this job. I'm prejudiced. A reviewer need not perhaps be as just as Aristides, but he should at least be able to see the good in books he

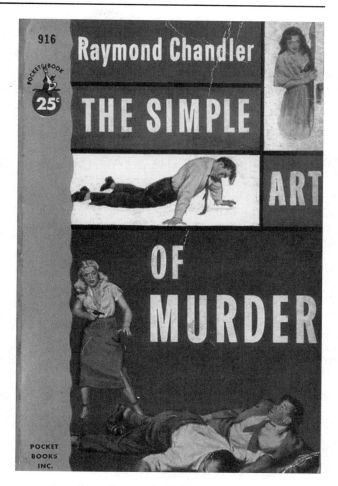

Cover for the first paperback edition, published in 1952

may not personally care for. If the editor of the book section of the TIMES knows the facts and offers the assignment deliberately to somebody who has just got a sharp knife waiting for the author, then the editor of the book section of the TIMES is not an honorable man. Of course that's a silly way to put it. He's most probably some frightened hack who won't have a job if he doesn't pull in enough full-page ads. And of course you publishers back him up. You think space is all that counts. You'd rather have a good review, but a bad one is better than none. A bad one that takes a column is better than a good one that takes a quarter of a column. And for all I know, you may be right. I don't know how much space the TIMES gave to this last job. I think they gave a column to THE LITTLE SISTER. But what I'm wondering is, did they give the space to Mr. John Dickson Carr, or did they give it to me, or did they give it to your full-page ad. Interesting thought, isn't it? God, what a sleazy business newspaper and magazine criticism has become. How many critics could you name whose opinions have any validity above the level of a fireside chat, or a tout for the lending libraries? How many who really know anything about writing beyond the fact that they pooped out at it themselves? How many could you name who could read a page of a man's book and know for sure whether he's a real writer, regardless of his opinions on the current social and political scene? Not very many I'm sure. Look what they've done to the old war horse, Hemingway, and what they've been doing to him for a good many years for that matter. He'd have quit writing a long time ago if he had the faintest suspicion that any of them knew what they were talking about, that they had no spite in their systems, and that they were not sniping at him just because he had made good. Let's face it. One of the penalties of any kind of success is to have the jackals snapping at your heels. They don't hate you because you're bad. They say you're bad because they want to hate you.

Yours always,

Ray

–Houghton Library, Harvard University

In response to Carr's review, several readers wrote letters to the editor of The New York Times Book Review, *defending Chandler's work. Three of these letters, along with Carr's response, were published in the 5 November 1950 issue.*

Detective Stories

TO THE EDITOR:

JOHN DICKSON CARR'S review of Raymond Chandler's "The Simple Art of Murder" is blurred by Carr's gratuitous defense of the kind of writing he does in company with nine-tenths of the detective story writers dependent on the nineteenth century originators and first developers of the form.

The facts would seem to be that Hammett, the first original since the nineteenth century forms were set, came along in the third decade with an awareness of the need for terseness and direct forcefulness similar to that experienced earlier by Pound, Hemingway, or by most other poets attuned to the twentieth century condition.

Chandler followed after Hammett, Hemingway, etc., but perhaps only in his slower comprehension of the twentieth century idiom, gotten as much through experience of today's tensions as from his reading. Compared to Chandler's, Carr's concoctions are unenviable rehashes of the nineteenth century modes hackneyed and hackneyed by unenviable pens. For this reason, he can't see Chandler for his preconception, which renders his perceptions of Chandler's virtues and defects negligible.

WADE DONAHOE.

Washington, D. C.

Sense of Realism

TO THE EDITOR:

ALTHOUGH I have always been an avid detective story fan, I formerly found that the detective story, no matter how clever and diverting, lacked a true sense of realism. Mr. Chandler's appearance was a welcome relief on the scene at a time when Dashiell Hammett seemed to have retired on his laurels and left detecting to a school which had made little, if any, progress beyond the Gold Bug and Sherlock Holmes era.

Mr. Carr is a clever writer in his field. He knows how to build a story around deduction gimmicks and needle-in-the-haystack clue seeking and uses them well. Unfortunately the reader of this type of mystery story is also subjected to page after page of dull reading to get at the eventual conclusion.

It seems that Mr. Chandler's critics, at best, can say only that his cardinal sin is failure to conform to a formula established by Poe and Stevenson. As such, even the severest criticism becomes a point in his favor creatively.

BILL DIEHL.

Atlanta, Ga.

Full of Envy?

TO THE EDITOR:

I THINK It would be easy to show that John Dickson Carr's review of Raymond Chandler's collection of stories is full of envy. Since Mr. Carr generalizes about all of Chandler's writing, and though I am always aware, in reading Chandler, of Hemingway's and Hammett's influences, may I as an ordinary reader point out that I read with intense interest: Simenon, Sayres, "The Lady In the Lake" and "Red Harvest," and cannot, for all my honest attempt, keep from puckering my mind over the insipidity of Carr, Queen and Gardner.

RENE BLANC-ROOS.

Philadelphia, Pa.

A Reply

TO THE EDITOR:

AM I prejudiced? Of course I am: against muddy writing and bad construction. Am I envious? Somehow I think not: few architects would envy a house designed by a fellow-architect who could not be bothered to put in the doors and the windows. Is my own work intolerably bad? Here I cheerfully confess they may be right, as must any writer whose conceit has not burst his hat.

Your correspondents seem to think that the detective story, invented in the nineteenth century, simply sat down and stayed there. * * * Mr. Dona-hoe, for instance, raises the old dismal cry for "terse-ness and direct forcefulness" of style. If he wants to know who really could write a swift, bone-terse, stabbing, colorful style, and in superb English as well, let him turn back to a book of detective short stories named "Uncle Abner," by an American named Melville Davisson Post. Yet "Uncle Abner" was published in 1918, before anybody had even heard of Mr. Hemingway.

JOHN DICKSON CARR.
Mamaroneck, N. Y.

Working on *Strangers on a Train*

At the end of his work on Strangers on a Train *Chandler got into a dispute with Warner Brothers over payment for the final days of his contract. His agents found the argument petty and not worth advancing, but Chandler was highly sensitive to issues of business integrity and was offended by what he considered dishonest treatment. He blamed Ray Stark, Brandt & Brandt's Hollywood representative, for much of the controversy, and as a result Chandler ended his association with Stark and returned to H. N. Swanson for representation in Hollywood. The following letter from Chandler to Finlay McDermid, head of the story department at Warner Brothers, lays out Chandler's complaint against the studio.*

TO FINLAY McDERMID

6005 Camino de la Costa
La Jolla, California
Nov. 2, 1950

Dear Mr. McDermid:

I am a cad not sooner to have made acknowledg-ment of your two letters dated July 7 and August 22. I remember very well the time when you (at the ungodly hour of 9:30 in the morning) conducted me to a projec-tion room where I sat alone and watched *The Big Sleep*. I was trying to do a script on *The Lady in the Lake* for M.G.M. then, and we were very anxious to be sure that we did not imitate any effect which Warners had got in the Howard Hawks' picture.

As to the week for which I did not receive pay-ment working on *Strangers on a Train*, was I a damn fool about that! I had had a touch of food poisoning, incurred in the course of duty at a lunch with Hitch-cock; and for three days I just sat around and gloomed, although I did work the rest of the week including Sat-

urday and Sunday. In fact I worked Saturdays and Sun-days all the time I was on this assignment. What strange delicacy of conscience induced me to give any weight to this, I wonder. It must have been that I thought I was dealing with people as precise as myself in these matters.

When I took this assignment, I was told by Mr. Hitchcock that there was no hurry–no hurry at all; no pressure–no pressure at all. About halfway through it I heard from his factotum that there was a shooting date of October 1, because Mr. Hitchcock had to go East before the leaves fall and he would have to have, or at least very greatly desired, the completed script some little time before that; and that there was even the possibility (although this may have been just talk) that if a page marked "The End" was not received by the studio before October 1, then Mr. Hitchcock might not be allowed to begin shooting. So I, as the phrase is, exerted myself to the full and perhaps a little more than to the full. I completed the script on the evening of Tuesday, September 26, mailed it to you special deliv-ery, and it must have been in your hands early the next day, because early the next day I had a wire from Ray Stark that I was off salary as of Monday night. Inciden-tally, or perhaps not incidentally, I was not paid for Tues-day, September 26. I have raised this point in several places and at several times, and still I am not paid for Tuesday, September 26.

Of course my thought had been that I would be paid for the whole week. In the circumstances surely this would have been only a minimum of decency. I could very easily have kept the work going until the end of the week. Almost any writer you would deal with would have done so. And in view of the way Hol-lywood treats writers, I think he would have been justi-fied in so doing. I am aggrieved about this, Mr. McDermid. I am not particularly greedy for money, but I am greedy for fair treatment.

Are you aware that this screenplay was written without one single consultation with Mr. Hitchcock after the writing of the screenplay began? Not even a telephone call. Not one word of criticism or apprecia-tion. Silence. Blank silence then and since. You are much too clever a man to believe that any writer will do his best in conditions like this. There are always things that need to be discussed. There are always places where a writer goes wrong, not being himself a master of the camera. There are always difficult little points which require the meeting of minds, the accommoda-tion of points of view. I had none of this. I find it rather strange. I find it rather ruthless. I find it almost incom-parably rude. And I think in your heart of hearts you would be very apt to agree with me.

Yours very sincerely,
Raymond Chandler

—Selected Letters of Raymond Chandler, pp. 232–234

One of Chandler's biggest challenges during the writing of Strangers on a Train *was with the essential implausibility of the plot, in which a tennis champion named Guy Haines meets Bruno Anthony on a train. Bruno proposes a plan in which he will murder Guy's estranged wife and Guy, in return, will murder Bruno's father. In his notebooks, Chandler recorded the following notes about the scene where Guy and Bruno meet.*

I nearly went crazy myself trying to block out this scene. I hate to say how many times I did it. It's darn near impossible to write, because consider what you have to put over:

(1) A perfectly decent young man agrees to murder a man he doesn't know, has never seen, in order to keep a maniac from giving himself away and from tormenting the nice young man.

(2) From a character point of view, the audience will not believe the nice young man is going to kill anybody, or has any idea of killing anybody.

(3) Nevertheless, the nice young man has to convince Bruno and a reasonable percentage of the audience that what he is about to do is logical and inevitable. This conviction may not outlast the scene, but it has to be there, or else what the hell are the boys talking about.

(4) While convincing Bruno of all this, he has yet to fail to convince him utterly so that some suspicion remains in Bruno's mind that Guy intends some kind of trick, rather than to go through with it in a literal sense.

(5) All through this scene (supposing it can be written this way) we are flirting with the ludicrous. If it is not written and played exactly right, it will be absurd. The reason for this is that the situation actually is ludicrous in its essence, and this can only be overcome by developing a sort of superficial menace, which really has nothing to do with the business in hand.

(6) Or am I still crazy?

The question I should really like to have answered, although I don't expect an answer to it in this lifetime, is why in the course of nailing the frame of a film together so much energy and thought are invariably expended, and have to be expended, in exactly this sort of contest between a superficial reasonableness and a fundamental idiocy. Why do film stories always have to have this element of the grotesque? Whose fault is it? Is it anybody's fault? Or is it something inseparable from the making of motion pictures? Is it the price you pay for trying to make a dream look as if it really happened? I think possibly it is. When you read a story, you accept its implausibilities and extravagances, because they are no more fantastic than the conventions of the medium itself. But when you look at real people, moving against a real background, and hear them speaking real words, your imagination is anaesthetized. You accept what you see and hear, but you do not complement it from the resources of your own imagination. The motion picture is like a picture of a lady in a half-piece bathing suit. If she wore a few more clothes, you might be intrigued. If she wore no clothes at all, you might be shocked. But the way it is, you are occupied with noticing that her knees are too bony and that her toenails are too large. The modern film tries too hard to be real. Its techniques of illusion are so perfect that it requires no contribution from the audience but a mouthful of popcorn.

Well, what has all this got to do with Guy and Bruno? What a silly question! You shouldn't have asked it. The more real you make Guy and Bruno, the more unreal you make their relationship, the more it stands in need of rationalization and justification. You would like to ignore this and pass on, but you can't. You have to face it, because you have deliberately brought the audience to the point of realizing that what this story is about is the horror of an absurdity become real—an absurdity (please notice because this is very important) which falls just short of being impossible. If you wrote a story about a man who woke up in the morning with three arms, your story would be about what happened to him as a result of this extra arm. You would not have to justify his having it. That would be the premise. But the premise of this story is not that a nice young man might in certain circumstances murder a total stranger just to appease a lunatic. That is the end result. The premise is that if you shake hands with a maniac, you may have sold your soul to the devil.

—Raymond Chandler Speaking, pp. 133–135

Poster for the 1951 movie written by Chandler, Whitfield Cook, Ben Hecht, and Czenzi Ormonde based on Patricia Highsmith's novel

Still from Strangers on a Train; *Farley Granger as Guy Haines and Robert Walker as Bruno Anthony*

The climactic scene from Strangers on a Train, *set on an out-of-control carousel*

Chandler's Critical Standing

By the early 1950s Chandler was aware that he had a much higher critical reputation in England than he did in the United States. The difference between his critical standing in the two countries is reflected in the following two articles, the first an academic article by the American critic Leslie Fielder and the second an appreciation from the British journal The Listener.

Raymond Chandler is, in the field of metaphor, the poor man's Mary McCarthy. It is hard to get past his own notions of what he is doing, especially since he has published in four separate places an essay called "The Simple Art of Murder," in which he claims to have rescued the detective story from commercialism and the "flippers of the trained seals of the critical fraternity"—for "Realism" as defined by Hemingway and Hammett. Taken on his own terms, Mr. Chandler is a little ridiculous in that sentimental, back-room vein that has come to be called "hard-boiled"; but understood as a popular pastoral poet, the creator of a world of the incredibly drunk and lush, and the untiringly nymphomaniac babe, through which the wise-cracking Swain as Private Eye walks to the inevitable beating he so richly deserves, Chandler is unsurpassable. To purvey his sadist pastorals, Chandler has contrived the most successfully atrocious prose style since Lyly's Euphues, but one which, we should realize, does for the reader to whom literature comes flanked by ads, for sure cures for piles and correspondence courses in becoming a detective, the work of poetry. "He looked about as inconspicuous as a tarantula on a slice of angel-food cake."

—Leslie A. Fielder, "Style and Anti-Style in the Short Story," *Kenyon Review,* 13 (Winter 1951): 166–167

* * *

The Whiskey of Affliction
H. A. L. Craig
The Listener (27 September 1951): 513–515

RAYMOND CHANDLER is a man up in the world. His thrillers, instead of going the furnace way of their flesh, might have a cool rest on any respectable shelf. They carry, indeed, their warrant against the fire; the imprimatur of the right authority. There is Elizabeth Bowen (for good taste), J. B. Priestley (for good companions), W. H. Auden, and Edmund Wilson. Already on their dust jackets Raymond Chandler's thrillers begin to entice, not by the silk legs and upset

bodies but by the choosey nodding of the best literary doormen. Mr. Chandler has—the word is *entrée*. For we feel, as the advertisement says of the baby food, that seven royal mothers cannot be wrong.

'Not Escape Literature'
Yet, this high critical opinion has an uneasy turn to it, a glance about, as if it needed to defend itself. Chandler's novels are marked as the exceptions that are literature of a rule that is not. 'His books', Auden says, 'should be judged not as escape literature but as works of art,' and Elizabeth Bowen, in *The Tatler:* 'No consideration of modern American literature ought, I think, to exclude him.' But, however conditional, this praise is still a dainty finger for a very rough neck.

In what he writes Raymond Chandler is neither apart nor original. Far from it. The glossy thriller, like the *bouillabaisse,* must follow its recipe or it is not itself. It is the way that Chandler writes that is original. No man is less lockjawed when it comes to using an image, none more cormorant. Without his images Chandler would be sludged and stuck; they are his way of progress and he pulls himself along by them. Indeed, he seems to have hooks instead of hands, and is forever gaffing up some Swiss-sea fish. Chandler's style is uncompromisingly of the typewriter—the heavy, flailing, office typewriter. His words are flung down and pressed down. His sentences, like the play of the machine, are staccato. Each tap is a separate letter and part of a separate word. They neither run on nor dally with each other, though sometimes they bite back at each other. They have beat, but not enough variation or changing of pace for rhythm. And, still in the abrupt way of the machine, Chandler (almost) does without conjunctions. It is wonderful to be a man and dare to do without conjunctions.

Yet Chandler's style, or rather, his manner of Hemingway and Dashiell Hammett born, is cut well to his subject. There is speed to it, and vitality, and structure. It is a functional style, without ornament, with all the hardness of its Californian glare. Chandler explodes by compression, he can ram a short story into a phrase or cram a man's character into half a line of description—'His faint smile seemed to slide off the end of his long nose'. Chandler's images are nearly all concrete, punched straight at the bag, with none of that elusive quality, that fringiness, of most European imagery. Underneath the neons, Chandler is never very subtle and never tries to be; the pace is wrong for it, and where the hip-pocket holds either a gun, a flask of rye, or the blackmailer's ten grand, the atmosphere is wrong too. But within this atmosphere, an atmosphere so dense that it has swing-doors to it, Chandler wisecracks, sidecracks, and blackjacks as few have done before him. Here even imagination is a form of violence and the image has a cauliflower ear. 'When his chin came

---

Repackaging Chandler

An edition titled Trouble is My Business, *which included five stories, was initially published by Penguin in England in 1950; the Pocket Books edition of the title included four tales—the title story and "Finger Man," Goldfish," and "Red Wind"—and was reprinted three times between 1951 and 1957.* Pick-Up on Noon Street, *originally published by Pocket in January 1952, included the title story and "Smart-Aleck Kill," "Guns at Cyrano's," and "Nevada Gas." This particular printing of the collection was brought out after the publication of* The Long Goodbye *in 1953.*

Covers for two paperback editions of Chandler's stories originally published in the early 1950s

down I hit, hit as if I were driving the last spike of the first continental railway'.

Raymond Chandler's first novel, *The Big Sleep*, established his reputation. That was in 1939. Since then he has published four other novels—*The Lady in the Lake, The High Window, Farewell My Lovely,* and *The Little Sister.* These last four are, in fact, variations on *The Big Sleep,* with one main character throughout, Philip Marlowe, and one scene, Chandler's California, a private world with a private detective in it. For all its pace it is an unchanging world; Marlowe gets no older and no wiser; he does not, like Sherlock Holmes, refer back nor, in the way of Proust, grow back. But this

ungrowth in a detective story or a thriller is part of the game. The big audience of crime want to be given the grace of a little stability, a tune they recognise with the kind of recognition that is ownership. And Philip Marlowe, at the wrong or right end of a gun, is a familiar and a possession. He tells the story in the first person, which leaves him shadowy enough for any reader to inhabit him, with survival assured. But Marlowe, like most 'I' characters, is never seen in the round; he never pauses at a mirror except, perhaps, to leer back at a hangover. And although you may have drunk and driven, cut and thrust your way through five books with him, if you saw him in the street he would be a stranger, while you would nod to every thug or corrupt policeman and know what it feels like to be hit by him.

For, surely enough, in these American crime thrillers the clout has replaced interrogation. Deduction, logic, motive, the, siftings of the orthodox detective story are in abeyance. There is no paper chase of clues, only a stockpile of corpses—and the funnybone, the hunch of the detective. The hunch, indeed, has taken the place of Sherlock Holmes' magnifying glass. So, Philip Marlowe, the detective, does not work by logical deduction. Philip Marlowe, detective, works by mysticism. He doesn't know why he plays a thing the way he does. He just feels like that. And he will play it alone. And alone Philip Marlowe will walk the barefoot way through fire, and drink the whisky of affliction. Raymond Chandler has set up Philip Marlowe; he is the hero of our time, our purification, our redemption, and he is bearing all our guilt in his punch-drunk stagger along some street with a number of L.A., U.S.A., going west. This mysticism of the detective is neither chance nor muddle; it is the awful finger of an unseen. For Raymond Chandler has set up Philip Marlowe.

In a disconcerting statement, in an essay called 'The Simple Art of Murder', Chandler gives his revelation of the detective:

> In everything that can be called art there is a quality of redemption. It may be pure tragedy, if it is high tragedy, and it may be pity and irony, and it may be the raucous laughter of a strong man. But down these mean streets a man must go who is not himself mean, who is neither tarnished nor afraid. The detective in this kind of story must be such a man. He is the hero, he is everything. He must be a complete man and a common man and yet an unusual man. He must be the best man in the world and a good enough man for any world.

And so on. Certainly, it seems that to scratch a tough guy is to find a sentimentalist. The bigger their chests, the more they wobble at the knees. No doubt private detective Marlowe has many things to recommend him above his companions-in-Chandler; he does not hit the women or kick the corpses.

Textbook Case of Love-Hate

But strapped under his arm is the bulge of beauty, the chastening rod of the mean city. The arguments for this contemporary Daniel can only be medieval, Borgian, or perhaps the smugness of the punisher—this hurts me more than it hurts you. Indeed, in point of masochism, Chandler is away on his own. His chosen hero achieves his mission at the cost of a tooth a book, bruises galore, and lumps on him like a dozen of eggs. Some of these manhandlings

are suffered in encounters with the official authority, the police with whom the detective figure has a relation as curious and as complicated as a love affair. His role is feminine: he half tells, half conceals, half promises, taunts, and eludes; he plays his lone hand, but in the end he capitulates. It is a textbook case of ambivalence, of love-hate. And as such it is important—the noblest estate of the heart—the only love in Chandler. There is lust and desire and fond violence, but no love. The soft moment, when it occurs at all, is sentimental and embarrassing. It lies too shallow for tears. The redemption that Chandler is so grand about is, after all, a self-deception—for how can there be redemption without love? As for the way of a private detective with a maid, it is to solicit her advances and then to slap her down. Marlowe among the girls is just a great big tease. But who would blame him, since, in these books, Chandler is so savage about women: they are bitches, man-eaters, spiders, drunks., nymphomaniacs and, of course, murderers. They are armed with teeth and pearly revolvers.

But alongside these figures of melodrama there are also real characters in Chandler, though mostly the riff-raff of the plot—the liftboy in a hotel, the girl in a shop, the landlady in the doorway, the moral rearmament cop. They are authentic, living their bewildered lives among the grandees of crime. They give the background and the power to these novels, and the realism that Chandler believes to be the intention of all fiction. But though all Chandler's people look different, they all sound the same—for the lingo of the wisecrack has about as many nuances as the ticking of a clock. It is a case of I know my love by his way of walking, but never by his way of talking. Nor have Chandler's characters a way of thinking. Their author's talent is visual and external; he is under the restriction of the visual, and the unseen remains unsaid. But what Chandler does see, he says brilliantly. If he cannot fill in his characters, he can certainly fill in the walls behind them. Out of his catalogue descriptions, his inventories and lists, he makes an atmosphere that has more tension and excitement than his brittle plots.

Chandler's claim that his novels are realistic—set out rather truculently in 'The Simple Art of Murder'—is a curious piece of self-justification. Indeed this claim for realism in the contemporary thriller is the counterpart of the moral pretensions that went with the Victorian thrills—'I know it's ugly, but I can't help it, it's true'—as though fact could disinfect the imagination. But is it so true? Murders do happen. There is violence, revenge, and cruelty beyond its third degree. But these, in life, do not have the density, the lavish concentration, that they have in

Chandler's childless world—even though every tusky gangster should lumber in to die in the graveyard of Bay City. It is not life. It is not realism. It is the romanticism of destruction, the 'nostalgia for mud'. The corpse becomes an exclamation mark not a question mark; and the killing is a kind of existentialist, wanton act. The logic, the motive are gone. You do not get a gun in order to shoot somebody: you just shoot somebody because you happen to be carrying a gun. The finger whitens on the trigger, and that is that.

But in this plethora of killings a saturation point is soon reached and, indeed, Chandler's novels themselves demonstrate the law of diminishing returns. He never wrote a better book than the first one you read. Yet the *rigor mortis* of the thriller-formula does not spread along every limb of this most curious D.P. of a writer; he is too full of the snap and sting of language to be ever entirely stiff. He has too many surprises of phrase to moulder, too many images to grow stale. Yes, Raymond Chandler is alive and monarch of his no man's land of literature, and he keeps a whisky state.

Fantastic Tales

As his income from past works grew more secure, Chandler was able to devote more of his writing time to non-mystery projects. He had a particular interest in fantastic stories—tales that were told realistically except for a magical plot twist such as teleportation or invisibility. As early as 1939 Chandler had planned to collect these stories into a book, but magazine publishers showed little interest in the tales and he never completed enough to make a book. Only two of these stories, "The Bronze Door" (Unknown, November 1939) and "Professor Bingo's Snuff" (Park East in June 1951), were published, and most critics have ignored them. In a 31 October letter to his friend James Sandoe, Chandler discussed "Professor Bingo's Snuff."

Anyhow I had fun writing the story, although it didn't turn out quite the way I expected. I started out to do a burlesque on the locked room mystery and somewhere along the line I lost interest in the burlesque angle and became preoccupied with the thought that a miracle is always a trap. As you know, good fantastic stories are extremely rare, and they are rare for a rather obvious reason, that in them it is almost impossible to turn the corner. Once you have exposed the situation, you have nowhere to go.

—Selected Letters of Raymond Chandler, p. 296

Cover of the first issue of Fantastic *magazine (Summer 1952), which reprinted Chandler's short story "Professor Bingo's Snuff," in which the gift of magical snuff that makes one invisible leads a man to murder*

Worries and Reflections

In 1951 Chandler had begun work on his next novel, which was published in 1953 as The Long Goodbye, *but he was distracted by the poor health of his wife, which he discussed in a letter to Hamish Hamilton.*

6005 Camino de la Costa
La Jolla, California
October 5th. 1951

Dear Jamie:

. . . .

I do hope to have a book in 1952, I hope very hard. But dammit I have a great deal of trouble getting on with it. The old zest is not there. I am worn down by worry over my wife, and that is why I am writing this myself and keeping no copy. We have a big house, rather, hard to take care of, and the help situation is damn near hopeless. For months after we lost our last cook, Cissy wore herself out trying to get someone, to endure what we got, to give up and start again. We cannot live here without help. Cissy can do very very little, she has lost a lot of ground in the last two years. She is a superb cook herself and we are both pretty much overfastidious, but we can't help it. I have thought that the sensible thing might be to get a small house and do for ourselves, but I'm afraid she is no longer capable even of that. When I get into work I am already tired and dispirited. I wake in the night with dreadful thoughts. Cissy has a constant cough which can only be kept down by drugs and the drugs destroy her vitality. It is not TB nor is it anything cancerous, but I am afraid it is chronic and may get worse instead of better. She has no strength and being of a buoyant disposition and a hard fighter, she fights herself to the point of exhaustion. I dread, and I am sure she does, although we try not to talk about it, a slow decline into invalidism. And what happens then I frankly do not know. There are people who enjoy being invalids, being unable to do anything, but not she. She hates hospitals, she hates nurses, and she does not greatly love doctors. In bad moods, which are not too infrequent, I feel the icy touch of despair. It is no mood in which to produce writing with any lift and vitality.

You say nice things about what I write and I know you mean them, but I have never felt important as a writer. In every generation there are incomplete writers, people who never seem to get much of them-

selves down on paper, men whose accomplishment seems always rather incidental. Often, but not always, they have begun too late and have an overdeveloped critical sense. Sometimes they just lack the necessary ruthlessness and think other people's lives as important as their own, other people's happiness more essential than the expression of their own personalities, if any. I guess maybe I belong in there. I have enough material success to see through it, and not enough sense of destiny to feel that what I do matters a great deal.

Don't think I worry about money, because I don't. There are always ways to make money if you really need it. I rather envy people who think art and literature worth any sacrifice, but I don't seem to feel that way. My salute to posterity is a thumb to the end of the nose and the fingers outspread. Publishers read too many critics, in the course of business, naturally. And just who are the critics after all? People of small accomplishment, mostly, whose dignity in life depends on the perpetuating of a set of artificial values conceived by other critics who were also people of small accomplishment. My standards are too high for me to admire the successful hacks very much, and too unorthodox for me to care what the pundits say. Also, I have blind spots. I admit it. I think your Nancy Mitford is probably a charming and clever woman but the stuff means nothing to me. The wit is not real, the satire is not of the vintage year, the whole performance tries to be something it is not capable of being. An absolutely trivial writer, but you don't agree and you shouldn't. This is strange (that I feel that way) because as a rule I admire the good second-raters, like Marquand and Irwin Shaw and Herman Wouk, etc. I like to read them and *while* I read them they seem very good. It is only afterwards that the quality fades. Same for Nicholas Montserrat. Or Priestley. Essentially one good chunk of Flaubert or Hemingway at their best is worth the whole pack of them. I had almost said Faulkner, but I think he is overrated. Well, all this matters nothing, except that a writer to be happy should be a good second-rater, not a starved genius like Laforgue. Not a sad lonely man like Heine, not a lunatic like Dostoevski. He should definitely not be a mystery writer with a touch of magic and a bad feeling about plots.

We still hope for "Europe in the spring," but is it more than hope now? Anyhow, Churchill will be in and I hope he doesn't make an ass of himself. These great men can be awfully silly in their dotage. It doesn't show in the rest of us. Nobody is looking.

I look upon you as a dear friend, Jamie. I am sorry to be such a depressing bore.

Ray
—*Selected Letters of Raymond Chandler,* pp. 291–293

Chandler on Agents

In February 1952 The Atlantic Monthly *published "Ten Percent of Your Life," Chandler's essay on literary agents. Though he made an effort to be balanced in his treatment, much of the essay reflects Chandler's complaints against Sydney Sanders, his first New York agent, and Ray Stark, his former Hollywood representative.*

Ten Percent of Your Life
Raymond Chandler
The Atlantic Monthly, 189 (February 1952): 48–51

1

AMONG all those quasi-professional businesses which like to refer to their customers as clients the business of literary agenting is probably the most enduring and the most adhesive. Technically, you can fire your agent; it is a sticky operation, but a determined man can achieve it. It really ends nothing. Year after you speak to him you will, if you are a writer for publication, be finding mud tracks across the carpet. He will have been there in the night doing what he calls "representing" you, and you will wake up in the morning with that tired feeling as if a Doberman pinscher had been sleeping on your chest. It was probably only a little old foreign book royalty that he nibbled at, a trivial matter in dollars and cents. But the nibbling goes on forever. Long after your agent has been gathered to his fathers, you may be paying commissions to his estate on some transaction with which he had hardly any contact, something purely automatic that arose out of something else long before.

There is nothing wrong with this. It is the way the agent gets his pay. But writers as a class are apt to be a cantankerous and not particularly lovable set of people; they have the egotism of actors without either the good looks or the charm. However much they are paid, they never think they are paid enough. They resent it that other people make money out of the work that they, the writers, do alone and unaided. The agent creates for himself a vested interest in the writer's entire professional career. However much you pay him, he is never paid off. He may collect a very large amount of money for what is essentially a very routine service. And of course you forget all that he does for which he receives no payment at all. What really galls you on the raw is not how much commission the agent collects, but that the account is never closed. The agent never receipts his bill, puts his hat on and bows himself out.

He stays around forever, not only for as long as you can write anything that anyone will buy, but as long as anyone will buy any portion of any right to anything that you ever did write. He just takes ten per cent of your life.

Perhaps the sensible thing is to get it over with and admit that throughout the history of commercial life nobody has ever quite liked the commission man. His function is too vague, his presence always seems one too many, his profit looks too easy, and even when you admit that he has a necessary function, you feel that this function is, as it were, a personification of something that in an ethical society would not need to exist. If people could deal with one another honestly, they would not need agents. The agent creates nothing, he manufactures nothing, he distributes nothing. All he does is cut himself a slice off the top. Possibly there are agents who dislike the commission method of payment as much as the most contentious writer, and would gladly change it into something else, if there were anything else to change it into. The writing profession itself is far too speculative and uncertain to permit of any system of fixed fees for the selling of its products. The struggling writer simply wouldn't have the money to pay the bill, and the successful one would very rapidly become aware that what he was charged was more nearly determined by the size of his income than by the amount of time and effort that went into the service rendered to him. That is obviously true of professions much more strictly administered than agency. Furthermore, the agent did not invent the percentage method of payment, nor does he monopolize it. He has a lot of company, including various taxing authorities and including the writer himself if he is a writer of books, since royalties are merely commissions by another name.

Perhaps the three most valuable attributes of an agent are his emotional detachment from a very emotional profession, his ability to organize the bargaining power of his clients, and his management of the business side of a writer's career. As to the first of these, I do not suggest that the agent is callous or hard-boiled, but merely that he is, and has to be, realistic in a thoroughly commercial sense. If you do a bad job, he will not tell you it is good; he will merely suggest its badness in the nicest possible way.

Next, the agent creates and maintains a competitive atmosphere without which the prices paid for literary material would be a mere fraction of what they are today. In Hollywood, where this is carried to its extreme limits, literary material is offered simultaneously to the entire market, and an offer received from one prospective purchaser is immediately used as a basis for needling all the others. The New York

FEBRUARY

ATLANTIC

Ninety-four years of continuous publication

VOLUME 189   1952   NUMBER 2

Reports: Hungary — Washington — The Soviet Family

Cover portrait of Governor Stevenson by Henry Kurt Stoessel

1 YEAR $6.00   2 YEARS $11.00   3 YEARS $16.00

THE ATLANTIC MONTHLY, February, 1952, Vol. 189, No. 2. Published monthly. Publication Office, 10 Ferry Street, Concord, N. H. Editorial and General Offices, 8 Arlington St., Boston 16, Mass. 50 cents a copy, $6.00 a year. Unsolicited manuscripts should be accompanied by return postage. Entered as second-class matter July 15, 1918, at the Post Office at Concord, N.H., under the Act of March 3, 1879. Printed in the U.S.A., by Rumford Press, Concord, N.H. Copyright 1952, by The Atlantic Monthly Company. All rights, including translation into other languages, reserved by the Publisher in the United States, Great Britain, Mexico, and all countries participating in the International Copyright Convention and the Pan-American Copyright Convention.

Table of contents of the February 1952 issue of The Atlantic Monthly, *which included Chandler's essay on literary agents*

literary agent has not carried the system this far; the book and magazine publishers still insist that what is offered to them for sale, while they consider it, shall for the time being be offered to no one else. The rule is not absolute; there are various genteel ways of evading it without causing too much acrimony. The more powerful the magazine, the more rigidly it can enforce the rule. But however rigidly it is enforced, the editor considering material submitted by an agent is aware that the agent knows the going price; the editor's offer must come within trading distance of this, or the material will be withdrawn. The agent knows how to say no without slamming the door. He can take risks, because his risks are averaged. And if, as I suppose occasionally happens, he loses a sale by pressing too hard, the client will never know why he lost it. There will always be another reason.

2

The truly commanding reason for any writer to deal through an agent nowadays is the enormous complexity of the literary business. A writer operating alone, even with the assistance of a secretary, would be so snowed under by correspondence and paper work, filing and digesting contracts, so confused by the ramifications of copyright, that either he wouldn't know where he stood or he wouldn't have any time left for writing. Many very successful writers have only the foggiest notion of what, legally and contractually speaking, has happened to the products of their brains. They don't know the elements of the financial side of their business. They don't know what they own, what they have sold, whom they have sold it to, nor on what terms, nor when the payments are due, nor whether in fact payments that are past due have been received. They trust their agents to took after all that and take what their agents send them without scrutiny or mistrust.

Such people would be very easy to swindle, and it is a high tribute to the agency profession that with so many suckers to deal with, so few agents have ever been caught doing anything dishonest. If the ethical standards of agency are declining, and I think they are, and I think it is inevitable that they should, it is remarkable that their dollars-and-cents honesty in dealing with their clients has so seldom been attacked. The decline I mentioned is not a question of individuals stealing money, but of something in the nature of a personal service profession turning into a hard-boiled business, and a pretty big business at that.

The old-line literary agent still exists, but he is slipping. He was a pretty useful fellow. In addition to his obvious functions of knowing markets and prices and having the tenacity to go through a long list of them before giving up, he acted as a clearing house for information. He was a postoffice, and he was a buffer. He guarded the writer in many matters of detail in connection with contracts and the sale of subsidiary rights. He gave fairly sound business advice. In those somewhat rare cases where he had the ability to recognize quality beyond mere salability, he encouraged and helped the writer to improve himself in his profession. If he made mistakes, they were usually not too costly, because his operations, taken one at a time, were rather modest. As a Hollywood operator of my acquaintance put it, "Those boys bring their lunch." The literary agent collected money, forwarded royalty reports, and kept the writer's affairs in some kind of order. Most writers were quite satisfied with this service.

This kind of agent, if I may say so without rancor, had inevitable faults, some of which were the price of his virtues. He was always persuading his writers to adapt themselves to the big smooth-paper magazines in which a few genuine talents have survived but far more have perished. The reason was not discreditable, since the agent had no security of tenure and demanded no contract for a term of years. If he wished to make money out of you, he would naturally try to channel your talents into the most immediately lucrative field. It would have been unfair to expect him to realize that this was not in the long run the most lucrative field for every writer. If he did realize this, the agent had no guarantee that he would be around when the long run paid off. He read himself half blind in a search for salable material and for talent which he might with good luck build into a money-making capacity; at which point some Hollywood agent would be very apt to steal it from him.

Another of his faults was that he took in rather too much territory. He demanded the right to represent you in fields which he did not understand and could not properly cover: motion picture, radio, television, the stage, and the lecture platform. In these he would make split-commission deals with specialists where he had to, but he would rather not, because he needed the money. When he did make split-commission deals, he was apt to select a second-rate practitioner not powerful enough to steal his client. This could, and did, result in serious mishandling of his client's interest. But against his faults must be set one commanding virtue: he spent a large part of his time and effort in the service of unknowns whose aggregate commissions would not pay his office rent. And he did so in the sure and certain knowledge that if and when they became known and successful, they were quite likely to slam the door in his face without so much as a thank you.

This type of agent has gradually been driven towards the fringes of his profession because of the same complexities which forced the working writer to have an agent in the first place. If the agent has the resource and ability to avoid this fate, he will be forced into a much more elaborate organization, and into a system of alliances with the high pressure specialists who operate in the other media to which writers contribute either directly or by the adaptation of their material to other forms. To stay even with these boys, the agent has to spend money and look as if he had it to spend. He has to have competent help and adequate space in a good office building. His life becomes expensive. His long distance telephone bills cost him as much as his entire overhead used to cost. And as his overhead rises, his availability to new or unknown writers decreases. He can still recognize talent without a name, but it takes an awful lot of it to convince him that he can afford the slow, expensive toil of a build-up. He will still, for sound reasons, handle a prestige writer who isn't making much money. But if you are just a promising beginner scratching a meager living from the tired soil, he will send you a polite note of regret. He can afford to wait until you have made a name, because when you do you will have to come to him anyway.

So, whether he likes it or not, the beginner will be forced to accept the services of a small agent as unsure and almost as uninformed as himself. Or he may even fall into the clutches of one of those racketeers of hope, calling themselves agents, whose real income is from reading fees and from such charges as they can impose on their "clients" for editing and revising work which any reputable commission man would know in the beginning to be hopeless.

The point about the small agent who is genuinely an agent is precisely that he is small. You take him only because you cannot get someone bigger and better. You know it, and he knows it. You will stay with him only as long as you cannot do better, and he will keep you as a client only as long as you are unimportant. There is no loyalty because there is no permanence. From the first your relationship with him will he ambiguous. And yet in later years, if you are what is known as successful, you may look back on this small agent with a touch of nostalgia. He was a simple fellow, insecure like yourself. A twenty dollar commission meant a lot to him, because he needed the money, and he couldn't afford to take chances. That story he sold to a pulp magazine might, with a little careful polishing, have made *Cosmopolitan* or *Red Book*. But the big market was a gamble, and here was a pulp magazine with money in its hand, and the agent's secretary bothering him for something on account of her overdue salary.

You didn't blame him and wouldn't have, even if you had known what was in his mind. You needed the money too. Besides, you rather liked the guy. More often than not he typed his own letters, just as you had to, and they were nice warm encouraging letters. In a simpler world you and he might have been good friends. But of course he could never have got you that deal with MGM.

3

This brings me, not too eagerly, to the orchid of the profession—the Hollywood agent—a sharper, shrewder, and a good deal less scrupulous practitioner. Here is a guy who really makes with the personality. He dresses well and drives a Cadillac—or someone drives it for him. He has an estate in Beverly Hills or Bel-Air. He has been known to own a yacht, and by yacht I don't mean a cabin cruiser. On the surface he has a good deal of charm, because he needs it in his business. Underneath he has a heart as big as an olive pit. He deals with large sums of money. His expenses are tremendous. He will buy you a meal at Romanoff's or Chasen's with no more hesitation than is necessary for him to tot up the commissions he has made out of you in the last six months. He controls expensive talent, since with rare exceptions he is not exclusively an agent for writers. This gives him prestige in dealing with people who are starved for talent in spite of having a great deal of money to buy it with.

He is rough and tough and he doesn't care who knows it. He may think up an entirely new kind of deal and put it over in the face of great opposition. He will seldom make a bad deal for fear of not making any deal at all. His prestige as a negotiator is at stake, and he is not moved by the consideration of earning a commission to the extent that he will allow himself to he beaten in a trade. He operates in a hard world.

The Hollywood agent pays a big price for his ability and toughness as a trader. He is a huckster of talent, but talent as such he seldom respects or even understands. He is concerned solely with its market value. Quality does not interest him, only the price tag. Even within the narrow limits of his own activities, he cannot tell the good from the bad, merely the expensive from the cheap. He scurries around the studios and the restaurants and the night clubs, his cars reaching for gossip and his eyes always restlessly seeking some new or important face. It is a part of his business to know what is going on, since many of his most successful operations have depended on a piece of inside information which was in effect nothing more than back-stairs gossip. If a studio wants to buy something, he must know why and for what purpose and on whose instructions, and whether the front office negotiator has a blank check or has been ordered not to purchase unless purchase is cheap.

No writer operating in his own interest could deal with this situation, even if the structure of the motion picture industry would allow him to, which it will not, because in Hollywood deals are made by word of mouth even though the elaborate contracts which embody them may take weeks to write. When made they must be final, although legally either party can withdraw up to the moment the contract is signed. To achieve finality the reputation and word of an agent must be involved. In the lush days of Hollywood there is no question but that many agents made far too much money. Ten per cent on the sale of a piece of literary property might be fair enough, but ten per cent of the salary earned during a seven-year employment contract came pretty close to larceny.

Since the same hard-boiled way of doing things prevailed in radio and prevails now in television, it was only natural that the once personal, kindly, and intimate relationship between an author and his commission man became a question of dealing more or less at arm's length with someone you never entirely trusted and often did not trust at all. The fat profits to be made in Hollywood and in radio brought a new kind or operator into the business—a sharpshooter with few scruples, whose activities spread over the whole field of entertainment. The law allowed him to incorporate, which, in my opinion, was a fatal mistake. It destroyed all semblance of the professional attitude and the professional responsibility to the individual client. It permitted a variety of subtle maneuvers whereby the agent could make a great deal more money after taxes, and it allowed him to slide, almost unobserved, into businesses which had nothing to do with agency. He could create packaging corporations which delivered complete shows to the networks or the advertising agencies, and he loaded them with talent which, sometimes under another corporate name, he represented as an agent. He took his commission for getting you a job, and then he sold the job itself for an additional profit. Sometimes you knew about this, sometimes you didn't. In any case the essential point was that this operator was no longer an agent except in name. His clients and their work became the raw material of a speculative business. He wasn't working for you, you were working for him. Sometimes he even became your employer and paid you a salary which he called an advance on future commissions. The agency part of his operations was still the basic ingredient, since without control of talent, he had no bricks to build his wall, but the individual meant nothing to him. The individual was just merchandise, and the "representing" of the individual was little more than a department of an entertainment trust—a congeries of powerful organizations which existed solely to exploit the commercial value of talent in every possible direction and with the utmost possible disregard for artistic or intellectual values.

Such trusts, and it is fair to call them that regardless of whether they meet an exact legal definition, cover the whole field of entertainment. Their clients include actors, singers, dancers, mouth organ players, trainers of chimpanzees and performing dogs, people who ride horses over cliffs or jump out of burning buildings, motion picture directors and producers, musical composers, and writers in every medium including those quaint old-fashioned productions known as books. These organizations maintain publicity departments, travel bureaus, hotel reservation facilities, and for a small additional commission (or perhaps for none if you are important enough to them) they will manage your private business affairs, keep your books, make out your income tax returns, and get you your next divorce. Of course you don't have to become their client, but the inducements are glittering. And if they reduce you to a robot, as eventually they will, they will usually be very pleasant about it, because they can always afford to employ well-dressed young men who smile and smile.

Old-line New York literary agents can hardly look forward with pleasure to the prospect of becoming department managers in some big, impersonal industry whose only motivating force is the fast buck. They have been for the most part serious and reputable people. Nevertheless, they have to eat, and preferably high on the joint where the meat is tasty. To do this, they must deal with the entertainment industry and with the talent trusts that feed it. And you can't deal with sharpers without becoming a little of a sharper yourself. The more distinguished practitioners may be able to keep their independence for a time; they may still deal scrupulously with their clients as individuals; they may still be the spark of successful and even distinguished literary careers. But the talent trusts are snapping at their heels in greed for commissions and in their desire for the control and manipulation of every ingredient that the increasingly vast entertainment industry must use. Where the money is, there will the jackals gather, and where the jackals gather something usually dies.

Probably the literary agents do not agree with my gloom. Having dealt in the past on fairly level terms with the big publishing combines and with the predatory but always uncertain and bewildered moguls of Hollywood, they think they can still deal on level terms with any and all concentrations of power. Naturally, I hope the agents are right. I pray they may be right. Any working writer who does otherwise is either an imbecile or already corrupted beyond repair.

6.
The Last Years, 1952–1959:
The Long Goodbye and *Playback*

A First Draft

In spring 1952 Chandler completed and sent a draft of
The Long Goodbye, *his most ambitious and longest novel, to*
Bernice Baumgarten in New York.

Raymond Chandler
6005 Camino de la Costa
La Jolla, California

May 14 1952

Dear Bernice:

I'm sending you today, probably by air express, a draft of a story which I have alled THE LONG GOODBYE. It runs 92,000 words. I'd be happy to have your comments and objections and so on. I haven't even read the thing,except to make a few corrections and check a number of details that my secretary queried. So I am not sending you any opinion on the opus. You may find it slow going.

It has been clear to me for some time that what is largely boring about mystery stories, at least on a literate plane, is that the characters get lost about a third of the way through. Often the opening, the mise en scene, the establishment of the background, is very good. Then the plot thickens and the people become mere names. A very good example of this is a current workncalled FIGURE by my friend Harry Kurnits, (Marco Page.) It begins so well, but RECLINING) in the end it is the same old hash. Well, what can you do to avoid this? You can write constant action and that is fine if you really enjoy it. But alas, one grows up, one becomes complicated and unsure, one becomes interested in moral dilemmas, rather than who cracked who on the head.And at that point perhaps one should retire and leave the field too younger and more simple men. I don't necessarily mean writers of comic books like Mickey Spillane.

Chandler in 1952

Anyhow I wrote this as I wanted to because I can do that now. I didn't care whether the mystery was fairly obvious, but I cared about the people, about this strange corrupt world we live in, and how any man who tried to be honest looks in the end either sentimental or plain foolish. Enough of that. There are more practical reasons. You write in a style that has been imitated, even plagiarised, to the point where you begin to look as if you were imitating your imitators. So you have to go where they can't follow you. The danger is that the reader won't either.

I promised Jamie a script about the middle of this month, but this did not mean submitting a script to him. It meant only a look at it so that he could see whether he was satisfied to go ahead. But of course I won't do anything to bother you. But please let him have a copy as soon as you can, with the understanding that the stuff may be revised quite a little, and that it could not go into print in any case except for corrected proof. They made some perfectly idiotic mistakes in The Little Sister. I'll write to him about it.

As to the Ballantine project I haven't figured it out yet. Have you? How ca n a publisher like HM put out a book for $1.50 or $2? Where do they make their money? What will the paper backs look like? Will they be subject to the same idiotic flaw in distribution as the current lot? By this I mean that in the end the guy who actually puts the books on the various display stands knows absolutely nothing about his merchandise. Say he puts out ten copies of a book and next week when he comes by seven of them are left. He decides it is a space-waster, leaves three copies, and when they are gone, does not replace them. A fellow I know, a druggist and magazine and paper book handler, gripes about it all the time. He says people are continually asking for books he hasn't got and feels he should have. The didn't sell fast enough to suit the distributor's man and there was always new stuff coming along. And the distributor's man, the ultimate judge of what is worth displaying, goes by quick turnover and nothing else. The retailer has nothing to say about it. He knows he can't have every book that someone might want and even ask for, but he also knows that the choice of what he has is not based on any principle he can understand. In the aggregate an enormous amount of business is being lost because the stuff is not available, but I don't presume to suggest how it can be changed. Perhaps stock lists ought to be posted. The Signet people send out mail order lists, but I don't know how many people actually bother to send them .30 for a quarter book. A great many don't take the trouble, think they'll pick it up somewhere else.

Yours ever,

Ray

—transcribed from original document, Houghton Library, Harvard University, bMS Am 1925 (347)

Baumgarten wrote to Chandler with Carl Brandt's and her reaction to the story and with suggestions for revisions.

May 22, 1952

airmail

Mr. Raymond Chandler
Box 128
La Jolla, California

Dear Ray:

Carl and I were immediately struck by the change in pace in THE LONG GOODBYE. The advantages are obvious, an opportunity for real characterization—exploration of character and the psychological reasons for the actions of your characters—and some of your best writing.

Both of us read it with complete attention, Carl at a single sitting.

Our only real concern was the change in Marlowe himself. His hardness was his great virtue and here he seems to have become almost Christlike. You put with great understanding his necessarily friendless state, and the great value he sets on having made a friend who wants nothing of him, but still we don't recognize the Marlowe we thought we knew. I can understand his being deeply moved by an unaccustomed friendship but I can't believe in him as a sentimentalist. We feel that Marlowe would suspect his own softness all the way through and deride it andhimself constantly.

Beyond this one important point, there are some minor things. Carl felt that there were too many beautiful woman, probably one too many. It would have been a relief to him to have one of them not beautiful but still tremendously attractive.

Why is Terry impotent? There does not seem to be any important reason in the story for this. It would have been much more reasonable to suspect him of killing Elaine if he were not impotent. We have to believe that underneath everything Terry's motive was to protect Eileen and since Eileen is really represented as frigid, the fact that he came back from the war impotent wouldn't have made her discard him. Indeed it's never quite clear why she would not take him back. Was she already married to Wade?

About Eileen. Why does she use the Peter Manning lure so blatantly? She was a clever woman and the pass she makes at Marlowe by the Peter Manning device is at all times deliberate. Therefore it must not be overdone, and would only be tried

Raymond Chandler

May 21, 1952

Corrections to be made on Copy 1 of THE LONG GOODBYE

✓Page 11, line 3--should read "into the police <u>car</u> and the--"

✓57, second line from end--gr<u>ay</u> suit, not gr<u>ey</u>

✓58, # 3, last line--be sure last sentence is "They chewed my
     tail off." Also second line from end of page--
     "They chewed my tail off." On page 58, line
     2--"They chew your tail off." 59
    (I think all these corrections were made on Copy 1)

✓72, last line--to paste in my scrapbook (not into)

✓73--next to last line--I didn't judge him or analyze hi<u>m</u> (not s)

✓88--Mark letter from Terry to be set in italics--no quotation marks.

✓96--line 12--push buttons should be two words

✓120--line 6--next to last word--change "The way he" to "The <u>road</u> he"

✓147--# 6, line 1--should be Dr. Vujanich

✓154--# 6--should be clo<u>th</u>es (not clothese)

✓165 line 4, second word from end end of #--should be for n<u>o</u>t four

✓183--# 2 should end "I shut it again and went back to my desk."
    (Eliminate remainder of #. I think this was done on
    original, but may not be quite correct. Paragraph
    ends as indicated on copy 2, enclosed.

✓191--line 2--word 7, should be here not her. "We never do
    any introducing around here."

✓194--line 2, third word from end of line--I've (not Ive)

✓196--# 7, last word in paragraph should be <u>that</u>. "But how
    could I be sure of that?"

✓232--line five--name is Juan Salvador <u>Garcia</u> de Soto y Sotomayor
    (Add Garcia)

✓233--line 12--last word is hi<u>m</u> (not his)

✓237--# 2, line 12, comma after bronze; line 13 comma after all
    (should be solid bronze, base and all, and heavy.

✓238--line 7--"The mystery was solved." (not They)

✓239--line 8--comma after event. (Should be In the event, I didn't--"

✓244--line 1--last two words should be "What's her" (not What her)
    (This may have been corrected.0

Chandler's corrections for a draft of his sixth novel (Bodleian Library, Oxford University)

RAYMOND CHANDLER
Mailing Address: Box 128   60.05 Camino de la Costa · La Jolla, California

May 29, 1952

Mr. Paul Brooks
Houghton Mifflin Company
2 Park Street
Boston 7, Mass.

Dear Mr. Brooks:

        Thanks very much for sending me your piece from
THE ATLANTIC. As it happens I read it when it originally
appeared, although I did not then know who you were. As
for my article on agents to which you referred and mentioned
that some New York agent was sputtering about it, well I
don't see what he had to sputter at. I think I let the
agents down pretty easy, much more easily than I should do
if I were writing the article now. Anyhow Charlie Morton
had to cut about two thousand words out of my original article, and the son of a bitch cut out some of the juiciest
parts. The idiotic thing about agents is that nobody likes
them, nobody wants them, and they don't really do their job
in all sorts of ways. Yet everybody is afraid to offend
them, including publishers and editors of considerable power
and prestige.

        I have a book finished. As a matter of fact I
actually sent it to Brandt & Brandt, and Bernice Baumgarten
wanted to show it to Dale Warren. But she made a number of
criticisms of it, which caused me to withdraw it for revision.
I am not sure I agree with any of her comments, and a couple
of them strike me as just plain silly. But the only thing
to do in a case like that is to put the thing aside for
awhile until you get perspective.

        I hope you have had a pleasant European trip.
We rather thought of going ourselves in the fall by boat
through the Canal, but it seems that we cannot get a reservation before September, if then, and September would be
just a month too late. So I guess it will have to go over
until next spring.

                With kindest regards,

                                              Yours very truly,

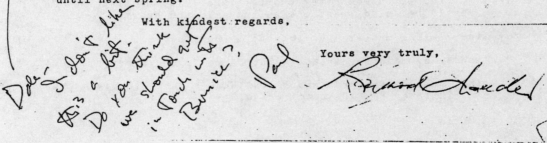

Letter from Chandler to Paul Brooks, president of Houghton Mifflin, announcing his decision to withdraw the draft of The Long Goodbye. *Brooks's handwritten comment in the margin reads, "Dale—I don't like this a bit. Do you think we should get in touch with Bernice?"*
(Houghton Library, Harvard University)

on at moments of great emotional strain for her. As we now have it, the reader begins to believe that Eileen is probably slightly mad and therefore immediately suspects that she must be the murderess.

It is not clear to us why Marlowe warmed to Wade. While Marlowe is attracted to Eileen, he seems to understand perfectly that she is driving Wade crazy but that one thing is surely not enough to arouse his sympathy. We never do know how Linda came to marry the dreadful little Doctor. With all that money and all that background it seems incredible.

Also, it's never clear whether the two racketeers are working for the girl's father or simply on their own. Is it possible that the old man himself was backing both the gambling setups?

Was Eileen really attracted to Candy or did she marry him because he was blackmailing her? We are never quite sure in the book whether Candy is faithful to Wade or to Eileen or is perfectly happy to betray them both.

Also, why shouldn't we know whether Terry really committed suicide and whether Eileen really murdered Elaine. I don't see that we gain anything by putting this into the lady or the tiger category.

One small thing which puzzled me because I think you did it deliberately. On page 6 Terry says to Marlowe "I don't remember where we met or how I got here." But on Page 11 he says "I never black out and I never forget." Was he lying the first time?

Carl thinks serial is uncertain, but of course he wants to show the manuscript. And I am very eager to have Houghton Mifflin's reaction. May I send this up to Dale now?

As ever,
Bernice

BB:SH

—transcribed from original document, Bodleian Library, Oxford University

Though in his cover letter he had asked his agents for their "comments and suggestions" on the draft of The Long Good-bye *and implied that the story needed considerable work, Chandler believed the novel was complete except for some minor polishing. Baumgarten's and Brandt's criticism of the draft came as a shock. As soon as he received Baumgarten's letter, he sent a telegram to his agents that read, "PLEASE RETURN ALL COPIES OF SCRIPT BY AIR MAIL A.M. WITHDRAWING BOOK FOR REVISION AND DO NOT WANT IT SHOWN TO ANYONE."*

Chandler in London

Chandler worked on revising the novel throughout the summer of 1952. In August he and Cissy traveled to England, a trip they had been planning for years. They sailed from Los Angeles on 20 August on the Guyana, *traveled through the Panama Canal, and arrived in London in the first week of September.*

Chandler was surprised to find himself received as a literary celebrity by the London press, and he was the subject of several interviews, including the following one in The Sunday Times *(London).*

The unconventional Mr. Chandler comes to Town
Cyril Ray
The Times (London), 21 September 1952, p. 8

As the photographer came in, Raymond Chandler put down his pipe and took out a cigarette. "I'm sick," he said, "of photographs of writers with pipes, looking thoughtful and sincere."

There was nothing affected about the lack of affectation, unless Chandler is more cunning than I think, and I more innocent. He respects his craft, but not many of the people who practise it ("I don't like writers much: do you? The nicest writers I know are hacks, because they know they're hacks.") And he has no inflated opinion of himself: "I'm not going to write the great American novel."

What he has written, though, and is still writing, is taut, fast American prose, in a series of novels that have earned the respect—often the enthusiasm—of serious literary critics such as no other writer of the kind commands, save Simenon.

It is an odd apotheosis for the Old Alleynian (Chandler was at Dulwich somewhere between P. G. Wodehouse's days and C. S. Forester's), who wrote notes and verses for the "Westminster Gazette" of Spender's time and the "Spectator" of Strachey's, gathering his material from the French and German newspapers at the National Liberal Club. Chandler sometimes earned as much at £3 a week in those days, the days when a week's bed and breakfast in his Bloomsbury boarding house cost him 9s. 6d.

It wasn't till after the first world war (and service in the Canadian infantry) that Chandler settled down in the America that was his own and his father's birthplace; and the anglicised young American who had "always wanted to be a writer" felt himself a foreigner at first in a country where the language was "fascinating, vigorous, alive; almost

Elizabethan in its freshness: wasn't stylised; hadn't become a 'class' language like literary English."

But Chandler was a late starter. It was a dozen years before he took again to writing–to writing so different from that of his literary days in London. A dozen years of being a salaried employee–"with a natural talent," he says, "for analytical accounting. Good training for a writer: taught me not to take anything for granted"–in a series of small Californian oil companies, till small Californian oil companies hit the skids, and Chandler set about learning a trade.

"I don't like interviews"

"I'd never been able to write fiction." he said. "Couldn't get a character into a room or out of it, or get him to put on his hat." Then, in the pulp magazines he was reading for fun–"Dime Detective" and "Black Mask," with their shoddy paper, shoddier illustrations, and advertisements for trusses–he recognised writing, he says, that was pretty honest compared with most magazines of the time and, more important still, a formula he thought he could work to. Dashiell Hammett was at his zenith: "I thought that perhaps I could go a little further, be a bit more humane, get a bit more interested in people than in sudden death."

It was at this point that Chandler said, "You know, I don't like this kind of thing, do you?" and "No," I said, which was true of interviewing in general, but not of this interview in particular. It was hard work for Chandler. He wanted to explain everything the way it had happened, and he has no glib line of patter to hand. He was worried lest I made a glamour boy of him, or a deep thinker with a pipe.

It would please him, I think, that I should say that his hair is grey and his neck muscles slack, that he looks something like a lightweight Lionel Barrymore. I please myself by recording that his smile is younger than his face and that only the young in heart could wear such a necktie.

It took him eight months to write his first short story. He rewrote it, all 18,000 words of it, five times and he sold it for $200. His first solid year of writing brought him in $1,500, "but I never had a story rejected. I stuck with every one of them till it sold." By the time he came to write his first novel, in 1938, he knocked off "The Big Sleep" in three months.

He poured me out another drink and said, "This sort of thing's hard work, and I'm getting lazier all the time." He complained of the cold. "I'm a soft cissy now. I'm only tough on paper."

Tough, though, with a difference. Chandler has as little liking for the novels he describes as "full of naked girls being tortured" as he has for the puzzle-plot in which (I quote his essay on "The Simple Art of Murder") "I have to go back to page 47 and refresh my memory about exactly what time the second gardener potted the prize-winning tea-rose begonia."

America, says Chandler, is still a pretty lawless place. Not every city's police force is corrupt, but "most are corrupt as hell because they're dominated by politicians, and politicians by the desire to make money. As a nation, we're just a bunch of chisellers We're frontiersmen still, and frontiersmen are greedy. What's more, we've got a habit of passing laws we can't enforce." So the Chandler novel is peopled with grifters and con men, and takes a sidelong glance at the Los Angeles that's "a neon-lighted slum," at what he calls a "decadent and corrupt and uneasy society" but one in which decency could exist, and down whose "mean streets a man must go who is not himself mean."

Finishing latest novel

The formula calls for that man to be a detective, but to Chandler he has the basic decency and the quality of the heart that is somewhere in most Americans, whatever their trade. And it didn't seem strange that at this point we found ourselves talking both of Eisenhower and of Stevenson. ("Stevenson'll get in hands down," says Chandler, "but whichever way it goes you'll get a man of character.")

Chandler lives not far from the neon-lighted slum, in a small suburb of San Diego, where his house cost him $40,000 (so much for the myth of the recluse in a shack) and he lives among "wealthy people and their parasites." It's there that he goes back next month to put the finishing touches to the latest novel, "Summer In Idle Valley," in which the same detective–"or one of the same name, anyhow"–faces a real moral problem, says his author, for the first time. A novel of suspense and action, as before, but "not so much murder in it. I suppose I'm mellowing, but not too much, I hope."

He broke off, and looked warily at me. "If you write that," he said, "you'll make me look as though I take myself too seriously."

"I'll try not to," I said.

"If I saw that sort of thing about some other writer I'd know what to call him," said Chandler.

And what he called him was a rude word.

After a month's stay in London, the Chandlers returned to the United States on the Mauretania, *arriving in New York on 7 October. After a short stay in the city, they returned by train home to La Jolla. In these two letters, the first to his English publisher Hamish Hamilton and the second to William Townend, an old friend from Dulwich College, Chandler provided summary accounts of his trip.*

6005 Camino de la Costa
La Jolla, California
November 5, 1952

Dear Jamie:

You people over there write one another so many little polite notes on all sorts of occasions that I suppose I was very stupid not to realize that I should not have waited until I had time to do a more substantial kind of letter. I am extremely sorry to have hurt your feelings inadvertently. There have been certain excuses but not any complete excuse. I could have written to you on the *Mauretania,* illegible as my writing is. I could have written to you from New York. I could have written to you on the train coming across the country. As soon as I got back here I wrote a couple of duty notes: one to Francis, who made me a present of a book just before I left and I had not time to thank him for it in person, the other to Leonard Russell. But these were short and not at all the kind of letter I should have liked to write to you. I think letter writing is more of a chore to me than it is to you, because I cannot write longhand so that anyone can read it. I don't like typing letters myself, because I don't type well enough, although I type rapidly, and I have fallen into the habit of dictating. But none of this is any adequate excuse for me to have been so neglectful that your feelings were hurt. And I do apologize most sincerely. As for my being offended about anything, you cannot use that word to me with impunity. *I just simply am not the type that gets offended,* even when there might be thought to be some justification and certainly there could never be from you. You were kindness itself, and I'm sure you spent far more hours worrying about me than you should have. I have had my feelings hurt, sometimes intentionally. Like most writers I have occasionally been sneered at and maligned. I don't say I have never been hurt and never discouraged, but I have never felt it a personal matter. I never sulk. I am never huffy. Sometimes, I admit, I can be pretty irritable, but this is perhaps more the fault of a nervous temperament than of any innate vice.

It seemed natural for Cissy to write to Roger, because he sent flowers to the boat and she certainly had to thank him, though if they had been sent to me, I might well have waited until I got home to do it. I can see now that that would have been wrong. So please, dear Jamie, try to understand that I think you and yours were all utterly kind and charming to us, and that even though certain things about our stay in London were a little annoying at the time, they are all very pleasant in retrospect. The annoying things were mostly things that could not be avoided. There was the desperate struggle on Cissy's part (when she was in no fit condition to do it) to find something to wear, and not merely something to wear to a dinner party but things which she badly needed and things which she simply could not find in the West End of London. She couldn't even find a decent pair of shoes to put on. At fantastic prices they were selling what we should over here regard as quite second-rate English goods. Of course I do understand why, but it was annoying just the same. I couldn't find a decent pair of woolen socks. The only things I found were fit for lumberjacks. I thought the hotel charges were pretty outrageous for a not too comfortable room. But all that is to be expected and I am sure as things go it is a pretty damn good hotel. Next time, however, I should like to try another, possibly Claridge's. And compared with New York, which is an abominable place in far too many ways, I think London is a paradise of charm and good manners. Soon after we reached London, although we said very little about it at the time, Cissy hurt herself getting into a taxi, just because the damn doorman wouldn't take the trouble to get the taxi up to the curb, and the strap on one of her shoes slipped. She developed a very serious bruise which should have been bandaged at once if we had realized how serious it was. But as a matter of fact it was not bandaged until she got on the *Mauretania.* She has been wearing bandages ever since. Evidently a large vein was broken and there was a great deal of subcutaneous hemorrhage which refused to absorb. On the way back on the train she developed some kind of infection, probably due to the use of harsh towels washed in detergent and insufficiently rinsed. I should say it was allergic in origin, but just the same it was bad and still is bad, very hard to shake off. I have been under the weather myself, but I'm all right now. And we were in such appalling difficulties from a domestic point of view that we had to ask Cissy's unfortunate sister to come right back and help us out, when she had been away from her own home for two months and was pretty fed up with being here. Also, I have been deeply depressed about my book. I felt, and I still feel, that Bernice was wrong in all but a few rather insignificant details. But there was always the chance that I was wrong and she was right. And when you're not feeling well, these things are apt to loom very large. After all I'm not getting any younger and I haven't turned out a book for quite a while and this sort of thing can't go on indefinitely. But I think I see now the answer to what problems there are, and that if we can have some peace in our home, things will start to move.

I didn't like the *Mauretania*. It wasn't a ship at all. It was just a damned floating hotel. I didn't like the hotel we stayed at in New York, and Cissy disliked it even more than I did. I suppose there is an amiable and pleasant side to New York we just didn't happen to see, except that I have one very good friend who took the trouble to come down from Old Chatham and meet us and stay several days with us. But frankly it seems to me a dirty, lawless, rude, hard-boiled place. It makes even Los Angeles seem fairly civilized. The New York taxi drivers were a bunch of hard-boiled, dirty-looking Jews except for an occasional grizzled and civilized Irishman. And most of them are crooks into the bargain. I have never been in any place that gave me such an acute feeling that no one had the time or inclination for even a modicum of good manners unless there was a quick buck in it for him. Oh yes, I will make one exception in favor of the customs inspectors. They are supposed to be tough. I found them charming and extremely clever. The one we got (after waiting an hour and a half because the Cunard people lost one of our suitcases and didn't even take the trouble to apologize when they finally found it) made a great to-do about the Berenson book, which I think was the only thing in our ten pieces of luggage he even looked at. But I had a very strong impression that his looking at it and talking about it and asking questions about it was simply a device for sizing up his customer, and that after a few moments of this he made up his mind what sort of people he was dealing with, and from then on he didn't want to see or know anything at all. He didn't even ask us to open our bags. I had declared this book on the customs declaration as a gift and put an estimated value on it, because it was the sort of expensive thing that I didn't want them to find without being told. But at the same time I wouldn't try to fool with these people. They caught a slick-looking Jew with a fine batch of very expensive looking French costume jewelry wrapped up in an old shirt. And they took no time at all in marching him off to a senior officer, the Jew remarking plaintively as he departed that he wasn't trying to get away with anything. Famous last words.

Well, Jamie, let's face it. We loved London and we had a lovely time there. What little inconveniences we happened to have suffered were all due to our own inexperience and probably would not happen again. All your people were wonderful to me. It was really extremely touching. I am just not used to being treated with that much consideration. There are things I regret, such as losing several days over my vaccination, such as not going to any of the picture galleries, such as only seeing one rather poor play, such as not having dinner at your home. I spent too much time talking about myself, which I don't enjoy, and too little time listening to other people talk about themselves, which I do enjoy. I missed seeing something of the English countryside. And childish as it may sound, I missed very much not having hired a Rolls Royce and a driver for a day and driven to Oxford or Cambridge or some place like that. But all in all there was a hell of a lot I did not miss, and all of it good. And for that you above all others are to be thanked. I'll be writing you again soon. In the meantime my best love to you and Yvonne, and that goes for Cissy too. I think the trip did her a lot of good. She had bad luck, but psychologically she was buoyed up no end.

Yours ever,

Ray

P. S. The Maugham book just came, and thanks ever so much for sending it. Francis had sent me a bound copy of the proof. I wish Maugham had taken the trouble to spell Marlowe's name right, and I don't agree with his thesis that the detective story is dying. That's just an elderly gentleman's point of view. Such predictions have been made periodically ever since one can remember. I'm sure I did thank you for the Berenson book, which I shall have a hard time getting away from Cissy, and for the *Journal* of Delacroix. But what's this about a Partridge book? You didn't send me a Partridge book, or if you did, I haven't received it.

R.

—*Selected Letters of Raymond Chandler,* pp. 323–327

* * *

In his 11 November letter to Townend, Chandler remarked that "The London of 1952 probably struck me as a much more amiable and attractive place than you found it, because I probably never saw it at its best, at least not since I was a very young man." He went on to describe some of his social activities.

Yes, I met a few of the literary and theatrical people who are big names in London. We had lunch with Priestley, and a very good lunch it was. We had dinner with Leonard Russell, and his wife, Dilys Powell. It wasn't much of a dinner, but it was elegantly served by a butler, and the company was very nice indeed. Dilys Powell I found charming; Leonard Russell, Cissy found charming. Not that I didn't like him, but I didn't go overboard for him the way she did. Also present were Val Gielgud, who is head of dramatic productions for BBC; Nicolas Bentley, the son of the fellow who wrote *Trent's Last Case,* his wife, who is the daughter of Sir Patrick Hastings; one of the daughters-in-law of H. J. Massingham, who used to edit the great liberal weekly, *The Saturday Review;* Campbell Dixon, who is some kind of a film reviewer and has been a foreign correspondent and a special feature writer in many places, and his wife, who also works for the BBC and has some connections with Korda. I had lunch with Eric Partridge, and we did happen to miss a dinner at which Cyril Connolly and Peter Ustinov were to have been present. I can't say I met all the bigwigs, even very many of them. But those I did meet were all very nice people and made an unnecessary amount of fuss over me.

—Selected Letters of Raymond Chandler, pp. 327–329

Hammett and Chandler

Three months before the publication of The Long Goodbye, *John Paterson in his article "A Cosmic View of the Private Eye" argued that hard-boiled detective fiction was a natural response to the conditions of life in twentieth-century America. Paterson's essay makes clear that by this point Chandler and Dashiell Hammett were considered the two American masters of the hard-boiled novel, the standard against which future writers would be compared. The critic also makes a charge that became a theme in some of the criticism of* The Long Goodbye—*that Marlowe had become soft.*

SAM SPADE, the hardboiled hero of Dashiell Hammett's "The Maltese Falcon," in a rare moment of weakness permitted his readers an oblique insight into his motivation as a human being. He told the story of Flitcraft. "Flitcraft," he said, "'had been a good citizen and a good husband and father, not by any outer compulsion, but simply because he was a man who was most comfortable in step with his surroundings." One day passing an office building under construction he was narrowly missed by a beam that fell ten stories. In the moment he realized that he had based his life on false assumptions. He had assumed that life "was a clean orderly sane responsible affair"; he now discovered that "he, the good citizen-husband-father, could be wiped out between office and restaurant by the accident of a falling beam." That afternoon he found it necessary suddenly and mysteriously to abandon his family, his business, and his community.

He had, of course, his reasons. He had seen life with the lid taken off and he had acted accordingly. He had dissociated himself from the clean orderly life he had known and begun his readjustment to a world in which beams fell.

This fable explains, I think, the revolt of the hard-boiled wing led by Hammett in the Twenties and Raymond Chandler in the Thirties against the practitioners of the historic detective story. For the society postulated by the older school, which flourished in the Twenties and which has continued to flourish in spite of the schism, resembles in its essentials the staid, comfortable, secure society of the pre-1914 period, the period before the beams begin to fall. In the age of the Boom, the Great Depression, flappers, gangsterism, and the Fascist Solution it recalls the sober gentility and crude optimism of an earlier and more complacent generation; it asserts the triumph of a social order and decorum that have all but passed away. It is the virtue of the insurgent wing, on the other hand, that it attempts more closely to approximate the central experience of the age, the experience of a war epoch, of an age of transition in which men are less confident of their values and their motives, less pleased with the society they have constructed.

. . . .

Dashiell Hammett is, I think, with so many of his literary contemporaries, protesting the horrors of a savagely competitive society, the horrors of an urban-industrial civilization. For when we scrape away the tough exterior of his hero we find not heart of stone and nerves of steel but the tortured sensibility of the Nineteen Twenties, its romantic isolation and its pessimism, its inability to find grounds for action. With Chandler's Philip Marlowe, however, we pass into another world, the world of the Depression. He retains, of course, many of the attitudes of his predecessor, his toughness, his irony, his loneliness. But he has none of

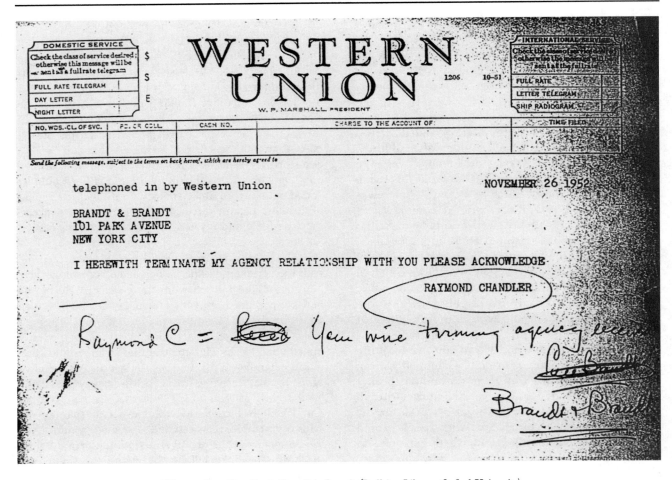

Telegram from Chandler to Brandt & Brandt (Bodleian Library, Oxford University)

Quitting Brandt & Brandt

Since receiving Baumgarten and Brandt's criticism of the first draft of The Long Goodbye, *Chandler had been brooding over what he considered his agents' overstepping their bounds and becoming editors. Though he was revising the novel, he increasingly felt that their suggestions were poor ones, and his letters to the agency remained cool and businesslike. Chandler neglected to visit Brandt & Brandt while in New York on the way home from England, and on 26 November 1952 he officially terminated his agreement with the agency.*

Spade's conviction of persisting failure, his sense of futility and defeat, none of his perhaps tragic implications. There is about him little of the spirit of a man who wins and does not win, who wins and cannot win. For he represents the moral and social ardor of the Depression years, the impulse towards reform; and he is frequently prone to feelings of boyish optimism.

In the first place, tough and brave though he may be, Marlowe is a much more respectable figure than Spade. He went to college and "can still," he asserts belligerently, "speak English if there's any demand for it." And if he is "a little bit of a cynic," as his client notes, he is no more so than is proper in one who aspires to knight errantry. For he does betray all the characteristics of the first-class crusader.

This is apparent in the deadly seriousness with which he takes his craft. "The first time we met," he says angrily, "I told you I was a detective. Get it through your lovely head. I work at it, lady, I don't play at it." Clearly the words of a man who knows what he means and what exactly he must do in the world, the words of a man who can, that is, afford social consciousness. We get another glimpse of this aspect of the private detective when we discover Marlowe in a jail cell pondering ruefully the two worlds, the nice, sane, comfortable world he has rejected and the ugly world to which he has committed himself. "I knew a girl," he meditates, "who lived on Twenty-fifth Street. It was a nice street. She was a nice girl. She liked Bay City. She wouldn't think about the Mexican and Negro slums stretched out on the dismal flats south of the old interurban tracks. Nor of the waterfront dives . . . the sweaty little dance-halls . . . the marihuana joints, the narrow fox faces watching over the tops of newspapers. . . ."

BUT Marlowe is not only the social crusader; he is also the moralist, almost the prude. Sam Spade could never have said, on discovering a nymphomaniac disposed in his bed, what Marlowe said. "It's so hard," he said, "for women—even nice women—to realize that their bodies are not irresistible." For Spade, in his grim odyssey through the underworld, was always too ambivalent a character to express an opinion one way or the other. He acted, but he acted inscrutably, almost without point of view. Marlowe, however, finds it difficult to conceal his contempt for the diseased world in which he must move.

Nevertheless he is, like the boy next door, a rather pleasant character and articulates the longing, universal in our day, for an honorable if not a pleasant world. Chandler describes him thus:

> He is a poor man or he would not be a detective. He is a common man or he would not go among common people; he has a sense of character or he would not know his job. He will take no man's money dishonestly and no man's insolence without a due and dispassionate revenge; he is a lonely man and his pride is that you will treat him as a proud man or be very sorry you ever saw him.

After this, he must indeed have seemed a wonderfully attractive symbol to the men who lost their pride in the bread lines and employment offices of that decade.

Unfortunately, the private detectives who succeed Sam Spade and Philip Marlowe represent a progressive deterioration of the type. We have noted the essentially romantic temperament of Hammett's Sam Spade. But where in him it has been implicit, in the lesser creations it is crudely explicit. The result is rather revolting sentimentality: the hardboiled novel turns soft at the center. There are signs even in Philip Marlowe of this contagion. "Knights have no meaning in this game," he muses, bitterly in love with himself. "It wasn't a game for knights."

—The Saturday Review (22 August 1953): 7, 32–33

The Publication of *The Long Goodbye*

After he had submitted the typescript of The Long Goodbye *to Hamish Hamilton in England, Chandler made a final series of revisions to the novel. Because of these changes, the novel has a complicated textual history, which is analyzed in the following article by Robert Henry Miller.*

The Publication of Raymond Chandler's *The Long Goodbye*

Robert Henry Miller

Papers of the Bibliographic Society of America, 63 (1969): 279–286

It is no secret to those who have read Raymond Chandler's published letters in *Raymond Chandler Speaking* (editors Dorothy Gardiner and Kathrine Sorley Walker [Boston 1962]) that he was concerned with securing accurate, polished printed texts of his works. The history of the composition and publication of *The Long Goodbye* reinforces this image of Chandler as a conscientious writer, and in addition it provides an unusual example of the difficulties that can occur when an American author in La Jolla, California, is trying to oversee the publication of his novel in London, England. Even more significantly, it provides us with an unusual example of textual revision between printings of an edition. Such an occurrence in modern texts is not uncommon, but the large number of changes involved in the printing of *The Long Goodbye* indicates the extent to which the text of a modern edition can be altered between printings.

I realize that Chandler is not one of the established writers in American fiction, but there seems to be some interest among scholars and critics of American literature in writers who deal with "crime" and "the city," and of this group the general consensus seems to be that Hammett and Chandler are the best, with Chandler perhaps holding a bit of an edge at the moment. Beyond this reason, however, I feel that the curious bibliographical problem involved here may be of interest to bibliographers in general.

The Long Goodbye, like many other American novels, was first issued in England, by Hamish Hamilton, Ltd., of London, in November 1953.[1] The first printing was quickly followed by a second printing in December of the same year. Between these two printings, eighty-six changes exist in the text of the novel (sixty-five substantives and twenty-one accidentals).[2] To complicate matters, the first printing of the United States edition, issued in March 1954 by Houghton Mifflin, not only contains

150
830

you bought a lot of me. For a smile and a nod and a few

drinks in a bar. For a little charm. For a gag in between

more expensive and more interesting moments. You bought

a lot of me, Terry. So long, amigo. Have fun in Mexico!"

"Goodbye," he said slowly. "If that's the way you

want it. I guess I just came around too late. I waited

too long. But I did come."

"Would you have told me who you were if I hadn't

known?"

He frowned and rubbed the tips of his fingers gently

along the side of his face, the way he used to do.

Suddenly there were tears in his eyes. He put the

dark glasses on quickly to hide them.

"I don't know. They didn't want me to. I wasn't sure.

I hadn't made up my mind."

Two intermediate draft versions of the ending for The Long Goodbye *(Bodleian Library, Oxford University)*

831

"You never will. But there will always be somebody around to do it for you. ~~Adios,~~ Well, goodbye Senor Maiorranos. ~~Vaya usted con dios.~~" Nice to have known you for a little while."

He turned quickly and walked out. I watched the door close. I listened to his steps going along the hall. ~~They died.~~ Then I just listened.

~~Slow curtain.~~

RC

6/24/53

331

"There's more of us than youthink. But the way you

said it is funny. Real funny. You bought a lot of me,

Terry. For a smile and a nod and a wave of the hand

and a few quiet drinks in a bar. For a little charm.

For a change of pace in between your more expensive

moments. So long, amigo. I won't say goodbye. I said

it to you when it meant something."

"I guess I came back too late," he said."But these

plastic jobs take time."

"Would you have come at all if I hadn't smoked you

out?"

He frowned and suddenly rubbed the tips of his fin

gers along the side of his face--the way he used to do

when it had no feeling, the way I had been doing myself

for a while. There was a glint of tears in his eyes.

101

(833)

"Don't you enjoy it ~~just~~ a little?"

He stood up. I stood up too. He put out his lean hand. I shook it.

"Goodbye, Senor Maioranos. Nice to have known you for a little while."

"Goodbye."

He turned ~~away quickly~~ and went out. I watched the door close and listened to his steps going away. ~~After a little while~~ *Then* I couldn't hear them, but I kept on listening *anyway. As if he might come* ~~back~~ ~~doitard~~

Don't ask me why. I ~~couldn't tell you.~~

but I told me ont get. as of I hope he would.

RC

Bitte ließ Not July 11,1953.

all the substantive variants in the second English printing but introduces sixty-four additional substantive changes into the text.[3] Such changes as these are the exception rather than the rule in modern texts, and between printings of an edition they are rarely so numerous. A close examination of the history of the novel's composition, however, and of the bibliographical evidence available can count for them and for the rather unusual manner in which they were made. Contrary to what one would expect, the revisions did not cumulate over the publication of the two English printings and the United States edition. They were made all at one time, in the galley proofs for the United States edition, and then some were incorporated in the second English printing, which also preceded the United States edition.

The revisions themselves do not alter the plot or overall tone of the novel; they are rather polishings that in some cases improve an expression, or in other cases remove serious inconsistencies within the text. For example, in the first English printing the caliber of the murder weapon is given in one place as a "Mauser. 63, Model P.P.K.," and in a later place as a "Mauser 7.65 P.P.K."; this was changed in both the second English printing and in the United States edition to the correct caliber, "Mauser 7.65 P.P.K." (pp. 194.1 and 200.20, respectively). In the first English printing, Marlowe, after spending close to three days in jail, says he has been in for "thirty-six hours"; in the second English printing and the United States edition the phrase is changed to "fifty-six hours" (50.29, 51.3). The proper name "Westerheym" is spelled in two different ways in the first English printing; in the second English printing and the United States edition it is corrected (67.36). In the first English printing, Terry Lennox says of Harlan Potter's two daughters, "Both his daughters are tramps." However, in the second English printing and in the United States edition the phrase is changed to "Sylvia is a tramp," perhaps to complement the more sympathetic picture which Chandler provides of Linda Loring later in the novel (19.19). In other places he carefully proofread the Spanish dialogue of both Candy and the disguised Terry Lennox and made minor corrections of it. Taken in the aggregate, the majority of revisions throughout the novel show that Chandler made stylistic changes which are minor but which are clearly improvements over the originals. A word is deleted here and there; an overwritten phrase is revised. Generally speaking, the revisions, especially the corrections of inconsistencies, show the work of an attentive author and editors and are improvements over the

originals, no matter how slight some of them may be.[4]

An explanation for these changes and the manner in which they occurred can be pieced together from Chandler's letters bearing on the novel, both published and unpublished, and from collations of (1) the existing typescript of the novel, (2) the two printings of the first English edition, and (3) the United States edition.

The typescript, which is now in the Raymond Chandler Collection at the University of California, Los Angeles, was used as setting copy for the United States edition. It is the final typed draft of the novel, as it carries the title "Summer in Idle Valley," corrected to "The Long Goodbye."[5] It consists of 425 pages of text and three sets of pages of revision inserted into the typescript. Notations appear in it in four different hands: (1) the Houghton Mifflin proofreader's notations, including galley divisions and directions on type style; (2) and (3), corrections and queries by two editors, Paul Brooks and Laurette Murdock of Houghton Mifflin; and (4) Chandler's comments, which consist of two small notations and one partly handwritten, partly typed reply to a query from Laurette Murdock.[6]

The letters reveal this brief chronology of the novel's composition. On 14 May 1995 Chandler sent the first draft of the novel, a typescript of about 92,000 words, titled "The Long Goodbye," to Bernice Baumgarten, of Brandt and Brandt, his literary agent (*Raymond Chandler Speaking*, pp. 232–33). After receiving her criticisms of it, he withdrew the script and decided to look through it again (letter of 25 May 1952 to Bernice Baumgarten, *Raymond Chandler Speaking*, pp. 233–34). On June 10 he wrote to Hamish Hamilton that he had changed the title to "Summer in Idle Valley," (*Raymond Chandler Speaking*, p. 234), but no further mention was made of the book until May of the next year, when he again wrote Hamish Hamilton that he was four-fifths of the way through "Summer in Idle Valley" but that he no longer liked the title, and that it had been almost completely re-written (*Raymond Chandler Speaking*, p. 236). By 12 June the first 69,000 words were sent to Hamish Hamilton Ltd., and the rest of the novel apparently followed by the week of 14 July (unpublished letters to Hamish Hamilton, 12 June and 11 July 1953, Chandler Collection).[7]

By 3 August Chandler had found it necessary to make some changes in the typescript and he mailed the corrected pages to Roger Machell, his editor at Hamish Hamilton Ltd., who was working on the script in England (unpublished letter of 3 August 1953, Chandler Collection). As the corrections were being made in the typescript in the United States, at least some of them were being relayed to London, where they were incorporated in the English copy of the typescript, since the three sets of inserted pages of revision in the typescript are followed in the first English printing, as are some of the pencil corrections in the typescript. They are few in number but they are important. In the uncorrected typescript, for example, Sylvia Lennox's first name was originally "Elaine," but it is corrected in pencil to "Sylvia" throughout the script, and she is called "Sylvia" in the first English printing. Likewise Terry Lennox's original name was "Paul Manning" in the uncorrected typescript, but was changed to "Paul Marston," as it appears in the first English printing.

Chandler expressed his concern about the matter of proofreading for the English edition in this same letter of 3 August to Roger Machell. He states that he wants to get corrected proofs to Hamish Hamilton, especially since he knows that English printers can make unusual mistakes when they attempt to deal with the American vernacular. On 24 October Chandler wrote to Hamish Hamilton, again on the same topic, commenting that since he has been reading the Houghton Mifflin galley proofs he realizes that there are a number of small things, matters of phrasing and logical consistency, that will need correcting (unpublished letter, Chandler Collection). At the same time he expresses firmly his own conviction that every author has a right to correct the proofs of his works. Since, according to this letter, Chandler was asking for proofs as late as 24 October he could not have had an opportunity to read proof for the English edition, issued on 1 November. This letter also indicates that by 24 October he was already correcting the galley proofs for the United States edition to be published in March of the next year. Thus the revisions which appear in the second English printing and in the United States editions must have been made in the galley proofs for the United States edition, and the first English printing, which did not include these corrections, was revised in the second printing to include some of the revisions already made in these proofs.

A close study of the existing typescript of the novel also supports the contention that the revisions were made in the United States galley proofs. It has already been noted that the English edition was set from a copy of this typescript, not from the typescript itself. The English edition follows in almost all instances the uncorrected text of the typescript and includes only a few of the numerous pencil emenda-

tions in it, and in some places it even follows what were typographical errors in the typescript. For example, at one point the typescript reads that Eileen Wade had a "half deductive smile"; the reading is followed in the first English printing, whereas in the second English printing and in the first United States edition it is corrected to "half-seductive smile" (251.13). In the second printing, two of the substantive pencil corrections in the typescript are adopted, while in the United States edition all the substantive pencil corrections are followed. However, none of the other revisions in the second English printing or in the United States edition appear in the corrected typescript. Therefore, they must have originated in the galley proofs for the United States edition. No information is available, to my knowledge, about the circumstances surrounding this arrangement. Roger Machell, who did the editorial work on the English edition, has informed me that he cannot recall exactly what the nature of the revisions in the second printing were but his recollection is that Hamish Hamilton Ltd. paid for the cost of the changes, and the only ones that he remembers were the result of either his or the printer's failure to understand Chandler's idiom (letter from Roger Machell, 8 December 1965).

To sum up, then, the changes in the text were initially made in the galley proofs for the United States edition. Of these 129 substantive changes made in the galley proofs sixty-five passed into the second English printing and appeared in print in England four months before they appeared in print in the United States.[8]

The subsequent publishing history of the English editions of *The Long Goodbye* is no less revealing of what can happen to any text. In England, there has been no edition available that contains a fully accurate text of the novel, even though Chandler has a larger reading audience there. In 1959 Penguin Books issued its paperback edition (the only edition still in print today), which is now in its fourth printing, but collation reveals that it is based on the second printing of the first English edition and therefore does not include all the revisions in the United States edition. Collation also shows that the most recent edition of the novel which appears in the collection *The Second Chandler Omnibus* published in 1962 by Hamish Hamilton Ltd., was set from the least accurate text available and the one which brought on all the above-mentioned complications in the beginning, the first printing of the first English edition issued in November 1953. By insisting on revisions in the second printing Chandler was trying to provide the English reader with a sound text, but one oversight has partly negated that effort. Such meticulousness and concern for his text again justifies an impression of Chandler as a craftsman, and the vicissitudes involved in the text of this novel are ample evidence of his concern for his works. But particularly, the unusual number of revisions between the printings of this first English edition and the unusual manner in which they passed into that edition are examples of a distinct possibility of slips that can occur in the printing of any modern text.

1 First English edition, first printing: The Long | Good-Bye | BY | RAYMOND CHANDLER| [Hamish Hamilton seal, tree rooted in an open book] | LONDON [1953]

Collation and pagination: [A] B-K¹⁶; [1-4] 5-319 [320].
The second printing is identical to the first, with the exception that at the top of the copyright page, p. [4], the second printing carries the statement *"Second Impression December, 1953."*

2 In order to accommodate these revisions, the printer had to make changes in ninety-five pages of the edition. Those pages in which revisions were made were changed, but in addition other pages in which no textual changes occurred had to be altered in order to accommodate the new readings. The second printing was probably produced by photo-offset, as the general appearance of the type impression in the second printing is too uniform to indicate changes in letterpress plates, some of which would have to have been cut apart and rejoined.

3 The Long | Goodbye | RAYMOND CHANDLER | [Houghton Mifflin seal, boy and dolphin] | HOUGHTON MIFFLIN COMPANY | BOSTON . . The Riverside Press Cambridge | 1954

Collation and pagination: [1²] [2-10]¹⁶ [11]⁸, [i-iv], [1] 2-316.

There were at least two printings of this edition. As is customary in Houghton Mifflin editions, the later printing does not have the year of publication printed on its title page.

4 Chandler's concern for his texts is well documented in his letters. In response to a proofreading job done on one of his articles for the *Atlantic Monthly,* Chandler angrily wrote the editor that "when I split an infinitive, God damn it, I split it so it will stay split, and when I interrupt the velvety smoothness of my more or less literate syntax with a few sudden words of bar-room vernacular, that is done with the eyes wide open and the mind relaxed but attentive" (*Raymond Chandler Speaking,* p. 77). In two instances in connection with *The Long Goodbye* he went beyond what could be called usual concern to point out textual errors. As late as 3 Feb. 1954, a few weeks before the United States edition was issued, he wrote to Laurette Murdock, his editor at Houghton Mifflin, that he had spotted a mistake in one of the Spanish phrases spoken by Candy, the Mexican houseboy (letter in the Raymond Chandler Collection, University of California, Los Angeles—hereafter cited as "Chandler Collection"). Still later, in 1955, after the publication of a paperback edition by Pocket Books, Inc., Chandler wrote Hardwick Moseley of Houghton Mifflin that he had discovered an error (and he was correct) in the paperback edition, on page 326, in the dialogue between Marlowe and the disguised Terry Lennox (letter of 3 March 1955, Chandler Collection).

5 The earliest typescript was titled "The Long Goodbye." See *Raymond Chandler Speaking,* pp. 232, 236.

6 Laurette Murdock signed her full name to three of her notations. She has since retired from the profession. Paul Brooks placed his initials after two of his queries, and they were identified for me by Mr. Brooks himself through Mr. Dale Warren of Houghton Mifflin's editorial staff. Mr. Brooks, now editor-in-chief of Houghton Mifflin, does not remember particular details of his work on *The Long Goodbye* (letter from Dale Warren, 11 July 1966).

At the present time the typescript used as setting copy for the English edition has not been located, but a collation of the existing typescript and the first English printing substantiates that setting copy for the English edition must have been a copy of this typescript, probably either a carbon or photographic copy. This is borne out by the fact that the first English printing follows faithfully the original readings of the typescript rather than the pencil corrections, to the point that even in matters of punctuation, in 169 instances the first English printing follows the uncorrected state of the typescript, while the first United States edition follows the corrections.

7 All letters cited are either from the published collection *Raymond Chandler Speaking,* or from unpublished typed copies, which were given to U.C.L.A. by Helga Greene, Chandler's literary agent and executor; the originals are still in private hands. All general references to the copies and their contents and to the typescript of the novel are given here with the permission of Brooke Whiting, Head of Special Collections, the University of California, Los Angeles. All quotes are given with the kind permission of the Helga Greene Literary Agency. The copies of the letters were made available to me through the gracious assistance of Philip Durham of the English Department of U.C.L.A.

8 *The Long Goodbye* incidentally provides some interesting examples of mistakes that can creep into the text of a work when the author does not have a chance to correct proof. The first printing of this first English edition contains thirty-nine readings that do not appear in either the original typescript or its corrections. A few examples will suffice. Lonny Morgan, a male reporter, is referred to as "her," while it is clear from the context that Lonny is a "he," not a "she" (p. 57.14). The phrase "like a ground mist," referring to our West Coast phenomenon, is changed to a "ground-like mist," even though the same phrase escaped emending at another point in the first English printing (198.10). Some American terms are given their British equivalents, so "levis" becomes "trousers" (142.28). Other changes are baffling, as for example "Mexico City" changed to "Mexican City" (310.37). The most revealing error is the substitution in the English edition of the British "wag" for the American slang term "vag," for vagrant (7.16). A tough Los Angeles cop says to hard-boiled Philip Marlowe, "I'd even say he was a wag and so maybe we ought to take him in." The error has never been corrected in any of the English editions to date, even though Chandler pointed it out to Roger Machell in a letter in 1956 (*Raymond Chandler Speaking,* p. 172). Of these thirty-nine substantive changes, only nine were corrected in the second printing, so that even though the second printing adopts eighty-six changes, it still contains thirty of these readings. Only the United States edition carries the corrected readings.

English Reviews of *The Long Goodbye*

Like The Little Sister, The Long Goodbye *was published in England before it was published in the United States. The novel sold well in the United Kingdom, with two printings released in the fall of 1953.*

The present fashion for treating Raymond Chandler as if he were Henry James should not prevent us from acclaiming his very real merits. Fuelled by endless supplies of gin and rye whisky, *The Long Goodbye* zips along at immense speed, and its standard cast of nymphomaniacs, racketeers, sadistic policemen and tough millionaires are given unusual depth and vigor. For addicts of the old-style crossword-puzzle detective stories there is a first-class surprise solution. There is also a good deal of radical social comment. ("Big money is big power, and big power gets used wrong. It's the system.")

What does it all add up to? One-third realism and two-thirds fantasy, with fantasy fully indulged in the impossibly virtuous, sentimental private eye Philip Marlowe, who keeps brushing away dirty money as if it were mud. Mr. Chandler's own virtues are a cunning artifice that is almost art, a power in ordering narrative, a terse style intelligently handled. Not Henry James, nor even Dashiell Hammett perhaps, but an uncommonly skilled creator of modern adventure stories, the best of his kind now writing.

J. S.

–"Criticism," *Punch,* 225 (30 December 1953): 800

* * *

Mr. Chandler's new novel is cast in much the same shape as its predecessors. Philip Marlowe, the private detective, tells the story, the scene is set in southern California and the familiar police officers, gangsters and lovely ladies make their usual impressive appearances. People continue to be horribly rude to each other and the style is still enlivened with brief and pungent similes. Still superficially disillusioned, Marlow is as altruistic as ever and at once gets into trouble by trying to prove that a brutal murder was not committed by the man accused of it. Once more he finds himself pitting his wits, his toughness and his rueful integrity against the old conspiracy of wealth and authority; police, racketeers, lawyers and rich folk try to silence and confuse him, but he solves his problem, and though justice is not seen to be done he has stood up for the truth and triumphed.

In early middle age now, Marlowe tends to reflect more frequently on the predicament of society, and his vision is sombre and violent as he thinks of the incessant evil and suffering of the big city. Wealth, as always, fascinates him, and he measures its dire effects on those who are possessed by it; the grave, sour multi-millionaire is another in the series of portraits of the unhappy rich which runs through all Mr. Chandler's novels. Marlowe is a connoisseur of men and women, a serious and involved student of moral fibre, in his own laconic and elliptical fashion, and there are one or two studies of weakness in the present book which should command respect.

Mr. Chandler is such an admirable story-teller, with such powers of making his scenes and situations palpable, that it is easy to overlook much that is improbable in their contrivance. In this book there are signs of strain when, for instance, he tries to explain just why a person who committed a murder should employ the very detective who is committed to solving it, and there are other matters which take a good deal of believing. But the illusion is still strong and the old mixture of realism and convention has lost little of its potency.

–"Mild and Bitter," *Times Literary Supplement,* 1 January 1954, p. 5

* * *

Mr. Chandler's style by now can be regarded as fixed: he has published no new work for the last four years, but *The Long Good-Bye* shows that nothing has happened in the interim to modify his evangelical outlook on life. Here comes Philip Marlowe again, crusading along the Californian coast against venal cops, corrupt politicians, ugly gangsters, and self-indulgent women, in fact the entire mammon of unrighteousness. "We are a big, rough, rich, wild people and crime is the price we pay for it." And all the reward Marlowe ever receives for his services is an occasional drink, an occasional woman, a succession of physical injuries and an addition to his embittered memories. He is a very remarkable creation: the perpetually crucified redeemer of all our modern sins. In *The Long Good-Bye* there is one jarring note of sentimentality; but Mr. Chandler's language has lost none of its impetus, the rhythm of his prose is superb, and the intensity of feeling he packs into his pages makes every other thriller-writer look utterly silly and superficial.

–"Detection and Thrillers," *The New Statesman and Nation,* 48 (9 January 1954): 47–48

IN *The Long Good-bye*, Mr. Chandler's first novel for four years, Philip Marlowe is shown to have lost none of the appetite for adventure and the contempt for authority and the over-privileged which make him a magnet for trouble. This is how he describes his life as a Private Investigator:

'So passed a day in the life of a P.I. Not exactly a typical day but not totally untypical either. What makes a man stay with it nobody knows. You don't get rich, you don't often have much fun. Sometimes you get beaten up or shot at or tossed into the jailhouse. Once in a long while you get dead. Every other month you decide to give it up and find some sensible occupation while you can still walk without shaking your head. Then the door buzzer rings and you open the inner door to the waiting-room and there stands a new face with a new problem, a new load of grief, and a small piece of money.'

But, as the reader of Mr. Chandler's earlier books won't have to be told, such casual encounters usually lead to a succession of curious and increasingly violent events. Suffice it to say that in *The Long Good-bye*, Mr. Chandler writes as brilliantly as ever and that the suspense, characterization, and description of people and places are of the first order. To give away more would be to spoil the reader's fun.

W. SOMERSET MAUGHAM (in *The Vagrant Mood*) writes: 'Chandler is the most brilliant author now writing this kind of story . . . he has an admirable aptitude for that typical product of the quick American mind, the wisecrack, and his sardonic humour has an engaging spontaneity'.

Jacket design by
FRITZ WEGNER

10s. 6d. net

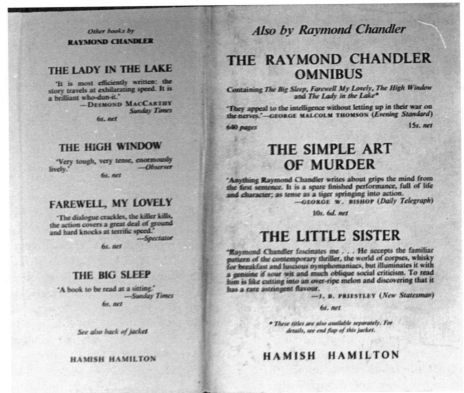

Other books by
RAYMOND CHANDLER

THE LADY IN THE LAKE

'It is most efficiently written: the story travels at exhilarating speed. It is a brilliant who-dun-it.'
—DESMOND MacCARTHY
Sunday Times
6s. net

THE HIGH WINDOW

'Very tough, very tense, enormously lively.'
—*Observer*
6s. net

FAREWELL, MY LOVELY

'The dialogue crackles, the killer kills, the action covers a great deal of ground and hard knocks at terrific speed.'
—*Spectator*
6s. net

THE BIG SLEEP

'A book to be read at a sitting.'
—*Sunday Times*
6s. net

See also back of jacket

HAMISH HAMILTON

Also by Raymond Chandler

THE RAYMOND CHANDLER OMNIBUS

Containing *The Big Sleep, Farewell My Lovely, The High Window* and *The Lady in the Lake**

'They appeal to the intelligence without letting up in their war on the nerves.'—GEORGE MALCOLM THOMSON (*Evening Standard*)
640 pages   15s. net

THE SIMPLE ART OF MURDER

'Anything Raymond Chandler writes about grips the mind from the first sentence. It is a spare finished performance, full of life and character; as tense as a tiger springing into action.
—GEORGE W. BISHOP (*Daily Telegraph*)
10s. 6d. net

THE LITTLE SISTER

'Raymond Chandler fascinates me . . . He accepts the familiar pattern of the contemporary thriller, the world of corpses, whisky for breakfast and luscious nymphomaniacs, but illuminates it with a genuine if sour wit and much oblique social criticism. To read him is like cutting into an over-ripe melon and discovering that it has a rare astringent flavour.
—J. B. PRIESTLEY (*New Statesman*)
6s. net

* These titles are also available separately. For details, see end flap of this jacket.

HAMISH HAMILTON

Dust jacket for the first edition of Chandler's sixth novel, published in England on 27 November 1953 (Bruccoli Collection, Kent State University)

The American Reception of *The Long Goodbye*

By the spring publication of the first American edition of
The Long Goodbye *by Houghton Mifflin, Chandler knew
that the novel had sold well in England, and he was fully aware
that his literary reputation was much better overseas than it was
at home. The book had not yet been reviewed widely in America
when Chandler wrote this letter to Hardwick Moseley discussing
his expectations for its reception in the United States.*

Box One Twenty Eight • La Jolla, California
                                        March 23rd. 1954

Dear Hardwicke:

I'm sick as a dog, thank you, with one of these
lousy virus infections the doctors have invented to cover up
their ignorance. But I know you want an answer. I missed
seeing Paul Brooks two weeks ago and I'm still rocking. I
also missed a Time photog who insisted on a picture.
(They said he was a Time photog but they intrinsically lied.
He was from the San Diego Union-Tribune and there is no
worse murderer than a newspaper flash gun artist. They
did one of me in London that made me look like Grandma
Moses and I swore I'dnever have another. (By the way
where did you got the beastly thing you put in your spring
list?) Of course Time doesn't matter because the fact that
they interview you or photograph you is no guarantee.
Imagine those lice in Newsweek not even paying for the
photographs they ordered!

You better do a damn sight better with The Long
Goodbye that you did with Little Sister. I realize the appalling situation but I also realize that the publishers are not
indefinitely going to be able to make their profits if any by
their share of the reprints. Writers of forgettable fiction will
simply be forced into the paperback market. How the hell
can you expect anyone to pay dollars three for a mystery
novel? I might be the best writer in this country, and with
two exceptionsx I very likely am, but I'm still a mystery
writer. For the first time in my life I was reviewed as a Novelist in the London Sunday Times (but Leonard Russell is a
friend of mine andmay have leaned a little out of kindness).
I was discussed on the BBC by as addled a group of
so-called intellectuals (among whom Dilys Powell hardly
got a word in) as ever had soup on their vests. But over
here? The New York Times which surely should know
what it is doing if any newspaper does has twice given
books of mine for review to mystery writers who had been
witing for years for the chance to knife me because I have
ridiculed the sort of thing they wite themselves (notmen-
tioning them by name in any sense nor even by suggestion). Neither had either the guts or the ability to make a
reply on the same level as theoriginal article. It could be
that the Times has it in for me because I have persistently
refused to review books forx them; on the other hand they
change personnel so often that they probably don't even

know I refused. But what I'm getting at is that if a paper of
that quality can't judge a book by its quality as a piece of
writing rather than by its news value or subject matter, how
in hell can one expect a semi-literate public to do anything
more intelligent? In the current list of the 20 best sellers (SR
version) there are two books worth reading as writing, one
abrave and handsome try but a muddle all the same, six
that are just a lot of fat pretentiousness, two that are first
class second class fiction of the quality of The Cruel Sea,
and the rest include a great subject not a great book, a piece
of scandal, a journalitic investigation, a piece of tiresome
religious yap, and one of those books that Americans and
English always fall for because they seem—while you are
reading them—to extend a touch of clarity in the direction
of the confused mystics of the lecture circuit suckers.

Well, to business. As to Pocket Books, the joint control clause was not important to me and there was no dispute over it. What you get from Pocket Books will be, as I
know, the best that can be got. So as to terms and even time
of publication I gladly leave the decision to you.

As to the other thing, and Mr. Runyon's letter is
herewith returned, I do think you should be informed of
the contents of the book, the total length, the names and
nature of theother contributions. I will not agree to any
condensation except on a specific basis. As a reader I won't
buy a condensed book and as a writer I won't sell one.
(Which reminds me to ask you if by any remote chance
you have a copy of James Ross's They Don't Dance Much,
originally published by you and reprinted not too unre-
cently in a condensed version, which I spit on. Dale Warren ought to know.) If, for instance, the total length of the
contents is not equal or greater to/than the length of LY, we
are getting horsed. We may be getting horsed in any case.
But if you don't know, who does?

It may interest and even sadden you to know that I
receive a larger income from Europe, especidlly England,
than from the USA. In spite of the exchange situation. Your
December statement was a whimper from the Morgue.
Your total sales of LS (which you hope to equal with this
last thing and have not at the timeof writing, obviously,) are
less than 17,000 copies. The English sales for the same
period were almost 30,000. Knopf sold about 15,000 copies
of Farewell MY Lovely and didn't reach that with any
other book. Do you think I could do any better if I wrote a
story which was not a mystery? I think I'd do worse. I
think a certain pattern of thinking has been established in
this monkky-culture of ours and only some violent accident
would change it.

We are still trying to sell this house, much as we like
it. My wife is far from well, domestic help is unobtainable
unless you have, as we have, a treasure. But we have her
only five days a week, she is not too well herself, and she
has troubles which may end her for us at almost any time.
If I get sick over a week end, it is a catastrophe. My wife

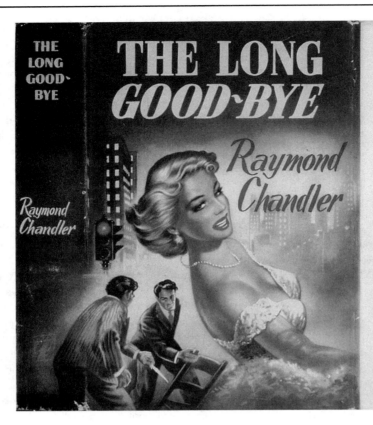

IN *The Long Good-bye*, Mr. Chandler's first novel for four years, Philip Marlowe is shown to have lost none of the appetite for adventure and the contempt for authority, and the over-privileged which make him a magnet for trouble. This is how he describes his life as a Private Investigator:

'So passed a day in the life of a P.I. Not exactly a typical day but not totally untypical either. What makes a man stay with it nobody knows. You don't get rich, you don't often have much fun. Sometimes you get beaten up or shot at or tossed into the jailhouse. Once in a long while you get dead. Every other month you decide to give it up and find some sensible occupation while you can still walk without shaking your head. Then the door buzzer rings and you open the inner door to the waiting-room and there stands a new face with a new problem, a new load of grief and a small piece of money.'

But, as the reader of Mr. Chandler's earlier books won't have to be told such casual encounters usually lead to a succession of curious and increasingly violent events. Suffice it to say that in *The Long Good-bye*, Mr. Chandler writes as brilliantly as ever and that the suspense, characterisation, and description of people and places are of the first order. To give away more would be to spoil the reader's fun.

Published by Hamish Hamilton at 10s. 6d.

THRILLER BOOK CLUB EDITION

THRILLER BOOK CLUB

President:
W. A. FOYLE

★ *Books by all these famous Authors have been issued by the Thriller Book Club:*

E. PHILLIPS OPPENHEIM
F. L. GREEN
FRANCIS BEEDING
AGATHA CHRISTIE
NIGEL MORLAND
JAMES HADLEY CHASE
GLADYS MITCHELL
GEORGE BELLAIRS
ERIC AMBLER
PETER CHEYNEY
JOHN CREASEY
GEORGES SIMENON
CHRISTOPHER BUSH
JONATHAN STAGGE
MICHAEL GILBERT
DELANO AMES
VERA CASPARY
SIMON HARVESTER
ERLE STANLEY GARDNER
MICKEY SPILLANE
NGAIO MARSH
GEORGE HARMON COXE

THE THRILLER BOOK CLUB
121 CHARING CROSS ROAD
LONDON, W.C.2

RECENT AND FORTHCOMING THRILLER BOOK CLUB SELECTIONS

FEAR TO TREAD
Michael Gilbert
Published at 10s. 6d.

★

WHISTLE UP THE DEVIL
Derek Smith
Published at 9s. 6d.

★

DETECTION UNLIMITED
Georgette Heyer
Published at 10s. 6d.

★

A POCKET FULL OF RYE
Agatha Christie
Published at 10s. 6d.

★

A KNIFE FOR HARRY DODD
George Bellairs
Published at 9s. 6d.

★

THRILLER BOOK CLUB EDITIONS
are issued at 3s. 6d.

Dust jacket for the book-club reprint of the first edition, published in 1954 (Bruccoli Collection, Kent State University)

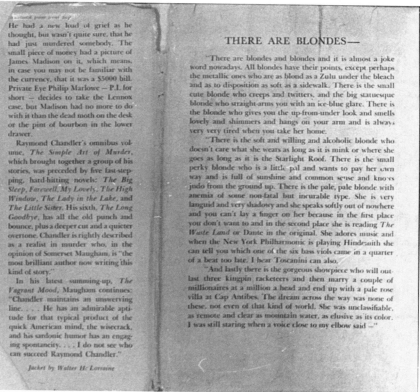

Dust jacket for the first American edition, of which ten thousand copies were published on 18 March 1954
(Bruccoli Collection, Kent State University)

Houghton Mifflin advertisement

almost fainted two or three times last weekend trying to take care of me. We can't live here indefinitely. We are thinking of the south of France. The climate would be good for Cissy. But it's a pretty risky adventure all the same. I have an operative working on it. What acquaintances tell you is no good unless you know their own standards. I'm not terribly fond of French people but I know the language and they at least do their own thinking and can express it in language. A stevedore on the docks is more articulate in France than most senators and Congressmen are here. And McCarthy would last over there about the length of time necessary to uncover the cesspool.

I salute you finally with two animal stories, one true, one not. A family on the street behind us has a black French poodle, small, toy size, I guess. The animal is taking piano lessons, $35 a month. As of now he can play Peter, Peter, Pumpkin eater, not technically very exactling, but one has to begin, n'est-ce pas? Little steps for little feet. Later one hopes he will make his debut in Carnegie Hall. The people can afford it and that's all it takes. One looks forward, perhaps a little hesitantly, to his scintillating performance of Chopin's Barcarolle, a difficult place seldom played and never played really well since de Pachmann. Rubinstein is supposed to be a Chopin virtuoso, but to me he is very in and out. The poodle has a pretty clear field there. It's nice to have ambitious neighbors, and to live in a milieu where money in spent on Art, not just on Cadillacs, Jaguars, and colored butlers. This is true. $35 a month for lessons. Black toy French poodle.

The other one is about a guy who went to the CINEMA (English accent please) and was annoyed by a large, tall and far too wide fur coat in front of him. Leaning over he perceived that the fur coat was a bear. He tapped the man beside the bear on the shoulder.

"I say, old man, is that your bear?"

"He's with me."

"Well get him out of here right away, old man. This is no place to bring a bear."

"I shall do nothing of the sort. He's paid for his ticket and he's enjoying himself."

Man subsides, very annoyed. Picture ends finally, lights go up, man with bear seems about to leave. Objecting man has a change of heart.

"I say, old man, sorry I spoke like that about your bear. Seems dashed well behaved. But why bring him to the pictures, old man?"

"Oh, he's very fond of the CINEMA, very fond indeed. And he particularly wanted to see this film. He liked the book so much."

                                                    Ray
                        —transcribed from original document,
                        Houghton Library, Harvard University

As Chandler expected, The Long Good-Bye *was generally relegated to the mystery review columns in American newspapers and magazines. The reviews were mixed, with some critics finding the novel a step backward for Chandler and others judging it one of his best performances.*

THE LONG GOODBYE, by Raymond Chandler (Houghton Mifflin) In this long book (316 pages), Mr. Chandler has practically abandoned anything resembling a coherent plot to devote himself to an exhaustive study of manners and morals in California, the status of both of which appears to be grotesque. The detective, Philip Marlowe, has an active time with lovely and acquiescent ladies, alcoholics, dope fiends, gangsters, sinister Mexicans, and all the other phenomena common to the locale, and the author's mannerisms have seldom been more pronounced; the story, which has to do with nymphomania in exalted circles as much as anything else, hardly seems worth all the bother.

—"Mystery and Crime," *The New Yorker,* 30
(27 March 1954): 135–136

* * *

Philip Marlowe is a kind (if gruff) man in an unkind world, a romantic in a world too rich for such illusions, a man of integrity whose acquaintance is sorted painfully from among vicious cops (and honest, less effectual ones), the hollow rich, and the wearily honest men caught between.

It is his compassion that catches Marlowe in this bloody mess—the chance that leads him to wretched Terry Lennox outside the terrace of The Dancers. Terry is a special sort of stray dog, and by helping him Marlowe finds himself thick in a vicious set of circumstances that leave murder a very simple art indeed.

The good by to Terry is spoken early and there is nothing much at first to suggest any connection with the puzzle of the distrait best-selling novelist. But Idle Valley (that retreat of the very rich from the vulgar inconveniences of Los Angeles) intervenes and Marlowe must work out the problems pretty much alone, beset by cops on one side and the influence of the very rich on the other. He works it out doggedly with all but absolute distaste, facing cops and blondes and the other more peculiar habitués of the Chandler world.

The consequence of all this is Mr. Chandler's longest novel to date, one of his most meticulously plotted and by some stretches his most corrosive. What he gives us here is painful if exciting pleasure.

—James Sandoe, "Mystery and Suspense," *New York Herald Tribune,* 4 April 1954, p. 13

* * *

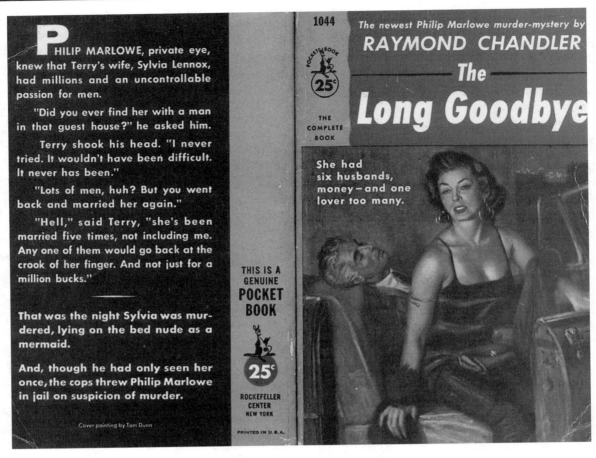

First paperback edition of Chandler's sixth novel, published in 1955

About ten years ago, a discerning friend urged me to read a mystery writer called **Raymond Chandler**, and since then I have been one of Chandler's more zealous *aficionados*. It sometimes saddens me to think that there are numerous persons of good taste who have not made the acquaintance of private detective Philip Marlowe, the hard-boiled *chevalier sans peur et sans reproche* who, with his trusty Oldsmobile, goes out to do battle with the hard boys and the crooked cops, the dope peddlers and blackmailers and murderous sirens of Los Angeles and surrounding California—and as often as not doesn't even collect his $25 per diem and expenses. To those who haven't bothered with Chandler out of a justifiable distaste for the run-of-the-mill murder mystery, I submit that his work is as superior to the aforesaid product as Beluga caviar is to salmon's eggs. If corroboration is wanted, I can cite, for one, Mr. Somerset Maugham, who has called Chandler "the most brilliant author now writing this kind of story."

Philip Marlowe has just showed up again in *The Long Goodbye* (Houghton Mifflin, $3.00)—a little older and more prone to bitter repartee, but still as tough as they come and as rudely chivalrous behind his mask of cynicism.

Marlowe's current troubles begin when he plays the good Samaritan to a polite drunk with a scarred face and an English accent who has been pushed out of a Rolls-Royce. There is a lost dog air about Terry Lennox that "gets" Marlowe. When Lennox shows up in a daze, not sure that he hasn't murdered his wife, a luscious tramp with millions, Marlowe helps him do a bunk to Mexico. The cops give Marlowe the treatment, and presently he learns that Lennox has shot himself and has signed a confession. A farewell letter from Mexico containing a $5000 bill makes it look as if the Lennox case were closed—except for the curious fact that a lot of people are going out of their way to impress upon Marlowe that the Lennox case had better *stay closed* or else. Before the whole truth comes to light, two more people die; Marlowe meets the loveliest woman he has ever seen and refuses to be seduced by her; he succumbs (for the first time on record) to another temptress, and he winds up with the flat taste of another disillusionment.

The Long Goodbye has not quite the same sparkle and bounce as Chandler's early novels, not quite the same profusion of similes that pucker the senses like an electric shock. But the somewhat quieter plotting makes for a more thoughtful tone, a deeper cut. I think that Mr. Chandler's fans will get their money's worth.

—Charles J. Rolo, "Philip Marlowe, Private Detective," *The Atlantic*, 193 (May 1954): 82–83

Cissy's Death

In the summer of 1954 Cissy Chandler's health worsened. She visited a succession of doctors in San Diego and Los Angeles before receiving a diagnosis of fibrosis of the lungs, a rare illness that causes the hardening of lung tissue. Cissy Chandler died on 12 December 1954. In writing to Hamish Hamilton, Chandler discusses plans and refers briefly to a proposal to serialize The Big Sleep, *but most of the letter is given over to a description of his wife's last days.*

Box One Twenty Eight
La Jolla, California
January 5, 1955

Dear Jamie:

It was nice to talk to you on the telephone. It was the first and probably the only time I shall ever permit myself the luxury of a trans-Atlantic telephone call. The occasion seemed somehow to justify it, and it did not cost as much as I expected. Thank you for your several kind letters and also for the books you sent. Please don't send me any more books, as they will only have to go into storage. I don't recall whether I told you that I have sold the house, but I have, and I will be out of here about March 15th or before. I don't think I can make it to New York early in February. In fact, I don't think that the trip would be worthwhile, because I am planning to take a Swedish boat through the Canal about the first or second week in April. The dates of sailings are not fixed yet so I can't be absolute. I'll let you know as soon as I know myself about when I shall be in London. I gather from your letter that you would like me to stay with you at your house for a little while. But if I may say so without sounding ungrateful, I should rather be on my own. I'd like to be at a hotel—any good hotel, even the Connaught—until you can help me find a service flat. And I don't want to spend a fortune. I should like to stay in Europe about six months, and spend as much time in England as I can without incurring the risk of being called a resident. I should also like to go to Paris, and perhaps though not certainly, to the South of France for part of the time. I don't want to be a burden or a nuisance to anyone. I am pretty badly broken up, and for me it may last a long time, as my emotions are not superficial. I have friends with me, and they are going to Europe with me, although I do not think that in the beginning they will go to England. We hope to come on one of the new Swedish cargo boats, which are about fifty per cent more expensive than the other ships of the type, and for that reason it is easier to get reservations on them. They probably go to Antwerp, Rotterdam and London, but God knows where in London, very likely the East India docks.

I hope the answer to your cable about *The Big Sleep* was satisfactory. I don't really care what they do with it. I assume the *Daily Sketch* is the type of paper you and I don't read.

Leonard Russell sent me a very touching letter which I have already answered. If it is convenient, you might telephone Eric Partridge and tell him that I know I owe him a letter, and tell him why I have not so far been able to write to him. You probably realized when we were in London that Cissy was in rather frail health. When we got back she looked and felt better than she had in a couple of years, but it didn't last. She got weaker and weaker and more and more tired. She tried to drive herself, and there were a few occasions when she actually drove her car out, and on several others I drove her somewhere she wanted to go, or just out of doors for the air, or to do some shopping for clothes she badly needed. But even that ceased. Usually, until about a month before she died, she was able to get up part of the day and to dinner. She had an obscure and rather rare ailment, I am told, called fibrosis of the lungs. I don't think they know very much about it or what causes it. It's a slow hardening of the lung tissue, starting at the bottom of the lungs and progressing upwards. The part that is fibrosed returns no oxygen to the blood, which of course puts more strain on the heart and the breathing. As far back as 1948 her X-rays showed the condition as existing, but it was quite a long time before I realized that it could only have one ending. I don't think that she herself ever quite gave up hope, or if so during the last weeks, she didn't let anyone else know that she had given up hope. We tried a number of doctors. Mostly they just gave up without saying why. Late in October we tried a Dr. Neber, whom we had known when we first came to La Jolla but had given up because his medicine had never seemed to agree with Cissy, and he started her on cortisone. We tried him principally because he had three or four cases of fibrosis of the lungs, which is unusual for one doctor to have in a

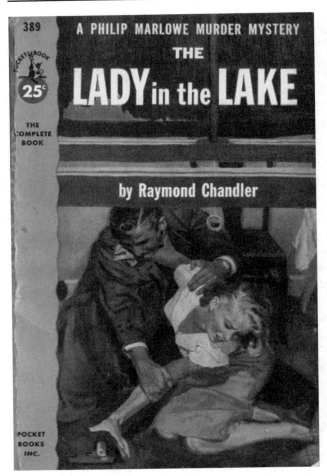 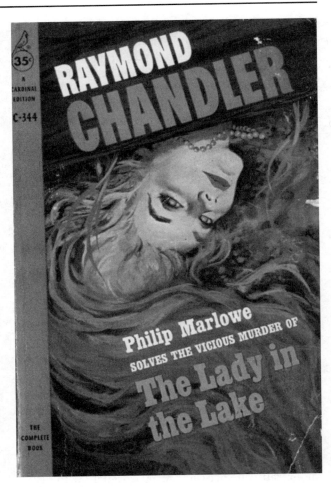

Covers for the last printing of the 1946 Pocket Books edition and the first printing of the Cardinal edition, both published in 1954

small place like La Jolla. With his other patients he had had great success with cortisone. A couple of them that had been bedridden had been able to get up and go about their business almost normally. But it is a very strong medicine, and Cissy was always peculiar about drugs. It affected her brain, and especially it affected her memory and made her very uncomfortable. She couldn't remember anything for five or ten minutes. I had to measure out all her medicines, or else she would take them twice or three times over without realizing she had already taken them. The cortisone didn't work, so at the end of the first week in November he took her off that and started her on ACTH, and this, after the first shots, I was able to give her myself hypodermically, as I had been used for several years to give her hypodermic shots of various vitamins. This didn't do very much good either. She got lower and lower and more and more depressed, and she was not an easily depressed person. On November 30 she developed pneumonia and had to be taken to the hospital in an ambulance. Early the next morning she was clamoring to be taken home in an absolute fury of indignation. From seven o'clock on she called repeatedly or had her nurse call. I managed to persuade her to stay there that day and until the following morning, and then her temperature being normal and the penicillin having apparently aborted the pneumonia, the doctor reluctantly allowed me to bring her home, which made her very happy. But the next day she had already forgotten about the horrors of the hospital—and no one ever hated hospitals more—and was wanting to go back again. The doctor furthermore wanted to try a medicine called ruwaulfia, or African snake root, which apparently has the property of inducing a condition of euphoria without any damage and can be taken indefinitely. He told me at the time that she would have to spend the rest of her life in a sanitarium and that he was hoping the ruwaulfia would put her in such a complaisant mood that she would accept that. The next morning again she called up early and demanded to be taken home.

So I got in touch with the doctor and I said I couldn't stand her mental suffering, and he again reluctantly allowed me to bring her home. By this time she was very ill and very weak, had to be helped to the bathroom, had to have someone stay there with her. Her sister Vinnie and I were just about done in, especially Vinnie, because we got very little sleep. I then managed to get nurses around the clock to take care of her, but she was very miserable, gasped all time, coughed violently, and said she was in great pain. By December 7th I realized she was dying. In the middle of the night she suddenly appeared in my room in her pajamas looking like a ghost, having evaded the nurse somehow. We got her back to bed and she tried it once more, but this time the nurse was watching. At three A.M. on the morning of December 8th her temperature was so low that the nurse got frightened and called the doctor, and once more the ambulance came and took her off to the hospital. She couldn't sleep and I knew it took a lot of stuff to put her under, so I would take her sleeping pills and she would tie them in the corner of her handkerchief so that she could swallow them surreptitiously when the nurse was out of the room. She was in an oxygen tent all the time, but she kept pulling it away so that she could hold my hand. She was quite vague in her mind about some things, but almost too desperately clear about other. Once she asked me where we lived, what town we lived in, and then asked me to describe the house. She didn't seem to know what it looked like. Then she would turn her head away and when I was no longer in her line of vision, she seemed to forget all about me. Whenever I went to see her she would reach her handkerchief out under the edge of the oxygen tent for me to give her the sleeping pills. I began to be worried about this and confessed to the doctor, and he said she was getting much stronger medicine than any sleeping pills. On the 11th when I went to see her I had none and she reached out under the edge of the oxygen tent with the handkerchief, and when I had nothing to give her she turned her head away and said, "Is this the way you wanted it?" About noon that day the doctor called me up and said I had better come over and talk to her as it might be the last chance I would have. When I got over there he was trying to find veins in her feet to inject *demerol*. What an irony that I should have written about *demerol* in my last book! He managed to get her asleep, but she was wide awake again that night. That is she seemed to be wide awake, but I'm not even sure that she knew me. She went to sleep again while I was there. A little after noon on December

12th, which was a Sunday, the nurse called up and said she was very low, which is about as drastic a statement as a nurse ever makes. Vinnie's son was here then with Vinnie, and he drove me over to the hospital at fifty miles an hour, breaking all the traffic regulations, which I told him to ignore as the La Jolla cops were friends of mine. When I got there they had taken the oxygen tent away and she was lying with her eyes half open. I think she was already dead. Another doctor had his stethoscope over her heart and was listening. After a while he stepped back and nodded. I closed her eyes and kissed her and went away.

Of course in a sense I had said goodbye to her long ago. In fact, many times during the past two years in the middle of the night I had realized that it was only a question of time until I lost her. But that is not the same thing as having it happen. Saying goodbye to your loved one in your mind is not the same thing as closing her eyes and knowing they will never open again. But I was glad that she died. To think of this proud, fearless bird caged in a room in some rotten sanitarium for the rest of her days was such an unbearable thought that I could hardly face it at all. I didn't really break until after the funeral, partly because I was in shock and partly because I had to hold her sister together. I am sleeping in her room. I thought I couldn't face that, and then I thought that if the room were empty it would just be haunted, and every time I went past the door I would have the horrors, and that the only thing was for me to come in here and fill it up with my junk and make it look the kind of mess I'm used to living in. It was the right decision. Her clothes are all around me, but they are in closets or hidden away in drawers. I have a couple of very old friends staying with me, and they are patient and kind beyond any expectation. But the horrors are all mine just the same. For thirty years, ten months and four days, she was the light of my life, my whole ambition. Anything else I did was just the fire for her to warm her hands at. That is all there is to say.

I'm afraid my Christmas orders were put in a little late, but I hope they arrived in time to cheer you all up a little. I don't know how things are over there now, but I gather from Roger that they are a lot better than they used to be.

Love to all,

Yours ever,

Ray

—*Selected Letters of Raymond Chandler,* pp. 374–379

After Cissy's death, Chandler fell into a depression and drank heavily. He threatened to kill himself several times during the two months after the funeral, and on 22 February 1955 he made an actual attempt. Neil Morgan, a reporter at the San Diego Tribune *and a longtime friend, came to Chandler's aid afterward, and he later described the incident in an article for* California *magazine.*

She died eight weeks before their thirty-first anniversary. Chandler was brusque. He stored her ashes at a San Diego mausoleum, and then he went home to La Jolla to look at the ocean and drink. He drank through their anniversary and for two weeks more. He had done this before, but not this big. He had married Cissy just fifteen days after the death of his mother, whom he had protected until her death. Now, for the first time, no one was dependent upon him. "All that is really the matter with me is that I have no home," he would later write, "and no one to care for in a home, if I had one."

The police were nearby one afternoon when two shots broke the quiet of the sea cliff. The police, who admired Chandler and had already helped him through three suicide threats, decided to lock him away in the county psycho ward. Their report read that he was sitting on the floor of his shower, trying to get his revolver into his mouth. When one officer asked Chandler for the gun, he laughed his hard cackle that came when he cared about someone or something and wanted it known that he did not care at all, and he handed it over. There were two holes in the shower ceiling. Neither bullet had been through Chandler.

It was simple to explain later that his act was theatrical, a classic cry for help. In *The Long Goodbye,* published just a year earlier, is this passage: "Then he opened his eyes and that weary smile played on his lips. 'Nobody hurt,' he muttered. 'Just a wild shot into the ceiling.'"

But Chandler's pain was real. I first learned of his pantomime through a small item in the next morning's *San Diego Union.* On a hunch that there had been no one else to do it, I stopped by the county hospital on my way to work. The superintendent waved me into his office, and I explained that I knew Chandler. He flipped through the night's admission sheets and whistled. He knew who Chandler was; he read. He got up and unlocked the white iron door and nodded to me to follow. It was an old hospital then, without any forced cheerfulness. It smelled of puke, and the eyes behind the heavy wire mesh were like those of caged animals.

Chandler stood among them like a wet puppy that had been bad. He had written of such places, but his pale face showed his shock at waking up in one.

"You want to get out of here?" I asked.

"I'd like that very much indeed," he said. The English public school accent stayed with Chandler throughout his American years, but it was not there that morning. He looked like a man about to cry again.

The superintendent nodded. This time with hope. "How do you feel now?" he asked.

"I feel like a bath," Chandler said, "and some decent coffee."

"I can't release you now unless you go to a private sanitorium under a doctor's care," he said.

"Why?" Chandler asked.

"The law. You were brought here as a suicide attempt."

Chandler managed a smile. "If you'll let me go I won't do that again."

I signed him out and drove him to a private sanitorium. It was just a trace more pleasant than the county hospital and cost a lot more. Chandler would have had considerable money except for his wife's long illness. As it was, he had enough. But this was not where he intended to spend it. He also knew the law. Six days later he released himself and called me to take him home. He was buoyant. Two pretty nurses slipped their arms through his and walked him to the car.

"If I am sufficiently sane to charm these ladies," he said, "I am weller than I have been in years."

So I drove him home, much like the reporter Lonnie Morgan, who drove Marlowe home one night in *The Long Goodbye.* Chandler said he remembered nothing and would never know whether he had meant to kill himself. He said he was sorry to trouble a friend. We didn't talk much. It was the kind of moment between people that is too revealing to risk small talk and too unsettling to permit much more. When we reached Camino de la Costa he asked me in for a drink. I felt not at all like drinking, but Chandler did, and the house was empty. We went in. He fixed drinks first and called a real estate agent second, to say he would sell the house to the first buyer.

−"The Long Goodbye," *California Magazine,* 7 (June 1982): 91

The "Long Nightmare" of Mourning

After selling his house on Camino de la Costa, Chandler put his furniture in storage and stayed at the Del Charro Hotel in La Jolla. In March 1955 he traveled by train to Chicago, then to Old Chatham, New York, where he stayed with Ralph Barrow, an old friend, formerly a lawyer in Los Angeles. Chandler intended to continue on to England, but in Old Chatham he developed a sinus ailment, and his trip was delayed by a stop in New York City for medical treatment. Chandler sailed for England on the Mauretania *on 12 April 1955 with plans to stay until September. Chandler was a literary celebrity in England, and his arrival was reported widely in British news. He gave several interviews, including the following one to Rene MacColl of the* Daily Express.

Raymond Chandler Now Says I Confess
'I've no special knowledge about the police . . .'
Rene MacColl
London Daily Express, 25 April 1955, p. 6

THE AUTHOR whose books are found in statesmen's suitcases, are read by bishops in trains—and devoured by millions of ordinary people—has just arrived in London. He has turned detective stories into literature, as well as gold mines. Over the past 16 years—in best-sellers and best-filmers such as "The Big Sleep," "The High Window," and "Lady in the Lake"—he has added his own creation, Philip Marlowe, to the gallery of unforgettable fictional detectives. Marlowe, of course, is a hardboiled, indestructible "private eye." And RENE MacCOLL decided to assume the Marlowe technique when he interviewed Chandler yesterday. Here is MacColl-Marlowe's report. . . .

RENE MacCOLL FINDS HIM IN
LONDON YESTERDAY

IT was about noon, and I was calling on a man who has slugged a million dollars out of a typewriter.

I was wearing my suit, the new one, and display handkerchief, brown suede shoes, matching socks with darns in them. I felt moderately healthy.

The rain had stopped and there was the clean, sharp smell of sparrows in the air. The place had a front-door, and I was standing there wondering if it opened outwards, when the commissionaire slid me a remote, ageless look, finished biting his nails, and went inside.

Chandler was sitting in the oak-panelled bar. He showed me dark glasses, grey hair, and a small face with a cigarette in it. His left hand moved imperceptibly, shifting a fawn-coloured trouser-leg upwards.

The canary-yellow socks were hand-made. So the pigskin monk's shoes. Figuring from knee-level to the ground alone, 30 guineas were on display.

I chance it
THE voice sounded as though it had been stabbed with an ice-pick. "How do you like your whisky?" it asked.

"With ginger-ale," I said. There was a long wedge of silence, and then the voice said softly, "You take chances, Mister."

He half-frowned at his gimlet, tasted it, and then frowned some more. I gave him the boyish smile and he started to talk.

"I won't tell you my age," he said, "because I never tell anyone that. I live in a suburb of San Diego, in Southern California. It likes to think itself exclusive.

"My mother was English, and when she divorced my father she brought me from Chicago, where I was born, back here, to London. We lived in Upper Norwood and I went to Dulwich College. I was a pretty good wing forward at Rugger. I bowled a fair off-break at cricket—a slow ball, but I didn't have proper control."

He paused, and I could feel the pulse in my throat starting to get faster. I waited for what was coming.

"Cricket," said Chandler—*and the hand holding my drink sweated a little bit as he spoke* – "has changed enormously since I was at Dulwich."

Jack-pot
CHANDLER refused to take a phone call, fought another cigarette into his mouth and lit it with an ivory-trimmed lighter that flared the first time.

"We returned to the States in 1912, and I went to work in oil in California.

"I started to wander up and down the Pacific coast after I quit oil. In the evenings I would read the pulp magazines under naked electric light bulbs in cheap rooming-houses and think 'This stuff is elementary enough for me to do too.' I had always wanted to write; it was just a question whether I could make a living out of it.

"I started writing full-time in 1933. After six years I hit the jack-pot with 'Big Sleep.'"

'Not Real'
CHANDLER turned and looked full at me, his face suddenly haggard. "I've got to tell you something," he almost whispered. "Something important.

"There are no people like Philip Marlowe. There couldn't be. Real life 'private eyes' in America are grubby little men who do wiretapping and divorce work and steal photos when they get the chance. They never work on murder cases.

"I have no special knowledge about the police or police methods. I have never been a crime reporter. I do know a couple of cops casually, and if I want a particular piece of information about police work I occasionally ask for it. I have never based a character on any person I have ever met. It's all imagination.

"Mostly the police in America are rather stupid people. And there is still a lot of police brutality and sadism in the large cities."

Chandler C/O
MRS. RALPH BARROW
RUSHWATER (You don't need this. It's
OLD CHATHAM, NEW YORK   just the name of
                                                        the estate)

Old Chatham 9-2114
                                                        March 23, 1955

Dear Hardwick:

        I spent hours trying to call you last night, but
you were out. Yours and Charlie Morton's were the
only telephone numbers and home addresses that I had.
I planned to come over to Boston but I have to go to
New York about April 1st and get my sinuses treated.
I also have an infected thumb which won't heal. A
broken big toe on my right foot is trivial by comparison. I leave for England on the Mauretania April 12th
and have a return leaving Southampton Sept 23rd if I
live that long. I also have half a book written and
hope to finish it over there. It is shorter and much
less introspective than LGB. In fact it is probably
worthless, but one never knows. Anyhow the scene is
La Jolla and a local columnist named Neil Morgan,
a Carolinian and very good friend of mine, has already
spilled the beans (why beans?) on that and the
citizenby are about equally divided between dragging
me behind a chariot and the more commonplace method
of shooting me with an arbalest. Unfortunately for
them the local police force is very much on my side.

        When the furniture had been moved out of the
house and I went through it checking doors and windows
I felt like the last man on a dead world. It was a
horror I could never describe. And yet I knew very well
how lucky I was to have sold it just when it happened.

        I am staying with friends here and am up to
my eyebrows in early American. It is a Cape Cod
house (I think) in a huge tract of over a hundred
acres of what was once farmland but is now all
trees and brooks and waterfalls. The weather up until
today has been lousy and I loved it. After the endless
calm of Southern California what a joy to slither
through snow and feel a biting wind. Love to all
                                                        Ray

Letter from Chandler to Hardwick Moseley, which he wrote while waiting to board a ship to England

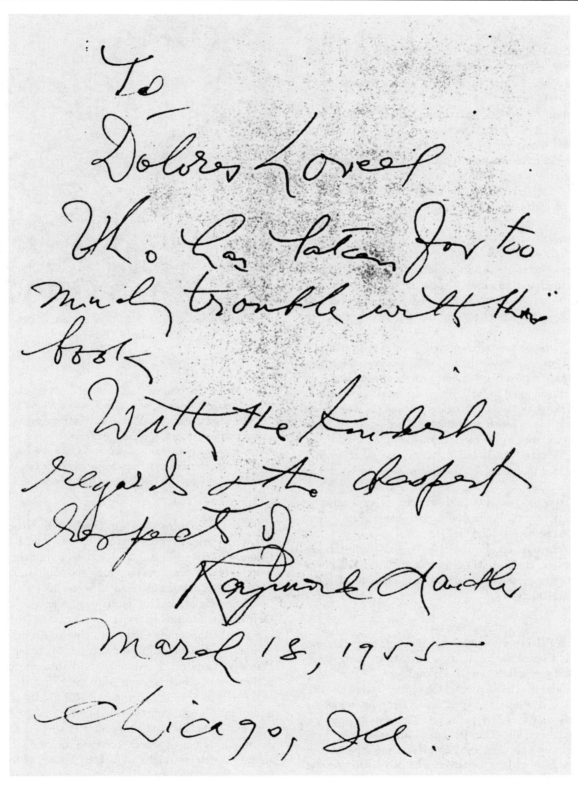

Chandler's inscription to a Chicago bookseller in Farewell, My Lovely. *Chandler traveled through the city on the first leg of a trip to England (Bruccoli Collection, Kent State University).*

Love? No

HE sat there brooding over the brutality and he bounced the cherry against the inside of his glass almost soundlessly. "Any questions?" he snapped.

I reached for my voice. "Why does Marlowe never quite fall for the girl?"

"Marlowe would lose something by being promiscuous. Some of these clucks, I mean some of the other writers, spend their time writing sex. Not me. But in his last case Marlowe did have an affair. It couldn't go on for ever, the way he always said no—the guy was human and he had to break down some time. I hated to see him do it, though. But the kind of affair he had, I'd like myself.

"Then came the films." He laughed with silence and no amusement.

"Hollywood," he said, and paused to listen to the small sound his cigarette butt made in the dregs of his gimlet, "is scared and insincere. It took me three years to get over one year of Hollywood. I had fights with the studio all the time. I was suspended for four months—very unusual for a writer.

"Of the actors who played Marlowe in films, I thought Dick Powell was best. Bogart is always superb as Bogart, but Powell seemed to me just right as Marlowe.

"I'm supposed to be finishing my next book here in London, but it looks like a hopeless proposition. Too many dinner parties, too much hospitality.

"I just work in the mornings, when I get up. I never revise. If I force myself and the stuff's no good when I re-read it, I throw it away. Always throw away what you don't like.

"I'm a good plain cook. I love jazz — but it must be wild jazz, not the commercial stuff. Jam sessions," he looked at me from far back behind his eyes.

"From now on, I write only books. TV is terribly hard work. So are films. My most successful book sold over a million copies, including paper backs, but not including the foreign translations."

And finally—

I MOVED my shoulders quietly inside my jacket and waited. There was one last thing to be said: one thing, inevitable as old age, pitiless as a slipped cartilage.

"After I left Dulwich," said Chandler, "I went to work on the *Daily Express* as a reporter. I was a complete flop, the worst man they ever had. Every time they sent me out on a story I would get lost. They fired me. I deserved it."

I got up and went away quickly, along the carpet in the lobby and out into the street. The pedestrian crossing looked as evil as the fine print in a hire-purchase contract. And when I called to the taxi at the head of the line the driver went on not hearing.

Natasha Spender

Despite the attention from the press and many social invitations, Chandler was lonely and unhappy during his stay in England. He established a warm friendship with Natasha Spender, a concert pianist and wife of poet Stephen Spender. Natasha Spender helped Chandler through his bouts of depression and drinking, and she described the experience in an essay titled "His Own Long Goodbye," which was included in The World of Raymond Chandler *(1977).*

A few months after the death of his wife, and a few weeks after his own first suicide attempt, Raymond Chandler arrived in England and settled into the Connaught Hotel, sixty-seven years old, still suicidal, ill, very alcoholic and absorbed in what he always called the 'long nightmare' of mourning. Knowing nothing then of this recent history, I found myself one day in late April 1955 sitting next to an elderly American gentleman at luncheon in the house of his publisher Hamish Hamilton. I saw only the lumbering courtesy and humour, which he seemed to force through an aura of despair to respond to the cheerful kindly conversation of his hostess. After luncheon when Yvonne Hamilton had told me the story, I tentatively suggested inviting him, which she encouraged me to do, though I supposed that he might well be in no mood for social life. However, he responded with apparent pleasure and gruff grace to my invitation for dinner in the following week, 'as long as there aren't any literary heavyweights around'. Hardly wishing to conduct a weighing-in of our friends, we invited younger non-literary ones, whom we knew to be intelligent enthusiasts for his books.

It was an amusing evening; he seemed delighted by compliments, and even rather exhilarated to deliver himself, with a certain flourish, of a far too deprecating reply. It seemed touching that, to quote Adlai Stevenson, he should allow himself to 'inhale some of the flattery' with a mixture of modesty and swagger, as if a long-immured hermit should be eagerly overjoyed at anyone even remembering his name. In his letter of thanks — which characteristically arrived by special messenger — he said that his hostess might be thought 'a rather over-enthusiastic appraiser of lowdown literature. I must insist that I am nothing but a glib and "quick-brained" character who chanced on a formula that would permit almost infinite experiment into the American vernacular.' Yet in spite of the pace of all our gaiety, and his sudden flights of glorious nonsense, his great brooding silences and the shadow of his desperation had hung in the air. Later, one of the guests, Jocelyn Rickards, talked to me of the alarm we both felt concerning his survival. She believed that his gentlemanly good manners would never permit him to implement his evidently strong suicidal impulses if he had an imminent social engagement with a lady. So in turn we each invited ourselves to a meal with him, or him to one with us, other friends joined in, and so began the 'shuttle service' by which our small group tried to ensure that he was never out of sight of an impending gentle and undemanding social engagement, and that he could at bad times telephone one of us at any time in the twenty-four hours.

Those telephone calls in the small hours (for he was particularly insomniac after his wife's death) could start out as long stretches of silence broken only by heavy breathing, followed by grim battles of his nihilism versus our spirit, but sooner or later he might be coaxed into feeling that there was not long to wait for the festivities of the following day; or his sardonic mockery of one's efforts to encourage him led to his being unable to resist making a joke, and then sudden delight at his own sally brought with it a resurgence of pleasure and hopefulness; he would ring off chuckling with triumph at having got the best of an argument and no doubt happily thinking up further volleys to shoot off at luncheon. Sometimes 'Hang on till breakfast-time' was the only way to deal with those early morning calls if all else failed, and then one or other of us would go to breakfast with him — 'The Dawn Patrol' as Alison Hooper called it.

The nucleus of the shuttle service was Jocelyn Rickards, Alec Murray. Alison Hooper and the Spenders. Others joined in, but some dropped out fairly quickly because of the 'emotional blackmail' he used in his suicidal state. Our motivation (as mine continued to be to the end, having been the last survivor of that group to continue responsibility) was to see him through to a point when he would want to go on living; where he could recognize and accept reality without its disrupting the fantasy into which all his psychic energy had been channelled when he was writing his novels; and above all where he would reverse the process of slowly killing himself with drink. But alternating with extremely alcoholic behaviour, his fantasy seemed entirely to be used in acting out romantic Don Quixote illusions, from the untoward effects of which we tried gently to deliver him, though at times it seemed far from easy or even advisable to do so, for the process would make him very ruffled. As we came to know him better, and to answer the many suicide threats or cries for help which seemed at one and the same time to be absolutely genuine, yet elaborately staged, it became no easier to judge the degree of his desperation, for you can't take chances with suicide, and any accompanying play-acting doesn't guarantee that the intention is less serious. So, as Alison remembers, if telephoned with the peremptory 'Unless you can get here in half-an-hour you'll find a mess like strawberry jam on the sidewalk', one was there in half-an-hour — though sometimes one might arrive to find a totally silent abstracted figure wrapped in gloom. The oscillation of his mood between exuberance and despair made one realize he was having a concealed nervous breakdown, concealed in that he could put up a good superficial show on social occasions, but in private he was resolutely and scornfully impervious to our suggestions that he consult medical advice for these extreme episodes. Indeed, he put up a very good show with us when he was in the mood, charming, considerate and wonderfully funny — 'sparkle' was one of his favourite words, and when he found his vein of good humour, it could be a Catherine-wheel display.

At first we didn't realize how muffled anxiety existed even at the cosy and undemanding social evenings he had in our company in ones or twos. At the Connaught, he would roll into the bar like a tough old Hemingway returning from a lonely battle at sea, he would hurl his order for 'gimlets' at the barman, and then slump flabbily into a chair—his gestures too expansive, his voice rather loud, the topic too boastful until, after a time, he began to feel more at ease. Our judicious delaying of more orders for drinks, combining with his increasing feeling of safety in the company of friends, brought out a gentler humour, yet curiously dissociated from what we knew to be his true state of mind. However, in both despairing and exuberant phases he seemed propelled by anxiety. Those virtuoso verbal improvisations at luncheon at the Connaught which, by their elegant outrageousness, both shocked and entranced the neighbours at the next tables into abandoning all pretence of attending to their own conversations, gave the impression that he was wound up to concert pitch, and after such cadenzas were over he was quite exhausted. (Later, under the title 'A Routine to Shock the Neighbours', he tried to write out some pieces in the same vein, but they emerged on paper as flat, laboured and sometimes, in their oddly automatic tone of 'porn', rather embarrassing.)

In his despairing times too, his anxiety rose as he talked of his wife's death, and it then seemed strange to us that *after* a traumatic loss a person could seem anxious rather than sad, almost as if still in anticipation of the shock. His imaginary misapprehensions about the circumstances of our lives were also at times suffused with unnecessary anxiety. I remember a whole luncheon taken up with his unrealistic fears for Jocelyn's safety during a two-week absence of her flat-mate, though Eaton Square was an eminently safe district in those days; furthermore, she had a wide circle of friends, and being of an independent temperament spent her days happily painting in her studio. But he clung obstinately to visions of a violent burglary or waylaying in spite of all reassurances.

. . . .

At the outset, we were too confident that his oscillations between euphoria and helpless suicidal gloom were no more than the temporary derangement consequent on bereavement. We thought only time was needed to end them. Raymond confided to Jocelyn during their first luncheon that he didn't have long to live as he had incurable cancer of the throat. After a tussle she persuaded him to consult a Harley Street physician, we saw him into the Westminster Hospital, whence after a few days he emerged with the diagnosis of smoker's laryngitis and a determination to ignore all instructions. After considerable provocation the distinguished physician withdrew politely from all responsibility for his wayward uncooperative patient; this being the first of many such relationships Raymond was to have but not to hold with English doctors. Who on earth could have persuaded him to seek psychiatric help, for he certainly wasn't a docile patient? Alison and I used to consult a friend Dr John Thompson (later of the Albert Einstein Hospital) as to how our friendly but unprofessional help could be most effective, but since it *was* only amateur, all one can say is that it was probably better than nothing. Soon afterwards there was liver trouble and a host of minor ailments, through all of which we nursed him or saw him into hospital, trying (when liver tests required *total* abstinence) to

extract the carefully hidden whisky bottles from his luggage without his spotting us.

What we admired was the courage and sporadic humour with which (even amid the egocentric self-pity) he fought his way through these alarming roller-coaster changes of mood, the plunging into loneliness and illness, the zooming up into deliciously irresistible sagas of outrageous nonsense; the bullying contentiousness swivelling suddenly to the disarming repartee, and all as if it was happening to him entirely outside of his control. Though he could at times be an intolerable cross-patch, we admired the courage (sometimes very dramatized courage) with which he undertook those gruesome drying-out cures, and the effort he often generously made to break out of his hopelessness in order to entertain us. Impossible as he could sometimes be, we all became fond of him.

Raymond's conversation swung with his mood. It ranged from the brilliantly fantastic to the serious, contentious or moralizing (for there were times when he found it impossible to be unreservedly appreciative of *anybody,* even his 'best friends'). At other times he would remain morose or sunk in silence. After which perhaps he might on rare occasions talk quietly of Cissy and his whole past life without the usual sentiment or pantomime, and about his reasons for refusing adamantly to admit that he had a future. These occasions were rare for he was a fantasist, so much so that it was often quite difficult to tell whether some story of exploits had not first been improvised and then congealed into permanent credence by frequent repetition. These stories would even sometimes be about one of us. We heard them with indulgent amazement at the kaleidoscopic change a perfectly ordinary event had undergone, emerging as dramatic or amusing with sometimes only a slender thread connecting it with the truth.

As far as we could see, he made no attempt to work in the first two years after Cissy's death and symptomatically his only publications were a letter to a newspaper to protest about the death of a woman by hanging, and an article (also for a newspaper) on his feelings about Cissy's death. But the fantasy which in health and seclusion had gone into novels, in this period of illness and disorientation in a strange country (for his homecoming to England had been unexpectedly fraught with culture-shock) was either acted out in extravaganzas of social behaviour or found its way into letters, of which he must have written hundreds. If one knew him well, one could winnow fact from fantasy in his letters, but since they read as plausibly as his novels it is impossible to imagine how a stranger would ever be able to do so. Although some parts were lucid, benevolent and even brilliantly reasoned, friends told me that they more or less ignored other parts of them as

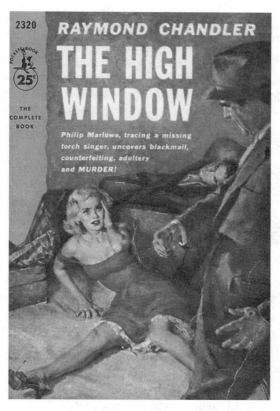

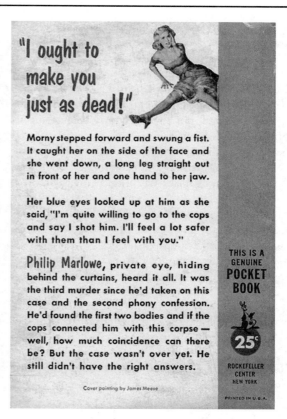

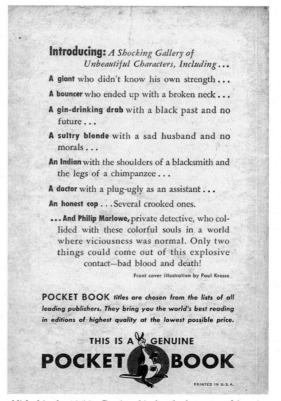

Front and back covers for Pocket Books paperback editions of Chandler's novels published in the 1950s. During this decade the covers of detective paperbacks in the United States emphasized violence and sexuality. Such packaging hindered the recognition of Chandler as a serious author in America.

alcoholic distortion, or, as I did, 'let it ride', interpreting their exaggerated accounts of people, whether approving or scurrilous, as symptoms of his disorientation and misery. Like Roger Wade, he seemed to be able to type equally well, whether sober or drunk.

His legacy from childhood of Victorian values was merely modified, not eliminated, by changes in his environment. They contributed to his deep distrust and disbelief in the generosity of human nature; people are always out to get something out of you and 'toughness' is the only weapon against corruption. This legacy was manifest in his repertoire of pejorative epithets. 'Snobbery' – yet he himself had vestiges of that Victorian middle-class attitude: 'Tradesmen come in by the back door'. He was too impressed by English titles ('blue blood' as he called it) and great family fortunes. 'Literary Pretentiousness' – he was always ready with suspicion of possible condescension towards the 'mystery writer', particularly that of any other writer whose classical education might be better than his own and, in addition, whose liberation from Victorian values might give him more intellectual adventurousness with new theories than Raymond's rigid ethic left him free to enjoy. 'Sham and Hypocrisy' – his sometimes harsh judgments of others were, one felt, also part of this legacy.

There were various perennial characters in his more elated fantasy conversation, all of whom could be understood as representing some anxiety of his (clearly related to this repertoire of pejorative epithets or to his hatred of his own Roger Wade alcoholism) which was allayed by the fantasy. For instance, there was the 'posh doctor' in striped trousers, whose urbanity or superiority were both mocked yet regarded as formidable; he was hated for 'having too much on the ball'. (Striped trousers were not only formal attire for Harley Street consultants in 1955, but in his youth in England an authoritative figure of a publishing house, also clad in striped trousers, had 'thrown him out', insulting him by suggesting he write cheap serial stories for a living, upon which Raymond had left England for ever.) The 'posh doctor' was always eclipsing Raymond in worldliness, success with women, money, and suavity of manners, and above all was always being condescendingly stringent, issuing warnings or challenges about Raymond's excessive drinking. But in these various fantasy encounters Raymond always got the best of it in the end with some brilliantly delivered insult, after which he would leave the 'posh doctor' with sagging jaw, and go on his way laughing.

There was an English 'duke' in his garden as magnificent as Kew, whose quietly-voiced, politely phrased rebukes to Raymond for his crude and racy American conversation would at first seem humiliating, but finally Raymond would lay a sophisticated verbal

trap, the duke would falter and fall headlong, the duchess would gaze in admiration, and Raymond would stroll away refusing all invitations brought by the footman who was sent hurrying after him.

Sometimes a fantasy figure was superimposed upon a real person to whom it bore not even a superficial resemblance, and it was utterly useless to protest about the transformation. Such a one was Cyril Connolly, who as a literary figure also had 'too much on the ball'. In fact, Raymond had been excessively grumpy the only time he was invited to Ian Fleming's house in Victoria Square precisely because we had all talked a little (but to his mind too much) of the pleasures of knowing Cyril who was in fact a brilliant classical scholar who had read more widely than Raymond, and whose conversation and writing could be a cornucopia of these treasures, together with surprising wit, instant parody, sharp aphorism. To Raymond our admiration of Connolly made him suspect him (quite wrongly) of despising a 'mystery writer'. 'Cyril Connolly' appeared in Raymond's fantasy as a curious mixture or hedonistic dilettante yet pedantic and censorious critic who knew nothing of the 'real' world of violence (nor of course did Raymond in his very secluded life) and who when finding himself in an alarming situation requiring instant tough physical action would be left helpless and gasping, whilst Raymond would stride in and master the whole dangerous predicament in a matter of minutes. This fantasy of Chandler's physical invincibility was particularly sad when one looked at the sick and shaky man who was entertaining one with these stories, the whole image having arisen out of a single moment of annoyance at feeling socially neglected.

Though, in fact, at that luncheon he had been very much the centre of attention. He had arrived pointing a finger of triumph at Ian and crowing, 'You *forgot* the glass of water. He had just read *Diamonds Are Forever,* prided himself on detecting all faults of detail, and was referring to the omission, in a scene at a short-order counter in Las Vegas, of the first object always to be placed before the customer; and Ian had amiably deferred to the colleague he so admired, and to whom he inscribed a book 'To Field Marshal Chandler from Private Ian Fleming'.

But, as often happens with alcoholics, Raymond was capable of seizing upon some chance remark of a person he hardly knew, brooding upon it, and transposing it into his own private fictional context, which then wholly determined his subsequent attitude towards that person. On the other hand he could be fiercely loyal to a friend if anyone else made what he thought to be an unjust or 'caddish' comment, never forgotten and forever held against the speaker, however unconsidered (and subsequently withdrawn) the remark may have been. At other times he could change his opinion within days, 'that slimy punk' having become 'that sweet sad man' or vice versa. He had a very clear eye for details but not for the realities of the lives around him; his novelist's selection and manipulation were always at work to fashion the characters he projected from within.

Another perennial fantasy/real-life composite figure who used to appear as an imaginary protagonist was the rich father of one of his 'girl-friends' whom Raymond, never having met him, imagined as a Harlan Potter. He would in imagination rehearse a session of hard bargaining which used to begin by the august and icy 'Mr Potter' saying: 'I can't put it out of my mind. Mr Chandler, that you wish to marry my daughter for her money' . . . 'That is certainly a factor.' Chandler would reply; after which with all royalty figures at his fingertips he would point out how much he was worth, and so on, reminiscent of his stories of his 'brutal bargaining with Hollywood moguls'. He himself later realized that this scene related to his inability to work during this time and fears about his continued earning power since he was very keen to lead a life of secure stylish luxury.

Later in May he moved from the Connaught to a spacious apartment overlooking the trees in Eaton Square, which Alison had found and helped him to arrange, though he was quite obstreperous about her suggestions for making it more comfortable. There must have been times when our help reminded him too sharply of his loss, for Cissy had been very fond of rearranging furniture. It was near to Jocelyn and to Alec Murray, also not far from Helga Greene, a new friend who also gave him as much attention as she could amid a busy life. For the next few weeks Eaton Square life became an amazing succession of contrasts: troughs of illness and misery, crests of exuberant festive gestures. After one of our all-day vigils by rota when he had been particularly ill and irritable, he could be suddenly jubilant or contrite, and lavish presents would appear – whole sprays of orchids to Jocelyn, red roses to me, or (most endearing, as Alison said) the four-page letter of apology typed in the small hours and sent by special messenger if his deportment and contentiousness had been, as he would own, intolerable, and he was afraid he had tried his friends too far.

He alternated not only in mood but also between a clear idea of his friends' desire to help and compulsions to test out their staying power by provoking them with intentionally outrageous behaviour into, as he thought and very much feared,

possibly deserting him. Sometimes he would totally ignore the 'only flowers or chocolates' rule and a box from a jeweller arrived and would be sent back to the shop. However he could on certain occasions become quite distraught no matter how tactfully one declined, and it became useless and even unkind to argue. Then we accepted happily, realizing that these lavish gestures were both pure gratitude and the fantasy of his novels rolled into one.

During a particularly bad bout of his illness, Jocelyn and I concealed from him that I was to play a concerto with the Bournemouth Symphony Orchestra since he was far too shaky to go. However he somehow had found out and when, after the concert was over, and a dinner with the mayor and council was in progress in the vast and otherwise deserted dining room of a large hotel, Raymond suddenly arrived white-faced and ghostly in full evening dress with white silk scarf, lurched towards the table and said he'd come to take me back to London. Lady Groves, who already knew from me a little of our patient's history and present plight, persuaded him to join us, and after dinner he was helped, almost carried, by the conductor Stanford Robinson to the waiting car – a very upright and ancient Rolls Royce the floor of which was covered with silver ice buckets full of champagne and carnations, a sight reminiscent of a scene from one of his novels. We three bowled off for London through the night – stopping at Raymond's insistence to drink champagne, the aged chauffeur making a fourth, and wild New Forest ponies wandering up towards the car. Soon Raymond was asleep and Stanford and I talked. Then Raymond, waking as we neared London, said very quietly and soberly: 'I know what you are all doing for me, and I thank you, but the truth is I really *want* to die.' It sounded simple, undramatic, and the natural inspiriting reply seemed suddenly impossible to utter.

Luncheons with each of us, dinners with other friends, or evenings when we battled for hours to lift his depressions continued. His various sagas of his tough-guy exploits or sexual encounters became even more incredible. There was the instant 'affair' with a bejewelled blonde he had met in the lift at the Connaught who was 'just resting' after her umpteenth divorce, and who silently followed him out of the lift to his room on the fourth floor; or there was his heroic, victorious punch-up by which he foiled the attempt by two hoodlums to snatch his wallet; and above all there were stories of rescuing ladies in distress when there was 'no one else around to do it, so I had to'. Some of these tales became part of his life story, congealed (like some of his pet hates

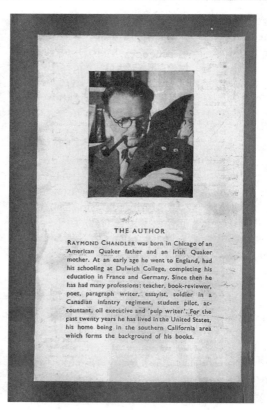

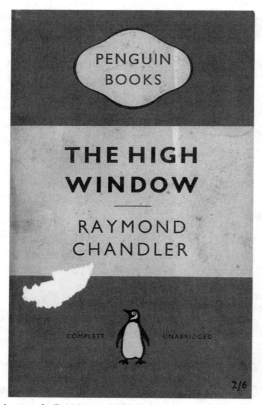

Front and back covers for British paperback editions of Chandler's novels published in the 1950s. In contrast to American paperback publishers, Penguin did not utilize sensationalism to sell mystery novels.

amongst acquaintances) into immutability. Though sometimes his hold on reality made him selective about the appropriate audience for certain stories (and his American friends, by some accounts, received an Arabian Nights version of his London life), at other times he could stick to his own account of a situation or even to the person who had actually been a witness of it. His highly dramatized views of our lives (for he treated all the shuttle service friends in a paternalistic manner) were often totally wide of the mark, and it was useless to argue against his strong desire to impose his interpretation. For him we became characters in one of his novels and to introduce our reality into his dream was to arouse his energetic opposition. He often didn't listen or, like a magpie, picked out only the bits which would fit his own picture, which was however always one of genuine solicitude for us and belligerency towards our imagined 'enemies'. He wished to deliver us from the 'hardships' of our lives, and thought of rescuing all of us because 'there was nobody around so I had to', though he could very well see some of the people who were around, but he discounted for rather arbitrary reasons their competence or concern. Nevertheless, his sympathy was genuine and abundant. To Alison he even offered to arrange to have somebody in America bumped off for having ill-treated her — 'It'll cost a thousand bucks!' he said, with a swagger, suggesting that he had only to raise a finger for the Mafia to act, and steadfastly ignoring that she thought this might be going a little *too* far.

Suddenly and rather dramatically he announced he was going to do a drying-out cure at home, and though it was going to be tough he was man enough to take it on. Indeed, in spite of the dramatics, he was. We nursed him on a rota system; I remember Jocelyn coming in one day to take over her turn, looking as fresh as paint, the sad old Raymond in the throes of it, gallantly trying to hurl outrageous witticisms at her, her smiling, droll, and spirited replies, and our most unhappy admiration of his courage and endurance, in which the doctor shared.

He was always immensely preoccupied with thoughts of illness, his own and that of all his friends about whom he became unduly over-anxious, and his letters were full of medical details, his or theirs. I thought it indiscreet of him to tell me such facts about others who might not like me to know them, but it clearly was an obsession of his. He looked for illness in all of us, he wished to return to the life of caring for an invalid, and felt utterly lost without the gentle round of devotion and simple errands he had been used to doing in the tragic previous year, when, he said, he had not been drinking. But by now his desire to care for any invalid could have fulfilment only in fantasy so long as his own health was so precarious. Thus it was, I now think, that of all the shuttle service friends, he wished to be of particular service to me, as the one who could be seen as having been recently ill, though leading the usual hard-working life of concerts, family, and looking after friends, including him. It is now clear that in the friendship which ensued, whilst I was in reality rather energetically organizing the nursing of an ailing Raymond, and Alison teased me about being 'our patrol leader', he was with genuine concern occupied with thoughts of rescuing an invalid; possibly this was satisfying at an unconscious level the search to restore the even tenor of life before his loss.

We were all happy that he had emerged from the drying-out cure relatively free of the big manic swings, our full-time rota was now tapered off, but he was helpless, seeming relieved to be in childlike dependence for a while. We all discussed how to keep him from resuming the solitary and social drinking, for the two were related in his London life, so we decided to suggest a holiday. Alec Murray had throughout this time always answered Raymond's summonses for night nursing, and at first he talked of accompanying Raymond, but a professional job intervened. Since Raymond was concerned for my health, he immediately took up the idea with Stephen and they arranged that I should act as nurse and travel-organizer whilst Raymond recuperated for two weeks at the hotel on Lake Garda where our family always stayed, and where I knew the local doctor well in case of Raymond's needing medical attention, and the friendly proprietor's wife could help if nursing were needed. As a non-drinker and hitherto without experience as nurse to alcoholics, my philosophy was simple: keeping on the move is keeping away from the drink. He was too weak to do any considerable walking, so I arranged local motoring expeditions including ones to Verona and even Venice. He returned to London much stronger, still not drinking, and in a calmer, sunnier state of mind.

He had begun making plans for his return to La Jolla; hitherto an unendurable prospect because of Cissy's lingering presence there. Thereafter he wavered between London and La Jolla.

—The World of Raymond Chandler, pp. 127–143

Chandler's residential permit expired in September 1955, and he returned to New York City on the Queen Elizabeth. *He stayed for a few weeks in New York and arrived in La Jolla in early November, where he took a room at the Del Charro Hotel. He was miserable and missed England, however, and in late November took a flight from Los Angeles to London. After only a few days he was traveling again, accompanying the Spenders to Madrid and Tangier for two weeks.*

Upon his return to England, Chandler was interviewed by Merrick Winn of the Daily Express *and discussed his wife's death and his subsequent depression.*

A Confession by Raymond Chandler
Merrick Winn
London Daily Express, 14 January 1956, p. 4

JUST about a year ago Raymond Chandler, one of the finest thriller writers of them all, put a revolver to his temple and pulled the trigger.

Nothing happened, and so began what was to be the bitterest year he has known.

Now he can talk about it, because the pain has eased and the year has ended. He talked to me at London's Ritz Hotel, in a room which, with brass bedstead, meals, and extras, costs £60 a week.

It is an expensive way of getting along without a real home. But Chandler has been a little afraid of homely things . . . because . . . "When you lose a home you've loved for 30 years it takes courage to start another."

GENTLE

HE sat, legs asprawl, in shirt sleeves, homely in spite of himself. This is the man who created Philip Marlowe, toughest detective in modern fiction. And this is one of the gentlest men I have ever met.

He lost his home when he lost his wife, Cecily, just about a year ago. Cecily *was* his home. They were married 30 years, and for the last two Chandler nursed her though the illness that ended her life.

"I loved her very much." It was a reflective statement, no longer emotional; it was a statement which looked back to that private drama when he tried to die.

'FARCE'

HE told me about that too, this man who wrote in his last published book, "The Long Good-

bye": "Suicides prepare themselves in all sorts of ways, some with liquor, some with elaborate champagne dinners. Some in evening clothes, some in no clothes. People have killed themselves on the tops of walls, in ditches, in bathrooms, in the water, over the water, on the water. . . ."

For Chandler, it was a bathroom. In an old dressing-gown. In the Californian home that was no longer a home without Cecily.

He pulled the trigger twice. It was old, damp ammunition. And nothing happened. Chandler kept his life and lost his dignity. He had muffed the simple job of killing himself.

"The successful suicide is tragedy," he told me. "The suicide failure is farce. For one thing people think you didn't mean it."

ONE FEAR

DID Chandler mean it? Yes, he did. Does he regret it? May he one day try again?

"I don't regret it. I don't think I was wicked. I believe every man has the right to end life when it gets too much for him.

"But I wouldn't try again. I can imagine only one circumstance in which I'd even want to—if I were flat broke. I'm afraid of poverty."

He said that lightly because he knows his fear is groundless. His first Philip Marlowe book, "The Big Sleep," alone has made him nearly £30,000 since it was published 17 years ago. He spends £100 a week and "I can go on, if I'm stupid enough, for the rest of my life so long as I don't live to be 100."

'DON'T KNOW'

HE offered me an expensive brand of cigarette, refused to smoke himself ("I stick to 10 or 12 a day") and told me about the weeks, the months, the year that came after his appointment with futility.

"I consider it takes two years to get over losing the person you love best—if you ever do completely. I've got through one and it's been pretty desperate.

"For the first week or two you're too numbed to feel anything. Then pain starts. Then gradually it doesn't hurt so much, and that's worst of all. It's hard to lose the woman you love. But it's harder still to face the fact that you can live without her, even forget her at times.

"I've reached that stage. Our life together seems like something enclosed in a crystal casket, precious but somehow remote and unreal."

Raymond Chandler has no religious faith to help him. Like many brave and gifted people he finds it impossible to accept beliefs for which there seems no evidence.

"I'm an agnostic—one of the don't-knowers. But I don't believe in a personal after-life. I don't believe I'll ever see my wife again."

Yet his life is still dominated by Cecily, more than even he knows. It shows in the little things. "I used to smoke a pipe but suddenly stopped enjoying it. When? I suppose about a year ago. . . ."

And: "I can't seem to write much now. I don't know why, something seems to be missing." He meant, of course, *someone*.

He has written hardly anything in this last year. His typewriter stands open beside a pile of half-sheets of yellow paper. But the new Marlowe book he began nearly two years ago is still half-finished.

COURAGE

WHAT kind of man is Raymond Chandler? Well, what kind of man is Philip Marlowe? For these two are head and tail of the same coin.

Take the tough, wise-cracking Marlowe and in reverse you have Chandler—tender, sensitive, hating all violence and cruelty.

Take Marlowe, the never-doubting man of instant action, and you have, again, the tortured, self-doubting writer who could have been a poet, who tears up an entire chapter to begin again, who writes 10 times more than is ever published.

That is why Chandler has written only six books since "The Big Sleep," and every one has been an agony. And still is in memory. For there is no consolation for Chandler even in the knowledge that each book has been as near as any writer could get to the perfection he strives for.

"I suppose Marlowe really is a sort of secret me," he said. "I wouldn't see it as clearly as other people, but I can see quite a lot of me in him. We're both lonely, sentimental, cynical—and we're both incorruptible. I am, as it happens, an extremely honest man."

I can vouch for that. Chandler is one of those rare people who have the courage to be honest with, and about, themselves.

For instance: "I like to show off a bit, when my friends let me. I'd still get a kick out of being seen with a pretty girl in a smart restaurant.

"But," with a grin, "I'm growing out of it. I used, like most people, to dramatise myself in all sorts of heroic situations. As a great athlete or war hero. Not now, I've come to terms with the real me."

'SO LAZY . . .'

HOW does Chandler see the "real me"?

Like this: "I'm a moody type, given to depressions. Probably due to my puritan conscience. I've got a quick temper, but don't sulk. And I'm surprised to find that, like most people, I've got more guts than I thought I had.

"I'd say my biggest fault was laziness, which a psychiatrist would probably say was really lack of confidence. Maybe.

"I'm very generous and a psychiatrist would say that was because I was afraid of not being liked. I admit it.

"I'm afraid of loneliness, crowds, insomnia (I get it badly) and telling my age." (He's "sixtyish.") "I don't know what a psychiatrist would say about all that. Anyhow, to hell with psychiatrists."

THE ANSWER

WHITHER Chandler now? He offered me another cigarette and this time joined me ("my seventh today"). He sat silent, perhaps thinking back to his year in the wilderness. And the year to come.

"I've no ambition, except perhaps to write one really good book. I don't consider I've done that yet. I must get working again, properly. I'm beginning. I'm writing a bit in the mornings.

"I'll live mostly in Britain. I'm American but I'm happier here. The friends I like best are British. I prefer British food, British clothes, even the way British publishers do my books.

"I've found a flat—it's time I had a home again. Alone. I don't think I'll ever remarry."

It was then that I asked him: Are you glad now that you failed to die?

I would have been easy for him, not wishing to shock, to answer Yes. He did not. He stubbed his cigarette, thinking, seeking the honest answer.

And it was a little while before he said: "I think so, yes. This will be a better year than last year."

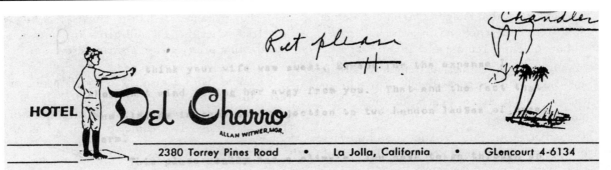

HOTEL **Del Charro**
ALLAN WITWER, MGR.

2380 Torrey Pines Road • La Jolla, California • GLencourt 4-6134

June 20,1956

Dear Harkdwick:

        Many thanks for your note. I'm sorry I fell downstairs,
but anyone as naturally careless and clumsy as I am could fall down
those stairs; They are a menace. But I think Barrow might have
waited to see whether I had cracked a rib before he began yankin-g
at me. It will be a hell of a long time before I go to Old Chatham
again. Also, this couple live such an ingrown, self-sufficient
life, in which I think they are perfectly happy, that it's a bit
of a bore to be there much, kind as they usually are. You can't
go out in a car with Jane Barrow without having every bloody tree
pointed out to you and hearing the history of every damnèd House
between Old Chatham and Bennington. And I'm such a lousy sightseer
that when I went to Italy with a lady who knows all about Italian
art and achitecture and wants to show you every trace of a Roman
ruin, every Palladian villa, every painting, mural or fresco,
every church in the whole damn place, I simply refused to look.
I preferred to sit at the Caffe Dante in Verona and drink Caffe gela
con latte, which is iced coffee with frozen cream.

        I have leased an apartment here, two bedrooms, unfurnished,
with the privilege of subleasing. It's in a good spot with that, for
being across the street from one of the few good beaches in
La Jolla. But mine is set well back and I think it will be quiet.
When I get enough furniture out of storage to overstuff it and get
smoothed out, I hope to find out whether I can still write a book.
PTO

Chandler's letter to Moseley in which he describes his new living arrangements in La Jolla (Houghton Library, Harvard University)

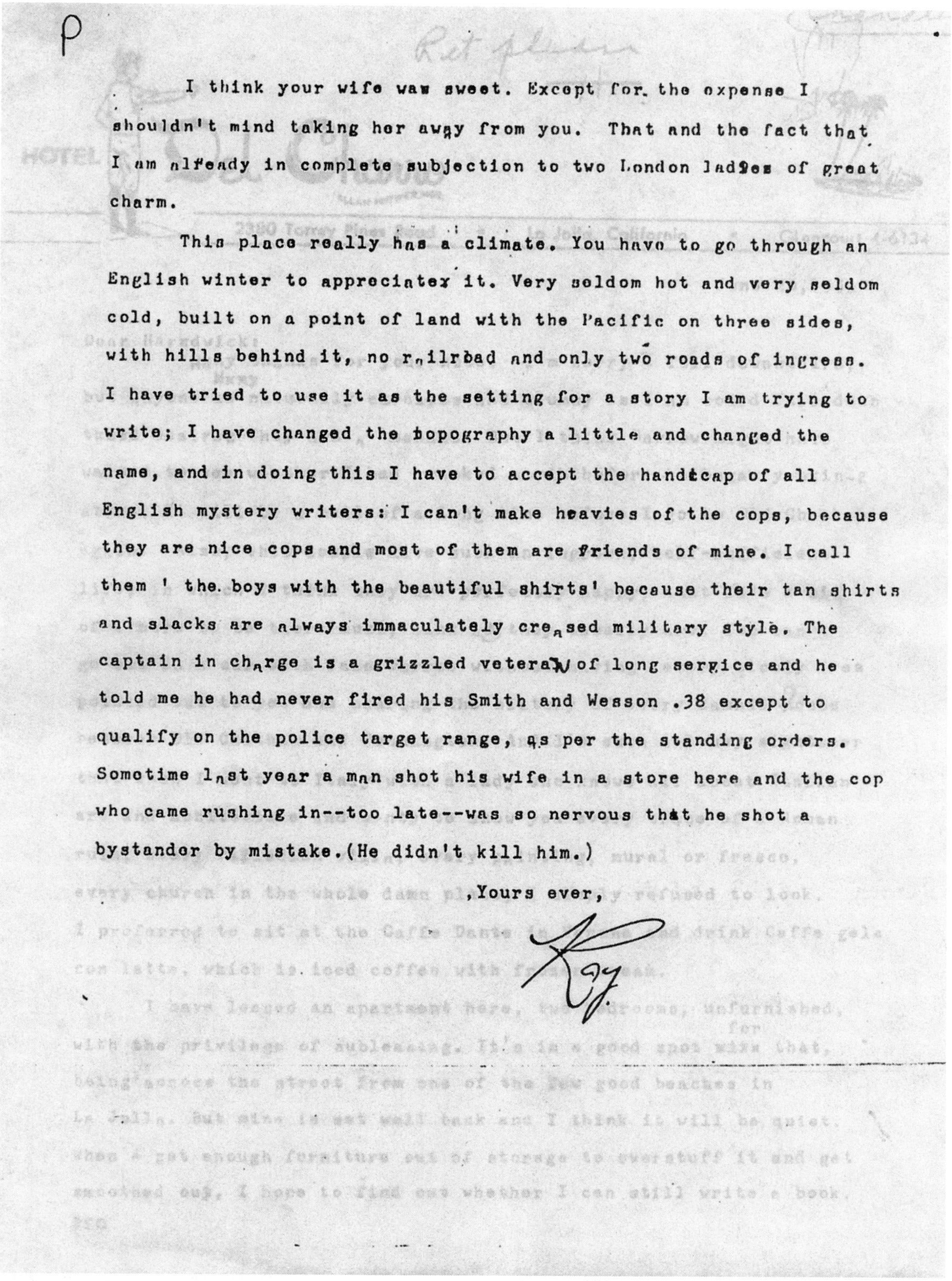

P   *Ret please*

I think your wife was sweet. Except for the expense I
shouldn't mind taking her away from you. That and the fact that
I am already in complete subjection to two London ladies of great
charm.

This place really has a climate. You have to go through an
English winter to appreciate it. Very seldom hot and very seldom
cold, built on a point of land with the Pacific on three sides,
with hills behind it, no railroad and only two roads of ingress.
I have tried to use it as the setting for a story I am trying to
write; I have changed the topography a little and changed the
name, and in doing this I have to accept the handicap of all
English mystery writers: I can't make heavies of the cops, because
they are nice cops and most of them are friends of mine. I call
them ' the boys with the beautiful shirts' because their tan shirts
and slacks are always immaculately creased military style. The
captain in charge is a grizzled veteran of long service and he
told me he had never fired his Smith and Wesson .38 except to
qualify on the police target range, as per the standing orders.
Sometime last year a man shot his wife in a store here and the cop
who came rushing in--too late--was so nervous that he shot a
bystander by mistake.(He didn't kill him.)

,Yours ever,

Ray

Chandler and Helga Greene dining in California. Greene, whom Chandler had met in England in 1955, was his literary agent during the late 1950s. Greene became Chandler's fiancée shortly before he died and served as his literary executor after his death. Chandler is wearing gloves because of a skin malady that caused his fingertips to split.

Return to the U.S. and *Playback*

In order to live more economically, Chandler left the Ritz Hotel and rented a small flat at 49 Carlton Hill in St. John's Wood. During the spring of 1956 he was drinking heavily and was often ill. Because he had stayed too long in England in 1955, Chandler had to pay a heavy penalty in income taxes in the U.K. To avoid the same situation in 1956, he left England in May.

Chandler flew to New York on 11 May and took a room at the Grosvenor Hotel, then traveled to Old Chatham to stay with Ralph Barrow again. He continued to drink and his health was poor. While at the Barrows' home he fell down a flight of stairs, and a few days later he had to be taken to New York Hospital in an ambulance. He was diagnosed as being mentally and physically exhausted and suffering from severe malnutrition that was caused by his drinking. He was put on a high-protein diet and within two weeks was strong enough to travel to La Jolla.

During the summer of 1956 Chandler continued drinking and was hospitalized several times. That fall, Natasha Spender traveled to the United States for a concert tour and visited Chandler in California.

Together they traveled to Arizona and Palm Springs, and the desert climate helped Chandler recuperate.

Chandler had a novel half-finished when his wife died, but he had been able to write very little for the next two years. In January 1957 he was determined to return to work. He considered writing a play for the English stage and a nonfiction book about fraud in the medical establishment, but he made little progress on either project. He soon resumed work on his seventh novel, *Playback*, which was based on the screenplay he had written for Universal in 1947.

Chandler had another bout of drinking in August and was admitted to a sanitarium with a broken wrist. After his release, he returned to work on *Playback* but struggled with the novel. On 20 October he wrote to Helga Greene, "I don't know how many times I have taken the Marlowe story out and looked at it and put it away again with a sigh, knowing all too well that my heart was too sad to let me capture the mood and gusto and impudence which is essential to that sort of writing." Disturbed by his evident despair, Greene decided to come to La Jolla and help take care of him while he finished the book.

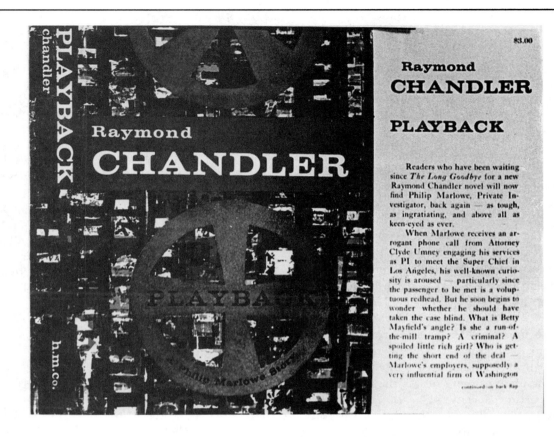

Dust jacket for the first American edition of Chandler's last novel (Bruccoli Collection, Kent State University)

The Reception of *Playback*

The general critical consensus in both England and the United States was that Playback, *though better than the average detective story, was a disappointing Chandler performance. The following notice in the* Times Literary Supplement *is representative of the reaction in England.*

When we had almost given him up for lost, Philip Marlowe has returned. Older, sadder perhaps, just as laconic, and wiser about women. If he has not actually gone up in the world he is reconciled to rising no higher. His new adventure starts as a very commonplace tailing job.

It seems that California in the 1950s offers his jaundiced and lascivious eye a scene far less fascinating than once it did. We miss the highly charged atmosphere of *Farewell my Lovely* and *The Big Sleep*, with its encompassing danger and promise forever on the brink of fulfilment. Now we move in the workaday world pursuing threads of truth, not stirring some fabulous hornet's nest in the upper brackets of a corrupt society. The Big Boy in the background is less of a tiger than his earlier counterparts, and we know we are not playing in the big leagues any more.

Marlowe's perceptions are still acute. His thinking is intuitive, his honesty impeccable as ever. But he is more concerned with the sheer technique of his trade—eavesdropping with a stethoscope, using a tire lever to break a gunman's wrist. His cynicism no longer has the flavour of piercing regret, and middle age has made him capable of corny sentiment. There is even a hint that he is on the brink of marriage.

Californian life still offers its macabre ironies. A bare step from the glittering boulevard Marlowe has a conversation with a Spanish-speaking parrot in a hanged man's hovel, with the owner present. "I sneered at him." Marlowe has kept his mannerisms, but he has moved with the times. The tension and symbolism of the great early Chandlers may not be so much in evidence in *Playback,* but still this is a good book.

　　　　　　　–"Death Comes As the End," *Times Literary Supplement* (11 July 1958): 395

* * *

When Playback *was published by Houghton Mifflin in the United States on 3 October 1958, even loyal support-ers of Chandler's previous work were hard pressed to praise the novel.*

Raymond Chandler's PLAYBACK (Houghton Mifflin, $3) is a brief, tight and ingenious narrative. As Chandler, it is unexpectedly relaxed and mellow. The old pent-up fury is now mildly sardonic, the bitter exchanges are brisk and thick with wisecracks and the abstemious Philip Marlowe climbs into bed twice with no sleepy purpose and is carrying a torch as the tale closes.

Chandler works as usual in a vivid, baffling thicket of incident but here allows himself reflective stretches. This is apparently interim Chandler but it is immensely welcome, surprisingly gentle in its wryness and far more concerned with the champagne than the spider in the cup.

　　　　　　　–James Sandoe, "Mystery and Suspense," *New York Herald Tribune Book Review,* 19 October 1958, p. 13

* * *

After a four-year absence, RAYMOND CHANDLER'S memorable private eye, Philip Marlowe, is back on the job in PLAYBACK (Houghton Mifflin, $3.00). His assignment is to meet the Super Chief in Los Angeles, identify among the passengers a shapely redhead named Eleanor King, tail her until she checks in somewhere, and simply report her address to his client, a famous attorney. Marlowe has no idea of what's behind this, and he is even more puzzled when he finds that the girl, whose real name is *not* King, is being pursued by a blackmailer, who is being shadowed by another private eye, who in turn has somebody's hired gunman on his trail. I'm afraid this plot is a bit too puzzling for its own good — what a mystery story is *about* should not be so much of a mystery. I missed, too, in *Playback* the climate of malevolence and danger, the exotic characterizations, the driving pace and imaginative mayhem that made Chandler's earlier books masterpieces of that kind. And the language — though it occasionally runs to a sentence like: "I've got friends who could cut you down so small you'd need a stepladder to put your shoes on" — isn't as electrifying as it used to be. But even though Chandler is nowhere near the top of his form, *Playback* is certainly several cuts above the run-of-the-mill thriller.

　　　　　　　–Charles Rolo, *The Atlantic Monthly,* 20 (November 1958): 176–177

Harlow Haier? More -   what a man!
Palm Springs,   *Please forward*   *Dec 28th 1957*
California   + return.

Raymond Chandler
6925 Neptune Place
La Jolla, California

Dear Paul:

Excuse my bloody handwriting, if you can. No typewriter here yet.

I am not going to Australia - legal reasons. So I shall come to Boston from New York, see you at arrival date uncertain.

By getting up at 6 a.m. and working 10 hours straight with no food but coffee and Scotch, I finished the new Love book. Haven't been over it yet, but I think it will stand up. I plan to dictate the whole thing - as an experiment - from my rough draft. Helga should have it within a month, unless I have made a mess of it somewhere. I don't really think so. I'll probably bring you a copy or two, but Helga is the boss.

Love,
Ray.

What a great life this man leads -

Chandler's letter to Paul Brooks reporting the completion of
Playback (Houghton Library, Harvard University)

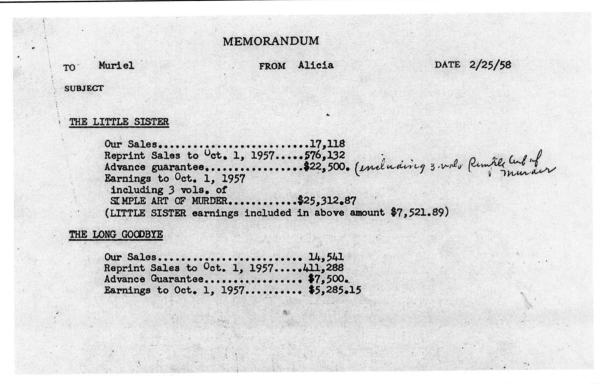

MEMORANDUM

TO   Muriel   FROM Alicia   DATE 2/25/58

SUBJECT

THE LITTLE SISTER

    Our Sales........................17,118
    Reprint Sales to Oct. 1, 1957.....576,132
    Advance guarantee................$22,500. *(including 3 vols Rumple art of murder)*
    Earnings to Oct. 1, 1957
     including 3 vols. of
    SIMPLE ART OF MURDER...........$25,312.87
    (LITTLE SISTER earnings included in above amount $7,521.89)

THE LONG GOODBYE

    Our Sales........................ 14,541
    Reprint Sales to Oct. 1, 1957.....411,288
    Advance Guarantee................ $7,500.
    Earnings to Oct. 1, 1957.......... $5,285.15

Houghton Mifflin memo showing the sales and reprint royalty figures for Chandler's books. The "Advance guarantee" was the money paid to Houghton Mifflin by Pocket Books for the reprint rights, which was split evenly between the firm and Chandler. The "Earnings" figures show the royalties earned on actual paperback sales. Based upon these figures, Houghton Mifflin decided to pay Chandler a $5,000 advance for Playback *against royalties of 15 percent (Houghton Library, Harvard University bMS Am 1925 [347]).*

In this excerpt from a critical article published two years after Chandler's death, "Raymond Chandler's Last Novel: Some Observations on the 'Private Eye' Tradition," Harold Orel not only identifies Playback *as Chandler's weakest novel but also suggests—inaccurately—that it marks the end of a vibrant literary tradition.*

The elegant stylization of the Marlowe novels is worth considering before we turn to *Playback*. What, then, are the conventions?

First: the dialogue is tough, the men are tough, the women are tough. "Toughness" means, simply, that the characters assume a great deal about the nature of society and the sinfulness of the individuals who compose it; they take so much for granted that they have no time for small talk. "I don't like your manners," a man named Kingsley says (*The Lady in the Lake*). Marlowe's answer is calculated to worsen relations: "That's all right. I'm not selling it." Gentle people would disintegrate in this world. Hence, there are few gentle people around.

Second: nobody ever tells the whole truth. In the old-fashioned detective story, characters would tell the truth: at least to the extent that they understood it. But Marlowe's client will not confide in him, those who have something to hide from the law will not be honest with him, and those who don't have anything to hide can hardly trust a man who operates in an ambiguous relationship to the forces of established law. Marlowe must fit in pieces and ends as best he can.

Third: The police are brutal or corruptible, or both; or stupid. Since the recognizable locale of Raymond Chandler's novels is Los Angeles, readers who live in that area must have felt uneasy for years about accidentally running afoul of the law. When Marlowe, on one occasion, admits to being a private operative, a policeman groans, "Cripes, that means everything will be all balled up." Marlowe, delighted that the cop has made a sensible remark, grins at him affectionately. His relations with the police are never easy. He discovers dead bodies under suspicious circumstances; he usually knows more than he tells; even if the police are unable to hang murder raps on him, they are not averse to trying to beat the truth out of him. They believe that the shortest distance between two points would be a straight line if only Marlowe did not interfere. Their theories about motivation and character are uncomplicated and simple-hearted. As mean-tempered men of action, they resent the intellectual approach to crime. Marlowe delays as long as he can any cooperation with the law. And he is never surprised by a policeman's delight in sadism.

Fourth: Marlowe cannot be bought. He once reveals why he refuses to spend a five-thousand-dollar bill in his safe (*The Long Goodbye*): there was something wrong with the way he got it. "I hear voices crying in the night," Marlowe says to Bernie Ohls, who has asked him what he does for eating money, "and I go see what's the matter. You don't make a dime that way. You got sense, you shut your windows and turn up more sound on the TV set. Or you shove down on the gas and get far away from there. Stay out of other people's troubles. All it can get you is the smear. . . ." But Bernie, not understanding, answers, "You know something, kid? You think you're cute but you're just stupid. You're a shadow on the wall." Marlowe will not do anything that he expects to be ashamed of at three o'clock in the morning.

Fifth: crime is a fact of life. "We do not live in a fragrant world – gangsters can rule cities, perhaps even nations; a screen star can be the fingerman of a mob; the mayor of your town may have condoned murder as an instrument of money-making. . . ." One eats, or one is eaten. The jungle is filled with lions looking for their prey. The night air trembles with the disregarded shrieks of the dying. No man is safe on the streets of a city. Crime is not a disease so much as a symptom, says Marlowe. "We're a big rough rich wild people and crime is the price we pay for it, and organized crime is the price we pay for organization." Knowing that, he can only scrape away at dirt on the underside of the sharp dollar. And he feels contempt for the courts which cooperate with the criminals. "Let the law enforcement people do their own dirty work. Let the lawyers work it out. They write the laws for other lawyers to dissect in front of other lawyers called judges so that other judges can say the first judges were wrong and the Supreme Court can say the second lot were wrong. Sure there's such a thing as law. We're up to our necks in it. About all it does is make business for lawyers. How long do you think the big-shot mobsters would last if the lawyers didn't show them how to operate?" To which his listener – unsurprised, not disagreeing, but annoyed by the irrelevance of Marlowe's speech to the problem he wants to talk about – protests, "That has nothing to do with it."

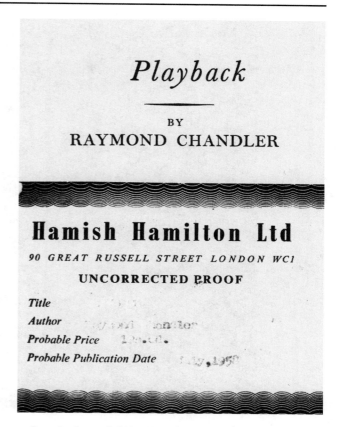

Cover for the proof of Chandler's seventh novel (Bruccoli Collection, Kent State University)

These attitudes make meaningful a great deal of the action, even if Raymond Chandler was in the business of providing entertainment. Marlowe, a shop-soiled Galahad, says these things because he believes them. Edmund Wilson, in that notorious attack on detective stories, "Who Cares Who Killed Roger Ackroyd?" correctly identified the subject-matter of Chandler's fiction as "a malaise conveyed to the reader, the horror of a hidden conspiracy that is continually turning up in the most varied and unlikely forms." What Wilson saw in *Farewell, My Lovely* was an American version of the Alfred Hitchcock-Graham Greene spy story. And Chandler himself argued in *The Simple Art of Murder* (1950) that a crime is not half so important as its effect on the characters, and that the reactions of the people to the crime are what makes the story. His concern was with the meaning of crime.

Playback, however, cruelly caricatures its predecessors. Its toughness is exaggerated and unconvincing. Chandler, some years ago, described how easy it is to fake the realistic style: "Brutality is not strength, flipness is not wit, edge-of-the-chair writing can be as boring as flat writing. . . ." Haste, lack

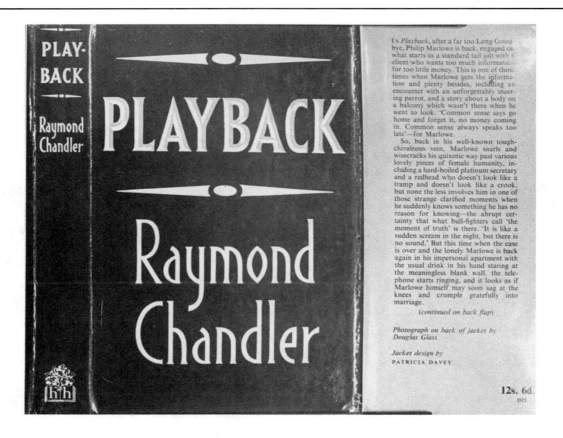

Dust jacket for the first edition of Chandler's novel that was published on 1 July 1958 (Bruccoli Collection, Kent State University)

of awareness, inability to bridge the chasm that lies between what a writer would like to be able to say and what he actually knows how to say, contribute to a decadent style. The plot is needlessly complicated, and the truth, even when we learn it, doesn't seem to matter. The murder is less interesting than we had hoped. The means of disposing of the body is tiresomely improbable; a helicopter, and the fact that a prime suspect knows how to fly one, are mentioned for the first time in the next-to-last chapter.

Chandler seems to be uncertain of his subject-matter. The police turn out to be efficient, lovable, honest, and polite. Marlowe even thanks them for the way they treat him. Captain Alessandro says, "We're not tough. We just have a job to do." Really, it is all too much.

Marlowe refuses $5,000 in American Express checks so many times, this reader lost count; he refuses money from other people for services he has rendered; he spends his own money for everything. But the worst is yet to come: the sex is gratuitous, and Marlowe turns out to be unexpectedly seedy. One chapter ends with the heroine sobbing, "Take me. I'm yours. Take me." It is dreary trash, and the reviewers, understandably, express their dismay. Anthony Boucher complains that after a wait of four and a half years, "It's a mousy labor from such a mountain" (*The New York Times*); Charles Rolo misses the climate of malevolence and danger, the exotic characterizations, the driving pace and imaginative mayhem that made Chandler's earlier books so interesting (*The Atlantic*); and W. L. Webb reports that the new Chandler "shows symptoms of a serious decline" (*The Manchester Guardian*).

The thing that went wrong, of course, is the fact that Marlowe no longer is up to date. Raymond Chandler, when he died on March 26, 1959, had already passed his threescore and ten, and his version of the "private eye" depended upon one's intimate knowledge of the decades of Depression, Fascism, and War. By the late 1950's, the Depression had worked itself out, and Marlowe's occupation, like Othello's, had gone. There is everywhere in *Playback* the suspicion that private detectives are unnecessary because the police know how to handle crime. Very early in the novel Marlowe asks a cab-driver to follow the car ahead of him. He is asked to prove that he is a private detective, officially licensed. The cab-driver reports the fact to his dispatcher, who in turn reports it to the Police Business Office. "That's the way it is here, chum," says the hack (all this for a tail job). It is now possible, in short, to see clear lines of demarcation between the criminals and the honest citizens. Indeed, sometimes it is hard to see the criminals because of the crowds of honest citizens. The pale-faced red-head with dead eyes who tries to ambush Marlowe is incompetent, and provides no trouble. The point is worth making more strongly: there is no trouble in the novel worth Marlowe's time.

Raymond Chandler, thinking out loud about the reasons he wrote low-life fiction, said that he refused to look at life as though it were a full-page ad in *Collier's* or the *Post;* he had gone to the pulps to study writing, and had been attracted to the kind of story-telling he found there; and third, "and possibly the best reason of all," "this elaborate over-tooled civilization of ours" had just struck him that way. "The story of our time to me," he said, "is not war nor atomic energy but the marriage of an idealist to a gangster and how their home life and children turned out." In *Playback* it is almost as if the children have grown up and are now attending college. One finds it difficult to accept the possibility that Philip Marlowe's adventures are becoming period pieces, but there will certainly be no more of them, and the atmosphere of the 1960's, despite all that we hear about atomic radiation, Cold War, and the population explosion, is considerably more relaxed, considerably more comfortable, for most Americans than the atmosphere of the 1930's and 1940's. A pity. For the "private eye," while he lasted, was one of the most exciting and original creations of our literature.

—Journal of the Central Mississippi Valley American Studies Association, 2 (Spring 1961): 61–63

A Last London Interview

In February 1958, as Hamish Hamilton and Houghton Mifflin were in the process of publishing Playback, *Chandler traveled again to England. He spent much of his time with Helga Greene, and he also renewed many of the social acquaintances he had made on earlier visits. Chandler accepted an assignment from* The Sunday Times *(London) to travel to Naples and interview Lucky Luciano, the American gangster who had been recently deported to his native Italy. Chandler enjoyed his visit with Luciano; but his article "My Friend Luco," which treated the gangster sympathetically as a scapegoat, was not published.*

After his trip to Italy, Chandler returned to England and stayed until September 1958, when he had to return to the United States or face another tax penalty. On his last night in London, he was interviewed by Derrick Sington, who published the following account of Chandler's views of crime and criminals.

Raymond Chandler on Crime and Punishment
Derrick Sington
Twentieth Century, 165 (May 1959): 502–504

I ONCE heard Raymond Chandler say about his villains, in a radio interview: 'They're human beings. I'm interested in them. I like them.' And when I met him on his last night in London (it was September 1958) I tried, a bit shamelessly, to discover whether this meant he had a set of convictions, a philosophy about the treatment of crime. Rather bear-like, in a loose tweed jacket and billowing flannel slacks, he rebuffed me with a grin that on a schoolboy face would have been called villainous.

'I know plenty of triggermen. I could get you killed in New York for a thousand dollars.'

But I persisted. After some exchanges on whether it was squeamish to flinch from killing either as executioner or soldier (he was extraordinarily proud of his service in the Canadian infantry) I wondered, was he just a romantic tough guy.

I asked him what he would do with his own murderers. Execute them? Shut them up for life?

'Carmen Sternwood the nymphomaniac in *The Big Sleep* who kills out of hurt pride is easily disposed of,' I said. 'You yourself get her taken to hospital in the last chapter.'

'Sure,' said Chandler, quickly serious, 'she was an epileptic. She should have been sent to hospital in Switzerland when she was about five. I wrote somewhere that "nobody was doing anything about her".'

'Would you extend the principle of treating rather than punishing the offender to other sorts of criminal? What about poisoners? What about Camino in *The Big Sleep*, the hired triggerman who kills with poison?'

Chandler got thoroughly condemnatory.

'He was hopeless. I wouldn't waste anything on him. He'd no sense of humanity at all.'

I half-thought I had found a proponent of selective capital punishment.

'No, I wouldn't execute Camino,' he said, and added with that impressive American seriousness: 'We degrade ourselves by arrogating to ourselves the right to take a human life. But society has to be protected.'

'Would you just keep such a person in ordinary prison for good?'

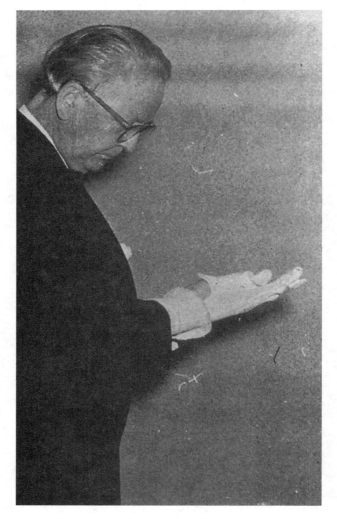

Chandler in 1958

'To transform a man like that by clinical treatment would take a long time – probably years,' he said. 'In any case would a Camino co-operate in, say, psychotherapy? Don't forget that men like him are probably too stupid to co-operate. And the expense to the public of treating them over a long period –'

I cut in with a comparison between the cost of treating an offender, expensively but perhaps successfully, for a limited number of years and the probably higher cost of keeping him in prison for long periods throughout a lifetime of alternate depredation and incarceration.

Chandler peered over his thick, horn-rimmed glasses. 'Unfortunately we're not that civilized. We don't take in that kind of proof,' he said.

He wanted to talk the thing through.

'I know that some peoples, the Swedes, for instance, go to a lot of trouble to redeem the criminal. But Sweden's a wealthy country with a comparatively small population.'

He paused.

'Of course, what we in the big countries lavish on guided missiles we should be spending on preventing crime by treatment. But will you sell that to the public in our time?'

The villainous grin returned, and Chandler hauled himself, in a curious lope, to the sideboard for another drink.

When I took the initiative again he seemed to enjoy describing his own characters in terms of their guilt or worth or what had made them. Of Vanier, the educated blackmailer and double murderer in *The High Window,* he said: 'He's not a very sweet character, but he must have had some human side at some time'; of Brandon, the gangster hotel-proprietor in *Playback:* 'I've a reasonable amount of sympathy for him. He was trying as well as he could to break out of it all.'

I had underlined a sentence in *The Big Sleep.* A cop says: 'I'd like to see the flashy well-dressed mugs spoiling their manicures in the rock quarry alongside of the poor little slum-bred hard guys that got knocked over on their first caper and never had a break since.'

'Are your own particular sympathies identified in that?' I asked.

'I certainly think far too many youngsters are sent to gaol who should be put on probation,' he answered, and told a story of his own charlady's sixteen-year-old son, who had got involved in a car theft. 'He was just going along with some others. What good does it do to put a kid like that in a reformatory? That's what they did.'

The revelation I remember best that evening, because it was such a vivid inconsistency beside Chandler's enthusiasm for the (presumably murderous) toughness of the Canadian infantry, concerned a motor drive he made frequently.

'I used to pass a packing plant, on the San Diego road, all lit up at night. It made me sick to feel that animals were slaughtered there. We must get beyond this killing of living creatures. But it'll take a long time.'

Concerns and Plans

During 1958 Chandler became increasingly involved in the affairs of Jean Fracasse, an Australian-born woman who he had hired as a secretary, and he was beginning to experience financial troubles. In early October, from his rented house in La Jolla, he wrote this letter to Hardwick Moseley at Houghton Mifflin and discussed his difficulties.

824 Prospect, La Jolla, Calif.

Dear Hardwick:

I have told Miss Rose of your publicity that I think your edition of Playback is the most elegant piece of bookmaking you have ever done for me. (Sorry forgot to double-space)

It makes the English edition look awfully damned cheap. The only consolation is that they sell far more books than you do, but their public is different. English people read books, and even if they get them from subscription libraries, Times Book Club, Harrods etc. these libraries work on annual subscriptions and pride themselves on filling all orders as requested. So they buy an awful lot of books. Also, English bookshops seem able to exist by selling books and not doilies, Christmas and other greeting cards, candles, knicknacks, giftes, and other items which have as much to do with books as I have with the Pope.

I still think American publishers are crazy not to bring out cheap editions from the original plates, but I suppose you have your reasons. One question I'd like to ask is why I never, but never, see any book of mine on the paper back stands. There is a tobacco shop in La Jolla that has two enormous stands with hundreds of paperbacks—but nothing by Chandler.People gripe to me all the time and I have to tell them the only way is to send the money plus mailing fee to Pocket Books in New York. I'M beginning to think that the goof in the panel truck, who seems to have absolute control of what he puts on the stands, doesn't like me. I can go into almost any bookstore in London and find a complete set of Penguins plus the paperbakcs Jamie Hamilton's firm now put out themselves. Here, only at very long intervals, do I ever see a book of mine. I know they have a system now of republishing at intervals with different cover designs, but how the hell can they sell the books to capacity, if there are not available to buyers?

I made a mistake in England. I was so disgusted with the pictures on Hamilton's dust jackets

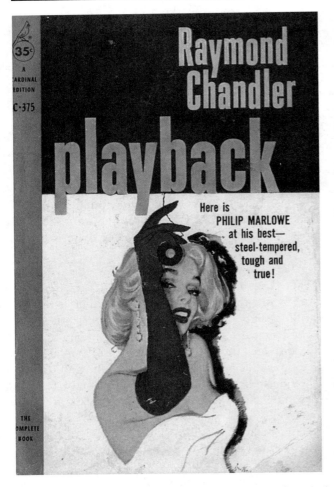
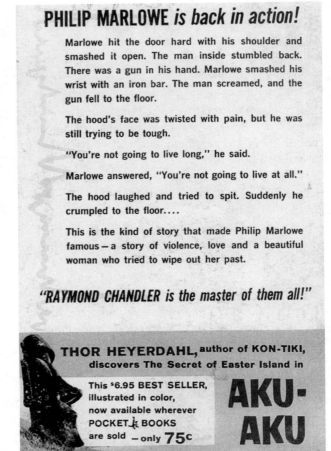

Front and back cover for the first paperback edition of Playback, *published in 1960*

that my agent, Helga Greene, demanded that I have the right to approve them. I've never needed that from Houghton Mifflin. I asked for a conventional cover and selected one with nothing but a black background, a couple of conventional decorations enclosing the title in white edged with red, and my name below. Then on the back the bastards put a perfectly loathsome photograph which, instead of portraying my almost classic features, made me look like a dishonest used-car salesman with jowls. Every line in my face, hardly noticeable to the naked eye, came out so over-emphasized that it was completely unnatural. And the book looks cheap while yours looks beautiful. I doubt that Hamilton could have got anyone competent to produce your dust jacket. The Australians refused to 'feature' Playback because they said a thriller must have a picture on the jacket. To hell with the Australians anyhow. Some magazine over there has pirated The

Big Sleep and advertised extensively over the radio. It happened when my Australian secretary and her children were over there on a visit, and the boy, who sees everything, spotted it at once. This will be the second fuss we have had with Australian magazines. The last one produced £1000 damages. This ought to go higher. Hamish Hamilton are very good at protecting their authors. Over here, for the most part, the publisher leaves it up to the author. When a bastard named James Hadley Chase, or Rene Raymond (and other names) lifted whole passages from me and Hammett and Jack Latimer they forced him to make a public apology in The Bookseller, under threat of issuing a writ.

Hardwick I need money, cash money, not assets. I need it because for a year and eight months I have been supporting my Australian secretary and her two children. She did a certain amount of work for me, but although she is a sweet girl and perfectly straightforward and honest, she is not by temperament the type to make an efficient secretary. Her swine of a husband walked out on his family after clearing out a joint back account and leaving them nothing. He was a doctor working in a clinic, a man with a vile temper and brutal behavior to his wife and children, who were terrified of him and loathed him. He was a manic-depressive and he was becoming a dangerous paranoiac. He went around telling people that his wife had been very cruel to him and lived by prostitution. He filed for divorce immediately and she, although a Catholic, was forced to file a defense and counter complaint to protect her children. I had to hold her together for the long months before the trial, organize the trial, assist the attorney, and I was even a witness, although I had never seen the man until the trial. I won't bother you with explaining how this happened. He took a beating. Jean's witnesses were very good. I decided they had to get out of the state, and I took them to New York, then to England (where I hoped they would like it, but they didn't like the weather—who does?— and then sent them to Australia. In August the man died after a heart operation which most probably should never have been performed. At that time my doctor, who is a top-flight neurologist, was gathering material to have him put away. So Jean came charging back from Australia, got a military funeral for the son of a bitch and paid for it, not the military part of course. All this has taken a small fortune from me, and I am very much against cashing in any securities, because at my age I must expect a time when I shall have to live on what I have, not what I earn. Hell, I even deeded the British and British Commonwealth rights in Playback to Jean, so I haven't had a cent from it over there. My agent Helga Greene bought the rights from Jean for a substantial sum of money, and she will make a profit, which will worry her, as she won't want to keep it. I made hardly any money in England for a reason I shall tell you. I got some fairly substantial royalties from former books, a fee for a review and several stints on BBC radio and TV. In the circumstances it wasn't nearly enough. I'd have been all right if I had only myself to think of, but the Fracasses can't live on less than $500 a month, and that is skimpy. Children, as you must know—growing children— cost a lot. I've even given Jean my car because she lives 15 miles away from me and there is no transportation to bring her to work.

Cover for a 1961 Australian edition of Chandler's last novel
(Bruccoli Collection, Thomas Cooper Library,
University of South Carolina)

Well, enough of moaning, but you can see that if you can scare up any advance for me and pay them into the Chase Manhattan, Rockefeller Center, I should be very grateful. I have good prospects. An English magazine has offerred me a fantastic sum (for England) for a Marlowe short story up to 10,000. I am not a short story writer by nature, so it will probably run to that. I have another book partly planned with a Palm Springs setting. And when I go back to England next April, or perhaps here, if it works out, I want to write a play. Chronologically I am getting pretty old, but many doctors have told me I have the body of a man of fifty or even less. But—

Jean and I both contracted acute infectious hepatitis, almost certainly in New York, because she was ill when she got to London and I felt rotten.

The English doctors failed to diagnose it in her or in me. It was perhaps excusable in my case, because, not knowing anything was wrong or rather what was wrong, I went happily on imbibing a fairly liberal quantity of Scotch, and that is poison to hepatitis. Jean was diagnosed by the ship's doctors immediately she got an board, but she had begun to turn yellow and that tipped them off. The minute I got back here, feeling lousy, my La Jolla doctor got an exhaustive blood analysis and there it was in the lymphocytes. I had all the classic symptoms, deep depression, weakness, an aversion to food, body itching, and vagueness of memory of recent things. I had all these in London. I even had a liver function test by a Harley Street pathologist, and he flunked. Here I had to have a blood transfusion and intravenous feeding. I am well now except for a weakness in the knees. But I can't touch alcohol, perhaps for a long time. The book says six months after you are cured. Physically I don't mind. I was nervous for a couple days, but not any more. But emotionally I hate it, I hate anything negative, any prohibition. It's against my nature.

I am terribly apologetic to write a busy man such a long letter. But you my friend and I am very fond of you and I thought you should understand why I am short of cash. I have about $7500 in banks, but with my obligations, it won't last very long. I ran short in London and I owe my agent probably £1000. Some of it I have paid back by giving Jean dollars on account of the purchase price of Playback. Otherwise it would be difficult for Helga to get dollars to send her, and probably illegal. It's not usual with me to owe anything to anyone except on current account. But Helga and I are not simply agent and client. She is my closest friend, and her father is immensely rich. She is an agent because she wants a life of her own. Anyhow everybody works in England. The sons of millionaires scramble for Christmas jobs at Harrods. I know a girl in a bookshop who is related to seven or eight dukes. If I were younger I'd try to talk Helga into marrying me, but as it is, it's better not. I'm not afraid of her money because I wouldn't touch it, except as an emergency loan. She actually went off to France for a couple of weeks leaving me a flock of signed blank checks. They made me pretty nervous, because she probably carries a bank balance of £10,000, or twice or three times that much. An Englishman is allowed overdrafts at interest; an American in England not, technically, but my bank would find some way to let me have one, if not too big. However, I haven't taken any that way. I've never taken any money I hadn't earned, and I don't ask you for any. I just bloody well wish some of the people I have lent money to had paid me back. Only one ever did.

I have a return ticket to London via TWA Transpolar, but I am almost sure I shall want to turn the return part in and go by way of New York and a jet plane. They may even have jets cross country by April.

This place is the best furnished apartment I ever saw, and quite reasonable for La Jolla. My former landlord is asking only $5 less than my rent for my former apartment unfurnished. I have a bedroom with two single, not twin, beds, a living room, a dining room, a good kitchen, an extra bedroom with a single bed, and a lavatory off the kitchen. I am so close to the business part of La Jolla that I can walk to any of the stores. If I need a car, I shall rent one, but I probably won't until I go to Palm Springs for a couple of weeks in November, December and January. I am very fond of Palms Springs and I am on a first name basis with a couple who run a very good, but not chi chi motor court. There I get an apartment over the garage, which is only used for storage. Nobody garages cars in Palm Springs. It is so dry that nothing can rust. This time I should go there for my health because I am a good swimmer and diver and once used to do fancy diving from the high board, but I haven't the spring in my legs to try the highboard (and there isn't one there). But I can still have a lot of fun on the low board. It will build me a lot. When I left there last January I was in top shape, and then I had to get this bloody hepatitis.

Try not to hate me for the length of this letter. I hope you are well and as full of bubbling good humor as always.

With love,
Ray

Helga calls me 'stinker' and says I am hell. I guess I am.

R

—transcribed from original document, Houghton Library, Harvard University

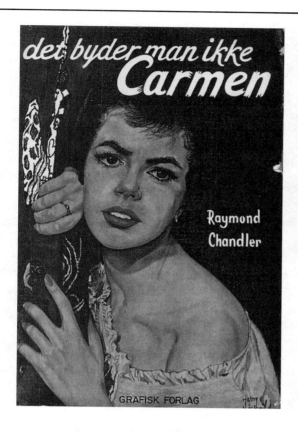

Covers for 1950s editions of The Big Sleep *translated into Danish, Italian, Norwegian, and Portuguese. Before his death Chandler had achieved a worldwide audience (Bruccoli Collection, Kent State University).*

A Final Honor

In January 1959 Chandler was elected president of the Mystery Writers of America (MWA), a largely ceremonial position that indicated the high regard in which Chandler was held by his fellow detective novelists. Chandler received the news of his election by telephone at the La Jolla Convalescent Hospital, where he was recovering from another bout of alcohol-related illness. His letter to the editor of The Third Degree, *the MWA's newsletter, was published in the February 1959 issue. Chandler died the next month.*

"February 7, 1959: . . . to speak on the telephone does not seem quite enough – especially as the real work has to be done by the Executive Vice President, Herbert Brean, and the Executive Committee, who seem to do all the work and get none of the praise.

"I am sure you realize that I take this honor as a token of a long career, and that I do not take it very personally. I wish it could mean more to the Mystery Writers of America. I feel very humble about this, but I suppose there must be reasons why I have been chosen, even if those reasons are obscure to me. After all, most of my life has been spent in trying to make something out of the mystery story – perhaps a little more than it was intended to be – but I am not at all sure that I have succeeded.

"I am enclosing a piece which might be of interest to you; if it is not, I shall not be in the least hurt if you deposit it in the wastepaper basket. I do not feel that we have made enough progress in promoting the dignity of the mystery story. I am sure every effort has been made, but somehow it seems always to end in frustration. This may be due to the fact that the organization does not have enough money at its disposal. My experience in Hollywood proved to me that you have to be very tough to get anywhere, that this toughness may be resented at first, but that in the end it will be accepted if it is backed up by a logical attitude.

"Now of course we face television, which is sometimes good but always poisoned by bad commercials. Therefore, I feel that as the titular head of an incomparable organization, I should make some effort to make our mutual endeavor seem as important as it really is. How to go about this requires assistance of other brains than mine. Mine, such as they are, are always at your disposal; but mine alone are not enough.

"I have reached a stage in my career where I have nothing to fear. Probably I shall get worse; possibly I shall get better. I have a feeling that hard-cover publication has become in this country rather silly; that you give too much away, and that the question of prestige is no longer important, since one already has it.

"I feel that any sort of discussion on these subjects would be something in which I should be vitally interested, and in which I should if possible desire to be of assistance. Yours cordially, (Signed) Raymond Chandler."

Raymond T. Chandler, Mystery Writer, 70, Dies

LA JOLLA, Calif., Mar. 26 (AP). — Raymond Thornton Chandler, seventy, writer of mystery novels, died today of bronchial pneumonia.

Philip Marlowe, Detective

Raymond Thornton Chandler was the creator of Philip Marlowe, a hardboiled private eye who tries to be kind in an unkind world. He has brutal moods and uses inelegant language, kisses ladies and later views their corpses with steely detachment. He dodges bullets fired by California police and underworld figures, and sometimes finds it necessary to fire back. Whatever he does, he does quickly.

The Hammett Tradition

A slick wise-cracking sleuth in the Dashiell Hammett (Sam Spade) tradition, Marlowe was born in Mr. Chandler's first novel, "The Big Sleep," published in 1939.

The detective's education in various, often exotic, forms of human depravity followed in "Farewell My Lovely," published in 1940; "The High Window," 1942; "The Lady in the Lake," 1943; "The Little Sister," 1949; "The Simple Art of Murder," 1950; "The Long Goodbye," 1954, and "Playback," 1958. A number of these novels were made into motion pictures and television plays.

Best Mystery of '54

The Mystery Writers of America, of which Mr. Chandler was a member, selected his "The Long Goodbye" as the best mystery novel published in this country in 1954.

Ironically, Mr. Chandler appeared to be almost a complete reverse of his tough, fast-talking creation. Unlike Phil Marlowe, Mr. Chandler impressed his acquaintances as a sensitive, almost tender man who hated violence and cruelty in any form.

Born in Chicago, he was brought to London as a boy by his English mother, and was educated at Dulwich College, near London. After service in the Canadian infantry during World War I, he settled in California and worked as an accountant for small oil companies.

He was forty-four years old when his first literary creation appeared—a short story entitled "Blackmailers Don't Shoot," which took him eight months to write.

"The Big Sleep"

He took only three months to knock out "The Big Sleep" which gained him immediate acclaim as a whodunit master.

In 1924, Mr. Chandler was married to Pearl Eugenia (Cecily) Hurlburt, with whom he lived a rather secluded life on the outskirts of Los Angeles. When she died in 1954, he took to drinking and one night put a revolver to his temple and pulled the trigger. Nothing happened, but the author was sent to a sanatorium for psychiatric treatment for a time thereafter. As he explained later: "When you've lost someone you've loved and lived with for thirty years, it's hard to begin again."

Associated Press

Raymond Chandler

Franz Blucher, Former Aid of Adenauer, Dies

BONN, Germany, Mar. 26 (AP).—Former West German Deputy Chancellor Franz Blucher, sixty-three, died today of a heart ailment in a clinic at Bad Godesberg, near here.

Mr. Blucher, a financial expert and one-time chairman of the right-wing Free Democratic party, was deputy to Chancellor Konrad Adenauer for eight years. At the same time, he held the post of a Marshall Plan minister and in that capacity was West Germany's chief representative at the Organization for European Economic co-operation.

In 1956, his party split over domestic and foreign policy issues. Mr. Blucher sided with Mr. Adenauer while the bulk of the Free Democrats went into opposition. In the 1957

Knickerbocker Artists Award Exhibit Prizes

The Knickerbocker Artists opened yesterday the group's annual exhibition of the works of the members at the National Arts Club, 15 Gramercy Park. The exhibition will continue, daily and Sunday, through April 8.

Takuma Kajiwara received the medal for oils, Ogden Pleissner the medal for watercolors and Grete Schuller the medal for sculpture. Knickerbocker prizes went to Mark Freeman for an oil and to William D. Gorman for a watercolor.

In addition, the Howe Memorial prize was given to Marjory Horn, for watercolor; the Brall Memorial prize to Domenico Facci, for sculpture; the Grumbacher prize to Arnold Hoffman, for an oil, and the Windsor & Newton prize to Robert W. Daley, for an oil.

Moissaye Marans won the Knickerbocker prize for sculp-

Obituary in the 27 March 1959 issue of the New York Herald Tribune

7.
Chandler's Popular and Literary Legacy

Popular interest in Raymond Chandler and his detective character has remained strong since Chandler's death. During the author's life, Marlowe was featured in the movies and on the radio; in the years since, Marlowe has appeared both on network and cable television and has continued to be featured in major motion pictures. Chandler has also exerted a strong influence upon writers—not only detective writers. While Chandler lived, poet W. H. Auden called his books works of art and novelist Elizabeth Bowen asserted that he was "a craftsman so brilliant that no consideration of modern American literature ought to exclude him." Critics and scholars have heeded Bowen's injunction and given Chandler's work serious attention.

* * *

Every time Chandler would have a new book published, I'd dash down to the lending library—I couldn't afford to buy books at that time—and read right through it the first night. I just can't overestimate the extent he influenced me at the time, turning me in the direction I took at that time as a writer.

–Ross Macdonald

Advertisement for the premiere of the **Philip Marlowe** *television series. The series debuted on 6 October 1959 on ABC and ran six months, ending in March 1960.*

Box cover of 1960 board game based on the Philip Marlowe *television series (© 1960 Bilmar Productions, Inc.; Collection of Robert F. Moss)*

Marlowe on Television

This review of the premier episode of Philip Marlowe *appeared in the 14 October 1959 issue of* Variety.

PHILIP MARLOWE
(Ugly Duckling)
With Philip Carey, Rhys Williams, Virginia Gregg, James Griffith, Barbara Bain, Addison Richards, Marc Towers, William Shallert, others
Producer: Gene Wang
Director: Robert Ellis Miller
Writer: Wang
30 Mins.; Tues., 9:30 p.m.
BROWN & WILLIAMSON, AMERICAN HOME PRODUCTS
ABC-TV (film)

(Ted Bates)

Up to the denouement, a clever and interesting whodunit was delivered by producer-writer Gene Wang, the scripter of the initial "Philip Marlowe" episode.

Story, as it unfolded, left a baffling array of clues, carried a number of surprises and maintained a good level of suspense. The story line was credible and not so jumbled, as in so many other private eyes, that the viewer couldn't follow the plot lines.

Philip Carey, a tall, handsome performer, carried the Philip Marlowe mantle well. He was given competent support by the featured players. Where the outing bogged

down was in the finale. The "heavy" in the situation turned out to be a character portrayed as a long friend of Carey, a hotel gumshoe. It was one of those cases where everybody but the real culprit is given a motive for the crime. Only when the "heavy" is unmasked by the super-sleuth is the triggering motive learned.

That the viewer may have felt cheated by the last few moments testifies to the episodes' interest. In so many other private eye series, it isn't a matter of whodunit. but who cares. Yet, if the denouement was as "logical" as the preceding portions of the plot, it would have been a far superior outing. Series is based on the character created by mystery writer Raymond Chandler.

Vet actor Rhys Williams played the hotel dick, the "heavy" in the murder, in pro style. His wasn't too big a part. Barbara Bain was okay as the femme fatale who's murdered. Virginia Gregg had a tough role as the all-forgiving wife and James Griffith, as the two-timing weakling husband, was all right.

This Goodson-Todman package production in association with NBC's California National Productions is up against some strong artillery of the other networks, "Red Skelton" on CBS and "Ford Theatre" on NBC. It probably won't make much rating noise in such a competitive vise, but based on the initialer, the skein should have some satisfied viewers among the private eye fans.

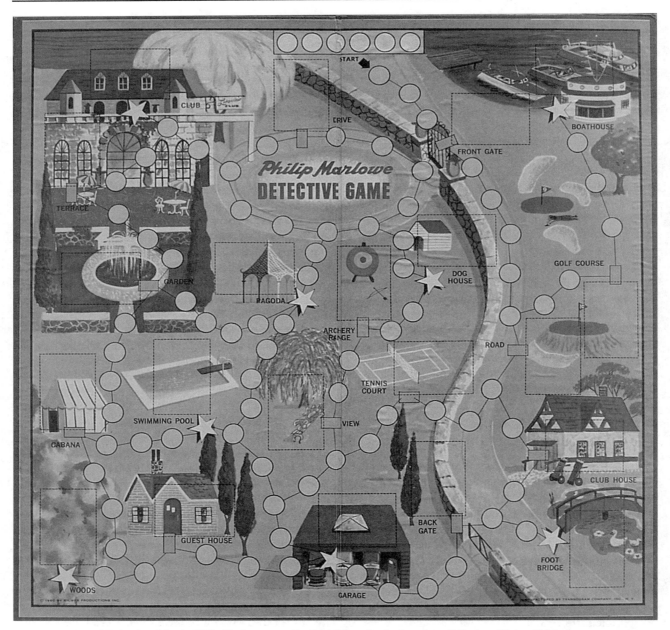

Playing board for the Philip Marlowe game (© 1960 Bilmar Productions, Inc.; Collection of Robert F. Moss)

A First Posthumous Work

In the summer of 1959, three months after Raymond Chandler's death, Houghton Mifflin investigated the possibility of publishing a posthumous collection of Chandler's writing. Hardwick Moseley, the sales manager of the firm, discussed the project in a memo to Paul Brooks, the president of the company.

Paul Brooks   Hardwick Moseley   10/2/59
Raymond Chandler

Since my long memo to you on 6/11/59 I inquired a bit around New York about the possibility of doing a posthumous volume of Raymond's works, and I also investigated to see whether there would be any reprint interest and I found that there is not. The odds are that Pocket Books, who has all the rest of the Chandler material in print, will not contract for this book when it is ready.

Except for the letters I would guess that we would find no material which Raymond in his lifetime thought was good enough to publish. Whatever he had could have been sold if it had Chandler quality. The best guess is that he left almost nothing and what little we could find he must have thought unpublishable.

I don't really want to go into the preparation of the book myself and feeling as I do I don't think I should be the one to select or work with an editor. I simply don't have time, nor in fact the interest. You will understand that I have grown cold on the project since my memo of mid-June. I know Dorothy Gardiner and have had some correspondence with her in the past and have watched her work with the Mystery Writers' Guild. A bulletin which she does for the Mystery Writers' Guild, I think monthly, is excellent. In it she herself writes very well. I happen to know that Dorothy Gardiner is a Chandler fan and I suspect she knows a good deal about Raymond, and if she doesn't she would know people who do. As I see it the choice of Gardiner would bet a good one. Best of all, of course, would be Dale or perhaps Gardiner and Dale could do the book together.

For the record: I don't think there is any money in it. If we are to do this one we should do it strictly for sentimental reasons or to please Helga or something of the sort.

—transcribed from original document, Houghton Library, Harvard University bMS Am 1925 (347)

Though it had only moderate sales, Raymond Chandler Speaking *was instrumental in the development of Chandler's literary reputation. For two decades it was the only published collection of Chandler's letters, and it was widely quoted in critical assessments of his work. Its publication was a catalyst for several articles in which reviewers evaluated Chandler's career and discussed his importance as a detective novelist and literary writer. These two essays, the first British and the second American, are typical of such assessments, and they clearly indicate the difference between Chandler's reputation in the two countries.*

Marlowe's Victim
Times Literary Supplement (23 March 1962): 200

In the early 1930s a small group of English readers looked eagerly each month for the American magazine *Black Mask,* and compared the style of its contributors with that of Ernest Hemingway. The admiration they felt for the laconic severity of the fiction in this pulp magazine was no doubt exaggerated: but still, it is true that Captain Joseph T. Shaw, who edited *Black Mask* during its "golden decade" from 1926 to 1936, imposed upon his writers a stylistic pattern as firmly fixed as that of the *New Yorker* under Harold Ross. He believed that the work of his best writers would effect a revolution in American literature. What captain Shaw wanted, as he told his

writers, was stories of violent action directly told, and he eliminated everything unconnected with the physical excitement he demanded, as rigorously as Ezra Pound blue-penciled the adjectives in the early work of Ernest Hemingway. He added, however, that "action is meaningless unless it involves recognizably human characters in three-dimensional form."

The stories in *Black Mask* had a corporate style. The men who wrote them were, with one exception, not easily distinguishable from one another, but their work was quite different from that appearing in any other magazine. The exception was Dashiell Hammett, who was almost immediately recognized by serious critics in England, although not in America, as a writer of high talent. Miss Laura Riding, writing in *Epilogue,* the periodical she edited with the assistance of Mr. Robert Graves, wrote about Hammett's *The Maltese Falcon* in 1936:

> The reader does not debate whether the girl was genuinely in love with Spade, or Spade with her; or stop to wonder whether Spade was an honest character or not.... There is no sentimental complexity, no architecture, no humour, no tragedy, no preoccupation this way or that—and yet the writing (writing of this kind), instead of being dull and careless, is impressive and definitive.

Among those who wrote for *Black Mask* during this period was Raymond Chandler, whose first story, "Blackmailers Don't Shoot", was published in the magazine in 1933. This crude story, and those that followed it in the next two or three years, seemed to be the work of a writer no more or less skilful than a dozen others who appeared in the magazine. It would have taken an extraordinary sensibility to discover in these stories the talent that was immediately evident when his first novel, *The Big Sleep,* was published in 1939. During the next five years Chandler wrote *Farewell, My Lovely, The High Window,* and *The Lady in the Lake.* These four books made him famous. During the fifteen years of life left to him he wrote three more crime novels, *The Little Sister, The Long Goodbye,* and *Playback.* When he died he was probably, with the exception of Agatha Christie, the most famous crime writer in the world.

* * *

Raymond Chandler's literary career was a curious one. He was born in America but went to school in England, and as a young man lived in Bloomsbury and contributed occasionally to *The Westminster Gazette, The Spectator,* and *The Academy.* After serving in the First World War with the Canadian Expeditionary Force he returned in 1919 to California, and there, by his own amount, did a variety of jobs from

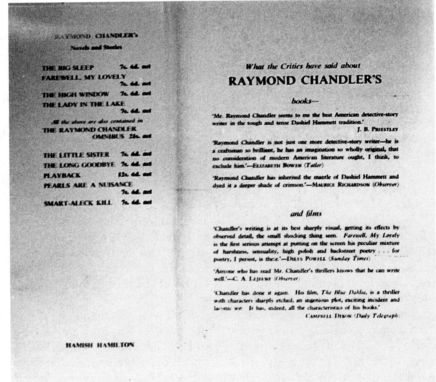

Dust jacket and table of contents for collection published 15 March 1962 (Bruccoli Collection, Kent State University)

CONTENTS

working on an apricot ranch to stringing tennis rackets. He did a three-year bookkeeping course in six weeks, and became an officer or director of a number of small oil companies. In the depression these companies were ruined, and Chandler lost his job. It was after their collapse, he says in a letter to Mr. Hamish Hamilton included in *Raymond Chandler Speaking*, that: "Wandering up and down the Pacific Coast in an automobile, I began to read pulp magazines" and "decided that this might be a good way to try to learn to write fiction and get paid a small amount of money at the same time." It was a brave, and perhaps a desperate, decision by a man who was then in his forties. When his first novel was published he was fifty years old.

Such a background made Chandler exceptional among the *Black Mask* writers. They were professional craftsmen, doing a job for money: Chandler was an amateur, who brought to writing a zest and freshness that never left him, and a desire that what he wrote should be as good in its kind as he could possibly make it. Acknowledging Hammett as his early master Chandler aspired to make the crime story a work of art. Much of the criticism, of his own the work and that of others, included in *Raymond Chandler Speaking*, is brilliantly intelligent. Nobody has said better things about the problems that must face any author who takes the writing of crime stories seriously:

> Dorothy Sayers tried to make the jump from the mystery to the novel of manners and take the mystery along with her. . . . She didn't really make it, because the novel of manners she aimed at was in itself too slight a thing to be important. It was just the substitution of one popular trivial kind of writing for another. I am not satisfied that the thing can't be done nor that sometime, somewhere, perhaps not now or by me, a novel cannot be written which, ostensibly a mystery and keeping the spice of mystery, will actually be a novel of character and atmosphere with an overtone of violence and fear.

Chandler's passionate concern with the sound and value of words is vividly illustrated in letters which express indignation about proof readers who were ready to improve his style, about novelists who used clichés by force of habit, about "the assumption on the part of some editorial hireling that he can write better than the man who sent the stuff in, that he knows more about phrase and cadence and the placing of words". He wished always to be judged by the standards of art, and was aware how often he fell short of them. Two years before his death he wrote, modestly enough, to his literary agent, Mrs. Helga Greene, that: "To accept a mediocre form and make

something like literature out of it is in itself rather an accomplishment. . . . We [artists] are not always nice people, but essentially we have an ideal that transcends ourselves."

Chandler's distinctive marks as a writer were the depth and sharpness of his observation, his power to create atmosphere, and the crackling wisecracks which, either in dialogue or in the first person comments of his detective Philip Marlowe, enliven almost every page of his novels. "Did I hurt your head much?" Marlowe asks the blonde with silver fingernails in *The Big Sleep*, after he has hit her with his gun. Her reply has the exact tone and timing that mark Chandler's jokes: "You and every other man I ever met." It is impossible to convey in a single quotation Chandler's ear for dialogue, but no reader of *The Second Chandler Omnibus*, which contains his last three books, can fail to hear, in the conversations of film stars and publicity agents, rich men and gangsters, both honest and corrupt, an ear for the form of speech such as few writers are lucky enough to possess.

His power to create atmosphere can be found in the very first scenes of his first novel, the interview Marlowe has in *The Big Sleep* with the old general who sits shivering in his orchid-filled conservatory, or in the almost equally brilliant opening of *The High Window*, or in a dozen scenes from the later novels. The sharpness of his observation is inseparable from his gift for the telling phrase, and from the indignation always roused in him by meanness and corruption. If one had to choose a single paragraph that showed most of Chandler's gifts, the care for words, the attention to what people look like and the clothes they wear, and the basic seriousness that underlay his violent entertainments, his description of two policemen in *The Little Sister* would do as well as any:

> They had the calm weathered faces of healthy men in hard condition. They had the eyes they always have, cloudy and grey like freezing water. The firm set mouth, the hard little wrinkles at the corners of the eyes, the hard hollow meaningless stare, not quite cruel and a thousand miles from kind. The dull ready-made clothes, worn without style, with a sort of contempt: the look of men who are poor and yet proud of their power, watching always for ways to make it felt, to shove it into you and twist it and grin and watch you squirm, ruthless without malice, cruel and yet not always unkind. What would you expect them to be? Civilization had no meaning for them. All they saw of it was the failures, the dirt, the dregs, the aberrations and the disgust.

The letters in *Raymond Chandler Speaking* show clearly, as Miss Dorothy Gardiner says, that he was a most prolific and original letter writer: but, editorially, this cannot be called a satisfactory book. Miss Gardiner and Miss Walker have filled nearly a quarter of it with bits and pieces from the workshop which we could have done without, including the opening of a new book which would certainly have been rewritten; and they have arranged the letters themselves in sections such as "Chandler on Chandler," "Chandler on the Film World and Television," "Chandler on Cats," so that snippets of a single letter may appear in two or three parts of the book. The earliest of the letters goes back no farther than 1939, and the publication of *The Big Sleep*. They are the letters of an increasingly successful literary man, and inevitably fail to give us a clear or complete portrait of Chandler as a person. We are not told whether letters from an earlier period exist. For lack of them we learn nothing of how poor Chandler really was during the depression, of his struggle to perfect a personal style in the early *Black Mask* stories: nor are we told how a photograph with the caption "A dinner of 'Black Mask' writers in the late twenties or early thirties" can refer to this period, when Chandler's first story in the magazine appeared in 1933. These omissions are important because Chandler's emotional life had a very great bearing upon his qualities and limitations as a writer.

* * *

From the four pages of biographical material printed before the letters it appears that Chandler's mother was divorced from his father when he was seven years old. He never saw his father again, but was brought up by his mother. After the First World War he accompanied her to California, and it was not until her death that he married, at the age of thirty-six, a woman who was seventeen years older than himself. They were married for thirty years, and during this time Chandler's devotion to her was unflawed. When she died he made an unsuccessful attempt to commit suicide.

It is not necessary to examine this background in detail to see that it must have played an important part in the development of ·Chandler's detective, Philip Marlowe. The crime novelist, Chandler said in his brilliant essay "The Simple Art of Murder," must be concerned with the sordid world of real crime and not with the country house murder beloved of lady detective story writers, yet to picture this world of real crime and criminals was not enough. "Down those mean streets a man must go who is not himself mean, who is neither tarnished nor afraid. The detective in this kind of story must be such a man. He is the hero, he is everything." This man was Philip Marlowe, who rapidly became an idealized expression of

the man Chandler would have liked to have been. Marlowe is tough, but he is strictly virtuous. He will not take more than his twenty-five (later forty) bucks a day. He is attracted to women, and immensely attractive to them, but not until *The Long Goodbye*, published in 1953, does he sleep with one. In fact, excessive sexuality in a woman often means that she is much worse than she should be. More than one woman eager to sleep with Marlowe, and denied that pleasure, has proved to be a murderess. He resists their wiles as easily as he resists attempts at bribery. His morality is as pure as his skull and teeth are insusceptible of damage. Perhaps it is not by accident that Chandler first called him Mallory, for he is at heart a perfect gentle knight.

How is it that Raymond Chandler, so intelligent and so sensitive, could not see that the figure of Marlowe was totally unreal, a concession to all that he had condemned in the orthodox detective story, a character deeply damaging to the artistic reality he set out to convey? He could not see it because this fragment of wish-fulfilment expressed the emotional weakness in his creator. Happily married to a woman old enough to be his mother, Chandler fulfilled in Marlowe dreams of violence and fabulous girls. There is an element of fantasy in all crime stories, but Marlowe is, when all allowances have been made, a disastrous piece of self-indulgence. Chandler is Marlowe's victim, much more than Conan Doyle was the victim of Sherlock Holmes. Under the spell of Marlowe even Chandler's dialogue becomes unreal, so that his women are liable to say things like "I wear black because I am beautiful and wicked–and lost", or "All these years I have kept myself for you". As time passed Chandler became more expert at constructing a plot, more clear about the sort of things he wanted to say, but when Marlowe took charge plot and reality moved farther and farther away. *Playback*, his last and weakest book, found Marlowe on the edge of marriage. In *The Poodle Springs Story* he was to have married Linda Loring, and there was to be conflict between them because "She won't like it that he insists on sticking to his own business and modest way of life. . . . I am writing him married to a rich woman and swamped by money, but I don't think it will last." Marlowe is Chandler's concession to himself and to the public, a measure of his inferiority to Hammett.

No doubt it is true that Hammett wrote just for the money, gave up when he thought he had enough, held no high opinion of his own books: yet there was in him a core of hardness which, combined with tact and taste, would have forbidden the creation of a Marlowe. The figure sketched in these brilliant, amusing, often touching letters (and one wishes very much that it was not a sketch merely, but a portrait done in the full colours of life) is that of a man on the surface contentious and strongly opinionated, beneath that surface basically shy, sentimental, longing to be loved. Yet in spite of the concessions to Marlowe, Chandler made out of this personality, with its considerable share of imbalance or maladjustment, a good deal of memorable fiction which is still not fully appreciated in his own country. "Over here [in England] I am not regarded as a mystery writer but as an American novelist of some importance", he wrote in 1955 to a fellow American crime writer, adding sadly: "I don't think somehow we shall ever reach that status in America." No doubt he was too pessimistic, but it is a pleasure to find ourselves, for once, in the vanguard of critical opinion.

* * *

Man With a Toy Gun
Wilson Pollock
The New Republic, 146 (7 May 1962): 21–22

Following in Dashiell Hammett's footsteps, Raymond Chandler brought a new vigor to detective fiction. His books sold in the millions but they were detective stories not serious literature, and so he was never invited to join the Boys in the Back Room, not even for a short beer. He died in La Jolla, California, March 26, 1959, at the age of 70. *Raymond Chandler Speaking* is a collection of excerpts from letters to friends, publishers, agents, and others during the forties and fifties. It also contains an unpublished short story, two articles, and the opening chapters of a new Philip Marlowe novel called *The Poodle Springs Story* which he did not live to finish.

Chandler began writing seriously in the thirties after losing a job with a California oil company. He wrote for money from the very beginning and he sold stories with titles like "Blackmailers Don't Shoot," "Nevada Gas," and "Guns at Cyrano's" to magazines with names like *Black Mask* and *Dime Detective Monthly*. In 1939 he published his first full-length book, *The Big Sleep,* and in 1943 he went to Hollywood. No one could accuse him of selling out.

He was no intellectual and although some of his work might seem to reveal a political conscience it wasn't there. "There was even a bird," he writes, "who informed me I could write a good proletarian novel; in my limited world there is no such animal, and if there were, I am the last mind in the world to like it, being by tradition and long study a complete snob." He merely believed that society was corrupt, that the only god was the fast easy buck, and that there was not very much any one could do about it. "The only difference I can see [between American big business and Russian Communism] is that in Russia

when you begin to slip a little they either shoot you or send you to a forced labor camp, whereas in the United States they ask you for your resignation or else force you to give it without being asked by humiliating you beyond endurance " He accepted Hollywood's big money without feeling anything like guilt; he seems to have liked the movies if not necessarily the men who made them. In one of the articles included here, "Writers in Hollywood " he tells the well-known story of the hamstrung screenwriter. "The impulse to perfection cannot exist where the definition of perfection is the arbitrary decision of authority. That which is born in loneliness and from the heart cannot be defended against the judgement of a committee of sycophants." He was in the thick of the celluloid at the time, but the tone was detached. "My agent was told by the Paramount story editor that it [the article] has done me a lot of harm with the producers at Paramount." He is not impressed. "Charlie Brackett said: 'Chandler's books are not good enough nor his pictures bad enough to justify that article' . . . I would reply to Mr. Brackett that if my books had been any worse I should not have been invited to Hollywood and that if they had been any better, I should not have come . . ."

He thought occasionally about writing serious novels, stories, and toward the end, a serious play, but he never did very much about it. The serious story included here is about a couple of people who slowly and painfully come to realize that they are not writers. It is like the work of a bright young man trying to break into the little magazines. Chandler wrote it when he was 63 and it is no wonder that it was never published. It was too late.

Drugstore literature of the kind he wrote is consumed by juvenile delinquent and dowager alike and Chandler knew it. It was pretty raw stuff sometimes, but he was never one of those "writers of comic strips like Mickey Spillane." Auden, in an article on the detective story called "The Guilty Vicarage" said that Chandler was "interested in writing serious studies of a criminal milieu." Chandler's comment on this was: "So now I look at everything I put down and say to myself, Remember, old boy, this has to be a serious study of a criminal milieu. Are you serious? No. Is this a criminal milieu? No, just average corrupt living with the melodramatic angle over-emphasized, not because I am crazy about melodrama for its own sake, but because I am realistic enought to know the rules of the game."

In a letter to one of his readers who wants to know more about Philip Marlowe he writes about his detective hero as if he were a very good friend. He describes

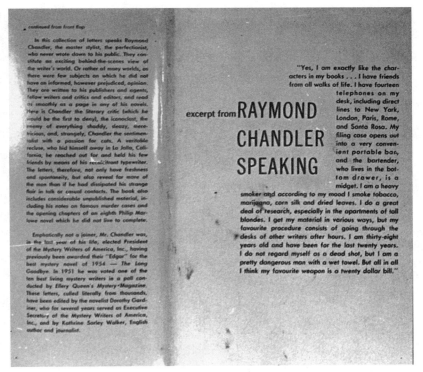

Dust jacket for the first American edition, published on 24 April 1962, on which Chandler is promoted not as a genre writer but as an author of literary distinction (Bruccoli Collection, Kent State University)

Marlowe's education, smoking and drinking habits, attitudes toward women, the lay-out of his apartment. Then in another letter he writes, ". . . if being in revolt against a corrupt society constitutes being immature, then Philip Marlowe is extremely immature. If seeing dirt where there is dirt constitutes an inadequate social adjustment, then Philip Marlowe has an inadequate social adjustment. Of course Marlowe is a failure and he knows it. He is a failure because he hasn't any money. A man who without physical handicaps cannot make a decent living is always a failure because their particular talents did not suit their time and place. In the long run we are all failures or we wouldn't have the kind of world we have." It comes as a letdown when Chandler writes, "But you must remember that Marlowe is not a real person. He is a creature of fantasy. He is in a false position because I put him there. In real life a man of his type would no more be a private detective then he would be a university don."

Chandler was interested in everything but what he cared about most was his wife Cissy who was 18 years younger than he was and died five years before he did. "She was the beat of my heart for 30 years. She was the music heard faintly at the edge of sound. It was my great and now useless regret that I never wrote anything really worth her attention, no book that I could dedicate to her. I planned it. I thought of it but I never wrote it. Perhaps I couldn't have written it." And three years later " . . . I wasn't faithful to my wife out of principal but because she was completely adorable, and the urge to stray which afflicts many men at a certain age, because they think they have been missing a lot of beautiful girls, never touched me. I already had perfection."

Chandler attempted suicide in 1955, a little more than a year after his wife's death. According to the editors of this book one of Chandler's friends described it as being "the most inefficient effort at suicide on record." He writes about it frankly here in one of these carefully edited letters. Too carefully edited. Chandler may not have been as hardboiled as Marlowe but he had guts, and it doesn't seem right that guts should be represented in a man's last work by three dots.

He knew the language of the underworld the way Ring Lardner knew the language of baseball. "How do you tell a man to go away in hard language? Scram, beat it, take off, take the air, on your way, dangle, hit the road, and so forth. All good enough. But give me the classic expression used by Spike O'Donnell (of the O'Donnell brothers of Chicago, the only small outfit to tell the Capone mob to go to hell and live). What he said was, 'Be missing'." And in the same letter Chandler says he is sure that O'Neill borrowed the phrase "the big sleep" for *The Iceman Cometh* thinking that it was an underworld expression. But Chandler had made it up.

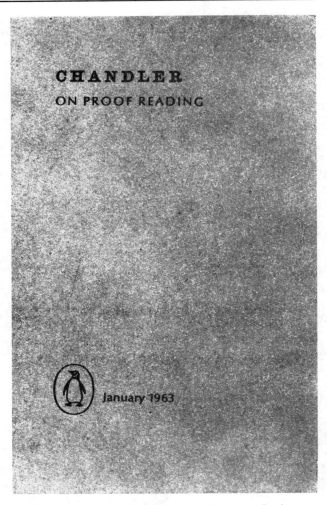

Cover for a keepsake that printed remarks about proofers from Chandler's 18 January 1948 letter to Edward Weeks of The Atlantic Monthly *(Bruccoli Collection, Kent State University)*

It is only natural that Hemingway's name should come up. Chandler defends *Across the River and Into the Trees* against what most people were saying about it at the time and are still saying. "Candidly, it's not the best thing he's done, but it's still a hell of a sight better than anything his detractors could do." Chandler and Hemingway had more in common than Humphrey Bogart. "The Killers" could almost be a "Black Mask" story except that the ending would probably have cost the author a rejection slip. *To Have and Have Not* is not very much better than *Farewell, My Lovely*. The biggest difference is that Hemingway also wrote *A Farewell to Arms*. It's too bad that Chandler and Hemingway never got together. But maybe they didn't have to.

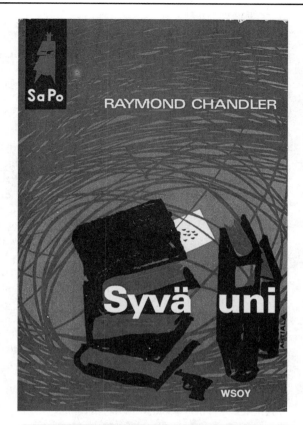

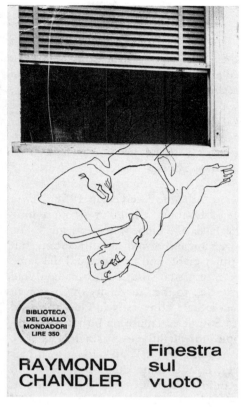

Foriegn translations of Chandler's books from the 1960s, clockwise from top left: The Big Sleep *in Finnish,* The High Window *in Italian,* The Long Goodbye *in Serbo-Croatian, and* Trouble is my Business *in German (Bruccoli Collection, Kent State Universtiy)*

Chandler's Knight

In 1963, the University of North Carolina Press published Philip Durham's Down these Mean Streets a Man Must Go: Raymond Chandler's Knight, *the first book-length scholarly treatment of Chandler's writing. Durham identified in the seven Philip Marlowe novels the central motif of a knight questing for justice in a corrupt world, and his analysis established the dominant critical interpretation of Chandler's work. Chapter 6 of Durham's book examines the character of Philip Marlowe.*

In answer to a letter, received in 1951 from a D. J. Ibberson of London, Chandler wrote a long account of "the facts of Philip Marlowe's life." The date of Marlowe's birth, he said, was uncertain, but he was about thirty-eight, and he remained the same age. He was born in Santa Rosa, California, and had gone two years either to the University of Oregon in Eugene or Oregon State University in Corvallis, and he had come to Southern California because eventually most people do. Slightly over six feet tall, he weighed thirteen stone eight. With dark brown hair and brown eyes, he was more than "passably good looking." He could be tough but he didn't look it. Cary Grant was the movie actor who came closest to the author's version of his own hero. The letter continued with such details as the kind of matches Marlowe used, the manner of his drinking, the effectiveness of his chess game, his interests in women, his knowledge of perfume, and his further likes and dislikes, interests and lack of them, in a variety of other areas. It was a long letter, but it gave Mr. Ibberson only the barest outline of the hero who had been developing through the years in Chandler's works.

When late in the depression year of 1933 a private investigator left his small agency in Chicago on an assignment that took him to Los Angeles, the man called Mallory successfully completed his job; but something happened to him while he was about it—for he did not return to Chicago. In the December issue of the old *Black Mask,* which had arrived on the newsstands while the country was accommodating itself to the shock of repeal, Mallory became an Angelino. In "Blackmailers Don't Shoot" Chandler created his hero, the hero—somewhat weathered and weaker—he was still writing about when he died twenty-six years later. Although the Chandler hero, frequently called the hard-boiled hero, became distinctive, he was by no means an original creation. Rather he was a part of a continuous tradition that had begun in American literature on the frontier in the 1830's. The American literary hard-boiled hero (suggested by Washington Irving's Brom Bones, the

"burly, roaring, roystering blade" who had "a mingled air of fun and arrogance" and "was always ready for either a fight or a frolic") originated in the tales of Augustus Longstreet, Charles Webber, and Joseph Baldwin, and he continued in *The Desperadoes of the South-West* by Alfred Arrington where he was one who "dares danger, laughs at pain, and challenges death." In 1860 the hero was taken over by the Beadle and Adams dime-novel writers and utilized by them until the 1890's. At the beginning of the twentieth century he was ready-made for such early "western" writers as Owen Wister and Zane Grey, and in the westerns he is still active. As a detective hero he first appeared in the pages of the *Black Mask* in the early 1920's where his creator was Carroll John Daly. Daly's private eye, Race Williams, arrived only a few months before Dashiell Hammett's Continental Op appeared in the same magazine. Thereafter the *Black Mask* became known, especially during the regime of Editor Joseph Shaw from 1926 through 1936, as the leader of the Hard-Boiled School of Detective Fiction. Into this group and into this tradition Raymond Chandler contributed his own version of the hard-boiled hero, the man who was to become Philip Marlowe. When Chandler began publishing detective stories, the characteristics of the hero were already clearly evident: courage, physical strength, indestructibility, indifference to danger and death, a knightly attitude, celibacy, a measure of violence, and a sense of justice were things that mattered. Chandler accepted these characteristics, and they became a part of Philip Marlowe.

When Editor Shaw received "Blackmailers Don't Shoot," from a man he had never heard of, he could not decide whether it was remarkably good or cleverly fraudulent, so he sent it to one of his established writers, W. T. Ballard, for an opinion. The answer was a vote for "remarkably good." Although the hero of the story, Mallory (or ten other names before he became Philip Marlowe), was at the outset rather sparsely drawn, he was gradually to evolve into a well-rounded character. Physically in the beginning he was a stock character, "tall, with wide-set gray eyes, a thin nose, a jaw of stone." His black hair was "ever so faintly touched with gray, as by an almost diffident hand." His distinction, that which set him apart from the stereotype detective, was that while he was a man of the people he wore clothes that "fitted him as though they had a soul of their own, not just a doubtful past." He was tough enough to handle a hood, strong enough to bounce back from the inevitable sapping, determined to take nothing from a couple of crooked cops, and sufficiently hard-boiled to kill when it came his turn. Mallory, essentially the same as a dozen or more pulp detectives, had found his destiny in the West.

Chandler's second Mallory story, "Smart-Aleck Kill," is hardly different from the first; but the third and fourth stories, both of which use a nameless first person narrator, show marked changes in the hero. For one thing he was beginning to develop an active resentment against social injustices, and for another he was making decisions that, although they may not have been strictly legal, were in his eyes honorably moral. Prohibition having been repealed, the criminal element was in city politics. The detective, having already become the traditional hero who was willing to contribute a portion of his time and risk a segment of his indestructible hide for good, made a voluntary play for the betterment of social conditions. He participated in the elimination of the political mobsters, so the city was better off. He also decided that because the lady was mixed up with the criminal element only through fear, she should not be subjected to the law, and he allowed her to escape saying, "I didn't mind very much if she got away." The knightly attitude, indigenous in the hard-boiled hero, had become a characteristic of Chandler's protagonist.

Coupled with attaining knighthood, the detective identified himself as being in the tradition of violence. Throughout a century of hard-boiled heroic fiction, the protagonist had been allowed to perpetrate acts of violence as evidence of his courage. Chandler did not use the technique of violence to the extent that many of the earlier writers had, and his hero never accomplished the brutally-smashing effects of, for example, Dashiell Hammett's hero; but he did use the technique, and in some of his early work it is quite evident. "Finger-Man" has several episodes that are intended to contribute to the detective's hard-boiled effectiveness. "But the big man was already sagging. My bullet had drilled through his neck. Ohls fired at him very carefully as he fell and the sixth and last slug from his gun caught the man in the chest and twisted him around. The side of his head slapped the curb with a sickening crunch." Obviously, too, the simple shooting of a man of this type was not adequate; the act needed literary emphasis—needed to be dwelt upon long enough to compensate for the evils the villain performed against society.

In 1935 in "Killer in the Rain" the detective clearly expressed his attitude toward the man in trouble. Making a little money on the case was obviously not as important as doing good. When the dumb but well-meaning Dravec could no longer handle his wild

daughter, the hero stepped in to protect him. Although Dravec broke a man's neck he was morally innocent because he was fighting such social evils as blackmailers, homosexuals, and dispensers of pornography. The detective, when accused by the police of being tough, made clear his feelings about people: "I'm not tough. I was working for Dravec and trying to save him from a little heartache. . . . I didn't care a lot about trash like Steiner or Joe Marty and his girl friend, and still don't."

On occasion Chandler turned from his detective hero to one of another sort. In "Nevada Gas"—a smooth, tough, sophisticated, first-rate story—Johnny De Ruse, the gambler, had all the characteristics of the detective hero. De Ruse was so competent and his girl friend was so considerate she felt obliged to warn his antagonist. "There isn't a guy in the world that doesn't rate a start on you, Johnny. It wouldn't do him any good, but he'd have to have it, if I knew him."

Shortly before his death Chandler wrote a newspaper column on cops in which he had several affectionate things to say about them. He knew, he said, that they were like most people—good and bad, ethical and greedy. Until his final novel, however, he was never very soft on them. True, there was an occasional cop like Bernie Ohls who was tough and efficient and honest. Frequently, though, they were dishonest and brutal, using their badges as an excuse for meanly-motivated desires and for taking advantage of the little man who could not protect himself. These cops served as a contrast or a foil for the detective. Some *Black Mask* writers, Thomas Walsh for one, used the cop as a hero. Chandler did this only once, in "Spanish Blood." Sam Delaguerra was a policeman with all the best characteristics of the private eye. Unlike the distasteful cop who was identified by his bad breath, Sam was honest and loyal and willing to sacrifice himself for good, beyond the requirements of his job. In true knightly fashion he allowed an old friend to cover up after killing her husband. As he sadly reviewed the toll of seven deaths, Sam told the lady, "Life seems to do nasty things to people."

In "Guns at Cyrano's" Chandler used as hero a man who had once been a private eye but was living on the money—dirty money—inherited from his father. The story is distinguished by the hero's attempt to make up to society for his father's acts against it. The girl expressed it to the hero: "You think you're hard-boiled but you're just a big slob that argues himself into a jam for the first tramp he finds in trouble."

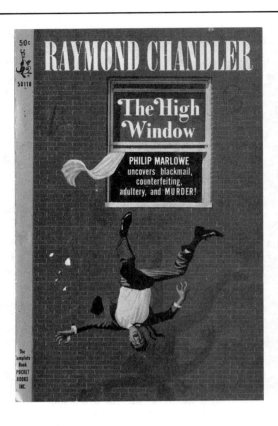

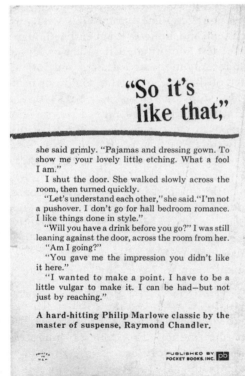

"So it's like that,"

she said grimly. "Pajamas and dressing gown. To show me your lovely little etching. What a fool I am."

I shut the door. She walked slowly across the room, then turned quickly.

"Let's understand each other," she said. "I'm not a pushover. I don't go for hall bedroom romance. I like things done in style."

"Will you have a drink before you go?" I was still leaning against the door, across the room from her.

"Am I going?"

"You gave me the impression you didn't like it here."

"I wanted to make a point. I have to be a little vulgar to make it. I can be had—but not just by reaching."

A hard-hitting Philip Marlowe classic by the master of suspense, Raymond Chandler.

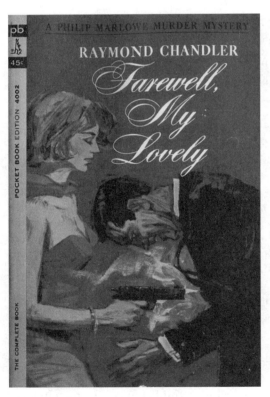

Covers for 1960s paperback editions of the first three Chandler novels. At the same time that scholars and Chandler's hard-bound publishers were making the case that his books should be treated as works of literature, the paperback editions continued to promote the sex and violence in the novels.

Carmady, the private investigator of "The Curtain," spent a great deal of time he didn't get paid for in finding out who "put the pencil" on his friend Larry Batzel and why Dud O'Mara had "pulled down the curtain." He discovered the hood who was responsible for the gunning of Larry, and that hood was taken care of in the course of a night's work. But discovering that Dud had not pulled down the curtain but had been shot by his eleven-year-old step-son presented a different kind of problem. How to curb a "crazy little sadist with an itchy trigger-finger" and how to prevent the dying general, the boy's grandfather, from learning that evil blood had developed in his family somewhat enlarged the role of the hero. But after solving the problems and clearing up all the loose ends, he said to the boy's mother, "Take him away. . . . He's young enough to be cured by the right handling. Take him to Europe. . . . It would kill the general out of hand to know his blood was in that." When the mother tried to thank him he said, "Forget it. I'm just an old workhorse. Put *your* work on the boy."

By 1937 the role of Chandler's detective had grown far beyond the limits of simple investigations. In looking for a missing husband in "Try the Girl," Carmady found himself in the middle of a nasty web of life in which many people were involved, the guilty and the innocent, the crumby ones and the decent ones. On his own time and money he set out to bring some order into the chaotic situation and to uncover any good he could find. One of his motives was to point up to the police that he, a free and independent man, had to do a job they appeared unable to cope with. He accomplished his self-appointed mission but only after coming dangerously close to violating his code of humanitarian decency. He shamelessly plied an old alcoholic widow with liquor in order to get her to talk, but he berated himself as he "went out into the fall sunlight." "I like knowing myself. I was the kind of guy who chiseled a sodden old wreck out of her life secrets to win a ten dollar bet."

Chandler's hero was always passionately ethical. To take a fee, no matter how little, for a job not done or not done well was unthinkable. John Dalmas in "Mandarin's Jade" hired out for fifty dollars to protect a client for an evening. Although Dalmas was badly smashed up, his client was killed, so the detective went looking for someone to whom he could return the money: "Even my mother wouldn't think I had earned it." A short time later he was sent for through a messenger bearing a hundred-dollar bill. Before discussing the problem he returned the money so he would be under no obligation. Only a

day or two later he walked into his office to find a blond who shoved a wad of bills in the amount of $467 across the desk to him. The fact that she was "a blond to make a bishop kick a hole in a stained-glass window" had no deterrent effect on his ethics—he refused the money. After having been knocked out three times in twenty-four hours and having been shot at from various angles, Dalmas was forced to spend ten days in the hospital at his own expense. Upon being released he went to the blond's mansion in Beverly Hills, not to collect his fee but just to let her know that although she had been cleared by the police he knew that she had had a man murdered. She obliged by shooting at him, as her millionaire husband strolled into the room with checkbook in hand asking, "How much will keep you quiet?" "Make it a million," Daimas said. "And she just took a shot at [me]. That will be four bits extra."

The theme of working not for money but to see justice done continued in "Red Wind." When Dalmas found a suspect, a girl in a printed bolero jacket, his impulse was to protect her until he had more facts. She could not believe there was this much voluntary good in people, especially in a private eye, and assumed he wanted money. His humanitarian gestures were frequently mistaken, and he, just as frequently, seemed dumbfounded at being misunderstood. Yet the hero went doggedly on risking life, reputation, and license to assure protection for those he believed worthy of it. In this story he spent extra time and money in covering up for a fourflusher in whom the girl had romantic faith, in fixing it so she need never discover the truth.

"Bay City Blues" was a study of violence in the American frontier tradition, for it accepted brutality in an effort to exhibit the virtues of courage and guts. The private eye complimented a doctor with an obviously unethical practice because "you in your quiet way have a lot of guts." A secondary character who "had his own brand of guts" was praised. Although somewhat qualified, there was also admiration for De Spain, the most brutal cop in Chandler's work. With an aching head and sick stomach, the detective watched De Spain slowly and methodically smash a mobster into senselessness. In the end, of course, De Spain got his, but even after his incredible display of sadism, after he had murdered and scratched the naked body of a girl, the detective said of him, "The hell of it is I liked De Spain. He had all the guts they ever made." This somehow echoes the dime novel days of the nineteenth century. When the famous border villain, Simon Girty, turned up in an Edward Ellis novel, he was called a "brave man for all he's such an inhuman brute."

Love, marriage, and sex were, until the end of the author's career, consistently denied the Chandler detective. Love and marriage were forbidden, partially, at least, because like Natty Bumppo the private eye had grown out of his class, but he was smart enough to know that he should not marry too far above it. More important, however, was the undeniable fact that a man is less capable of freely offering his life in defense of others while he has a family at home depending on his continuance as a provider. Sex without marriage was impossible, for the detective was operating within the heroic code of the frontiersman. Almost any aspect of the code could, under certain conditions, be forgiven except that of "violating" a white woman. In "Trouble Is My Business," Dalmas was tempted by a redhead with "bedroom eyes" who was once in the social register. He went out with or saw her four times but then recognized his own strength and place. "It was nice, but I didn't have the money, the clothes, the time or the manners."

Shortly before his death at the end of the 1950's, Lester Dent wrote of the days when Captain Joe Shaw was editor of the old *Black Mask,* "the brief wonderful time when American literature was endowed with the most effective training ground of all history–the pulp magazine." The pulp media were Raymond Chandler's training ground. From December, 1933, until October 14, 1939, Chandler published twenty short stories: eleven in the *Black Mask,* seven in *Dime Detective Magazine,* one in *Detective Fiction Weekly,* and one in *Saturday Evening Post;* one slick and nineteen pulps. (Editor Shaw, incidentally, could never bring himself to say "slick" or "pulp" but always "smooth paper" or "rough paper.") In the twenty stories the hero had ten different names and was twice nameless. In fifteen stories he was a private eye; in five he had such assorted roles as gambler, detective lieutenant, and hotel dick. But using the pulps as a training ground for developing his hero, Chandler was eventually ready to use that hero in sustained fiction, so the short story writer became a novelist, with Philip Marlowe as his detective. The year was 1939 and the first novel was *The Big Sleep.*

In mid-October, on a morning with a "look of hard wet rain in the clearness of the foothills," a "neat, clean, shaved and sober" private investigator drove along the streets of Los Angeles on his way to a mansion in the Hollywood Hills where he would discuss a job with a prospective client. The unmarried detective was thirty-three years old, had been to college, and could still speak English when there was a "demand for it." He was proud of testing "very high on insubordination." As Philip Marlowe, who had just begun his career as a knight-errant for the citizens of Los Angeles, entered General Sternwood's mansion, he looked above the entrance door at a stained-glass panel on which a knight in dark armor was trying to rescue a lady who was tied to a tree, a lady covered only by her long and convenient hair. Standing there looking at the scene, the detective thought: "if I lived in the house I would sooner or later have to climb up there and help him. He didn't seem to be really trying."

Throughout *The Big Sleep* the hero played the characteristic role he had learned to act so well. He turned his talents against blackmailers who preyed on society. In nineteenth-century Western style he threw his gun on the ground and fought the kid with nature's weapons, albeit the kid was a pansy, and "a pansy has no iron in his bones." He said "To hell with the rich" for they made him sick, yet he worked for them and protected them because they seemed unable to take care of themselves. In one evening he turned down two lovely ladies, each of whom offered her all. To one he explained that it was a case of "professional pride," that he was a loyal detective trying to do a job for her father; "I work at it, lady. I don't play at it." The other, whose beautiful, nude body beckoned him from his own bed, was refused because promiscuous cohabitation would have violated the sanctity of his home: ". . . this was the room I had to live in. It was all I had in the way of a home. In it was everything that was mine, that had any association with me, any past, anything that took the place of a family. Not much; a few books, pictures, radio, chessmen, old letters, stuff like that. Nothing. Such as they were they had all my memories."

Once the district attorney and the city police took a dim view of Marlowe's activities, telling him that had he not held back information a life (of a blackmailer) might have been saved, and after all "a life is a life." "Right," Marlowe said. "Tell that to your coppers next time they shoot down some scared petty larceny crook running up an alley with a stolen spare." When asked by the district attorney why he was jeopardizing his life and his future for twenty-five dollars a day and expense money, Marlowe answered, "I'm selling what I have to sell to make a living. What little guts and intelligence the Lord gave me and a willingness to get pushed around in order to protect a client." When he finished the job he offered to return his fee to the General, for he felt his work had been unsatisfactory.

Although he was a simple man trying to mete out simple justice, as he saw it, the hero clearly recognized the complex realities in a human society. He thought at times that "fate stage-managed the whole

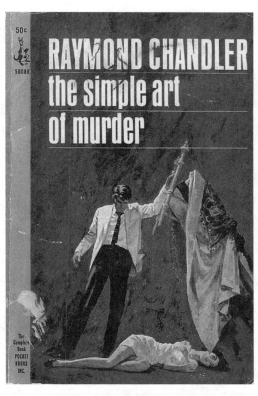

can be found almost any place. If you like proof, just follow the tough babies who stagger, batter, and bully their unlovely ways through these blistering pages. You'll find:

SLAUGHTER A shabby apartment with a pull-down bed. Under the bed a dame with a broken neck. Outside her door a guy pumping lead into a big thug's belly.

BRUTALITY Henry plodded into the hotel room and Gage hit him with everything he had. The punch would have stopped a bull. But Henry was bigger than a bull. He blinked then muttered, "So you want to play for keeps."

HOMICIDE Johnny Ralls had a long standing engagement with a redhead. Johnny never kept his date. When he walked out toward Wilshire the "trouble boys" were waiting . . . with an invitation to the morgue.

Here in one volume are four complete novelettes, plus that very famous essay—THE SIMPLE ART OF MURDER —by the all-time master of the tough crime story, RAYMOND CHANDLER.

PUBLISHED BY POCKET BOOKS, INC. PRINTED IN U.S.A.

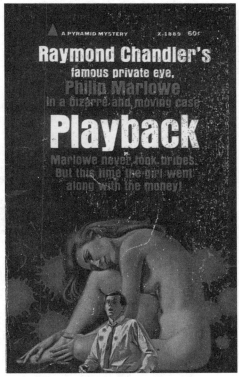

Front and back covers for 1960s paperback editions of Chandler's 1950 short-story collection and his 1958 novel

thing." When a problem looked too easy, too pat, it was time to become suspicious; beware if it "had the austere simplicity of fiction rather than the tangled woof of fact."

In his lonely hours Marlowe relaxed his body, tested his mind, and provided himself with some knotty philosophical situations by playing solo chess against set problems. Having on one occasion made an unwise move with a knight, he returned the knight to its original position. As he made the move he thought of the analogy to the human situation in which he was involved: "Knights had no meaning in this game. It wasn't a game for knights." The irony of the contemplation was, of course, that from the beginning of the novel until its conclusion it was a story being played by a knight.

With the publication of *Farewell, My Lovely*, Chandler was approaching the peak of his creative ability. Although never quite real–as a symbol could not be–the hero simulated reality with believable ease. Marlowe was indestructible, as all private eyes must be, but he was not a superman, as so many of them are. His closest neighbor in terms of literary realism is the private investigator of Dashiell Hammett's *The Dain Curse*. Chandler's knight, the protector of society, the dispenser of justice, had acquired a bit of humility, and to prove that he was really human he admitted to being scared. When, at the end of the novel, he confessed to having a touch of sentiment, he was the complete man. He was the hero that men in their feckless souls imagine themselves being; he was the hero that women in their optimistic hearts hope they have married.

Having achieved all the characteristics the Americans have traditionally approved of in their literary heroes, Marlowe moved with easy confidence through *The High Window*. Now that he had proved himself hard-boiled, he could say, "I'm not tough. Just virile." Being called a "shop-soiled Galahad" meant only that he was the conscience of, and protector of, the people, and as such he was willing to suffer for them and represent for them the symbol of right against the forces of injustice.

In the Galahad role Marlowe went to the police to let them know that they must deal with him as the representative of society. Detective Lieutenant Breeze, the leader of "force," tried to push Marlowe around because he was the leader of the unorganized social group. Marlowe would not be pushed. The private eye explained to the cops that he had been around town for fifteen years and had seen a lot of murder cases. Some were solved, some couldn't be, some were solved wrong, and some were arranged for another to take the rap. In order to "make a

point" he presented a "hypothetical" case: A rich young man killed his secretary and then shot himself. To protect their name, the family arranged it to look like the secretary had done the killing. The cops knew what had been done but let it go. Breeze was unimpressed with the story because both men were dead; but to Marlowe it was not that simple for no thought was given to the family or friends of the secretary. And then the hero spelled out his "point." "Until you guys own your own souls you don't own mine. Until you guys can be trusted every time and always, in all times and conditions, to seek the truth out and find it and let the chips fall where they may–until that time comes, I have a right to listen to my own conscience, and protect my client the best way I can. Until I'm sure you won't do him more harm than you'll do the truth good."

When society's legal agencies were unable, although not necessarily through faults of their own, to protect society adequately, when these agencies discriminated between the little man and the big man, when they no longer took a precise stand for right against wrong, the literary hero came to the rescue–"to seek the truth out and find it and let the chips fall where they may." But it was a rarely appreciated role and a lonely life. With "another day drawing to its end, the air dull and tired," Marlowe returned to his dingy office. "I filled and lit my pipe and sat there smoking. Nobody came in, nobody called, nothing happened, nobody cared whether I died or went to El Paso."

There was no obvious change in the hero in the next novel, *The Lady in the Lake*, but there was, however, the implication that Chandler, through Marlowe, was disillusioned by the acts of mankind–the story was written during the height of World War II. Throughout the book the hero traveled between Santa Monica, on the edge of the Pacific, and Big Bear Lake, high in the mountains above Los Angeles. The unsaintly Santa Monica, the town of brutality and evil, was contrasted with the purity of the mountains, where the Sierra Madres cast their spell on the man of action: "The air was peaceful and calm and sunny and held a quiet you don't get in cities. I could have stayed there for hours doing nothing." Nature appeared superior to human nature when a "bluejay squawked on a branch and a squirrel scolded at me and beat one paw angrily on the pine cone it was holding. A scarlet-topped woodpecker stopped probing in the bark long enough to look at me with one beady eye and then dodge behind the trunk to look at me with the other one." Near sundown a "robin sat on the spike top of a hundred foot pine and waited for it to be dark enough for him to sing his goodnight song," but it was time for the detective to return to the city where he had a job to do. The corrupt police of the city were contrasted with the sheriff of the mountains—a large, primitive, friendly man who represented the goodness of nature. True, there was murder in the mountains, but it was done by city people to city people; and the perpetrators of the crime did not rightly calculate the combined effect of the city hero and the mountain hero.

At this point in Raymond Chandler's literary career his hero had reached the apex of his development—so much so that Chandler could carefully delineate him in "The Simple Art of Murder." For one who had read through Chandler's stories and novels from 1933 to 1944, this description came as no surprise, yet the clarity with which the author listed the hero's characteristics had a uniqueness.

"But down these mean streets a man must go who is not himself mean, who is neither tarnished nor afraid. . . . He is the hero; he is everything. He must be a complete man and a common man and yet an unusual man. He must be, to use a rather weathered phrase, a man of honor—by instinct, by inevitability, without thought of it, and certainly without saying it. He must be the best man in his world and a good enough man for any world. I do not care much about his private life; he is neither a eunuch nor a satyr; I think he might seduce a duchess and I am quite sure he would not spoil a virgin; if he is a man of honor in one thing, he is that in all things.

"He is a relatively poor man, or he would not be a detective at all. He is a common man or he could not go among common people; he has a sense of character, or he would not know his job. He will take no man's money dishonestly and no man's insolence without a due and dispassionate revenge; he is a lonely man and his pride is that you will treat him as a proud man or be very sorry you ever saw him. He talks as the man of his age talks—that is, with rude wit, a lively sense of the grotesque, a disgust for sham, and a contempt for pettiness.

"The story is this man's adventure in search of a hidden truth, and it would be no adventure if it did not happen to a man fit for adventure."

Not only had Chandler described his detective hero, he had, and as artfully as it had ever been done, presented the American hero—the one who had been evolving in American fiction for more than a hundred years. It must be emphasized, however, that the detective hero was only a literary one. Never for a moment did Chandler imply that he was real except on paper. In California, in fact, the private investigator is licensed only to investigate, and it is doubtful that ever in his career would he have anything to do with murder. The fictional private eye caught the public fancy because he allowed both sexes to dream, but he was only what his creator intended him to be—pure fantasy. As a symbol the detective hero was superb, but as a symbol he could never achieve reality. The result was that Chandler was actually writing romantic fiction, but by simulating reality through a hard-boiled attitude he could stay within an American literary tradition. The action and violence more or less covered up the fact that everything came out all right in the end.

Although Chandler probably did not know it at the time, his hero was never again to reach the rarified mountain air. Marlowe in *The Little Sister* was still the traditional hero, but he had become a little jaded. It was springtime in Los Angeles and the jacarandas were in bloom, but it was also the "year the all-tile bathroom became the basis of civilization." The once exciting city had now become the home of screen stars. "Screen stars, phooey. The veterans of a thousand beds." The once beautiful ocean had become the "great fat solid Pacific trudging into shore like a scrubwoman going home." He found it necessary to remind himself with automatic frequency, "You're not human tonight, Marlowe." He was five years older, which was beginning to tell, and he had upped his fee to forty dollars a day, to compensate for the increased cost of living.

Yet as a knight, Marlowe was working for good rather than for money. When he went out to risk his life and reputation and to spend days of his time for a token amount of twenty dollars, it obviously was not for a fee but for a girl in trouble. In the end he gave back the twenty dollars and drove the little sister all the way home to Manhattan, Kansas, neither of which she deserved. The big sister received his sympathy and protection because although she had free-and-easy Hollywood morals she was not the "blood-money" type and she had "bedrock guts."

What had really happened to Marlowe was that he had lost some of his common touch. He had, for example, no sympathy for those women who work in municipal offices: "They are what human beings turn into when they trade life for existence and ambition for security." In his true role the hero had stoically accepted loneliness as a part of his character. Yet in his disillusionment at the end of the 1940's he could not take it: "Let the telephone ring, please. Let there be somebody to call up and plug me into the human race again. Even a cop. Nobody has to like me. I just want to get off this frozen star."

—Down these Mean Streets a Man Must Go:
Raymond Chandler's Knight, pp. 79–98

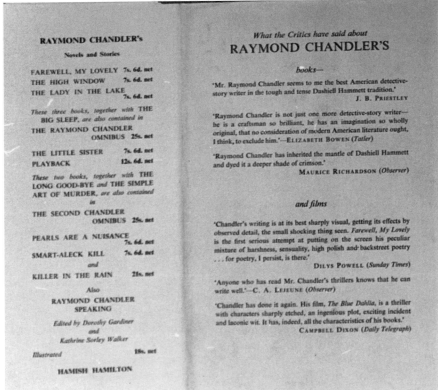

British and American dust jackets for the first book publication of the eight pulp stories that Chandler had "cannibalized" and incorporated into his novels (Bruccoli Collection, Kent State University)

New Editions and Collections

During his lifetime Chandler refused to reprint the eight stories he had used in writing his novels because he felt it dishonest to sell the same work twice. In the preface to Killer in the Rain, *however, Philip Durham argued that the stories should be published because of their scholarly importance. In 1964–the same year* Killer in the Rain *was released–Alfred A. Knopf published Chandler's first four novels together in a hardbound edition titled* The Raymond Chandler Omnibus. *This volume is an indication of both the continuing public interest in Chandler's novels and the growing academic respect for his writing. In 1967 the publication of* Farewell, My Lovely *and* The Lady in the Lake *in the Modern Library series marked another important milestone in the growth of Chandler's literary reputation. The series aimed to publish "the best of the world's best books in modern fiction," and Chandler appeared in it along William Faulkner, James Joyce, Jean-Paul Sartre, and Thomas Mann.*

* * *

In his foreword to The Raymond Chandler Omnibus *Lawrence Clark Powell, the special collections librarian at the University of California at Los Angeles, emphasized Chandler's documentation of life in Los Angeles during the 1940s and 1950s in his novels.*

Throwing brickbats at Los Angeles has been a favorite sport of writers for as long as Los Angeles has been a city. There is even an anthology of anti-L.A. literature, compiled by W. W. Robinson, called *What They Say about the Angels.* San Francisco frequently serves as a vantage point for throwers, although New York and London have known strong-armed critics who could land on target from a long way off.

As an old-timer in Los Angeles, dating from 1910, I have been critical of the shower of novels about my home town, finding them mostly shallow and not rooted in reality. Admittedly it's a hard place in which to root, and it's getting harder as the blacktop thickens. Also, every time a layer of cultural humus accumulates, along comes a new wave of immigration to wash it away; all of which makes it tough for writers, who need the nourishment that comes from being rooted. The high mobility of the inhabitants makes it difficult to keep one's eye on the facts. Besides, just where is L.A.? Unlike San Francisco, packed on its peninsula, yours in a glance, Los Angeles is dispersed over a wide expanse of the coastal plain.

Among the many novels about Los Angeles there have been a few memorable ones, from *Merton of the Movies* (1922), *The Postman Always Rings Twice* (1934), and *The Day of the Locust* (1939) to *What Makes Sammy Run?* (1941) and *The Loved One* (1948). Almost everything written about La Reina de Los Angeles, however, has been by those revolted by her, intent on satirizing her follies, and hot with scorn that blinds a writer to details of the local scene.

Whatever's to be said about L.A., there's a lot of her; the queen of the Angels' robes are spreading wide and high. At the present rate of growth, another generation will find Los Angeles the most populous city in the United States.

Which brings us to Raymond Chandler.

As a genre, mystery novels are not usually regarded by critics as literature, and they are often reviewed together in a special department. Yet, to my taste, of all the hundreds of novels thus far written about the city, the truest to the mobile, violent, foolish and fantastic metropolis of Los Angeles, erstwhile Queen of the Cow Counties, are those by Raymond Chandler and particularly the "big four" of his brief prime, collected in this volume: *The Big Sleep* (1939), *Farewell, My Lovely* (1940), *The High Window* (1942), and *The Lady in the Lake* (1943).

What makes them so good? Why are they among the few mystery stories of our time, and among the few novels about Los Angeles, that have achieved the distinction of literature? The answer is contained in a single word: *style.* Chandler's prose style has what he said Dashiell Hammett's lacks–overtones, echoes, images.

"When a book, any sort of book," Chandler wrote to Erle Stanley Gardner, "reaches a certain intensity of artistic performance it becomes literature. That intensity may be a matter of style, situation, character, emotional tone, or idea, or half a dozen other things. It may also be a perfection of control over the movement of a story similar to the control a great pitcher has over the ball."

These are indeed the very qualities that characterize these triumphs of Raymond Chandler; and high among them is the absolute control the writer has over his setting. Chandler brought Los Angeles into focus; he stopped the kaleidoscope, so that we see the brilliant bits and pieces in perfect register; no random movements, no distortion, no blur; all appears the way the city does on a December night after the Santa Ana winds have broomed away the smog and the million lights sparkle like jewels in a queen's robe.

Chandler wrote with classical dispassion of a romantic and violent society. He was neither for nor against L.A.; his vision was not dazzled by the neons which rainbow the Southern California night. He had the X-ray eye that penetrates blacktop and fog (smog didn't come until the 1940's–Chandler's L.A. is of the two earlier decades). He had the gift of tongue; he was a poet. Metaphors flowered for him in language utterly suited to the exotic people and places he was describing with Flaubertian meticulousness. Chandler didn't moralize, satirize, deplore, or lament; he saw, selected, and said, in language that lives. The reader is left to his own conclusions about the morality of the Southern California milieu.

The inhabitants are all there to the life–garage men, room clerks, carhops, grifters, grafters, and house dicks, the idle rich and their butlers, houseboys, and chauffeurs–a marvelous menagerie of Southern Californians, differentiated in appearance and speech, pitilessly portrayed yet without malice. Chandler had lived among them most of his life—he *was* one of them, he and his alter ego, Philip Marlowe—and he memorialized their brutal and violent actions with redeeming compassion.

If it can't be said that Chandler loved Los Angeles, it is true nevertheless that he never left her for long; and by Los Angeles I mean that monster of men and machines that is ravaging the countryside from Santa Barbara to San Diego. Why did he choose Los Angeles? Why not Chicago, where he was born in 1888? Or London, in whose Dulwich College he was classically educated? Why not Paris, where he lived briefly after service in the Canadian Army during World War I? Or Vancouver or San Francisco, where he worked in banks?

Why L.A., whose laureate he became? The question is unanswerable, at least in the short space of a foreword. He went there for the first time in 1912, when he was twenty-four, and lived on Bunker Hill, a little escarpment in the heart of the city, in an apartment-hotel at the top of the tiny funicular railway known as the Angels Flight. In those years Bunker Hill was genteel. By the time Chandler came to write about it, decay had set in; the old dwellings and hotels had become cheap boardinghouses, the seamy setting of many incidents in his novels.

In 1919 he returned to Southern California for good, living in Pasadena, Palm Springs, Hollywood, and finally La Jolla, where he died in 1959. He knew the region about which he wrote down to the smallest details of its topography, flora, and weather. As no other novelist has done, he perceived the differences between, for example, Azusa, Rialto, Hueneme, and Escondido. Chandler is just as truly Southern California's poet as Robinson Jeffers is the laureate of Carmel and the Big Sur.

Up until the Depression and his mid-forties, Chandler was a prosperous businessman, a good example of the unpredictability of the who, when, and where of literary genius. "Wandering up and down the Pacific Coast in an automobile," he wrote in 1950 to Hamish Hamilton, his English publisher, "I began to read pulp magazines, because they were cheap enough to throw away and because I never had at any time any taste for the kind of thing which is known as women's magazines. This was in the great days of the *Black Mask* (if I may call them great days) and it struck me that some of the writing was pretty forceful and honest, even though it had its crude aspect. I decided that this might be a good way to try to learn to write fiction and get paid a small amount of money at the same time. I spent five months over an 18,000 word novelette and sold it for $180. After that I never looked back, although I had a good many uneasy periods looking forward."

Chandler had reached the age of fifty-one when he wrote, in three months, *The Big Sleep,* the first of his four masterpieces; the others followed in a machine-gun burst of

creativity. In that brief time of high noon, all his gifts, all his preparation, all that he had been and done and seen, coalesced in his writing. Perceptive vision, absorptive capacity, creative stamina, were his and he emptied them out in these books. He proved finally to have the three S's that, joined in a writer, mean literature: the power to see, to sense, and to say.

Two women in Raymond Chandler's life gave him anchorage—his Irish mother, with whom he lived until she died when he was thirty-six, and then his wife, a woman eighteen years older than he was, with whom he knew a long and faithful marriage. When she died in 1954, Chandler survived her for five years in a kind of living death. "She was the beat of my heart for thirty years," he wrote to Leonard Russell. "She was the music heard faintly at the edge of sound. It was my great and now useless regret that I never wrote anything really worth her attention, no book that I could dedicate to her."

Now that he is dead and all his work published, we can look back over the seventy-one years of Chandler's life and plot the arc of his creative career; we can see how it rose slowly at first, then soared and remained at zenith for the duration of these four miraculous books, before it fell fast and sputtered out in *The Little Sister* (1949) and *The Long Goodbye* (1954). In addition to his novels and stories there are other sources for study: *Raymond Chandler Speaking,* a posthumous collection of letters and essays on writing which reveal him as an intellectual craftsman, and *Down These Mean Streets a Man Must Go,* a critical study by Philip Durham, based on the Chandler papers that were left to the UCLA Library, thanks to a friendship that flowered between Chandler and Wilbur Smith, a member of the Library's staff.

Now it is the mid-1960's and the Southern California of a generation ago, mirrored so faithfully by Chandler, is going fast, torn apart by freeways, lost in a pall of smog, the groves of orange and lemon, walnut and avocado, ripped out by the roots to make way for tract houses, factories, auto parks. Urban renewal is returning Bunker Hill to its lost gentility, earth-movers push around the Hollywood hills, Westwood rises high, Bel Air's dwellings have all but disappeared in a jungle of subtropical vegetation, while Pacific Palisades presents a solid stucco face to the sea and even far-out Malibu begins to feel the hot breath of the bulldozer. And the rash spreads along the coast and out onto the air-conditioned desert, as the widening stain of the city is carried by freeways and their off-ramps.

None of this happens in the enchanted world of Raymond Chandler. In his books the city and country stay as they were, once and for all. This writer fixed his world in prose that cannot be touched by time. Such was his supreme achievement.

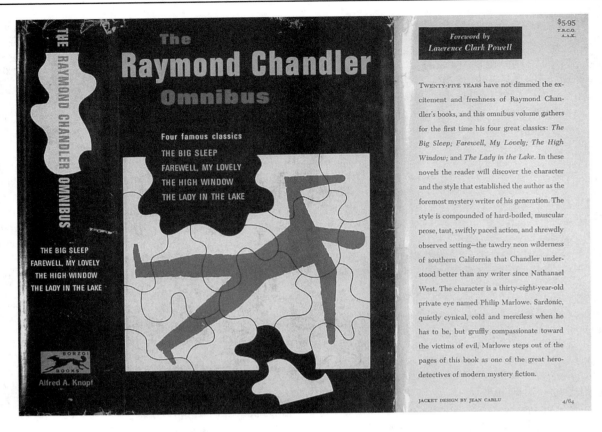

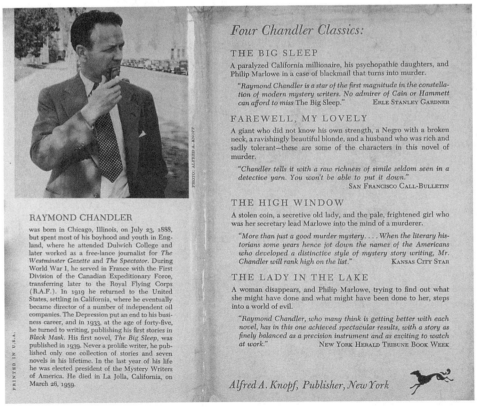

Dust jacket for the 1964 collection of Chandler's first four novels

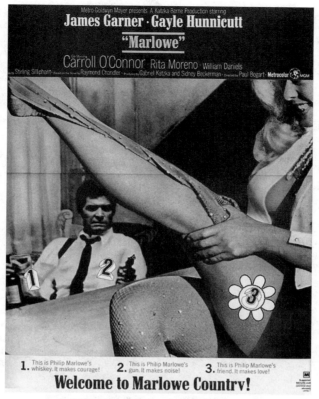

Poster and cover of the paperpack tie-in for Marlowe *(MGM, 1969), the only movie version of* The Little Sister

Covers for early 1970s paperback editions of three novels and a collection. Beginning in 1971, Ballantine became the American paperback publisher of Chandler's books and promoted him with lurid artwork.

Altman's *Long Goodbye*

In 1973 United Artists released The Long Goodbye, *which was directed by Robert Altman and starred Elliot Gould as Philip Marlowe. Altman set the movie in contemporary Los Angeles and recast the story as a parody of the detective as a lone hero. With a few exceptions, the movie was panned by critics. Charles Gregory, who wrote the review for* Film Quarterly, *was one of many critics who condemned Altman for his approach to the material.*

Robert Altman is the first major director to attempt Raymond Chandler/Phillip Marlowe since Howard Hawks made *The Big Sleep* in 1946. Unlike Hawks, however, Altman has come to bury Marlowe, not to have fun with him. At first, Altman seems a perfectly compatible choice to depict the highly stylized, often bizarre Southern California-based world of Marlowe, which Chandler described in simile filled paragraphs that resemble nothing so much as the layers and layers of witty images and lines from *M*A*S*H, Brewster McCloud,* and *Images.* Hawks's dialogue pacing in *The Big Sleep,* as well as in his comedies (especially *His Girl Friday*), resembles the snap, crackle, and pop of *M*A*S*H.* Even the weaker films in the Marlowe series have some of the touches that Altman might be expected to appreciate: the pure Chandlerese of the voice-over in *Murder, My Sweet, Lady in the Lake,* and even *The Brasher Doubloon;* the a-psychedelic drug scene in *Murder, My Sweet;* the camera eye in *Lady In The Lake;* Mike Mazurki's soft-spoken but inhumanly strong giant in *Murder, My Sweet;* Florence Bates's homicidal old matriarch in *The Brasher Doubloon;* and a general assortment of Hollywood residents who are by nature more bizarre than actors can dream of in their philosophy.

But as Chandler remarked in his 1953 novel *The Long Goodbye,* "in Hollywood anything can happen, anything at all." Altman has proven this with a series of public statements announcing that his new film version of that very novel will "put Marlowe to rest for good." The first step toward this rather unusual goal for the sixth Phillip Marlowe movie was the casting of Elliott Gould as Marlowe. Altman has said that he is out to cast doubt on the continuing validity of the values that Marlowe embodies: *loyalty, honor, duty.* Altman does not believe in Chandler's hero "who is not himself mean, who is neither tarnished or afraid." The Gould/Altman Marlowe looks remarkably lonely and silly for having held on so long to such platonic ideals. The rest of Altman's cast seems more in the Chandler tradition, where reality and fiction blur uneasily on the front pages of newspapers. Nina Van Pallandt, famous mainly as hoaxer Clifford Irving's

mistress, in the central rote of Eileen Wade; Henry Gibson, the flower poet from TV's *Laugh-In* as Dr. Verringer; Jim Bouton, former baseball player and author turned TV commentator, as Marlowe's friend Terry Lennox; and film director Mark Rydell as a mod, Hollywood-Vegas syndicate boss provide Gould/Marlowe with a density of sensationalism proper to the Chandler world. *Bonanza's* Dan Blocker was originally scheduled as the writer Roger Wade, but died. A bearded Sterling Hayden replaced him and gives a marvelous performance as a virulently virile alcoholic writer who can no longer write. (Altman putting out to pasture still another American hero linked to the tough guy literary tradition.)

This unusual cast is supplemented by bit players creating the rich textural background for which Altman is justifiably famous. For instance, there are four or five nubile, yoga-addicted girls who live next to Marlowe and exercise naked to the waist on their terrace; a black grocery clerk who engages Marlowe in some enigmatic exchanges about cats and girls; David Carradine as Marlowe's hippie cellmate; Mark Rydell's gang which consists of one member of each ethnic minority, including an over-developed refugee from Muscle Beach; cocktail party guests who sin-

Still from The Long Goodbye; *Elliot Gould as Philip Marlowe and Nina Van Pallandt as Eileen Wade.*

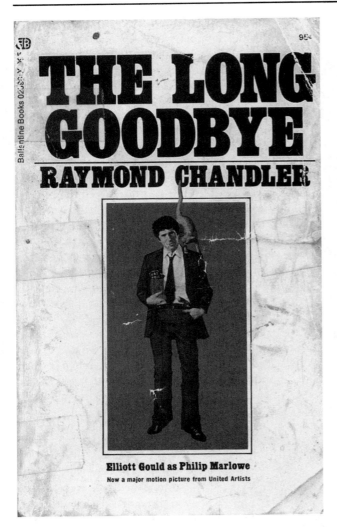

Front and back cover for the paperback tie-in for Robert Altman's movie, part of the promotional campaign that accompanied the release of the movie in the spring of 1973

cerely chatter the most awful banalities; and a girl whose only importance is to be hit across the face with a bottle—one of the three shockingly violent moments in a film curiously devoid of action.

Leigh Brackett, who had collaborated on the tough, cynical, and cynically romantic script of *The Big Sleep,* has failed to bring character, motivation, or plot into crisp focus. Perhaps Altman's love of the edges of things makes this impossible. Altman credits Brackett with the controversial ending that reverses the events, motivation, and moral tone of the Chandler novel, but this certainly suits Altman's destructive purposes. Plot was never Chandler's strong point except as it suited his general vision of hopeless entanglement solved only by obeying certain basic principles. Yet here in this movie the principles are gone and so is the hope for motivation. The

all-important Terry Lennox character who disappears at the beginning fails to maintain a presence in the film; both of the Wades are opaque in the way that all suburban agony is to me but shouldn't be in art; the villainous Mark Rydell gangster is simply unmotivated violence and threat in the current style. Only Marlowe remains to provide some center, some direction, but he lacks either the aggressive curiosity of the private eye or that hidden moral center that separates Sam Spade, Phillip Marlowe, and Lew Archer from the confusions and amorality within which they move.

A lack of aggression and arrogance is at the heart of the Altman/Gould detective. Their Marlowe is passive, moving in nebbish bewilderment from one scene to the next, never observing or detecting, never dominating a scene as the previous Marlowes did

Poster designed by Jack Davis of MAD *magazine, part of a revised promotional campaign mounted in the fall of 1973 that presented the movie as a parody. After the poor critical and box office reception, United Artists decided that their original publicity had led audiences to expect a traditional private-detective movie.*

even when they too were ignorant and baffled (but only in the earlier parts of their respective pictures, naturally). Altman's publicly declared premise is putting Marlowe, a forties hero with forties values, in the disillusioned seventies. Gould wears the same blue serge with whiter-than-white arrow shirt and narrow tie in every scene. He even drives a 1948 Lincoln Continental–Gould's own car (one of those blurrings of reality and fiction that Altman loves.) Altman says, "The picture is a commentary on the fifties and seventies–on beliefs then and now." In other words, how does a man with honor appear in a world without honor? Altman's answer lies in the *Raymond Chandler Speaking* collection of letters that he had the entire cast read: "the best thing for getting a sense of Chandler." Undoubtedly, Altman had in mind the lines about "how any man who tried to be honest looks in the end either sentimental or plain foolish." Altman's Marlowe is plainly foolish and foolishly dangerous, but he is not Hollywood's Marlowe, nor Chandler's. Altman seems to have confused Marlowe imitations with Marlowe himself.

The significant word in the Chandler quote is "looks," not "is." Only the corrupt eyes of an amoral world would see Marlowe as sentimental and foolish. To feel sentiment and to be honest, to have honor are clearly worthy ideals. But Altman fears what has been done in the name of honor, national and private, in the last decade. He fears the tendency in Marlowe (and for that matter in Hammett's Sam Spade and Continental Op and MacDonald's I.ew Archer) to act as judge and jury punishing and freeing according to his own private code. Western fans, as well as mystery buffs, know that feeling of dramatic release and psychological climax when the hero finally triumphs in the name of good, when righteousness prevails, and evil is thwarted, even crushed. Although these are justifiable in art, Altman is calling them into question in life–unfortunately through his art.

Chandler's Marlowe accepts the bizarre quality of daily life in Southern California. In the film, Gould/Marlowe is at a total loss. He goes through the film muttering, "I don't know, I don't know, but it's OK with me" whenever faced with still another example of the seventies that he can not comprehend, whether it is the yoga-loving candle-makers next door, the earnest ecology freak with her petition in the bar, or the wealthy Wades whose lives are so entwined with violence, money, and secret sex. Gould embodies perfectly Altman's conception of Marlowe as a bewildered, sincere anachronism who willingly goes to the supermarket at three in the morning to buy the special brand of canned food that his cat prefers.

In other words, Altman envisions Marlowe in the seventies as another McCabe, with the same purposes in mind. Gould's Marlowe does not need to strut the pretensions that McCabe does because he comes with a built-in reputation. Yet they are the same character, the naive nebbish with unsought pretensions due to a completely unwarranted reputation, a man trying to live by an earlier or never-was ethic, a foolish but lovable schmuck who explodes into unexpected violence. The qualitative difference lies in the complexities in *McCabe and Mrs. Miller,* developed through the richness of the Mrs. Miller character and the careful plot and image structuring influenced by Altman's love of the Leonard Cohen sound track, which documents a modern hero's journey and the role that the sisters of mercy play.

Despite the creation of the Southern California ambience and the lovely contrasts between nebbish Marlowe and the glamorous clichés that swirl around him, *The Long Goodbye* fails to suggest the heroic attraction in the detective character. In *McCabe and Mrs. Miller* Altman maintains the tension by having the townspeople consistently believe in McCabe's superiority, by having McCabe believe in it, by having Mrs. Miller dismiss it, by having McCabe act against it, and by having so many McCabe images (riding into town alone on horseback, winning the gunfight, his success in town) reinforce it. In *The Long Goodbye* nothing suggests Marlowe's equality, let alone his superiority. One can not satirize or destroy a hero image until one defines it and shows it functioning.

Altman's Marlowe film begins deliberately in the opposite vein. While earlier Marlowe films like *Murder, My Sweet, Lady in the Lake,* and *The Brasher Doubloon* open with deliberate repetitions of Chandler monologue to establish the hero's alienation, loneliness, toughness and cynicism, Altman's film opens by undercutting Marlowe by showing him in an unequal battle with his cat. Nothing contradicts that opening until the very end of the film.

Robert Altman has established himself as an important American auteur, and even a failure as obvious as *The Long Goodbye* reflects a large and ambitious talent. Here, however, in his anxiety to express his own disillusionment with a mistrustful decade lacking in ideals and heroes, he relentlessly attacks before he has shown what he wants to attack. Thus Philip Marlowe is not only a nebbish, but a victim in the hands of Robert Altman.

Respect Grows in the 1970s

Chandler's academic reputation flowered in the 1970s. Volumes published during this decade included Chandler Before Marlowe: Raymond Chandler's Early Prose and Poetry, 1908–1912, *edited by Matthew J. Bruccoli (1973);* Frank MacShane's The Life of Raymond Chandler *(1976);* The Notebooks of Raymond Chandler and English Summer, *edited by MacShane (1976); and Bruccoli's* Raymond Chandler: A Descriptive Bibliography *(1979). These books were reviewed widely in the American press and influenced popular interest in Chandler's works. The ending of the following favorable review of MacShane's critical biography suggests the role of such scholarly works in drawing new attention to Chandler.*

Tender is the Tough Guy
Priscilla L. Buckley
National Review (12 November 1976): 1246–1247

There is little in Raymond Chandler's background, upbringing, or training that would account for his extraor-dinary success as a writer of well-crafted, hard-boiled American detective novels. Although born in America, he was raised and educated in England by a Victorian uncle who did his Victorian least by his penniless sister and her son. He never saw California, about whose seedy undersides he wrote so graphically, until a grown man. It wasn't until after he had been fired from a good job for prolonged and very public drunkenness that he turned to writing as one way to make some money. ("The best way to find out if you have friends," he was later to write, "is to go broke. The ones that hang on the longest are your friends.") He was then forty-five.

The creator of Philip Marlowe, private eye and tough guy, was an incurable romantic. He married a woman nearly twenty years older than himself—the wife of a good friend—and, while not above an occasional infidel-ity, remained true to her, was her constant companion, friend and nurse, until her death. He was pathologically shy, could be inordinately rude, was off and on, mostly on as he grew older, a drunkard. He was a difficult friend, a spiny business associate, suspicious, arrogant, and subject to deep suicidal depressions. But to the weak and the help-

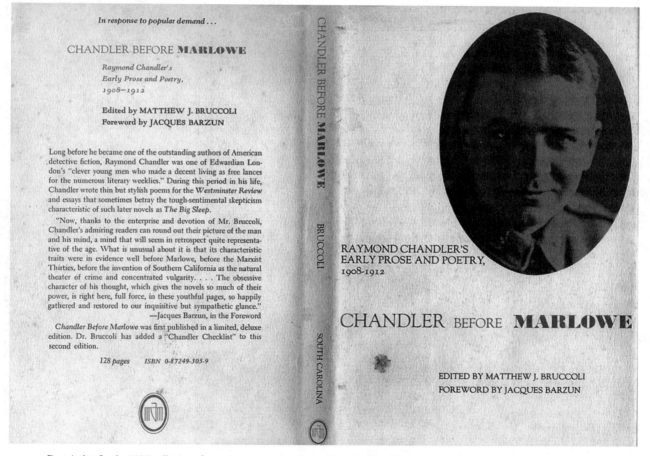

Dust jacket for the 1973 collection of poems, essays, and reviews written by Chandler as a young man in London. It was the first of several scholarly volumes on the author and his work that were published in the 1970s.

less—his mother, his wife, a hopeless secretary-housekeeper who attached herself to him after his wife's death—he was a thoughtful and a tender man.

Frank MacShane has managed the impossible. Any one with reasonable skills could have made a life of Raymond Chandler interesting simply by unrolling the facts. Mr. MacShane has done more; he shows us every wart there is, yet Chandler comes across as an attractive and sympathetic character largely because of the seriousness with which he pursued his craft as a writer and because of an irrepressible humor from which no one, most particularly himself, was ever safe. It was this seriousness of purpose and his habit of self-deprecation that saved Chandler from being the self-indulgent monster his closest friends must at times have thought him.

Frank MacShane was given access to Raymond Chandler's papers and letters and has put them to skillful use. He quotes just enough from Chandler's early writing to show what it was that would eventually distinguish his work (and that of Dashiell Hammett) from other graduates of *Black Mask* and *Dime Detective*. Hammett had, as Chandler once said, taken "murder out of the Venetian vase and dropped it in the alley." To Chandler it was important to do more, to have those alley characters taken seriously, to write serious fiction, not detective stories. He returns to that theme time and again.

> I am not satisfied that the thing can't be done [he wrote shortly after the publication of *Little Sister*], nor that sometime, somewhere, perhaps not now nor by me, a novel cannot be written which, ostensibly a mystery and keeping the spice of mystery, will actually be a novel of character and atmosphere with an overtone of violence or fear.

His frustration in trying to transcend the genre is amusingly demonstrated in a letter to Blanche Knopf:

> . . . the thing that rather gets me down is that when I write something that is tough and fast and full of mayhem and murder, I get panned for being tough and fast and full of mayhem and murder, and then when I try to tone down a bit and develop the mental and emotional side of a situation, I get panned for leaving out what I was panned for putting in the first time.

He was a stickler about his writing.

> . . . Convey my compliments [he wrote Edward Weeks of the *Atlantic*] to the purist who reads your proofs and tell him or her that I write in a sort of broken-down patois which is something like the way a Swiss waiter talks, and that when I split an infinitive, God damn it, I split it so it will stay split, and when I interrupt the velvety smoothness of my more or less literate syntax with a few words of barroom vernacular, this is done with the eyes open and the mind relaxed but attentive.

He tosses out one book on which he had spent six months because it was not good enough, which will leave him "with possibly nothing to eat for the next six. But it also leaves the world a far, far better place to live in than if I had not thrown it away." Literature he once described as "any sort of writing at all that reaches sufficient intensity of performance to glow with its own heat." He could not agree with the popular dictum that has it that writers hate to write. "How can you hate the magic which makes a paragraph or a sentence or a line of dialogue or a description something in the nature of a new creation?" he asked.

To his craft, as to his wife, Raymond Chandler remained true to the end. But did he succeed in his only real ambition? Will he be remembered as a novelist rather than as a writer of detective potboilers? Frank MacShane gives us the facts. He quotes from what others had to say about Chandler's work, but he makes no final judgment himself. What his book will do is to send other readers, as it will send me, back to *The Big Sleep*, *Farewell, My Lovely*, and the others, to decide for themselves.

Dust jacket for the first full-length biography of Chandler, published in 1976

During the 1970s and 1980s, dozens of articles on the works of Raymond Chandler were published in scholarly journals. The following essay by Peter J. Rabinowitz is an important response to the main critical line laid down by Philip Durham in the 1960s. Rabinowitz argues that Chandler was a writer who challenged the conventions of the traditional detective novel and, in doing so, made a political statement about the nature of evil in society.

Rats Behind the Wainscoting:
Politics, Convention, and Chandler's *The Big Sleep*
Peter J. Rabinowitz
Texas Studies in Language and Literature, 22 (1980): 224–245

Despite New Critical claims that works of art are "autonomous," most critics today would probably agree that it is impossible to make adequate sense of a literary text without knowing the assumptions and beliefs controlling it. As the structuralists have demonstrated, literature–like language–operates through signs with no inherent meaning; we can "recover the meaning" of a text only when we have grasped the system of norms behind the signs, a system of norms which comes in part not only from outside the work in question, but even from outside the sphere of art as a whole.

That system, to be sure, is vast; Jonathan Culler, for instance, delineates five separate levels on which such norms operate to allow literature to become "intelligible" to us.[1] But even Culler's elaborate analysis seems to accept implicitly the assumption that there is a clear-cut distinction between those levels which are intrinsic to art and those which are extrinsic. At first glance, that assumption–surely a familiar one[2]–may appear unquestionable. We all recognize that *some* of the norms which allow us to decipher a text come from prior experiences with the world and society, rather than with literature per se; intelligent reading of Tolstoy's *War and Peace* depends in part on knowledge of nineteenth-century history, without which we would miss, for instance, the inevitability of Napoleon's defeat and hence much of the novel's irony. And just as certainly, *some* norms appear purely literary; the pleasure we get when a poem fulfills certain expectations of meter and rhyme requires prior experience with conventions of poetry, conventions which have little to do with the world outside the poem.

But is this distinction really that sharp? To be sure, Culler recognizes that there might be some overlap, that there might be a relationship between some literary conventions and some social attitudes, but he continually backs off from discussing it: "We could, of course, speak of such conventions as theories or views

of the world, as if it were the task of novels to express them, but such an approach would do scant justice to the novels themselves."[3] And given Culler's critical goal ("to specify how we go about making sense of texts, what are the interpretive operations on which literature itself, as an institution, is based"[4]), the New Critical bias of the extrinsic/intrinsic distinction and of the phrase "the novels themselves" is probably appropriate, perhaps even necessary. But such an approach oversimplifies the interrelation between literary and extraliterary norms. While it is a useful postulate for certain kinds of inquiry, the assumption that artistic conventions can be treated in purely formal terms obscures the social dynamics at work when real audiences confront art. A formal study of the techniques of the minstrel show might have some explanatory power; but unless you look at the social implications of the genre's conventions, you will never understand why minstrel shows have all but disappeared. The "rules" for reading literature may be similar to the "rules" for playing chess; but they are not entirely analogous because of the very close relationship between the literary conventions of texts and the social and cultural attitudes of readers.

The relationship, needless to say, is complex. To a certain extent, social attitudes create literary conventions. The novel, at any rate, is a largely mimetic form, and not only its content, but even its formal characteristics, originate partly in social conditions.[5] But the influence runs simultaneously the other way. Literature, like language, provides one frame through which we come to understand the world, and, as John Cawelti has put it, "Our artistic experiences over a period of time work on the structure of our imaginations and feelings and thereby have long-term effects on the way in which we understand and respond to reality."[6] Indeed, the corruption of the "innocent" reader by literary conventions has been a major theme of literature itself: *Eugene Onegin, Madame Bovary,* Lisa Alther's *Kinflicks.* In sum, art and life imitate each other; conventions appear both to reflect (sometimes obscurely) and to affect (sometimes indirectly) the ways we interact with the world.

This essay is an exploration of the relationship between literary conventions and social attitudes. Specifically, I shall show that some conventions that appear to be purely literary have, in fact, deep social roots and that authors who want to challenge popular political assumptions may find a suitable battleground on the field of literary conventions. My case in point is Raymond Chandler's first novel, *The Big Sleep* (1939), a work which makes a serious political argument by vigorously overturning what are generally considered purely aesthetic conventions. I have chosen this book

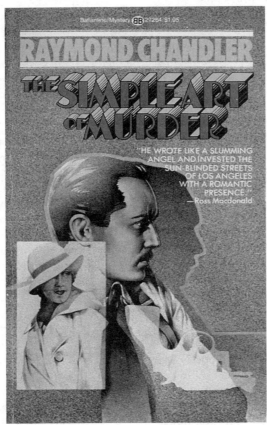

Covers for Chandler books published by Ballantine in the mid 1970s. Ross Macdonald is considered by many to be the third major writer of the hard-boiled detective novel tradition following Hammett and Chandler.

for a variety of reasons: first, because the detective story is a highly conventionalized genre, with specific rules which have been accepted by readers, critics, and writers alike; second, because in the Howard Hawks film based on it, we have what amounts to a re-conventionalized version of the novel, a version which underscores the social and political implications of Chandler's original attack on the tradition; and third, because the novel itself is far better than its academic reputation suggests and is worthy of more critical scrutiny than it has received.

II

Critics from W. H. Auden to S. S. Van Dine have long delighted in tabulating the laws which govern the classic detective story. But most of them view the genre—and criticism of it—as a diversion, and consequently treat the rules like those for any other game. There have been so many of these rules—many of them extremely silly (such as Knox's dictum that "Not more than one secret room or passage is allowable")[7]—that one is apt to agree that they are arbitrary. But if we do a little pruning, if we take off some excess foliage to look for the essential rules which show up explicitly or implicitly on every list, then we begin to see that their ramifications extend beyond game playing.

The genre, in fact, hinges on three primary conventions; most of the other rules that critics and authors have enunciated are trivial or else are elaborations or consequences of these three. First of all, as S. S. Van Dine puts it, "There must be but one culprit." Second, the detective must always triumph by restoring order in the end; as Van Dine archly notes, "The detective novel must have a detective in it; and a detective is not a detective unless he detects." Finally, the crime must turn out to be the result of some idiosyncratic aberration, succeeding temporarily only because it operates under a veil of falsehood; the criminal, therefore, can always be uncovered through simple rational procedures—what Van Dine calls "logical deductions."[8] Although there are violations of these rules, they are rather rare, for many apparent exceptions turn out to be mere variations. For instance, Christie's *Murder in the Calais Coach* (*Murder on the Orient Express*) appears to have twelve criminals, not one, and they remain unpunished. Actually, though, those twelve are justly avenging a previous crime; it is the victim himself who is the "real criminal," and Poirot's final explanation demonstrates that justice has indeed been served and order restored.

Now these three rules are *not* "purely literary." As soon as we examine the kind of imaginative uni-

verse which such rules generate, we can begin to see social underpinnings. For convenience, I will limit myself primarily to the works of Agatha Christie. Of course, there are other practitioners who might serve to represent the genre; but Christie, if not the most accomplished of them, is surely the most widely read, and it seems appropriate to assume that her works have been particularly effective in catching readers. Most of the remarks which follow, however, would apply with only slight modification to Ellery Queen, John Dickson Carr, Ngaio Marsh, and others.

What sort of world *do* the conventions lead to in the novels of Agatha Christie? What are the beliefs at the root of her imaginative landscape? What views of society, politics, and humanity might lead her to construct it, and what social attitudes would such a world foster and encourage? John Cawelti, one of the few critics to have seriously posed such questions, gives us an extremely valuable point of departure. Christie, he claims, develops "the moral fantasy that human actions have a simple and rational explanation and that guilt is specific and not ambiguous."[9] If we push this insight further, we can see that Christie's world entails a definite political vision; it reflects particular political biases and encourages readers to take certain political stances. And to those she convinces, her invented world offers a special form of political comfort.

Christie's novels always open with the same conflict: the peaceful, natural social order (often a small country village) is threatened by disruption through a murder or series of murders that seems bizarre and inexplicable. But this specter of social disruption is always laid to rest in the same way. According to the first rule of the genre, the threat always turns out to come from an individual rather than from a social failing; the restoration of order guaranteed by the second rule thus never requires a serious alteration—or even examination—of society. Furthermore, according to the third rule, evil can operate only as long as "the truth" remains concealed. This, of course, simplifies the detective's task of restoration, for once the deviant individual is unmasked, he or she is powerless to operate further. No wonder Poirot can claim, "I have only one duty—to discover the truth."[10] Rarely is physical force required in Christie's world; once the truth is revealed through reason, justice follows as a matter of course. As Harrison R. Steeves puts it, "There is nothing in art . . . more unswervingly optimistic" than a detective story.[11]

Viewing the conventions of the genre in this light helps explain why the detective story has been so popular: whatever their other virtues, Christie's novels also have a cathartic effect. Indeed, her work can be seen as a trivialization of Aristotelian tragedy. Writing for a bourgeois audience tormented by the possibility of social upheaval, she arouses its worst fears and then purges this emotion with the affirmation of both the justice and the strength of the status quo. Since evil springs not from social inadequacies but from antisocial individuals with "a little kink in the brain somewhere,"[12] the existence of evil does not necessitate a change in the social order. The sympathetic reader closes Christie's novels with a sense of profound peace; if anything goes wrong there is no reason to vote the government out of power—just call in Poirot. It is appropriate that so many of her novels take place on country estates, an excellent symbol of the society she wishes to convince us is both desirable and eternal.

Christie's political vision emerges most clearly in her overtly political novels, especially such early potboilers as *The Secret Adversary* (1922). This implausible tale concerns a Labour Party attempt to oust the Conservatives. Catastrophic as this would be, it is but the tip of the iceberg. As her spokesman soberly informs us, "A Labour Government at this juncture would . . . be a grave disability for British trade, but that is a mere nothing to the real danger. . . . Bolshevist gold is pouring into this country for the specific purpose of procuring a Revolution."[13]

Absurd as this sounds today, it probably struck a sympathetic chord in the conservative middle class of 1922. That such a claim was believable is demonstrated by an incident which occurred only two years later. *The Daily Mail* published a letter—supposedly from Zinoviev, but probably a fake—in which the British Communist Party was ordered to start preparations for a military insurrection;[14] and the public's consequent outrage contributed to the conservative backlash of the October 1924 elections. Given the political atmosphere in 1922, such gullibility is not really surprising. The collapse of the British economy following the war had resulted in a virtual depression by 1921; the Empire was threatened by radical agitation in Ireland, and by Gandhi's civil disobedience in India, leading to his arrest in 1922; the labor union movement, moderately sympathetic to the Soviet cause, had grown so substantially that the Labour Party was able, in the 1922 elections, replace the Liberals as the official opposition. No wonder there was "widespread mistrust and . . . fear" of the Labour Party in the early twenties.[15]

Christie's novel capitalizes on this mistrust and fear; but once she unleashes the threatening prospect of imminent revolution, she reassures us that we really have nothing to fear. She does this with a masterstroke as ingenious as it is naive—she reveals that there is a *single man* behind the "Bolshies." The Revolution can thus be forestalled without recourse either to social reorganization or to political repression. Once this individual is found out—unmasked by a bunch of amateurs at that—the power of the truth is so great that even the abashed Labour Party falls into line to support the status quo.[16]

Needless to say, in her better novels Christie complicates and refines this basic scheme. Her criminals occasionally have accomplices; noncriminals often tell lies in order to protect their loved ones or to cover minor inadequacies which are not quite "crimes"; occasionally, some genteel violence is called for. But her outlook remains generally as I have described it: confident that logic and justice will prevail.

The detective story is simultaneously a reflection of such attitudes and a cause of them, although not in any simpleminded way. Thus, the conventions of the classical English detective story cannot be considered simply a direct reflection of the attitudes of its actual readers. Detective stories are enthusiastically read by readers who are equally at home with genres built on substantially different conventions; there is nothing unusual about a person who enjoys both Christie and writers whose sociopolitical ideas are thoroughly subversive. Our attitudes are complex, ambiguous, even internally inconsistent enough for us to respond to a variety of works mirroring different strands of our personalities. On the other hand, certain sociopolitical currents—and consequently, certain widespread beliefs—probably made especially fertile ground for the detective story to flourish. The genre, in fact, first took form in the 1840s, at a time when many people felt threatened by the social unrest that produced the *Communist Manifesto,* and it reached its golden age between the two world wars, when fear of the Bolshevik threat was at one of its crests.

Nor could one realistically argue that traditional detective novels "created" the attitudes that led to such events as the execution of Sacco and Vanzetti. And yet, readers who worried about social disruption did find an echo of their fears in these novels; and these novels probably helped reinforce the conservative tendencies in their thoughts, since everything in the novels' imaginative world would nourish the belief that killing the archvillains disguised as simple, innocent men would push back the encroaching chaos.

III

Chandler himself criticized the genteel English school for its lack of mimetic realism,[17] but as sympathetic as we might find that argument, it is really a

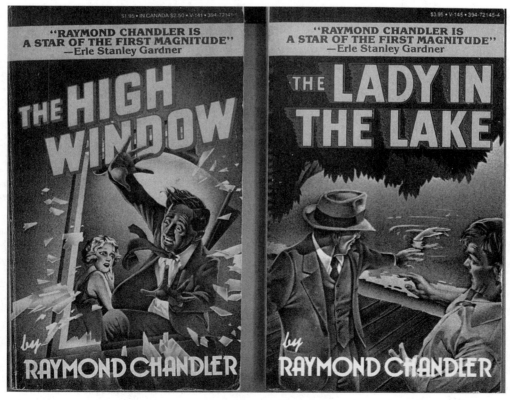

Covers for Chandler novels that Random House began republishing in 1976 in its Vintage paperback line. Erle Stanley Gardner was the creator of the Perry Mason character.

false issue. After all, Christie's novels are as true to her view of reality as Chandler's are to his; and neither of them portrays a world particularly close to the day-to-day one in which most of us live. What is more interesting than the question of photographic accuracy is the way that Chandler's angle of vision influences his art. He sees the world not from a country estate, but rather from the Los Angeles of the union-busting Merchants and Manufacturers Association, a city ruled by what Frank MacShane, in his excellent biography of Chandler, calls a "right wing coalition so repressive that it had no equal elsewhere in the country."[18] This background, and the typically thirties cynicism that went with it, clashed violently with the conventions of the genre and helped make *The Big Sleep* the extraordinary novel that it is. At first, the critics were so impressed with the brutality and degeneracy of the novel's subject matter (it made Hammett "seem as innocuous as Winnie-the-Pooh," quipped the New Yorker),[19] that they overlooked just how far *The Big Sleep* subverted the conventions of the classics. Yet the subversion was serious indeed, for the novel breaks all three of the cardinal rules of the genre. There are many criminals, some of them introduced as such from the beginning; despite both logical explanation and physical carnage, the detective cannot eliminate them; and most important, their crimes cannot be explained away as individual, nonsocial quirks or abnormalities. Thus, the novel ends not with the soothing conservative affirmation of order, but with something more politically unsettling: loose ends, a detective who fails, and a pervasive sense of individual despair, social chaos, and the triumph of evil. While MacShane is correct when he says that Chandler uses "the formulas of detective fiction,"[20] there is a twist to his use of them that MacShane misses.

The events in *The Big Sleep* are so intricate that even Chandler later had difficulty recalling all the details. "I remember," he wrote to Hamish Hamilton, "several years ago when Howard Hawks was making *The Big Sleep,* the movie, he and Bogart got into an argument as to whether one of the characters was murdered or committed suicide. They sent me a wire asking me, and dammit I didn't know either."[21]

The rough outline of the story is as follows. Detective Philip Marlowe is hired by the wealthy, aging General Sternwood to "take care of" Arthur Gwynn Geiger, a pornography dealer, blackmailer, and bisexual who is putting the screws on the General's younger daughter, Carmen. Marlowe eventually learns, however, that the General really wants to track down the husband of his older daughter, Vivian, a former bootlegger named Rusty Regan. Regan has mysteriously disappeared, apparently in the company

of Mona Grant, the wife of gambler and local racketeer Eddie Mars. Several seduction attempts by the Sternwood sisters, three or four murders (depending on how you count that ambiguous death), and countless other sensational events take place before Marlowe can discover Mona; in the process, he is himself captured by Lash Canino, Mars gunman. With the help of Mona—to whom he has given the pet name "Silver-Wig"—he escapes and kills Canino; and he returns to the Sternwood mansion where the denouement takes place. Carmen, furious that Marlowe has resisted her advances, tries to kill him; we learn that she had shot Regan for similar reasons some time ago. Mars and Canino, who had helped dispose of the body in a sump, had been using their knowledge to blackmail Vivian. At Marlowe's insistence, Vivian agrees to put her sister in an institution.

If Christie's country mansions symbolize the essential innocence of her world, and the glass key symbolizes for Hammett the impossibility of returning to that innocence once you have been corrupted, then Raymond Chandler's vision can be crystallized in a phrase Marlowe twice uses to describe Carmen's sinister, moronic giggles: "rats behind the wainscoting."[22] The apparent respectability of the world masks a fundamental core of horror: corruption, perversity, death. Marlowe's world is not one where it is lost, as in Hammett's. In Chandler's world, innocence simply does not exist.

Given that Chandler did not share the political vision implied in the classical detective story, one might well ask why he chose to revamp the genre rather than to write in another genre, such as that of *The Day of the Locust, To Have and Have Not, U.S.A.* One reason may have been the reciprocal relationship between convention and attitude. That the conventions of a genre are morally or politically unsound is reason enough to challenge them on their home ground. Jane Austen began her string of realistic novels with the upside-down gothic of *Northanger Abbey*. And surely similar considerations influenced Pushkin's decision to challenge the moral assumptions of the sentimental novels of his day by his parody of them in *The Belkin Tales* (especially "The Station Master").

Although *The Big Sleep* is not a traditional parody, it does, as I have said, topple all the fundamental conventions of the genre. Most obvious is Chandler's violation of our first rule. In a Christie novel, a string of crimes always has a single source. But here, the number of criminals seems endless; as Harry Jones remarks, "We're all grifters. So we sell each other out for a nickel" (p. 156). Geiger, Brody, Taylor, Lundgren, Canino, Carmen, and Mars: that's enough to populate an entire decade of Christie productions. Guilt is thus impossible to localize in Chandler's urban jungle—and we shall see later on why this is so important.

More startling still is Chandler's violation of the second rule: the detective fails to bring the most vicious of these criminals to justice. To be sure, the novel opens with the promise of his success, for against the grim background of California degeneracy, the virtues of Philip Marlowe stand out in bold relief. With his vigorous intelligence and unusual (although not superhuman) physical stamina, with his honesty, integrity, justice, and even chastity, he is—as Chandler himself often stressed—a modern knight. Marlowe first appears in *The Big Sleep*[23] and the knighthood theme is announced in the second paragraph, which foreshadows Marlowe's later "rescue" of the nude Carmen: "There was a broad stained-glass panel showing a knight in dark armor rescuing a lady who was tied to a tree and didn't have any clothes on but some very long and convenient hair. The knight had pushed the vizor of his helmet back to be sociable, and he was fiddling with the knots on the ropes that tied the lady to the tree and not getting anywhere. I stood there and thought that if I lived in the house, I would sooner or later have to climb up there and help him. He didn't seem to be really trying" (p. 1).

But while few readers miss the promises held out by the imagery of Marlowe's knighthood, a curious number have failed to realize that they are never fulfilled. Thus, for instance, Philip Durham argues that Marlowe is the traditional American man of action who brings "fair play and justice where it could not be or had not been administered,"[24] and R. W. Lid claims that he is "Chandler's knight, righting the balance in a wronged and fallen universe. He corrects injustices, stands up for the underdog, speaks out for the little guy."[25] But *The Big Sleep* does not depict the triumph of justice and fair play; to the contrary, it traces Marlowe's descent from moderately optimistic knighthood to a despairing recognition of his own impotence. For in contrast to the similar virtues of Poirot, Marlowe's virtues are powerless against the vastly superior forces of evil. He may be able to perform a few good acts, such as protecting General Sternwood from heartbreak and avenging Harry Jones's death. But this is a far cry from the administration of justice, which Marlowe comes to realize is no longer possible for an individual in our urban society.

In order to understand how Marlowe fails, we must first understand the plot—no mean feat. Specifically, we must recognize the central villain. Actually, this is more of a problem than might appear. As we have noted, Chandler's world is infected with far more widespread guilt than Christie's; and certainly, many of the evildoers are punished, even overpunished. Geiger, Brody, and Owen Taylor are just as dead for their crimes as the far more vicious Canino is for his; Carol Lundgren is in jail; and Carmen, the kind of traditional "aberrant individual" that Christie would have made the villain (which may explain why so many readers falsely see her as such)[26] is about to be institutionalized. Don't we have enough retribution for a dozen novels?

Chandler's world is more vicious than Christie's, and it is not surprising that his novels end in more bloodshed. But this should not fool us. Chandler, in order to stress the theme of widespread evil, may have given us a large number of criminals; but in order to stress the note of despair, he has made one of them stand out above the rest and has left him quite untouched at the end. This is not a trivial point; it is this structural twist which keeps the plot from resolution and which consequently provides much of its political force. Since so many readers and critics, however, have misread the novel's denouement, it may be necessary to demonstrate that Eddie Mars and not Carmen is, in fact, the closest thing to a central villain in the novel; that Chandler has purposefully structured his novel to make him the evil counterpart to Marlowe's virtue (in effect, he plays the dragon to Marlowe's knight); and that by leaving him unpunished, Chandler puts the capstone on the theme of failure he builds throughout the entire novel.

IV

Besides the novel itself, there are three sources which cast light on the role of Eddie Mars and the significance of his continued power at the end of *The Big Sleep*: "Killer in the Rain" and "The Curtain," two short stories which Chandler "cannibalized" (to use his word) when he wrote the novel; and the film that Howard Hawks made of *The Big Sleep* in the 1940s.

The two stories can be considered as a draft of the novel. As such, they provide the kind of evidence which any draft provides when compared to a polished artistic whole. They are especially revealing with regard to two aspects of the novel: the prose style (which sharpened considerably between 1934, when "Killer" was written, and 1939) and, more relevant to our concerns, the plot structure. Specifically, aside from Marlowe (unnamed in "Killer," Carmady in "The Curtain"), the only character in the novel with an equivalent in both stories is Eddie Mars, who replaced the one-armed Guy Slade from "Killer" and Joe Messarvey from "The Curtain."[27] Mars, then, like Marlowe, is a common denominator of the two old

Dust jacket for the first English edition, published 24 October 1977, of the volume that includes previously unpublished selections from Chandler's writing

plots—one of the two screws holding the pieces of the new construction together.

But Chandler did more than use Mars' character as a unifying thread; he also increased his importance by shifting the moral responsibility. In the stories, Slade and Messarvey are vicious and disreputable, but they are largely innocent of the actual crimes committed. In *The Big Sleep* Mars, while not a literal killer, is behind most of the violence that takes place. It is Mars' stranglehold on Vivian which makes the blackmail and its consequences possible; it is the need to protect Mars' position that results in Canino's murder of Jones (the second most honorable character in the novel) and his attempted murder of Marlowe.

Marlowe himself is quite aware of the special position of Mars. In the course of the novel, he criticizes the police, the rich, and the racketeers. But of his moral outbursts, the most bitter is the one against Eddie Mars:

> "You think he's just a gambler. I think he is a pornographer, a blackmailer, a hot car broker, a killer by remote control, and a suborner of crooked cops. He's whatever looks good to him, whatever has the cabbage pinned to it. . . . [Jones is] a dead little bird now, with his feathers ruffled and his neck limp and a pearl of blood on his beak. Canino killed him. But Eddie Mars wouldn't do that, would he, Silver-Wig? He never killed anybody. He just hires it done." (pp. 179–80, 182)

Marlowe delivers this speech to Silver-Wig, and its vehemence—which Chandler made far stronger than in the parallel scene from "The Curtain"—is partly due to his growing involvement with her. This is no reason, however, to dismiss his words as anything less than sincere. Indeed, the competition for Silver-Wig's affections, which the novel also develops more fully than does "The Curtain," serves to underscore the adversary relationship between the two men. It is not uncommon in mythology for hero and dragon to compete for the same woman, nor is it uncommon for the wife or daughter of the ogre to become the ally of the hero (e.g., Ariadne and Theseus).[28] Significantly, Chandler emphasizes Marlowe's failure by inverting the traditional heroic pattern. Although Silver-Wig helps Marlowe escape, he is unable to win her away from her husband. Thus, in the last sentences of both *The Big Sleep* and "The Curtain" we are presented with a Theseus abandoned by his Ariadne: "On the way downtown I stopped at a bar and had a couple of double scotches.[29] They didn't do me any good. All they did was make me think of Silver-Wig, and I never saw her again" (p. 214).

Comparison of the source stories and the final text, then, confirms that Chandler saw Mars as a primary thread linking the disparate plots, and made whatever alterations were necessary to point up his function as Marlowe's antagonist. As a final touch, he gave hero and villain new names to emphasize their respective roles—another sign of his extreme care in writing. The theme of the individual's weakness in the face of evil is doubly reinforced by Marlowe's name, which is surely *not* the "coincidence" MacShane claims it is.[30] First, while *The Big Sleep* is not modeled on *Heart of Darkness* in the same way that Robbe-Grillet's *Les Gommes* is modeled on *Oedipus,* British-educated Chandler must have had Conrad in mind when he finally chose the name of his detective, for the general drift of the two novels is strikingly parallel. Both tell of idealists whose adventures seem destined to bring them in contact with some kind of truth, but who in fact find only a hollowness and a horror. Significantly, both these lovers of truth learn that the only way to deal with the horror they have exposed is to bury it once again with a lie, a lie that leaves the hero perhaps wiser, but also more bitter; and a lie that leaves the evil fundamentally untouched.

In addition, the name harks back to E. C. Bentley's famous detective novel, *Trent's Last Case*. This is a classic, but one that breaks several traditions of the genre: most important, there are two people who act as "detectives," both of whom come up with "solutions," neither of which is correct, as we learn only when the real killer confesses. The names of these two flawed detectives? Philip Trent and Marlowe!

Similarly, as the central force behind the novel's violence, Mars is of course well-named after the god of war; likewise, his position as Marlowe's antagonist is emphasized by having their names begin in the same way. He "mars" everything decent around him. Given all this, it is a delightful coincidence—if coincidence it be—that Kurtz, Marlow's antagonist in *Heart of Darkness,* is associated too with the planet Mars.[31]

V

While many readers have failed to appreciate Eddie Mars' function in the novel, there is evidence—indirect but compelling—that Hollywood was not so deceived. Indeed, by comparing the novel with Hawks' film version, we can learn something about both politics and the aesthetics of the novel's ending.

Hawks's film, despite its romantic elaboration of Marlowe's relationship with Vivian, is largely faithful to the plot of the novel; yet the ending is altered significantly. Why? A general familiarity with popular films of the period suggests an answer. As Chandler—briefly a film writer himself—has remarked, cinematic decisions often result from the need to submit to conservative ethical norms: "Of course most motion pictures are bad. Why shouldn't they be? Apart from its own intrinsic handicaps of excessive cost, hypercritical blue-nosed censorship, and the lack of any single-minded controlling force in the making, the motion picture is bad because 90 percent of its source material is tripe, and the other 10 percent is a little too virile and plain-spoken for the putty-minded clerics, the elderly ingénues of the women's clubs, and the tender guardians of that godawful mixture of boredom and bad manners known more eloquently as the Impressionable Age."[32] Thus, even the best popular films, at least before the 1960s, were hampered by studio pressure to conform to simplistic ethical patterns to which few sophisticated novels subscribe. Hollywood, for instance, found it difficult to express the notion that crime *should* be punished without failing into the notion that crime always *is* punished. Consequently, when a novel ended with an unpunished criminal, the film version tended to correct the "error," even if it made total hash of the original conception. The film version of Daphne du Maurier's *Rebecca* could not portray a murderer who goes free,[33] yet the alternative solution of killing Maxim was equally unthinkable, for it would require the execution of Laurence Olivier and would bring undeserved suffering upon a stranded Joan Fontaine. Since punishment could not be added to the plot, the only alternative was to remove the crime. Thus the film blithely transformed Rebecca's murder into an unfortunate accident, trivializing the story but preserving the viewers' purity. A similar outrage was perpetrated on the ending of Frances Iles's *Before the Fact* when it was turned into the film *Suspicion*.

The ending of the film of *The Big Sleep* is not so jarring aesthetically; in fact, it is quite effective. But it exemplifies the same mental set. To avoid any hint of immorality, the death of Mars was inserted into the story and made to serve as the movie's climax.[34] Simultaneously, Hawks absolved Carmen, and—more important—expunged the novel's bitterness toward the police, going so far as to use the sound of sirens as a symbol of a return to order at the film's conclusion. The moral universe of Hawks's film is consequently much more soothing than that of the novel; no wonder that Chandler preferred the first half of the film to the second.[35]

Although the film is useful as a demonstration of how Hollywood interpreted the function of Eddie Mars, it is even more valuable as a demonstration of what Chandler had to sacrifice in order to keep his unresolved ending. The killing of Mars is cathartic: Chandler was doubtlessly fully aware of this potential

and quite capable of ending his novel with the same dramatic triumph. In ending *The Big Sleep* as he did, then, he consciously sacrificed an audience reaction which would be both powerful and satisfying. Knowing well that a detective story with an unpunished criminal is "like an unresolved chord in music,"[36] he deliberately chose to conclude on a jarring note of irritation.

VI

Both the multiplicity of the evildoers and Marlowe's failure to restore order are echoed in Chandler's disruption of the third rule of the genre: for the evil in the world of the novel comes less from the quirks of deviant individuals like Carmen than from society itself. Chandler emphasizes this point by his grim portrayal of the environment of his tale: Christie's genteel countryside has been replaced by the dirty sump where the "horrible decayed" (p.

Dust jacket for a 1977 collection of essays about Chandler's life and career, which includes personal accounts by Billy Wilder, John Houseman, and Natasha Spender and critical essays by Julian Symons and Jacques Barzun

Poster and cover of the paperback tie-in for the 1975 movie starring Robert Mitchum as Philip Marlowe

212) body of Regan lies. Chandler himself would argue that his portrayal was more "realistic" than Christie's, but as I have suggested, behind that claim lies a particular view of reality: only if you start with a socially critical attitude toward crime are you likely to view Chandler as more "realistic." And it is to encourage that attitude that he draws the picture he does.

Just as Chandler's reversal of the detective-as-victor convention begins with the traditional image of the hero-as-knight, so his reversal of the convention of individual evil begins with a traditional symbol. At first glance, the Sternwood mansion is reminiscent of the sprawling estates so familiar from Christie's countryside. But from the moment that Carmen enters and throws herself at Marlowe, the image begins to distort. We soon realize that this mansion cannot represent the smooth ordering of society; there are rats behind the wainscoting, and everything is infected.

More important, Chandler's world turns out to be neither logical nor orderly; Poirot's key tool would be useless in this version of Los Angeles, where virtually *everything* is false. Many of Chandler's images for this falsity are comic; he is, despite his gloom, a witty writer. Thus, Marlowe can't be sure whether cavalry pennants are bullet-torn or simply moth-eaten (p. 2); Mexican musicians try to impress audiences with their toughness by pretending the mineral water they gulp is really tequila (p. 125); cheap gangsters studiously imitate their Hollywood counterparts (pp. 72, 172). Nothing is solid in California in 1939, as Marlowe ruefully notes while breaking into Geiger's home: "I gave the front door the heavy shoulder. This was foolish. About the only part of a California house you can't put your foot through is the front door" (p. 30).

But were it not for Chandler's stylistic maneuvers, there would be little to laugh about in this Los Angeles where wealth and success stink both liter-

Poster and cover of the paperback tie-in for the second movie in which Mitchum played Marlowe. The movie, unaccountably, was set in England, not Chandler's Los Angeles.

ally (Sternwood's foul oilwells) and figuratively (Geiger's smut bookstore). It is a society where both the legitimate rich and the gangsters have lines into police headquarters, and where the law routinely provides protection for blackmail rackets and a personal guard service for Eddie Mars when he opens his safe each morning (p. 121). And yet the same cops who so oblige the big-timers are likely to "shoot down some petty larceny crook running up an alley with a stolen spare" (p. 101). The police are not embarrassed by their corruption: they see it simply as keeping in step with the rotten times. As Captain Gregory puts it, quite sincerely, "I'm a copper . . . Just a plain ordinary copper. Reasonably honest. As honest as you could expect a man to be in a world where it's out of style" (p. 189). Finally, in contrast to Christie's close-knit and chatty environment, Chandler's California is a world of solitary, disconnected individuals; people are so alienated from their neighbors that gunshots in a building go unnoticed, and corruption spreads unimpeded.

VII

Chandler's disruption of the three basic conventions of the genre, then, correlates with a vision of the world far less comforting than Christie's. Evil cannot be uprooted by logic alone: there is simply too much of it; it is too well organized and too well protected by "legitimate" institutions. It is hard, sometimes impossible, to capture the wrongdoers—and even if you can, society is such that it will continue to spawn them.

Marlowe's journey in the course of the novel is a journey toward the recognition of these social truths. At first, like Poirot, he has confidence in right and justice, and his optimism provides an antidote to the cynicism expressed, for instance, by Vivian Regan and Bernie Ohls. When Vivian notes that Owen "didn't know the right people. That's all a police record means in this rotten crime-ridden country," Marlowe replies, "I wouldn't go that far" (p. 52). And short while later, he bluntly suggests to Ohls, "You ought to stop some of that flash gambling"—a remark that Ohls finds

Still from the 1978 movie version of The Big Sleep; *Jimmy Stewart as General Sternwood, Robert Mitchum as Philip Marlowe.*

appallingly naive. "With the syndicate we got in this country? Be your age, Marlowe" (p. 56).

But from the beginning of the novel, there is also a nagging undercurrent of despair. The weather reflects it: the novel opens "with the sun not shining and a look of hard wet rain" (p. 1); the inaction of the knight in the stained-glass window reflects it; even Marlowe's dreams reflect it: "I went to bed full of whiskey and frustration and dreamed about a man in a bloody Chinese coat who chased a naked girl with long jade earrings while I ran after them and tried to take a photograph with an empty camera" (p. 38). And as the novel progresses, Marlowe's thoughts—and in consequence, the whole tone of the narrative—grow more and more somber. Midway through the case he notes, "I was thinking about going out to lunch and that life was pretty flat and that it would probably be just as flat if I took a drink and that taking a drink all alone at this time of day wouldn't be any fun anyway" (p. 117). When Vivian wonders aloud whether there really is a "wrong side of the law" (p. 137), Marlowe is no longer impelled to contradict her. The key moment, however, comes when Marlowe returns to his room to find Carmen waiting impatiently in his bed. Ignoring her, he turns to his chess board: "There was a problem laid out on the board, a six-mover. I couldn't solve it, like a lot of my problems" (p. 143). Symbolically, he tries a knight move, but a few moments later, he recognizes his mistake—both in his game and, by extension, in his perception of the world: "Knights had no meaning in this game. It wasn't a game for knights" (p. 145). He becomes more and more repelled by the society around him: the police, who turn out to be both corrupt and powerless, make him sick; women make him sick (p. 148); the rich make him sick (p. 168). By the end of the book, he doesn't even have an answer to Gregory's cynical defense of his own corruption: "I'd like you to believe that, being a copper I like to see the law win. I'd like to see the flashy well-dressed muggs like Eddie Mars spoiling their manicures in the rock quarry at Folsom alongside of the poor little slumbered hard guys that got knocked over on their first caper and never had a break since. That's what I'd like. You and me both lived too long to think I'm likely to see it happen. Not in this town, not in any town half this size, in any part of this wide, green and beautiful U.S.A. We just don't run our country that way" (pp. 189-90).

On his final visit to the Sternwood residence, Marlowe notes that "the knight on the stained-glass window still wasn't getting anywhere untying the naked damsel from the tree" (p. 194); but this time, he doesn't offer to help. On the contrary, he refuses payment for "an unsatisfactory job" (p. 195). By pointing out that he is neither a Sherlock Holmes nor a Philo Vance (p. 197), Marlowe seems to admit that the conventional detective has no place in the real world. One might, perhaps, interpret this as the darkness before the light, for it is just before Carmen, trying to kill him, reenacts her murder of Regan. Such an interpretation, however, would distort the story. First of all, Marlowe has already "solved" the mystery and has set the stage for proving it by putting blanks in Carmen's gun. More significant, however, the discovery of the truth does no good whatever. Unlike the last-chapter fireside revelations of Hercule Poirot, this truth is insufficiently powerful to overcome the evil. Nor, for that matter, does this discovery really tell him—or us—anything he did not already know: it only confirms our belief that the rats behind Carmen's wainscoting are predatory, even rabid. Marlowe can now suggest that Carmen be institutionalized—but we have known for some time that this was necessary. What effect does this revelation have on all the questions the book has raised? Since Mars is still free to act, the plague has not been cured. Besides, for Chandler, the perpetrator of evil is not the cause of evil. Even if Marlowe could eliminate Mars, would that make Los Angeles a significantly better place to live? Would it eradicate gambling, murder, and blackmail? Would it reduce the influence that the racketeers and the rich have over the law? In Chandler's world, evil is fundamentally tied to an overwhelming sickness in the society at large; the capture and punishment of deranged individuals has only a minimal effect.

Ironically, at the end of the novel the best Marlowe can do with this truth is conceal it. Like Conrad's Marlow, he becomes a preserver of illusion—specifically, General Sternwood's illusion that "his blood is not poison, and that although these two little girls are a trifle wild, as many nice girls are these days, they are not perverts or killers" (p. 211). Far from freeing him, the truth simply helps imprison Marlowe in the nastiness of the world. Rather than bringing Mars to justice, Marlowe finds himself an accomplice—the knight defending the dragon.

The darkest pages of the novel are the last two, where Marlowe contemplates the meaning of death and decides that this world is so ugly that death can only be seen as a liberation. This thought had momentarily flickered through his mind earlier, when he looked an the dead body of Harry Jones, reeking of cyanide and "the sour smell of vomit" (p. 166). The morbidity becomes far stronger, though, when he thinks of Rusty Regan lying in the sump: "What did it matter where you lay once you were dead? In a dirty sump or in a marble tower on top of a high hill? You were dead, you were sleeping the big sleep, you were not bothered by things like that. Oil and water were the same as wind and air to you. You just slept the big sleep, not caring about the nastiness of how you died or where you fell. Me, I was part of the nastiness now. Far more a part of it than Rusty Regan was" (pp. 213-14). Once again, we hear the voice of Conrad's Marlow, this time from "Youth": "You simply can do nothing, neither great nor little—not a thing in the world. . . . Youth, strength, genius, thoughts, achievements, simple hearts—all dies. . . . No matter."[37]

VIII

The conventions of the detective novel, then—like most artistic conventions—can profitably be studied in a social and political context. They serve a formal aesthetic function, but they also serve political ends through their reciprocal relationship with social attitudes. The structure of Christie's novels reflects a passive form of conservatism and encourages us to believe that the problems of violence and social disruption can be eliminated without changing the structure of society. Hers is a soothing voice which holds out promises of harmonious resolution if only we will sit still and let the experts take charge. Chandler's reversal of those conventions reverses the effect. His emphasis on the social origins of crime, and his consequent refusal to resolve his plot in traditional fashion, challenges those conservative assumptions. Instead of calming us, Chandler purposely irritates us, disrupts our peace; at the end of *The Big Sleep* we feel dissatisfied. Chandler forces us to disapprove of the world we live in and demands that we reexamine our political outlook.

Does this make Chandler a "political" writer? Many critics have insisted that he is not, because he does not offer any solutions. As Wilson Pollock puts it, "although some of his works might seem to reveal a political consciousness, it wasn't there. . . . He merely believed that society was corrupt, that the only god was the fast and easy buck, and that that there was not very much anyone could do about it."[38] In a sense, this is true. Although Marlowe's continuing battle against corruption offers a model of behavior which is not as passive as Pollock implies, it certainly is possible to read Chandler's novels as essays in mere negativity, cynical suggestions that things are so bad that there is no point in trying to change them.

But Marlowe as a model of behavior—indeed, the whole question of "solutions"—is really beside the point. Chandler is a political writer, not because he promotes a particular political line, but because his novels challenge, in a dynamic and forceful way, the hidden political assumptions of other novels which have been widely read and extremely influential. Such an intellectual challenge may or may not be more important than a political program, but it probably has to precede one, and in many ways, it is the most valuable and important work that a writer can do.

Hamilton College
Clinton, New York

1. Jonathan Culler, *Structuralist Poetics: Structuralism, Linguistics, and the Study of Literature* (Ithaca: Cornell Univ. Press, 1975), pp. 140–60.

2. The extrinsic/intrinsic distinction is, of course, a critical commonplace; one major source of its currency is the enormously influential book by René Welek and Austin Warren, *Theory of Literature,* 3rd ed. (New York: Harcourt, 1956).

3. Culler, p. 146.

4. Ibid, p. viii.

5. See, for instance, Ian Watt, *The Rise of the Novel* (Berkeley and Los Angeles: Univ. of California Press, 1957), esp. ch. 2.

6. John G. Cawelti, *Adventure, Mystery, and Romance* (Chicago: Univ. of Chicago Press, 1976), p. 24.

7. Ronald Knox, "Detective Stories," in *Literary Distractions* (New York: Sheed and Ward, 1958), pp. 180–98. Among the countless other critics who see detective stories as a game is Fredric Jameson: "The detective story, as a form without ideological content, without any overt political or social or philosophical point, permits . . . pure stylistic experimentation." ("On Raymond Chandler," *Southern Review,* n.s. 6, no. 3 [July 1970], 625.) E. M. Beekman concurs: "The traditional detective novel is not a novel at all, but an intellectual game on the level of acrostics or checkers." ("Raymond Chandler and an American Genre," *Massachusetts Review,* 14 [1973], 149.) So does Jacques Barzun in "Detection and the Literary Art," in Barzun, ed., *The Delights of Detection* (New York: Criterion, 1961), pp. 9–23.

8. S. S. Van Dine, "Twenty Rules for Writing Detective Stories," in *The Art of the Mystery Story: A Collection of Critical Essays,* ed. Howard Haycraft (New York: Grossett and Dunlap Universal Library, 1947), pp. 190–91. My formulation is quite close to that enunciated by W. H. Auden: "The basic formula is this: a murder occurs; many are suspected; all but one suspect, who is the murderer, are eliminated; the murderer is arrested or dies," ("The Guilty Vicarage," in *The Dyer's Hand and Other Essays* [New York: Vintage, 1948], p. 147.)

9. Cawelti, p. 132. See also John M. Reilly's remark: "The 'classic' mystery conveys the notion that a developed human mind, coupled with will, can maintain order, because, it is implied, society is an aggregate of personal relationships." ("The Politics of Tough Guy Mysteries," *University of Dayton Review,* 10 [1973], 25.) There is much of interest in Reilly's discussion of the role of disillusioned populism in the tough mysteries, and especially in the genre's latent tendencies toward fascism; he does not dwell, however, on our concern here—the relation between politics and convention. See also Mark Gidley's claim that "classic detective fiction . . . usually restores the reader's faith in the ultimate efficacy of justice, in the stability of the social order." ("Elements of the Detective Story in William Faulkner's Fiction," *Journal of Popular Culture,* no. 1 [Summer 1973] 7, 106.) Finally, note Michael Holquist's study of the convention and its inverse function in contemporary literature: "Whodunit and Other Questions: Metaphysical Detective Stories in Post Modern Fiction," *New Literary History,* 3 (Autumn 1971), 135–56.

10. Agatha Christie, *The Mystery of the Blue Train* (New York: Pocket Books, 1940), p. 204. Originally published in 1928.

11. Harrison R. Steeves, "A Sober Word on the Detective Story," in *The Art of the Mystery Story,* p. 520.

12. Christie, *Mystery of the Blue Train,* p. 172. John Dickson Carr's Dr. Fell elaborates: "This is not, of course, to say that all murderers are mad. But they are in a fantastic state of mind, or they would not be murderers. And they do fantastic things." (*To Wake the Dead* [New York: Collier, 1965], pp. 201–02.

13. Agatha Christie, *The Secret Adversary* (New York: Bantam, 1967), p. 29. Originally published in 1922.

14. R. K. Webb, *Modern England from the Eighteenth Century to the Present* (New York: Dodd, Mead, 1968), p. 511. For a good summary of the immediate postwar years, see pp. 486–514.

15. Henry Pelling, *Modern Britain* (1885–1955) (New York: Norton, 1966), pp. 99–100.

16. The notion that a few masterminds control international events underlies a whole subgenre of literature. For decades, Sax Rohmer charged Dr. Fu Manchu with all the upheavals in the Mysterious East. In fact, in *President Fu Manchu* (1936), the archfiend engineers the assassination of Huey Long (called Harvey Bragg) and nearly succeeds in stealing the 1936 election. Some of Ian Fleming's novels fit this mold, as does Richard Prather's remarkable *The Trojan Hearse* (1964) which seriously argues that Hubert Humphrey (called Horatio Humble) is about to rape the nation with the help of the Communist Party, the Mafia, and an unusually venal impresario. National virtue is preserved only by the individual heroism of Shell Scott, who barrels through the wall of a secret hideout on the steel ball of a wrecking machine. Phallic bravado can go no further.

17. See, especially, Raymond Chandler, "The Simple Art of Murder," [1944] in *The Simple Art of Murder* (New York: Pocket Books, 1952), pp. 177–94.

18. Frank MacShane, *The Life of Raymond Chandler* (New York: Dutton, 1976), p. 64.

19. "Mysteries," *New Yorker,* 11 February 1939, p. 84.

20. MacShane, p. 63. Beekman recognizes that Chandler's novels "use elements of a particular fictional tradition, and in so doing either amplify or destroy established constrictions, not for malice but from superior artistic imagination" ("Chandler and an American Genre," p. 150), but neither examines these changes in detail nor investigates their political implications.

21. "Letter to Hamish Hamilton, March 21, 1949," in *Raymond Chandler Speaking,* ed. Dorothy Gardiner and Kathrine Sorley Walker (Freeport, N.Y.: Books for Libraries Press, 1971), p. 221.

22. Raymond Chandler, *The Big Sleep* (New York: Pocket Books, 1950), pp. 60, 143. All further references to this edition are made in the text.

23. Once the character caught on, Chandler renamed the hero in some of his earlier stories "Marlowe."

24. Philip Durham, *Down These Mean Streets a Man Must Go: Raymond Chandler's Knight* (Chapel Hill: Univ. of North Carolina Press, 1963), p. 32.

25. R. W. Lid, "Philip Marlowe Speaking," *Kenyon Review,* 31, no. 2, (1969), 159. Later he seems to back off slightly from this position, but he never really follows through on his retreat.

26. Even Cawelti suggests as much, implicitly (Cawelti, p. 174). Philip Durham, in listing the "villains" of the book, includes Geiger, Brody, and Canino—all of whom are dead at the end; but he neglects to mention Mars. ("The Black Mask School," in *Tough Guy Writers of the Thirties,* ed. David Madden [Carbondale: Southern Illinois Univ. Press, Crosscurrents: Modern Critiques, 1968] pp. 78–79.) Similarly, Herbert Fuhm refers to Carmen as "the villainess" ("Raymond Chandler: From Bloomsbury to the Jungle—and Beyond," in *Tough Guy Writers,* p. 181).

27. Two others—General Sternwood and Carmen—are involved in incidents from both stories; but as characters, they only have equivalents in one or the other. Thus, for example, the General takes over some of the plot function of Tony Dravec in "Killer," but in no sense is there any continuity of character between the two.

28. A detailed examination of these themes in the context of the "combat myth" can be found in Joseph Fontenrose, *Python* (Berkeley: Univ. of California Press, 1957).

29. "Double scotches" was originally simply "drinks." (Raymond Chandler, "Curtain" [1934], in *Killer in the Rain* [New York: Pocket Books, 1965], p. 127.)

30. MacShane, p. 69.

31. The names of the other characters in *The Big Sleep* have been carefully chosen as well. Almost all have been rechristened from the original stories, and almost all of the names are evocative. Carmen, a literal man-killer, is obviously named after Mérimée:

Carmen was one of Chandler's favorite stories. ("Letter to Hamish Hamilton, December 4, 1949," in *Chandler Speaking*, p. 84). Lash Canino conjures up images of whips and knives, and he is as vicious a dog as literature has produced. Mona Grant, enigmatic as the Mona Lisa, "grants" Marlowe his freedom. And the name Sternwood resounds with quality and solidity, even if we learn that the wood is rotten. Amid all these names full of character, the name of Harry Jones stands out–for he is the nonentity in this world, the little guy with nothing going for him.

32. Raymond Chandler, "Oscar Night in Hollywood," *Atlantic Monthly,* March 1948, p. 25.

33. Of course, Maxim de Winter is "punished" in the novel; but by film-world standards, the destruction of Manderley and the years of miserable wandering were too subtle a retribution for murder.

34. Hollywood's quid pro quo morality is often applied with disarming ingenuity. Marlowe has seen Canino kill Jones–it is therefore acceptable for him to kill Canino in return. But since Marlowe has not seen Mars himself kill anyone, it would not be cricket for Marlowe himself to kill him. Moral scruples are preserved when Marlowe forces Mars out a door and his own men gun him down. There is, apparently, yet a third–and perhaps a fourth–version of the scene as well; see MacShane, p. 125. MacShane's description, however, is confusing, for he seems to have forgotten how the film actually ends.

35. "Letter to Hamish Hamilton, May 30, 1946," in *Chandler Speaking*, p. 216.

36. "Casual Notes on the Mystery Novel" (1949), in *Chandler Speaking*, p. 66. Chandler insists that this is a purely formal matter, having nothing to do with morality; but his dichotomy is a false one. The punishment of the criminal is formally "satisfying" because it is morally lulling–that is, because it allows the novel to perform its social function of arousing and then purging our fears of social chaos. In any case, the unresolved conclusion of *The Big Sleep* is a conscious irritant.

37. Joseph Conrad, "Youth," in *The Norton Anthology of English Literature,* ed. M. H. Abrams et al. (New York: Norton, 1968), 2: 1502, 1504.

38. Wilson Pollock, "Man with a Toy Gun," *New Republic,* 7 May 1962, p. 21.

Marlowe's Los Angeles

At the same time that Chandler's work was gaining acceptance within college English departments, he was becoming an icon of popular culture. Many readers found in his novels nostalgic representations of life in the 1940s and took pleasure in the images of the tough-talking private detective in a trench coat. This pop-culture image of Chandler is reflected in the following article from Mystery *magazine, which describes a 1980 tour of Los Angeles locations from Chandler's novels.*

**The Longest Goodbye:
or the Search for Chandler's Los Angeles**
Paul Bishop
Mystery, 1 (March/April 1980): 33–36

It is difficult, if not impossible, to write an article concerning Raymond Chandler or his famous detective creation, Phillip Marlowe, without mentioning those well-quoted "mean streets:"

"Down these mean streets a man must go who is not himself mean, who is neither tarnished nor afraid. The detective in this kind of story must be such a man. He is the hero, he is everything. He must be a complete man and a common man and yet an unusual man."

Those 'mean streets' belong to the city of Los Angeles. A city that Chandler felt he helped to shape and yet could not control. It was at once a city of inspiration to him and a one of pain. In his later years Chandler would write a letter to his friend John Houseman that would state in part:

"But I have lost Los Angeles. It is no longer the place I knew so well and was among the first to put on paper. I have a feeling that I helped create the town and was then pushed out of it by the operators. I can hardly find my way around it any longer."

But when Chandler wrote about the Los Angeles he knew, he drew a vivid picture of the city as it moved through the decades of the 30's and 40's. His buildings were real buildings, his streets existed, his suburbs portrayed behind thinly veiled aliases.

Like everything else, L.A. has changed with the passage of time. Neighborhoods have changed from white to black to brown and back again. Progress has made the city more garish, more rushed and the air more tainted. The bums, the prostitutes, pimps and hypes that prowl its back streets and alleyways pass on leaving only a legacy of filth and despair for the new boy on the block.

The city has changed, of that there is no doubt, but its heart still remains the same. The city still retains that indefinable quality that makes it L.A. – quality that is as far removed from the quaintness of San Francisco as it is from the vacation vistas of San Diego. It is a quality that no song could ever capture, that no phrase could ever coin. A quality that makes L.A. the drawing point for all the young hopefuls looking for a starting break, the gathering spot for weirdos of every description from all over the country, and a haven or hell for executives who have broken out of the staunch regimes of New York and Chicago. It is still the land of endless sunshine and still the testing ground for every new fad trying out its first steps.

And as the city has changed, so have the people. The cops no longer use heat lamps and rubber hoses, as in Marlowe's experience. They have been replaced with college degrees, computers and a growing paranoia of 'us against them'.

The private shamus has changed too. He is no longer the loner with a bottle in his bottom desk drawer and a leggy blond secretary he can't afford to pay. In his place has appeared the full-service security agencies that have all the angles covered from private rent-a-cops, surveillance, car repo's, bodyguards and drivers to industrial espionage and all the sophisticated equipment that goes with it.

But through all its changes Los Angeles is still L.A., "City Of Angels." Its heart might be a little blacker now but that indefinable something still remains the same as when Chandler first put pen to paper.

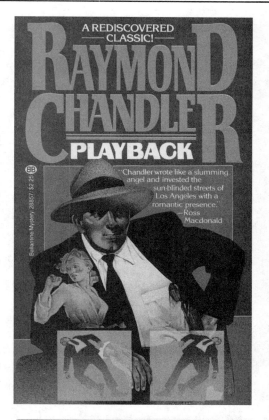
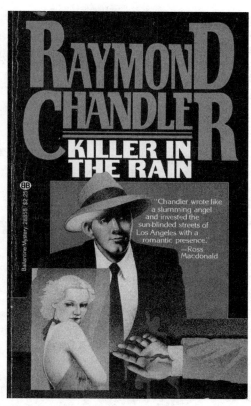
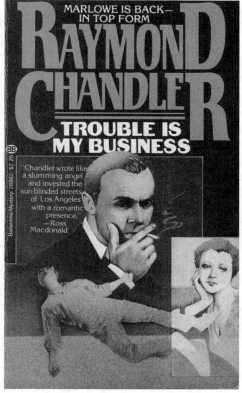

Covers for four paperbacks published by Ballantine in 1980

And yes, Chandler's "mean streets" are still there, as are many of the old haunts that Marlowe gumshoed. With the changes of time and Chandler's liberal sprinkling of poetic licenses, four-story buildings become six-story buildings, the lobby of one building is placed in that of another, the location of a building is moved up or down a street or maybe two streets over. The finished product becomes an intriguing puzzle for the true aficionado who wishes to revisit the scenes of Chandler's Los Angeles.

For a partial solution to this puzzle I gathered with fifty other assorted Chandler/Marlowe fans to search out those "mean streets" and the still existing scenes of Marlowe's cases. Scenes that are hidden behind new facades and above the street level modernization.

The morning of November 24th dawned bright and clear. The air was filled with an almost touchable stillness and a warmth that belied the coming of winter and the presence of autumn. The guides for our tour, as well as the people behind the volumes of research used to put the tour together, were none other than Phillip Marlowe himself (as portrayed by Michael Pritchard, complete with creased fedora and crumpled trench coat) and Ruth Windfeldt (owner of the Scene Of The Crime bookstore on Ventura Blvd. in Sherman Oaks where we were all gathered to start our search).

As encouraged by our hosts, many in our group had dressed for the occasion in styles from the 30's and 40's, with pearls, veiled hats, anklets and black-seamed stockings, trenchcoats and padded shoulders. To help us get in the right frame of mind to turn back the years, two musicians, Charles Orena on sax and Bill Fowler on guitar, treated us to soft standards from the past as we boarded our time machine—a large tour bus. The musicians were with us throughout the tour.

We started down Ventura Blvd. east bound from the Scene Of The Crime, in the opposite direction taken by Marlowe in *The Little Sister*:

> ". . . down on to Ventura Blvd. past Studio City, Sherman Oaks and Encino, there was nothing lonely about that trip. There never is on that road. Fast boys in stripped down Fords shot in and out of traffic streams missing fenders by a 16th of an inch . . ."

We gained entrance to the Hollywood Freeway and headed for downtown L.A., passing the Sheraton Universal Hotel where mystery fans had recently been treated to the pleasures of Bouchercon X. There had been but one

Dust jackets for two novels published in the 1980s in which the hero is named Raymond Chandler

Powers Boothe, who played Chandler's detective in one-hour HBO productions of Philip Marlowe, Private Eye *in 1983 and 1986*

group presented an odd sight as we made our way through the Saturday morning workers to the Los Angeles Athletic Club. This was where Marlowe again meets with Derace Kingsley to get more information on Kingsley's missing wife in *Lady In The Lake.*

At 315 W. 9th we find Chandler's Belfont Building from *High Window.* Today it is the Coastal Federal Building and there is still an auto park located next door on the left and just down the street. On the other side is the Eastern Columbian Building the green and chromium structure that Chandler describes as being next door. Unfortunately, Elisa Morningstar is no longer in residence.

Back on our bus we passed the Hotel Chandler, on Main St. just past 8th and stopped across the street from the Hotel Barclay at 163 4th St. The VN, for Van Nuys, can still be seen intertwined in the etched glass, left over from a time when it was known as the Van Nuys Hotel, and George Hicks was murdered by the business end of an ice pick in *The Big Sleep.* A chess set is encased in glass in the seedy lobby as a tribute to Marlowe.

At Broadway and 2nd our group moved into the overwhelming opulance of the Bradbury Building to search for the office used by James Garner as Marlowe in

freeway in Chandler's day, the Pasadena which like the streets of Beverly Hills, were closed to tour buses.

Our first stop was at the Oviate Building located at 617 Olive St. In *Lady In The Lake,* Chandler uses the Oviate as the model for the Trealor Building where Marlowe has his first encounter with Derace Kingsley. Surprisingly free from vandalism since its closing a decade ago, the Oviate stands as a monument to craftsmanship. With all materials used to build it shipped to L.A. from Paris in the largest shipment (200 tons) to ever pass through the Panama Canal at that time. The Oviate, like the pyramids, can almost overwhelm you with the vision of its architects. Marble walls from southern France, a foyer ceiling crafted from 30 tons of glass and hand carvings in the solid wood pillars gave us all a feel for a time that has been lost behind modern chrome and glass. Now being renovated, the Oviate Building is set to re-open sometime in the 1980's.

From the Oviate we walked the couple of blocks to the Bank of America Building at Olive and 7th, where Chandler worked for the Davney Oil syndicate as Chief Accountant in 1927 when it was known as the Bank of Italy. On the large sign outside proclaiming Bank of America, you can still discern the logo of the Bank of Italy in small print.

Strung with cameras, dressed for the 30's and chattering like a group of stereotype Japanese tourists, our

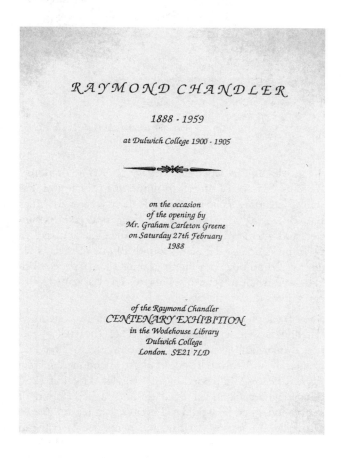

RAYMOND CHANDLER

1888 - 1959

at Dulwich College 1900 - 1905

on the occasion of the opening by Mr. Graham Carleton Greene on Saturday 27th February 1988

of the Raymond Chandler CENTENARY EXHIBITION in the Wodehouse Library Dulwich College London. SE21 7LD

Announcement for Chandler Centenary exhibition at Dulwich College

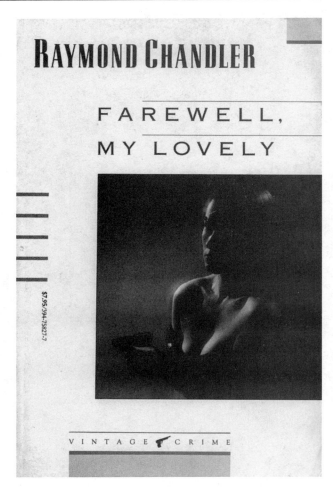

Covers for paperbacks that Random House published in 1988 in its Vintage paperback line

the movie *Marlowe* based on *The Little Sister*. The Bradbury Building has been featured in numerous private eye TV series, including *Banyon* starring Robert Forster as Miles Banyon, *City Of Angels* with Wayne Rogers as Jake Axminster, and *The Lonely Profession* with Harry Guardino as Lee Gordon. Amongst the lilting sounds of our musicians we discovered a door with the inscription 'Sam Spade – Private Investigations' lettered on its frosted glass panel. Who cares if it is the wrong city?

Back on the bus we drove past numerous sights of Chandler's writings including City Hall, the Hall of Justice, Bunker Hill (so changed by the ravages of time and progress), and through little Tokyo (mentioned in *The High Window*). We passed by the Mayfair Hotel at 1256 7th St. where Chandler lived through a bad period of depression when he would call friends with tearful threats of suicide, the Bryson Apartments, mentioned by name in *Lady In The Lake* and Bullock's Wilshire where Marlowe had a late night, rendezvous with Agnes Lozelle, at the east entrance to the parking lot, to pay for information on Derace Kingsley's missing wife (*Lady In The Lake* again):

"Give me the money."

The motor of the gray plymouth throbbed under her voice and the rain pounded above it. The light at the top of the Bullock's green-tinged tower was far above us, serene and withdrawn from the dark dripping city.

Union Station seems almost unchanged since Marlowe spent time there in *The Little Sister* and *Playback*: the trains still run late and the atmosphere brought us closer to the L.A. we were looking for.

With our wanderings for the morning complete, it was time for lunch. We made our way across Hollywood towards Musso and Frank's Grill where we had reservations. Along the way it was inevitable that we would pass more sites from the Marlowe canon–the Fulwider Building at Santa Monica and Western where in *The Big Sleep* Harry Jones died of drinking arsenic. On Hollywood Blvd. we passed another Bank of America building that in *High Window* became the Cahuenga Building and in *The*

 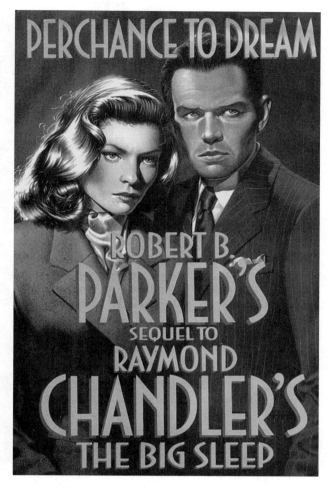

Dust jackets for two novels that Robert B. Parker based on Chandler's material. The first four chapters of Poodle Springs *(1989) were written by Chandler; Parker completed the novel, in which Marlowe has married wealthy Linda Loring, a character from* The Long Goodbye. Perchance to Dream *(1991), which was written wholly by Parker, is a sequel to* The Big Sleep *and details Marlowe's attempts to find Carmen Sternwood after she disappears from a sanatorium.*

Big Sleep was the home of Marlowe's 7th floor office. Pritchard, still staying in character as Marlowe, also pointed out the Hollywood Library at 1623 Ivar St. where, in *The Big Sleep,* "I do some research prior to my visit to Geiger's Bookstore."

Lunch at Musso and Frank's, mentioned by name in *The Long Goodbye,* was most enjoyable. Starting with gimlets, with Rose's Lime Juice of course, we drank a toast to Chandler and also, as Marlowe would have wanted, to the memory of Terry Lennox (*The Long Goodbye*). Musso and Frank's Grill has been around since 1919 and still, as in Chandler's day, is a hangout for many major writers.

After lunch we walked casually down the street from Musso and Frank's to the Book Treasury located at 6707 Hollywood Blvd. This bookstore was at one time quite possibly known as Geiger's Bookstore which Marlowe investigates in *The Big Sleep.* Due to the store's possi-bly sordid past—Geiger's was a front for pornographers—the new owners are not letting on one way or the other as to the truth of our assumptions.

Reboarding our bus we made the short trip to Camrose and Hightower Dr., where back on foot again we walked up Hightower to view the apartment complex featured in the Elliot Gould version of *The Long Goodbye* filmed in 1973. Also at the top of Hightower Dr. is the magnificent tower Chandler used as the home of Jules Amthor in *Farewell My Lovely.*

Following the trail of pornography, after Geiger's murder in Laurel Canyon, Marlowe ends up at Joe Brody's residence in the apartment complex now located on a jutting finger of land at the corner of Kenmore and Palmerson. The arched garage entrance is just as Chandler described. The building is known as the Chateau Delaware. Marlowe moves into these apartments after events in

Farewell My Lovely when they were known as the Bristol Apts. Marlowe lived there until he moved to Yucca, off Laurel, in *The Long Goodbye*.

Moving through the streets again we passed by the Hobart Arms on Franklin where Moose finally catches up with Velma in *Farewell My Lovely*. Now it is known as the Solana Apartments and has lost much of its original sparkle.

At 5400 Marathon St. we passed the gates of Paramount Pictures. Here Ruth Windfeldt told us about Chandler's struggles as a screenwriter, with Paramount being the only studio at which he felt happy.

With more jazz supplied by Orena and Fowler, we left L.A. behind and made our way out towards Santa Monica, or as Marlowe knew it, Bay City. It was here that I really began to feel in tune with Marlowe and Chandler. On the corner of Highway 1 and Sunset, the Standard gas station where Marlowe stops to fill his tank on the way to Lindsay Marriott's house, still stands, still pumping gas even if it is only to half the population at a time due to the present day odd/even gas rationing.

Leaving the bus parked alongside the highway, we traversed the pedestrian overcrossing that would lead us to the home of Lindsay Marriott in Montemar Vista, a Chandlerism for Pacific Palisades. As we got to the bottom of the 280 steps that led to our destination it was with a feeling of deja vu that I noted it was exactly as Marlowe described it:

> "I got down to Montemar Vista as the light began to fade but there was still a fine sparkle on the water and the surf was breaking far out in long, smooth curves . . . Above the beach the highway ran under a wide concrete arch which was in fact a pedestrian bridge . . . I walked back through the arch and started up the steps, It was a nice walk if you like grunting. There were 280 steps to Cabrillo Street. They were drifted over with windblown sand and the handrail was as cold and wet as a toad's belly . . ."

The description was so vivid it was almost spooky. It was with reluctance that I rejoined my fellow fans and made my way back to the highway for the short trip to the Santa Monica Pier.

The trance I had fallen under was intensified by the pier. It was from here that Marlowe rented a boat to take him out to the gambling ship Montecito, which in *Farewell My Lovely* is owned and operated by Laird Brunette. With the sun slowly setting and the music of a sad sax wafting softly through the still air, I felt the years slip away until I was no longer a part of Santa Monica 1979. It was now Bay City in the 1930's. The city hall jail is again not the place to spend the night if you're a shabby shamus who doesn't get along with the crooked cops of the era. Dr. Sonderberg's sanitorium is

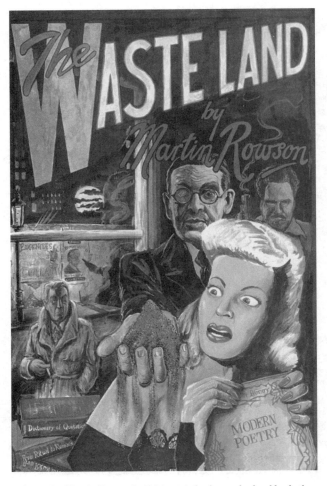

Cover for Martin Rowson's 1990 comic-book parody that blends the Marlowe novels with T. S. Eliot's The Waste Land *(1922)*

just around the corner, and on 25th St. at number 819 is the safety and sanctuary of Annie Riordan's house.

It was the end of a 10-hour day for us and I folded my trenchcoat carefully across my knees as we started home through the early evening traffic. There were still many Chandlerisms that remained unviewed that we would have to seek out on our own: The "Dancers" nightclub and the Sternwood mansion (now the Doheny mansion and open for public view) in Beverly Hills, the sites of Marlowe's cases that take him to Pasadena, and the beauty of Esmerelda, masquerading now as La Jolla, where Chandler retired. For me though, none of these would bring back the same glow that I got as I stood halfway up those 280 stairs, looking out at "A lonely yacht tacking towards the yacht harbor at Bay City" and gripping that galvanized handrail that was still as "wet and cold as a toad's belly."

Chandler in France

Chandler's books have been translated into all of the major languages. His work has been especially popular in France, where an interest in the American hard-boiled novel has been keen since the 1950s. The term roman noir, *or black novel, was originally used by the French in the eighteenth century to describe the English Gothic novel, but the phrase in the twentieth century became a term that encompassed the hard-boiled genre, beginning with John Carroll Daly, Dashiell Hammett, Raymond Chandler, and the* Black Mask *writers of the 1920s and 1930s. The marked interest of the French in Chandler's writing is indicated by this French reader.*

---

132   *Raymond Chandler*

BIG JOHN MASTERS was large, fat, oily. He had sleek blue jowls and very thick fingers on which the knuckles were dimples. His brown hair was combed straight back from his forehead and he wore a wine-colored suit with patch pockets, a wine-colored tie, a tan silk shirt. There was a lot of red and gold band around the thick brown cigar between his lips.

He wrinkled his nose, peeped at his hole card again, tried not to grin. He said: "Hit me again, Dave—and 10 don't hit me with the City Hall."

A four and a deuce showed. Dave Aage looked at them solemnly across the table, looked down at his own hand. He was very tall and thin, with a long bony face and hair the color of wet sand. He held the deck flat on the palm of his hand, turned the top card slowly, and flicked it across the table. It was the queen of spades.

Big John Masters opened his mouth wide, waved his cigar about, chuckled.

"Pay me, Dave. For once a lady was right." He 20 turned his hole card with a flourish. A five.

Dave Aage smiled politely, didn't move. A muted telephone bell rang close to him, behind long silk drapes that bordered the very high lancet windows. He took a cigarette out of his mouth and laid it carefully on the edge of a tray on a tabouret beside the card table, reached behind the curtain for the phone.

He spoke into the cup with a cool, almost whispering voice, then listened for a long time. Nothing changed in his greenish eyes, no flicker of emotion showed on his 30 narrow face. Masters squirmed, bit hard on his cigar.

After a long time Aage said, "Okey, you'll hear from us." He pronged the instrument and put it back behind

Spanish Blood   133

large: massive □ **fat** ≠ meagre □ **oily:** greasy □ **sleek:** lustrous **jowls:** sides of the face □ **thick:** big □ **knuckle(s):** articulation of the finger □ **dimple(s):** small cavity □ **combed:** arranged **forehead:** top of his face □ **wore:** had on □ **suit:** costume **patch:** appliqué □ **tan:** ochre **a lot of:** an ostentatious □ **thick:** large

wrinkled his nose: grimaced □ **peeped:** looked briefly □ **hole card:** secret card □ **grin:** smile □ **hit me again:** give me another card □ **hit me with City Hall:** give me a card of high value **deuce:** two □ **showed:** were exposed **across:** to the other side of □ **own hand:** cards he had in his hand □ **tall:** high in stature □ **thin** ≠ thick □ **bony:** very meagre □ **wet:** humid □ **held the deck flat:** maintained the pack of cards horizontal □ **top:** first □ **slowly** ≠ rapidly **flicked:** directed, sent rapidly □ **spades:** *pique* **wide:** completely □ **waved... about:** brandished, moved... in the air □ **chuckled:** exulted, laughed **once:** one time □ **right:** just, correct **flourish:** impressive gesture **muted:** practically silent **rang (ring, ~, rung):** resounded □ **close to:** near □ **drapes:** curtains □ **lancet:** ogival **laid (lay, ~, laid):** placed □ **carefully:** meticulously **edge:** border □ **tray:** ashtray, to place cinders of cigarettes **reached... for:** extended his arm to seize **cup:** telephone receiver □ **cool:** calm □ **whispering:** murmuring

no flicker: not a trace **narrow:** pointed □ **squirmed:** moved nervously □ **bit hard on:** masticated vigorously □ **you'll hear from us:** we will contact you □ **pronged:** attached □ **back:** where it was before

Cover for and pages from a 1993 reader for French students learning the American language (Bruccoli Collection, Thomas Cooper Library, University of South Carolina)

Many critics praised Chandler's fiction for his realistic and evocative treatment of Los Angeles and the surrounding region. Charles Wasserburg discusses Chandler's view of the city and how it is reflected in his novels.

Raymond Chandler's Great Wrong Place

Charles Wasserburg

Southwest Review, 74 (Autumn 1989): 534–545

Raymond Chandler is as closely identified with the Los Angeles of the thirties and forties as Dickens is with Victorian London or Joyce with Dublin. Devotees obsessively map out his terrain, providing photographs of exotic, often sleazy Southern California landmarks opposite descriptions lifted from the novels or stories. Thus we get dreary black-and-white shots of the Bradbury Building's wrought-iron balconies and grille elevators facing a description of "The Belfont Building" in *The Little Sister,* or, alongside a shot of a frosted glass door, almost any one of Marlowe's descriptions of his office. But Los Angeles nourished Chandler as much metaphorically as physically, as London did Dickens or Dublin Joyce. While Chandler is hardly a Dickens or Joyce, he is—more than any mystery writer of his time—an artist. In "The Guilty Vicarage," an essay that at once flattered Chandler with its praise and embarrassed him with its unabashedly literary tone, W. H. Auden speculates on the significance of locale in the detective novel generally:

> In the detective story, as in its mirror image, the Quest for the Grail, . . . Nature should reflect its human inhabitants, *i.e.,* it should be the Great Good Place; for the more Eden-like it is, the greater the contradiction of murder.

Auden is of course writing about drawing rooms and monasteries, typically English locations, in which corpses shockingly turn up. But thinking in Auden's terms, what better place for crime than boom-time Los

"Raymond Chandler Square," at the intersection of Hollywood and Cahuenga Boulevards, was named an Historic-Cultural Monument in 1994 by the City of Los Angeles. This square is the site of the Pacific Security Bank building, the likely model for Chandler's Cahuenga Building, where Philip Marlowe leased a sixth-floor office (photograph courtesy of Jess Bravin).

The Library of America Edition

In 1995, a two-volume collection of Chandler's novels and other writings was published in the Library of America. His inclusion in this series—which publishes canonical works of America's most respected authors—indicates the degree to which Chandler had achieved recognition as a classic American writer. The publication of the volumes was the catalyst for several retrospective essays that reassessed the work of Raymond Chandler and his place in American literature.

Angeles, a type of Great Good Place ready to lose its illusory innocence? For in Chandler's time, the city was still being touted as the new Eden, though the deception was becoming clear: Los Angeles had grown fast, but not naturally. By all rights it still ought to have been a desert town. From their beginning at the turn of the century, the valley's proliferating lawns and palmtrees were fed by water filched from Owens Lake, two hundred and fifty miles away near the Sierras. Meanwhile, city father Harrison Gray Otis advertised the new paradise in his newspaper, the *Los Angeles Times.* Realtors' prices were unbelievably low, as the newly arrived Midwesterners discovered, on finding that their dream lots lay at the bottom of the Los Angeles River. Deception, of course, is a theme as old as writing itself. But Chandler's use of this specific region to embody it is distinctive. For this English-bred outsider forced by monetary considerations into "popular" writing, the physical city is emblematic of the pastless, valueless society it con-

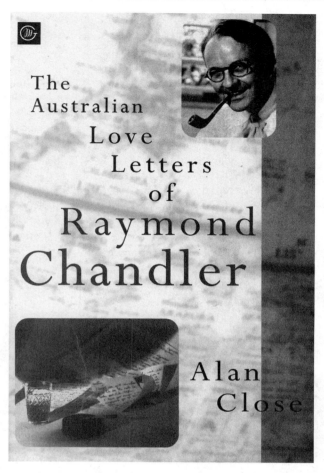

Cover for Close's 1995 book that combines fiction and biography; it was inspired by Chandler's letters to Diedre Gartrell, a young woman who had written to him when she read of his depression.

tains, with as much cultural as criminal deception taking place within its bounds. And it is Marlowe's job to ferret out both.

The great architecture writer Reyner Banham, like Chandler a displaced Englishman who became fascinated with Los Angeles, insists that the sheer oddity of many of Los Angeles' buildings shows

the convulsions in building style that follow when traditional cultural and social restraints have been overthrown and replaced by the preferences of a mobile . . . society, in which 'cultural values' and ancient symbols are handled primarily as methods of claiming or establishing status.

Present at the heyday of this society, Marlowe is not delighted but profoundly disturbed by its absence of tradition and concommitant lack of social restraints. Chandler's quarry, more often than not, are in Southern California because it's the one place where they can

fabricate a past for themselves and begin anew. Mrs. Grayle, the millionairess in *Farewell, My Lovely,* who has concealed her seamy lounge singer past, is part melodramatic character, part personification of Los Angeles. When her secret is unveiled we are not surprised, having been prepared by Marlowe's description of her mock-antique mansion. After zeroing in on her chauffeur's Russian tunic (why not merely "chauffeur's uniform"?) Marlowe notes:

The entrance was barred by a wrought-iron gate with a flying cupid in the middle. There were busts on light pillars and a stone seat with crouching griffins at each end . . . And far over to the left there was a wild garden, not very large, with a sundial in the corner near an angle of wall that was built to look like a ruin.

The notion of ruins, with their associated historical grandeur, in this newest of cities is preposterous, as is Mrs. Grayle's life story, a similarly elaborate fabrication. In *The Long Goodbye,* Terry Lennox's presumed murder is less intriguing, finally, than the circumstances of his European past that Marlowe digs up in the course

Diedre Gartrell in 1957 (from the January–February issue of The Australian Magazine)

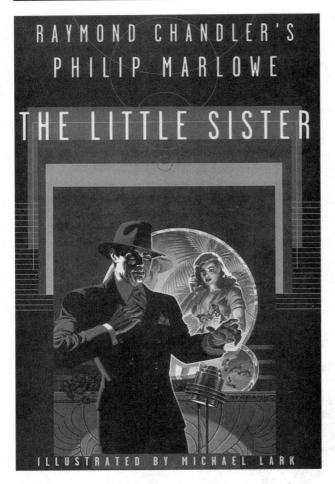

Cover for Michael Lark's 1997 graphic-novel version of
The Little Sister

Psychologically, as architecturally, Chandler is less interested in exposing his criminals' two-facedness than he is in exploring its nature. The detective story, he once reminded a friend, wasn't just a lot of fisticuffs and womanizing, but a story of detection—how was the façade created, and why? "Who am I cutting my throat for this time?" Marlowe asks himself in *The Little Sister.* "All I know is that something isn't what it seems." Nicholas Schenk, president of the Loew's theater chain, reportedly once lamented while wandering the outdoor sets at MGM, "false fronts! Nothing behind them! They are like Hollywood people." The same could be said for most of Chandler's characters and their culture. As Marlowe observes on a drive past some cheap hamburger joints' "false fronts," "There ought to be a monument to the man who invented neon lights . . . There's a boy who really made something out of nothing."

Otto Friedrich and others who have tried to see Los Angeles through Chandler's eyes attribute the atmosphere of bitterness and decay that permeates

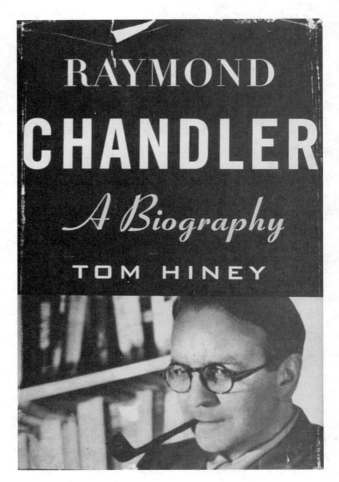

*Dust jacket for the second book-length biography
of Chandler, published in 1997*

of his investigation. Skepticism toward the new is one key to Marlowe's identity. In this light, money, well- or ill-gained, is only an accessory to the crime. As Chandler once remarked, "Marlowe and I do not despise the upper classes because they take baths and have money. We despise them because they are phoney." Thus in *The Long Goodbye* Marlowe sardonically remarks on the architectural bombast of Los Angeles aristocrat Harlan Potter's mansion:

> It was the damndest-looking house I ever saw. It was a square gray box three stories high, with a mansard roof, steeply sloped and broken by twenty or thirty double dormer windows with a lot of wedding cake decoration around and between them. . . . There were all sorts of ornamental trees in clumps here and there and they didn't look like California trees. Imported stuff. Whoever built that place was trying to drag the Atlantic seaboard over the Rockies. He was trying hard, but he hadn't made it.

LA JOLLA FESTIVAL X/1998

International Imitation Raymond Chandler Writing Competition

The La Jolla Festival 1998 will center upon an INTERNATIONAL IMITATION RAYMOND CHANDLER WRITING COMPETITION. The object is to imitate or parody the writing style of the man who invented the hard-boiled whodunit and left the world the fictional character Philip Marlowe, a tough, witty and honorable detective. Contestants should make use of typical Chandler locales, interests, and subject matter as appropriate. Chandler lived and wrote in La Jolla, California, from 1946 until his death in 1959.

The judges will select the best imitation Chandler entry, i.e. good "bad" Chandler. Three winning entries will be selected to receive either a $500 first prize, a $300 second prize, or a $200 third prize. Students, non-professional and professional writers are encouraged to make submissions. Awards will be announced August 26, 1998.

HOW TO ENTER

- ✔ All entries must be typewritten, double spaced on 8 1/2" x 11" plain, white paper.

- ✔ All entries must be approximately 500 words in length.

- ✔ All entries must mention La Jolla.

- ✔ All entries must include an original and four (4) copies.

- ✔ All entries must be identified—on each back—with the author's name, address, and phone number.

- ✔ All entries must be received by August 1, 1998.

- ✔ All entries must be titled.

- ✔ Each contestant will be limited to one entry.

- ✔ No entries will be returned.

- ✔ All entries must be unpublished submissions.

- ✔ All entries become property of the Friends of the La Jolla Library and are subject to release to other media.

- ✔ Members of the La Jolla Festival Committee are not eligible, nor are their relatives.

- ✔ The decision of the Judging Committee will be final.

LA JOLLA FESTIVAL

FRIENDS OF THE LA JOLLA LIBRARY

Send entries to:
International Imitation
Raymond Chandler Writing Competition
c/o Friends of the La Jolla Library
6632 Avenida Manana
La Jolla, CA 92037, USA

©1998 Friends of the La Jolla Library

Advertising flyer for an annual event begun in 1989 by the Friends of the La Jolla Public Library

Chandler's work to his disgust with the unrelenting sprawl that Los Angeles had become by the late forties, quoting Marlowe's diatribe in *The Little Sister:*

> I used to like this town . . . There were trees along Wilshire Boulevard. Beverly Hills was a country town. Westwood was bare hills and lots offering at eleven hundred dollars and no takers . . . Los Angeles was just a big dry sunny place with ugly homes and no style, but goodhearted and peaceful. It had the climate they just yap about now . . . it wasn't a neon-lighted slum either.

But nostalgia for the big dry sunny place was only part of the novelist's vision. Chandler was fascinated by the psychology and culture of the migration itself, of the urban sprawl in the making. He almost compulsively explored the layers of deception characteristic of the thirties and forties, when new arrivals, lured initially by false promises, were then duped by a second set of hucksters. Marlowe, who desires no miracle cure and no money, has little patience for these types. The bogus mystic, Amthor, in *Farewell, My Lovely,* keeps an Indian assistant to lend his pseudo-rituals credibility—although, as Marlowe rightly suspects, he serves double duty as a bodyguard. When the Indian arrives to fetch Marlowe, the detective immediately deflates his act:

> "Huh. Me Second Planting. Me Hollywood Indian."
> "Have a chair, Mr. Planting."
> " . . . Name Second Planting. Name no Mister Planting."
> "What can I do for you?"
> He lifted his voice and began to intone in a deep-chested sonorous boom. "He say come quick. Great white father say come quick. He say me bring you in fiery chariot. He say—
> "Yeah. Cut out the pig Latin," I said. "I'm no school-marm at the snake dances."
> "Nuts," the Indian said.

This borrowing from the Old West for the purpose of disguise is reminiscent of Nathanael West's Earle, the Hollywood cowboy in *The Day of the Locust,* whose conversation is limited to laconically "western" catch phrases—"lo thar" is his standard greeting—because he truly has nothing to say. In Chandler's novels, though, there's a more insidious turn to such fakery. His crooks dress themselves in old culture for the express purpose of taking advantage of, and often brutalizing, the innocents who take the cultural borrowing seriously. When, in *The Long Goodbye,* Marlowe tracks the feelgood doctor Verringer to his "hospital" in Sepulveda Canyon, he encounters the doctor's psychopathic bodyguard Earle, who is dressed in a gaucho-style getup—flat black hat, fringed scarf, skintight black pants, patent-leather dancing pumps—whose showiness suggests a burlesquing of the cowboy tradition. Earle's language is a similarly discomfiting clash of western slang and modern city banter:

> "The bank owns the place. They done foreclosed it or it's in escrow or something. I forget the details."
> " . . . Which bank would that be?"
> "You don't know, you don't come from there. You don't come from there, you don't have any business here. Hit the trail, sweetie. Buzz off but fast."

Marlowe's suspicions are verified when Earle attacks him with a pair of brass knuckles. "Just what bothers you about Earle?" Dr. Verringer innocently asks. Marlowe, in a statement reminiscent of Chandler's about the rich, snaps back: "He's so obviously a phoney . . . The guy's a manic-depressive, isn't he? Right now he's on the upswing." One often wonders whether any doctors in the Marlowe novels *aren't* sinister dope peddlers. "I looked hard at him," Marlowe remarks of another fake doctor suggestively named Lagardie in *The Little Sister*. It didn't buy me a way into his soul. He was quiet, dark, and shuttered." Why is the doctor practicing in Santa Monica (which Chandler calls Bay City)? "Because of something that happened years ago—in another city," he tells Marlowe. New beginning indeed.

As Frank MacShane's biography of him suggests, Chandler's own new beginnings in Los Angeles had little to do with writing, but say a good deal about the cultural tensions he shared with some of his characters. Born in Chicago, he had arrived in Southern California in his early twenties looking and sounding like an Englishman. He had, in fact, been reared in London and schooled in Greek and Latin at the Dulwich Academy. Like a lot of people, he'd come to Los Angeles on a lark, invited by someone he'd met on an English cruise ship headed for New York. A series of bookkeeping jobs finally landed him work in the Dabney Oil Syndicate, where by his late thirties he'd ascended to the company vice-presidency. Those were heady times to be in the California oil business. Second only to Shell, Dabney was the major developer of the largest oil field in California history on Signal Hill in Long Beach. But in the early thirties, Chandler was fired. The Depression may have been a factor, but there are various accounts of his on-the-job philandering and drunkenness, as well as corporate infighting. Whatever it was, at the age of forty-four, a man with amorphous literary ambitions who, as he put it in a letter, preferred "a conservative atmosphere and a sense of the past" found himself like the average arrival from the midwest: job-

James Caan as Marlowe and Dina Meyer as his wife in the 1998 HBO cable movie version of Poodle Springs

less and at loose ends in the perfect weather and high promise of Southern California.

The crisis forced Chandler's writerly hand, and he turned the aspirations he'd always harbored to money-making by imitating the only stories he knew that paid: the pulp detective tales in *Black Mask* magazine. Chandler admitted that nearly all of what he read in the pulps, with the exception of Hammett, was deplorable stuff—predictable and misleading and lacking in tonal variety and characterization. He saw the detective novel, like the movies he would later write for, as a medium capable of at once reaching the widest audience and allowing for a maximum degree of artistry, with formal requirements as tight as any sonnet. His letters are peppered with comments on the similarities between Elizabethan drama and the detective story. Whether he makes these comparisons in earnest or because he was slightly embarrassed to be practicing such a popular form of writing is sometimes difficult to tell. He was, at any rate, a snob who couldn't help making self-conscious references to his English education. He claimed he heard American English with the ear of a foreigner, picking out slang, colloquialisms, snide talk, and solecisms and working them into dialogues in the same self-conscious manner he'd once worked exercises in Greek or Latin. He experimented endlessly with these Americanisms until he achieved the snap he was after. His obsession with American rhythm and diction surely accounts not just for the memorable dialogue in

the novels, but for the Chinese-firecracker exchanges between Barbara Stanwyck and Fred MacMurray in his screenplay for *Double Indemnity*. In one of the movie's most famous scenes, MacMurray's Walter Neff and Stanwyck's Phyllis Dietrichson engage in an aggressive, sexy, and funny dialogue—and though Dietrichson seems to want to slow down Neff's wisecracking attempt at seduction, her responses actually propel the exchange forward:

Phyllis: There's a speed limit in this state, Mr. Neff: forty-five miles an hour.

Neff: How fast was I going, officer?

P.D.: I'd say around ninety.

W.N.: Suppose you get down off your motorcycle and give me a ticket?

P.D.: Suppose I let you off with a warning this time?

W.N.: Suppose it doesn't take?

P.D.: Suppose I have to wack you over the knuckles?

W.N.: Suppose I bust out crying and put my head on your shoulder?

Is it possible to talk without smirking about stichomythic dialogue in Hollywood movies? Surely this is an example of it.

If you drive down Melrose Avenue in east Hollywood today, you pass through a lively, if somewhat run-down neighborhood where most of the store signs are in Spanish. Unwatered lawns and agave dry in the sun in front of small frame houses whose paint is chipping off from heat, smog, and too little money for repair. Suddenly, on your left, white and pristine, rise the walls of Paramount Studios. Through the giant wrought-iron gates, on unsmoggy days, you can just make out the white HOLLYWOOD sign on the hills behind. This insular, fortress-like construction seemingly dropped in the middle of the teeming city suggests the relationship between the Hollywood dream factory of producers, directors, and actors and the Los Angeles around it with which it's often conflated. Marlowe remarks on this rather peculiar relationship between the two communities in *The Little Sister:*

> Real cities have something else, some individual bony structure under the muck. Los Angeles has Hollywood . . . It ought to consider itself damn lucky. Without Hollywood it would be a mail-order city. Everything in the catalogue you could get better somewhere else.

David O. Selznick once observed that phony accounting built Hollywood. Phony accounts had their place too, and not only in Hollywood, but throughout

Southern California. The sudden and rather contrived creation of the Los Angeles paradise, in fact, was not unlike the process by which Hollywood manufactured some of its most famous employees: Emmanuel Goldenberg, Margarita Cansino, Harlean Carpenter, Betty Perske. Of these, only Goldenberg kept a private treaty with his past by retaining the *G* from his surname. *Edward G. Robinson,* after all, sounded sufficiently aristocratic and safely non-ethnic. The identities the others chose have even less to do with personal or cultural background: the child of Mexican parents, Cansino dyed her black hair red as one of the steps toward becoming Rita Hayworth. Only a slight echo of vowels reminds us that Harlean Carpenter was a castoff of Jean Harlowe. And though she changed her last name from Perske before arriving in Hollywood, Betty Bacall took Howard Hawks' advice and not only changed her first name to Lauren, but practiced lowering her voice to achieve the famous "put your lips together and blow" huskiness. Moreover, as not only Otto Friedrich but, more recently, Neal Gabler has pointed out, in *An Empire of their Own,* most of the studio tyrants of the thirties and forties were Eastern European immigrants who knew and feared poverty and so saw assimilation as a way to success. Louis Mayer was a scrap metal merchant who managed theaters in the East until he controlled enough distribution rights to create his own studio in Hollywood; Samuel Goldwyn was a glove salesman from Lodz; Lewis Selznick, a jewelry dealer from Kiev. And none of them admitted to their pasts. Friedrich recounts the bet that screenwriter Ben Hecht made with David O. Selznick, in which Hecht challenged Selznick to find one person who considered the producer an American and not a Jew. Despite Selznick's certainty that he had erased his ethnic past, he could not find a single person who agreed. As Marlowe acidly remarks in *The Little Sister,* "Wonderful what Hollywood will do for a nobody. It will make a radiant glamour queen out of a drab little wench . . . a he-man hero . . . out of some overgrown kid who was meant to go to work with a lunchbox."

When Chandler was summoned by Paramount in 1944 to work on a script of James M. Cain's novel *Double Indemnity,* he was living, almost literally, around the corner from the studio and had been in Los Angeles for nearly thirty years. He and his wife Cissy had moved restlessly around Southern California—Arcadia, Bel Air, Hollywood, Palm Springs, Riverside, Santa Monica—for most of their life together. In doing so, Chandler had familiarized himself with the variousness of the area. If Hollywood created personalities devoid of ethnicity, Chandler wrote frequently (though many times with a mean-spirited shallowness bordering on caricature) about the Hispanics and blacks who had poured into the area to build ships and airplanes, as part of Los Angeles's "other" major industries at the time. Deception is so pervasive in Chandler's Los Angeles, that occasionally even Marlowe is fooled into thinking the worst about a fundamentally decent man simply because of his ethnicity. Candy, the houseboy at the Wade mansion, has all the earmarks of a hoodlum and yet never attacks Marlowe. Marlowe goes so far as to suggest that part of Candy's appeal to the Wades is his ethnicity, which Candy takes pains to exaggerate. At the police station, Marlowe observes Candy telling his side of the story of Roger Wade's murder "with very little accent. It seemed as if he could turn that on and off at will." Absolved of Wade's murder at the end of the novel, Candy confronts Marlowe with a switchblade, thinking Marlowe is about to threaten Mrs. Wade. But the detective reveals a rare streak of sympathy and admonishes the Mexican to leave town while he still can:

> They'd hang it [the murder] onto you and love it. Just the kind of smoke screen that would make them grin with delight . . . They fouled it up so bad that they couldn't straighten it out now if they wanted to. They'd blast a confession out of you so quickly you wouldn't even have time to tell them your full name.

The contrast between the city that he knew and the sanitized creations of Hollywood could only have exacerbated the bitterness already inherent in Chandler's vision. As Banham reminds us, if Los Angeles is mythologized as the land of gratification, then Hollywood brought the technical skill and resources to convert these fantastic notions of gratification into physical realities through the construction of exotic sets:

> The movies were thus a peerless school for building fantasy as fact, and the facts often survived one movie to live again in another . . . [to] survive as cities of romantic illusion . . . elevated to the status of a kind of cultural monument.

Reversing the fantasy, Chandler's only collaboration with that other emigré, Billy Wilder (who claimed he loved nothing better than setting Hollywood back on its heels) led to one of the grimmest portrayals of Los Angeles society ever, in their movie of *Double Indemnity.* There's a sense of overripeness edging into decay in *Double Indemnity,* not just in the hurried, violent sexuality, but in the scenery, for Wilder and Chandler spent much time scouting the seedier areas of Los Angeles, its train stations and vacant lots. This was the city Wilder had found when he'd arrived a penniless emigré from Berlin in 1934, to try his luck against the hundreds of other screenwriters in Hollywood. Thus, at Wilder's insistence, Stanwyck, as Phyllis Dietrichson, wears a blonde wig

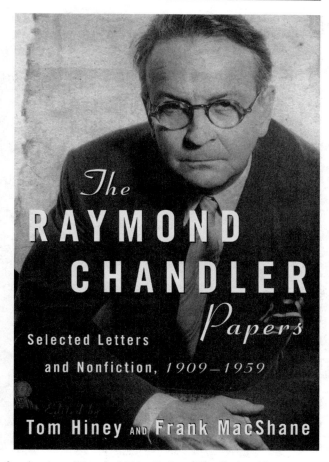

Dust jackets for the first edition (left), published in Britain, and the first American edition of a 2000 collection of Chandler's writings

to took as sleazy as possible, though at first glance she appears to be a typical California blonde. Her voluptuousness is shot through with corruption, in good *noir* manner, from the moment Neff leaves her house for the first time and thinks back on her perfume: "Honeysuckle. How could I know that death smelled of honeysuckle." Phyllis' greed, disguised as erotic interest in MacMurray's slick, confident Walter Neff, is what ensnares Neff and exposes his sexual greed. This underlying corruption in the city of promise would five years later lead Wilder in *Sunset Boulevard* to home in just as mercilessly on Hollywood itself, where everyone had a price. It's the screenwriter Joe Gillis's desperation for money, after all, that compels him to stay on with the aging Norma Desmond and maintain her illusion of youth and fame. Chandler, while not as desperate monetarily as Gillis, still suffered the miseries of forced collaboration his whole time in Hollywood. "If you can go it alone, what do you need me for?" he would later fume at Hitchcock, who had suggested a few changes for the *Strangers on a Train* script. But Chandler's collaboration with Hitchcock sounds civil compared with the trials he and Wilder put each other through. Wilder later called the writing of *Double Indemnity* the most miserable job he'd ever been involved in.

Chandler hated Wilder's arrogance even more than he hated Cain's writing. Yet something rotting in the core of the orange fascinated the two outsiders enough to finish the job and to limit a vision of their adopted city that no one had seen in the movies.

At the time that Wilder received an Academy Award for *Sunset Boulevard,* Chandler was living in La Jolla and nearly through with screenwriting. He was to have one last fling, with Hitchcock's version of *Strangers on a Train,* which he turned over to another writer to finish, and write one more good detective story, *The Long Goodbye. The Long Goodbye* is certainly Chandler's most ambitious and in many ways most psychologically penetrating novel. But it suffers from the sprawl of Los Angeles itself—too much smart-alecky dialogue, too much unneeded commentary from Marlowe, and a number of lengthy set speeches that, while often finely written, seem stapled to the larger narrative structure of the novel. In terms of sheer economy of style, *Farewell, My Lovely* may be his finest book: all the beliefs regarding trust, friendship, and ethics that Chandler wished to explore in *The Long Goodbye* appear in this earlier novel, but with a terse precision that belies the complex emotions underlying the characters' exchanges. Anne Rior-

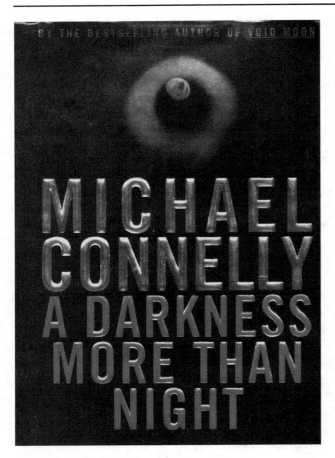

Dust jacket for Connelly's 2001 novel, set in Los Angeles, that takes its title from a Chandler line in his introduction to The Simple Art of Murder

din is perhaps one of Chandler's most compelling female characters, if not simply one of his most compelling overall: independent, direct, and able to parley a wisecrack while still showing great compassion.

Disgruntled as he was with Hollywood, Chandler knew he'd lost his focus by settling permanently in La Jolla. To one of his friends he wrote, "I know what is the matter with my writing or not writing. I've lost any affinity for my background. Los Angeles is no longer my city . . . I know damn well I sound like a bitter and disappointed man. I guess I am that." It may be surprising to hear Chandler, who had once snobbishly mourned his separation from English culture, now mourning the loss of this city. But maybe not. For the last two decades, while living in Los Angeles, he had been inventing the city for himself even as it was developing on its own into a metropolis. He had articulated its speed and garishness, its need to make promises that proved more often than not illusory, and chronicled its culture, which shifted as uneasily as the earth below it.

Chandler's work is still compelling, but not because of its "whodunnit" qualities, for which he cared very little.

(Asked by Howard Hawks in a telegram who killed the Sternwood chauffeur in *The Big Sleep,* Chandler wrote back "I don't know.") What Auden defined as Chandler's "serious studies of a criminal milieu," and Edmund Wilson as Chandler's ability to convey the "malaise" of a place are perhaps his most significant virtues, in that their application cannot simply be limited to criminality. It's unfortunate that Wilson was unable to include Chandler in what was in many ways a groundbreaking study of California writers, *The Boys in the Back Room.* Published in 1941 when Chandler was still a relative unknown, its essays discuss novelists as diverse as John O'Hara, James M. Cain, and Nathanael West. Wilson introduces his eloquent, if sometimes squeamishly xenophobic collection with "The Playwright in Paradise," a satirical poem in jogging rhymed couplets about life in the Golden State. Since he had just numbered his friend Scott Fitzgerald among the lost in Hollywood's "record of talent depraved and wasted," Wilson's sarcasm at the expense of Southern California in the poem is heartfelt, but finally misdirected. Singling out a number of cliches still associated with the area—eternal sunshine, orange juice, avocadoes that drop into one's lap—Wilson satirizes its superficiality through the shade of a failed screenwriter who depicts this place

"Where billows, blue and brineless, glide and glisten—
And there we dance in bougainvillea wreathes,
Speeding the golden day with golden shoes"

Wilson evidently chooses the bougainvillea, a plant ubiquitous in Southern California, for its brilliant violet bracts suggestive to him of the gorgeous shallowness of California life. But for all his sophistication, Wilson makes a botanical error that allies him with others deceived throughout history by Los Angeles' enchanting surfaces. Anyone familiar with the tropical vine knows that its lush purples mask a tangle of thorny branches that can shred flesh. Knowing this, it's hard to imagine the Californians in Wilson's poem taking too much pleasure in wearing such wreathes on their heads—though to an outsider, doing so must look lovely and appealing.

At the end of his acknowledgments for his novel, Connelly wrote of his title.

Lastly, special thanks to Raymond Chandler for inspiring the title of the book. Describing in 1950 the time and place from which he drew his early crime stories, Chandler wrote, "The streets were dark with something more than night."
Sometimes they still are.

For Further Reading and Reference

BIBLIOGRAPHIES

Matthew J. Bruccoli, *Raymond Chandler: A Checklist* (Kent, Ohio: Kent State University Press, 1968).

Bruccoli, *Raymond Chandler: A Descriptive Bibliography* (Pittsburgh: University of Pittsburgh Press, 1979).

Skinner, Robert E. *The Hard-Boiled Explicator: A Guide to the Study of Dashiell Hammett, Raymond Chandler, and Ross Macdonald* (Metuchen, N.J.: Scarecrow Press, 1985).

BIOGRAPHIES

Frank MacShane, *The Life of Raymond Chandler* (New York: Dutton, 1976).

Tom Hiney, *Raymond Chandler: A Biography* (New York: Atlantic Monthly Press, 1997).

REFERENCES

Leon Arden, "A Knock at the Backdoor of Art: The Entrance of Raymond Chandler," in *Art in Crime Writing: Essays on Detective Fiction,* edited by Benstock Bernard (New York: St. Martin's Press, 1983), pp. 73–96.

W. H. Auden, "The Guilty Vicarage," *Harper's* (May 1948): 406–412.

Liahna K. Babener, "Raymond Chandler's City of Lies," in *Los Angeles in Fiction: A Collection of Original Essays,* edited by David Fine (Albuquerque: University of New Mexico Press, 1984), pp. 109–131.

Jacques Barzun, "The Aesthetics of the Criminious," *American Scholar,* 53 (1984): 239–241.

E. M. Beekman, "Raymond Chandler and an American Genre," *Massachusetts Review,* 14 (1973): 149–173.

Paul Bishop, "The Longest Goodbye or the Search for Raymond Chandler's Los Angeles," *Mystery,* 1 (March/April 1980): 33–36.

Gay Brewer, *A Detective in Distress: Philip Marlowe's Domestic Dream* (San Bernardino, Cal.: Borgo, 1989).

John G. Cawelti, "Hammett, Chandler, and Spillane," in *Adventure, Mystery and Romance: Formula Stories as Art and Popular Culture* (Chicago: University of Chicago Press, 1976), pp. 162–191.

Al Clark, *Raymond Chandler in Hollywood* (New York: Proteus, 1982).

Alan Close, *The Australian Love Letters of Raymond Chandler* (Ringwood, Australia: McPhee Gribble, 1995).

Philip Durham, *Down These Mean Streets a Man Must Go: Raymond Chandler's Knight* (Chapel Hill: University of North Carolina Press, 1963).

George P. Elliot, "A Country Full of Blondes," *Nation* (23 April 1960): 354–360.

David Fine, "Nathanael West, Raymond Chandler, and the Los Angeles Novel," *California History,* 68 (Winter 1989–1990): 196–201.

Fine, "Raymond Chandler and The Great California Road Show," *Californians,* 9 (1991): 22–25.

Ian Fleming, "Raymond Chandler," *London Magazine,* 6 (December 1959): 43–54.

R. W. Flint, "A Cato of Cruelties," *Partisan Review,* 14 (1947): 328.

Ernest Fontana, "Chivalry and Modernity in Raymond Chandler's *The Big Sleep,*" *Western American Literature,* 19 (1984): 179–186.

Brian Gallagher, "Howard Hawks's 'The Big Sleep: A Paradigm for the Postwar American Family'," *North Dakota Quarterly,* 51 (1983): 78–91. Reprinted in *The Critical Responses to Raymond Chandler,* edited by J. K. Van Dover (Westport, Conn.: Greenwood Press, 1995), pp. 145–157.

George Grella, "Murder and the Mean Streets," *Contempora,* 1 (March 1970): 6–15.

Miriam Gross, ed., *The World of Raymond Chandler* (London: Weidenfeld & Nicolson, 1977).

James Guetti, "Aggressive Reading: Detective Fiction and Realistic Narrative," *Raritan,* 2 (1982): 133–154.

Frederic Jameson, "On Raymond Chandler," *The Southern Review,* 6 (1970): 624–650.

R. W. Lid, "Philip Marlowe Speaking," *The Kenyon Review,* 31 (1969): 153–178.

Rick Lott, "A Matter of Style: Chandler's Hardboiled Disguise," *Journal of Popular Culture,* 23 (1989): 65–75.

William Luhr, *Raymond Chandler and Film* (New York: Ungar, 1982).

William Marling, *Raymond Chandler* (Boston: Twayne, 1986).

W. Somerset Maugham, "The Decline and Fall of the Detective Story," in *The Vagrant Muse* (London: Heinemann, 1952), pp. 91–122.

Roy Meador, "Chandler in the Thirties: Apprenticeship of an Angry Man," *Book Forum,* 6 (1982): 143–153.

Robert H. Miller, "The Publication of Raymond Chandler's *The Long Goodbye,*" *Papers of the Bibliographical Society of America,* 63 (1969): 279–290.

Neil Morgan, "The Long Goodbye," *California* (June 1982): 81, 159, 161–162, 164.

Joyce Carol Oates, "The Simple Art of Murder," *New York Review of Books,* 21 (December 1995).

Luke Parsons, "On the Novels of Raymond Chandler," *The Fortnightly,* 175 (1954): 346–351.

John Paterson, "A Cosmic View of the Private Eye," *Saturday Review* (22 August 1953): 7–8, 31–33.

Stephen Pendo, *Raymond Chandler on Screen* (Metuchen, N. J.: Scarecrow Press, 1976).

Gene D. Philips, *Creatures of Darkness: Raymond Chandler, Detective Fiction, and Film Noir* (Lexington: University of Kentucky Press, 2000).

Wilson Pollock, "Man with a Toy Gun," *New Republic* (7 May 1962): 21–22.

Peter J. Rabinowitz, "Rats Behind the Wainscoting: Politics, Convention, and Chandler's 'The Big Sleep'," *Texas Studies in Literature and Language,* 22 (1980): 224–245.

Tom S. Reck, "Raymond Chandler's Los Angeles," *Nation,* 221 (20 December 1975): 661–663.

Richard Schickel, "Raymond Chandler, Private Eye," *Commentary,* 352 (Feb 1963): 158–161.

Johanna M. Smith, "Raymond Chandler and the Business of Literature," *Texas Studies in Language and Literature,* 31 (1989): 592–610. Reprinted in *The Critical Responses to Raymond Chandler,* edited by J. K. Van Dover (Westport, Conn.: Greenwood Press, 1995), pp. 183–201.

Jerry Speir, *Raymond Chandler* (New York: Ungar, 1981).

Lawrence D. Stewart, "The Dust Jackets of *The Great Gatsby* and *The Long Goodbye,*" *Mystery and Detection Annual* (1973): 331–334.

Julian Symons, "The Case of Raymond Chandler," *New York Times Magazine* (23 December 1973): 13, 22, 25, 27.

Symons, "Marlowe's Victim," *Times Literary Supplement* (23 March 1962): 200.

Stephen L. Tanner, "The Function of Simile in Raymond Chandler's Novels," *Studies in American Humor,* 3 (1984/85): 337–346.

J. K. Van Dover, ed., *The Critical Responses to Raymond Chandler* (Westport, Conn.: Greenwood Press, 1995).

Charles Wasserburg, "Raymond Chandler's Great Wrong Place," *Southwest Review,* 74 (1989): 534–545.

James Wolcott, "Raymond Chandler's Smoking Gun," *New Yorker* (25 Sep 1995): 62–69.

Peter Wolfe, *Something More Than Night: The Case of Raymond Chandler* (Bowling Green, Ohio: Popular, 1985).

PAPERS

The two major collections of Raymond Chandler's papers are held by the University of California, Los Angeles Library and the Bodleian Library, Oxford.

Cumulative Index

Dictionary of Literary Biography, Volumes 1-253
Dictionary of Literary Biography Yearbook, 1980-2000
Dictionary of Literary Biography Documentary Series, Volumes 1-19
Concise Dictionary of American Literary Biography, Volumes 1-7
Concise Dictionary of British Literary Biography, Volumes 1-8
Concise Dictionary of World Literary Biography, Volumes 1-4

Cumulative Index

DLB before number: *Dictionary of Literary Biography*, Volumes 1-252
Y before number: *Dictionary of Literary Biography Yearbook*, 1980-2000
DS before number: *Dictionary of Literary Biography Documentary Series*, Volumes 1-19
CDALB before number: *Concise Dictionary of American Literary Biography*, Volumes 1-7
CDBLB before number: *Concise Dictionary of British Literary Biography*, Volumes 1-8
CDWLB before number: *Concise Dictionary of World Literary Biography*, Volumes 1-4

F

J

K

L

N

O

U

ISBN 0-7876-5247-4

90000

9 780787 652470